Figure 2.8. Daniel Maclise, *The Origin of the Harp,* engraved by F. P. Becker from *Moore's Irish Melodies* (1866). Photograph courtesy of Linda Phyllis Austern.

Music of the Sirens

Music of the Sirens

Edited by
Linda Phyllis Austern and
Inna Naroditskaya

Indiana University Press

BLOOMINGTON AND INDIANAPOLIS

This book is a publication of
Indiana University Press
601 North Morton Street
Bloomington, IN 47404-3797 USA

http://iupress.indiana.edu

Telephone orders   800-842-6796
Fax orders   812-855-7931
Orders by e-mail   iuporder@indiana.edu

MANUFACTURED IN THE UNITED STATES OF AMERICA

Library of Congress Cataloging-in-Publication Data

Music of the sirens / edited by Linda Phyllis Austern and Inna Naroditskaya.
p. cm.
Includes bibliographical references and index.
ISBN 0-253-34736-X (cloth : alk. paper) — ISBN 0-253-21846-2 (pbk. : alk. paper)
1. Feminism and music. 2. Women in music. 3. Sex in music. 4. Sirens (Mythology)
I. Austern, Linda Phyllis, date II. Naroditskaya, Inna, date
ML3838.M9495 2006
780.82—dc22
2005034293

1 2 3 4 5   11 10 09 08 07 06

CONTENTS

ACKNOWLEDGMENTS

The Editors wish to thank all of the following, without whom this book would not have been possible: Megan Guenther and Stephen Houbeck for assisting tirelessly and cheerfully with preparation of the final version of the manuscript on top of their own teaching and graduate study; our husbands, James Borland and Anthony Elmendorf, for offering continual personal support and occasional research assistance; each other for complementary intellectual insight and editorial styles; and finally and most importantly, all of our contributing authors for letting us have such fascinating articles.

Singing Each to Each

Inna Naroditskaya and Linda Phyllis Austern

The siren and her sisters are the most elusive and paradoxical of all creatures. Neither fish, fowl, nor long-tressed mammal, they are impossible combinations of any of these, or none at all. Most often female, they may sometimes be male. Mortal or eternal, they may deliver death or bestow the kiss of everlasting life. They haunt the forests of Russia and the mountains of Bolivia, the foggy coasts of Norway and the warm seas of the East Indies. Sirens are beings of foam and fantasy, insubstantial as the play of moonlight across the surface of a pool, born of the desires of simple river-folk and ancient sailors. But they have also been subject to scientific scrutiny, carefully documented alongside other fauna by learned men. They are the disembodied demons of dark watery depths, nightclub performers of the modern city, celluloid angels, zoological finds, carved capitals, consorts of Chinese sky-gods, and the frame for the strings of an Irish harp. Spirit-being or knowing body, they seem to be everywhere and nowhere at once, dwelling in the liminal spaces between earth, sea, and sky, between life and death, between imagination and the senses. One of the few qualities that draws them together is their music, the subject of this book.

The impetus for this collection of essays came, like the siren and her kin, from multiple places and traditions. In July 1998, two British music-scholars, one a historian of Western music and the other an ethnomusicologist, organized an international symposium on "Knowledge, Seduction and Danger: Music and the Sirens" at Darwin College, Cambridge. Several of the present essays were born from this conference. Some time later, an ocean and a half-continent away from Cambridge, another contrasting pair of scholars began a dialogue about culturally divergent aerial and aquatic musical beings who shared a surprising number of traits and who, in turn, inspired an astonishing array of narrative and visual representations.

In this interdisciplinary and cross-cultural collection, the term "siren" has several specific meanings. It indicates a particular mythological or folkloric figure whose name, in various languages, is drawn from the ancient Greek term *siren,* such as the Russian *sirin,* the Italian *sirena,* and the Andean *sirinu.* The term also incorporates a range of archetypal beings dwelling in or near water, at once human-like and inhuman, recognized by different names in contrasting ethnic traditions, myths, folk legends, and rituals. Furthermore, as portrayed in this book, the siren is a human being whose particular musical abilities have led her to be referred to as one of these creatures, or who has chosen to usurp such a title or the behavioral signifiers that would mark her as one. Naiad or nixie, mermaid or merrow, undine or Lorelei or *mami wata,* she has many names and many homes across human time and geography. Her alluring vocal powers and other distinctive traits have been borrowed by nightclub singers and MTV stars many years and half-a-world apart.

Sirens appear here in a number of guises as well as in varied forms and with many names: artifacts of living hybrid aquatic-human creatures, images in oral and literary narrative, specific individuals referred to as sirens, or works of music or the visual arts that pay homage to any or all of these. Virtually all human cultures seem to have invented myths or tales of enchantment that involve fairy-like stories of water-beings, or at least the cosmic love between some water-woman and an earthly or celestial man.[1] The existence of "real" or biological sirens has often seemed as plausible as the existence of a spirit world or the peoples and traditions of unfamiliar cultures, as real as any other creature from air, land, or sea. Scholars, adventurers, and entrepreneurs have sought traces of the siren and her kin not only through myth and folklore but also in the realm of the natural and human sciences. The salty blood beneath our skin and the manner of our conception and gestation indicate the ancient aquatic origin of our species and all of earthly life. Although never widely accepted, a mid-twentieth-century theory of evolution even suggested that our more immediate predecessors—to whom we owe our smooth skin, strategically distributed layers of fat, and "emotional" salty tears—had returned from land to water before giving rise to us. The human ability to speak and thus to sing was particularly connected to this aquatic hypothesis, as if some siren-like being could have been our foremother, some missing link in our evolution.[2] Siren figures from myth and folklore stare at us to this day from gallery walls, popular films, mass-market art-books, children's toys, and even mass advertising. They sing on compact discs and in film and music video, as explored by several contrasting essays in this volume. Widespread fascination with the idea of living sirens also continues to the present day; fake mermaids still materialize in major museums and collections, where they stare mutely back at viewers along with stuffed ibises and empty nautilus shells.[3] Modern science has silenced the siren even more effectively than Franz Kafka's famous retelling of the adventure of Odysseus, which several of our authors mention in differing contexts.

More than any other quality, it is the siren's music that positions her in the flowing spaces between the human, animal, and spirit worlds, between past and present, danger and delight. These spaces are the substance of myth and the arts, severed from Western-style science by the "Scientific Revolution" of the seventeenth century, and even more so since the "Age of Enlightenment" a century later. The song of the siren belongs to the threshold between time and eternity, the plane of reference for the metaphors of myth.[4]

From the seaside meadow-dwellers of Homeric epic to the mechanical cry of the emergency vehicle across the modern landscape, from the lochs of Scotland to the Amazon basin, sirens have been overwhelmingly associated with the acoustic world and the powers of sound. To consider the sirens is thus largely to consider cultural constructs of performance and audition, diverse links between sounding body and hearing body. Narrative and absolute musics from many cultures and for many sorts of performance have further envoiced even the otherwise most silent of those beings, as Henry John Drewal with Charles Gore and Michelle Kisliuk and Inna Naroditskaya show in their essay. However diffuse or improbable their bodies, with or without souls, the song of the sirens has often been the most memorable aspect and principal locus of their tremendous power. In the words of a global favorite of today, an English playwright from the age of colonial expansion:

> . . . once I sat upon a promontory
> And heard a mermaid on a dolphin's back
> Uttering such dulcet and harmonious breath

> That the rude sea grew civil at her song.
> And certain stars shot madly from their spheres
> To hear the sea-maid's music.[5]

The siren's acoustic power and its capacity to affect the external world span centuries and cultures, ultimately encompassing both genders. In some ethnic myths and legends, the mermaid and other siren-like figures (such as the Germanic nixie and the Andean *sirinu*) can adopt male or female form and seduce earthly women as well as men; the regional prototypes of the Russian *rusalka* are male-female couples.[6] The classical triton was the male equivalent of the water-nymph or the siren, with his loud military instrument the counterpart to her singing voice. But his was never the realm of seduction or death, enchantment or prophecy, between his mythic space and the human world. The positive, productive musical powers of legendary male figures, such as the mythic Orpheus or Arion and the biblical David, have been rendered strongly masculine by artists and exegetes, often set in opposition to the destructive powers and false promises of the sirens.[7] In the transition from folk tale to literary narrative and back again, siren prototypes were often gendered and their "natural" feminine qualities were reinforced. The most famous musical figures of this type are nearly always female; men who borrow the power of sirens' music to charm or corrupt may be labeled "effeminate," as in an English poem of 1600:

> Who with a mayden voice, and mincing pace,
> Quaint lookes, curl'd locks, perfumes and painted face,
> Base coward hart, and wanton soft array,
> Their manhood onely by their beard bewray,
> *Are* cleanly call'd, who likeliest greedy Goates
> Brothell from bed to bed; whose Syren notes
> Inchaunt chast *Susans*. . . .[8]

Coupled with the siren's aquatic habitat and her nebulous and often grotesque form, music has, for many peoples, specifically helped to position her within the domain of femininity. Water has long suggested bodily interiority to many peoples, the ebb and flow of female cycles, the realms of conception and birth, and male heterosexual satisfaction. In Western cultures, where the siren has most often been a dangerously seductive water-woman whose song envelops its listener in an open void, both space and the immaterial art of music have most often been conceived as feminine.[9] The woman musician becomes a siren, becomes sexually available, as discussed in contrasting ways by several of the essays in this collection; sometimes the body is imagined or imaginary, but the music is real. Where vision has often been associated with male privilege, hearing and vocality have been linked to women's interiority and invitation to comfort or seduction. The siren and her sisters may therefore be creatures whose vocal beauty obscures the perils and dangers of embodied union, serving as a metaphor against trusting the ear above the eye. One of the tensions presented throughout this book is between constructions of the siren that emphasize unity or disjunction between sight and hearing, and the concomitant danger of loss of self or utter dissolution for those who misread the "true" sensory signifier. The listener's body is as subject to disintegration as the performer's, if not more so.

Like many of the world's sirens and similar beings, those in this book may trace their primal ancestry, often removed by great distance and mutated many times, to the ancient Mediterranean. As Linda Phyllis Austern points out, the earliest sirens who have left traces in visual art and written reference are probably descended from pre-Olympian and Semitic aquatic deities of creation and destruction. These proto-sirens also gave rise to other progeny, such as the apocryphal Lilith, Adam's first wife, banished to the depths of the sea and forever wedded to the water; Venus, the sea-born classical goddess of love and desire; and even the biblical Eve, whose voice inveigled Adam and brought death to the world, and who is often visually merged with the serpent of sin in Christian iconography.[10] Leofranc Holford-Strevens shows that there was little agreement even among the earliest written descriptions as to the form and powers of the sirens, nor even on their numbers or parentage. His essay provides a catalogue of the classics, each describing a slightly different sort of being: the nameless and deadly sirens in their bone-strewn seaside meadow in Book XII of Homer's *Odyssey*, whose form is never given; the eight beneficent celestial dwellers of the myth of Er in Book X of Plato's *Republic*; Heraclites' siren with the body of a woman and the legs of a bird; Virgil's hybrid bird-maidens born of the Achelous River and the muse Calliope; Ovid's metamorphosed maidens, soaring above land and sea at the behest of the harvest-goddess; and the first fishtailed sirens of written description, dating from the eighth century CE. These are the creatures that most influenced later visual and written narratives, directly as in the case of the sixteenth- and seventeenth-century classically influenced works described by Stephen Buhler and Elena Laura Calogero, and less immediately as in the more distant hybrids discussed by Henry John Drewal (with Charles Gore and Michelle Kisliuk) and by Henry Stobart.

Like a siren's song, sung to each listener alone, or like the siren's hair—braided, bedecked with pearls and coral, curled or streaming, tied or loosened—literary and visual representations of this creature have been woven from mythology, sacred ritual, written traditions, and gossip. Neither the siren's body nor her music have been consistent, and her dwellings have varied as well; she lives above the earth or within the water as woman-bird, woman-fish, both, or neither. Sometimes she is a serpent, sometimes a woman-spirit, a fairy, or the whisper of a dream. Sometimes, as Stephen Buhler emphasizes, the poetry of praise or earthly fame is like a siren; or, as Thomasin LaMay and Robin Armstrong explain, a corporate record executive's promises to a rising star render him a siren. The siren, mermaid, *rusalka,* or their sisters in this book may drown sailors or dwell among suicides. Or they may sing eternal harmony and bestow everlasting life. The only constancy is a human-like voice. In some cases, up to three physical forms converged within the same body, feathered, finned, and female-faced; in others, assorted human hybrids with scales and/or wings formed small bands in which they were depicted as performing the contrasting musics of string, wind, and voice, which, to Europeans before the classification-obsessed eighteenth century, simply signified all musics. Their bodily form mattered far less than their diverse musical capacities:

> Then there were the Sirens . . . one of them sang, the second played a flute, and the third a harp. They made such melodious harmony that they enchanted poor admiring sailors, who were wrecked upon the rocks of Sicily. Ulysses, sailing that way, tied himself fast to the mast of his ship, & his crew put wax in their ears, so that the Sirens, deprived of their prey, threw themselves into the sea, where their lower bodies were changed into fish. But Servius thinks they were part bird, & not fish at all; this opinion is supported by Ovid and by Claudian. Boccaccio says that the sirens lived in pleasant fields with the bones of the dead scattered around them, but Xenophon writes that the Sirens sang the praises to people of conspicuous merit whose virtues had gained them universal approbation.[11]

The sirens have long been creatures of mystery and paradox, whose music has unusual power. They have sung and played instruments associated with men and with women, transgressing male territory to play instruments used exclusively in war or for masculine erotic or civic display, and reaffirming femininity on others linked to women's spaces and pursuits. In the Bolivian Andes, music may be traced originally to them. "They are by the Greeks called *Tractatoriae,* as by attracting and insinuating into the ears of man," says an early cataloguer of outstanding women of myth and history, who also explains that sirens sing and play winds and strings in a trio.[12] The improbable amalgamation of body parts or contrasting habitat often relates to far more than musical performance or uncertain narrative ancestry. Elena Laura Calogero contrasts heavenly and earthly sirens in a tradition that draws from the contrasting neo-Platonic and Homeric heritage. Naroditskaya shows how the water-spirit *rusalka* became more artistically significant than the bird-like *sirin* during the historical transition from the old landlocked *Rus* of the time before Peter the Great (1672–1725) to the great naval empire of Russia. John O'Connell observes that the ancient visual dichotomy between bird-like and fishtailed sirens was brought to relate to the geo-ethnic identities of terrestrial Turkey and maritime Greece in the twentieth century. In fact, with their ability to traverse disparate geographical areas and allure travelers, sirens and their sisters have often served as emblems of empire and dominion. Many sailing ships from the age of global exploration and colonialism bore the image of the sea-siren as their figurehead. *Rusalka*s entered the literary world at the end of the eighteenth century as inhabitants of lakes, rivers, and seas, becoming markers of territory and political expansion. In Germany, the birth of the literary Lorelei signifies the beginning of romanticism and the rise of nationalism. A woman with a fish tail, the Polish *syrenka*, carries a shield and raised sword on the Warsaw coat of arms, embodying Polish nationalism. The siren Parthenope serves a similar purpose for Naples, to which she also serves as mythic protector.

In the transition from oral to written narrative, or between various forms and styles of either, writers and other creative artists have continually modeled their sirens on others, combining physical and intentional elements at will. The siren therefore epitomizes hybridity, both in her physical body and in her role as the traversor of cultural, ethnic, and regional spaces. As early as the fourteenth century, narrative poet Geoffrey Chaucer drew together several layers of English folklore, French literary romance, Christian oral tradition, and ancient natural history in his brief reference to the paranatural birdsong which was "lyke to be / Songe of meremaydens of the see."[13] The African *mami wata* discussed by Drewal, Gore, and Kisliuk in the present collection is a particularly derivative figure, uniting such disparate influences as ancient indigenous African images of serpents and aquatic creatures, fourteenth- and fifteenth-century European mermaids, nineteenth-century German prints of snake charmers, and a plethora of twentieth-century visual images from prints of Hindu gods and goddesses to movie posters advertising the Walt Disney Company's *Splash*. Her music is no less hybrid, combining African music with various non-African styles of melody, rhythm, instrumentation, and performance. The *sirinu* of the Bolivian Andes are in some ways reminiscent to their Iberian counterparts but have clearly indigenous ancestry;

the same can be said of the Russian *sirin* and her Greek bird-bodied namesake. The literary Lorelei of the nineteenth century has German folkloric roots and American popular cultural descendents, as Annegret Fauser demonstrates. Even the most evidently consistent group of sirens, Buhler's seventeenth-century English literary ones, draw together several previous traditions. Many of the beings in these pages, often counterparts or adaptations of the multiply hybridized Greek sirens, can be deathly or angelic, Christian or pagan—or some paradoxical combination of all at once. Nonetheless, they share an essential feature—their powerful voices—which render them desirable objects for poets, visual artists, and musicians to describe or emulate.

Just as the siren has most often been female, until the twentieth century, when women reclaimed her image in unprecedented numbers, the artists who accomplished her transmission from the oral to the written realm were, for the most part, men. Describing her—with hair blue, green, or blond, with or without a tail, with skin smooth like milk or with fish scales, with a song like a mother's lullaby or a lover's ecstatic cry—translating her story, painting her image, and writing her song, the male artist acquired an often uneasy ownership of the siren and her various relations, especially during the nineteenth and twentieth centuries.

Fashioned into an innocent, lonely Lorelei, a soul-seeking Little Mermaid, or a morbid *rusalka,* the sirens of this book often provide their creators with as much angst as desire, offering dreams of virgin-whores to make the men who market or consume them feel intensely alive, aroused by sex, fear, and music. Across many cultures, the siren has been a sort of hallucinogenic stimulant that gives the sensitive man a feeling of fullness in life—by paradoxically killing him. A virtually undefeated seductress, she rarely completes her sexual act, and her promises are usually unfulfilled. For her lover, fulfillment would mean a loss of hope, the end of the road, everlasting depression, and the extinguishing of desire as well as his mortal body. But it is not the sweet pleasure of love that the siren bestows upon her men. An embodiment of man's deepest fantasies, the siren gives no sexual satisfaction without demanding his life in return. Does he die because sexual fulfillment would leave him no dreams, or because he realizes that his desire will never be fulfilled? "Suffice it to say that in those [siren] embraces I enjoyed both the highest forms of spiritual pleasure and that elemental one," says the narrator of one of the twentieth century's many siren stories, "felt by our lonely shepherds on the hills when they couple with their own goats."[14] No human woman's love can compare with the rich and unattainable paradox of siren-love. Acting as both sweet angelic bird and courtesan *femme fatale* in Calogero's essay, the siren personifies death. But, according to sixteenth- and seventeenth-century musical and literary conventions, death also signifies the completion of the sexual game. Austern further suggests that the siren brings together the child's primal desire to return to the womb and the man's drive toward sexual climax, unifying the incomprehensible vocalise of the lullaby and (female) orgasmic ecstasy. The siren epitomizes the love-death of romanticism, as Kramer and Naroditskaya show in these pages.

But an encounter with a siren is not always about sex. It may be about creativity, the dream, artistic transgression—or the nature of music itself. Buhler and Calogero emphasize that the (conventionally) erotic dimension of the siren legend is absent in Homer's ancient version. The hero of the Homeric *Odyssey* is, in fact, first told of the sirens by one of his female lovers, the mighty sorceress Circe, who turned many men to beasts. By that point in his narrative, he had already been seduced by a seaside musical enchantress, the semi-immortal Calypso, whose body he had enjoyed along with her song. By failing to fill his ears with "honey-sweet wax" as he instructs his men to do, it becomes clear that it is, in fact, the sirens' song he desires—a song that challenges man's sexual and creative potency. The song itself, and its poetic promise, embodies prophetic knowledge and the meaning of life and death. *She,* the song, may be the key to immortality and omniscience. But we don't know the original. Homer's epic gives us the words the sirens sang to Odysseus, once performed with music by a long-dead bard, and subsequently lost in the mists of oral transmission. The voice of Orpheus drowned the same song for Jason's Argonauts in Apollonius of Rhodes's tale of the latter hero. Victorious Odysseus, surviving his encounter with sirens, maintains silence about their music. Did he actually hear nothing? Perhaps the sirens did not bother to charm the self-restrained hero. Perhaps, tied to the symbolically explicit mast, he is metaphorically turned into a woman, "all ears," vulnerable to the penetration of seductive voices, as one twentieth-century scholar suggests.[15] Did he forget the song when he sailed to the land of the dead or upon his return to his faithful wife? Kramer registers the modern disappointment with Odysseus through the poets and philosophers of a skeptical era: Adorno and Horkheimer, Kafka and Nietzsche and Rilke, all men concerned with the power of sound and word, and with male usurpation of the creative process.

So sometimes there is no song as there is no siren. Sometimes there is a man, who, swimming in his dream, reinvents himself as a siren. Both Holford-Strevens and Buhler point out that Homer referred to the best male bard as an "ambrosial Siren"—perhaps the bard who could emulate the sirens' song in his performance of their promise to Odysseus before an enraptured audience. Spanish-American poet Rubén Darío (1867–1916), referred to as a siren many centuries later, writes:

> . . . fatal, cosmopolitan,
> universal, immense, unique, one
> and all; mysterious and erudite;
> she—sea and cloud, spume and wave—loves me.[16]

The poet, the composer, the painter, the visionary who (re)presents the song of the siren in his own terms usurps her power. He thus disarms her, and emerges victorious in what becomes a battle for the power of creativity, of artistic expression; her performance is not heard without his mediation. Reinventing themselves as the *truest* sirens, men, especially Romantic poets and musicians, recite, sing, and dance, dreaming of their own clean-sounding voices—not framed by beards and bulging muscles, but flowing from smoothly beautiful female bodies, half in the water and half in the sky. He—creator, critic, owner, and lover—is the siren himself. "The discourse one might call the poetry of transgression is also knowledge," writes Susan Sontag in a famous essay on the pornographic imagination. "He who transgresses not only breaks a rule. He goes somewhere that others are not; and he knows something that the others don't know."[17] Not every creator of siren-art is a man; nor are siren-powers usurped by men alone. Especially during the nineteenth and twentieth centuries, when Western men most made the siren their own creature, women came to re-claim her as their heritage. Women's re-appropriation of the male-created siren increased steadily throughout both centuries, perhaps as part of the global reclamation of femininity from male dominance and impersonation.[18] Those at the forefront of the political struggles for women's rights and women's equality particularly found inspiration in the sirens. In her heyday in 1870, suffragist Victoria Woodhull (1838–1927), called "the queen of the prostitutes" and paying "the pioneer's penalty of misrepresentation," borrowed siren imagery as old as the moralizing works discussed by Austern, Buhler, and Calogero. She adapted classic male siren rhetoric to herself and her ideals as she wrote in the *New York Evening Post*:

> The terrible syren has defeated you
> And charmed your cohorts and
> Battalions to silence and inacton.[19]

This same image of the Terrible Siren inspired the title to Sachs's biographical novel about Woodhull, who, born and bred in poverty in Homer, Ohio, ended her life as the "esteemed by the estimable" widow of a wealthy English banker.[20]

Almost exactly a century after Woodhull, during the heyday of the Women's Liberation Movement, assorted sketches of sirens appeared on newspapers and letters of the Women's Liberation Committee. And the powerfully feminine elemental creature loaned her name to a journal of "anarcho-feminism" which first appeared in Chicago in 1971. On the cover of the group's manifesto and its title issues was the image of an angry siren, her mouth wide, her song like the harpies' scream.[21]

Even more than their sisters in politics, women creative and performing artists of the late nineteenth and twentieth centuries learned to bring the siren to life. Among those directly referred to as a siren was the shining star Sarah Bernhardt (1844–1923), actor, singer, writer, and sculptor, who, driven by passion, seduced a whole generation and admitted that "her heart demands more excitement than anybody can give it." Like other sirens who mediated the spaces between differing elements, and the realms of the living and the dead, she traversed performance art and "real" life, and slept in a coffin.[22] O'Connell writes about another self-manufactured "daughter of the sea"—Deniz Kizi Eftalia Hanum of Turkey, who was able to adjust the mermaid imagery to her own aspiration and to the sociopolitical circumstances in Turkey at the fall of the Ottoman Empire and the formation of Ataturk's modern state. As Fauser reminds us, no less than the mid-twentieth-century American movie icon Marilyn Monroe became a siren, a lorelei, in one of her most famous roles.

Twentieth-century women musicians and lyricists of many sorts were especially adept at re-claiming the siren from their earlier male counterparts and making her their own. They not only sang as sirens but also invented their own words, notes, or sometimes both. Among the many woman composers of Western art-music who created works depicting sirens, mermaids, sea-fairies, and their ilk was the incomparable Lili Boulanger (1893–1918), who, on July 5, 1913, became the first woman to win the coveted *Prix de Rome* with a cantata for three-part chorus of mixed voices and soprano solo with piano accompaniment entitled "Les Sirènes."[23] Irish singer-songwriter Sinéad Lohan, who particularly "want[s] to express things that are very internal," rejects the external imposition of myth on the self in favor of "a reality that's more fantastic than fiction" in her 1998 hit "I Am No Mermaid."[24] Here, toying with convention in both ironic and emotive ways, she finds new means to evoke aquatic and passionate imagery in a free-spirited female voice. In a different but no less expressive medium, contemporary poet Amy Gerstler describes a siren as a self-portrait, teasing and ridiculing convention:

> I have a fish's tail, so I am not qualified to love you
> But I do. Pale as an August sky, pale as flour milled
> a thousand times, pale as the icebergs I have never seen,
> and twice as numb—my skin is such a contrast to the rough
> rocks I lie on.[25]

In their article for this book, LaMay and Armstrong introduce even more recent sirens who enamor and electrify the hordes willing to listen to their dangerous songs—Shania Twain, Mariah Carey, and Lil' Kim, each of whom mastered (and created) her own mythology based on the tales and musics of many sorts of siren.

This collection does not attempt to be comprehensive, but it includes glimpses of sirens from many cultures over thousands of years. It embraces the siren, Lorelei, mermaid, *rusalka, mami wata,* and other similar figures. The collection begins with the narratives of ancient Greece, and goes through such regions as Africa, Bolivia, and Turkey before ending with American film. Our sirens come from contrasting oral and written traditions from many languages and expressive media, but they are all capable of enchantment.

NOTES

1. For particularly good summaries of some of these, see Gabriele Bessler, *Von Nixen und Wasserfrauen* (Köln: DuMont Buchverlag, 1995); Gwen Benwell and Arthur Waugh, *Sea Enchantress: The Tale of the Mermaid and Her Kin* (London: Hutchinson and Co., 1961); Adeline Bulteau, *Les Sirènes* (Puiseau: Éditions Parades, 1995); Michel Bulteau, *Les filles des eaux* (Monaco: Éditions du Rocher, 1997); Francoise Morvan, *La douce vie des fées des eaux* (N.p.: Actes Sud, 1999); Géza Róheim, "The Song of the Sirens," *Psychiatric Quarterly* 22 (1948): 18–44; and John Vinycomb, *Fictitious and Symbolic Creatures in Art* (London: Chapman and Hall, 1906), 247. Simone de Beauvoir speaks about how sun and fire are generally male divinities, and she says that the sea, one of the most universal symbols of femininity and maternity, is often personified in creation legends as wife of the sun, *The Second Sex,* trans. and ed. H. M. Parshley (New York: Alfred A. Knopf, 1971), 144.

2. See Elaine Morgan *The Descent of Woman* (New York: Stein and Day, 1972), 91, 102–104.

3. See Jan Bondeson, *The Fejee Mermaid* (Ithaca, N.Y.: Cornell University

Press, 1999), 40–41 and 58–59; and Norman Douglas, *Siren Land* (London: Secker and Warburg, 1923), 3.

4. See Joseph Campbell, *The Inner Reaches of Outer Space: Metaphor as Myth and as Religion* (New York: Alfred van der Marck Editions, 1986), 69; Philip Kuberski, *The Persistence of Memory: Organism, Myth, Text* (Berkeley: University of California Press, 1992), 95; and George Lakoff and Mark Johnson, *Metaphors We Live By* (Chicago: University of Chicago Press, 1980), 40. Lawrence Kramer's essay in the present collection emphasizes that the nineteenth-century European siren reappeared in force after an Enlightenment banishment, which Austern shows was primarily due to the silence of scientific inquiry.

5. William Shakespeare, *A Midsummer Night's Dream*, Act II, scene 1, lines 149–54.

6. In addition to the essays in the present collection by Fauser, Naroditskaya, and Stobart, see W. L. Hanchant, "The Truth About Mermaids: A Warning to Sailors," *Lilliput* (March 1945): 215; and Róheim, "The Song of the Sirens," 19, 28, and 32–33. Linda J. Ivanits writes about the half-fish, half-man *vodianoi* (*voda*, water) and his lesser-known spouse *vodianikha*, and also about the *beregina* (*bereg*, shore), who at times appears with the *beregovoi*, all of them related to the *rusalka*; see Ivanits, *Russian Folk Belief* (Armonk, N.Y.: M. E. Sharp, 1989), 64–82. See also *Korinfskii Narodnaya Rus'* [Folk Russia] (1901; reprint ed., Moscow: Laborer, 1995), 44–55; and Róheim, "The Song of the Sirens," 19–20.

7. See, for example, Linda Phyllis Austern, "Love, Death and Ideas of Music in the English Renaissance," in *Love and Death in the Renaissance,* ed. Kenneth R. Bartlett, Konrad Eisenbichler, and Janice Liedl, Dovehouse Studies in Literature 3 (Ottawa: Dovehouse Editions, 1991), 29–30; and Pollard, "Muses and Sirens," 61.

8. Robert Allott, *Englands Parnassus: or the choysest Flowers of our Modern Poets* (London: N.L. C.B. and T.H., 1600), 180. The poem, entitled "Of Lovers," is attributed by the compiler to J. Sylvester.

9. See Sue Best, "Sexualizing Space," in Elizabeth Grosz and Elspeth Probyn, eds., *Sexy Bodies: The Strange Carnalities of Feminism* (London: Routledge, 1995), 181–85; and Luce Irigaray, *Speculum of the Other Woman,* trans. Gillian C. Gill (Ithaca, N.Y.: Cornell University Press, 1985), 239.

10. See H. David Brumble, *Classical Myths and Legends of the Middle Ages and Renaissance: A Dictionary of Allegorical Meanings* (Westport, Conn.: Greenwood Press, 1998), 339–40; Bulteau, *Les Filles des eaux,* 7–26 and 136–83; Silla Consoli, *La Candeur d'un monstre: essai psychoanalytique sur le mythe de la sirène* (Paris: Éditions du Centurion, 1980), 12–13; Louis Ginzberg, *The Legends of the Jews* (Baltimore: Johns Hopkins University Press, 1998), 5:147–48; Robert Graves and Raphael Patai, *Hebrew Myths: The Book of Genesis* (New York: Doubleday, 1964), 65–69; Buffie Johnson, *Lady of the Beasts: Ancient Images of the Goddess and Her Sacred Animals* (San Francisco: Harper and Row, 1988), 239–40; Meri Lao, *Sirens: Symbols of Seduction,* trans. John Oliphant of Rossie in collaboration with the author (Rochester, Vt.: Park Street Press, 1998), 10 and 57; John R. T. Pollard, "Muses and Sirens," *The Classical Review* n.s., 2, no. 12 (1952): 63; and Diane

Wolkstein and Samuel Noah Kramer, *Inanna: Queen of Heaven and Earth* (New York: Harper and Row, 1983), 8.

11. Edward Herbert, Lord Cherbury, *Pagan Religion,* ed. John Anthony Butler (Ottawa: Dovehouse Editions; and Binghamton, N.Y.: Medieval and Renaissance Texts and Studies, 1996), 177. For a more modern summation that says much the same thing, see Jorge Luis Borges with Margarita Guerrero, *The Book of Imaginary Beings,* revised, enlarged, and translated by Norman Thomas di Giovanni in collaboration with the author (New York: E. P. Dutton, 1970), 206.

12. Thomas Heywood, *Gynaikeion* (London: Adam Islip, 1624), 364–65.

13. Geoffrey Chaucer, *The Romaunt of the Rose* in *The Romaunt of the Rose and La Roman de la Rose: A Parallel-Text Edition,* ed. Ronald Sutherland (Berkeley: University of California Press, 1968), 14.

14. Giuseppe di Lampedusa, *Two Stories and a Memory,* trans. Archibald Colquhoun (London: Collins and Harvill Press, 1962), 101.

15. Thomas G. Pavel, "In Praise of the Ear (Gloss's Glosses)," in *The Female Body in Western Culture: Contemporary Perspectives,* ed. Susan Rubin Suleiman (Cambridge, Mass.: Harvard University Press, 1986), 48, n. 1.

16. As cited in Octavio Paz, *The Siren and the Seashell,* trans. Lisander Kemp (Austin: University of Texas Press, 1976), 39.

17. Susan Sontag, "The Pornographic Imagination," in *Styles of Radical Will* (New York: Farrar, Straus, and Giroux, 1969), 71.

18. For centuries, Japanese female actors and other women entertainers have studied the art of being a woman from *onnagatas,* the female impersonators in Kabuki theater and the *true* women. The Takarazuka Revue, existing since 1920, introduced an all-female troupe, starring an *okayaku* (male impersonator). See Ayako Kano, *Acting Like a Woman in Modern Japan: Theater, Gender, and Nationalism* (New York: Palgrave, 2001), 56 and 16–26; and Jennifer Ellen Robertson, *Takarazuka: Sexual Politics and Popular Culture in Modern Japan* (Berkeley: University of California Press, 1998).

19. The citation is credited by Victoria Woodhull Martin to William Cullen Bryant in *The New York Evening Post,* January 9, 1873.

20. See Emanie Louise Sachs, *The Terrible Siren: Victoria Woodhull (1828–1927)* (New York: Harper and Brothers, 1928), cover page. In Lois Beachy Underhill's biography, Woodhull is *The Woman Who Ran for President: The Many Lives of Victoria Woodhull* (Bridgehampton, N.Y.: Bridge Works Publications, 1995).

21. The two articles, "Anarcho-Feminist Manifesto" and "Blood of the Roses," first appeared in *Siren—A Journal of Anarcho-Feminism* 1, no. 1 (1971), and were later published as a pamphlet in Seattle and London (Seattle: Black Bear, 1977). Different sketches of sirens appear on newspapers and letters of the Women's Liberation Committee and on the cover page of the journal. Moreover, a siren conducts the correspondence, gives advice, and argues with readers.

22. Arthur Gold and Robert Fizdale, *Divine Sarah: A Life of Sarah Bernhardt* (New York: Albert A. Knopf, 1991), 171. For a photograph of Bernhardt sleeping in the coffin, see ibid., fig. 27 and also 115.

23. Lili Boulanger, "Les Sirènes" (New York: G. Schirmer, Inc., 1918, 1981; and Paris: Société Anonyme des Éditions Ricordi, 1919), written in 1911–1912 on a text by Charles Grandmougin. Boulanger was the first female winner, but fourth female to compete for, the coveted *Prix de Rome,* following Juliette Toutain, Hélène Fleury, and sister Nadia Boulanger, whose choral entry had been entitled "La Sirène," and who had previously set Grandmougin's poem "Les Sirènes" in 1905. Competitors each entered an instrumental fugue on a subject written by one of the jury members, and a choral piece setting a poem chosen by the jury just before each one received it, so the figure of the siren must have been on the minds of the judges just as women were starting to compete for the prize. For more information about the early entry of women into the competition, and the Boulanger sisters in particular, see Annegret Fauser, "La guerre en dentelles: Women and the Prix de Rome in French Cultural Politics," *Journal of the American Musicological Society* 51 (1998): 83–86 and 112–29; and Caroline Potter, "Nadia and Lili Boulanger: Sister Composers," *The Musical Quarterly* 83 (1999): 526–56.

24. www.sineadlohan.com/biography, accessed April 12, 2004; and Sinéad Lohan, *No Mermaid* (Los Angeles: Interscape Records, 1998).

25. Amy Gerstler, "Siren," in *The Extraordinary Tide: New Poetry by American Women,* ed. Susan Aizenberg and Erin Belieu (New York: Columbia University Press, 2001), 122.

ONE

Sirens in Antiquity and the Middle Ages

Leofranc Holford-Strevens

The first and still most famous manifestation of the Sirens in Greek literature is in the twelfth book of the *Odyssey*.[1] In lines 39–54, Circe warns Odysseus at his departure:

> First you will come to the Sirens, who beguile all mortals, any who comes their way. Whoso draws near in ignorance and hears the sound of the Sirens, him wife and innocent children shall not meet on his returning home, nor shall they have joy of him, but the Sirens beguile him with clear-voiced song, sitting in their meadow; but all about is a great heap of the bones of rotting men, and their hides waste away around them. But make speed past them, and knead honey-sweet wax and smear it over your comrades' ears, lest any should hear among the others; but if you yourself wish to hear, let them bind you in the swift ship hand and foot, upright at the foot of the mast, and let cords be attached to you, so that you may hear and enjoy the two Sirens' voice. But if you beseech your comrades and bid them release you, let them bind you then with all the more bonds.

Odysseus, forewarned against this and other perils, warns the sailors: "First, she bade us avoid the sound of the supernatural Sirens and the flowery meadow" (158–159). He repeats the instructions that he is to be tied up; soon the ship has reached "the two Sirens' island" with a fair wind behind her, "but thereupon the wind ceased and there was a windless calm, and a god lulled the waves" (167–169). The sailors get ready to row, but first Odysseus prepares the wax and applies it to their ears; in turn they tie him up before resuming the voyage.

> But when we were as far away as one who shouts may be heard, sailing with all speed, they did not overlook our swift-leaping ship as she rose up near them, but broke into clear song:
> "Come hither, much-praised Odysseus, great glory of the Achaeans, draw up your ship, that you may hear the voice of us two. For no one yet has passed this way in his black ship before hearing the honeyed voice from our mouths, but he goes home having rejoiced and knowing more. For we know all the things that in broad Troy the Argives and Trojans endured by the will of the gods; and we know all things that happen on the many-nurturing earth." (181–191)

Odysseus wished to hear them, but his crew rowed on; two of the men tied him up even tighter. Only when the Sirens were no longer audible did the sailors release him.

In the original Greek, the verses are markedly euphonious, and also close to the *Iliad* in diction, as if they were a blasphemy upon it, a sinister parody of the epic praise inspired by the all-knowing Muses that perpetuates the hero's memory; the Sirens also know, for they call Odysseus by his name, but they give only inglorious death in remote wastes of the sea.[2] The windless calm recalls the approach to Lamos (*Odyssey* 10.93–94), home of the cannibal Laestrygones, but even more sinisterly the departure from the Underworld, which must first be executed by rowing, and only afterwards with a fair breeze (11.640); that adventure, followed immediately by the voyage being narrated, is so fresh in the mind that the meadow on which the Sirens sit evokes the "asphodel mead" bestridden by Achilles' ghost (11.539). Unlike the island, the Sirens are not described; they are voices whose embodiment we must imagine for ourselves. This commends the proposed etymology of *Seirēn* from a West Semitic (Phoenician?) *šîr-ḥēn*, "bewitching song," parallel to Hebrew *'eben-ḥēn*, "magic stone, talisman, charm" (Prov. 17:8).[3]

From the seventh century BCE, Greek visual art presents us with human-headed birds known and sometimes labeled as Sirens;[4] Odysseus does not join them till the sixth, and at first they are not always female.[5] Unlike Homer's Sirens, which sit in a meadow, these Sirens fly through the air and perch on rocks. Their number varies: in Homer there are two,[6] and

Figure 1.1. Attic *stamnos* from Vulci, ca. 475–460 BCE. London, British Museum, 1843.11–3.31 [E 440]. © Copyright The British Museum.

paired Sirens are to be found on early vases,[7] but three soon appear. Likewise, a mythological poem of the sixth century BCE, the *Catalogue of Women* formerly ascribed to Hesiod, which reviewed the heroines of mythology, each with her parents, consorts, and offspring, seems to have recognized three Sirens—in another recension, four—who were daughters of the Aetolian river-god Achelous and the local heroine Sterope. Having offended Aphrodite by choosing to live as virgins, they grew wings and flew to an island in the Tyrrhene Sea called Anthemoessa ("Flowery"), where Zeus assigned them a home; as implicitly as in Homer, they had power to lay the winds.[8]

By the end of the century the Sirens have acquired human torsos, and with them arms that permit them to play musical instruments. When there are only two, one may have an *aulos* and the other a *kithara*,[9] which she plays in accompaniment to her own singing; when there are three, one may

[18]

sing, another play on the *aulos,* and the third on the *kithara.* This soon became the more favored number, for instance, on an Attic *stamnos* made circa 475–460 BCE and exported to Vulci in Italy (fig. 1.1),[10] on which two Sirens, one with spread wings and labeled Himeropa, "Of Delightful Speech," the other with folding wings and unnamed, perch on rocks astern and ahead of Odysseus's ship, while a third dives into the sea.[11]

Although their parentage varies from author to author, Achelous was their most frequent father;[12] their mother was usually not Sterope but one or other of the Muses.[13] This did not prevent their challenging the latter to a competition, allegedly at Hera's instigation:[14] the Muses won and humiliated them by plucking out their feathers to wear themselves;[15] alternatively (since sportsmanship in defeat was no more a Greek virtue than in victory), they themselves tore off their feathers and jumped into the sea off Aptara in Crete (now Palaíkastro), whose name was adjusted in literary sources to Aptera ("Featherless").[16] But in the more normal account, their suicide resulted from their failure to seduce Odysseus; on the Vulci vase one Siren is shown diving into the sea. Their pique fulfilled the fate decreed for them by an oracle, to die when a ship sailed by unscathed.[17]

Being associated with death,[18] Sirens were frequently represented on graves, and as such constituted a poetic commonplace, being made into mourners themselves: "Having lacerated ourselves in our weeping, we stand here on your tomb, stones in the image of Sirens"; "Gravestones and Sirens mine, and mournful urn."[19] They were even located in the Underworld, whence Euripides' Helen, in the play of that name (412 BCE), bids the "feathered maidens, virgin daughters of Earth, Sirens" come to join in her lamentations on their instruments.[20]

From the fifth century BCE a polite term, *Kēlēdones* ("Soothers"), is attested for beings indistinguishable from Sirens. Pindar (ca. 520–ca. 440 BCE) speaks of a previous temple at Delphi, buried in an earthquake brought on by divine wrath at the six golden Soothers above the pediment, who caused strangers to waste away "far from their children and consorts, hanging up their spirits (in dedication) to the voice that honeyed the mind";[21] Sophocles' grave was marked, according to a late-antique biography, "with a Siren, some say a bronze Soother."[22] The simplest explanation is that these are two names for the same thing; the Greeks understood the value of euphemism in dealing with superior powers.

Siren Land

Despite the claims of Aptera, and the prolonged scholarly debate whether Odysseus's wanderings took place in the Mediterranean, the Atlantic, or a purely imaginary world,[23] the location of the Sirens off the west coast of Italy became no less canonical than that of Scylla and Charybdis (his next ordeal after passing the Sirens) in the Straits of Messina.[24] Local patriotism found them several homes: some placed them at Cape Peloron (now Faro), others off Paestum. Complexity and refinement are (as usual) found in Apollonius Rhodius, who about the middle of the third century BCE composed a learned and sophisticated epic, the *Argonautica*, describing the voyage of Jason and companions in quest of the Golden Fleece, and their wanderings afterwards. That raised a problem: since their voyage had taken place in the generation preceding the Trojan War, what had happened when the Argo encountered the Sirens in the Tyrrhene Sea? Apollonius met the challenge by making Orpheus, a participant in the expedition, drown out the Sirens' song with one of his own, sung to the lyre; nevertheless, one of the company, called Boutes, leapt overboard and swam toward their island of Anthemoessa, but was rescued by Aphrodite and resettled in Lilybaeum (now Marsala) in Sicily.[25]

Apollonius's learned reader is expected to recall that Aphrodite was the foe of the Sirens, and that by Boutes she would bear a son, Eryx, who built her a great temple on the mountain of that name.[26] However, Boutes's leap also saved the Sirens from singing in vain, and hence from committing suicide as they did when frustrated by Odysseus.[27] The story was to be told at length in the Greek colonies of southern Italy (Magna Graecia)—where the Sirens were given the names Parthenope ("Maiden-Voiced"), Leukosia ("White"), and Ligeia ("Soprano"); some said they dwelt on islands called Seirenoussai (Li Galli),[28] others that Parthenope had been washed ashore and buried at Naples, Leukosia at or off Punta Licosa, and Ligeia at Terina, a city destroyed by Hannibal near Sant'Eufemia Lamezia.

The association of Parthenope with Naples proved enduring. In the late fifth century BCE an Athenian naval commander called Diotimus put in there, sacrificed to Parthenope in accordance with an oracle, and instituted an annual torch race in her honor;[29] in Roman times her tomb was pointed out to visitors, and Parthenope became a poetic name for the city, even being taken for the original appellation.[30] Modern Naples has remained proud of her Siren: in 1799 the rebels installed in power on French bayonets styled their régime the Repubblica Partenopea; one stretch of road beside the sea is known as the Lungomare Partenope.

Temptation

When, in a play written circa 425 BCE, Hermione blames her plan to murder her husband Neoptolemus's concubine Andromache on female visitors who had encouraged her not to put up with her rival's presence, Euripides makes her confess: "And I, hearing these words of Sirens, was swept off my feet by folly."[31] Siren words are temptations that ought to have been resisted. Likewise Aeschines, in a political prosecution of 330 BCE, claims to have heard that his enemy Demosthenes will liken him to the Sirens for his flowing eloquence that brings harm upon his hearers.[32] The theme is taken up by Latin writers. Horace (65–68 BCE) speaks of "the evil Siren Laziness";[33] the miscellanist Aulus Gellius (ca. 180 CE), displaying the typically Roman suspicion of intellectualism, warns against excessive interest in propositional logic: "if you do not set a limit to it, there will be no common danger that like many others you too will grow old in those twists and turns of dialectic as if on the Sirens' rocks" (*Attic Nights* 16.8.7).

More generally, the Siren is the symbol of the false and the trivial,[34] sometimes contrasted with the truthful and serious Muses: Plutarch (early second century CE) makes his brother Lamprias conclude a dialogue on degenerate music by declaring that "whenever we fall among the Sirens, we must invoke the Muses and take refuge on the Helicon of the ancients"; Porphyry (d. ca. 305 CE) makes Pythagoras liken the pleasures of gluttony and venery to the "man-slaying songs" of the Sirens, but those of righteousness and justice to the harmony of the Muses; however, in Boethius (ca. 523 CE) Philosophy calls the poetical Muses "harlots of the stage" and "deadly sweet" Sirens, bidding them leave him to be cured and cared for by muses of her own.[35]

This theme is particularly congenial to writers with a message too austere for general taste. Seneca (d. 65 CE) urged Lucilius (the recipient of his morally instructive letters) to ignore Siren voices that would distract him from the pursuit of virtue;[36] Christians would make it their commonplace. At most the more enlightened spirits will allow that an Odysseus will derive some benefit from hearing the Sirens' song: Clement of Alexandria (150—after 210 CE), having in his *Protrepticus* likened the way of the world to the Sirens' island, heaped up with bones and corpses, on which a pretty little whore sings and takes delight in popular music, elsewhere writes that the good Christian teacher will use Greek learning insofar as it will assist his hearers: "However, they must in no way dwell on these things, but only on what is useful in them, so that, having taken it and made it their own, they may return home to the true philosophy."[37]

It is no surprise if Christians see in the Sirens the symbol of the world, the flesh, and the devil; more striking is the interpretation of Odysseus's mast as standing for Christ's Cross:

Therefore our ears are not to be closed, but opened, that Christ's voice may be heard; he that has received it will not fear shipwreck, and is not to be tied like Ulysses with bodily cords to the mast, but his soul is to be bound to the wood of the Cross with spiritual bonds lest he be moved by the enticements of sinful enjoyments and pervert the course of nature into the danger of delight.[38]

Sweet Music, Sweet Speech

Notwithstanding all this, the deadliness of the Sirens' song was accidental, its sweetness essential; there are numerous mentions that are neutral or even favorable. In the seventh century BCE, Alcman seems to have equated them with the Muses, at one place calling them goddesses, at another writing "The Muse has spoken, the clear-voiced Siren."[39] A chorus in Euripides (d. 407/6 BCE) sings: "Golden wings have I on my back, and I have put on the Sirens' feathered shoes; and I shall journey to the aether to the company of Zeus."[40] Xenophon recalls, or affects to recall, hearing Socrates (executed 399 BCE) liken the means for gaining a friend to the Sirens' invitations, always matched to their hearer, and contrast them with the violence of the sea-monster Scylla.[41] The Neapolitan poet Statius, writing circa 90 CE, by agreeable exaggeration makes the Siren leave her nearby rocks for the superior songs of Pollius Felix;[42] for Christodorus of Egyptian Thebes (ca. 500 CE) "Siren" and "Muse" are synonymous.[43]

By extension, a persuasive speaker or a first-class poet could be called a Siren. The lyric poet Simonides of Ceos reportedly so described the Athenian strong man Peisistratus (d. 527 BCE);[44] his continued service to the family suggests that this was a compliment. The Siren on the tomb of the orator Isocrates (437–338 BCE) was reinterpreted as a tribute to his eloquence.[45] In the mid-first century BCE the Roman critic C. Valerius Cato was called in a famous epigram *Cato grammaticus, Latina Siren;*[46] later Greek writers use the noun of Homer, Bacchylides, and Menander.[47] When the same Aulus Gellius who likens logic to the Sirens' rocks declares that he had never visited the great orator and stylist Fronto without coming away better educated and more learned, it is hard not to think of the Sirens' promise.[48]

The Platonic Sirens

In the myth of Er (a report from the afterlife) that closes Plato's *Republic* (first half of fourth century BCE), round the spindle of Necessity there revolve eight concentric whorls representing the fixed stars and the planets; "and (he reported) that on top of each of its rings stood a Siren, who was borne along with it, singing a single sound, a single note; but from all eight of them there sounded in concord a single harmony."[49] The puzzlement to which this passage gave rise may be seen in Plutarch, when the *Republic* is brought into a debate on the number of the Muses. One speaker notes that Plato assigns the eight spheres to Sirens, not Muses; another is surprised at his bestowing "the eternal and divine revolutions" on the malevolent Sirens; but Plutarch's teacher Ammonius, having canvassed the notion that the music of Homer's Sirens imparted to departed souls a love of the heavenly world, from which a faint echo reached us on earth that only the more refined soul perceived, prefers to make Plato call the Muses Sirens as uttering (*eirousas*) things divine in Homer,[50] the ninth Muse being assigned to the earth.

However, this is not Plato's only reference to the Sirens: his Socrates bids Phaedrus talk on over the chatter of the cicadas, "sailing past them as if they were Sirens, unbeguiled," that the admiring insects may report favorably on them to the Muses;[51] elsewhere he, like Euripides, speaks of Sirens in the underworld, which they are unwilling to leave, so charmed are even they by Pluto's conversation.[52] In order to harmonize these passages, Proclus (d. 485 CE) posited three kinds of Sirens: those in the *Republic* are heavenly Sirens in the realm of Zeus, souls living the intellectual life, whose rational activities, simple and all of a piece, are not compelled to infer and guess like ours in order to know reality; the Homeric Sirens, in the realm of Poseidon, are generative beings; and those in Hades effect purgation. Nevertheless, all three kinds attune only the body, whereas the Muses attune the mind; therefore the Muses have the beating of the Sirens, and deprive them of their feathers.[53]

Such subtleties were not for all; some expositors simply devised etymologies equating the Sirens with stars, namely the planets, either as blazing bright or as generating music with their motions;[54] Macrobius (fl. 430 CE) assured the Latin Middle Ages that "Siren" was Greek for "singing to God."[55] From this it was easy to develop the angelic Siren who underlies Petrarch's description of Laura as "this Siren of heaven who alone is amongst us,"[56] who holds him back from dying; the notion is perpetuated in the Christian Neoplatonism of Milton's "At a Solemn Music."

Explanations and Rationalizations

Apollonius's Sirens had been companions of Persephone before she was abducted by Hades; in Ovid, having searched diligently for her by land, they persuade the gods to give them wings so that the sea too might be subject to their quest.[57] The mythography ascribed to "Hyginus," by contrast, made their metamorphosis a punishment for not helping her in time of need; it gave them hen's feet (because the older Greek word for "bird," like English "fowl," had been narrowed down to poultry), and reported the oracle already mentioned, that they should live for so long as no mortal heard their song and sailed by.[58]

Others tried different approaches. Some detected an allegory for magic;[59] but a rationalistic writer called Heraclitus, perhaps of the third century BCE, accounted for the Sirens as follows:

> Mythology gives them two natures, having the legs of birds and the bodies of women, and says that they wrecked those who sailed by. They were harlots outstanding in both instrumental music and sweetness of voice, very beautiful; those who approached them found their property eaten up. They were said to have birds' legs because they departed with speed from those who had lost their money.

Such reductive explanations of "what really happened" are especially associated with the perhaps contemporary author Palaephatus, who gave a similar account of the Sirens.[60] The story also found its way into Servius's commentary on Vergil, compiled soon after 400 CE:

> The Sirens, according to myth (secundum fabulam), were three part-maidens part-birds, daughters of the river Achelous and the muse Calliope. One of them sang, another played the double aulos, the other third the lyre;[61] at first they dwelt near Pelorum, later on Capri. Those whom they enticed by their music they led into shipwreck. But in fact (secundum ueritatem) they were harlots; it was because they reduced passers-by to beggary that the fiction arose of their causing shipwrecks. Ulysses, by scorning them, brought them to death.[62]

This account was repeated in similar words by Isidore of Seville (d. 636), Etymologiae 11.3.30–31, adding that they were said to have wings and claws because love flies and wounds, and were located in the sea because the waves had begotten Venus.

The "Tales from Ovid" (Narrationes fabularum Ovidianarum), compiled in the second/third century CE, combined Ovid's account with some details from Hyginus:

> The Sirens, daughters of Achelous and the muse Melpomene, having searched for the abducted Proserpina [the Latin name of Persephone] but been completely unable to find her, finally persuaded the gods to turn them into birds so that they could pursue the search for her not

only on land, but even by sea. Eventually they reached the rock of Mars,[63] which overhung the sea from close at hand. They were destined to remain invulnerable so long as their voices should not have been heard by mortals.[64] It so happened that Ulysses, on Circe's advice, passed them by; then they drowned themselves.[65]

In the late fifth century, Fulgentius brought his characteristic mixture of learning, error, and invention to the topic:

> Sirens mean "female hauliers" (*tractoriae*) in Greek, for the enticement of love is hauled in by three ways, song, sight, or habit. For some women are loved for the sweetness of their voice,[66] others for the charm of their appearance, others again have custom for their go-between. Ulysses' companions passed them by with blocked-up ears, he himself tied up. For Ulysses is called in Greek as it were *olonxenos*, that is "stranger of all"; and since wisdom is a stranger to all the things of the world, he was said to be very clever. Finally, as to the Sirens, that is the enticements of pleasures, he both saw them and heard them, that is knew them and judged them, and yet passed them by. Nevertheless, precisely because they were heard, they died, for in the wise man's sense every passion dies. They fly, because lovers' minds swiftly pervade each other's breast?;[67] they have hens' feet because the passion of lust scatters everything it has; and lastly they were called Sirens because *syrein* is the Greek for "to haul."[68]

Biblical Sirens

There are seven verses in the Greek version of the Old Testament (the Septuagint, abbreviated LXX) where reference is made to Sirens. One from 4 Maccabees 15:21, "Neither the melodies of Sirens nor the songs of swans attract the attention of their hearers as did the voices of the children in torture calling to their mother" (RSV), is unproblematic, for this book was composed in a high literary Greek; but the other six all occur in translations from the Hebrew, and all in contexts of desolation. Isaiah's prophecy on the fall of Babylon includes the prediction that foul creatures shall inhabit her walls (13:21–22); but what these creatures are is by no means clear. In third place are *bənôt ya'ănāh*, "daughters of *ya'ănāh*," most commonly taken to mean "ostriches," but in LXX rendered "sirens" here and at Jeremiah 27:39 (corresponding to 60:27 in Hebrew, Latin, and English Bibles) and Micah 1:8 ("daughters of sirens").[69] At Job 30:29, Isaiah 34:13, 43:20 the sirens correspond to Hebrew *tannîm*, "jackals"; these are coupled with *bənôt ya'ănāh*, which now in LXX become ostriches. St. Jerome, in the Vulgate, turned the *tannîm* into snakes (*dra-*

cones) and the *bənôt ya'ănāh* once again into ostriches (*strutiones*); but at Isaiah 13:22, where LXX had taken *tannîm* for hedgehogs, he followed later Greek translators to write "et respondebunt ibi ululae in aedibus eius et sirenae in delubris uoluptatis," in Richard Challoner's revision of the Vulgate-based Douay version "And owls shall answer one another there, in the houses thereof, and sirens in the temples of pleasure."

Precisely what the translators had in mind when they spoke of sirens is hard to say; certain Church Fathers such as Eusebius and Ambrose (respectively of the early and late fourth century CE) invoked the mythical maidens,[70] but the first passage from Isaiah created an opportunity for the Physiologus or Naturalist, whose allegorical interpretations of almost entirely bogus phenomena were first recorded in the second century CE:

> Isaiah the prophet said that "demons and sirens and hedgehogs shall dance in Babylon." The Physiologus spoke of the sirens and hippocentaurs: "There are beasts in the sea called sirens; like the Muses they sing melodiously with their voices, and passing sailors, if they hear their singing, throw themselves into the sea and are lost. For half their bodies, down to the navel they have human form, but for the other half thereafter that of a goose; similarly hippocentaurs have one half of a human being, the other, from the breast downwards, of a horse."[71]

This work became extraordinarily popular, being revised and expanded at will and translated into numerous languages. In some manuscripts, on which the Latin adaptations were based, the goose becomes a more generalized flying creature, or the hippocentaurs become onocentaurs with the lower half of an ass;[72] however, all these mixed creatures symbolize persons in the Church who are outwardly pious but harbor heretical and godless thoughts with which they mislead the innocent. St. Jerome too associates sirens with heretics in his commentary on Micah:

> And they shall weep like the daughters of sirens, for sweet are the songs of the heretics, and with their pleasant voice they deceive the people. Nor can any pass by their singing, but he who has stopped his ear and as it were gone deaf.[73]

However, he understands his own sirens at Isaiah 13:22 as "either demons or some kind of monsters, or indeed great snakes (*dracones magnos*) that have crests and fly."[74] It may be these flying snakes that underlie Isidore's assertion: "In Arabia there are winged serpents called sirens that outrun horses but are also said to fly; so poisonous are they that death follows sooner on their bite than pain (*quorum tantum uirus est ut morsum ante mors insequatur quam dolor*)."[75]

The Latin *Physiologus,* which came into existence circa 600, survives in more than one recension:[76] short versions make the sirens shriek with loud or different voices and symbolize hypocrites or heretics,[77] but the best-known ("version B") is more expansive:

> Isaiah the prophet says: "Demons and sirens shall dance in Babylon, and hedgehogs and onocentaurs shall dwell in their houses." The Physiologus has set forth the nature of each as follows: Sirens (he says) are deadly animals that from head to navel have human form, but their end-part down to the feet has the shape of a flying creature (*volatilis*); and they sing a certain musical and very sweet song of melody;[78] so that through the sweetness of their voice they delight the ears of sailors from afar and draw them to themselves, and by the excessive sweetness of their long-drawn-out melody (*nimia suavitate modulationis prolixae*) they soothe their ears and senses and send them to sleep. Then, when they see them lulled into the deepest slumber, they attack them and tear their flesh apart, and thus by the persuasion of the voice[79] deceive the ignorant and unwise men and make them dead to themselves.
>
> Thus then are they too deceived who take pleasure in the delights of this world and its pomps and shows (*pompis et theatralibus voluptatibus*), and undone and as it were weighed down by tragedies and diverse musical melodies, are lulled with sleep and made the prey of their enemies.[80]

There follows a description of onocentaurs, to which in many manuscripts is appended Isidore's accounts of these creatures; such composite texts are known as bestiaries.

The Medieval Siren

Familiar as it was with Isidore and the Physiologus, the medieval West also had sources of information about the classical Sirens in late-antique summaries of learning. The process of transmission and adaptation may be studied in the three so-called Vatican Mythographers. The First, who according to his latest editor wrote "environ entre 875 et 1075," devotes two chapters to the Sirens; the first (1.42) follows Servius, the second (2.84) the *Narrationes fabularum Ovidianarum,* but omitting the absurd negative that condemned them to sing unheard.[81] The Second, in the late eleventh century, combined these accounts, in reverse order, with matter from Fulgentius; he also states that the Sirens ate their victims, and describes Ulysses' ruse for avoiding them in greater detail.[82] The Third—the mid-twelfth-century canon of St. Paul's, Master Alberic of London—presents a similar blend, but moralizes Ulysses's precaution as follows:

The wise man stops up the ears of his dependants, less they hear [the Sirens'] melodies, that is he instructs them with salutary teachings, lest they become entangled in secular delights. But he himself passes by bound to the mast, that is, supported by virtue, although he feels the enticements of the mutable world, yet he despises them and makes course for his fatherland of eternal bliss.[83]

All this was small potatoes beside the Greek learning of Alberic's contemporary, the Homeric commentator Eustathius, metropolitan of Thessalonica, who finds in the "honey-sweet wax" that Odysseus infuses into his sailors' ears an allegory for philosophical teaching; the philosopher himself will give heed to the Sirens' song, that is, "histories, ancient tales, literary compositions, collections of myths, especially if philosophically presented, then gather what is useful from them and blend their beauty into his own writings, and thus become a kind of inspired Siren himself; the great sages had done likewise. The complete philosopher will combine speculation (by listening to them) with action (by sailing on). Eustathius then offers alternative treatments:

> Others, more concerned with a factual basis, supposed that the Sirens were lyre-playing harlots who deprived passers-by of their travel goods; they did not kill them (that being a mythical exaggeration) but rendered them poor and thus made them come to grief. Others say they were places that emitted a continuous stream of air from the ground; auloi, placed next to them by the locals, produced a melody that attracted passers-by, astonished them, and made them stay, though the myth exaggerates in saying that their provisions ran out and they died.

He goes on to speak of the pleasant sound of waves beating on the shore, or hollow cliffs.[84]

As in antiquity, not all references are pejorative. In the thirteenth century, Guillaume de Lorris declares that birdsong at the castle of Deduit resembled that of the Sirens of the sea, so called from their pure and serene voices;[85] Gottfried von Straßburg, praising Îsôt (Isolde), writes, "To whom may I compare the beautiful and blessed lady but to one of the Sirens, who with the magnet-stone draw ships to themselves?"[86] Again as in antiquity, the same writer may take different views: thus, in the fourteenth century, Dante, who twice represents the Sirens as temptresses,[87] and even makes the dream-siren of *Purgatorio* XIX mendaciously claim to have diverted Ulysses from his course,[88] in *Paradiso* considers only the beauty of their singing, comparable with that of the Muses but yet no match for that of the heavenly trumpets which surpasses it as much as primary light surpasses reflected;[89] Petrarch, who as we have seen makes Laura a heavenly Siren in a sonnet, in a canzone confesses that he should have closed his ears to the Sirens' call—though he is not ready to repent.[90]

In the late fifteenth century, Johannes Tinctoris, long resident in Naples, calls the city Parthenope[91] at the close of a work in whose prologue he had implicitly likened the polyphony of his great contemporaries to the song of the Sirens.[92] His interest in Sirens is confirmed by a disquisition in *De inventione et usu musicae*,[93] even though he piously cites Jerome's exhortation, at the end of his prologue to Joshua, to sail past them on the way to our heavenly fatherland.

Tailpiece: Sirens and Mermaids

The marine creature with the upper parts of a woman and the tail of a fish is known from ancient art, and called a tritoness; sporadic conflation with Sirens is attested. On a bowl of the third century BCE two such mermaids enclose a boat in which Odysseus is lashed to the mast;[94] a tritoness plays the lyre on a lamp from Volubilis (near Moulay Idriss in Morocco) dated to the second century CE.[95] But although the mermaids just mentioned are attractive and seductive like Sirens, not ferocious like Scylla, who had acquired a fishtail in classical art and two in Etruscan, nevertheless, yet Sirens and Scylla were neighbors, as the poetess Hedyle had remarked in the third century BCE,[96] both preyed upon sailors, and they may appear together in the visual arts as in literature.[97] They could even be made to collaborate for this purpose: Jerome observed that the sirens found in other translations at Isaiah 43:20, where he preferred snakes, were "monstrous beasts (*animalia portentosa*) that by their sweet and deadly song hurled sailors to be torn apart by Scylla's hounds; and this means that those who were previously given over to pleasure and luxury are converted to the service of the Lord."[98]

Nevertheless, it is not until the *Liber monstrorum* of the early eighth century, composed in the circle of Aldhelm, that Sirens are given fishtails in writing:

> Sirens are sea-girls, who deceive sailors with the outstanding beauty of their appearance and the sweetness of their song, and are most like human beings from the head to the navel, with the body of a maiden, but have scaly fishes' tails, with which they always lurk in the sea.[99]

They thus resemble Scylla except in relying on deceit where she employs brute force;[100] they also serve the author as a similitude for his own

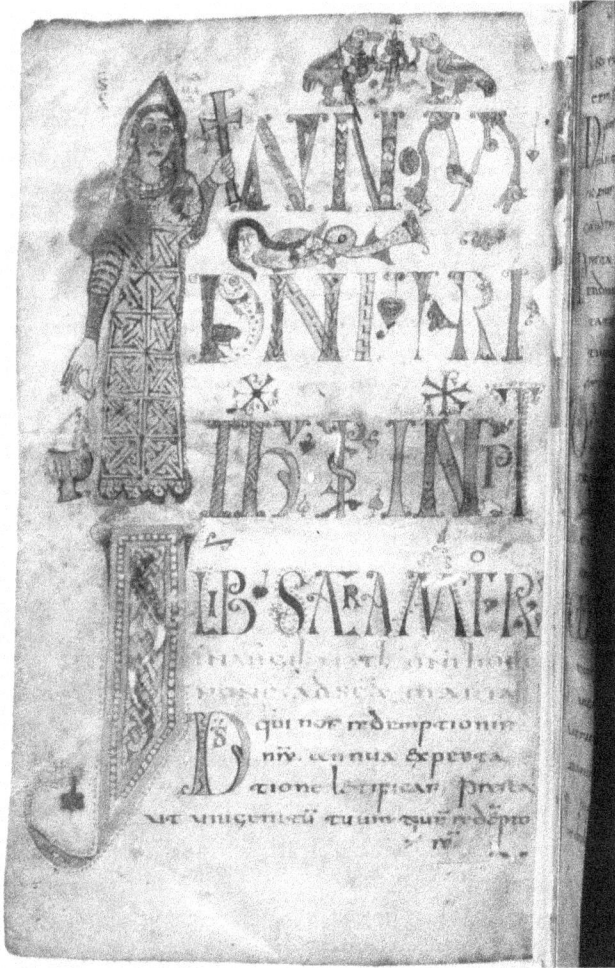

Figure 1.2. Gellone Sacramentary, ca. 780, diocese of Meaux.
Paris, Bibliothèque nationale de France, ms. lat. 12048, fol. 1v.
Cliché Bibliothèque nationale de France, Paris.

work, in which the rational element leads off, but "shaggy and scaly" stories follow (*hispidae squamosaeque sequuntur fabulae*).[101]

A creature of this type forms the titulus above the *nomen sacrum* DÑI in the Gellone Sacramentary, written in the diocese of Meaux circa 780 (fig. 1.2).[102] Not far distant in time are the "Corpus Glosses" of Cambridge, Corpus Christi College, MS 144, in which Latin words are translated into the Mercian dialect of Old English;[103] one entry runs "sirina meremenin."[104] Until the thirteenth century the latter word, meaning

Figure 1.3. Bestiary,
Oxford, s. xiiex, England.
Oxford, Bodleian Library,
MS Bodley 602, fol. 10r.
By permission of the
Bodleian Library,
University of Oxford.

"sea-wench," was the regular equivalent of Late Latin *sirena* and Old French *seraine*, in some instances clearly denoting the fishtailed creature that since Chaucer we have called a mermaid,[105] but evoking beliefs and traditions independent of either classical or patristic writers that in Western Europe would bring about the triumph of fish over bird.[106] From the twelfth century onwards the two were in conflict; the fish scored an early victory in the biblical commentary known as the *Glossa ordinaria* at Isaiah 13:22, in which the marginal gloss offered a choice of Jerome's flying serpents and "sea-fish in woman's shape, or monsters of the Devil that deceive folk with sweet singing if they do not pass by the shipwreck of this world with closed ears" (the interlinear gloss has "who lead their hearers to death"). The objection raised by Nicholas of Lyra (early fourteenth century) that even if such fish existed, they lived in the sea and not ruined cities, had not troubled those who introduced the mermaid into the Latin *Physiologus* and the bestiaries thence derived: while in Oxford, Bodleian Library, MS Bodley 602, fol. 10r, the Sirens are illustrated as bird-maids in accordance with the text (fig. 1.3),[107] in MS Bodley 764, fol. 74v, though the text still declares *volatilis habet figuram,* they are portrayed with

Figure 1.4. Bestiary, s.
xiiimed, France? Oxford,
Bodleian Library, MS
Bodley 764, fol. 74v. By
permission of the
Bodleian Library,
University of Oxford.

fishtails (fig. 1.4).[108] This appurtenance invades the treatise *De bestiis et
aliis rebus* by Hugh of St. Victor (d. 1142), whose account of sirens begins
by approximating the quotation from Isaiah to the Vulgate:

> Whereas Isaiah says of Babylon, "Sirens shall dwell in the temples of
> pleasure thereof," sirens are animals deadly to those who acquiesce (in
> their power) that as the Physiologus describes them have a woman's
> form above down to the navel, but their lower part down to the feet has
> the shape of a fish.

The rest of the Physiologus' account ensued; then come excerpts from
Servius and Isidore, but adapted to fishtails:

> They feign that there were three Sirens, part maids, part fishes, with
> the scales and tail of a fish, of whom one sang, another played the pipes,
> and the third the lyre; by the attractions of their music they caused
> careless sailors in those parts to run the risk of shipwreck. But in truth
> they were harlots who reduced passers-by to poverty, and were therefore
> said to shipwreck them; they are said to have had scales, and lived in the
> waves, because the waves gave birth to Venus.[109]

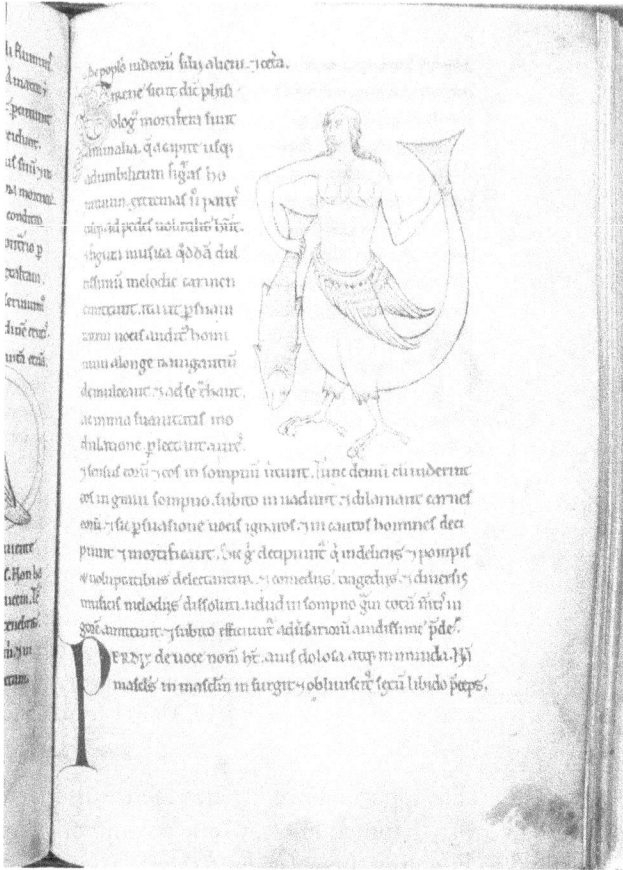

Figure 1.5. Bestiary, s. xiii, England. Cambridge University Library, MS Ii. 4. 26, fol. 39r. By permission of the Syndics of Cambridge University Library.

Similarly, whereas the versified Physiologus of Theobaldus (early eleventh century) makes the Siren a bird below,[110] some late manuscripts, and a related German version, change bird to fish,[111] as does the Middle English Physiologus, whose *mereman,* described under the heading *Natura sirene,* is "half man [= human being] & half fis [*sic*]," symbolizing hypocrites of pious speech and wicked action.[112]

At times bird-woman and fish-woman coexist, either within the same body or as two distinct species.[113] At Cambridge University Library, MS Ii. 4. 26, fol. 39r the text retains *volatilis,* but the illustration shows a hybrid Siren with wings hanging from her waist and bird-like feet, but an enormous fish-tail held in her left hand and a whole fish dangling from her right (fig. 1.5).[114]

[33]

Figure 1.6. Brunetto Latini, *Li livres dou tresor,* s. xiv, France. London, British Library, MS Yates Thompson 19, fol. 50v. By permission of the British Library.

Philippe de Thaün, in a bestiary dedicated to Queen Alice of England, since 1121 the second wife of Henry I, makes the Sirens women down to the girdle, with falcon's feet and a fish's tail.[115] In 1215 Gervase of Tilbury informed the emperor Otto IV that off the coast of Britain there were Sirens resembling women down to the navel, but fish beyond it, who lured sailors to shipwreck with their singing.[116] Thomas de Cantimpré, in the thirteenth century, also gave his Sirens a fish's tail, but an eagle's talons; unlike other writers, who emphasize the beauty of the female portion, he assigns them a hideous face and very long filthy hair. He also makes them suckle their young on their great breasts; when sailors see them they are sore afraid, but distract them by throwing them an empty jug to play with while the ship sails past.[117]

On the other hand, an expanded recension of Pierre le Picard's *Bestiaire* (originally written ca. 1200) divides the Sirens into three types (*manieres*): two half-women, half-fish, one half-woman, half-bird: and all three kinds make music (*chantent*), the ones on the trumpet, the others on harps, the third by singing (*en droite vois*); an illustration shows two mermaids in the sea, one singing, one playing a harp, and one bird-siren in the air playing a trumpet.[118] This accounts for the statement in some texts of Brunetto Latini's *Livres dou tresor* (which was written between 1260 and 1266), that Sirens "sont de iij manieres"; others simply say "sont iij." In any case, Brunetto not only blends Servius with Isidore, but fish with birds:

> Sirens, say the authors, are of three kinds: they had the semblance of a woman as far as the thighs [i.e., where the thighs would begin], but from that place downwards they had the semblance of a fish, and had wings and claws. The first sang marvelously with her mouth like the voice of a woman, the second with the sound of flute and canon, the third of a citole,[119] and by their sweet songs they brought death to ignorant sailors. But in truth, the sirens were three harlots who deceived

Figure 1.7. Brunetto Latini, *Li livres dou tresor*, Thérouanne, ca. 1310. St. Petersburg, National Library of Russia, MS Fr. F. v. III, 4, fol. 47r. Photograph: National Library of Russia.

all the passers-by and made them poor. The story says that they had wings and claws as a symbol of love, which flies and smites; and they dwelt in the water because lechery was made out of moisture.[120]

These three-natured Sirens posed a problem for artists called upon to illustrate them. In British Library, MS Yates Thompson 19, fol. 50v, the fishtails are unmistakable, and the shawm-playing siren in the middle has a fin besides, but the singing siren on the right has a wing and a bird's foot (fig. 1.6). By contrast, in a Thérouanne manuscript of circa 1310 the Sirens' nether parts are clearly avian; the rightmost, who has taken over the shawm so that her colleague can play the canon, has two wings (fig. 1.7).[121]

In the fourteenth century, Boccaccio summarized all the information on the Sirens that he had; confusedly citing Ovid and Alberic, he combines fishtails and hens' feet. His Greek informant Leontius Pilatus reckoned with four sirens, "Aglaosi, Telciepi, Pisonoi et Iligi,"[122] daughters of Achelous and Terpsichore, of whom the fourth played the drum and to whom Boccaccio added a fifth, Parthenope, whose tomb he knew from the elder Pliny to have bestowed her name on Naples. Leontius supposed them to commemorate the origin of prostitution in Aetolia; after a long

Figure 1.8. Book of Hours, France, ca. 1400. Oxford, Bodleian Library, MS Douce 62, fol. 51r. By permission of the Bodleian Library, University of Oxford.

allegorization on this theme, Boccaccio adduces Isaiah's prophecy, "Sirens and demons shall dance in Babylon," with the comment, "which perhaps we have seen happen in our own day in the new Babylon," meaning papal Avignon.[123] Some two centuries later political relevance was found in the classical Sirens by expositors who allegorized them as the flatterers who kept Italy divided by giving princes evil counsel.[124]

Gervase of Tilbury had singled out for mention the Sirens' gleaming long hair (*capillos lucidos et proceros*). Such hair requires grooming; as the Siren became more regularly equated with the mermaid familiar from folk tradition and heraldry, she exchanged her musical instrument (though not her lovely voice) for comb and glass (fig. 1.8).[125] The bird-maiden fought back: in the margin of a late-thirteenth-century psalter from Artois, a Siren with the feet and tail of a bird (but no visible wings) holds up a mirror and combs her abundant hair (fig. 1.9);[126] but in the long term not even Renaissance learning could restore her in Romance-speaking countries, where *sirène* or *sirena* remained the standard word for "mermaid."[127] A book of madrigals printed at Rome in 1533 under the title *Libro Primo de la Serena* displays not a bird-woman but a mermaid with a double fishtail;[128] single-tailed mermaids represent the siren in the emblem books of Alciato and Camerarius;[129] even the dictionary of Calepine,

Figure 1.9. Psalter, Artois, late s. xiii. Oxford, Bodleian Library, MS Douce 118, fol. 9r. By permission of the Bodleian Library, University of Oxford.

the standard Renaissance work of reference, continued to state through various revisions and expansions that sirens were maidens in countenance and down to the pubic region, but in the rest of the body fishes (*ore et pube tenus virgines, reliqua parte corporis pisces*).[130] In Parthenope's own city of Naples, it was a mermaid with two intertwining tails that the learned author, printer, and publisher Antonio Bulifon (1649–1707) used as his mark "a l'impresa de la Sirena" with the motto "Non sempre nuoce" (fig. 1.10).[131] But in England, although Spenser let Boccaccio's five mermaids contend with the Muses and entice sailors,[132] the confusion did not last: Spenser's frequent imitator William Browne of Tavistock, in his *Inner Temple Masque* presented on 13 January 1614/5, introduces "two *Syrens* as they are described by *Hyginus* and *Servius*, with their upper parts like women to the navell and the rest like a hen."[133] The social order has been restored: mermaids are for sailors, Sirens for scholars.

IL PENTAMERONE
Del Caualier
GIOVAN BATTISTA BASILE,
Ouero
LO CVNTO DE LI CVNTE
Trattenemiento de li Peccerille

DI GIAN ALESIO ABBATTVTIS.
Nouamente reſtampato, e co tutte
le zeremonie corrietto.

All'Illuſtriſſimo Sig. e Padron Oſſ.
IL SIGNOR
PIETRO EMILIO GVASCHI
Dottor delle leggi, e degniſſimo
Eletto del Popolo
Della Fedeliſſima Città di Napoli.

IN NAPOLI. Ad iſtanza di
ANTONIO BVLIFON Libraro
all'Inſegna della Sirena M. DC. LXXIV.

Con Licenʒa de' Superiori, e Priuilegio.

Figure 1.10. Title page, G. B. Basile, *Il pentamerone* (Naples: Antonio Bulifon, 1674). Oxford, Bodleian Library, Fic. 27423 f. 2. By permission of the Bodleian Library, University of Oxford.

NOTES

The Greek term for "siren" is *seirēn;* variant spellings show that the first vowel was a long close [e:] like German *eh* that by the Hellenistic period (and sporadically earlier) had become [i:] like German *ie.* In Latin the name was borrowed as *siren;* but the more popular gender-marked form *sirena* forced itself into the written language in the fourth century CE.

In accordance with modern scholarly practice in writing English, I use the Greek name Odysseus with reference to Greek literature, but in Latin contexts replace the classical *Ulixes* with the medieval *Ulysses* used (with stress on the second syllable) by poets from Golding to Pope.

All unacknowledged translations are my own.

1. This assumes the widely held belief that a poem capable of being considered "the same" as the *Odyssey* known to us was composed not much later than 700 BCE, though it may have taken some three generations to become widely diffused among the Greeks at large. For convenience I call its author "Homer," a name attached in archaic Greece to epic poetry in general; by the late fifth century BCE critical minds were restricting it to the *Iliad* and *Odyssey*. In modern times many use it either of the *Iliad* poet alone, or of no one.

2. The point is well made by Charles Segal, *Singers, Heroes, and Gods in the Odyssey* (Ithaca, N.Y.: Cornell University Press, 1994), 100–106; cf. Wolfgang Schadewaldt, *Von Homers Welt und Werk,* 4th ed. (Stuttgart: K. F. Koehler Verlag, 1965), 85. For what follows cf. Siegfried de Rachewiltz, *De Sirenibus: An Inquiry into Sirens from Homer to Shakespeare,* Harvard Dissertations in Comparative Literature (New York: Garland, 1987); Jacqueline Leclercq-Marx, *La Sirène dans la pensée et dans l'art de l'Antiquité et du Moyen Âge: Du mythe païen au symbole chrétien* (Brussels, 1997); other works found useful are Bernard Andreae, "L'immagine di Ulisse" in *Ulisse: il mito e la memoria,* ed. Bernard Andreae and Claudio Parisi Presicce (Rome: Progetti museali, 1996), 55–57, 141–47; G. C. Druce, "Some Abnormal and Composite Forms in English Church Architecture," *Architectural Journal* 72 (1915): 169–78; Georges Kastner, *Les Sirènes* (Paris: Brandus and Dufour, 1858) (a vast repertoire of comparative information, rounded off by a "grande symphonie dramatique" of his own composition, *Le Rêve d'Oswald,* words by Francis Maillan); *LIMC* [Lexicon Iconographicum Mythologiae Classicae, 8 vols., ed. Hans Christoph Ackermann and Jean-Robert Gisler (Zurich: Artemis, 1981–97)] 6/1/1:962–64, 6/2:632–51, 8/1:1093–1104, 8/2:734–44; Oxford Classical Dictionary, 3d ed., ed. Simon Hornblower and Anthony Spawforth (Oxford: Oxford University Press, 1996), 1413 (N. J. Richardson); Jane Davidson Reid, *The Oxford Guide to Classical Mythology in the Arts, 1300–1990s* (New York: Oxford University Press, 1993), 2:1004–1008.

3. Heinrich Lewy, *Die semitischen Fremdwörter im Griechischen* (Berlin: R. Gaertners Verlagsbuchhandlung, 1895; reprint, Hildesheim: G. Olms, 1970), 205; M. L. West, *The East Face of Helicon: West Asiatic Elements in Greek Poetry and Myth* (Oxford: Oxford University Press, 1997), 428. No plausible Greek etymology exists.

4. They are not always easy to distinguish from Harpies (Emily Vermeule, *Aspects of Death in Early Greek Art and Poetry,* Sather Classical Lectures 46 [Berkeley: University of California Press, 1979], 201–202); in Lycophron's riddling *Alexandra* (third century BCE, some say later) they are called "Harpy-kneed nightingales" (l.653). On their relation to the Homeric Sirens see the survey of opinions in John R. T. Pollard, *Seers, Shrines and Sirens: The Greek Religious Revolution in the Sixth Century B.C.,* Unwin University Books 21 (London: Unwin University Books 21, Allen and Unwin, 1965), 137–45.

5. Beards apart, note the masculine gender for the silver Siren dedicated to Hera at Samos ca. 580–570 BCE (*Supplementum Epigraphicum Graecum* 12:391).

6. This is indicated twice with the genitive dual *Seirēnoïn,* "of the two Sirens," once with *nōïterēn,* "of us two."

7. But also later: see Peter H. von Blanckenhagen and Christine Alexander, *The Augustan Villa at Boscotrecase,* Deutsches Archäologisches Institut Rom, Sonderschriften 8 (Mainz: P. von Zabern, 1990), pls. 38–41. There are birds that hunt in pairs: two vultures tear at Tityos' liver in *Odyssey* 11. 278, " 'twa corbies" or carrion-crows feast on the slain knight in a Scottish ballad (The Oxford Book of English Verse, 3d ed., ed. Christopher Ricks [Oxford: Oxford University Press, 1999], 295, #355).

8. R. Merkelbach and M. L. West, eds., *Fragmenta Hesiodea* (Oxford: Clarendon Press, 1967), frags. .##27–28 with apparatus. The three Sirens were called Thelxiope ("Beguiling of Speech") or Thelxinoe ("Beguiling the Mind"), Molpe ("Song"), and Aglaophonos ("Illustrious of Voice"), the four Aglaopheme ("Illustrious of Utterance"), Thelxiepeia ("Beguiling with Her Words"), Peisinoe ("Persuading the Mind"), and Ligeia ("Soprano"). It was the latter account that reached Boccaccio; cf. below at n. 113. Later writers took "Flowery" as the island's name, but it may have been meant as a description. See now Martina Hirschberger, *Gynaikōn Katalogos und Megalai Ēhoiai: Ein Kommentar zu den Fragmenten zweier hesiodeischer Epen. Beiträge zur Altertumskunde 198* (Munich and Leipzig: K. G. Saur, 2004); Hirschberger, *Gynaikōn Katalogos,* 229–31, on frag. #18.

9. The *aulos* is a wind instrument with a double reed; the plural is *auloi,* and in fact the performer generally plays two *auloi* simultaneously. The *kithara* is a stringed instrument (technically a box lyre) played with a plectrum.

10. A *stamnos* is a wide-mouthed, short-necked pot. Although Vulci is in modern Lazio, it pertains to the ancient Etruscan civilization, which avidly imported pottery from Athens.

11. British Museum 1843.11–3.31; *LIMC,* Odysseus no. 155. To be sure, some have suggested that the diving Siren is Himeropa over again.

12. But Sophocles (ca. 496–406 BCE), in a lost tragedy, makes Odysseus say: "I came to the Sirens, the daughters of Phorcys, the two that sing the lays of Hades" (*Tragicorum Graecorum fragmenta 4: Sophocles,* ed. Stefan Radt [Göttingen: Vandenhoeck & Ruprecht, 1977], TrGF 4, frag. #861); Phorcys, the Old Man of the Sea, was the father of the Gorgons and other monsters. Another writer, masquerading as Epimenides the Cretan seer, apparently made them daughters of Ocean and Earth: see Robert L. Fowler, *Early Greek Mythography,* 1 (Oxford: Oxford University Press, 2000), 1:96, frag. #8.

13. Terpsichore (e.g., Apollonius), Melpomene (e.g., Hyginus), or Calliope (e.g., Servius); but another story had them born of Earth from the blood that flowed when Heracles, wrestling the river-god as his rival in love, wrenched off one of his horns (e.g., Libanius, *Progymnasmata,* narratio 1 4).

14. Pausanias, *Description of Greece* 9.34.3: a statue at Coroneia by Pythodorus of Thebes showed Hera with Sirens in her hand; this was some five miles from Mount Libethrion, which was sacred to the Muses. The silver man / Siren of n. 5 was also dedicated to Hera.

SIRENS IN ANTIQUITY AND THE MIDDLE AGES

15. Tzetzes on Lycophron 653, ed. Scheer, 2:218 (Eduard Scheer, *Alexandra Lycophronis,* 2 vols. [Berlin: Weidmann, 1881, 1908]) (Terpsichore, their mother, refraining). The scene is illustrated (Terpsichore not refraining) on a marble sarcophagus of the second or third century CE, New York, Metropolitan Museum of Art, New York, 10.104, Rogers Fund 1910; see *LIMC* vii/2:219, pl. 219; Janetta Rebold Benton, *The Medieval Menagerie* (New York: Abbeville Press, 1992), 36–37, ill. 24.

16. Stephanus of Byzantium, ed. August Meineke, *Stephani Byzantii Eth-nicorum quae supersunt* (Berlin: G. Reimer, 1849; repr. Chicago: Ares Publishers, 1992), s.v. [in Greek] Aptera.

17. See, e.g., "Epimenides" (n. 12), and cf. below at n. 56. In consequence, Aeneas does not need to take precautions against them; on the other hand, without their calming influence the sea is rough (Virgil, *Aeneid,* 5.864–86).

18. See, e.g., Vermeule, *Aspects of Death,* 201–206; Pierre Courcelle, "Quel-ques symboles funéraires du néo-platonisme latin: Le vol de Dédale—Ulysse et les Sirènes," *Revue des études anciennes* 46 (1944): 6575–93 at 75–93. But it is no longer fashionable to believe with Weicker, *Der Seelenvogel* and "Seirenen," fol-lowed by Zwicker, "Sirenen," that they are descended from the Egyptian soul-bird or *ba* (cf. Vermeule, *Aspects of Death,* 69).

19. Respectively, *Palatine Anthology* 7.491.3–4 = *HE* 2641–42 (Mnasalces), 7.710.1 = *HE* 1781 (Erinna?), both probably third century BCE. They weep to-gether with halcyon birds in Werner Peek, *Griechische Vers-Inschriften I: Grab-Epigramme* (Berlin: Akademie-Verlag, 1954), no.1: 923, 11211. 3–5; Leon's or-phan child weeps like a Siren in Werner Peek, *Griechische Grabedichte, griechisch und deutsch,* Schriften und Quellen der alten Welt 7 (Berlin: Akademie-Verlag, 1960), 445, 11.11.2:17–18.

20. Lines 167–72; for "daughters of Earth" see n. 13. The transmitted text speaks of "the African lotos [i.e., aulos] or the panpipes or lyres," but meter requires that either the lyres or the panpipes be eliminated; preferably the former, since Helen's lament is called "lyreless" at l.1.1851. 185, and the plural is unex-pected for that instrument). See C. W. Willink, "The Parodos of Euripides' *Helen* (164–90)," *Classical Quarterly,* n.s. 40, no. 1 (1990): 77–99, 83–84, 87–88.

21. *Paean* B2. 109?–116?, ed. Rutherford, 211 with commentary 219–20 (Ian Rutherford, *Pindar's Paeans: A Reading of the Fragments with a Survey of the Genre* [Oxford: Oxford University Press, 2001]). A mere imitation of the Sirens, sniffs Pausanias, *Description of Greece* 10.5.12. "They made their hearers forget to eat in the same way as the Sirens," comments Athenaeus, *Deipnosophists* 7.290 E; the Sirens, again called nightingales (cf. n. 4), thus kill the Centaurs at Lycophron, *Alexandra* 670–72.

22. *Life of Sophocles* §15 (to be found in most editions of Sophocles).

23. Rehearsed at length in the first book of Strabo's *Geography.*

24. Hence the title of Douglas, *Siren Land.*

25. For the episode see Book 4, ll. 891–919. The story of Orpheus's victory had already been told by Herodorus of Heraclea (ca. 400 BCE): see Fowler, *Early*

Greek Mythography, 1:292 (Pherecydes of Athens, frag. 26). In the fourth century BCE a terracotta group from Taranto representing "Orpheus and two baffled-looking Sirens," see West, *The Orphic Poems,* 25, 32, and pl. 4 appears to have denoted the initiate's defeat of Death (see M. L. West, The Orphic Poems [Oxford: Clarendon Press, 1983], 25, 32, and pl. 4).

26. Now called Monte San Giuliano; the city on its summit regained the name of Erice in 1934. For Aphrodite's hostility to the Sirens, see n. 8.

27. Aphrodite's intervention was no more a slight to their powers than her rescue of Paris is a slight on Menelaus's prowess at *Iliad* 3. 373–82. By contrast, in the *Orphic Argonautica* of the fifth century CE the two Sirens, of whom one plays the *aulos,* the other sings to the *kithara,* on being defeated by Orpheus fling themselves into the sea and are turned to rocks (11.1264–90).

28. See, e.g., Pseudo-Aristotle, *De mirabilibus auditionibus* 103.

29. Timaeus (third century BCE), *Die Fragmente der griechischen Historiker,* ed. F. Jacoby (Berlin: Weidmannsche Buchhandlung, 1923– ; Leiden: E. J. Brill, 1957), no. 566 F 98; this was the Diotimus who was sent to Corcyra in the prelude to the Peloponnesian War (Thucydides 1.43.1).

30. Virgil, *Georgics* 4.563–64; Solinus (third century CE), *Collectanea* 2. 9, cf. the elder Pliny, *Natural History* 3. 62.

31. *Andromache* 936, 938 (l.937 is spurious).

32. *In Ctesiphontem* 228.

33. *Sermones* 2.3.14–15: "improba Siren Desidia." It is this Siren with whom Ulysses disputes in Samuel Daniel's poem (ca. 1611) "Ulisses and the Syren," *OBEV*³71–72, #81.

34. Observe Rabelais's parody of this theme, as well as of allegorical reading, in *Gargantua,* "Prologe [thus!] de l'auteur": "Et, posé le cas qu'au sens literal vous trouvez matieres assez joyeuses et bien correspondents au nom, toutesfois pas demourer là ne fault, comme au chant de Sirenes, ains a plus hault sens interpreter ce que par adventure cuidiez dict en gayeté de cueur" ("And, put the case that in the literal sense you find matters merry enough and well matching the name, all the same you should not stop there, as at the Sirens' song, but interpret in a higher sense what perhaps you think was said in gaiety of spirit").

35. Plutarch, *Symposiaca* 7.5.4, 706 D; Porphyry, *Vita Pythagorae* 39; Boethius, *De consolatione Philosophiae* 1, pr. 1. For the Sirens as harlots, see below.

36. *Epistulae morales* 31.2, 123.12.

37. *Protrepticus* 12.118.2; *Stromateis* 6.11.89.3.

38. Ambrose, *Expositio in evangelium secundum Lucam* 4.2; "bound to the Cross" already at Clement of Alexandria, *Protrepticus* 12.118.4. See in general Erich Kaiser, "Odyssee-Szenen als Topoi," *Museum Helveticum* 21 (1995): 109–36 (temptation), 132–36 (Odysseus's escape), and for Christian interpretations Hugo Rahner, *Griechische Mythen in christlicher Deutung,* 3d ed. (Zurich: Rhein-Verlag, 1957), 298–315.

39. PMGF Poetarum melicorum Graecorum fragmenta, ed. Malcolm Davies

(Oxford: Oxford University Press, 1991), frags. ##1, ll. 96–98 and 30, respectively. Ernst Buschor, *Die Musen des Jenseits* (Munich: F. Bruckmann, 1944), maintained that the Sirens were the Muses of the Other World, and not originally sinister; but see John R. T. Pollard, "Muses and Sirens," *The Classical Review* n.s. 2, no. 12 (1952): 60–63.

40. TGF Tragicorum Graecorum fragmenta 5: Euripides, ed. Richard Kannicht (Göttingen: Vandenhoeck & Ruprecht, 2005), Euripides, frag. #911 from an unknown play.

41. *Memorabilia* 2.6.12, 31; the extent to which these recollections are factual or fictitious cannot be determined. A comic chef boasts that the odors of his cooking attract passers-by as the Sirens did of old (Hegesippus, *PCG* [= Poetae comici Graeci, ed. Rudolf Kassel and Colin Austin, 8 vols. (Berlin: de Gruyter, 1983–2001)], frag. #1, 11.20–21).

42. *Silvae* 2.2.116–17.

43. *Palatine Anthology* 2.303–305 (Apuleius, who contemplated the secrets of the "Latin Muse," was nurtured by the "Ausonian Siren"), 350 ("Pierian Siren"). See in general Kaiser, "Odysee-Szenen," 113–21, cf. Kaster, *Suetonius,* 152–53.

44. *PMG*, #Poetae melici Graeci, ed. D. L. Page. Oxford: Clarendon Press, 1962), fr. 607. Peisistratus governed Athens for some twenty years; despite the illegal violence by which he came to power, Athens flourished under his rule, not least culturally. The city was governed by his sons for another sixteen years.

45. Philostratus, *Vitae sophistarum* 1.17.1.

46. Cited anonymously by Suetonius, *Gramm.* 11.1; commonly attributed to Furius Bibaculus, whose fragment 6 (but marked "dubium") it is Edward Courtney, *The Fragmentary Latin Poets* (Oxford: Oxford University Press, 1993), 195, but see Robert A. Kaster, *Suetonius: De grammaticis et rhetoribus* (Oxford: Oxford University Press, 1995), 152.

47. H. W. Parke and D. E. W. Wormell, *The Delphic Oracle* (Oxford: Basil Blackwell, 1956), 2:188, item #465; *Palatine Anthology;* 9.184. 1–2 = *FGE* Further Greek Epigrams, ed. D. L. Page (Cambridge: Cambridge University Press, 1981), 1194–96 (anon.); Luigi Moretti, *Inscriptiones Graecae urbis Romae* (Rome: Istituto italiano per la storia antica, 1968–90), no. #1526, l.6.

48. *Attic Nights* 19.8.1; the notion had been used ironically by Terence, *Eunuchus* 790–91, probably following Menander's *Flatterer.*

49. Book 10:617 B 4–7.

50. *Symposiaca* 9.4.6, 745 F; the verb is itself Homeric.

51. *Phaedrus* 259 A–D.

52. *Cratylus* 403 D 6–E 2.

53. See his commentaries on the *Republic,* ed. Kroll, 2:238.15–239.14, and *Cratylus,* ed. Pasquali, 88, para. CLVIII; cf. Robert Lamberton, *Homer the Theologian: Neoplatonist Allegorical Reading and the Growth of the Epic Tradition* (Berkeley: University of California Press, 1986), 230–32. Other ancient expositions are listed in Cherniss's note, 335–39, on Plutarch, *De generatione animae* 32, 1029 C–

D; Pythagorean origin (which might be guessed) is indicated by Iamblichus, *De vita Pythagorica*, 82. Zeus, Poseidon, and Hades were brother gods, who ruled respectively the sky, the sea, and the underworld, holding the earth in common.

54. Theon of Smyrna, *Expositio* 146.8–146.6 Hiller; cf. Philo Judaeus, *Quaest. in Gen.* 3.3.

55. *Commentum in Somnium Scipionis* 2.3.1; for the reading see Regali's commentary, 2:144.

56. "Questa sola fra noi del ciel sirena," *Rime in vita di Madonna Laura*, 167.14.

57. *Metamorphoses* 5.551–63 (beginning of first century CE).

58. *Fabulae* 125 ("Odyssea"), 13; 141 ("Sirenes"). The present form of this work probably belongs to the third or fourth century CE.

59. To the elder Pliny's scorn (*Natural History* 30.6; before 79 CE).

60. Eusebius, *Chronicle*, tr. Jerome, ed. Helm, 62, ll.24–26; on this explanation see Courcelle, "L'interprétation evhémériste [sic]" (but there is no evidence for ascribing it to Euhemerus). At about the same time, three ladies of the profession are described as "more malevolent than the Sirens" at *Palatine Anthology* 5.161. 6 = *HE* 1001 (Hedylus or Asclepiades); for an earlier comic use of the theme see Anaxilas, *PCG* 2, frag. #22, ll.20–21. The equation was transvalued in Nicolò Franco's letter "*a le puttane,*" declaring that courtesans are the true Sirens, drawing sailors with sweetness to their delights; evenUlysses's prudence recognized in the end that it was greater wisdom to let himself be defeated than to seek victory over people ("essere sapienza maggiore il farsi uincere, che uoler uincere si fatta gente"): Nicolò Franco, *Le pistole vulgari* (Venice: Antonio Gardane, 1542; repr. ed. Francesca Romana de' Angelis, "Libri di Lettere" del Cinquecento [Ferrara: Arnaldo Forni, 1986], no. *Pistole volgari,* #256, fol. 220v, kindly brought to my attention by Dr. Melanie Marshal.

61. "Harum una uoce, altera tibiis, alia lyra canebat": in Latin the same word means both "sing" and "play" (on an instrument). This usage is regular in the Latin and Old French texts cited below, but cannot be reproduced in English.

62. On *Aeneid* 5.864. The subsequent recension known as Deutero-Servius, which normally expands the original, has only slight verbal variants here. On the Siren as songstress-temptress see Elizabeth Eva Leach, "'The little pipe sings sweetly while the fowler deceives the bird': Sirens in the Later Middle Ages," *Music & Letters* (forthcoming).

63. Probably a corruption for "a rock in the (Sicilian) sea (*maris*)."

64. "quamdiu earum vox audita non esset mortalibus": a misunderstanding of Hyginus's Hyginus' "quam diu earum cantum mortalis audiens nemo praetervectus esset" (*Fabulae* 125.13; "so long as no mortal should have sailed past hearing their song").

65. Ed. Magnus, 656–57. On this work see Richard J. Tarrant, "The Narrationes of 'Lactantius' and the Transmission of Ovid's Metamorphoses," in *Formative Stages of Classical Traditions: Latin Texts from Antiquity to the Renaissance*, ed. Oronzo Pecere and Michael D. Reeve, 83–115, Biblioteca del "Centro per

ilcollegamento degli studi medievali e umanistici in Umbria" 15 (Spoleto: Centro italiano di studi sull'alto medioevo, 1995), 83–115.

66. The words are missing in the text, but something of the kind must have been said. Alan Cameron, *Greek Mythography in the Roman World*, American Philological Association, Classical Studies 48 (New York: Oxford University Press, 2004), esp. 14–24 for the date.

67. The text has "quia amantum mentes celeriter permeant": the overall structure precludes understanding *mentes* as accusative ("they swiftly pervade lovers' minds"), but if it is nominative, what is the object of *permeant*? The Second Vatican Mythographer (see below) changed it to *mutantur,* "are changed," Alberic to *pereunt,* "perish."

68. *Mitologiae* 2.8; see Fabii Planciadis Fulgentii V.C. opera, ed. Rudolf Helm (Leipzig: B. G. Teubner, 1898), 48–49.

69. Kaiser, "Odyssee-Szenen," 112 suggests a play on šā'îr, pl. š'îrîm "hairy one(s)," the fourth creature in Isa. 13: 21 and rendered "demon(s)" there and at 34:13.

70. Eusebius, *In Isaiam* 2. 25 on Isa. 49:19–21; cf. Ambrose, *Expositio psalmi XLIII,* 75.

71. Chap. 13, ed. Sbordone, 51–54, cf. chap. 13 bis, 54, where the hippocentaurs are male and the sirens female; other recensions ed. Dieter Offermanns, *Der Physiologus nach den Handschriften G und M.*, Beiträge zur klassischen Philologie 22 (Meisenheim am Glan: Hain, 1966), 58–59; ed. Dimitris Kaimakis, *Der Physiologus nach der ersten Redaktion,* Beiträge zur klassischen Philologie 63 (Meisenheim am Glan: Hain, 1974), 42. On the Physiologus complex see, besides the various editors, Perry, "Physiologus."

72. These appear in LXX at this point, representing *'iyyîm,* which are owls in Jerome; some interpreters take them for hyenas.

73. *In Michaeam* 1, on Micah 1:6–9.

74. *In Esaiam* 5, on Isa. 13:21–22.

75. *Etymologiae* 12.4.29. Note too the (masculine) *seirēn* for a bee- or wasp-like insect (Aristotle, *Natural History* 9. 40, 623a11–12), on which see Malcom Davies and Jeyaraney Kathirithamby, *Greek Insects* (London: Duckworth; New York: Oxford University Press, 1986), 73–75.

76. See Nikolaus Henkel, *Studien zum Physiologus im Mittelalter,* Hermaea, germanistische Forschungen, neue Folge 38 (Tübingen: Niemeyer, 1976), *Studien,* 25–42.

77. "Version Y," chap. 15, ed. Francis J. Carmody, "Physiologus Latinus Versio Y," University of California Publications in Classical Philology 12/7 (1941): 93–134 at 113–14 (*clamitantia uocibus altis*); *clamitant uocibus diuersis*: MS Bern, Burgerbibliothek 318, ed., Charles Cahier, "Le Physiologus ou Bestiaire," in *Mélanges d'archéologie, d'histoire et de littéerature,* ed. Charles Cahier and Arthur Martin, 4 vols. (Paris: Mme Vᶜ Poussielgue-Rusand, 1847–56), 2:173–74. Note that other scholars call this version A and use Y for the lost common source of A and B.

78. This unnatural English renders the no more natural Latin *dulcissimum melodiae carmen;* one would have expected *dulcissimae melodiae carmen,* "a song of very sweet melody," but the concord with *carmen* is firmly attested even when, as in some of the revisions to be studied below, the epithet is changed to *dulcisonum.*

79. Reading *per suasionem vocis* (cf. Carmody's apparatus) rather than, as edited, *persuasionis vocis,* "[ignorant of] the voice of persuasion"; other attempts at correction are *persuasionis voce,* "by the voice of persuasion," in the Cambridge MS considered below, *per suavis soni vocem* ("by their sweet-sounding voice") in Oxford, Bodleian Library, MS Laud Misc. 247 (s. xii), fol. 147ʳ (which also portrays a fishtailed siren).

80. Ed. Francis J. Carmody, *Physiologus Latinus*: Éditions préliminaires, versio B (Paris: E. Droz, 1939), ed. Carmody, 25–26, chap. 12.

81. Nevio Zorzetti, *Le Premier Mythographe du Vatican,* Association Guillaume Budé, Collection des Universités de France (Paris: Les Belles Lettres, 1995), xii, 27, 100–101 (needlessly restoring the negative).

82. Chap. 123, ed. Péter Kulcsár, *Mythographi Vaticani I et II,* Corpus Christianorum, Ser. Latina 91C (Turnhout: Brepols, 1987), 189–90.

83. Vat. Myth. III 11.9, ed. Bode, 233–34.

84. Ed. Gottfried Stallbaum, *Eustathii archiepiscopi Thessalonicensis commentarii ad Homeri Odysseam* (Leipzig: J. A. G. Weigel, 1825–26; reprint, Hildesheim: G. Olms, 1970), 2:3–5 (1707–1709).

85. "Tant estoit li chans dous et biaus / Qu'il ne sembloit pas chans d'oisiaus, / Ainz le peüst l'en aesmer / A chant de serainne de mer, / Qui por lor vois qu'elles ont sainnes / Et serines ont non seraines":Guillaume de Lorris et Jean de Meun, Le Roman de la Rose, ed. Daniel Poiron (Paris: Garmier-Flammarion, 1974), 59, ll. *Roman de la Rose,* in Geoffrey Chaucer, *The Romaunt of the Rose and La Roman de la Rose: A Parallel-Text Edition,* ed. Ronald Sutherland (Berkeley and Los Angeles: University of California Press, 1968), 669–74.

86. *Tristan* 8089–93; and see the whole passage down to 8135.

87. *Purgatorio* XXXI 45, *Epistulae* 5.13.

88. Ll. 22–3: "Io volsi Ulisse del suo cammin vago / Al canto mio"; there is no need to posit either a misreading of Cicero, *De finibus* 5.50 (in which the Sirens' song is translated into Latin, and the attraction of knowledge for great men considered) or a confusion of the Sirens with Circe and Calypso.

89. *Paradiso* XII 7–9: "canto che tanto vince nostre muse, / nostre serene in quelle dolci tube, / quanto primo splendor quel ch'e' refuse."

90. *Rime* 207, 81–84.

91. *Liber de arte contrapuncti* 3.9.9, ed. Albert Seay, Johannis Tinctoris opera theoretica, 2 vols. *Corpus Scriptorum de Musica* 22 (N.p.: American Institute of Musicology, 1975), ed. Seay 2:156–57: "dulcique Parthenope, qua se vatum lumen splendidissimum, Virgilius olim poetice studentem nutritum fuisse gloriatur."

92. See Leofranc Holford-Strevens, "Tinctoris on the Great Composers," *Plainsong and Medieval Music* 5, no. 2 (1996): 193–99. I can now confirm that, as

suggested there in n. 12, FranciscusAretinus's translation of *Od.* 12. 187–88 was that published by Übelin in 1510: "Nemo enim unquam hic iter fecit quin nostri cantus suauitate demulceretur: qua oblectatus et plura doctus a nobis dimittitur."

93. Karl Weinmann, *Johannes Tinctoris (1445–1511) und sein unbekannter Traktat "De inventione et usu musicae": Historisch-kritische Untersuchung,* rev. Wilhelm Fischer. (Tutzing: Hans Schneider, 1961), 30–31.

94. Athens, Agora, P. 18640; see Susan L. Rotroff, *Hellenistic Painted Pottery: Athenian and Imported Moldmade Bowls, The Athenian Agora* 22 (Princeton, N.J.: American School of Classical Studies at Athens, 1982), 67, #190 (cf. pls. 35, 80).

95. Michel Ponsich, *Les Lampes romaines en terre cuite de la Maurétanie Tingitane,* Publications du Service des Antiquités du Maroc 15 (Rabat: N.p., 1961), 54 with fig. 16, #176; pl. xvi, #177. Purported Roman lamps show a member of Odysseus's crew removing the wax from his ears as he gazes on a fishtailed Siren in the water; but see Gerald Heres, "Odysseus und die Tritonin, zu einer Gruppe gefälschter Tonlampen," *Eirene* 12 (1974): 63–68.

96. *Supplementum Hellenisticum,* ed. Hugh Lloyd-Jones and Peter Parsons (Berlin and New York: Walter de Gruyter, 1983), frag. SH # 456, 11.4–5.

97. Odysseus, a Siren on a raft, and Scylla appear together on a Vatican mosaic (*LIMC,* vol. 6, Odysseus, no. #163; Sirens and Scylla decorate the statue Athens, Agora S 2039 (Odette Touchefeu-Meynier, *Thèmes odysséens dans l'art antique* [Paris: E. de Boccard, 1968], 163, #289). The beautiful woman above who turns into a dark and ugly fish below in Horace, *Ars poetica* 3–4, is presented, not as a mythological monster, but as an artistic absurdity.

98. *In Esaiam* 12. In a similar spirit two centuries later Leander of Seville (Isidore's brother), in warning nuns to avoid the company of laywomen: "Flee the Sirens' songs, my sister: lest while with itching ears you take pleasure in hearing earthly delights you be turned aside from the true course, and either be smashed on the right against the rock of Scylla [reading *Scyllae illidaris scopulo* to balance *Charybdis deglutiaris rictu*] or swallowed up on the left in Charybdis' gape. Flee the Sirens' songs, and block your ears against the tongue of her that urges ill": *De institutione virginum,* ed. Ángel Custodio Vega, *El "De Institutione Virginum" de San Leandro de Sevilla,* Scriptores Hispano-Latini Veteris et Medii Aevi 16–17 (Madrid: Real Monasterio de S. Lorenzo de El Escorial, 1948), 101.

99. Book 1, chap. 6, trans. Andy Orchard, *Pride and Prodigies: Studies in the Monsters of the "Beowulf" Manuscript* (Cambridge: D. S. Brewer, 1995), 263 (text 262).

100. Ibid., chap. 14 (266, trans. 267).

101. Ibid., Prologue (256, trans. 257).

102. Paris, Bibliothèque nationale de France, MS lat. 12048, fol. 1ᵛ. On this MS, extremely rich in representations of animals, see E. Heinrich Zimmermann, *Vorkarolingische Miniaturen* (Berlin: Deutscher Verein für Kunstwissenschaft, 1916), text vol., 9, 11, 14, 24, 89–90, 228–30, and pls. 153–59. A *nomen sacrum* is a religious term (in this case *domini,* "the Lord's") written for reverential reasons in abbreviated form.

103. By contrast, there are no sirens in King Alfred's adaptation of Boethius (late ninth century), nor in the bestiary fragment of the Exeter Book (copied ca. 940).

104. Henry Sweet, rev. and T. F. Hoad, *A Second Anglo-Saxon Reader: Archaic and Dialectal* (Oxford: Clarendon Press, 1978), 87, gloss #1864.

105. Chaucer notes that "mermaydens" is the English for "sereyns" (Chaucer, *Romaunt of the Rose,* 682–84), and so renders Boethius's *Sirenes* in *Boece;* see too L. A. J. R. Houwen, "Flattery and the Mermaid in Chaucer's Nun's Priest's Tale," in Animals and the Symbolic in Mediaeval Art and Literature, ed. L. A. J. R. Houwen, 77–92, Mediaevalia Groningana 20 (Groningen: Egbert Forsten, 1997), Houwen, "Flattery and the Mermaid," kindly brought to my attention by Dr. Dorothy McCarthy.

106. In the Byzantine world the Sirens remained avian. There are two splendid (though unfortunately damaged) bird-women, very much in the classical tradition, together with an ostrich, at Oxford, Bodleian Library, MS Barocci 201, fol. 187^v, a catena on Job at 30:29, which in LXX reads "I am become the brother of sirens, and the companion of ostriches." The comment, from Olympiodorus (see *PG* 93:317 D–320 A), interprets the sirens as singing birds, "halcyons or owls, for both are mourners."

107. On this MS see Montague Rhodes James, *The Bestiary: Being a Reproduction in Full of the Manuscript Ii. 4. 26 in the University Library, Cambridge, with Supplementary Plates from Other Manuscripts of English Origin, and a Preliminary Study of the Latin Bestiary as Current in England* (London: Roxburghe Club, 1928), 10–11.

108. Examples could be multiplied: for instance, the *Liber bestiarum* of the Archdeacon of Cambrai (1469), Biblioteca Apostolica Vaticana, MS Rossiana 22, xx, retains the Physiologus's *volatilis* and Isidore's *volucres,* but the illustration on xx is of a fishtailed siren.

109. *De bestiis et aliis rebus* 2.32 (*PL* 177:78). The work is sometimes ascribed to Hugh of Fouilloy ("de Folieto," d. ca. 1172), whose treatise on birds (*Avicularius*) was prefixed to book 1 in manuscripts.

110. Ed. P. T. Eden, *Theobaldi "Physiologus,"* Mittellateinische Studien und Texte 6 (Leiden: E. J. Brill, 1972), 60; l.8 runs "quodque facit monstrum, uolucres sunt inde deorsum" ("and—what makes them monsters—from there downwards they are birds," 61).

111. See Eden's apparatus and Henkel, *Studien,* 125, from Munich, Bayerische Staatsbibliothek, Clm 5594 (s. xv), fol. 323^r: "Obenn mensch vnd vndenn visch-lich," with note ad loc. Contrast the twelfth-century Millstätter Physiologus edited from MS Klagenfurt, Landesmuseum für Kärnten VI/19 by Peter F. Ganz, *Geistliche Dichtung des 12. Jahrhunderts. Eine Textauswahl* (Berlin: Erich Schmidt, 1960), 47–58 at 56, l. 580: "getan sam die vogele."

112. Ed. Hanneke Wirtjes, *The Middle English Physiologus,* Early English Text Society, orig. ser. 200 (Oxford: Oxford University Press, 1991), 15–16, ll.391–422 (quotation l.406), with discussion lxxxvii f., and for the regular *fis* " 'fish," xxi.

Note that *mereman* still represents Old English *meremenin,* not the modern English masculine "merman" for a triton.

113. For a more detailed analysis see Edmond Faral, "La queue de poisson des sirèenes," *Romania* 74 (1953): 453–506; Faral, "La queue de poisson," 478–506; see too Henkel, *Studien,* 173–74 for a list of passages concerning Sirens.

114. For hybrid Sirens cf. the Worksop Breviary, England, s. xii, New York, Pierpont Morgan Library, MS M81, fol. 17ʳ, illustrated by Benton, *Medieval Menagerie,* 19; Bestiary, England, ca. 1255, British Library, MS Harley 3244, fol. 55r, illustrated by Ann Payne, *Medieval Beasts* (London: British Library, 1990), 74.

115. "E de feme at faiture / Entresqu'a la ceinture, / E les piez de falcun / E cue de peissun": ed.in Emmanuel Walberg, *Le Bestiaire de Philippe de Thaün* (Lund: H. Möller, 1900; reprint, Geneva: Slatkine, 1970), 51, ll.1365–68. Guillaume le Clerc, in 1211, recognizes both types: "De la centure en amont / Est la plus bele rien del mond, / En guise de femme est formee; / L'altre partie est figuree / Come peisson u cum oisel"; see Cahier, "Physiologus," 175–77; cf. Faral, "La queue de poisson," 491, and in general McCulloch, *Mediaeval Latin and French Bestiaries,* 166–70.

116. *Otia imperialia* 3.64, ed. Banks and Binns, 680–83.

117. Faral, "La queue de poisson," 471–76; hence Vincent of Beauvais, *Speculum naturale* 17.129 (*Speculum quadruplex,* 4 vols. [Douai: B. Beller, 1624], 1:1314).

118. See Faral, "La queue de poisson," 487–91; Cahier, "Physiologus," 172–73 with pl. XX, Fig. Z from Paris, MS Bibliothèque de l'Arsenal 3516 (*olim* B.F. 283; misprinted "3156" in Faral,"La queue de poisson," 487 n. 2). The Picard is followed by Richard de Fournival in his *Bestiaire d'Amour* (Faral,"La queue depoisson," 497). The *Ovide moralisé* overturns the majority: "Forme humaine et forme d'oisiaus / Ont les deus, l'autre de poisson": 5.3471–72, ed. de Boer, 2:261. See too Benton, *Medieval Menagerie,* 36–38.

119. "Dont la premiere chantoit merveilleusement de la bouche comme vois de feme, l'autre en vois de flaüt et de canon; la tierce de citole." For the canon (a form of zither) and the citole (the precursor of the cittern) see *New Grove II* 5:6 (Joan Rimmer/Nelly van Ree Bernard), 5:672–76 (Lawrence Wright).

120. Book 1, chap. 136, "Des Sieraines," ed. Francis J. Carmody, *Physiologus Latinus: Éditions préliminaires, versio B.* (Paris: E. Droz, 1939), Brunetto Latini, *Li livres dou tresor,* University of California Publications in Modern Philology 22 (Berkeley and Los Angeles: University of California Press, 1948), 131–32; my translation. Lechery (*luxure*) is Isidore's *Venerem* taken as a common noun (Faral, "La queue de poisson," 501) and read in the light of humoral pathology. For good measure Brunetto throws in Isidore's poisonous serpents to bridge his transition from fish to reptiles, which "sont plus resamblables as poissons de maintes proprietes": ed. Carmody, 132.

121. St. Petersburg, National Library of Russia, Fr. F. v. iii. 4, fol. 47ʳ, kindly brought to my attention by Dr. Wendelien van Welie-Vink.

122. Cf. above, n. 8.

123. *Genealogie deorum gentilium libri* 7.20, ed. Vincenzo Romano, *Genealogie deorum gentilium libri* by Giovanni Boccaccio: Opere, 10, Scrittori d'Italia 200–201 (Bari: Laterza, 1951), 1:334–37; for Pliny see *Natural History* 3.62.

124. Natalis Comes, *Mythologiae sive explicationum fabularum libri decem* 7.13. Comes himself preferred to see them as pleasures; likewise Hans Sachs, "Ulisses mit den meerwundern der Syrenen, den leibs-wollust andeutent" (Nov. 27, 1557; ed. Adelbert von Keller, *Hans Sachs: Werke,* 7/2, Bibliothek des litterarischen Vereins in Stuttgart 115 [Tübingen, 1873; reprint, Hildesheim: G. Olms, 1964], 410–14: "Ulysses with the marine marvels of the Sirens, signifying bodily pleasure").

125. Marginale from a French book of hours, ca. 1400, Oxford, Bodleian Library, MS Douce 62, fol. 51^r; so in the same library MS Buchanan e. 18, fol. 60^r. Not indeed that these accoutrements are *de rigueur* (e.g., same library, MS Canon. Liturg. 242, fol. 186r); musical instruments may be preferred, e.g., the fiddle of Baltimore, Walters Art Galley, W 440, fol. 91^r (Lilian M. C. Randall, *Medieval and Renaissance Manuscripts in the Walters Art Gallery* [Baltimore: Johns Hopkins University Press, 1997], pl. XLIIa). There is a Siren Hair Salon in New York, and a Sirene Hair Salon in Oxford; the latter has a mermaid as its logo.

126. Bodleian Library, MS Douce 118, fol. 9^r; note too the grotesque of the Ormesby Psalter, s. xiii–xiv, with the nether parts of a quadruped. For assistance with my research into Bodleian Sirens my thanks are due to Mrs. Rigmor Båtvig.

127. Charles Moïse Briquet, *Les Filigranes,* ed. Allan Stevenson (Amsterdam: Paper Publications Society, 1968), 2:684–85 with i. *80 and illustrations in vol. 4, records two types of "Sirène" used as a watermark, both fishtailed: single tail nos. 13852–62 (with round mirror in all but 13852–53), of French origin ("probablement champenoise"); two tails nos. 13863–902, Italian, used throughout the Seicento. There is no mention of bird-sirens, but cf. #1411 (from Brünn/Brno, 1595), called a harpy at 1:114 but to my eye too inviting.

128. RISM 1534^{15}, illustrated in Suzanne G. Cusick, *Valerio Dorico: Music Printer in Sixteenth-Century Rome,* Studies in Musicology 43 (Ann Arbor: UMI Research Press, 1981), described 166–67, and see 35, 41–50, 163; no title page has survived from the first edition of 1530 (RISM 1530^2). I thank Dr. Bonnie Blackburn for the reference.

129. Andrea Alciato, *Emblemata* (Paris: Jean Richer, 1960), no. #115; Joachim Camerarius, *Symbola = Symbolorum et emblematum centuriae tres . . . Accessit noviter Centuria IV. ex aquatilibus et reptilibus,* 2d ed. (Nuremberg: Voegelin, 1605), cent. IV, #63 (with reasons for choosing this type and not the other).

130. Cf. DeWitt Talmage Starnes and Ernest William Talbert, *Classical Myth and Legend in Renaissance Dictionaries* (Chapel Hill: University of North Carolina Press, 1955; reprint, Westport, Conn.: Greenwood Press, 1973), 108–10. Natalis Comes describes the Sirens as having the nether parts of birds, but cites among his bogus authorities two writers "de Piscibus"; the expanded 1581 ed. includes a repudiation of creatures half-human and half-fish (499), but the woodcut found in illustrated editions shows three standing bird-women. Hans Sachs fol-

lows Homer so closely as to offer no physical description, but expands a detail from the Physiologus: "Als denn umbkeren sie die schieff / Und stürtzen sie zu grunde tieff. / Als denn erwürgen sie die lewt, / Fressens, ziehen in ab ir hewt, / Die irem singen hören zu" (411, ll. 2–6: "Then they capsize the ships, and send them down to the bottom, then choke those who listen to their singing; they devour them and tear off their skin"). See n. 1254.

131. "She does not always harm." On Bulifon see *DBI* 15:57–61. The Sirena fountain in Piazza Sannazzaro is in mermaid form.

132. *The Faerie Queene* 2.12.30–34. For figures in the Lord Mayor's pageant of 1612 called "Mer-maides" in English and *Sirenen* in German see Werner, "A German Eye-Witness," 262.

133. Ed. Gwyn Jones, *William Browne: Circe and Ulysses, the Inner Temple Masque* (London: Golden Cockerel Press, 1954), 7; as befits the authorities cited, these Sirens offer love.

TWO

"Teach Me to Heare Mermaides Singing"

Embodiments of (Acoustic) Pleasure and Danger in the Modern West

Linda Phyllis Austern

And everyone was listening. . . . [A]s the mist swirled and
parted and joined and parted again in flying diaphanous
banners, [Colin] could see the other men, still where they
should be working, spellbound gray-blurred ghosts listening
so intently that even the steersman had abandoned the steering, leaning over the wheel, ears straining.
        "How sweet she sings!" whispered Neddy.
        "Ah, there never was one to sing sweeter," sighed the
second officer.
        "I'd no idea you all knew her," Colin said with amaze-
ment. "You certainly didn't mention it when I was telling you
about her."
        "Quiet! Can't you hear Mother singing me favorite nur-
sery rhyme?" . . .
        "Your MOTHER? She's young enough to be your
grandchild!" They were about to pitch him overboard when
he finally made out the words Maggie sang. It was a tender
love song, personally addressed to him. . . .
        It was Pinchpurse who first came to his senses and
shook off the enchantment, and he wasted no time at wrest-
ing the wheel from the spellbound steersman. "Siren, you
lubbers! To your stations!" he hollered, every sinew straining
as he pulled the wheel hard to the right, away from the rock
that suddenly loomed up at them from the sea.
                —Elizabeth Scarborough, *Song of Sorcery* [1]

Elizabeth Scarborough's charming fantasy novel of 1982, *Song of Sorcery*,
offers a brief encounter with thousands of years of Western siren-lore,
brought together with a light, comedic touch. The fabled creature enters

the work and the reader's consciousness as softly as she strokes the sailors' ears: a hypnotic thing of mist and memory, with no more substance than a half-forgotten dream. She is but a sound upon the water, whispering secrets from some distant place. There is little room aboard the tiny ship for privacy or contemplation. Yet the siren's voice addresses each man alone. To the young lover, it is the rhapsodic call of the beloved, carried impossibly across the miles. To the ancient wanderer, her voice is the long-lost comfort of the mother's lullaby. To the jaded salt in a world of crude strength and mercenary bargaining, it bestows an inconceivable moment of pure acoustic sweetness. By the time the listeners recognize the true source of this wondrous song, it is too late. Total destruction seems imminent.

For centuries, the Western siren has inhabited this same liminal space between sea, sky, the solid manifestation of civilized artifice, and the human psyche. Hers remains the voice of desire, transplanted to a body invisible or monstrous. Hers is the power to force men to listen, to abandon themselves against rational judgment to the insubstantial pleasures of things heard. From classical myth through its Christian retellings and into the era of scientific inquiry and psychoanalysis, the siren has continued to signify the paradoxes of pleasure and danger in ways that suggest enduring cultural connections between Woman and both the natural and eternal worlds. In contrasting visions founded on a tangled web of oral and written traditions, the siren envoiced has represented for the postclassical West the metamorphic gateway from love to death, and sometimes beyond these to the promise of life everlasting.

The Ecstatic Call of Nature: Mother/Water/Soul/Music

> Sea, wind, leaves, thunder, waters, cows lowing, the cattle market, cocks, hens don't crow, snakes hissss. There's music everywhere. . . .
> That's joyful I can feel. Never have written it. Why? My joy is other joy. But both are joys. Yes, joy it must be. Mere fact of music shows you are.
> —Bloom's meditation on the sirens, in James Joyce,
> *Ulysses*[2]

From Homer through Joyce and beyond, the siren has been connected to the ungovernable infinitudes of nature that menace civil artifice and self-restraint. The act of listening to music has likewise been linked to subjective displacement, to personal decentering, and to an ecstatic connection to the infinite polyphony of the world that threatens to engulf the self. *"There's music everywhere."* For Joyce's Bloom, the natural and the cultural merge in the music he hears at the Ormond bar, evoking a longstanding Western tradition through which art reveals a connection to inner truth or to external substance—or sometimes paradoxically to both.[3]

> But wait. But hear. Chords dark. Lugugugubrious. Low. In a cave of the dark middle earth. Embedded ore. Lumpmusic.
>
> The voice of dark age, of unlove, earth's fatigue made grave approach, and painful, come from afar, from hoary mountains, called on good men and true. The priest he sought, with him would he speak a word.
>
> Tap.
>
> . . .
>
> The priest's at home. A false priest's servant bade him welcome. Step in. The holy father. Curlycues of chords.
>
> Ruin them. Wreck their lives. Then build them cubicles to end their days in. Hushaby. Lullaby. Die, dog. Little dog, die.
>
> The voice of warning, solemn warning, told them the youth had entered a lonely hall, told them how solemn fell his footstep there, told them the gloomy chamber, the vested priest, sitting to shrive.[4]

For Bloom, as for many who encounter siren sound, the sensory and the musical merge with death and spirituality, with the (remembered) maternal voice, against a shifting, forbidding landscape neither fully physical nor metaphysical. Bloom remains uneasy at being emotionally touched by music against his will or his control. It has set his mind wandering freely while his senses attend to what has become the customary abode of urban sirens.[5] Like other musical contemplatives before him, Bloom acknowledges the connection between music and sexual attraction, and ultimately positions the aesthetic and the erotic in the swirling spaces between nature and culture. "Flood of warm jimjam likitup secretness flowed to flow in music out, in desire, dark to lick flow, invading," reflects Bloom not long after he recognizes that it is "Love that is singing: Love's old sweet song."[6]

The siren and her music conventionally belong to the most fluid elements of the natural world, air and water, embodying femininity to the West for as long as solid earth and fire have suggested manhood. Even the modern siren of the cocktail lounge represents the call of Nature and its promise of erotic freedom, drawing her wandering suitor away from his mundane home and domesticated Penelope.[7] Love, too, and the swirling, whirling shapes of desire take on the nebulous liquescence of water, particularly in nineteenth-century visions and in (post-)Freudian psychology.[8] "Woman is the siren who lures sailors upon the rocks," writes Simone de Beauvoir, she is Circe, who changes her lovers into beasts, the Undine who draws fishermen into the depths of pools. The man captivated by her charms no longer has will-power, enterprise, future; he is no longer a citizen, but mere flesh enslaved to its desires, cut off from the community, bound to the moment, tossed passively back and forth between torture and pleasure. The perverse sorceress arrays passion against duty, the present moment against all time to come; she detains the traveller far from home, she pours him the drink of forgetfulness.[9]

Across cultures, across time, Woman has been perceived to be closer than Man to nature. Her physiology alone has brought her to that point, her passions linked to the rhythms of moon and tide. But Woman cannot be consigned fully to the shifting, uncontrollable world of the natural because she has a human consciousness.[10] Nonetheless, as Beauvoir points out, "Man seeks in Woman the Other as Nature and as his fellow being,"

But we know what ambivalent feelings Nature inspires in man. He exploits her, but she crushes him, he is born of her and dies in her; she is the source of his being and the realm that he subjugates to his will; Nature is a vein of gross material in which the soul is imprisoned, and she is the supreme reality; she is continence and Idea, the finite and the whole. She is what opposes the Spirit, and the Spirit itself. Now ally, now enemy, she appears as the dark chaos from whence life wells up, as this life itself, and as the over-yonder toward which life tends.[11]

Whether fish, seaside bird, maiden, or some strange mixture of all three, the siren belongs essentially to the aquatic realm—as human women have often been presented in mythology, folklore, and psychoanalytic thought. The aquatic theory of evolution, so beloved by feminist writers of the 1970s, emphasizes that the particular fat deposits of the feminine form make Womankind further removed from terrestrial simians and more suited to water-dwelling than her male counterpart.[12] Earthly Venus, the carnal goddess of love, belongs to the same sea as the sirens, fecund wellspring of life in its myriad forms.[13] Water serves as blood for the earth and its inhabitants, which become parched and dry without its steady flow. It is literally the source of vitality, the uterine environment of embryonic growth, seminal fluid, the blood beneath the skin. Ancient and traditional Western medicine have called for diverse applications and preparations of seawater, which provide not only healing but also numerous vital minerals to sustain terrestrial life.[14] The sea is the prototypical mother of all, moody and deep, the recipient of fiery rays of light that spawn teeming life. Yet she gives domicile to monsters and pirates as well as to the beautiful and useful. She is as capable of destruction as of creation, allied through feminine form not only to birth and erotic desire but also to death. Psychoanalytical and ethnographic data suggest a widespread connection between the perception of the mother and the fear of mortality, a longing for death as a return to the womb.[15]

"In the depths of the sea, it is night," says Beauvoir,

> Woman is the *Mare tenebrarum*, dreaded by navigators of old; it is night in the entrails of the earth. Man is frightened of this night, the reverse of fecundity, which threatens to swallow him up. . . . under his feet there is a moist, warm, and darkling gulf ready to draw him down; in many a legend do we see the hero lost forever as he falls back into the maternal shadows—cave, abyss, hell.[16]

Arthur Rackham's exquisite illustration of 1912 for Aesop's fable, "The Shipwrecked Man and the Sea" (fig. 2.1), typically unites the womanly and the dreadful, *Mare tenebrarum,* the dark sea. She is Nature unrestrained, the maternal shadow between life and death. Looming cold and gray against the fading sunset that blends into the wreckage of a once-tall ship, she dwarfs the tiny, ravaged figure of a man who faces her from behind a shallow barricade of water-worn rock. Seafoam and spray drip from her outstretched arms, raised in a gesture of unconscious power, to merge with the wild waves below. Frenzied waters caress her loins (or are they of them?), but her high, firm breasts, flat belly, and smooth, expressionless face suggest the perfect, youthful beauty of Desire. She is cold, uncaring, and impossibly out of reach. Yet she is fecund and beautiful, the sea, the mother of sirens. She rises with the Night.

The thoroughly modern mermaid of H. G. Wells's *The Sea Lady* (1902) is superficially far more civilized, becoming on land a lady of fashion and polite manners. No more wildly oceanic than the shallow water of her "bath chair," she is still in essence a creature of dark depth and primal nature, whispering blissfully of the unknown:

> ". . . what no one seems to understand, is that she comes—"
> "Out of the sea."
> "Out of some other world. She comes, whispering that this life is a phantom life, unreal, flimsy, limited, casting upon everything a spell of disillusionment—"
> "So that *he*—"
> "Yes, and then she whispers, 'there are better dreams'. . . . She is a mermaid, she is a thing of dreams and desires, a siren, a whisper and a seduction. She will lure him with her—"
> He stopped.

Figure 2.1. Arthur Rackham, *The Shipwrecked Man and the Sea* (1912). © V&A Images/Victoria and Albert Museum.

"Where?" she whispered.
"Into the deeps."
"The deeps?"[17]

Elation flows metaphorically as streams and tides through psychological and philosophical descriptions of human emotive states.[18] In this case, however, the wonders of the sea, "the deeps," further function as an ancient metaphor for the pleasures, the dangers, and the mystery of the feminine realm: the place of birth, of death, of transfiguration. Feminine erotic energy in particular has been perceived in modern psychoanalytic theory as fluid, flowing, always in flux, destroyer of the permanence of hardness.[19] It is substantially of nature, unceasingly threatening male artifice. The fatal embrace of the siren has been explained similarly as a childhood fantasy return to the dark waters of the womb, the "primal incest."[20] Orgasm is likewise a fall into the abyss, the "little death" with its loss of boundary between self and other, and its fragmentary ecstatic cries. *"Hushaby. Lullaby. Die, dog. Little dog, die."*

The mother's lullaby and the lover's exaltation share the essence of the siren's song. All are emotive and sometimes paralinguistic vocalizations from some primal place. The sirenic fantasy relies largely, as Joyce demonstrates, on conceptions of hearing as a passive, feminine sense, and on the links between woman, water and the insubstantial, affective flow of music. The legend's extraordinary vitality through centuries of epistemological and cultural change, and across the margins of the arts and sciences, has suggested that it serves some deep-seated psychological or even spiritual longing. It is undoubtedly tied as much to the nature of hearing and the hearing of Nature as to the shapes and shades of Desire. Human speech is evolutionarily grafted onto a phylogenetically older vocal call system that was used mainly for affective and social signaling; it remains unclear to what extent the development of language might have been constrained by this affective signaling system. What is apparent, however, is that in at least some cases the use of a particular acoustic feature in spoken language limits its use for communication of emotion.[21] *"Sea, wind, leaves, thunder, waters, cows lowing, the cattle market, cocks, hens don't crow, snakes hissss. There's music everywhere. . . . That's joyful I can feel."*

Beyond the clichés of human agency, sounds become music when they are made meaningful to the listener, when they are sustained and acted upon by the ear and the mind. This happens when the listener is driven to care, whether voluntarily or (as in the case of Joyce's Bloom) through the involuntary relinquishment of acoustic freedom.[22] Music carries with it the ability to fascinate, to stimulate the imagination, in a way that mere sound does not. *"That's joyful I can feel."* Says the first title character as he remembers the second in Giuseppe di Lampedusa's short story "The Professor and the Siren" (1961):

> She spoke: and so after her smile and her smell I was submerged by the third and greatest of [her] charms, that of voice. It was slightly gutteral, veiled, reverberating with innumerable harmonies; behind the words could be sensed the lazy surf of summer seas, last spray rustling on a beach, winds passing on lunar rays. The song of the Sirens does not exist, Corbera: the music from which there is no escaping is that of their voices.[23]

Asks the even more besotted Melville of his siren seductress in Wells's *Sea Lady,* " '. . . who could tell the quality that makes me *swim* in the sound of her voice[?].' "[24] The vocality and signification of Venus, water-born goddess of love and desire, was linked to siren song in a tradition that lasted well beyond the demise of classical religion.[25] A similar confluence of convention bestowed seductive voices on the water-sprites of contrasting folkloric traditions from one end of Europe to the other well into the modern era.[26]

In the modern, visually oriented West, hearing has been considered the second sense in the traditions of ancient custom and modern laboratory science. It is particularly associated with memory, teaching, learning, and feminine ways of knowing.[27] Noteworthy in this context is the central deception of Franz Kafka's short story "The Silence of the Sirens" (written between 1917 and 1923), which relies on the mime of emotive musical performance, with the title characters' "throats rising and falling, their breasts lifting, their eyes filled with tears, their lips half parted." Ulysses does not perceive their silence, but believes that he alone had not heard the sirens.[28] Perception through the ear becomes equated with true (re)cognition.

"Hearing is the organ of understanding," writes the early modern English thinker, Richard Brathwaite, "by it we conceive, by the memorie we conserve, and by our judgement we revelve; as many rivers have their confluence, by small streames," he continues with aquatic analogy, "so knowledge her essence by the accent of the *eare*. As our *eare* can best judge of sounds, so hath it a distinct power to sound into the center of the heart."[29] More recently, modern music-scholar David Schwartz has explained "the all-around pleasure of listening to music" as an "oceanic" fantasy, akin to sleeping, swimming, and having sex or being absorbed by a movie, religious experience, or landscape.[30] What these contrasting practices share is the dissolution of some boundary separating the self and its senses from the external world. They are also what the Medieval Church warned against in the guise of sirens in moralizing bestiaries and fantastical representations. The voice of the siren comes from a monstrous body, an invisible body, or an unknown and therefore doubly frightening body. Such freakish forms have been associated in folklore and psychoanalysis with fear of sexuality and its tremendous complexities.[31] But siren song is a thing of rapturous beauty. One feature of vocal expression is that it is optimally suited to relatively indirect communication over long distances; visual contact between listener and the sonic source is not necessary.[32] "All poets unanimously," begins an anonymous seventeenth-century English editor of René Descartes, "have made the *Magick* of *Sirens* to consist only in the *Sweet Accents* and *Melotheticall Modulation* of their *Voices*."[33] The myth of the sirens therefore reminds us of the *jouissance* of music, the pleasures of surrender and engulfment, and the fears of making bad choices under the influence of uncontrollable substances—and the dangers of dissolving a safe distance between self and other.

The same terms used to delineate the sort of temporal and spatial experience that is music are also applied to other oceanic occurrences and to feeling in general: overlap, penetration, expansiveness, tightness . . . .[34] These are also words used to describe the male experience of sex, particularly in a heteroerotic context. For centuries, the ear—the organ of hearing—has been equated with the vagina, the listener with the receptive female body.[35] *"Hearing is the organ of understanding, by it we conceive."* The intimacy of speaking (or singing) and listening may resemble that of erotic exchange in a culture that once acknowledged the possibility of divine conception through the ear.[36] The voice penetrates and touches the most pliant and receptive organ of the listening body, seat of primal emotive response, softening and opening it to delight. After sound enters the heart, wrote Brathwaite in the early seventeenth century,

> [the heart] is open to receive, ministering matter sufficient for the mind to digest; some things it relisheth pleasantly, apprehending them with a kinde of enforced delight . . . [yet] in affaires conferring delight, the voluptuous man hath an excellent *eare;* in matters of profit . . . The eare is best delighted, when any thing is treated on, which the minde fancieth: and it is soon cloyed, when the minde is not satisfied with the *subject* whereof it treateth.[37]

The siren's is a fetishized voice, severed from the (expected) body and equated by modern psychoanalysis to the female phallus, the penetrating voice of fearsome, aggressive love. It is the acoustic embodiment of mother-love in all its allurement, but with the grim promise of death.[38] It is truly the voice of "enforced delight." The body of the siren in either of its standard forms suggests smothering, engulfment, ephemerality, and swift motion beyond the human element of solid earth.[39] Its upper parts, source of the infantile delights of nourishment and soothing sound, of maternal caress, are monstrously joined to scales or feathers at the primary locus of sexual pleasure. As a sea-maid in particular, with her cold, pulsing tail, the siren clearly embodies the fearsome phallic mother of psychoanalytic theory, she "of whom we are afraid."[40] Even the siren's nutritive breasts, maidenly face, and sweet voice cannot conceal her barren coldness or sexual inaccessibility. Schwartz further links acoustic receptivity to the sonorous envelope of the maternal voice, the pleasurable sonic womb of the newborn.[41] Both ideas are already clearly evident in the siren fantasy of the thirteenth-century English Franciscan friar and natural historian, Bartholomeus Anglicus:

> The mermaide[n] is called *Sirena,* and *hael Siren, sirenis* . . . is a beaste of the sea wonderfully shapen as a maide from the navell upward, and a fish from the navell downward, and this wonderfull beast is gladde and merrie in tempest, and sadde and heavie in fayre weather. With sweetnesse of song this beast maketh shipmen to sleepe, and when shee seeth that they be a sleepe, she goeth into the ship, and ravisheth which she may take with her, and bringeth him into a drye place, and maketh him first lye by her, and doe the deede of lechery, and if he will not or may not, then she slaieth him and eateth his flesh.[42]

From ship-womb to cave-tomb, this horrifying image of siren aggression truly embodies the irresistible, forceful, and deadly power of her music. From the pen of a celibate friar, the link between maiden-voice, abduction, and the choice between "the deede of lechery" and female cannibalism is particularly significant as well as grotesque. Mother-lover crooning the lullaby of ecstatic death, she reaches from memory to unknown future with a song Bartholomeus's reader can only imagine. For centuries, the only safe siren has been the one rendered voiceless, whether by her own mischief or the act of another. "The song of the Sirens could pierce through everything," writes Kafka with phallic metaphor, "and the longing of those they seduced could have broken far stronger bonds than chains and masts."[43] Most famous, perhaps, is Hans Christian Andersen's beloved Little Mermaid; as her first step toward salvation, she is required to sacrifice her alluring tongue with "its means to charm the prince."[44]

Musical representations of sirens throughout the era of tonality and beyond have made use of synesthetic acoustic metaphors for aquatic comfort and the pleasures of surrender and engulfment, as well as the incessant ebb and flow of water. The Sirens of John Dryden's *King Arthur: or, The British Worthy. A Dramatic Opera* (1691), with music by Henry Purcell, provide an early example with conventions already in place. In Act IV, scene ii, redolent of the sorcerous magic of the title character's evil enemy, the Sirens attempt to lead the heroic monarch from his dual quest to free his captive beloved and his kingdom. Rising bare-breasted from a stream in an enchanted wood, they sing a languorous duet in an attempt to catch his fancy through aural delight (ex. 2.1). Their music washes over the listener in a slow, sweet G minor, rich with expressive melisma and modulation. It suggests the gentle caress and overlap of waves, in a lingering imitation that fades to brief solos or expands to the luxuriousness of parallel thirds. Both text and music swell to all-encompassing circles, ripples that surround and sustain, after rising and falling carefully around a series of promissory climaxes in a variety of keys. As "a lazie pleasure

Example 2.1. Beginning of "Two Daughters of this Aged Stream" by Henry Purcell from Act IV, scene ii of John Dryden's *King Arthur: or, The British Worthy* (1691).

13
comb'd and both our sea - green locks have comb'd have comb'd for ye
locks have comb'd for ye, and both our sea - green locks have comb'd for ye
13
17
Come, come, come, come, bathe with us an hour or two;
Come, come, bathe with us an hour or two;
17
21
Come, come, come, come na - ked in for we are so
Come, come, come, come na - ked in for we are so.
21
25
What dan - ger what dan - ger from a na - ked foe?
What dan - ger from a na - ked foe?
25

Come, come, bathe with us, come, come

Come, come, come, come, bathe with us, come, come

bathe and share What plea sures in the floods ap- pear (etc.)

bathe, and share What plea - - - - sures in the floods ap - pear (etc.)

(etc.)

trickles through [his] veins," Arthur, unlike a more voluptuous man, heeds the call of honor. With a cry of "farewell, with half my Soul I stagger off," the king tears himself from what he knows are dangerous aquatic demons raised by a supernatural power.[45]

Such captivating representations of the fantastic serve as reminders that allegorical forms propose fixed meanings based on the sensible cosmos: water, earth, the woman's voice, the verdant things of nature . . . Mythologies differ from science in that they posit a vast series of correspondences between the visible universe, its mysterious creators, and the human psyche.[46] Stories of monstrous matings, whether threatened or consummated, are often linked to fear of sexual surrender or erotic disorder.[47] And Western culture has long linked soul, death, and (male) genitals in an unholy trinity.[48] Like a shell, that other fabled object that links land, sea, and the contrasting domains of sight and hearing, the ear (like the mouth or vagina to which it is analogized) folds inward past lips, past an epithelial sleekness, into a fluid realm of metabolic tides and circulations.[49]

John William Waterhouse's famous painting *A Mermaid* (1900), his final diploma work from the Royal Academy of Arts, unifies these ideas seamlessly (fig. 2.2). The exquisite title character's mouth is open in song as she combs her long auburn hair. The gentle waves, with an evident undertow and a plethora of rocks and flotsam in the foreground, suggest the ebbing tide at its lowest, the time when all is drawn out to sea and the concealed becomes revealed. Behind the enchantress, to the right of her

Figure 2.2. John William Waterhouse, *A Mermaid* (1900). Royal Academy of Arts, London. By permission of the Royal Academy of Arts.

head and its parted lips, gapes a slender fissure in a sea-worn cliff. Here, water flows suggestively through narrowing layer upon layer of enfolded rock to and from the boundless ocean, a vaginal portal to the mysteries beyond. In front of the curvaceous mermaid, echoing the shape of her glistening, scale-clad buttocks, sits an open shell, spilling lustrous pearls and other treasure from its nacreous interior. It is no coincidence that such a shell serves as a chariot to the foam-born embodiment of love from classical myth, guiding her from water to earth, from the realm of gods to that of men—and male desire. "Bloom through the bardoor saw a shell held at their ears," writes Joyce in *Ulysses:*

He heard more faintly that that they heard, each for herself alone, then each for other, hearing the plash of waves, loudly, a silent roar.

Bronze by a weary gold, anear, afar, they listened.

Her ear too is a shell, the peeping lobe there. Been to the seaside. Lovely seaside girls. . . . Hair braided over: shell with seaweed. Why do they hide their ears with seaweed hair? And Turks their mouth, why? Her eyes over the sheet, a yashmak. Find the way in. A cave. No admittance except on business.

The sea they think they hear. Singing. A roar. The blood is it.[50]

Anatomy and Destiny: [Un]Natural History of the Siren

> There are more things in heaven and earth, Horatio,
> Than are dreamt of in your philosophy.
> —William Shakespeare, *Hamlet*, Act I, scene v

> If you want to know more about femininity, enquire from your own experiences of life, or turn to poets, or wait until science can give you deeper and more coherent information.
> —Sigmund Freud, "Femininity," in
> *Introductory Lectures on Psychoanalysis*[51]

Nowhere have the contrasting quests for literal and allegorical truth over-lapped more thoroughly than in pursuit of the siren. The ancient, shifting forms of such creatures gaze at us silently from tombstones, the tops of capitals, illustrated books, fluttering banners, and the carved silence of misericords, where they are condemned to listen eternally to the transcen-dental music of a rival power. They have their own natural history. Yet this history and the description of the siren's nature and habits have also been claimed by religion, literature, visual arts, and the interpretive branches of mythography and psychoanalysis. The search for the siren has been as varied and venerable as her song. "The natural history of mermaids can-not be understood by the methods of natural science alone," writes a mid-twentieth-century member of the profession for which he apologizes. "These hauntingly beautiful goddesses of the sea, full of mystery and danger," he continues, "were surely conjured from the chaos of the waters in answer to some primal human need."[52] An account of British heraldic beasts published only four years after Wells's *The Sea Lady* includes an observation that "there is still a lingering belief in the existence of the mermaid."[53] And a natural history of the manatees of British Guiana published two years after Lampedusa's narrative of *The Professor and the Siren* is entitled *In Search of Mermaids*.[54]

The siren is a creature of myth and of science through whom we discover aspects of ourselves. One was canonized as a saint in the sixth century CE when she left the waters to live among Welshmen and their women.[55] Another was driven through a breach in the dike of Edam in the Netherlands during a storm in 1401, after which she learned the art of spinning and became a good Catholic.[56] Others became eighteenth- and nineteenth-century specimens for zoological study.[57] Woman's constitution and bodily capacities for love and nurturance are explained through the myth of Venus as well as the aquatic theory of evolution. Such metamorphic tales as those traditionally surrounding the siren and her kin in fact provide "first drafts of a general evolutionary theory of life" as well as reflections of our own human nature.[58] The disjunction between siren form and siren song further reminds us that metaphor is largely bounded by the relationship of bodies to language.[59] Whether musical beast-woman or gentle sea-mammal of the order *sirenia,* the anatomy and habitual characteristics of the sirens have long been the objects of careful human scrutiny.

In what is generally accounted as the main source of subsequent understanding, Book XII of Homer's *Odyssey,* the deadly Sirens are assigned no bodily traits, no marks by which they may be known. Theirs is the intangible power of ear and mind. We first meet them through the voice of Circe, another female embodiment of music, dark magic, bestial passion, and unearthly knowledge:

> First, to the *Sirens* ye shall come, that taint
> The minds of all men, whom they acquaint
> With their attractions. Whosoever shall
> (For want of knowledge mov'd) but heare the call
> Of any *Siren:* he will so despise
> Both wife and children, for their sorceries,
> That never home turnes his affections streame;
> Nor they take joy in him, nor he in them.
> The *Sirens* will so soften with their song
> (Shrill, and in sensuall appetite so strong)
> His loose affections, that he gives them he[e]d.
> And then observe: They sit amidst a meade:
> And round about it runnes a hedge or wall
> Of dead mens bones: their withered skins and all
> Hung all along upon it; and these men
> Were such as they had fawnd into their Fen,
> And then their skins hung on the hedge of bones.[60]

They are known by sound and deed, and may lay claim to something like omniscience. Theirs is a primary power over mind, the power of oral suggestion. Their leavings are truly ghastly, especially to any culture that emphasizes ritual consecration and elaborate burial of the dead. We never see them.[61] Homer's brief poetic narrative draws together the paradoxes by which sirens are recognized, rendered all the more terrifying by the creatures' amorphousness. They permeate and envelop as sound, like air or water. The open orifice of the ear cannot shake them out, enabling them to invade consciousness and the whole body. They are things feared and desired, things unknown and hoped for, banished to the liminal spaces between life and death, memory and renewal, briny sea and blooming meadow. Already in this ancient portrayal they pass the very threshold of ways of knowing, pitting sense against sensibility, perception against received wisdom, and sound against sight. How might such creatures be embodied? How might they fascinate, terrify, and remind us tamely of their lethal song?

There has been much debate over the origin and proper form of the siren, made more complicated by the fact that each new expert since the ancient Greeks has tended to be familiar with prior portrayals. Furthermore, there was scant agreement even among early describers as to the number of sirens, their form, their parentage, their precise relationship to the muses, or even whether they were beneficent or malign; the seven empyrean sirens of Plato's *Republic,* for instance, were extraordinarily different creatures from their seaside Homeric homologues.[62] Such beings clearly have widespread multicultural roots and many contradictory antecedents, even in the West. Perhaps originally connected to pre-Olympian and ancient Semitic divinities of sun, moon, and sea, sirens also acquired association with underworld cults and Dionysian revelry on ancient artifacts and literary works known to later eras.[63] They were creatures of afternoon delirium, of twilight, and of midnight darkness. They were of the shifting lunar light that returns to water. Sirens belonged to ancient and later Christian hours of phantasms, and to the realm of nightmares.[64] Greek artists most often conceived of them as birds with women's heads, perched on rocks overlooking the ocean. As their semantic and symbolic field expanded more deeply into psychology and mysticism, they came closer and closer to the sea and to heterosexual male fantasies of flowing desire. They acquired arms, breasts, and scales, cold blood and mysterious depth.[65] The Aristotelian science and Galenic medicine that dominated European thought for millennia associated cold and moisture with the feminine sex. From the Enlightenment music history of Charles Burney through contemporary feminist theology, many have noted the parallel between the Homeric siren, her scaly piscine sister, and the Hebraic serpent of Eden, particularly as interpreted by Christian artists and moralizing exegetes.[66] This tradition is only partly offset by the neo-Platonic celestial sirens, embodiments of heavenly harmony and universal order, particularly beloved by sixteenth-century cognoscenti.[67] Linguistically, the same root meaning enflame, burn, or illuminate is shared between "seraphim" and "siren."[68] In the postclassical West, however, only the angel has remained truly sublime. No matter how benign, the "pagan" siren was always somehow suspect, if only for the graceless limits of her power. "If you want to know more about femininity, enquire from your own experiences of life, or turn to poets, or wait until science can give you deeper and more coherent information."

Natural historians from ancient Rome well into the nineteenth century classified sirens and their kin among other beasts of earthly ecosystems, whether as scientists, philosophers, theologians, or mixtures of all three. Science and philosophy were rarely far from art and legend, nor was experience far from poetry. The case of the siren and her siblings particularly shows how supposedly competing forms of Western knowledge work in parallel as part of the need to explain ourselves and our experiences. The Roman historian and cavalry officer Pliny (Caius Plinius Secundus, 23–79 CE), whose natural history served as the primary Western text on the subject until the Enlightenment, acknowledges visual art and poetics in his careful descriptions of questionable creatures. "As for the meremaids called Nereides," says Pliny in early modern English translation

> it is no fabulous tale that goeth of them: for looke how painters draw them, so they are indeed . . . For such a Mermaid was seene and beheld plainely upon the same coast neere to the shore: and the inhabitants dwelling neer, heard it a farre off when it was a dying, to make pitteous mone, crying and chattering very heavily. Moreover, a lieutenant or governour under *Augustus Caesar* in Gaule, advertised him by his letters, That many of these Nereides or Mermaids were seene cast upon the sands, and lying dead. I am able to bring forth for mine authors divers knights of Rome, right worshipfull persons and of good credite, who testifie that in the coast of the Spanish Ocean neere unto Gades, they have seene a Meere-man, in every respect resembling a man as perfectly in all parts of the bodie as might bee.[69]

On the other hand, the beings called sirens are relegated by the great Roman natural historian to the chapter titled "Of new birds, and such as are holden for fabulous," where he also positions griffons and pegasi:

> As touching the birds Syrenes, I will never beleeve there be any such, let
> *Dino* the father of *Clitarchus* that renowmed writer, say what he will:
> who avoucheth for a trugh, that they be in India: and that with their
> singing they will bring folke asleepe, and then flie upon them and teare
> them in peeces.[70]

Here we see the confluence of myth, folklore, and observation, linked by a
strong reliance on written records supplemented by oral reporting. This
was the way Western knowledge of the sirens was transmitted by the
literate for centuries. It was always somebody else who had witnessed the
fabled creatures, most often far away in some colonized or otherwise
dangerously exotic place. But, as with Pliny, the reliability of the observer,
and the quality of the information, were of paramount importance.

Late antique and medieval commentators on sirens in the natural
world were less concerned with demonstrating the existence or delineating
the geographical territory of such beings than with their moral meaning
to the lives of men. Within this tradition, sirens belonged as much to
metaphysics and theology as to the sensate world within which they were
depicted. Such writers as Fulgentius, Isodore of Seville, and the authors of
the *Physiologus* and the medieval bestiaries which drew on it (such as
Bartholomeus's) were more concerned with the mystical transcendence of
the natural world, with reading the divine text of symbols that God had set
within the universe. Whether winged, scaled, or both, what figured most
about these monsters (and the universe was full of monsters and other
marvels) was their femaleness and their song—and the danger posed by
both to good Christian men. From species descriptions, presented and
interpreted along with such others of God's wonders as peacocks, pan-
thers, and dragons, sirens were allegorized into ever-present dangers that
could be met in other forms. Theology and naturalism here joined with
parallel traditions of folklore and mythography; for readers who sought
simple natural history, Pliny remained widely available and widely respected.[71] Nonetheless, such books were usually organized according to
general categories of animals (such as "aquatic animals"), and particular
descriptions almost invariably begin with a physical definition. The siren
of the medieval bestiary demonstrated the ingenuity of visual and verbal
thought in seemingly limitless combinations of monstrous features from
dwellers of air and sea and those of human women:

> Syrenas (sirens), popularized in poetic fable, are marine monsters whose
> upper body has the figure of a woman with long pendulous breasts with
> which it suckles its young; its face is horrible and it has a mane of long
> free-flowing hair; below they have eagle's claws, and above are aquiline

wings, and behind a scaly tail used as a rudder to guide their swimming. Upon making an appearance, they hold out their young in full view, emit some sweet alluring sounds by which they lull their hearers to sleep, and then tear the sleepers to pieces. However, wise sailors plug their ears as they pass, all the while throwing overboard empty bottles to divert the sirens' attention, until their ships are out of danger.[72]

Nonetheless, the "classic" siren of the Middle Ages, whose image is carved and drawn in a multitude of media, faces the viewer with a pair of fishtails spread to expose her vulva and sometimes emphasize her high, firm breasts and smooth, youthful face.[73] In such a pose, her mouth is almost always sealed, leaving no doubt as to the ultimate attraction of her song: "... and [she] bringeth him into a drye place, and maketh him first lye by her, and doe the deede of lechery, and if he will not or may not, then she slaieth him and eateth his flesh."

With the colonial and materialist impulses of the early modern era came a renewed interest in describing, identifying, categorizing, and mapping the territory of sirens and their kin. This was not only the era of the "scientific revolution," but also a time of extraordinary redefinition of women's social and professional roles and of an artistic and theatrical obsession with the sorceress, particularly singing on the operatic stage in works by such composers as Handel and Mozart. The double hybrid and bird-sirens lived on in artistic and mythographic tradition, but the one who survived into early scientific work was a water-dweller. (Her operatic counterpart—the musically virtuosic enchantress along the lines of Alcina, Armida, Medea, or the Queen of the Night—was, by contrast, physically all woman, "diva" of the theatrical world.) In the era of global travel and the birth of scientific collecting, explorers brought back tales and classifiable memorabilia of all sorts of exotic creatures: people of unfamiliar cultures, valuable flora, domesticable animals—and mer-people.[74] Like a latter-day Pliny, Erik Pontoppidan, author of an eighteenth-century natural history of his native Norway, dismisses as mythic those accounts of mer-folk he deems untrue while assembling an "accurate" natural history of the genus. He scoffs at reports of their fabulous voices, prophetic abilities, and multilinguistic fluency, demoting them to the uncommunicative and pre-rational realm of mere animals, in spite of their form.[75] In contrast, Dutch colonizers of the East Indies of the same era, sailors to sparkling seas no less distant or exotic to their world than the isle of sirens had been to Homer's, made scientific observations of "Zee-menschen" and "Zee-wyven," at least one of whom of the latter was captured and observed in a barrel until she died. Samuel Fallours, official painter to the Dutch

East India Company, included a typically eroticized image of such a "sea-wife" in his 1718 book on marine creatures of the region, as part of a group of scientific sketches of (other) fish. Colonial chaplain François Valentijn's natural history of Dutch East Indian Amboina, published in 1726, not only republished Fallours's image but also suggests that Fallours had encountered a different species of mermaid from those with which he had become familiar through reliable descriptive accounts.[76] None of these naturalists' sea-folk were remarked for their voices.

In contrast, Enlightenment historian and philologist Charles Burney (1726–1814), with his extreme interest in music and his encyclopedic habits, instead tried to trace the natural history of the siren from legends of her music. "The name, according to Bochart, who derives it from the Phoenician language," he writes, "implies a *songstress*. Hence it is probable, that in ancient times there may have been excellent singers, but of corrupt morals, on the coast of Sicily, who by seducing voyagers, gave rise to this fable."[77] Burney's older contemporary Jean-Jacques Rousseau (1712–1778) more subtly evokes the fable of the sirens to illustrate the disjunction between auditory attraction and visual repulsion in his *Confessions*. Neither the natural nor cultural history of these creatures figures in his account; instead, he suggests the acoustic beauty that conceals an underlying malformation as had fascinated earlier moralists. The music-loving traveler gives a sensuous account of the young cloistered singing-girls of one of the *Scuole*s which he visited in Italy in 1743–1744, whose "voluptuous and affecting" voices aroused his passions when they performed invisibly, modestly hidden by a grille. He longed to see them, the hidden source of such extreme pleasure. He became obsessed by their sound, trembling with amorous delight at the prospect of meeting them face to face. Finally, when introduced by a friend, he describes the exquisite singers as hideous to a one, disfigured by injury and disease.[78]

Thus the siren's body and voice were severed by scholars during the eighteenth century as completely as her literary and natural scientific histories. Careful observers such as Pontoppidan and Valentijn followed the course of the growing natural sciences and rendered her into an object of silent scrutiny. Others like Burney, who were more interested in the human sciences, instead made the siren the subject of historical or cultural inquiry, often fixating on legends of her voice and power over the human psyche. This bifurcation into silenced object of systematic inquiry or creature of the human imagination has continued to this day. Modern science has banished the siren's song to the fields of history, folklore, and the manifold realms of poetics and the mind.

During the nineteenth century, even as public and private exhibitions showed such paintings as Waterhouse's and countless images of scaled and winged sirens, other venues displayed desiccated "mermaid" bodies to interested observers.[79] The century of Hans Christian Andersen was also the century of Charles Darwin. The elusive unicorn had been banished to the fictions of poetics and fable, but the siren (in mermaid form) remained a subject of interest to many zoologists. As in the previous two centuries, trustworthy travelers to distant seas or to isolated coastal regions on the outskirts of Europe returned with matter-of-fact observations of mer-people; even reliable newspapers reported sightings well after Darwin's voyage of the H.M.S. *Beagle*.[80] As late as 1906, folklorists reported that older people in some rural regions of western Europe had been raised to believe that mermaids and their kin posed a danger to travelers who passed particular lonely shoreline spots at twilight.[81]

By and large, however, the twentieth-century West banished sirens from the observable realms of heaven and earth to vanished philosophies and fantasy fiction. Natural historians and physicians of recent times have tended to attribute centuries of prior belief to the appearance and habits of such curious marine mammals as seals and manatees, or to rare birth-defects that fuse the lower limbs of developing fetuses into a single, tail-like appendage.[82] Gentle dugongs mate face-to-face as do human beings; and, along the Red Sea, there remains an oral tradition that, in former centuries, sex-starved sailors who found the large-breasted female of the species lazing in shallow waters learned by experience that the dugong vagina is rather similar to the human one.[83] Taking Burney's impulse one step further, twentieth-century investigators have explained the source of the fabled song of the siren to be seaside nightingales whose exquisite voices carried further than their image across the waters.[84] The siren's voice, body, and legendary powers over the human psyche have thus been neatly dissected and parceled out to different academic specialists for study.

These attempts to fully separate fact from fable say as much about the way in which twentieth-century science has dealt with competing epistemologies as about the (natural) history of the siren. It beggars belief to accept that millennia of sailors, whose lives and professions depended on extraordinarily keen powers of visual and auditory observation, would have mistaken bloated, bald sirenians or pinnipeds for long-tressed maidens, or the twittering of birds for personally addressed prognostications in their native languages. The fact that sirens have belonged to so many parallel Western intellectual systems demonstrates the cultural complexities of the search for knowledge and the reflection of who and what we are. The publisher of the vernacular Nuremberg Bible (1483) presumes no exegetical paradox by including an exquisite, full-color image of a

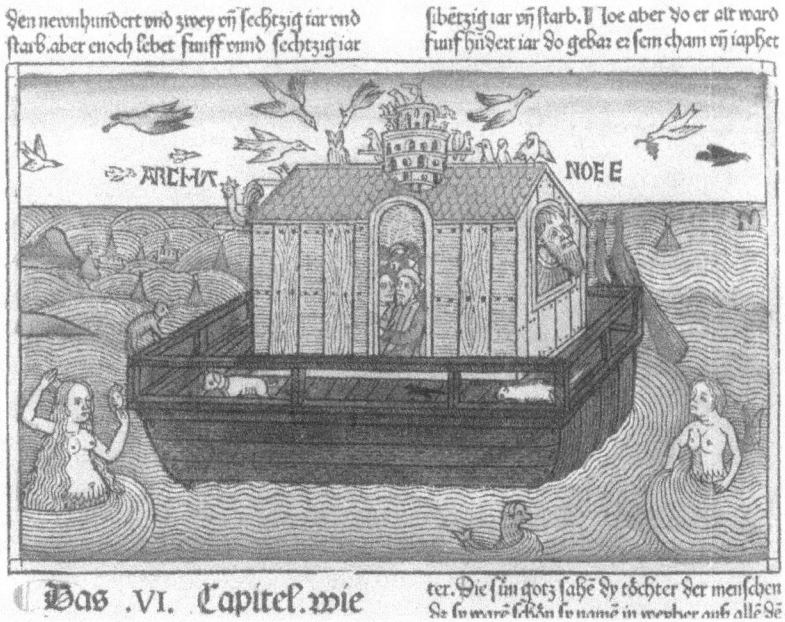

Figure 2.3. Woodcut from the Nuremberg Bible (1483). © V&A Images/Victoria and Albert Museum.

mermaid, merman, and mer-puppy swimming beside Noah's ark (fig. 2.3). This early German Reformation work was intended to enable direct individual access to the Word of God in all its meaning. It was presumably in this same spirit of intellectual syncretism that the seventeenth-century German Jesuit philosopher Athanasius Kircher drew together the fields of optics, mathematics, engineering, and zoology with mystical theology in his enormous work *Arca Noë* (1675). In this book, complete with a fold-out diagram of Noah's ark as zoological museum, the siren is described after the tortoise ("Testudo") and seal ("Phoca") as the last of the "Amphibia," creatures who live between land and water and which also include the beaver. Kircher describes the "Syrena" as a sea-monster ("Monstrum marinum") who sings, called by the Greeks of his day a "siren" and by the Spanish and Italians a "woman fish" ("pesce Mugier" and "Pesce donna," respectively). He also assures us that, in spite of some controversy over the issue, this creature had been granted a place on Noah's ark, in vats of water.[85]

As to the siren's body across the centuries and competing epistemolo-

Figure 2.4. Siren from Athanasius Kircher, *Arca Noë* (1675). By permission of the Newberry Library, Chicago.

gies, it was in mermaid form that Kircher showed her (fig. 2.4). It was in the same shape that forgeries were made of fish- and monkey-parts earlier in the scientific era, and displayed throughout Europe and North America with tales of exotic origin and mysterious prognostications before death.[86] Yet, as we shall see, the original bird-siren lived on, bringing the creature closer to the mystical swan of prophetic utterance, and allowing artists a wide range of vision in presenting a monster whose power is aural. The tradition that sirens are depicted with chicken's feet "because whatever they hold is sprinkled with the emotion of passion" survived medieval mythography to influence Arnold Böcklin's *Sirenen* (1875), in which hens' feathery softness has metamorphosed into a horrifying image of deadly music (fig. 2.5).[87] By the late nineteenth century, when the greatest threats to humankind were revealed most clearly through the microscope and when behavioral science largely explained what had previously been left to allegory, the siren no longer needed monstrous form. The most frightening beast lurked just beneath the exquisite beauty of feminine flesh. Dante Gabriel Rossetti's *A Sea Spell* (1877), framed with the author's accompanying poem at its bottom, presents an exquisite red-haired harpist with an entirely human form, surrounded by fruit and blossoms in varying shades from blush to blood (fig. 2.6).

Figure 2.5. Arnold Böcklin, *Sirenen* (1875). National-Galerie, Berlin. Photo credit: Bildarchiv Preussischer Kulturbesitz / Art Resource, New York.

Figure 2.6. Dante Gabriel Rossetti, *A Sea Spell* (1877). Courtesy of the Fogg Art Museum, Harvard University Art Museums, Gift of Grenville L. Winthrop, Class of 1886. Photo Credit: Katya Kallsen. Image Credit: © 2004 President and Fellows of Harvard College.

Her lute hangs shadowed in the apple-tree.
While flashing fingers weave the sweet-strung spell
Between its chords: and as the wild notes swell
The sea-bird for those branches leaves the sea.
But to what sound her listening ear stoops she?
What netherworld gulf-whispers doth she hear,
In answering echoes from what planisphere,
Along the wind, along the estuary?
She sinks into her spell; and when full soon
Her lips move and she soars into her song
What creatures of the midmost main shall throng
In furrowed self-clouds to the summoning rune,
Till he, the fated mariner, hears her cry,
And up her rock, bare breasted, comes to die?[88]

The sirens' barren, bone-strewn meadow has here become a florid paradise, her avian origins relegated to her song and to a gull hovering like some secular embodiment of the Holy Spirit; her "Sea Spell" has become irresistible in an age of empire and mercantile wanderings. Yet always has the siren been some sort of impossible hybrid, a riddle, an anomalous vessel for the music of dangerous rapture. "Birds without wings, and girls without legs, and fish without a mouth, they nevertheless sing with their lips," writes the influential sixteenth-century Italian emblematist, Andrea Alciati, "because lust carries itself with many monsters."[89] The torment of the sirens' song had become the cold flame of desire.

The Siren and the Soul

> Every evening the young Fisherman went out upon the sea, and called the Mermaid, and she rose out of the water and sang to him. Round and round her swam the dolphins, and the wild gulls wheeled above her head. . . .
>
> And each day the sound of her voice became sweeter to his ears. So sweet was her voice that he forgot his nets and his cunning, and had no care of his craft. . . . His spear lay by his side unused, and his baskets of plaited osier were empty. With lips parted, and eyes dim with wonder, he sat idle in his boat and listened, listening till the sea-mists crept around him, and the wandering moon stained his brown limbs with silver.
>
> And one evening he called to her, and said, "Little Mermaid, little Mermaid, I love thee. Take me for thy bridegroom for I love thee."
>
> But the Mermaid shook her head. "Thou hast a human soul," she answered. "If only thou wouldst send away thy soul, then could I love thee."
>
> —Oscar Wilde, "The Fisherman and His Soul," in
> *A House of Pomegranates*[90]

To the Christian culture that has dominated Western thought for close to 1,500 years, even the most fantastic tales and fabulous creatures could be drawn into the eternal drama of sin and salvation. The most pervasive myths and folktales of earlier Western cultures have been handed to the modern era through the filters of a religion founded on universalism and on the revelation of spiritual truths through (humanly) inexplicable wonders. The Christian siren from Medieval legend through Romantic fairy-tale is a strange, soulless creature of exquisite voice and bestial behavior. Every strict adherent to the early faith knew that she had been fashioned alongside winged fowl, with "the great sea-monsters and every living creature . . . wherewith the waters swarmed," on the fourth day of creation. The Greek Septuagint and Latin Vulgate Bibles positioned her among the voluptuaries in Babylon in Isaiah's bleak vision of destruction.[91] The similitude between the promise of wisdom made by the Sirens to Ulysses and that between the Serpent and "our first parents" in the Book of Genesis was as remarkable as the monstrous forms of both.[92] Holy writ itself thus emphasized the siren's utterly alien character directly and through inference, further underscored by image after image in moralizing bestiaries and in churches. She belonged to the moiety of sorcery and the company of demons; she embodied pagan literature and heretic speech, particularly figured through her tempting song.[93]

Especially in mermaid form, with genitals exposed between a split tail or with a single phallic appendage, the siren gained a number of other meanings in a Christianized culture of orality, misogyny, and fear of the sexualized female body. She was particularly associated with lust and earthly pleasure, but also with fame, flattery, and all vain pursuits.[94] A summary by seventeenth-century English mythographer Richard Linche draws on a wealth of earlier native and continental material:

> But howsoever the Poets varie their opinions, they generally understand by those Syrens the delicate purenesse of beautie, wantonnesse, pleasure, and enticing allurements to the daliance of amorous embracements. And it is read, that they sing so melodiously, and with such a sence-besotting sweetnesse, that the suspectlessly inchaunted sea-travellers are infinitely beguiled and lulled asleepe with the harmony and pleasing blandishment thereof, and by that meanes are murthered and devoured by them, as indeed it often times befalleth unto those miserable and unfortunate men, who bewitched aith the illecebrous and honny-dewed tongues of harlots, suffer themselves to be (as it were) cast into a sleep, shutting the eyes of understanding and reason, and by that meanes are made a pretty to those devouring & greedie vulturs . . . unclouding thereby the assurednesse of ruine, decay, and perishment to those that so voluptuously addict themselves to the unbridled affection of such lascivious and soule-hazarding concupiscence.[95]

The mer-siren was the cold *femme fatale* from the depths of a watery Hell, come to seduce the Christian soul as easily as she might catch a fish. She was piscine sister to the foam-born Venus whose erotic predilections she shared in many accounts, an earthly Stella Maris with a barren womb. As such, she figured prominently in many religious and moralizing works from Clement of Alexandria well into the modern era. "Mer-mayds or *Syrens* . . . would allure Saylers to them, and afterward destroy them; being first brought asleepe with harkening to their sweete singing . . . wherefore sometime alluring women are said to be *Syrens*," explains an early-seventeenth-century English dictionary written for the female gender.[96] Sir Thomas Wyatt's translation of Psalm VI, "Domine, ne in furore," metaphorically embodies secular distractions as "mermaids, and their baits of error" from which David the Psalmist stops his ears with the help of divine goodness.[97] Her perfect breasts and open mouth were the visual manifestation of the attractive dangers of her voice, and her loose hair signified potentially dangerous magical powers, linked by ancient tradition to her song. Her mirror, comb, and shell were not simply images of vanity; the latter two had longstanding association with the female pudenda.[98] Her tail was homologous to the Edenic serpent whose sibilant utterance had caused death and disease to enter the world. She was literally banished to the margins in the context of the sacred Word of illuminated manuscripts and illustrated bibles, her unheard song the brazen flourish of eternal doom.

What signifies most about the siren in Christian theology and mythography is her femaleness, her song presumably as feminine as her upper body. Taxonomically speaking, she is all beast, and as such she figures prominently in the bestiaries and naturalist studies of the Middle Ages and early modern era. Virtually each and every one of these, extending back to the *Physiologus* and even to Pliny, emphasizes the power of her song in text if not in image. But here its sound has been moralized into the lure of all unchristian pleasures. Should the soul rest even for a moment, like a weary sailor lulled by her sweet song, it would be torn to pieces in her savage grasp. Hers are the spiritually unintelligible words against the Word. To enter the sonic envelope of *jouissance* and to be softly enraptured by methods and messages that rivaled the Church was to be lost eternally, to sink into a forbidden world of death and darkness. The siren was thus accounted the patron demoness not only of secular music, theater, pagan poetry, and the worldly lusts for flesh and fame but also of all heretic speech and distractions from the contemplative or moral life, as Wyatt presents her.[99] "Lewd and unchast [songs and] verses, notwithstanding that they be very elegant and made in good Latin," exclaims Peter Martyr Vermigli among his commonplaces, "may well be called the Syrens of mens minds, wherein yong men being trained, can hardly escape shipwrack."[100]

Like Wilde's sweetly sentimental mermaid, the Christian siren was a hunter of fish, ancient icon of the Christian soul, which she often grasps in triumph, flopping phallic trophies of the power of her song (fig. 2.7).[101] Tradition had further reduced the creature to a common whore, luring men to the shipwreck of (sexual) sin. This pragmatic connection became even clearer under the shadow of the Ovidian evocation of the sirens as embodiments of the erotic power available to any woman who would acquire musical skill.[102] By the close of the nineteenth century, in such images as Edward Coley Burne-Jones's *The Depths of the Sea*, the phallus-fish had become a man, dragged downward to a watery grave as her song

re qulbz dr. popls quem non co
uro m. & malio ppha.vocabo n p
plebem meam. & non dilectam. b

Figure 2.7. Siren from manuscript St. John's 61, folio 47. St. John's College, Oxford. By permission of the Library, St. John's College, Oxford.

became a silent smile of triumph (fig. 6.1). Her work done, her lure accepted, the cold, soulless being had no more need of music. The un-reasoning, amoral danger of siren-song—whatever that encompassed—transferred easily from an era of Christian spirituality to one of psycho-analysis. Hans Zender's brief chamber piece "Les Sirènes chantent quand la raison s'endort" ("The Sirens Sing When Reason Sleeps," 1966), scored for soprano, flute, clarinet in B, cello, vibraphone, and piano toys with rationality and expectation on several levels. Written as an homage to Surrealist artist Max Ernst, the piece toys horizontally and vertically with the listener's presumptions as much as any from its era. Melody, harmony, tone-color, rhythmic units, and performance techniques are all presented in ever-shifting ways that defy expectation; without careful analysis—the ultimate triumph of silent, rational control over music—it is virtually im-possible to determine the organizational principles underlying the piece. Perhaps most importantly, the virtuosic soprano line—with its mixture of song and *sprechstimme*, of sound through open and closed lips—vocalizes wordlessly in short, irregular phrases for most of the piece between the reference to siren-song and its stated antithesis to reason. The sirens do indeed sing when "reason" sleeps—but in a single, surreal voice, defiant of rational expectation.[103]

By ancient tradition, not all siren-beings were unreasonable creatures, deliberate destroyers of men's lives and souls. According to the sixteenth-century German physician and occult philosopher, Paracelsus (Theophrastus Bombastus von Hohenheim), such water-women were redeemable through marriage to a man from Adam's seed and his transfigurative love. The divine Creator of All had peopled the world not only with human beings, animals, and all matter of spirits but also with those who were midway between flesh and spirit and who lived within each of the four elements. They communed with spirit-beings, sensed and ate like humans, but died like animals, for they were born without souls. "This happens with the water people," he writes,

> They come out of their waters to us, make themselves known, act and deal with us, go back to their water, come again—all this to allow man the contemplation of divine works. From this it follows that they marry men. A water woman takes a man from Adam, and keeps house for him, and gives birth to children. Of the children, we know that they follow after the father. Because the father is a man from Adam, a soul is given to the child, and it becomes like a regular man, who has an eternal soul. Furthermore, this also is well known and must be considered, that such women also receive souls by becoming married, so that they are saved before God and by God like other women. . . . This is demonstrated by them also: they have no soul, unless they enter into a union with men, and now they have the soul. They die, and nothing remains of them but the beast. And a man who is not in divine union is just like them. Just as the condition of these people is, when they are in union with man, so is the condition of man, when he is in union with God. And thus they demonstrate that they are beasts without man, and like them man without divine union is nothing. The union of two things with each other can achieve so much, that the inferior benefits from the superior and acquires its powers.[104]

Long before Paracelsus's day, historians had chronicled sirens and their kin who had left the water, joined communities on land, and become good Christians; one had taken her place among the beatified as Saint Murgen.[105] But it was particularly during the eighteenth and nineteenth centuries, even as many of her kind were depicted as amoral hookers of the souls of men, that the sweetest of sirens sought true immortality through Christian marriage. This promise of ensoulment through love, of an immortal ascent from sea to sky for all eternity from a blessed union with one man, ultimately unifies the Homeric and Platonic sirens within a Christian context. Such sanctified sacramental love promises the true immortality of a Christian soul, transcendence from Eve's loquacity to Mary's spiritual grace. But the undertaking is not without peril for either participant. "Mr. Melville," asks Wells's uncomprehending Sea Lady some time before he follows her into the aquatic depths from which there is no return, "what *is* a soul?"[106] It is only in the transfigurative silence of death and the prior loss of his own soul that Wilde's Fisherman attains union with his beloved Mermaid, who lies dead and voiceless in his net. Baron Friedrich de la Motte Fouqué's spurned Undine returns to land to grant her beloved Uldbrand a watery death as she weeps away her hard-won immortality in the famous tale that bears her name (1811).[107] "There must be something very precious, but also very dreadful about a soul," she remarks to the priest who suggests that she try to tune hers in harmony with the husband who ultimately betrays her.[108] "*For a man who is not in divine union is just like them.*"

For all of these women of the water, the price of a soul is silence, the very virtue enjoined to her human counterparts by holy scripture and traditional Christian values. With the loss of her musical voice and removal from her fluid natural element comes (metaphorical) chastity, the foundation of Christian marriage. The silenced siren, the tamed seductress, or the woman removed from her wild habitat to the realm of men is fit for matrimony. "'Why have not *we* immortal souls?'" asks the most famous of all, Andersen's Little Mermaid, of her wise old grandmother.

> "I would willingly give up my three hundred years to be a human being for only one day, thus to become entitled to that heavenly world above."
>
> "You must not think of that," answered her grandmother, "it is much better as it is; we live longer and are far happier than human beings."
>
> "So I must die, and be dashed like foam over the sea, never to rise again and hear the gentle murmur of the ocean, never again see the beautiful flowers and the bright sun! Tell me, dear grandmother, are there no means by which I may obtain an immortal soul?"
>
> "No!" replied the old lady, "it is true that if thou coudst so win the affections of a human being as to become dearer to him than either father or mother; if he loved thee with all his heart, and promised whilst the priest joined his hands with thine to be always faithful to thee; then his soul would flow into thine, and thou wouldst then become partaker of human bliss."[109]

The grandmother's response clearly links soul to semen, even while protecting the beloved child's virginity. The Mermaid, of course, sacrifices her (potentially seductive) voice to the Sea-Witch's knife, and ultimately loses all she had and all for which she hoped. However, with her death and the loss of the magically impaired mer-body that had never quite become human, she once again acquires a voice, antithetical to the traditional song of the siren:

> The sun rose from his watery bed; his beams fell so softly and warmly upon her, that our little mermaid was scarcely sensible of dying. She still saw the glorious sun; and over her head hovered a thousand beautiful transparent forms; . . . the voices of those airy creatures above her had a melody so sweet and soothing, that a human ear would be as little able to catch the sound as her eye was capable of distinguishing their forms. . . .
>
> "Where are you taking me?" asked she, and her words sounded just like the voices of those heavenly beings.[110]

The idea of the beneficent, bodiless siren Christianized is perhaps presented in most extreme form in an American publication from around the time of Andersen's famous story. "The Siren, *A Collection of* Sacred Music," proclaims the title page of an anthology of Protestant devotional music, "Suitable for Sunday Evening's Recreation, and Public or Private Devotion, *Consisting of the most Celebrated* Psalm and Hymn Tunes &c. adapted and arranged for One, two, three or four Voices and Piano Forte *or Organ.*"[111] Severed from her body, and granted not her own seductive voice but loaning her name to the old songs of salvation for the Sabbath, this siren becomes the ultimate power of the soul.

Death and Metamorphosis

> Full fathom five thy father lies;
> Of his bones are coral made;
> Those are pearls that were his eyes;
> Nothing of him that doth fade,
> But doth suffer a sea-change
> Into something rich and strange.
> —William Shakespeare, *The Tempest*, Act I, scene ii

The Western siren, relegated to the flowing reaches between air and sea, life and death, noon and night, and body and soul, has been granted numerous metamorphic qualities since ancient times. Finned, fleshed, or feathered, she has taken many shapes and shades of morality. She has loaned her form to men's ships and to musical instruments, her voice to prophecy and doom. She has been the lulling mother, and the shriek of the storm. One of the most ancient and vital aspects of the siren has been her role as mediatrix between states of being, or her airy fluidity between physical forms. Where there are sirens, there are sea-changes. Andersen's humane Little Mermaid dissolves not to foam, but into a gentle, transparent angel-being of sound and light. Undine, ensouled and then scorned by the knight she had loved, becomes a silvery spring embracing his grave for all eternity.[112] The banished Soul re-enters Wilde's Fisherman as he recognizes the transcendent power of love which breaks his heart as the sea engulfs his body in the arms of his Mermaid. On a holy day, three years after their death and burial in a single unconsecrated grave, grow curiously beautiful and deeply affecting flowers.[113] Long before the time of Andersen, Motte Fouqué, or Wilde, culminating in the era of Paracelsus, the siren had a vital place in alchemy, the ultimate science of transmutation. Here, she stood for the supreme conjunction of opposites, bringing together the cool, moist, "first matter" of life (alchemical mercury) and the hot, dry, active principle (alchemical sulfur), rendering spiritual that which was corporeal, metaphysical that which was of nature, and external that which was interior. Her very paradoxical nature and hybridity—a unity of the potent symbols of the fish and the virgin—embodied the divine knowledge or wisdom sought by alchemy. She was the very power of transformation.[114] According to a tradition memorialized by Ovid, the sirens were granted their strange form, with wings and claws to skim the seas but with girlish face and voice, by Ceres after they witnessed the abduction of her daughter from their flowery meadow.[115] Thus they stood, like Proserpina, at the juncture between florid growth and the land of the dead. "Why were sirens, hyenas and certain other monsters given harmonies and alluring voices by nature?" asks the sixteenth-century neo-Platonist and music theorist John Case,

> just as in sirens and hyenas is a human face: so it is not to be wondered that there is here also an imitation of the human voice: for just as a heavenly modulation is conceded to humans in particular, so those who bear the form and likeness of a human are often given sweet voices and (musical) concord.[116]

Throughout European lore, no creature has been granted a celestial and often prophetic voice more often than the swan. A widespread tradition with roots in ancient natural history links swan-song to the evident silence of death. The uncanny cry of the wild swan, her shifting habitat between air and smooth water, and her preference for lonely, unpopulated shores further connected her to the siren. Yet unlike the more loquacious and potentially dangerous siren, the swan was often silent to the end, metamorphosing between a fully human and an avian form through dark magic. Her cry signified not only the beginning and end to her flight but also its metaphysical extension between forms, between body and soul. In visual symbolism, the abundant, loose hair of the siren also corresponds to the feathered headdress of the enchanted swan-maiden and represents a similar connection to the metaphysically linked wilderness and Otherworld, both opposed to familiar human domain.[117] In the widespread ballad called "The Twa Sisters" by nineteenth-century English collector Francis James Child (Child #10), a woman drowned by her jealous sister undergoes a brief metamorphosis from human victim to mermaid to swan in the eyes of the person who finds her body. It is only after death, rescue, and a final gruesome metamorphosis into a musical instrument (most often a harp) in the hands of a traveling musician that she gains a voice to denounce her killer.[118]

During the nineteenth century, on the heels of stories like Andersen's, in which the siren serves as rescuer and humane force instead of traditional *femme fatale,* and under the influence of the increased interest in collecting such ballads and folk-tales as "The Twa Sisters," the forms and varieties of siren metamorphosis became more diverse than ever. Layer upon layer of old legends continued to mix together to create new myths and extraordinary new images.[119] Daniel Maclise's exquisite woodcut for Thomas Moore's 1846 poem, "The Origin of the Harp," clearly owes a great deal to the sort of metamorphic tradition as "The Twa Sisters," as well as to the Celtic revival and Irish nationalist movements of the period (fig. 2.8).

Tis believ'd that this Harp, which I now wake for thee,
Was a Siren of old, who sung under the sea;
And who often, at eve, thro' the bright waters rov'd
To meet, on the green shore, a youth whom she lov'd.

But she lov'd him in vain, for he left her to weep,
And in tears, all the night her gold tresses to steep:
Till heav'n look'd with pity on true-love so warm,
And chang'd to this soft Harp the sea-maiden's form.

Still her bosom rose fair—still her cheeks smiled the same
While her sea-beauties gracefully form'd the light frame;
And her hair, as let loose, o'er her white arm it fell,
Was changed to bright chords, utt'ring melody's spell.

Figure 2.9. Parthenope from Giulio Cesare Capaccio, *Delle imprese trattato* (1592), folio 23v. By permission of the Newberry Library, Chicago.

Hence it came, that this soft harp so long hath been known
To mingle love's language with sorrow's sad tone;
Till thou didst divide them, and teach the fond lay
To speak love when I'm near thee, and grief when away.[120]

The four-stanza poem not only explains the human head carved onto so many European instruments (including, but not limited to, traditional Irish harps) but also grants supernatural power to the music that would have accompanied it. Flowing over the ears like seawater, like the sound from the shells shown around the siren's body (mostly facing outward for the viewer to grasp them in imagination), this is music that touches the hearer powerfully and beyond rational response. From death to life, from sorrow to joy, from aquatic charmer to earthly musician, this is the music of enchantment, of change from one state to another at the touch of a finger, that "doth suffer a sea-change / Into something rich and strange."

The representation of superior power of enchantment on musical instruments already had a long history in Europe before the mid-nineteenth century. Sirens in particular had long held an important place in this craft, as figures of the power of music for good or ill. The *lira da braccio*, instrument of courtly poet-musicians and metaphor for persuasive speech in Renaissance Italy, is nourished by the milk of the siren Parthenope,

Figure 2.10. Sirens and aquatic demigoddesses spellbound by Arion, from the lid of an Italian octave spinet (ca. 1600). Victoria and Albert Museum, Keyboard Catalogue Number 11. © V&A Images/Victoria and Albert Museum.

mythical founder and protectress of the city of Naples, in a visual allegory of civic concord from 1592 (fig. 2.9).[121] In contrast, the interior lid of a sixteenth-century Italian spinet now housed in the Victoria and Albert Museum (fig. 2.10) shows sirens and shell-born demigoddesses held spellbound by the song of Arion, perhaps giving the performer equal power over less honorable musical impulses. For in the Christianized mythography of early modern Europe, if the siren was the demonic Eve of temptation, huntress of the ichthyoid soul, Arion with his tamed dolphin and more powerful, lifesaving song, like Orpheus, was Christ.[122]

Yet in the liminal spaces between life and death, sea and sky, light and darkness, the siren has also retained her more gentle power over the soul in transit. She crosses the barrier between ancient legend and deep psychic desire in Herbert Draper's 1898 *Lament for Icarus* (fig. 2.11), in which the pale, glowing bodies of the three sirens recall ancient legends of their kind as gentle lights upon the waters to guide human souls to eternity.[123] Objects of nurturance and desire, they could hardly contrast more with the

Figure 2.11. Herbert Draper, *Lament for Icarus* (1898). Tate Britain, London. By permission of Tate Enterprises Ltd.

exquisite form of Icarus. Scion of an earthly wizard, he lies dead from his flight above the earth on artificial wings. Where the sirens stand for the deep mysteries of nature and forbidden knowledge, the son of Daedalus represents the failure of civilized artifice. His was a foolish quest for forbidden knowledge, brought to its tragic end by the scorching heat of unattainable enlightenment. Cool beauties of aquatic depth, the sirens rise to cradle the sun-kissed body on its bier of eagle wings, so gently that they barely disturb the water. As the sunlight leaves his broken form, they sing. Where he is darkly chiseled with all the physical virtues of masculinity, they are pale and soft, caressing him not as lovers would, but as a mother might shift her sleeping child into a more comfortable position. We imagine their music from their forms, soft, lush, unaccompanied, richly twined with pleasing harmony, rising upward like the dead hero's soul. The highest one, her golden hair illuminated like a halo by the dying sun, holds aside a shining harp, unplayed. They have no need of artificial instruments

Example 2.2. Opening of "The Mermaid's Evening Song" by Chas. D. Blake (1881).

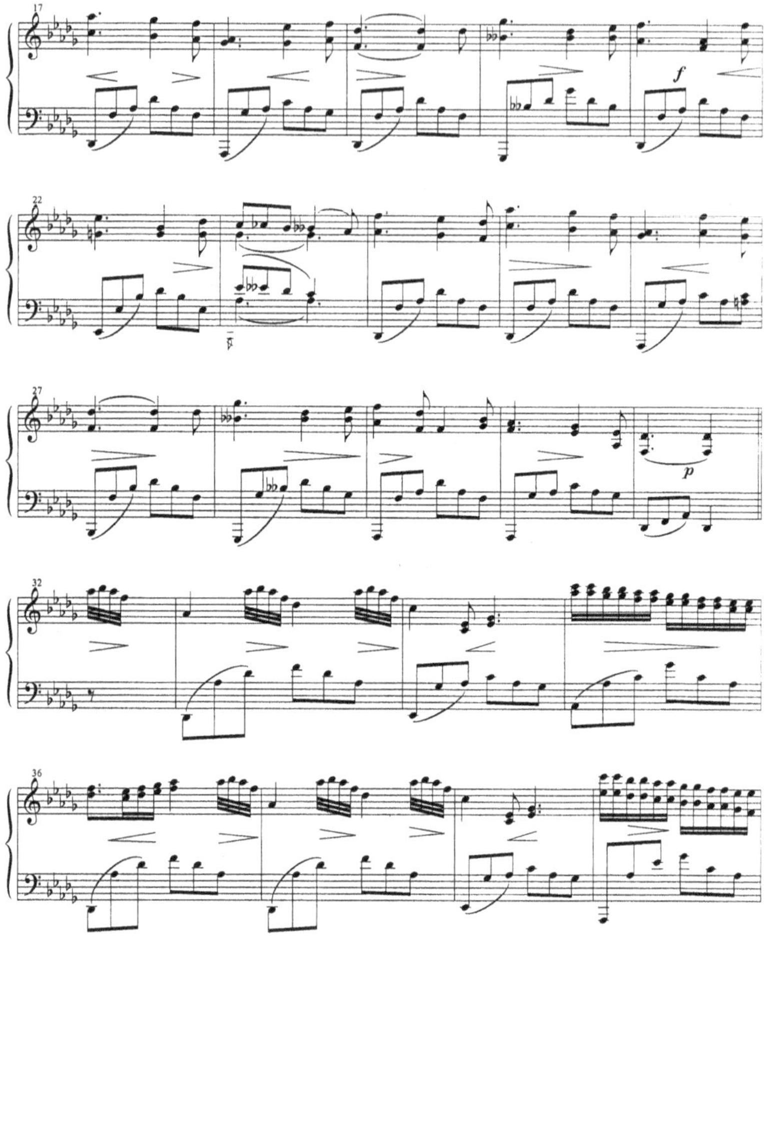

in their lament. They have become aquatic angels from below whose song guides home the soul of a fallen member of another tribe. Here the demonic, Christian fish-huntress and the grasping, knowing hooker of the depths have come full circle to become the sapient possessor of eternal secrets and the soul's beloved.

In the first volume of his *History of Music,* published in 1776, Charles Burney suggests that it is not only muses who live in every era. Sirens, too, he tells us, appear whenever beauty and talent come together to attract us with their music.[124] In 1962, British novelist E. M. Forster, who himself had created a cosmic siren whose song would destroy silence, primness, cruelty, and save the world, wondered what would happen to the topos in an era in which the sea was no longer untamable or eternal, but had been

Figure 2.12. Cover of Chas. D. Blake, *The Mermaid's Evening Song. A Souvenir of the Great Lakes* (1881). By permission of the Newberry Library, Chicago.

polluted and destroyed by "the mightiness of Man."[125] The alternating ebb and flow, the gentle waves of siren music, still remain a metaphor for the unfathomable, the infinite, and the ever-changing, even in an era of eco-logical ruin. The siren's music and all that it affects remains the same. A lovely "souvenir of the Great Lakes," an evocative piece of sheet music for piano of 1881, reminds us of this over a century after its creation. This "Mermaid's Evening Song," dedicated to one "Mrs. Wm. Flagg of Chicago, Ill." (ex. 2.2), was first published and sold in an era in which the instru-ment served as both a vehicle for the display of female beauty and talent and an iconographic reminder of the dangerous links between women, desire, and death.[126] The piece still retains its power to charm and enrap-ture. Written in the abstruse key of D-flat major and full of rising and falling motives that evoke water, the piece is to be played "Andante Mis-terioso" in alternating duple and compound meter and without the intel-lectual specificity of text. It borrows centuries-old musical and cultural clichés of siren seduction, pieced together in unexpected ways. Yet it is perhaps the cover that performs the most evident siren magic: floating past jagged rocks and engaged in feminine grooming rituals in front of a

[94]

palm tree, three large-eyed mermaids (blonde, brunette, and redhead) and their swimming sisters have metamorphosed the cold waters and flat, industrialized shoreline of Chicago into an exciting tropical paradise (fig. 2.12).[127] Both nature and reason have been transformed "into something rich and strange" by their wordless music. As English writer John Donne commands in one of his most famous poems, if only facetiously, "teach me to heare Mermaides singing."[128]

NOTES

1. Elizabeth Scarborough, *Song of Sorcery* (New York: Bantam Books, 1982), 170–71. As part of this delightful pastiche of Western folklore, fairy tale, balladry, and literary classics, the siren character is given the name of Lorelei; see 182–85.

2. James Joyce, *Ulysses* (New York: Vintage Books, 1961), 282.

3. See Cheryl Herr, "Nature and Culture in the 'Sirens' Episode of Joyce's *Ulysses*," in *James Joyce's Ulysses: Modern Critical Interpretations* (New York: Chelsea House Publishers, 1987), 134 and 143; and Lawrence Kramer, *After the Lovedeath: Sexual Violence and the Making of Culture* (Berkeley and Los Angeles: University of California Press, 1997), 110–11.

4. Joyce, *Ulysses*, 283.

5. For further information about the bar or cocktail lounge as the abode of the twentieth-century siren, see Joseph Lanza, *The Cocktail: The Influence of Spirits on the American Psyche* (New York: St. Martin's Press, 1995), 78–87.

6. Joyce, *Ulysses*, 274. See also Herr, "Nature and Culture in the 'Sirens' Episode of Joyce's *Ulysses*," 135–37; and Kramer, *After the Lovedeath*, 109–10.

7. Lanza, *The Cocktail*, 79–81.

8. See Karen Horney, *Feminine Psychology* (New York: W.W. Norton and Co., 1967), 134; and Klaus Theweleit, *Male Fantasies*, trans. Stephen Conway in collaboration with Erica Carter and Chris Turner, vol. 1, *Women, Floods, Bodies, History*, foreword by Barbara Ehrenreich (Minneapolis: University of Minnesota, 1987), 252–53 and 283–84.

9. Simone de Beauvoir, *The Second Sex*, trans. and ed. H. M. Parshley (New York: Alfred A. Knopf, 1971), 165.

10. See ibid., 603; and Sherry B. Ortner, "Is Female to Male as Nature Is to Culture?" in *Woman, Culture and Society*, ed. Michelle Zimbalist Rosaldo and Louise Lamphere (Stanford: Stanford University Press, 1974), 71–79.

11. Beauvoir, *The Second Sex*, 144.

12. See Elaine Morgan, *The Descent of Woman* (New York: Stein and Day, 1972), 22–55; and Theweleit, *Male Fantasies*, 288–92. It is worth noting that nineteenth-century iconography, which included numerous eroticized images of sirens and other water-dwelling women, linked female sexuality to the same over-

development of the buttocks that is particularly emphasized in the image of the mermaid, Kramer, *After the Lovedeath,* 260. Even apart from evolutionary biology and Romantic fantasy, Woman in her culturally constructed, passive eroticism "feels that she is surrounded by waves, radiations, mystic fluids," Beauvoir, *The Second Sex,* 599.

13. See Patrick Bade, *Femme Fatale: Images of Evil and Fascinating Women* (New York: Mayflower Books, 1979), 8; Beauvoir, *The Second Sex,* 144; H. David Brumble, *Classical Myths and Legends in the Middle Ages and Renaissance: A Dictionary of Allegorical Meanings* (Westport, Conn.: Greenwood Press, 1998), 39–40; Buffie Johnson, *Lady of the Beasts: Ancient Images of the Goddess and Her Sacred Animals* (San Francisco: Harper and Row, 1988), 239–40; and Ann Moss, *Poetry and Fable: Studies on Mythological Narrative in Sixteenth-Century France* (Cambridge: Cambridge University Press, 1984), 33–34. "And every one of those flowing places goes by the name of Woman," writes Klaus Theweleit of the waters of the earth, *Male Fantasies,* 284.

14. Michel Bulteau, *Les Filles des eaux* (Monaco: Éditions du Rocher, 1997), 10–11; and Johnson, *Lady of the Beasts,* 36.

15. See Henry Alden Bunker, "The Voice as (Female) Phallus," *The Psychoanalytic Quarterly* 3 (1934): 426–27; Horney, *Feminine Psychology,* 117; and Theweleit, *Male Fantasies,* 273–74. Sigmund Freud points out that "men also picture death as a return to the womb (to the water)," "Revision of Dream Theory," in *The Complete Introductory Lectures on Psychoanalysis,* trans. and ed. James Strachey (New York: W. W. Norton, 1966), 488.

16. Beauvoir, *The Second Sex,* 147; see also ibid., 165; and Horney, *Feminine Psychology,* 134.

17. H. G. Wells, *The Sea Lady* (New York: D. Appleton and Co., 1902), 238–39.

18. See Theweleit, *Male Fantasies,* 249–54.

19. See Meri Lao, *Sirens: Symbols of Seduction,* trans. John Oliphant of Rossi in collaboration with the author (Rochester, Vt.: Park Street Press, 1998), 34–35; and Theweleit, *Male Fantasies,* 258–62.

20. See Bunker, "The Voice as (Female) Phallus," 429; Silla Consoli, *La Candeur d'un monstre: essai psychanalytique sur le mythe de la Sirène* (Paris: Éditions du Centurion, 1980), 69; and Géza Roheim, "The Song of the Sirens," *Psychiatric Quarterly* 22 (1946): 25–26 and 38. For further information about the voice as part of primal infantile fantasy, see Roheim, "The Song of the Sirens," 26; and Guy Rosolato, "La Voix," in *Essais sur le symbolique* (Paris: Éditions Gallimard, 1969), 295; and for more about death as a return to the womb, see Freud, "Revision of Dream Theory" in *The Complete Introductory Lectures on Psychoanalysis,* 488.

21. Tom Johnstone and Klaus R. Scherer, "Vocal Communication of Emotion," in *Handbook of Emotions,* 2d ed., ed. Michael Lewis and Jeannette M. Haviland-Jones (New York: Guilford Press, 2000), 223.

22. Thomas Clifton, *Music as Heard: A Study in Applied Phenomenology* (New Haven, Conn.: Yale University Press, 1983), 277–78.

23. Giuseppe di Lampedusa, "The Professor and the Siren," in *Two Stories and a Memory*, trans. Archibald Colquhoun, intro. E. M. Forster (London: Collins and Harvill Press, 1962), 100.

24. Wells, *The Sea Lady*, 273.

25. See Moss, *Poetry and Fable*, 33–34.

26. Roheim, "The Song of the Sirens," 18–20.

27. See Linda Phyllis Austern, "The Siren, the Muse, and the God of Love: Music and Gender in Seventeenth-Century English Emblem Books," *Journal of Musicological Research* 18 (1999): 102–103; Kramer, *After the Lovedeath*, 110–11 and 202; Thomas G. Pavel, "In Praise of the Ear (Gloss's Glosses)," in *The Female Body in Western Culture: Contemporary Perspectives*, ed. Susan Rubin Suleiman (Cambridge, Mass. and London: Harvard University Press, 1986), 47–49; Rosolato, "La voix," 290–91; and John Shepherd, *Music as Social Text* (Cambridge: Polity Press, 1991), 154–58.

28. Franz Kafka, "The Silence of the Sirens," in *The Complete Stories*, ed. Nahum N. Glazer with a new foreword by John Updike (New York: Schocken Books, 1983), 431. "The Silence of the Sirens" is part of a group of stories written between 1917 and 1923; see 474.

29. Richard Brathwait, *Essays Upon the Five Senses* (London: N.p., 1625), 6.

30. David Schwartz, *Listening Subjects: Music, Psychoanalysis, Culture* (Durham, N.C.: Duke University Press, 1997), 7–8.

31. See Norman O. Brown, *Love's Body* (New York: Random House, 1966; reprint ed., Berkeley and Los Angeles: University of California Press, 1990), 128–31; Dorothy Dinnerstein, *The Mermaid and the Minotaur: Sexual Arrangements and Human Malaise* (New York: Harper and Row, 1976), 2 and 5; James Gollnick, *Love and the Soul: Psychological Interpretations of the Eros and Psyche Myth* (Waterloo, Ont.: Wilfrid Laurier University Press, 1992), 40–48; and Roheim, "The Song of the Sirens," 25.

32. Johnstone and Scherer, "Vocal Communication of Emotion," 223.

33. "The stationer to the ingenious reader" of René Descartes (Renatus Descartes), *Compendium of Musick*, trans. and ed. by a person of honour (London: Thomas Harper for Humphrey Moseley, 1653), sig. A3v. For a more modern iteration of the same precept, see Gill Saunders, *A Book of Sea Creatures* (London: Victoria and Albert Museum, 1992), in which the reader is reminded that "a mermaid's beauty is seductive but it is her singing which lures sailors to their doom," n.p; and James Anderson Winn, *The Pale of Words: Reflections on the Humanities and Performance* (New Haven: Yale University Press, 1998), 4–5.

34. See Clifton, *Music as Heard*, 272.

35. See Austern, "The Siren, the Muse, and the God of Love," 111–12, especially the illustration on 111; Philip Kuberski, *The Persistence of Memory: Organism, Myth, Text* (Berkeley: University of California Press, 1992), 85; and Pavel, "In Praise of the Ear," 45–50.

36. See Roland Barthes, "The Grain of the Voice," in *Image, Music, Text*, trans. Stephen Heath (New York: Farrar, Straus and Giroux, 1977), 188; Barthes, *The*

Pleasure of the Text, trans. Richard Miller (New York: Farrar, Straus and Giroux, 1975), 66–67; Pavel, "In Praise of the Ear," 44 and 47–48; and Rosolato, "La voix," 295.

37. Brathwait, *Essays Upon the Five Senses,* 6–7.

38. Bunker, "Voice as (Female) Phallus," 392 and 427–28.

39. The bird-form, through the ability to fly, is considered in psychoanalytic anthropology to symbolize especially the eroticism of such beings, while their beaks and claws indicate castration anxiety, Roheim, "The Song of the Sirens," 25; see also Bunker, "The Voice as (Female) Phallus," 413.

40. Freud, "Revision of Dream Theory," in *The Complete Introductory Lectures to Psychoanalysis,* 488. See also Géza Roheim, *The Gates of the Dream* (New York: International Universities Press, 1952), 334–35.

41. Schwartz, *Listening Subjects,* 7–8. The nurturing maternal voice has especially been linked to the mother's milk in a longstanding Western tradition; see Linda Phyllis Austern, " 'My Mother Musicke': Music and Early Modern Fantasies of Embodiment,' " in *Maternal Measures: Figuring Caregivers in the Early Modern Period,* ed. Naomi J. Miller and Naomi Yavneh (Aldershot: Ashgate, 2000), 240–44.

42. Bartholomeus Anglicus, *De proprietatibus rerum,* trans Stephen Batman (London: Thomas East, 1582), 379–80.

43. Kafka, "The Silence of the Sirens," 431.

44. Hans [Christian] Andersen, "The Little Mermaid," in *Fairy Tales* (New York: Henry Holt and Co., 1913), 151.

45. John Dryden, *King Arthur; or, the British Worthy,* Act IV, scene ii, in *The Works,* vol. 8 (Edinburgh: William Paterson, 1884), 183–84.

46. See Kuberski, *The Persistence of Memory,* 95; Amy Schuman, "Gender and Genre," in *Feminist Theory and the Study of Folklore,* ed. Susan Tower Hollis, Linda Pershing, and M. Jane Young (Urbana and Chicago: University of Illinois Press, 1993), 80; and Stephen Toulmin, *The Return to Cosmology: Postmodern Science and the Theology of Nature* (Berkeley: University of California Press, 1982), 23–24.

47. See Dinnerstein, *The Mermaid and the Minotaur,* 5; Gollnick, *Love and the Soul,* 40–48; and Donna J. Haraway, *Simians, Cyborgs, and Women: The Reinvention of Nature* (London: Free Association Books, 1991), 180.

48. Brown, *Love's Body,* 128–31.

49. See Kuberski, *The Persistence of Memory,* 78–80 and 85.

50. Joyce, *Ulysses,* 281.

51. Freud, *The Complete Introductory Lectures on Psychoanalysis,* 599.

52. Richard Carrington, *Mermaids and Mastodons: A Book of Natural and Unnatural History* (London: Chatto and Windus, 1957), 19.

53. John Vinycomb, *Fictitious and Symbolic Creatures in Art with Special Reference for Their Use in British Heraldry* (London: Chapman and Hall, 1906), 226.

54. Colin Bertram, *In Search of Mermaids: The Manatees of Guiana* (New York: Thomas Y. Crowell Co., 1963). It is noteworthy that, in spite of the book's

title, its author disclaims in his introduction any scholarly investigation of the link between the gentle sea-cows and the legendary sea-women "but it is possible that manatees and the related dugongs, more than any other particular species, may have seemed to corroborate earlier flights of fancy," ix.

55. Jorge Luis Borges with Margarita Guerrero, *The Book of Imaginary Beings*, rev., enl., and trans. Norman Thomas di Giovanni in collaboration with the author (New York: E. P. Dutton and Co., 1970), 207.

56. About this famous and often-recounted tale, see Clair, *Unnatural History*, 223; and Norman Douglas, *Siren Land* (London: Secker and Warburg, 1923), 3.

57. See Carrington, *Mermaids and Mastodons*, 10–15.

58. Kuberski, *The Persistence of Memory*, 94.

59. Haraway, *Simians, Cyborgs, and Women*, 185.

60. Homer, *The Whole Works*, trans. George Chapman (London: Nathaniell Butter, [1616?]), 180–81. For a more literal modern prose translation of the same passage, and for more detailed information about the Homeric and other ancient Greek sirens, please see Leofranc Holford-Strevens, "Sirens in Antiquity and the Middle Ages," in the present volume, chapter 1.

61. See Borges, *The Book of Imaginary Beings*, 206; Ann Payne, *Medieval Beasts* (London: British Library, 1990), 74; John R. T. Pollard, "Muses and Sirens," *The Classical Review* 2, no. 12 (1952), 61–62; and Siegfried de Rachewiltz, *De Sirenibus: An Inquiry into Sirens from Homer to Shakespeare* (New York: Garland, 1987), 9–21. The image of death that accompanies Circe's description of the sirens belongs to a tradition whereby death in the masculine sense, as symbolized by Thanatos, signifies the passing away of the hero in the eternally beautiful flower of his youth, while death in the feminine sense is characterized by the corpse and decomposition, Lao, *Sirens*, 16–17.

62. For a list of classical sources of information about the sirens, see Jane Davidson Reid, *The Oxford Guide to Classical Mythology in the Arts, 1300–1990s* (New York: Oxford University Press, 1993), s.v. "Sirens," vol. 2, 1004. See also Gwen Benwell and Arthur Waugh, *Sea Enchantress: The Tale of the Mermaid and Her Kin* (London: Hutchinson and Co., 1961), 14; Borges, *The Book of Imaginary Beings*, 206–208; Brumble, *Classical Myths and Legends in the Middle Ages and Renaissance*, 312–15; Michel Bulteau, *Mythologie des filles des eaux* (Monaco: Éditions du Rocher, 1982), 37–39; Consoli, *Candeur d'un monstre*, 12–13; Holford-Strevens, "Sirens in Antiquity and the Middle Ages"; Pollard, "Muses and Sirens," 60–61; and Guy de Tervarent, *Les Enigmes de l'art: l'heritage antique* (Paris: Les Éditions d'art et d'histoire, 1946), 29–30.

63. See Benwell and Waugh, *Sea Enchantress*, 14; Bulteau, *Les Filles des eaux*, 7–26 and 136–83; Bunker, "The Voice as (Female) Phallus," 412; Carrington, *Mermaids and Mastodons*, 5–9; Consoli, *Candeur d'un monstre*, 12; Lao, *Sirens*, 16–17; and Pollard, "Muses and Sirens," 60 and 63.

64. See Bulteau, *Les Filles des eaux*, 9–10; Lao, *Sirens*, 16; and Roheim, *The Gates of the Dream*, 337.

65. See Borges, *The Book of Imaginary Beings*, 206; Bulteau, *Mythologie des*

filles des eaux, 39–45; Adeline Bulteau, *Les Sirènes* (Puiseau: Éditions Pardès, 1995), 8–9; Carrington, *Mermaids and Mastodons,* 8; Consoli, *Candeur d'un monstre,* 22–26; Payne, *Medieval Beasts,* 74; Pollard, "Muses and Sirens," 60; Rachewiltz, *De Sirenibus,* 85–86; and T. H. White, ed., *The Book of Beasts* (New York: G. P. Putnam's Sons, 1954), p. 135.

66. See Charles Burney, *A General History of Music from the Earliest Ages to the Present Period,* vol. 1 (London: N.p., 1776; reprint, New York: Harcourt, Brace and Co., 1935), 252; Bernard D. Prusak, "Woman: Seductive Siren and Source of Sin? Pseudo-epigraphal Myth and Christian Origins," in *Religion and Sexism: Images of Women in the Jewish and Christian Traditions,* ed. Rosemary Radford Ruether (New York: Simon and Schuster, 1974), 89; and Rachewiltz, *De Sirenibus,* 98–99.

67. See Rachewiltz, *De Sirenibus,* 145–58. For more information about a few of the many adaptations of this early modern neo-Platonist siren, often linked to the idea of the muse, see the chapters by Henry Stobart and Elena Laura Calogero in the current volume, chapters 3 and 4.

68. Lao, *Sirens,* 54–55.

69. Pliny [Plinius Secundus], *The Historie of the World Called the Natural Historie,* trans. Philemon Holland (London: Adam Islip, 1601), 236.

70. Ibid., 296.

71. See Brumble, *Classical Myths and Legends in the Middle Ages and Renaissance,* 312–13; Albert Stansborough Cook, ed. and trans., *The Old English Physiologus* (New Haven, Conn.: Yale University Press and Oxford: Oxford University Press, 1921), Introduction, iii–iv; Michael J. Curley, Introduction to *Physiologus,* trans. Michael J. Curley (Austin: University of Texas Press, 1979), ix–xii, xv, and xxix–xxx; Florence McCullough, *Medieval Latin and French Bestiaries, University of North Carolina Studies in the Romance Languages and Literatures,* no. 33 (Chapel Hill: University of North Carolina Press, 1960), 15–35, 47–69, and 168; Rachewiltz, *De Sirenibus,* 81–100; and John M. Steadman, *Nature into Myth: Medieval and Renaissance Moral Symbols* (Pittsburgh: Duquesne University Press, 1979), 24–25. Some bestiaries also considered the siren to be a fast-moving and deadly venomous (Arabian) serpent, sometimes with a sweet song that linked it to the sea-siren; see, for instance, Albertus Magnus [Albert the Great], *Man and the Beasts: De Animalibus (Books 22–26),* trans. James J. Scanlan, in *Medieval and Renaissance Texts and Studies* 47 (Binghamton, N.Y.: Medieval and Renaissance Texts and Studies, 1987), 412.; and Isidore of Seville [Isidore de Séville], *Etymologies,* livre XII *Des animaux* (Paris: Societé d'Édition "*Les Belles Lettres,*" 1986), 157.

72. Albertus Magnus, *Man and the Beasts,* Book 24, "The Nature of Aquatic Animals in General Followed by Their Listing in Latin Alphabetical Order," chap. 55, "Syrenas," 373. See also Beauvais, *Bestaire,* 24–25 and 68; McCullough, *Medieval Latin and French Bestiaries,* 168–69; and White, trans. and ed., *The Book of Beasts,* 134–35.

73. See Rachewiltz, *De Sirenibus,* 95–96.

74. See Carrington, *Mermaids and Mastodons,* 9–10. For more information

about sixteenth- and seventeenth-century collectors and collections and the types of collections later referred to as museums, see Arthur MacGregor, "Collectors and Collections of Rarities in the Sixteenth and Seventeenth Centuries," in Mac-Gregor, ed., *Tradescant's Rarities: Essays on the Foundation of the Ashmolean Museum 1683* (Oxford: Clarendon Press, 1983), 70–97.

75. See Carrington, *Mermaids and Mastodons,* 12.

76. See ibid., 10–11; and Colin Clair, *Unnatural History: An Illustrated Bestiary* (London, New York, and Toronto: Abelard-Schuman, 1967), 222–23.

77. Burney, *A General History of Music,* vol. 1, 253.

78. Jean Jacques Rousseau, *The Confessions* (London: William Glaisher, 1883), 262–63. ". . . after having seen the girls," he tells us, "the danger was lessened. I still found their singing delightful; and their voices so much embellished their persons that, in spite of my eyes, I obstinately continued to think them beautiful," 263.

79. See Bade, *Femme Fatale,* 6; Carrington, *Mermaids and Mastodons,* 13; and Harriet Ritvo, *The Platypus and the Mermaid and Other Figures of the Classifying Imagination* (Cambridge, Mass.: Harvard University Press, 1997), 178–83.

80. See Carrington, *Mermaids and Mastodons,* 3–4; Ritvo, *The Platypus and the Mermaid,* 181–82; and Vinycomb, *Fictitious and Symbolic Creatures,* 248.

81. Vinycomb, *Fictitious and Symbolic Creatures,* 247–48.

82. See Benwell and Waugh, *Sea Enchantress,* 13–22; and Lao, *Sirens,* 168.

83. Morgan, *The Descent of Woman,* 54–55.

84. See White, *The Book of Beasts,* n. on 135.

85. Athanasius Kircher [Athanasii Kircheri, S.J.], *Arca Noë* (Amsterdam: Apud Joannem Jansonium à Waesberge, 1675), 73.

86. Benwell and Waugh, *Sea Enchantress,* 14; and Carrington, *Mermaids and Mastodons,* 13–15.

87. See Jane Chance, *Medieval Mythography* (Gainesville: University Press of Florida, 1994), 587–88; and also Fabius Planciades Fulgentius, *The Mythologies,* in Leslie George Whitbread, ed. and trans., *Fulgentius the Mythographer* (Columbus: Ohio State University Press, 1971), 73–74. Such hybrid monsters, half-female and half-animal, took on new life through the infinite vision of Romantic artists, who even joined women's heads and breasts to insects, reptiles, vultures, and assorted felines in addition to more traditional piscine and avian life-forms; see Bade, *Femme Fatale,* 8; and Bram Dijkstra, *Evil Sisters: The Threat of Female Sexuality and the Cult of Manhood* (New York: Alfred A. Knopf, 1996), 178–81 and 214–17.

88. Dante Gabriel Rossetti, *Collected Writings,* ed. Jan Marsh (London: J. M. Dent, 1999), 411.

89. Alciati [Andreus Alciatus], *Emblems,* 116.

90. Oscar Wilde, "The Fisherman and His Soul," in *A House of Pomegranates* (London: Methuen & Co., 1891; 3d ed., 1909), 73.

91. The siren is linked in the relevant passage in Isaiah with the onocentaur, another hybrid creature redolent of unrepressed animal sexuality with its human head and chest, and its ass's hindquarters; medieval bestiaries in the tradition of

the Physiologus often discuss this male monster with the siren for this reason. See Curley, Introduction to *Physiologus,* 76–77; Holford-Strevens, "Sirens in Antiquity and the Middle Ages,"; McCullough, *Medieval Latin and French Bestiaries,* 166–67; Payne, *Medieval Beasts,* 75; *Physiologus,* 23–24; *Physiologus Latinus,* ed. Francis J. Carmody (Paris: Librarie E. Droz, 1939), 25–26; and Rachewiltz, *De Sirenibus,* 64–69 and 84–85.

92. Burney, *A General History of Music,* vol. 1, 252.

93. See Bulteau, *Les Filles des eaux,* 14–15; Jacqueline Leclerq-Marx, *La Sirène dans la pensée et dans l'art de l'Antiquité et du Moyen Age: Du myth païen au symbole chrétien* (Bruxelles: Academie Royale de Balgique, 1997), 41–65; Lao, *Sirens,* 54–55; Payne, *Medieval Beasts,* 74; and Rachewiltz, *De Sirenibus,* 74–78.

94. See Brumble, *Classical Myths and Legends,* 313–14; Edward Lucie-Smith, *Sexuality in Western Art* (London: Thames and Hudson, 1991), 31 and 34–38; Rachewiltz, *De Sirenibus,* 102–106; and Theweleit, *Male Fantasies,* 296.

95. Richard Linche, *The Fountaine of Ancient Fiction. Wherein is Lively Depictured the Images and Statues of the Gods of the Ancients, with Their Proper and Perticular [sic] Expositions* (London: Adam Islip, 1599), sig. Ov.

96. Bullokar, *An English Expositor,* sig. N8v.

97. Sir Thomas Wyatt, *The Poetical Works* (Boston: Little, Brown and Co., 1856), 209.

98. See Rachewiltz, *De Sirenibus,* 109–11.

99. Ibid., 78–85 and 100–103.

100. Peter Martyr Vermigli, *The Common Places,* trans. Anthonie Marten (London, 1583), 312.

101. See Lucie-Smith, *Sexuality in Western Art,* 252.

102. See Ovid, *De arte amandi or The Art of Love* (Amsterdam: Nicholas Janz Vissher, n.d.), Book IV, 78.

103. Hans Zender, *Les Sirènes chantent quand la raison s'endort* (Berlin: Boosey and Hawkes Bote and Bock, 1966). The piece received its premier on December 6, 1966 in Berlin, performed by the Freiberger Ensemble für Neue Musik.

104. Theophrastus von Hohenheim (Paracelsus), *A Book on Nymphs, Sylphs, Pygmies, and Salamanders, and on the Other Spirits,* trans. Henry E. Sigerist, in *Four Treatises of Theophrastus von Hohenheim called Paracelsus,* trans. C. Lilian Temkin, George Rosen, Gregory Zilboorg, and Henry E. Sigerist, ed. Henry E. Sigerist (Baltimore: Johns Hopkins University Press, 1941), 238.

105. See Borges, *The Book of Imaginary Beings,* 207.

106. Wells, *Sea Lady,* 151.

107. Friederich Heinrich Karl de la Motte Fouqué, *Undine,* trans. Paul Turner (London: John Calder, 1960), 125. It is striking in context that Undine and Huldbrand both dissolve in tears, symbolic orgasm, drowning, and surrender of the soul at once. Motte Fouqué was evidently familiar with Paracelsus, as Undine's disquisition on elemental beings, including herself, to her new husband makes

clear as she explains how she has received a soul through loving union with him, 63–65.

108. Ibid., 56–57. Undine does not lose her exquisite voice upon marriage, or cast aside her music, presumably a clear signal that she will return to her native water and ultimately bring death to Huldbrand, 78–81.

109. Andersen, "The Little Mermaid," 146–47.

110. Ibid., 161–62.

111. James Aykroyd, ed. and arranger, *The Siren: A Collection of Sacred Music* (Philadelphia: G. E. Blake, 1822), title page.

112. Motte Fouqué, *Undine,* 128.

113. Wilde, "The Fisherman and his Soul," 141–42.

114. See Lyndy Abraham, *A Dictionary of Alchemical Imagery* (Cambridge: Cambridge University Press, 1998), 210–11 and 213; Bulteau, *Les Sirènes,* 69–75; Bulteau, *Mythologie des filles des eaux,* 56–60; and Lao, *Sirens,* 105–108.

115. See Ovid, *Metamorphoses,* trans. George Chapman (London, 1632), Book 5, 103.

116. Case, *Apologia musices* (Oxford: Joseph Barnes, 1588), 72. "*Cur syrenibus, hyenis, aliisque quibusdam monstris harmonicas & alledtratrices voces natura dedit?* . . . ut in syrene & hyena est facis humana: ite aminus mirandum est siis quoque insit humanae vocis imitatio: nam ut praecipue hominibus coelestis modulatio conceditur, ita gerentibus formam & similitudinem hominis dulces voces & concentus saepissimè concedantur."

117. See Georges Kastner, *Les Sirènes: Essai sur les principaux mythes relatifs a l'incantation* (Paris: and London: Barthès et Lowell, 1858), 130–57; Rachewiltz, *De Sirenibus,* 109–10; and Vinycomb, *Fictitious and Symbolic Creatures,* 246–47.

118. Francis James Child, ed. and collector, *The English and Scottish Popular Ballads* (1882–1898; reprint ed., New York: Dover Publications, 1965), vol. 1, 118–41. Forms of this ballad were written down as early as 1656, and have been found from the British Isles through Scandinavia and Eastern Europe.

119. Jim Higgins, *Irish Mermaids: Sirens, Temptresses and Their Symbolism in Art, Architecture and Folklore* (Galway: Crow's Rock Press, 1995), 30.

120. [Thomas Moore,] *Moore's Irish Melodies,* new ed. (London: Longman and Co., [1866]), 60–61. For further information about this woodcut and Maclise's ca. 1842 oil painting on which it is based, particularly in relation to the harp as a symbol of eighteenth- and early-nineteenth-century Irish Romantic nationalism, see Barra Boydell, "The Female Harp: The Irish Harp in 18th- and Early 19th-Century Romantic Nationalism," *RIdIM/RCMI Newsletter* 20/1 (Spring 1995): 13–16.

121. Giulio Cesare Capaccio, *Delle imprese trattato* (Napoli: Gio[vanni] Carlion & Antonio Pace, 1592), fol. 23v. See also Borges, *The Book of Imaginary Beings,* 206; and, for more information on Parthenope's longstanding position as the mythical protectress of Naples and an inspiration for music, Dinko Fabris, "La Città della Sirena. Le origini del mito musicale di Napoli nell'età spagnola," in

Napoli viceregno Spagnolo: Una capitale della cultura alle origini dell'Europa moderna, ed. Monika Bosse and André Stoll (Napoli: Vivarum, 2001), vol. 2, 473–501.

122. See Linda Phyllis Austern, "Love, Death and Ideas of Music in the English Renaissance," in *Love and Death in the Renaissance,* ed. Kenneth R. Bartlett, Konrad Eisenbichler, and Janice Liedl, *Dovehouse Studies in Literature* 3 (Ottawa: Dovehouse Editions, Inc., 1991), 29–30; Bulteau, *Les Sirènes,* 9–10; Pollard, "Muses and Sirens," 61; and Sanders, *Sea Creatures,* n.p. For further information about early modern musical-instrument design that incorporates sirens, see A. J. Hipkins, *Musical Instruments Historic, Rare, and Unique* (London, 1888; reprint ed., London: A. & C. Black, Ltd., 1921), 28–29.

123. See Consoli, *Candeur d'un monstre,* 27–28; Lao, *Sirens,* 14–16; and Roheim, "The Song of the Sirens," 25.

124. Burney, *A General History of Music,* vol. 1, 253.

125. E[dward] M[organ] Forster, Introduction to Lampedusa, *Two Stories and a Memory,* 6–7. It is striking in this retrospective context that the last line spoken to the narrator by the central character in Forster's siren story of forty-two years earlier is: "It may be a hundred or a thousand years, but the sea lasts longer, and she [the siren] shall come out of it and sing," Forster, *The Story of the Siren* (Richmond, England: Printed by Leonard and Virginia Woolf at the Hogarth Press, 1920), 14.

126. See Richard Leppert, *The Sight of Sound: Music, Representation, and the History of the Body* (Berkeley and Los Angeles: University of California Press, 1993), 139–51.

127. Cha[rle]s D. Blake, "The Mermaid's Evening Song: A Souvenir of the Great Lakes" (Chicago, Ill.: White, Smith and Co., 1881).

128. John Donne, "A Songe," *The Complete Poetry, The Stuart Editions,* ed. John T. Shawcross (New York: New York University Press; and London: University of London Press, 1968), 90. The complete first stanza reads

> *Goe, and catche a falling starre,*
> *Get with child a mandrake root,*
> *Tell me, where all past yeares are,*
> *Or who cleft the Divels foot,*
> *Teach me to heare Mermaides singing,*
> *Or to keep off Envies stinging*
> *And finde*
> *What winde*
> *Serves to advance an honest minde.*

A musical setting of this famous song is preserved in British Library MS Egerton 2013, f. 586, and is transcribed in *The Complete Poetry,* 91.

Devils, Daydreams, and Desire

Siren Traditions and Musical Creation in the Central-Southern Andes

Henry Stobart

The high Andes, especially southern Peru, Bolivia, and northern Chile, are home to an immensely rich and diverse range of traditions concerning dangerous siren-type beings associated with musical enchantment and creativity.[1] These beings are typically said to reside in waterfalls, springs, lakes, rivers, or rocks, and they are widely referred to by Quechua and Aymara speakers with the Spanish loan-word *sirena* (siren/mermaid)[2] or *sirinu.* This latter term, more commonly heard in southerly regions, might be interpreted as a less gender-specific version of *sirena,* beings which in the Andes are by no means exclusively female.[3] In addition, the word *sirinu* may incorporate aspects of the semantic space of the identically pronounced Spanish *sereno,* which dictionaries variously gloss as "night watchman," "evening dew," "serene," or a "clear sky."[4] The widespread use of these Spanish loan words among indigenous language speakers suggests that collective imaginings about musical creativity and enchantment in these parts of the Andes are likely to have developed in dialogue with European cultural traditions.

Both the ubiquity and variety in local and regional practices and beliefs involving siren-type beings in the Andes is evident from a number

Map 1. Map of central-southern Andes showing places and locations of ethnic groups mentioned in the text.

of ethnographic accounts published over the last few decades.[5] In this chapter I shall explore and develop some of this material, drawing on my own fieldwork in various parts of the Bolivian Andes. My principal point of reference, however, will be the community of Quechua-speaking agriculturalists and herders of Kalankira (*cayanquira*), who form part of the ethnic group *ayllu* Macha, Northern Potosí, Bolivia. I draw on a total of over two years of fieldwork in Kalankira, spread over more than a decade, and over a year in other regions of rural Bolivia. In Kalankira, as in many other parts of the Andean highlands, musical performance is closely linked to agriculture, courtship, and a range of collective rituals. Discourse about *sirinus* is centrally important to local ideas about musical enchantment, creativity, and aesthetics and to music's role in agricultural production.[6] However, although the links between Andean siren-type beings and "love magic"[7] have received considerable attention in the literature, as have their association with musical creation[8] and flowing water,[9] their connection with agricultural production is less well known. My own research in a range of locations suggests that this probably reflects regional differences in tradition rather than oversights on the part of other researchers. Thus, my aim in this chapter is both to provide a comparative overview of Andean traditions and to examine local discourse and practices surrounding *sirinus* for the specific case of Kalankira—where everyone is a musician.[10] I will begin by briefly exploring the European siren-mermaid legacy, certain aspects of which have been somewhat overlooked in musical approaches to the study of Andean sirens.

Siren Mermaids: European Resonances

The *sirena* or siren-mermaid had long been a familiar European cultural trope when Europeans began to flood into the Andes following Pizarro's initial invasion of 1532. Given the immense danger of the Atlantic and Pacific voyages undertaken to reach this new world, sirens and other monsters may have loomed particularly large in the colonists' imaginations—informed by the fantastical descriptions from such popular and widely circulated texts as *Mandervilles Travels*.[11] In 1547, just fifteen years after the Spanish arrival, Enrique de Valderrabano published a collection of vihuela music in Spain entitled *silva de sirenas* ("whistling sirens"), suggesting that sirens were far from out of fashion on the Iberian Peninsula. Indeed the contemporary fascination with sirens and sea nymphs, perhaps catalyzed by the exploration and discoveries of the time, was to leave deep traces in many parts of Europe—as evident from other chapters in this volume. In addition, the writings of a group of neo-Platonic scholars around 1500 brought the idea of the classical celestial sirens to prominence through arguing for closer connections between celestial and human music than had usually been accepted by medieval writers.[12] As his title *silva de sirenas* ("whistling sirens") suggests, Valderrabano was evidently well aware of these humanistic developments. Accordingly, in his dedication he invokes the writings of Socrates, Plato, and Pythagoras and compares the passions and affects of the reasoned human soul to the music of the celestial spheres. He observes that:[13]

> This music is caused and perfected by the seven Sirens which exist in the soul, which are seven virtues, those which awaken the spirit with its concord and harmony, to feel and know divine and human things, and the great good that follows from this knowledge. In no terrestrial creature has god placed such reason and perfection as in man, nor in string instruments as in the vihuela. And thus from what the ancient scholars =and all the others have written concerning music, it appears clear that with most reason this must be attributed to the vihuela, in which is [to be found] the most perfect consonance of strings.[14]

Valderrabano's identification of the benign celestial sirens with the soul, reason, and the vihuela, invoking the perfect proportions between strings, are particularly notable. His reference to celestial sirens clearly draws on reworkings of Plato's myth of Er, from the *Republic*, although Plato actually refers to eight sirens.[15] This contrasts vividly with Homer's seductive sirens, and their maritime associations, which were linked with the power of music and feminine enchantment to ensnare men and lead them to moral corruption and disaster.[16] Both of these contradictory yet interrelated constructions of the siren would undoubtedly have made the journey to the Andes, carving out spaces for themselves and becoming reinterpreted in new contexts.

Representations of *sirena* (siren-mermaid) figures holding a plucked-string instrument (vihuela, guitar, or lute), dating from between about 1618 and 1800, appear in the architecture, sculpture, or mural painting of some eighteen Peruvian and Bolivian churches.[17] This motif, which has been interpreted as "a fine example of the mixture of indigenous and Spanish elements in the imagery of mestizo art," is also found in certain eighteenth-century textiles and the decoration of *keru* drinking beakers.[18] Teresa Gisbert has observed that 70 percent of the *sirena* representations in church art are located around Lake Titicaca or the water systems that feed or drain it.[19] She argues that this iconographic motif can be related to a pre-Columbian tradition surrounding the Andean creator god Tunupa and his seduction by two mermaid-like beings called Quesintuu and Umantuu in Lake Titicaca. Although the evidence for this specific case is sketchy, there seems to be wide acceptance for the idea that "pre-Columbian water spirits"—possibly associated with music—syncretized with the European siren-mermaid concept and image.[20]

An intriguing drawing by Guaman Poma de Ayala (ca. 1615) provides some of the most compelling evidence for pre-Hispanic water spirits associated with music.[21] This image (fig. 3.1), entitled "Songs and Music" (*canciones y música*) for which no explanation is provided in the main text, introduces the section dedicated to pre-Hispanic music in Guaman Poma's 1,189-page chronicle intended for the king of Spain.[22] The drawing depicts two male flute players, carrying on their backs sheaves of harvested cornstalks or grass for thatching, perched high on a cliff. Lower down, n the opposite margin, two naked women, who are evidently singing, are shown submerged in fast-flowing water or a waterfall. Between these sharply contrasted representations of solidity (male flute players) and fluidity (female singers) are depicted gently rolling hills suggesting agricultural land.[23] This imagery not only implies that the male flute players acquire musical inspiration from seductive beings associated with flowing

Figure 3.1. *Canciones y música* (ca. 1615) by Guaman Poma de Ayala, from *Nueva Corónica y Buen Gobierno* (codex péruvien illustré). Ed. P. Rivet. Paris: Institut d'Ethnologie (1936), f. 316.

water but also suggests that this musical interaction—mediating between solid and fluid elements—might be linked to the growth of crops in the fields. Indeed, the women's pointing fingers suggest that their fluid essence both travels upward, to become clouds and rain, and communicates directly with the male flute players to be expressed as musical sound. As we hall see, parallels between the flow of music and water, where "sound, like water, vivifies the cosmos," have been widely reported in Andean ethnography.[24]

However, considerable caution is necessary in approaching this image, because the drawing conventions used by Guaman Poma were intro-

[109]

duced from Spain, making it hard to disentangle indigenous musical beliefs from Spanish semiotic language. This leads us to wonder how much
the medium of representation and Guaman Poma's expectations of the
cultural knowledge of the Spanish reader shaped this highly structured
image. Would this drawing have had resonances for indigenous Andean
musicians of the time? We are not in a position to answer this question
today, but I did show this picture to my hosts in Kalankira. They examined
it with some hilarity and described the river as both a *wayq'u* (ravine) and
p'akcha (waterfall). Although *sirinu* were often said to inhabit such places,
nobody associated the naked women with music or *sirinus,* instead describing them as *nina q'ara* ("naked fire") or *q'ara yaku* ("naked water"), dangerous demonic spirits that can enter a person's stomach, via the
mouth, leading to death.[25] Despite my Bolivian hosts' lack of recognition,
I still feel that this drawing might fruitfully be viewed as a fascinating
and immensely creative exercise in cultural translation; this task remains
one of the ethnographer's principal challenges.[26] Whether or not this
image represents definitive evidence for the existence of a pre-Hispanic
Andean siren-mermaid tradition, its resonances with contemporary siren
accounts are striking. For example, further aspects that are relevant to
themes discussed later in this chapter include:

    (1) the idea of the natural world as a source of musical creativity;
    (2) the presence of flutes (rather than other instruments);
    (3) the trance-like expressions of the flute players;
    (4) the juxtaposition between water and rock.

Mermaids and Guitars

Thomas Turino has suggested that "the strict association of the *sirena* with
stringed instruments" evident from both colonial art and modern practice
in parts of southern Peru, "appears to be original for Latin America, from
the colonial period."[27] He also observes that many of these images of siren-
mermaids with guitars appear on churches where in European tradition angels would have been expected, and he interprets the "blending of
the European "angel band" motif and the "Andean *sirena*" as one of the
sources for the *sirena*/string association.[28] This is a compelling hypothesis,
and the iconographic tradition of depicting mermaid-sirens with string
instruments may indeed be a uniquely Andean phenomenon. However, I
wonder whether the search for a source of inspiration should be entirely confined to some notion of an indigenous "Andean *sirena*"; perhaps
Turino's suggestion that there has never been "a consistent association of

Figure 3.2. Sculpted celestial siren from the façade of the church of San Lorenzo, Potosi, Bolivia (ca. 1728–44). Photograph by Henry Stobart.

strings with the European mermaid"[29] overlooks the importance of neo-Platonic celestial sirens and their close association with string instruments, dating back to classical times.

The idea of the celestial sirens (from the myth of Er in Plato's *Republic*) would seem to be vividly expressed in the image from the sculpted portal of the church of San Lorenzo in Potosí, Bolivia (fig. 3.2). In this famous image, the siren-mermaid holds a small guitar/vihuela and is depicted with stars and the sun.[30] This juxtaposition is reminiscent of the link, noted above, between celestial sirens and string instruments evident from Valderrabano's 1547 collection of vihuela music entitled *silva de sirenas*. In addition, a number of highly influential stage works from the Renaissance feature Plato's celestial sirens and associate them with string instruments. For example, the *Pellegrina intermedi,* performed in Florence in 1589 for the wedding of Ferdinand de Medici and Christine of Lorraine, opens with Harmony playing the lute while she sings in praise of her escort of celestial sirens. The backdrop falls away to reveal a host of sirens on clouds playing a range of string instruments: harps, viols, lutes, and a theorbo.[31]

The Andean mermaid-siren image of the colonial period, depicting

[111]

her holding a guitar (or harp), has been presented as an example of syncretism between European and indigenous Andean culture, resulting when mestizo or indigenous artisans worked without supervision.[32] In addition, Durkin suggests that a close association of this motif with pre-Columbian gods may have functioned as a form of covert propaganda in the resurgence of mestizo nationalism and insurrection against the Spanish colonial authorities.[33] While not denying potential indigenous contributions to this image, I wish to suggest that it might also be understood in terms of a creative crystallization of European Humanist ideas—with potential input and supervision from the clergy. After all, a culture's ideas are often most vividly and literally realized when transported to colonial settings or expatriate communities. It remains unclear whether the siren-mermaid with her guitar also expressed resistance (a) to the colonial Spanish authorities as an indigenous emblem and/or (b) to the more conservative religious climate of mainland Spain as a radical, neo-Platonic one. What is for sure is that the neo-Platonic associations of the sirens, alongside the more familiar Homeric and seafaring ones, found a welcome home in the Andes and have been influential to its various cultural expressions.

Themes and Variations

In addition to the depiction of mermaids playing guitar-type instruments in church art during the colonial period, Thomas Turino has described a rich folk tradition linking the siren-mermaid with *charango* performance in courtship songs of the Cusco and Puno regions of southern Peru.[34] Several local people—mestizos and peasants alike—described to Turino how, for example, new instruments were taken to the *sirena* at a spring or waterfall late at night and offerings were made. When collected several hours later, the instrument would have acquired the power of the *sirena* and typically be said (1) to be perfectly in tune, (2) to sound more beautiful than before, and (3) to have the power to attract girls, making the man who played it irresistible. Turino also observes that certain individuals considered that the "*sirenas* are the source of all music."[35]

Turino's account of the nocturnal practice of usurping the *sirenas'* powers in order to render the sound of men's musical instruments exquisitely beautiful, perfectly tuned, and irresistible to girls has striking similarities with those I have encountered in many parts of the Bolivian highlands. Similarly, I have frequently heard individuals claim that these dangerous and mysterious beings are the "source of all music," even the source of those melodies acquired through copying commercial recordings. But although Turino notes that his informants typically described the *sirena* as "a beautiful woman with a fish tail,"[36] none of the rural musicians I have spoken to over some fifteen years of regular visits to Bolivia has ever related the form of the *sirena* or *sirinu* to a mermaid.[37] In addition, I did not encounter "the strict association of the *sirena* with stringed instruments" and never with the "wind and percussion instruments" identified by Turino for the case of southern Peru.[38] Instead, I found that the places "inhabited" by siren-type beings were associated with specific wind or string instruments—or with an unspecified range of instruments, including percussion. For example, the rock situated beside a siren spring near Sacaca, northern Potosí, Bolivia—where bands of pan-pipe players sometimes magically tune their instruments—was referred to as *bombito,* meaning "bass drum" (fig. 3.3), and according to Ester Grebe Vicuña the *serenos* (*sirinus*) of the Tarapacá region of Chile are closely associated with *sikura* panpipes.[39] However, my hosts in Kalankira were unanimous in the conviction that *sirinus* sound like *pinkillu* flutes. Indeed, one evening whilst playing a new set of these flutes, a neighbor arrived to investigate, exclaiming that the music was so beautiful that he thought it must have been the *sirinus* playing.

Another important regional difference between accounts of sirens is the aspect of seasonality and their integration into agricultural practices. Turino does not mention this for the case of southern Peru, nor did it feature in the various testimonies I have collected in northern Bolivia. By contrast, people in Kalankira specified that bands of *sirinus* emerge from the earth and roam the hillsides during the nights between the Feast of Saint Sebastian (January 20) and the end of Carnival (February–March). Springs, waterfalls, and rocks inhabited by *sirinus* may be visited at other times of year to collect melodies or "tune" instruments in much the same way as described by Turino and other writers, but—as we shall see later—the emergence of the *sirinus* and their presence during the Carnival season was of key importance to my hosts' understanding of agricultural production. From these examples, it is evident that Andean siren traditions are subject to considerable variation, and this relates to such factors as region, locality, ethnic group, class, and age group. However, it is also possible to recognize a number of common themes, these include:

(1) Aesthetics: the ability to render the sound of an instrument or group of instruments especially beautiful, in terms of tuning, expression, timbre, and ensemble.
(2) Seduction: the ability to "enchant" with their music, or to render the sound of (usually men's) instruments irresistible to women.[40]

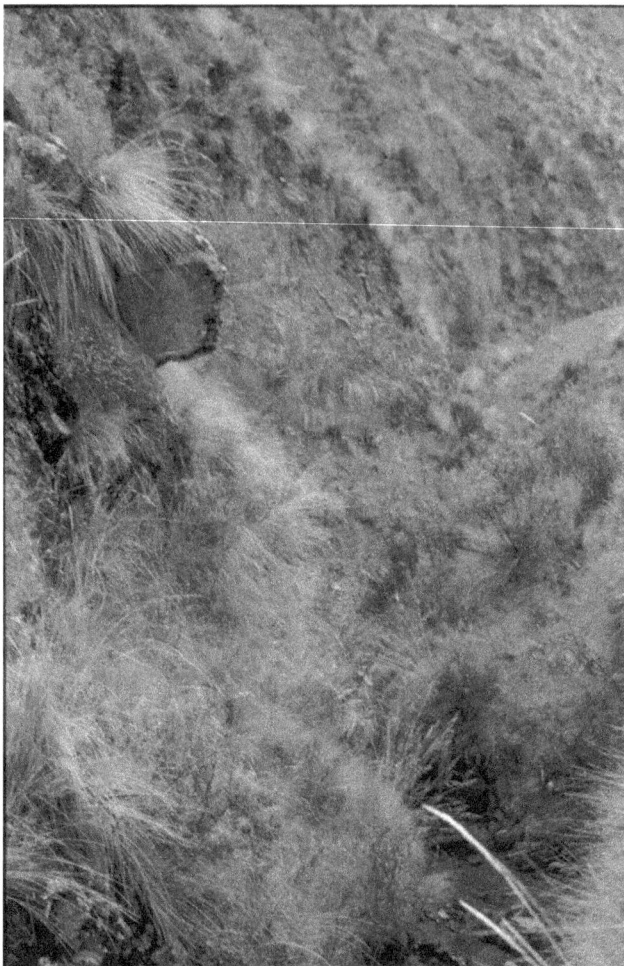

Figure 3.3. A *sirinu* ("siren spring") where instruments are "tuned" near Sacaca, northern Potosi, Bolivia. The large rock was referred to as *bombito* ("bass drum"). Photograph by Henry Stobart.

(3) Knowledge: the source of musical inspiration and creativity (usually in the form of new melodies), but also sometimes of understanding and knowledge more generally.[41]

(4) Danger: the ability to cause illness, death, or insanity unless sirens are approached with adequate care, respect, courage and strength.

(5) Exchange/Contract: the acquisition of the sirens' powers is contractual; it requires some form or offering or sacrifice in return.

(6) Demonic powers: the association with Andeanized "devils," darkness, night, and the inner earth.

(7) Natural world/Landscape: the association with places in the natural world, rather than human habitation.

(8) Altered consciousness: encounters with sirens, especially the acquisition of new melodies, often involve the listener entering into a dream- or sleep-like state and/or being intoxicated.

(9) Water (or Rocks): association with clear (*ch'uwa*), flowing water, such as springs and waterfalls, or with rocks.

Many of these themes have strong resonances or parallels with Greco-European traditions. For example, the "honey-sweet music" of Homer's sirens led hearers to death and destruction, while promising delights and knowledge of "all things that come to pass on the fruitful earth."[42] Similarly, the Swedish water sprite or *näck* provided fiddlers with bewitching new tunes and virtuosic techniques.[43] For the case of the Andes, I will develop some of these themes in varied depth over the coming pages. I will also explore the specific case of Kalankira, where a connection with agriculture, Carnival, and the miraculous powers of Saint Sebastian prove particularly important.

Satanic Sirens

Although a number of Bolivian colonial-period churches include images of mermaids holding a guitar, as noted above, I have not heard local people describe *sirenas* or *sirinus* as women with fishtails. For example, my hosts in Kalankira stated that *sirinus* look just like humans, dressed in Carnival costume. They live in their own *llajta* ("village" or "country") in families and, unlike the exclusively female mermaid, they may be male, female, or *q'iwa* (half-male, half-female). Other people from the region considered that *sirinus* were the size of small children, like European pixies or fairies, or they observed their ability to transform between human and a variety of animal forms. For example, one man observed that they might take the form of a dog, toad, lizard, *urqulla* snake, *yaka yaka* bird, or owl—creatures associated with *supay,* the devil.

In my own experience and throughout the literature, Andean siren-type beings are almost always classified as a form of *supay* or "devil" (*diablo*), "demon" (*demonio*), or "satan" (*satano*): powerful, ambiguous, and creative beings that inhabit the hidden realms of *ukhu pacha,* the inner earth. Andean approaches to these ambiguous beings tend to focus on their creative aspects, as well as the destructive and corrupting associa-

tions that dominate orthodox Christianity.[44] Although a few people described the *sirinus* as *buenos* ("good"), for the most part they were characterized as "evil" (*sajra* or *saxra*).[45]

In Kalankira the term *satanu* ("satan") was sometimes used where I
would have expected *sirinu*. More generally, siren-like musical powers may
be attributed to other diabolical characters. For example, in the Tarabuco
area of southern Bolivia, *Tata Pujllay* is said to arrive a few weeks before
Carnival galloping through the night on a silver horse, playing the *pinkillu*
flute, and providing the enchanted new Carnival melodies for the year.
This dangerous demon, whose gender is ambiguous and sexual appetite
insatiable, may lure men or women away to drown in the river.[46] In another account, reminiscent of Stravinsky's *Soldier's Tale,* from near Porco,
southern Bolivia, the devil appears to a young *charango* player as a gentleman with a tie. After enchanting the *charango,* so that it tunes itself and
renders the young man irresistible to girls, the lad sickens and is only saved
by a healer who supplies the devil with the soul of a sacrificed animal in his
place.[47] This story, in which musical powers are acquired from the devil,
has parallels with numerous European, central Asian, and other traditions.[48] It is notable that in both these examples, which share many similarities with tales of Andean sirens, the acquisition of music powers is
associated with elite social groups who, from a peasant perspective, represent sources of both immense wealth and danger. As I shall suggest below,
the distinction between Andean sirens and other forms of devils is by no
means clear-cut. However, in rural settings the terms *sirena* or *sirinu*
almost always carry musical connotations.

Fatally Seductive Sounds

Accounts of sirens in the Andes, as elsewhere, highlight the beauty of their
music and its ability to enrapture or seduce the listener, who is attracted
irresistibly and sometimes fatally toward the source of sound. In Kalankira, *sirinus* were said to emerge from the earth during the nights of the
Carnival season and to wander the mountainsides in groups (*tropas*),
playing flutes, singing, and dancing. I was warned not to walk outside
alone at these times, as I could easily be lured away by one of these groups,
as once happened to my friend Asencio Jara while he was drunk during
Carnival. He told me that the group of *sirinu* were extremely friendly, like
normal people, and gave him corn beer, but then suddenly disappeared.
He awoke outside on a mountainside the following morning, frozen to the
bone, far from home and completely lost. Another friend was also lured
away one night during Carnival by a childlike cry resembling the voice of

his infant daughter. He would have been a victim of the *sirinu*, I was told the next morning, had he not been spotted and dragged home by a group of friends. Several other ethnographers working in northern Potosí have mentioned the danger of being lured away by Carnival devils. However these are often classified as *saxras* ("evil ones") or *yawlus* ("devils") and differentiated from the strictly musical associations of sirens.[49]

As is also evident from Turino's research in Peru,[50] beliefs and tales about sirens are not entirely restricted to *campesino* ("peasant") communities; although some mestizos ridiculed these as backward or ignorant, others offered me vivid descriptions. For example, Don Garnica, a mestizo shopkeeper from the town of Macha, told me how just before Carnival each year he visits the *sirinu* that lives in a gully (*wayq'u*) near the road to Colquechaka in order to collect new tunes. A few years previously, he had witnessed the cold and lifeless body of a young man lying in this gully, with no signs of injury besides grass stuffed in the mouth. Apparently, the youth had been seen in Macha the previous evening, extremely drunk and celebrating *tentación*, the final night of the feast of Carnival. There was no doubt in Don Garnica's mind; the young man must have wandered off alone and been lured away to this dangerous place by the *sirinus*.

Rather than bands of sirens roaming the countryside at Carnival, as in the case of Kalankira, much of the ethnography implies that the danger of Andean sirens is usually restricted to visiting the places they are believed to inhabit, either accidentally or intentionally, in order to harness their musical powers. In northern Potosí, such places were often described as *fyiru*, which Thomas Solomon suggests combines two Spanish loan words: *feo* ("ugly") and *fiero* ("fierce," "wild").[51] The sirens' powers are usurped for two main purposes: firstly to enchant or tune musical instruments, especially for use in courtship, and secondly to provide a source of new, powerful melodies. I will briefly consider these two contexts for visiting the sirens in turn.

Enchanting Instruments

Accounts abound of young men visiting sirens' springs, waterfalls, or rocks late at night to "tune" a new string instrument or to prepare instruments for a fiesta. We have already heard how an instrument tuned in this way is claimed to be perfectly in tune, to sound enchantingly beautiful, and to render the male player irresistible to girls. According to my many Bolivian consultants, other types of instruments may also be tuned in this way, and whole consorts of flute or panpipe players sometimes visit sirens' springs on the eve of an important feast.[52] For example, in the instrument-making village of Walata Grande (Department La Paz), I was told that consorts of wind instruments are placed beside the *sirena's* spring together with offerings. The players withdraw to a safe distance and listen out for the tuning note that initiates each piece. The moment the *sirenas* sound this note, a man from the group hurls a tin can in order to startle and frighten them back into the earth, whereupon the players retrieve their instruments which are then claimed to be "perfectly in tune" and to outshine all other consorts played in the feast.

I have heard almost identical descriptions in northern Potosí, where— near Sacaca—I was told that it was essential for the group of players to remain together after tuning their instruments at the *sirinu,* or its power would be lost. More generally it seems to be believed that the sirens endow instruments with a form of animating energy or essence. In Sonqo, southern Peru this energy is termed *sami,* which Catherine Allen has characterized as "a kind of genius or ebullient spirit, when possessed by a person, object or phenomenon."[53] She also observes how a Sonqo man, to whom she had given a harmonica, planned to "leave it at midnight in a hole leading to an underground stream, where a *sirena* (siren) would play it, endowing the instrument with *sami.*"[54] According to some accounts, once an instrument has been endowed with the siren's enchanting power, it must not be placed on the ground because the siren would be likely to escape and return back to the inner earth.[55]

Offerings to Andean sirens, as a form of exchange, are deemed essential if instruments are to sound beautiful and players to perform well. Even in large towns, such as the mining center of Oruro, brass-band players sometimes sacrifice a red cockerel to the *sereno* (*sirinu*) and spill its blood on the instruments before an important performance.[56] Similarly, I witnessed a red guinea pig sacrificed and its blood spilt on a new set of *tarka* flutes in Walata Grande.[57] According to some makers, from this village famed for instrument construction, the offerings to the local *sirenas* are so frequent and abundant that they often have no appetite. This failure to consume offerings means that musicians are not provided assistance. However, "very hungry" *sirenas* could be found, I was assured, at remote places in the tropical lowlands, involving a five-hour lorry ride and a three-day walk. These ravenous *sirenas,* it was explained, inhabit immensely deep holes stinking of sulfur, called *chinkanas,* where "many demons" (*demonios*) and ten-year-old snakes are to be found. Grebe also documents two oral testimonies of a former tradition of human sacrifice (children and sometimes adults) to the *sereno* (*sirinu*) from two parts of the Tarapacá region of Chile.[58]

These accounts highlight the sirens' common requirement for some form of exchange, sacrifice, or contract if humans are to be granted musical assistance. Significantly, in northern Potosí, *sirinu* were sometimes referred to as *juchan*, a word that means both "sin" and "contract," suggesting that relations with them may be seen as both potentially corrupting and a form of negotiation. The idea that the provision of musical powers requires some form of compensation is also evident from many European folktales, as well as from later classical representations of Ulysses's encounter with the sirens. When the hero and his ship succeed in passing the sirens unscathed, the bird-women are depicted falling from their cliff-top perches, as if committing suicide. Without compensation for the pleasure and knowledge of their music, the sirens and their music cannot survive—music demands a sacrifice.[59]

Twisting New Melodies

While the acquisition of musical powers from siren- or devil-like beings would seem to have much continuity with European folklore, the practice of acquiring new melodies each year would seem to be more indigenous in character. Indeed, the collection of new *wayñu* melodies (the genre played throughout the rainy growing season) for the feast of Carnival was one of the most widespread contexts in which *sirinus* were discussed in Kalankira. Melodies from previous years were described as *q'ayma* ("tasteless, insipid") and, as my host Paulino Jara put it, did not have the power to "do/make anything."

In order to collect new Carnival *wayñu* melodies, players were often said to visit waterfalls, inhabited by *sirinus*, with their *pinkillu* flutes or local guitars (*kitarras*). After leaving offerings and pouring libations of alcohol, men would listen to the sounds of the water. Don Adrian Chura, the oldest man in the Kalankira district, vocalized this rumbling of the waterfall as "*booooo boooo*," invoking the sense of a deep and constant mass of harmonics—suggestive of the fundamental drone in overtone singing.[60] It was from this deep and constant sound, he explained, that patterns and forms would gradually begin to emerge, "as if in a dream," and then new melodies would enter your head. Chilean archaeologist and musicologist Claudio Mercado has beautifully described this shift in consciousness brought about through listening to water, where the *sirinu's* melodies initially emerge in the form of "metasounds."[61] Don Adrian observed that these phantom melodies were "indistinct" (*charpu*), and he described their perception with the verb *q'iwiy*, meaning "to twist."[62] In other contexts, this verb (*q'iwiy*) is associated with spinning thread from raw wool; in other words, the creation of form from a mass of disconnected strands, beautifully evoking the way in which a melody emerges from the mass of harmonics and sonic textures at a waterfall.[63]

Encounters with visual manifestations of the sirens, like those of the aural, often focus on the indistinctness of their forms. For example, Doña Asunta Beltrán (my host's mother) encountered a band of *sirinus* while herding on the mountain one day during Carnival, and she described her experience as follows:

> Yes, I saw the *sirinu*. Just like that, as I was sitting there in the rain as though day-dreaming. Then *wuuu . . . wuu wuu miiii* the *wayñu* came completely filling that hollow. Honestly, as indefinite colour I saw them, on that slope as though indeterminate colour. There by Lorenzo's [llama] mating [corral] in a cave I sat, while it was raining, as though carried off in sleep, day dreaming *wuu.. wuu.. aaaata* the *pinkillu* flutes sounded *uj*. From that hollow it sounded during Carnival.[64]

Doña Asunta's description emphasizes the dreamlike nature of such encounters; she described her state as *chuturkurikasqani,* evoking the idea of being "removed" in some way or perhaps in trance. Her son, Paulino Jara, glossed this as "asleep when awake." More generally, musical inspiration from the sirens is widely associated with contemplation of the natural or supernatural world and entering a receptive, dreamlike state. As one man from near Sacaca explained: "*Wayñus* cannot be made up in the house, but only in special places. Often they come to you beside a river—perhaps overnight while resting, as if in a dream."

The idea of being lulled into a soporific or trance-like state, while attentive to the dreamlike and creative emergence of melodies is common to many accounts. Such descriptions are also suggestive of the siren's sleep-inducing song described in a number of early European sources,[65] or the musical vision quests of certain north American Amerindian groups.[66] Indeed, some of my consultants insisted that the *sirinus'* waterfalls must be visited alone, as a form of personal quest. However, others described how the siren's new melodies fell under their fingers as they played flute consorts together at a waterfall or in other places. Similarly, Olivia Harris notes that "the tune is communicated either in a dream to the owner of the instrument, or directly through the instrument which plays in a new way."[67]

Although I met many people who claimed to have visited and acquired musical powers or melodies from *sirinus,* the majority claimed to be unable to do this or to have lost the knowledge. Instead, new melodies were typically copied from musicians who, by preference, were from other ethnic groups (*ayllus*). For example, the Kalankiras, who form part of *ayllu* Macha, ideally chose to copy melodies from members of *ayllu* Laymi during the feast of Candelaria (February 2) in Pocoata.[68] According to Olivia Harris, the Laymis also consider that one of the *sirenas* for the best *wayñus* is located in Pukwata (Pocoata) territory. However, she observes that in practice the Laymis have lost their *sirenas* and now travel to the fiesta of Candelaria in Chayanta to learn *wayñus* from the Chayantakas, Sikuyas, and Jukumanis.[69] Wálter Sánchez has interpreted this widespread practice of appropriating music from other ethnic groups, or favoring their *sirinus,* as a form of circulation or articulation between upper (cold) and lower (warm) ecological zones.[70] In turn, Thomas Solomon describes this in terms of establishing "a network of relationships between relatively higher and lower levels"—comparable to the cosmological circulation of water.[71] It is significant in this context that people in Kalankira considered that melodies collected from the *chawpirana,* the middle-altitude territory (a kind of fulcrum between the highlands and the valleys), had no power and were *q'ayma* ("insipid").

I was told on several occasions that the *sirinus* are the source of "all music," including, for example, the commercial recordings made by professional artists. This connection with recorded media has been highlighted in recent years by the annual production of commercial cassette recordings of Carnival *wayñus* by local artists. These are released a few months before Carnival so as to allow time for local musicians to imitate and learn the new melodies on their own instruments for the feast. The locally famous recording artist Gregorio Mamani, who was brought up in Tomaykuri (just a two hours' walk from Kalankira), appears to have been the first to identify this potential market. Significantly, the group with whom he has made these recordings is called *ZURA ZURA,* the name of a powerful *sirinu* near Tomaykuri. As Solomon has also observed for the case of *ayllu* Chayantaka, although the advent of recording technology has reduced "the immediacy of *sirina* as powerful landscapes" it does not seem to have entirely displaced their association with musical creation, but rather "to increase people's access to music associated with *sirinas.*"[72]

Water Music and Rock Music

The sirens' close association with springs, caves, and gullies—points of communication between the inner earth (*ukhu pacha*) and the realm of humans (*kay pacha*)—highlights both their ability to pass between these worlds and their fluidity of form. Several accounts of sirens from central Bolivia have identified their association with the cosmological circulation of water.[73] In this hydraulic cycle, water descends from the world of the living (*kay pacha*) to the underworld, inhabited by the souls of the dead. It then passes upward via a subterranean river to mountain lakes, from where it either evaporates to form clouds in the upper world (*janaq pacha*) and falls as rain, or is channeled downward via rivers and irrigation canals.[74] In a fascinating extension of this cosmological circulation of water, based on fieldwork among the Bolivian Qaqachakas, Arnold and Yapita note that through evaporation and rising clouds, water also travels to the eternal dark lakes of the Milky Way. They also observe that at the end of the rains the sirens return to the celestial ocean (*lamara*) of the black lakes of the sky and to their respective stars, *sirin istrilla* ("siren star") or *lamar istrilla* ("ocean star"), which contrast with the darkness of the Milky Way.[75] These accounts are tantalizingly evocative of the neo-Platonic celestial sirens, but it must be stressed that developed discourse concerning astronomic phenomena has been documented in several parts of the rural Andes.[76]

Nobody in Kalankira mentioned such celestial associations, but they did invoke the cosmological circulation of water in musical terms. I was told how the performance of *pinkillu* flutes, combined with women's voices, made clouds gather and release rain; the resulting water flows downward to *lamar* ("the inner ocean") and to the *sirinus*. In addition, I was told that the *sirinus* pass up from deep within the earth through "little pipes"—"just like water." Working with the Chayantakas of northern Potosí, Solomon has interpreted *sirinas* as "a kind of disruption in the hydraulic cycle, returning water directly to the land of the living from the underground domain of the dead" enabling people to "tap directly into the energy of the underworld through water."[77] The music acquired in this way might thus be seen to embody the dangerous and generative forces of the demons and ancestors of the inner earth, where the sirens represent a direct line of communication with the ancestral world. As we shall see, the role of the *sirinus* in conveying souls or soul substance between the realms of the living and ancestors was vividly played out during the Carnival rites of Kalankira.

Although springs, caves, and gullies highlight the idea of communication with the inner earth, the places most widely associated with sirens, or claimed to be inhabited by them, are waterfalls. Such places are notable as sources of sound, as highlighted in the Quechua/Aymara term for a waterfall, *p'akcha*, which stresses the onomatopoeic sound of splashing water. According to an analysis of Pastaza Quechua sound symbolism by Janis Nuckolds, *pak* "describes the moment of contact or the idea of a sound of contact made by an object or substance that falls on a surface and is reconfigured or changed by the fall."[78] I have already discussed how people listen to waterfalls and enter into a trance-like state in order to acquire new melodies from the sirens. However, here I wish to stress the symbolism of the waterfall as a point of transition, where falling water is temporarily released from the spatiotemporal constraints of its riverine pathway, before being reconfigured and finding its way along another riverbed. Indeed, the meandering river or pathway is a common motif in local weaving and knitting, and an important metaphor for the journey through life.[79] In this context the waterfall may be seen to symbolize a point of disjunction and reconfiguration of life substances communicating between distinct generations as life pathways. On similar lines, people in Kalankira told me that while abroad during the nights of Carnival, the *sirinus* do not follow the footpaths trodden by normal living people. Instead, they freely roam the landscape, unfettered by the spatiotemporal constraints of defined pathways. This freedom from constraint, alongside the idea of phantom melodies emerging from the sound of crashing water, might in part explain the widespread association between waterfalls and sirens.

The aquatic associations of Andean sirens are well known, but I have also often found them associated with dry places or rocks, a point rarely mentioned in the literature. For example, in the hills around the important instrument-making village of Walata Grande in northern Bolivia, several *sirenas* were said to be located in dry hollows and rocks, in addition to those of springs and waterfalls. In another part of northern Bolivia, I was told that besides visiting sirens at a waterfall in the river, men also take their *charangos* to be tuned by a *sirena* that inhabits three large rocks in the hills above the village of Sullka Titi Titiri.[80] Apparently a drunken man who had fallen asleep in this place one night was found dead there the next morning. The boulders were described as *encanto* ("enchanted"); in Aymara they are called *wali munañaniw*, conveying notions of both intense desire and power.[81] In addition, people in Kalankira, insisted that melodies could be collected from certain boulders (*qaqa*). For example, during a Carnival ceremony for the male llamas on a mountain peak, my friend Asencio Jara briefly left the family group to collect a "new" *wayñu* song from a nearby rock. He returned some four minutes later singing a song to the strummed accompaniment of a local rainy-season guitar (*kitarra*), which the rest of the family insisted was indeed "new." Asencio later remarked to me that an offering of alcohol must be made to the *sirinu* of the rock and that collecting such *wayñu* songs must be accomplished alone. In addition, I was told that *jula jula* panpipe melodies were formerly collected from a "white rock" (*yuraq qaqa*) in the highlands, although more recently they tend to be collected from *sirinus* in the valleys, near to the places where the canes grow that are used to make these instruments.

[123]

These various examples suggest that an exclusive association between sirens and water should not always be assumed. Rocks, which are sometimes presented as living beings in a state of lithomorphosis or slumber, often possess strong associations with musical creativity and enchantment. Some such rocks are claimed to come alive or awaken at particular times, often linked with the lunar cycle. As some of the most permanent features of the landscape, rocks may be seen to represent depositories of certain forms of ancestral knowledge and power. Suggestively, dictionaries from the early colonial period and some of my consultants in northern Bolivia have glossed the Aymara word *salla* as both (1) a large boulder and (2) a beautiful (or high-pitched) voice, or an exceptionally good musical ensemble.[82] It is notable in this context that musical creativity and enchantment should be associated with water, on the one hand, and with rock, on the other—a contrast in media that was especially prominent in Guaman Poma's drawing (ca. 1615) titled "Songs and Music" (fig. 3.1). These contrasted media are again identified in a much more recent sketch depicting musical composition from a community near Yura (Southern Potosí), elicited by Michelle Bigenho. Beneath the depiction of a solitary flute player sitting on a slope in a hilly landscape, alongside water, a footpath, and wind, there are the words *agua* (water), *peña* (rock), and *camino del viento* ("path of the wind").[83] These two drawings highlight the importance of both water and rock—and perhaps their very juxtaposition, as representations of contrast between solidity (dryness, structure, durability) and fluidity (lack of form, circulation). As evident from the rolling hills, suggesting agricultural land, in the centre of Guaman Poma's drawing, life and (vegetative) growth depend on the mediation of these contrasts. Guaman Poma seems to be telling us that these creative processes are heralded by music, as it "makes audible the new world that will gradually become visible."[84] In the remainder of this chapter, I will focus on the agriculturally centered practices of Kalankira and examine some of the ways in which *sirinus* and their music contribute to bringing the new world into being.

The Siren's Flute and Dancing Souls

Although sirens are widely associated with the magical "tuning" of string instruments in northern Potosí, it is with *pinkillu* flutes that they are most closely linked. These wooden duct flutes are played in consorts of four to six sizes and closely resemble the recorders used in church music during the colonial era. While it is likely that these *pinkillus* were modeled on Spanish renaissance recorders, the preferred timbre is considerably more strident than that usually sought by recorder players today.[85] In Kalankira, these instruments were explicitly linked with *sirinus*. On several occasions, I enquired, "What do *sirinus* sound like?" The answer, without hesitation or reflection, was always, "Like *pinkillu* flutes." One clue to this association is suggested by the green plastic whistles, called *sirinus*, which were played by men representing sirens during the final rites of Carnival. Like duct flutes, these instruments require no embouchure; the player simply blows, and sound is created by the instrument itself. In short, the instrument has its own "magical" voice.[86] The introduction of recorders to this part of the Andes, where very few if any duct flutes have emerged from the pre-Hispanic archaeological record, may have helped this instrument to acquire associations with supernatural siren-type beings. Similarly, for the case of southern Peru, Thomas Turino has suggested that indigenous people must have found certain aspects of European string instruments "truly wondrous," such as their power to sustain sound for a relatively long time.[87] The fact that one of Turino's consultants directly related this sustaining quality to the presence of a *sirena* within the instrument helps us to appreciate how a connection between new "wondrous" music technologies from Europe and the magical powers of siren-type musical beings might have developed.[88] However, Guaman Poma's "Songs and Music" (fig. 3.1), with its two *pincollo* flute players, suggests that we should not entirely discount the possibility of a pre-Hispanic association between flutes and seductive, siren-like musical beings.

The view expressed to me in Kalankira—that humans originally acquired and learned to play *pinkillu* flutes by imitating the *sirip'itas* ("crickets")—again highlights an association with sustained sound. These insects are common in the trees and vegetation of the warm valleys of the region, where *pinkillu* flutes are constructed, and their voices provide a constant background hum during the nights of the rainy growing season. In turn, these seasonal associations were linked with performance practice: *pinkillu* flute music was widely claimed to "call the rain" and to "help the crops grow" and was almost exclusively restricted to the rainy growing season, between November and Carnival (February/March). I was also told that these flutes are played by the souls of the dead, as they constantly sing and dance *wayñu* music in *alma llajta* ("land of the souls"), a hidden realm situated just out of sight to the west.[89] Descriptions of the abundant vegetation, flowers, and weeping willows of *alma llajta* contrasted vividly with the barren, treeless landscape of Kalankira, especially during the dry winter months. As my hosts confirmed, performing *wayñu* music with *pinkillu* flutes was a means to invoke the ancestors' verdant landscape in the world of the living, thereby encouraging the crops to grow during the rains. For this reason it is crucial that following the dispatch of the *pin-killu* flutes, toward the end of Carnival—the ritual climax of the growing season—these instruments are packed away and remain silent until the start of the next growing season. To continue performing *wayñu* music after these rites of dispatch, or to even play back a tape recording of them, would draw the dangerous Carnival devils and souls of the dead back to the world of the living.[90]

In these various accounts we discover that through the performance of *wayñu* music a close conjunction is invoked between the souls of the dead, the flow of rain, and the growth of vegetation. The anthropologist Olivia Harris, working with the nearby Lamis, has also identified the key importance of *wayñu* music to understanding this conjunction. "Only through music," she remarks, "did it become clear that the dead remain in the world of the living throughout the season of rains."[91] For the case of Kalankira, *wayñu* music began to be played as the souls of the dead were invited back to the world of the living to be feasted on All Saints' Day (November 1), which was related to the start of the rains. In particular, ceremonial activity and music-making was focused on the homes of families that had suffered the death of an adult man over the past year, as though harnessing this power for the growth of crops through the rains. As we shall see, during Carnival these same souls were ritually dispatched by a group of *sirinu* dancers, playing the new Carnival *wayñus* of the year, to join the community of ancestors; their participation in the growth of the year's crops now complete.

Saint Sebastian, Patron of the Sirens

In Kalankira, the arrival of the new *wayñu* melodies for the year was related to the Feast of Saint Sebastian (January 20), which occurs at the climax of the rainy growing season when many cultivated and wild plants are in flower.[92] From this date, the *sirinus* were claimed to emerge from inside the earth with their new tunes and to remain abroad each night until *Tentación*, the final night of Carnival, when they must be ritually dispatched back into the earth once more. Antonia Caballero, to whose memory this chapter is dedicated, described Saint Sebastian as *paracero*—he "makes things appear."[93] Not only do the *sirinus* and the year's *wayñu* tunes arrive with his feast, but also the new "offspring" (*uña*) potatoes miraculously appear on the roots of the parent plants. Similarly, Padre Manzano—a priest from Sucre—observed that the Feast of Saint Sebastian was widely known in the countryside as *yarqa kacharpaya* ("dispatch/departure of hunger").

When I attended the Feast of Saint Sebastian in the nearby rural church of Titiri in January 1991, I was astonished to be told that this saint was the patron of the *sirinus*. From my Eurocentric perspective I initially found it difficult see how *sirinus*, which everybody classed as "devils" or "satans," could possibly have a patron saint. In order to convince me that Saint Sebastian was indeed the "saint of the *sirinus*" (*santo de sirinu*), Hilarion Gallego—a resident of the community—led me to the saint's statue, which had just been carried back into the church. Pointing to the statue, Hilarion triumphantly said: "He's got a *pinkillu* flute, see? The saint has a *pinkillu*." I couldn't see a flute anywhere. But Hilarion insisted: "It's at his back." Sure enough, the saint was tied to a large bass *pinkillu* flute. A little later I was told that the new *wayñus* for the year were now coming up through the floor of the church. At that moment, right on cue, a band of intoxicated flute players lurched into the church, dancing as they played what was presumably a new *wayñu*.

According to legend, Saint Sebastian was a Roman soldier who, after professing his Christianity, was tied up and shot with arrows. However, he survived this ordeal and was nursed back to life. The many depictions of this saint usually show him tied to a tree, wearing little more than a loincloth, his body pierced with arrows (fig. 3.4). The substitution of the flute for a tree in Titiri's statue of Saint Sebastian emphasizes his link with the *sirinus* and the way in which both flutes and trees communicate be-tween the inner earth and other cosmological levels.[94] Indeed, the flute literally is a tree—typically a *sawku* branch (*Sambucus peruviana*) from which the core is burnt away—which through performance may be seen to metaphorically come to life, flower, and bear fruit.

Tragically, this statue of Saint Sebastian, which I did not photograph at the time for fear of causing offense, was destroyed—with the rest of the church—in a fire a few months after this feast. My memory of the statue's details is hazy, but statues of Saint Sebastian in the regional capitals of Sucre and Potosí typically depict the saint as wearing nothing but a skirt (*pollera*), suggesting a sense of androgyny, but also of perpetual youth—an Adonis.[95] People mentioned the saint's special association with indigenous people and his powers to provide release from suffering and hardship—or even to hasten the end of a jail term. The important point here seems to be that Saint Sebastian is associated with overcoming danger, illness, and hardship, thereby enabling the continuity of life. As Hilarion Gallego put it during the feast in Titiri: "This is what Sebastian gives. He gives perma-nence to the people.... If he didn't give, [things] wouldn't be complete.... In this way we are alive, aren't we?"[96] For the people of Kalankira and neighboring Titiri, Saint Sebastian would seem to represent overcoming

Figure 3.4. Saint Sebastian bound to the tree and shot with arrows, by Albrecht Dürer (ca. 1501). By permission of the Fine Arts Museums of San Francisco, Achenbach Foundation for Graphic Arts, 1963.30.19.

the labors, dangers, and proximity of the dead during the rainy season, enabling the miraculous arrival of new life suggested by his own perpetual youth.

Carnival and the Sirinus

In Kalankira the significance of the *sirinu* was made most explicit during Carnival, the annual feast of agricultural abundance that marks the symbolic end of the rainy growing season, after which the year's new fruits may be eaten. On the Monday night of Carnival, in a ceremony called *alma kacharpaya* ("dispatch of the soul"), *sirinu* dancers from each hamlet visit any house where a man has died over the past year, the so-called *wañuq wasi* ("house of the dead"). This time the *sirinus* take the form of living men and women in Carnival dress—the traditional woolen jackets,

Figure 3.5. *Alma kacharpaya* ("dispatch of the soul") ceremony on the Monday night of Carnival (February 11, 1991). Two men with white flags act out the soul's dance followed by a band of *sirinu* dancers with *pinkillu* flutes. Photograph by Henry Stobart.

trousers, and embroidered dresses and backcloths (*aksu*) of *ayllu* Macha. The groups dance from one *wañuq wasi* to the next, singing the new *wayñu* melodies of the year to *pinkillu* flutes or local rainy-season guitars (*kitarras*). When I took part in this nocturnal series of visitations, as a *sirinu* dancer and flute player, we danced and scrambled through the night, traversing some ten miles of hillsides—avoiding footpaths in the same way as the *sirinus.*

At each *wañuq wasi* we danced and were offered corn beer and numerous plates of food. Just before we departed, a man from our party would pick up, and sometimes wear, the clothes or fighting helmet of the dead man. He would then circle left around the ritual table and perform a halting dance with a white flag, followed by the *sirinu* dancers, playing *wayñu* on *pinkillu* flutes (fig. 3.5). At the end of the dance, the man would circle the ritual table to the left once more and then replace the dead man's clothes and helmet. This, it was stated, is the only time in the year that a dance begins and ends with movement to the left. In this way the soul of the dead man was dispatched along his appropriate pathway, which is said to be *lluq'i* ("left"), the reverse to that of the living, who travel to the right.

This performance highlights the way that the powers of recently deceased adult men are harnessed to promote agricultural production. The majority of the ceremonial activity surrounding these men's deaths is reserved until the start of the rainy growing season in November, and their souls are only finally dispatched to join the community of ancestors when the crops have fully grown, flowered, and begun to bear fruit. Potatoes are Kalankira's primary crop and staple, and the emergence of the *sirinus* and their new *wayñu* melodies for the year, from the time of the feast of Saint Sebastian, coincides with the appearance of the "offspring" potato tubers on the roots of the parent plant.[97] In short, the new *wayñu* melodies mark the arrival of a new generation of potatoes beneath the soil, which grow in strength with the decline of the parent plant. An invocation of this turning point and particular form of vegetative reproduction, where one generation arrives and another departs, was vividly acted out in the *alma kacharpaya* ("dispatch of the soul") ceremony described above. While the *sirinu* dancers, with their new *wayñus* and clothing woven especially for Carnival, richly evoked the arrival of new life. The male dancer with his white, flower-like flag conveyed the sense that the departing soul was now descending from the ultimate flowering of his life cycle.

A few nights later, on Friday night of the Carnival, the *pinkillu* flutes were ritually silenced and packed away to be replaced by the small, dry-season, mandolin-like *charangos* and finally, on Sunday night, the *sirinus* and *satanos colorados* ("colored satans") were dispatched.[98] On this occasion, the parts of these various devils were acted out by two pairs of cross-dressed men and women. At the climax of the ceremony, following much singing and dancing, these actors leapt into a gully below the hamlet and emerged a few minutes later in their own gender-specific clothing. As several people later explained, the *sirinus* had entered back into the earth and would not emerge again until the height of the following growing season, at the feast of Saint Sebastian some eleven months later. However, their Carnival *wayñus,* so intimately connected with the new generation of potato tubers, would be sounded once more some eight months later in November, when the *pinkillu* flutes are brought out again at the start of the rainy growing season. These same melodies would incite the now-mature seed potatoes to sprout, grow, flower, and, in turn, give rise to a new generation.

These practices not only highlight the way that *wayñu* melodies are closely identified with specific generations of food crops, as if representing their very soul substance or animating energy,[99] but also emphasize the role of the *sirinu* in enabling the creation of new life. The *sirinus* appear at the critical moment when one generation gives way to the next, through musical sound spinning new life from the remnants of the previous generation. In the same way as the waterfall, discussed above, they act as a transition between distinct life pathways, their seductive powers musically connecting the generations of foodcrops, the ancestors and the living and inciting amorous relations between men and women.

Conclusion

Despite the immense variety in local traditions, a generalized geographical pattern seems to emerge in the ethnography of sirens in the central-southern Andes. In Southern Peru, these beings have been reported to take the form of the mermaid (*sirena*) and to be "exclusively" associated with string instruments,[100] neither of which appear to be defining characteristics as we move southward into Bolivia. As we continue further southward, into central-southern Bolivia and westward into northern Chile, the name *sirena* (*sirina*) is frequently substituted with *sirinu,* and closer links often seem to emerge between sirens and agricultural practices, especially surrounding Carnival.[101]

It might be tempting to view this association with agriculture, which seems relatively rare in European accounts, as a uniquely Andean phenomenon. Certainly, people's experience and understanding of, for example, potato cultivation in this part of the world is shaped by distinctive environmental and seasonal phenomena and experience. However, I would not want to characterize such practices as somehow "more indigenous" than, for example, the mermaid-guitar association of southern Peru. After all, Greco-European ideas about sirens arrived in the Andes over 450 years ago. Rather than alien grafts or prostheses, they are fully digested and integral aspects of a living and perpetually transforming Andean cultural body with its shifting modes of expression.

The mermaid-guitar (vihuela) association, as a motif in colonial church art, has been widely interpreted as an example of syncretism with existing Andean beliefs in water spirits associated with music. While far from discounting such processes, I have also stressed the neo-Platonic identification between celestial sirens and string instruments as an important and under-recognized contribution to this equation. A relationship between string instruments and celestial harmony was not only widespread in Renaissance Europe but also dates back to classical times.[102] In Latin America's almost unprecedented colonial program of church building, it is intriguing to wonder to what degree images of mermaids with string instruments might have expressed the creative distillation of Renaissance Humanist ideals. At the same time, indigenous fascination with new European music technology and timbres—especially the ability to sustain sound and to tune strings—is also likely to have heightened existing associations of music with potent powers of other imaginary worlds.

In these Andean examples, we have discovered many close parallels with the fatally seductive and often aqueous associations of European sirens and devils, but also a stress on musical creativity and knowledge, and its connection with cosmology and shifts in consciousness. Despite close associations of Andean sirens with flowing water and rocks in the landscape, we find—at least in northern Potosí, Bolivia—that recording technology and the local recording industry seems to have reconfigured rather than eclipsed people's views of sirens as a source of music. In the case study from the community of agriculturalists and herders of Kalankira, the *sirinus* and their music emerge as critical to agricultural production. Commencing with the feast of their patron, Saint Sebastian (January 20), the *sirinus* emerge from the earth with the new *wayñu* melodies for the year at the very moment that the new generation of potato tubers begin to be formed on the roots of the parent plant; cycles of music and potato cultivation go hand in hand. The *sirinus* and their melodies connect the generations and mediate seasonally shifting relations between the worlds of the living and the ancestors, announcing new life and escorting the dead to *alma llajta* ("land of the souls").

Is it more than pure coincidence that, according to certain Greek traditions, the sirens were originally daughters of the Earth, escorts of the dead, and companions of Persephone on her season-shaping journey to and from the underworld?[103] Even if not a salient feature of the European legacy, in both ancient Greece and Kalankira today, the sirens have close associations with guiding the rotation of the seasons and with all that comes to pass on the "fruitful earth."[104] In addition, Plato's celestial sirens were originally presented in the *Republic* in the context of the myth of Er, the story of a warrior killed in battle who returns from the afterlife to tell the living what awaits them following death. It is a tale of the continuity of the soul, where after its spell in purgatory or heaven, it returns to the sphere of the living to take a new form. At the point when the soul is about to acquire a new life form, it approaches Mother Necessity, who is spinning with a spindle whorl on her knee—precisely like those used daily by people in Kalankira to spin yarn from raw wool. Mother Necessity's cosmic spindle—a rainbow-like pillar stretching through heaven and earth—includes eight whorls, with a siren singing a different note on each.[105] This metaphor of spinning or "twisting" new life from disconnected strands, mediated by the sirens and their music, is identical to that which I encountered in Kalankira and finds resonances in other siren traditions discussed in this book.[106] But how much should such shared metaphors be attributed to the flow of ideas and imagery across time and space, and how much to the myths and metaphors that emerge from the practices of everyday life?

Like many of their Greco-European counterparts, what unifies most accounts of Andean sirens seems to be the way they inhabit boundaries and embody the idea of transition, transformation, or communication between different realms of being. This creative potential for transformation, enabling the emergence of new forms, knowledge of understandings, may—like the sirens and their music—be seen as both intensely desirable and dangerous.

NOTES

1. This chapter is dedicated to the memory of Antonia Cabellero, originally from the community of Titiri, who died in childbirth in 2000. She and her husband were both close friends during my time in Kalankira and Antonia, in particular, was a rich source of knowledge about Sirens and their local patron, Saint Sebastian.

2. No separate word exists in Spanish for "mermaid," so the word *sirena* implies the compound "siren-mermaid." *Sirina,* a spelling that sometimes appears in this chapter, is the Spanish *sirena* written using standard Quechua and Aymara orthography.

3. While the Spanish *sireno* is a masculine form, it is not exclusively masculine (in the same way as *sirena* is exclusively female) and would be applied to a group of sirens of mixed gender.

4. As *sirinu* are closely associated with the night and clear or crystalline water—evocative of dew—these Spanish meanings may, at least in part, be relevant to local understanding of *sirinu.*

5. *Sirena* traditions have been reported from several other parts of Latin America, including Amazonian Peru, where shamans sometimes make aquatic journeys with the *sirena* wives (personal communication, Francoise Barbira-Freedman). For Mexico see Nadine Béligand, "Les trois âges d'un couple de déités lacustres: Éclosion, renaissance et deparition des sirènes du lac de Chicnahua-pan, vallée de Tolluca (Mexique)," *Journal de la Société des Américanistes* 84, no. 1 (1998): 45–72, and for Venezuela see Rafael Salazar, *The Arab World in Our Music* (Caracas: Fundación Tradiciones Caraqueñas, OPEC Summit, PDVSA, 2000), 131.

6. See Henry Stobart, *Music and the Poetics of Production in the Bolivian Andes* (Aldershot: Ashgate, in press).

7. Thomas Turino, "The Charango and the Sirena: Music, Magic and the Power of Love," *Latin American Music Review* 4 (Spring/Summer 1983): 81–119.

8. Wálter Sánchez C., "El Proceso de Creación Musical (Música Autoctona del Norte de Potosí)," Centro Pedagogico y Cultural de Portales/Centro de Documentacion de Música Boliviana, *Boletin,* no. 7 (Octubre 1988): 1–18; Claudio Mercado, "Detrás del sonido, el mundo," *Takiwasi* (Tarapoto, Peru) 4 (año 2, 1996): 46–61.

9. Thomas Solomon, "Mountains of Song: Musical Constructions of Ecology, Place, and Identity in the Bolivian Andes" (Ph.D. diss., University of Texas at Austin, 1997).

10. See Stobart, *Music and the Poetics of Production.*

11. Stephen Greenblatt, *Marvelous Possessions: The Wonder of the New World* (Oxford: Clarendon Press 1992), 26.

12. Gary Tomlinson, *Music in Renaissance Magic: Toward a Historiography of Others* (Chicago: University of Chicago Press, 1993), 67–100.

13. Esta music se causa y perfeciona de siete Sirenas que ay enel alma, que son siete virtudes, las quales despiertan el spiritu con su concordia y armonia, para sentir y conoscer las cosas divinas y humanas, y el gran bien que deste conoscimiento se sigue. Esta en ninguna criatura terrena la puso dios con tanta razon y perfection como enel hombre, nien los instrumentos de cuerdas como enel de la vihuela. Y assi es/que lo que los sabios antiguos y todos las demas en loor de la musica escriuieron, parece claro que con mas razon se deue attribuir a la vihuela, en que es las mas perfecta consonancia de cuerdas. (My translation.)

14. Enrriquez de Valderrabano, *Libro de musica de vihuela intitulado Silva de Sirenas* (facsimile) (Geneva: Minkoff, [1547] 1981).

15. Herbert Schueller, *The Idea of Music* (Kalamazoo: Medieval Institute Publications, Western Michigan University, 1988), 32–33.

16. Valderrabano makes only one fleeting reference to the Homeric sirens, among other classical references, noting their "consonant voices and verses" and promise of immortal knowledge. Valderrabano, *Libro de musica de vihuela intitulado Silva de Sirenas.*

17. Teresa Gisbert, *Iconografia y Mitos Indiginas en el Arte* (La Paz: Gisbert y Cia, 1980), 50. Gisbert further mentions fourteen siren-mermaid representations from church iconography that do not include a musical instrument.

18. Jennifer Durkin, "The Iconography of Insurrection: The British Museum Tapestry No 1913 3–11 and the symbolism of 18th century Peruvian Nationalism" (M.A. diss., Department of Art History and Theory, University of Essex, 1989), 51.

19. Gisbert, *Iconografia,* 51.

20. Turino, "Charango and Sirena," 97

21. Felipe Guaman Poma de Ayala, *El Primer Nueva Corónica y Buen Gobierno* (ca. 1615). Ed. J. Murra and R. Adorno (Mexico City: Siglo Veintiuno, 1980), f. 316; Turino, "Charango and Sirena," 111–12.

22. For an analysis of the (mainly Quechua) words in the drawing, see Veronica Cereceda, "Aproximaciones a una estetica andina: de la belleza al *tinku,*" in *Tres reflexiones sobre el pensamiento andino,* ed. T. Bouysse-Cassagne, O. Harris, T. Platt, V. Cereceda (La Paz: Hisbol, 1987), 151.

23. For further discussion of this drawing see Thomas Turino, "Charango

and Sirena" 1983), 111–13; Veronica Cereceda, "Aproximaciones a una estetica andina," 151; and Henry Stobart, "Interlocking Realms: Knowing Music and Musical Knowing in the Bolivian Andes," in *Knowledge and Learning in the Andes: Ethnographic Perspectives,* ed. H. Stobart and R. Howard (Liverpool: University of Liverpool Press, 2002), 83–85.

24. Constance Classen, "Creation by Sound/Creation by Light: A Sensory Analysis of Two South American Cosmologies," in *The Varieties of Sensory Experience,* ed. D. Howes (Toronto: University of Toronto Press, 1991), 241.

25. I have not had the opportunity to show this drawing to people in southern Peru where *sirenas* are widely associated with mermaids. It may have provoked rather different responses.

26. Marilyn Strathern, "Out of Context: The Persuasive Fictions of Anthropology," *Current Anthropology* 28, no. 3 (1987): 260

27. Turino, "Charango and Sirena," 96.

28. Ibid., 113.

29. Ibid., 96.

30. Teresa Gisbert has also identified a possible association with Platonic celestial sirens in this image and a few others from Andean churches (Gisbert, *Iconografía,* 49).

31. D. P. Walker, ed., *Musique des intermèdes de "la pellegrina": Les fêtes de Florence—1589,* score and notes (Paris: Cente National de la Recherche Scientifique, 1986), xxxvi–xxxvii; Jamie James, *The Music of the Spheres: Music, Science and the Natural Order of the Universe* (London: Abacus, 1993), 103–104.

32. Durkin, *Iconography of Insurrection,* 59.

33. Ibid., 59.

34. Turino, "Charango and Sirena."

35. Ibid., 96–97.

36. Ibid., 96.

37. See also Solomon, *Mountains of Song,* 245.

38. Turino, "Charango and Sirena," 96.

39. María Ester Grebe Vicuña, "Generative Models, Symbolic Structures and Acculturation in the Panpipe Music of the Aymara of Tarapaca," Chile (Ph.D. diss., The Queen's University, Belfast, 1980), 161–62.

40. Accounts of women visiting siren-type beings to acquire their powers are relatively rare.

41. See Henry Stobart, "Interlocking Realms."

42. Homer, *The Odyssey* [ca. 800 BC], trans. W. Shewring (Oxford: Oxford University Press, 1980), 147.

43. Anna Johnson, "The Sprite in the Water and the Siren of the Woods: On Swedish Folk Music and Gender," in *Music, Gender, and Culture,* ed. M. Herndon and S. Ziegler (Wilhelmshaven: Florian Noetzel Verlag, 1990), 27.

44. See, e.g., Regina Harrison, *Signs, Songs, and Memory in the Andes: Translating Quechua Language and Culture* (Austin: University of Texas Press, 1989), 47–48.

45. Olivia Harris, "The Power of Signs: Gender, Culture and the Wild in the Bolivian Andes," in *Nature, Culture and Gender,* ed. C. McCormack and M. Strathern (Cambridge: Cambridge University Press, 1981), 81.

46. Rosalia Martinez, "Musique et démons: Carnaval chez les Tarabuco (Bolivie)," *Journal de la Société de des Américanistes* 76 (1990): 157–58.

47. Xosé Ramón Mariño Ferro, *"Muerte, religion y simbolos en una comunidad quechua* (Universidade de Santiago de Compestella, Spain, 1989), 136–37.

48. Slowomira Zeranska-Kominek (with Arnold Lebeuf), *The Tale of the Crazy Harman* (Warsaw: Dialog Academic Publications, 1997), 187–89.

49. Harris, "The Power of Signs," 81.

50. Turino, "Charango and Sirena."

51. Solomon, *Mountains of Song,* 249.

52. In certain local traditions it is maintained that panpipes cannot be tuned in this way although in others panpipes are included. See Vicuña, *Generative Models,* 162.

53. I provide a detailed account of a similar concept of musical energy, referred to as *animu.* See Henry Stobart, "Bodies of Sound and Landscapes of Music: A View from the Bolivian Andes," in *Musical Healing in Cultural Context,* ed. P. Gouk (Aldershot: Ashgate, 2000), 26–45.

54. Catherine Allen, *The Hold Life Has: Coca and Cultural Identity in an Andean Community* (Washington, D.C.: Smithsonian Institution, 1988), 50.

55. Sánchez, "El Proceso de Creación Musical," 7.

56. Miranda van der Spek, *The Devil's Horn: A Documentary about Brass Bands in the Andes of Bolivia* (video) (Amsterdam 1994).

57. A guinea pig was used on this occasion because a red cockerel was not available. The guinea pig was made to squeak immediately before it was dispatched.

58. Vicuña, *Generative Models,* 162.

59. Compare, e.g., Jacques Attali, *Noise: The Political Economy of Music,* trans. B. Massumi (Manchester: Manchester University Press, 1985), 29.

60. See Carole Pegg, *Mongolian Music, Dance, & Oral Narrative* (Seattle: University of Washington Press, 2001), 60.

61. Claudio Mercado, "Detrás del sonido, el mundo," *Takiwasi* (Tarapoto, Peru) 4, año 2 (1996): 49. Mercado has also independently identified the similarity with overtone singing noted above.

62. Henry Stobart, "Lo recto y lo torcido: La música andina y la espiral de la descendencia," in *Gente de carne y hueso: las tramas de parentesco en los andes,* ed. D. Arnold (La Paz: ILCA/CIASE, 1998), 581–604; Wálter Sánchez also cites a local consultant from Northern Potosí who refers to the perception of new melodies at the *sirinu*'s waterfall with the word *k'uyu,* also meaning "twist." See Sánchez, "El Proceso de Creación Musical," 16.

63. Arnold and Yapita have written evocatively about the *jira maykus* of *ayllu* Qaqachaka, which are closely associated with *sirenas.* They characterize the *jira maykus* as the spinning warrior spirits of Carnival, who might be thought of as the

spinners of life and death. Denise Arnold and J. Yapita, *Río de vellón, río de canto: Cantar a los animales, una poética andina de la creacion* (La Paz: Hisbol, 1998), 51, 500.

64. *Sirinu nuqa rikuni a. Ajina parapi chuqurkuspa. Ajina puñuyta chuturqurikasqani. Chaymanta wuuu.. wu . . . miiii.. wayñu junt' arkurimushasqa chay mirkata. Libristuta! Challtikujina rikuq kani, challku kay kinray kay kinray challkujina. Chay Lurin arqiñan, chaypi, kuywapi parapi chukusaq kani, chaypi jinapi puñuyta chutushasqani, puñuta chutushaqtirqa wuu . . . wuu . . . aaaata. pinkillus "uj." Chay mirkamantaq sunarqamun kanpaq, karnawalqa.* Full account and recording in Stobart, *Music and the Poetics of Production* (Appendix II).

65. E.g., by Bartholemeus Anglicus ca. 1230. See Rodney Dennys, *The Heraldic Imagination* (London: Barrie & Jenkins, 1975), 122.

66. E.g., Alan Merriam, *Ethnomusicology of the Flathead Indians* (Chicago: Aldine Publishing Co., 1967), 3–8.

67. Harris, "The Power of Signs," 83.

68. At this feast I met several people who had recently visited the *sirinus* at waterfalls to collect new melodies, but nobody else from Kalankira actually attended the feast. Also, there seemed to be very few people from *ayllu* Laymi at this fiesta, which took place in *ayllu* Pukwata territory.

69. Olivia Harris, "Etnomúsica en el Norte de Potosí." *Jayma,* Año 6, nos. 26–27 (1988): 4.

70. Wálter Sánchez C., "Circuitos Musicales (Música Autoctona del Norte de Potosí)." Centro Pedagogico y Cultural de Portales/Centro de Documentacion de Música Boliviana. *Boletin,* no. 11 (Marzo 1989): 7.

71. Solomon, *Mountains of Song,* 265.

72. Ibid., 268

73. Sánchez, "El Proceso de Creación Musical"; Solomon, *Mountains of Song;* Arnold and Yapita, *Río de vellón.*

74. Solomon, *Mountains of Song,* 248

75. Arnold and Yapita, *Río de vellón,* 195–96.

76. See, e.g., Gary Urton, *At the Crossroads of the Earth and the Sky: An Andean Cosmology* (Austin: University of Texas Press, 1981).

77. Solomon, *Mountains of Song,* 248–49.

78. Janis Nuckolls, *Sounds Like Life: Sound-Symbolic Grammar, Performance, and Cognition in Pastaza Quechua* (New York: Oxford University Press, 1996), 222.

79. For illustrations and discussion of these meandering images, see Henry Stobart, "Lo recto y lo torcido: La música andina y la espiral de la descendencia," in *Gente de carne y hueso: las tramas de parentesco en los andes,* ed. D. Arnold (La Paz: ILCA/CIASE 1998); and Stobart, *Music and the Poetics of Production,* esp. chap. 4. Also see Thomas Abercombie, *Pathways of Memory and Power: Ethnography and History among an Andean People* (Madison: University of Wisconsin Press, 1998), 371 for an extensive discussion of the idea of "pathways" (*t"akis*) in ritual drinking.

80. Near Jesús de Machaca, Ingavi Province, La Paz, Bolivia.

81. I am grateful to Astvaldur Astvaldsson for this Aymara gloss and for introducing me to Sullka Titi Titiri. For more details about rocks in this community, see Astvaldur Astvaldsson, "The Powers of Hard Rock: Meaning, Transformation and Continuity in Cultural Symbols in the Andes," *Journal of Latin American Cultural Studies* 7, no. 2 (1998).

82. Ludovico Bertonio, *Vocabulario de la lengua Aymara* [1612] (facsimile) (Cochabamba, Bolivia: CERES, 1984), 2:305.

83. Michelle Bigenho, *Sounding Indigenous: Authenticity in Bolivian Music Performance* (New York: Palgrave Macmillan, 2002), 211.

84. Attali, *Noise,* 11.

85. Henry Stobart, "Flourishing Horns and Enchanted Tubers: Music and Potatoes in Highland Bolivia," *British Journal of Ethnomusicology* 3, 1994: 35–48; Henry Stobart, "The Llama's Flute: Musical Misunderstandings in the Andes," *Early Music* 24, no. 3 (August 1996): 470–82.

86. Stobart, "The Llama's Flute," 473–74.

87. Thomas Turino, "The Charango and the Sirena," 96.

88. Despite apparent European influences in the construction and playing tradition of the *pinkillu* flute, it is also tempting to identify a number of indigenous elements (Henry Stobart, "The Llama's Flute"). Flute-playing cults are widespread in South America, especially in Amazonia. See, e.g., Stephen Hugh-Jones, *The Palm and the Pleiades: Initiation and Cosmology in Northwest Amazonia* (Cambridge: Cambridge University Press, 1979), 134.

89. Stobart, "The Llama's Flute," 475.

90. Harris, "Dead and Devils," 58.

91. Ibid.

92. See also INDICEP, "El Carnival en las Comunidades Aymaras del Departamento de Oruro," *INDICEP (Instituto de Investigación Cultural para Educación Popular)*, Doc. 10, Serie. A, Oruro, Bolivia, *Año* 4, no. 7 (Octubre 1973): 4; and Sánchez, "El Proceso de Creación Musical," 12. In some cases the emergence of the *sirinus* with the new *wayñu* melodies for the year is related to the feast of Candelaria (February 2).

93. From the Spanish *aparecer* "to appear." Antonia spoke very little Spanish.

94. Tristan Platt, "The Andean Soldiers of Christ: Confraternity Organization, The Mass of the Sun and Regenerative Warfare in Rural Potosí (18th–20th Centuries)," *Journal de la Société des Américanistes* 73 (1987), 145–46.

95. Accordingly to religious canons, only Saint Sebastian (besides Christ on the cross and as an infant), was permitted to be depicted as a nude (Durkin, *Iconography of Insurrection,* 100). This saint's nakedness and "beautiful boy" image has led to many homoerotic associations in Europe, but I have no evidence that these were relevant to people in Kalankira. See, e.g., Camille Paglia, *Sexual Personae: Art and Decadence from Nefertiti to Emily Dickinson* (London: Penguin, 1992), 148.

96. *El Sebastian dar esa. Esta permincia dar el a la gente. Por eso, como eso es completo . . . Si no da, no completo . . . Como eso estamos vivo, no!?*

97. Stobart, "Flourishing Horns and Enchanted Tubers," 45.

98. In other parts of northern Potosí and the neighboring Oruro department, it is common for the *pinkillu* flutes and Carnival devils to be dispatched in a single rite.

99. Food crops were considered to be endowed with *animu,* the energy or soul substance that animates all living things and which may be expressed as musical sound. They were also widely attributed human-like sentiments, and claimed to weep "like human babies" if abandoned or mistreated. See Henry Stobart, "Bodies of Sound, Landscapes of Music," 31 and Henry Stobart, "Flourishing Horns and Enchanted Tubers," 43–44.

100. Turino, "Charango and Sirena."

101. Without much more ethnographic data this geographic distribution remains extremely provisional. For example, although the term *sirena* (*sirina*) appears more common in northern regions around Lake Titicaca, in his study of devil-type beings of the Bolivian altiplano (south of Lake Titicaca) Gerardo Fernández uses the term *sirinu.* See Gerardo Fernández Juárez, "*Iqiqu y achanchu:* enanos, demonios y metales en el altiplano aymara," *Journal de la Societé des Américanistes* 84, no. 1 (1998): 148.

102. Schueller, *The Idea of Music,* 35; Tomlinson, *Music in Renaissance Magic,* 85–86.

103. Betty Radice, *Who's Who in the Ancient World* (London: Penguin, 1973), 222.

104. The destinies of men and plants also intermingle in Homer's account of the sirens, who sat in a "meadow" surrounded by men's decaying corpses and claimed to know all that comes to pass on the "fruitful earth" (Homer, *The Odyssey,* 1980), 144, 147.

105. James, *Music of the Spheres,* 53–54; Schueller, *The Idea of Music,* 32–33.

106. See Inna Naroditskaya's discussion of Russian *rusalkas* in chapter 7 of this volume.

FOUR

"Sweet aluring harmony"

Heavenly and Earthly Sirens in Sixteenth- and Seventeenth-Century Literary and Visual Culture

Elena Laura Calogero

Sixteenth- and seventeenth-century love-poetry includes many references to music and, in particular, the praise of a lady's accomplishments
often including her skills in singing or playing a musical instrument.[1]
Poems exclusively dedicated to or describing female musicians tend to take
one of two directions: the effects of music are either ennobling, elevating
the (male) listener to spiritual contemplation and love; or they achieve the
result of further inflaming love and passion, bringing death or perdition.
Both trends have roots in ancient and medieval traditions offering two
paradigmatic models of sirens' music: one can be traced back to Platonic
views of world harmony, the latter and more familiar one to a famous
episode in Homer's *Odyssey*.[2] The following study explores how the treatment of female musicians in some sixteenth- and seventeenth-century
Italian and English poems is dependent on either tradition. This poetic
image acquires further meanings in the light of models or parallels in
contemporary visual culture, where the representation of sirens has a
place not only in paintings but also in widely circulating emblem books,
iconographies, and mythographies.

Although the poetic voice tends to remain passive in reference to an angelic siren/woman, when the beloved lady or other female musician is cast in the role of one of the mythological Sirens, the same voice adapts the role of Ulysses, devising or suggesting ways of escape from the aural and visual threat of female enticement. The two variants of angelic and earthly Sirens are usually kept distinct as touchstones for the woman, but they are sometimes intentionally conflated, and in these instances the result is a particularly meaningful "dual" image reflecting the ambivalent attitude toward female music that is so typical of this period.[3]

Heavenly Sirens

In a sonnet of the *Canzoniere* in praise of Laura's song, Petrarch (1304–1374) uses the parallel between Laura and a siren, in the following terms:

> Quando Amor i belli occhi a terra inclina,
> e i vaghi spirti in un sospiro accoglie
> co le sue mani, et poi in voce gli scioglie
> chiara, soave, angelica, divina,
>
> sento far del mio cor dolce rapina,
> et sì sento cangiar penseri et voglie
> ch'i' dico: "Or fien di me l'ultime spoglie:
> se'l ciel sì honesta morte mi destina."
>
> Ma'l suon, che di dolcezza i sensi lega
> col gran desir d'udendo esser beata
> l'anima al dipartir presta raffrena;
>
> così mi vivo, et così avolge et spiega
> lo stame de la vita che m'è data
> questa sola fra noi del ciel sirena.

(When Love bends her lovely eyes to the ground and with his own hands gathers together her wandering breath into a sigh and then looses it in a clear, soft, angelic, divine voice, I feel my heart sweetly stolen away and my thoughts and desires so change within me that I say: "Now comes the final plundering of me, if Heaven reserves me for so virtuous a death." But the sound that binds my senses with its sweetness, reins in my soul, though ready to depart, with the great desire for the blessedness of listening; so I live on, and thus she both threads and unwinds the spool of my appointed life, this only heavenly Siren among us.)[4]

This image of Laura as an angelic Siren is derived from ancient authority: the poet is elaborating on Plato's treatment of heavenly music in a passage of the *Republic* that refers to sirens sitting on and accompanying with a sound the motion of each of the eight spheres turning around the spindle of Necessity, and singing in unison with the Fates.[5] The sound of Laura's song has the effect of "binding the senses" and keeping the listener's soul from leaving his body. The age-old belief that music could draw the soul from the body and make it return to heaven—earthly music reminding the soul of heavenly music—is the basis of this allusion, and it would be often repeated and varied in sixteenth- and seventeenth-century poems in praise of music or of particular musicians.[6] But Laura herself, both a siren and one of the Fates, spinning the thread of the poet's life, remains passive, modestly keeping her eyes averted from him. Literary memories and actual experience merge in this case: in fact the latter picture is in line with some contemporary prescriptions for female musical practice. Francesco da Barberino (1264–1348), for example, giving advice on the proper behavior for a young woman, remarks that when requested to sing, she must perform without moving and with her eyes cast toward the ground:

> E se avien talora le convegna cantare per detto del signore o della madre o dalle sue compagne pregata un poco prima, d'una maniera bassa soavemente canti, ferma, cortese e cogli occhi chinati, e stando volta a chi magior vi siede. E questo canto basso, chiamato camerale, è quel che piace e che passa ne' cuori.

> (And if it sometimes befits her to sing, when requested and prayed a little by her father or mother or her companions, she should sing sweetly in a low tone, still, courteous, and with her eyes bent downward, and turned toward the oldest person sitting there. And this soft song, called chamber song, is the one that pleases and enters the hearts.)[7]

Petrarch's influence on later treatments of the angelic Siren in verse is clearly evident in a *ballata* by Bembo (1470–1547):

> La mia leggiadra e candida angioletta,
> cantando a par de le Sirene antiche,
> con altre d'onestade e pregio amiche
> sedersi a l'ombra in grembo de l'erbetta
> vid'io pien di spavento:
> perch'esser mi parea pur su nel cielo,
> tal di dolcezza velo
> avolto avea quel punto agli occhi miei.

> (I saw my lovely and innocent little angel, singing like the ancient sirens, with other friends of honesty and worth, sitting in the shade on the grass, and I was full of awe. Because I thought I was in heaven, such was the veil of sweetness that moment had wrapped around my eyes.)[8]

Here, too, the scene of female music-making is given through the poet's narrative of his visual experience, but the act of seeing the beloved lady sing is soon surpassed by the prevailing of sounds almost blinding the poet by enveloping him in a veil of sweetness and giving him the impression of being in heaven. The frame of reference is world harmony again; Bembo's comparison of his "little angel" to the "ancient sirens" is not unusual or original, since long before him the Platonic Sirens had been associated in the Christian tradition with the nine hierarchies of angels governing the celestial spheres, sometimes singing to their motion.[9]

In the same tradition, Du Bartas (1544–1590), for example, relates that:

> D'autant, comme l'on dit, que la Voix souueraine
> Logea dans chaque ciel vne douce Syrene
> Comme sur-intendante: à fin que ces bas corps
> Empruntassent des hauts leurs plus parfaits accords,
> Et qu'vn Chœur aime-bal auec le chœur des Anges
> Dans sa chapelle ardente entonnast ses louanges.

> (For [as they say] for super-Intendent there,
> The supreme Voice placed in every Spheare
> A *Syrene* sweet; that from Heav'ns Harmonie
> Inferiour things might learne best Melodie:
> And their rare Quier with th'Angels Quier accord
> To sing aloud the praises of the Lord.)[10]

If God is the supreme Voice, the voices of celestial Sirens, blended with those of angels, acquire the role of guides and models for men's sacred music within the well-ordered universe described by the French poet. But the angel-siren connection would be also used for mainly eulogistic purposes in nonreligious poems. Although the name of Pietro Aretino (1492–1556) is not usually associated with Petrarchan themes, he was able to exploit angelic siren imagery to his own ends by playing on his dedicatee's name, Angela Serena ("serena" being both a Christian or family name and an archaic spelling for the Italian *sirena*), in a sequence of refined love poems:

> Stelle, vostra mercé l'eccelse sfere
> dette del Ciel Sirene hanno concesso
> a lei non solo in belle note altere,
> come titol gradito, il nome istesso,
> ma de le lor perfette armonie vere
> con suprema dolcezza il suono impresso

ne le sue chiare e nette voci: ond'ella
quasi in lingua de gli Angioli favella.

(It is thanks to you, stars, that the lofty spheres, called the heavenly
Sirens, not only granted her their name itself as an agreeable title, with
beautiful proud notes; they even imprinted the sound of their perfect
true harmonies on her clear and neat voice, with sublime sweetness, so
that she speaks almost in the language of angels.)[11]

While the emphasis in these lines is again on heavenly notes and angelic
voices, the importance of the poet's gaze in his experience of ecstatic
contemplation is rendered in a sense by the frontispiece of the first edition
of the *Stanze*, probably designed by no less an artist than Titian. Here the
reader, twice removed, could see Angela Serena in the form of a double-
tailed Siren in the sky worshipped by a kneeling shepherd with the features
of the poet himself (fig. 4.1).[12]

These poems on women's inspirational song, lingering on the interaction between sight and hearing, have an immediate background in Neo-
platonic theories alluding to the link between music and love. For orthodox Neoplatonists, sight usually has first place in the hierarchy of the
senses, particularly in the transmission and reception of love. Some writers, as Gretchen Finney noticed, stress the notion that musical sounds, by
penetrating the body through the ears, contribute to the spread of love.[13]
Guido Casoni (1561–1642), expounding on a passage by Ficino (1433–
1499), explains "How Love is a musician," and interprets music as a "min-
ister" of Love, that is, as an instrument by which love can "increase the
flames in a lover's breast and make them more ardent."[14]

The same ideas were made popular through the *Book of the Courtier* by
Baldassar Castiglione (1478–1529), in which male musical practice is exalted for its power to please the listener's soul and, implicitly, to arouse love.
One of the main speakers, the Count, praises music not only for its recre-
ational qualities, but because "many things are taken in hand to please
women withall, whose tender and soft breastes are soone pierced with
melodie, and filled with sweetnesse."[15] Later in the same work Bembo, in his
role of authority on spiritual love, considers the link between love, female
beauty, and female music:

And as a man heareth not with his mouth, nor smelleth with his eares:
no more can he also in any manner wise enjoy beautie, nor satisfie
the desire that she stirreth up in our mindes, with feeling, but with the
sense, unto whom beautie is the very butte to level at: namely, the vertue
of seeing.

Figure 4.1. *I Mondi del Doni* (Venice: Francesco Marcolini, 1552), fol.71^r. By permission of the Biblioteca Nazionale Centrale, Rome.

Let him lay aside therefore the blinde judgement of the sense, and enjoy with his eyes ye brightenesse, the comelinesse, the loving sparkels, laughters, gestures, and all the other pleasant furnitures of beautie: especially with hearing the sweetnesse of her voice, the tunablenesse of her wordes, the melody of her singing and playing on instruments (in case the woman beloved bee a musitian) and so shall he with most daintie foode feede the soule through the meanes of these two senses, which have litle bodily substance in them, and be the ministers of reason, without entring farther towarde the bodie, with coveting unto any longing otherwise than honest.[16]

Within this context, sight and hearing are steps on the "stayre of love,"[17] that is, in the gradual progress from terrestrial to divine love, which explains the emphasis on incorporeal experience. Other works were less concerned with the philosophical aspects of falling in love and, while still drawing on this tradition, also recurred to other frames of reference for the treatment of love and music, giving the musical sirens a different shape.

Earthly Sirens

The attention to the place of sight and hearing in love can be also related to the topos of the five senses in the visual arts of the sixteenth- and seventeenth-centuries. Personified versions of this theme are sometimes accompanied by moralizing comments. In a Dutch engraving, for example, Hearing is presented by an apparently idyllic picture of a woman and a man making music; nevertheless, the inscribed Latin verses warn against lending open ears to the sweet song of "alluring sirens."[18] In fact, the Neoplatonic ladder of love could turn into what some scholars call the "ladder of lechery," a figure describing the five steps from visual and aural to material fruition of love. The text of a famous Elizabethan lute song exploits and varies this scheme in mentioning the lover's request "to see, to hear, to touch, to kiss, to die" with the lady,[19] and even when poets stop at the two "noblest" senses, the experience of a material enthrallment by looks and sounds can be emphasized, as in a poem by Andrew Marvell (1621–1678), praising a "fair singer":

> I
> To make a final conquest of all me,
> Love did compose so sweet an Enemy,
> In whom both Beauties to my death agree,
> Joyning themselves in fatal Harmony;
> That while she with her Eyes my Heart does bind,
> She with her Voice might captivate my Mind.
>
> II
> I could have fled from One but singly fair:
> My dis-intangled Soul it self might save,
> Breaking the curled trammels of her hair.
> But how should I avoid to be her Slave,
> Whose subtle Art invisibly can wreath
> My Fetters of the very Air I breath?[20]

The conceit of a military conquest here further transforms the poem into a witty piece in which even the traditional theme of the soul's ravishment by music is renewed. If in Petrarch Laura's breath turned into ethereal music, here the vocal sounds of an unnamed virtuoso female singer become the actual chains of the listener's enslavement.

Similarly Giambattista Marino (1569–1625), in a poem dedicated to a *"bella cantatrice,"* had insisted on the double attraction of eyes and song. He imagines to ask the angels confirmation about the heavenliness of the woman herself, but in lingering on his doubt, he shows that the opposite—that she might be an earthly Siren—could be equally possible:

> Piacciaui à me di dir quest'Angeletta,
> E Sirena del Ciel, ò de la terra,
> Che sì col canto, e co' begli occhi alletta?
> Dir v'odo già (se'l mio pensier non erra)
> In quel ciel di beltà vera e perfetta,
> Sappi, che d'alma in vece Angel si serra.

(Please tell me: is this little angel a heavenly or an earthly Siren, alluring so much with her song and fair eyes? I already hear you say [if my thought is not amiss]: "you must know that an angel, not a soul, is enclosed in that sky of true and perfect beauty.")[21]

The latter examples take to the other frame of reference for women's music in this period. In early modern culture, the Sirens of Homeric memory served as the favorite touchstone in references to women musicians, seducing by the beauty of their song as well as by their more physical charms. The similitude woman/siren reveals ambivalence: if, on the one hand, the comparison is useful to underline the affective, rhetorical power of words and song, so important both in Humanist and in Baroque aesthetical thought, it also recalls the idea of dangerous deception already present in older versions of the myth.[22]

The frequent references to women's music as performed in sixteenth- and seventeenth-century literature is surely related to its growing importance in the social life of the period, particularly in Italy.[23] Among the female musicians performing at some sixteenth-century Italian courts, the most renowned for their virtuosic vocal skills was the *concerto delle donne,* a group hired to offer chamber-music concerts at the court of Duke Alfonso II in Ferrara. In addition, music acquired particular significance in certain convents in northern Italy, where half-hidden nuns performed in rites and ceremonies for the public, although these musical activities did not escape objections and restrictions.[24] Some women—such as Maddalena Casulana in the second half of the sixteenth century and Francesca Caccini and Barbara Strozzi in the early seventeenth century—

gradually emerged as independent composers of printed music, both sacred and secular.

The lute seems to have been the preferred instrument of Italian noblewomen, and it involved not only the ability to read music, but also the improvisation of both music and words. In fact, music was seen by many as one of the desirable accomplishments for noble or upper-class girls, but only to be pursued in the inner spaces of home or court, and soon to be sacrificed to the occupations of married life. Even Bembo, who advocated music in the context of Platonic love, did not allow his daughter to learn to play instruments, thinking this pursuit was fit for "a vain and shallow woman" and preferring other subjects for her curriculum.[25] Rules concerning the kinds of music women could perform, as well as the instruments most appropriate for them, are sometimes explicitly mentioned in those books giving advice on the proper conduct in society. Castiglione's guidelines for a decorous female musical performance, including behavioral prescriptions, read:

> Imagin with your selfe what an unsightly matter it were to see a woman play upon a tabour or drum, or blow in a flute or trumpet, or any like instrument: and this because the boistrousnesse of them doth both cover and take away that sweete mildnesse which setteth so forth everie deede that a woman doth.
>
> Therefore when she commeth to daunce, or to shew any kind of musicke, she ought to be brought to it with suffring her selfe somewhat to be prayed, and with a certain bashfulnesse, that may declare the noble shamefastnesse that is contrarie to headinesse.[26]

Castiglione excludes drums and trumpets, as well as wind instruments, from his choices for women. The former were usually associated with the masculine field of war. His opposition to the latter recalls an ancient tradition, still well known in this period, according to which the goddess Minerva had cast away an *aulos* (linked in the era to the recorder and similarly held instruments) once she learned that it deformed her face.[27]

Although writing more than two centuries later than Barberino, Castiglione and many of his contemporaries still thought that reputable women should make music and dance only when requested.[28] Outside of fixed boundaries, female musicians could evoke the uneasy image of alluring sirens. Erotic implications are absent in Homer's episode, but they developed soon afterward, and were emphasized by another classical authority, Ovid, who had clearly interpreted music not as a means for spiritual elevation when used by women, but as a "weapon" for seduction. The *Art of Love* provides a long similitude between women skilled in music and the Sirens, who are in turn jokingly compared to mythical male musicians/magicians such as Orpheus, Arion, and Amphion:

> The Sirens were wondrous creatures of the sea, who with tuneful voice detained vessels, how sweet soe'er they sailed. Hearing them the son of Sisyphus all but unloosed his body; for his comrades' ears were stopped with wax. A persuasive thing is song: let women learn to sing; with many voice instead of face has been their procuress. Let them repeat now ditties heard in the marble theatres, now songs acted in the fashion of Nyle; nor should a woman skilled as I would have her be ignorant how to hold the quill in her right hand and the lyre in her left. With his lyre did Orpheus of Rhodope move rocks and hearts, and the lakes of Tartarus and the three-headed dog. At thy strains, most just avenger of thy mother, the stones with ready service formed new walls. A fish though dumb is believed to have shown favour to the voice in the well-known fable of Arion's lyre. Learn also to sweep with both hands the genial Phoenician harp; suitable is it to merry-making.[29]

Ovid's concise reference to these three mythical male musicians would have been easily grasped by his readers: their stories were often cited by writers from antiquity onward as examples of the civilizing effects of music, working its effects on the animate and inanimate world.[30] In contrast, the Sirens' music led listeners to loss of rational control and death, and it is mentioned in this context with a specific erotic application.

The Ovidian picture of women/sirens for some people took actual shape in what was seen as a "strategic" practice of music by courtesans. Far from being mere prostitutes, as they were bound to become later, Italian sixteenth-century *cortigiane* were beautiful, elegant women often accomplished in witty conversation, literary arts, and music. They were in touch with noblemen, artists, and men of letters, and sometimes they organized or joined literary circles. The Italian cities in which courtesans were most prominent were Rome, Florence, and Venice, and writers connected with Venice especially described courtesans' music.[31] In fact, some of these women were particularly renowned for their musical skills. They were praised by writers and artists of the period, although it is not always easy to determine the exact social position of the musical women mentioned in contemporary writings, who are also sometimes associated with courtesans in modern criticism. Aretino, for example, in a letter expressed his warm admiration for the musical abilities of one Franceschina Bellamano; she was also the dedicatee of a poem by Domenico Venier (1517–1582),[32] who praised her through the usual touchstones for musical excellence—the swan, Orpheus, and, more interestingly, both the sea-Sirens and angels in heaven:

Nè cantar di Sirene in mezzo l'acque;
Nè degli angioli in ciel fu mai, nè sia
Dolce sì, che s'agguagli a l'harmonia,
C'hoggi a uoi farmi udir per gratia piacque.

(Neither the song of sirens in the waters, nor of angels in heaven ever was
or will be so sweet as the harmony that by your grace you were pleased to
let me hear today.)[33]

A sixteenth-century Venetian who left a deeper trace than Bellamano
was the Petrarchist poet Gaspara Stampa (fl. 1523–1554), whose status as
a courtesan is again unclear, and who was also the object of similar associations. Parabosco (d. ca. 1557) in a letter refers to her "angelica voce,"
remarking that it acted "a guisa di Sirena," while Perissone Cambio (ca.
1520–?), in dedicating his first book of madrigals to her, makes the reference to angelic Sirens clearer when he records that Gasparina was defined
by her listeners as a "divina sirena."[34]

But apart from occasional works of praise, references to musical
women in Venice could be totally different. Thomas Coryat (1577–1617),
an English traveler to Italy, warns his fellow countrymen to beware of the
accomplishments of courtesans, including their musical skills on the lute.
He associates their skills with the allurements of a Calypso, and indirectly
of a Circe, when he advises his reader to provide himself with the herb
moly before going close to them; of another "remedy" he recommends
against Venetian Sirens, more will be said later.[35] Even the courtesan in
literary fictions is subjected to no encomiastic treatments. Aretino again,
for example, has some of his characters note how the courtesans' musical
skills are nothing but means to enthrall their lovers,[36] an interpretation
confirmed by the courtesan's voice itself when mediated through male
authorial vision. In an Italian dialogue by Francesco Pona (fl. 1595–1655),
a soul describes its various passages through metempsychosis before its
final embodiment into a lamp. When referring of its experience in the
guise of a courtesan, it boasts of her musical skills as a precious instrument
for the job, by typically referring to the Sirens' myth:

Ma, per tornarmene alla cortigiana che già informai, fra l'altre reti ch'io
tesi agli uomini fu questa delle più forti: la musica. Già la forza di questa
manifestan le favole degli Arioni, che trassero i pesci a fare del proprio
dorso nelle liquide piagge sostegno al peso; degli Anfioni, che chiama-
rono le pietre a formar le mura a Tebe; degli Orfei, che seppero raddol-
cir Dite e ricondurre da que' neri alberghi la dolce sposa; ma sovra
ogn'altra, delle Sirene, che seppero i naviganti col soavissimo canto
addormentare per ucciderli e divorarseli. Canto dunque di sirena era

il mio, perché con sì fatta vivezza e spirito mi faceva udire toccando un'arpa, un leuto o una chitariglia e cantando, che avrei fatto languir d'amore un Senocrate, anzi il Disamore. Non toccava corda che i cuori non si sentissero intenerire, non scioglieva accento che l'aure non si fermassero per udirlo. I sospiri degli uditori, uscendo dall'intimo delle viscere, portavano le mie voci dietro alle anime che svaniscono. Non ti narro iperboli, Eurota. Fu più d'una volta che si scordarono gli ascoltanti di respirare e di dar il naturale rinfrescamento all'arterie, tanto teneva la dolcezza delle mie voci ogni sentimento loro occupato.

(Going back to the courtesan I shaped, among the traps I laid for men one of the greatest was music. The force of which was already shown by the fables of Arion, inducing fish to make of their back a prop to his weight on the water lands; of Amphion, bidding the stones to form the walls of Thebes; of Orpheus, who was able to mellow Dis and to take away his spouse from that dark abode; but, above all, of the Sirens, who were able to induce sailors to sleep by their very sweet song, to kill and devour them. Therefore my song was that of a Siren, because with such a liveliness and spirit it made me realize that by touching a harp, a lute, or a little guitar and singing, I would make a Xenocrates, or even Estrangement pine away from love. I did not touch a string but the hearts felt softening, I did not pronounce a word but the winds themselves were stilled to listen. The listeners' sighs, going out of their bowels, brought my voices after their vanishing souls. I am not telling hyperbolical tales, Eurotas. More than once listeners forgot to breathe and refresh their arteries, so much the sweetness of my voice kept each of their feelings engaged.)[37]

Early modern readers would easily recognize a mocking quotation from Ovid in the comparison of this siren to the musical heroes of the classical tradition, but they would also associate this passage with the widespread moralization of the Sirens in countless allegorical versions in literature and the visual arts.

Emblems and Myths

In sixteenth- and seventeenth-century Italian painting, the representation of Ulysses and the Sirens is often connected with the treatment of virtues and vices, in which the Sirens serve as symbols of lechery while Ulysses stands for Temperance, Intelligence, or other "manly" qualities permanently associated with him in centuries of allegorical readings.[38] The practice of interpreting classical mythology in the light of moral teachings went back to late antiquity and had been transmitted through the Middle

Ages up to the early modern period.[39] The episode of Ulysses and the Sirens as an example of a moral dilemma was perceptively similar to another paradigmatic story of choice between virtue and vice, personified as two contrasting women: that of Hercules at the crossroads, which was revived in sixteenth- and seventeenth-century literary and visual culture. In fact, in the representation of vice in the visual arts, musical instruments are sometimes included, and used as attributes of Vice, as in a celebrated painting by Annibale Carracci (1560–1609).[40] A particularly striking English example shows that the tales of Ulysses and Hercules could be conflated. In the emblematic frontispiece of a conduct book for seventeenth-century gentlemen, one of the vignettes, headed "Youth," shows an elegant young man poised between two female personifications of Virtue and Vice or Pleasure, the first a modestly attired woman holding a palm branch, the latter a graceful sea-siren with comb and mirror.[41]

Emblem books from the same period often acted as a useful stock of the most common interpretations of mythology for writers and artists, as well as for common readers. The emblem, the subject of a number of recent theories and studies, can be briefly defined as a particular genre mixing word and image in a compound structure of three or more interrelated parts. At the center of it is usually a woodcut or engraving presenting an image, the symbolical meaning of which is clarified and expounded on by related texts in verse or prose. In its earliest form, as it appeared in 1531 in the first printed emblem collection by the Italian jurist Andrea Alciato (1492–1550), the textual parts consist of a brief motto or *inscriptio* above and a verse epigram or *subscriptio* beneath the picture. Later developments of the emblem include other verse or prose parts joined in more complex structures. Emblem writers drew their subjects from such diverse sources as ancient literature, natural history, collections of proverbs, and popular lore to entertain their readers by involving them in a game to decode their intended meanings but often, at the same time, to convey through the emblem moral or explicitly religious lessons, as in the case of many emblem books published in the seventeenth century, when the genre was appropriated both by Catholic and Protestant authors for their own didactic ends.[42]

As to the presence of the Sirens in emblems, Alciato's collection recurs to the usual interpretation of them as symbols of seduction, charming by looks and words, literally showing them as prostitutes with whom the wise, like Ulysses, must not mix.[43] The sixteenth- and seventeenth-century revival of the equation of sirens with prostitutes surely received a contribution from the popularity of Alciato's work, which spread throughout

Europe in a number of translated editions. The motif can be found in several European emblem books, showing iconographic variations in the pictures, but often sticking to the implicit or explicit equation of sirens with sexually provoking women, and warning readers against their danger.[44]

Some Italian mythographic handbooks were equally influential and repeat similar readings. Vincenzo Cartari (ca. 1500) also provides in word and image the two possible iconographic variants of fishtailed and bird-like sirens:

> Ma o pesci, come dissi, o uccelli che fossero le Sirene, basta, che sono cosa in tutto finta: onde vogliono alcuni, che per loro sia intesa la bellezza, la lascivia, e gli allettamenti delle meretrici, et che fosse finto, che cantando addormentassero i naviganti, & che accostatesi alle navi, gli uccidessero poi: perche così intraviene a quelli miseri, li quali vinti dalle piacevolezze delle rapaci donne, chiudono gli occhi dell'intelleto si, che elle poi ne fanno ricca preda, & quasi se gli divorano.

> (But were the Sirens fish, as I said, or birds, that is enough, as this is a totally feigned thing. In fact some people say they signify beauty, lechery, and the allurements of prostitutes, and that it is not true they induced sailors to sleep by song and when they drew near their ships they killed them. Because this happens to those wretches that, won by the pleasant manners of predatory women, close the eyes of intellect so as to become a profitable prey, and to be almost devoured by them.)[45]

The siren model is also at work in ambiguous moralizations of female beauty, as in a personification in another popular manual for artists by Cesare Ripa (ca. 1560–ca. 1625), which was later readapted in a collection of emblems by Henry Peacham the Younger (1576?–1643?).[46] The figure created by the English emblematist after directions from the Italian handbook shows a naked woman sitting on, and almost merging with, a dragon (fig. 4.2). This beast, denoting "love's poison," is depicted with bird-claws and a long tail, conflating the two conventional shapes of sirens. The woman holds a mirror, a traditional symbol of vanity and an attribute of Sight in representations of the five senses, which here, in fact, indicates "how we by sight are mooud to loue."[47] This tool provides another link with siren imagery as it could be often found in visual representations of mermaids, but Peacham's picture of female beauty could also evoke in his readers associations with other disquieting hybrid creatures.

Before emblem books, medieval bestiaries had handed down legends about aggressive animals who exploited the senses of sight and hearing in men's destruction. These were works about the nature of real and fabulous

A VIRGIN naked, on a Dragon fits,
One hand out-ftretch'd, a chriftall glaffe doth fhow:
The other beares a dart, that deadly hits;
Vpon her head, a garland white as fnow,
Of * print and Lillies. Beautie moft defir'd,
Were I her painter, fhould be thus attir'd.

Her nakednes vs tells, fhe needes no art:
Her glaffe, how we by fight are mooud to loue,
The woundes vnfelt, that's giuen by the Dart
At firft, (though deadly we it after prooue)
The Dragon notes loues poifon: and the flowers,
The frailtie (Ladies) of that pride of yours.

Cumque aliquis dicet, fuit hæc formofa, dolebis:
Et fpeculum mendax, effe querère tuum.

Nec femper violæ, nec femper Lilia florent:
Et riget amiffa fpina relicta rofa.

K 1.

Figure 4.2. Henry Peacham, *Minerva Britanna or a Garden of
Heroical Deuises* (London: Wa. Dight [1612]), 58. By
permission of Glasgow University Library, Department of
Special Collections.

beings, in which animal lore drawn from such ancient writers as Aristotle
and Pliny, and from the Bible and biblical commentators, was symbolically interpreted in order to give moral precepts. In the *Bestiaire d'Amour*
by Richard de Fournival (fl. 1246–1260), the genre was specifically
adapted to the theme of love. Here, animal examples are applied to the
literary, fictive male voice wooing a lady, parallel to the way in which
medieval love-poems employ similar bestial figures.[48]

In this tradition the siren was described as a lustful beast inducing to sleep by song only to capture and kill men. Early modern authors, bringing "scientific" and literary traditions together, would again blur any possible distinction between fact and fiction, old and new sirens:

> The Poets fein there were three *Mer-maids* or *Sirens;* in their upper parts like maidens, and in their lower part fishes: which dwelling in the sea of Sicilie would allure sailers to them, and afterwards devoure them; being first brought asleep with hearkening to their sweet singing. Their names (they say) were *Parthenope, Lygia,* and *Leucasia;* wherefore sometime alluring women are said to be *Sirens.*[49]

Another mythical monster, the basilisk, a bird-reptile notorious for its poisonous stare, was often mentioned, and was sometimes figured, like the siren, looking into a mirror, involuntarily killing itself by this act. This mythical beast, too, became associated with "dangerous" women.[50] Picinelli (1604–ca. 1667), in his monumental compendium of symbolic lore, refers to a man who had made the basilisk his *impresa,* or personal device, to remind himself of the caution he had to use with a beautiful female singer:

> Vn Mondano, osseruando, che questo perniciosissimo animale, offende, e col fiato pestifero, ò sia col fischio, ed anco con la malignità dello sguardo, ne fece vn imagine, segnata con le parole: E DA GLI OCCHI, E DAL CANTO, e ciò per inferire ch'egli doueua procedere con questa doppia circospettione, e cautela, per non soggiacere alla forza, & energia efficace di bella Cantatrice.

> (A worldling, observing that this most pernicious animal offends, both by its pestiferous breath, that is by its hiss, and by its malicious stare, made of it an image marked by the words: "by the eyes, and by song," to mean that he had to proceed with a double circumspection and caution, not to be subject to the force and effective energy of a beautiful female singer.)[51]

In a travesty of the Neoplatonic itinerary of love through sight and hearing, the Elizabethan Michael Drayton (1563–1631) could use this traditional lore with overt negative connotations, in a sonnet "describing" the lady:

> Three sorts of Serpents doe resemble thee,
> That daungerous eye-killing Cockatrice,
> Th'inchaunting Syren, which doth so entice,
> The weeping Crocodile: these vile pernicious three.

> The Basiliske his nature takes from thee,
> Who for my life in secrete waite do'st lye,
> And to my hart send'st poyson from thine eye,
> Thus do I feele the paine, the cause, yet cannot see.
>
> Faire-mayd no more, but Mayr-maid be thy name,
> Who with thy sweet aluring harmony
> Hast played the thiefe, and stolne my hart from me,
> And like a Tyrant mak'st my griefe thy game.
> Thou Crocodile, who when thou hast me slaine,
> Lament'st my death, with teares of thy disdaine.[52]

If in the Petrarchan tradition the different qualities of a woman were usually listed and praised by comparison with precious objects, here fatal eyes and voice prevail, and the conventional "pearls" falling from the lady's eyes turn into uncomplimentary crocodile tears.

The Scottish Drummond of Hawthornden (1585–1649) may be re-echoing Drayton:

> Is it not too too much
> Thou late didst to mee prove
> A *Basiliske* of Loue?
> And didst my Wits bewitch:
> Vnlesse (to cause more Harme)
> Made *Syrene* too thou with thy Voyce mee charme?
> Ah! though thou so my *Reason* didst controule,
> That to thy Lookes I could not proue a *Mole*:
> Yet doe mee not that Wrong,
> As not to let mee turne *Aspe* to thy Song.[53]

In addition to the basilisk and the siren, Drummond exploits two other images by mentioning a possible metamorphosis into a mole or an asp, creatures believed respectively blind and deaf. The figure of the asp has further implications, as the poet's concise reference grants other features that must have been recalled by readers familiar with animal symbolism. The adder or asp in medieval bestiaries was said to avoid the dangerous songs of the enchanter by deafening itself, plugging one of its ears with its tail, and rubbing the other on the ground. The original moral application to men who are unresponsive to Christian teachings had already been forgotten by Fournival, in whose work the male lover says he should have blocked his ears like the asp to the siren incantation of the lady's voice.[54] Many early modern works concerned with sirens give similar practical advice on how to escape their danger.

Ulysses's Remedy

Antidotes to the threat of beautiful, siren-like looks and voice could be either keeping open the eyes of intellect mentioned by Cartari, or closing bodily eyes or ears, or sometimes both. The English emblematist Whitney (1548–1601) warned against trusting on appearances, for Ulysses's example teaches the reader "That he shoulde flie, and shoulde in time beware, / And not on lookes, his fickle fancie feede."[55] Considering that this and many others of his emblems are readaptations from Alciato for an English-reading public, and that his collection is linked to the English campaign in the Low Countries of 1585,[56] his emblem could be especially meant to give advice on the risks of meeting foreign women.

Similar warnings were given to Englishmen traveling to Italy, as shown by the final suggestion Coryat gives prospective visitors to Venetian courtesans:

> Therefore for auoiding of these inconueniences, I will giue thee the same counsell that *Lipsius* did to a friend of his that was to trauell into Italy, even to furnish thy selfe with a double armour, the one for thine eyes, the other for thine eares. As for thine eyes, shut them and turne them aside from these venereous Venetian objects. For they are the double windowes that conueigh them to thine heart. Also thou must fortifie thine eares against the attractiue inchauntments of their plausible speeches. Therefore euen as wrestlers were wont heretofore to fence their eares against al exterior annoyances, by putting to them certaine instruments called *amphotides:* so doe thou take vnto thy selfe this firme foundation against the amorous woundes of the Venetian Cortezans, to heare none of their wanton toyes; or if thou wilt needes both see and heare them, do thou only cast thy breath vpon them in that manner as we do vpon steele, which is no sooner on but incontinent it falleth off againe: so doe thou only breath a few words vpon them, and presently be gone from them: for if thou dost linger with them thou wilt finde their poyson to be more pernicious then that of the scorpion, aspe, or cocatrice.[57]

The stopping of the ears developed as a meaningful variation of the Ulysses and the Sirens episode.[58] The material closure of the way of aural temptations, transferring Ulysses's remedy for his mariners to the hero himself, goes back to Patristic warnings against the dangers of either Greek philosophy, heresy, or just the allurements of *belles-lettres.*[59] In the early modern period this figure found different fields of application, both in literary and in visual culture.

In a French illustrated edition of Ovid's *Metamorphoses*, the episodes are summarized in word and image by woodcuts, accompanied by titles

QVINTO.   8

Serene compagne di Proserpina
con l'alie si precipitano
in mare.   73

Le compagne à Proserpina Serene
Poi che gia molto in van cercata l'hanno,
Desiose passar le molli arene,
Et prender di cercarla in mar l'affanno,
Chieggon da volar penne, & tosto piene
Di penne han l'alie,& dentro al mar s'en vanno,
Doue ogn'una di lor par che perisse,
Poi che il lor canto vdir non volle Vlisse.

f 3

Figure 4.3. Gabriello Simeoni, *La Vita e Metamorfoseo d'Ovidio* (Lyons: Jean de Tournes, 1559), 85. By permission of the Biblioteca Nazionale Centrale, Rome.

and verse epigrams in Italian, bringing each chapter close to a tripartite emblem. One of them conflates the tale of the transformation of Persephone's companions into sirens related by Ovid[60] with a version of Ulysses's purported unwillingness to hear the Sirens, also mentioning the subsequent suicide of the latter. The corresponding picture represents a few warriors on a ship stopping their ears (one in the foreground is presumably Ulysses) when they are confronted with five fishtailed and winged gesticulating sirens in the sea (fig. 4.3).[61] The same motif is repeated in a celebrated series of illustrations by the Italian engraver Antonio Tempesta (1555–1630), a source that was used in its turn as a model in Italian paintings of the period.[62]

This *topos* also found its way into Italian heroical poems.[63] Boiardo (ca. 1440–1494) in *Orlando Innamorato* attributes the application of the remedy to his hero. The warrior approaches a siren after putting rose petals into his helmet to shelter his ears, so as to become invulnerable to her song:

> Via ne va lui per quelle erbe odorose,
> E poi che alquanto via fu caminato,
> Lelmo a lorecchie empì dentro di rose,
> Delle qual tutto adorno era quel prato.
> Chiuse l'orecchie, ad ascoltar si pose
> Gli occei, ch'erano intorno ad ogni lato:
> Mover li vede il collo e 'l becco aprire,
> Voce non ode e non potrebbe odire,
>
> Perché chiuso se aveva in tal maniera
> L'orecchie entrambe a quelle rose folte,
> Che non odiva, al loco dove egli era,
> Cosa del mondo, ben che attento ascolte;
> E caminando gionse alla rivera,
> Che ha molte gente al suo fondo sepolte.
> Questo era un lago piccolo e iocondo
> D'acque tranquille e chiare insino al fondo.
>
> Non gionse il conte in su la ripa apena,
> Che cominciò quell'acqua a gorgoliare;
> Cantando venne a sommo la Sirena.
> Una donzella è quel che sopra appare,
> Ma quel che sotto l'acqua se dimena
> Tutto è di pesce e non si può mirare,
> Ché sta nel lago da la furca in gioso;
> E mostra il vago, e il brutto tiene ascoso.

(He went away across the fragrant grass, and when he had walked a little way, he filled his helmet at his ears with the roses of which the meadow was all adorned. He blocked his ears and started listening to the birds that were all around on every side. He saw them move their necks and open their beaks, but he did not, nor could hear any voice, because he had closed both his ears in such a way with those thick roses, that where he was he did not hear anything coming from the world, although he listened attentively. And walking he came to the stream that kept many people buried on its bottom. This was a little, joyous lake, with calm and clear waters to the bottom. As soon as the Count came on its shore the water became to gurgle. The Siren, singing, came on the surface. What appeared above was of a maid, but what moved beneath the waters was all of a fish, and could not be looked at, because her lower parts remained within the lake: she showed the fair and hid the ugly.)[64]

Successive stanzas reveal a gendered opposition of nature versus culture in the form of female voice versus male text. The siren, a parodic Orpheus attracting birds and other animals to her song only to induce them to sleep, is a "nasty beast," a monstrous half-woman and half-fish hybrid, coming directly from the older bestiaries. Her only weapon is a song of undefined content or perhaps a wordless song, the initial pleasantness of which is soon transformed into a loud sound of defense. On the other hand, the "learned" Orlando, following the instructions of a little book he read before, turns a deaf ear to the voice of nature, in the form both of the siren's song and of bird music.[65] The monster can be easily undone in this way as the knight, by pretending to yield to her song and fall asleep, is able to capture and, Perseus-like, behead her:

> Lei comincia a cantar sì dolcemente,
> Che uccelli e fiere vennero ad odire:
> Ma, come erano gionti, incontinente
> Per la dolcezza convenian dormire.
> Il conte non odìa de ciò niente,
> Ma, stando attento, mostra di sentire.
> Come era dal libretto amaestrato,
> Sopra la riva se colcò nel prato.

> E' mostrava dormir ronfando forte:
> La mala bestia il tratto non intese,
> E venne a terra per donarli morte;
> Ma il conte per le chiome ne la prese.
> Lei, quanto più puotea, cantava forte,
> Ché non sapeva fare altre diffese,
> Ma la sua voce al conte non attiene,
> Che ambe l'orecchie avea di rose piene.
> Per le chiome la prese il conte Orlando,
> Fuor di quel lago la trasse nel prato,
> E via la testa gli tagliò col brando,
> Come gli aveva il libro dimostrato.

(She began to sing so sweetly that birds and beasts came to listen: but as soon as they had come, suddenly they fell asleep by that sweetness. The Count could not hear anything of that, but he pretended to listen attentively. As the small book had instructed him, he laid himself on the meadow by the river. He pretended to sleep, snoring loud; the nasty beast did not understand that move, and she came ashore to kill him. The Count grabbed her by her hair, she sang as loud as she could, because she could not defend herself otherwise, but her voice did not reach the Count, who had both his ears full of roses. The Count Orlando grabbed her by her hair, he took her out of the lake onto the meadow and cut her head off with his sword, as the book had showed him.)[66]

Later Tasso (1544–1595) would keep the moralizing tradition in mind, devising two variations on the usual scheme. Rinaldo, approaching bare-eared the ghostly shape of a siren, a double for Armida, is easily induced to slumber and then caught by the enchantress.[67] In contrast, the two warriors who will rescue Rinaldo from Armida are saved by the metaphorical application of Ulysses's antidote. Before entering Armida's garden, Carlo and Ubaldo meet two nymphs bathing in a spring, referred to, even before their description, as "false sirens of pleasure." The men, advised here by a male magician, are ready to resist:

> Or qui tener a fren nostro desio
> ed esser cauti molto a noi conviene:
> chiudiam l'orecchie al dolce canto e rio
> di queste del piacer false sirene.

> (Here fond desire must by faire gouerning
> Be rulde, our lust bridled with wisedomes raine,
> Our eares be stopped while these Syrens sing,
> Their notes entising man to pleasure vaine.)[68]

The beautiful nymphs' musical offer of otiose pleasure is rejected and their destiny is close to the death by water imagined by some mythographers for the Sirens disappointed by their failure with Ulysses:

> L'una disse così, l'altra concorde
> l'invito accompagnò d'atti e di sguardi,
> sì come al suon de le canore corde
> s'accompagnano i passi or presti or tardi.
> Ma i cavalieri hanno indurate e sorde
> l'alme a que' vezzi perfidi e bugiardi,
> e'l lusinghiero aspetto e'l parlar dolce
> di fuor s'aggira e solo i sensi molce.

E se di tal dolcezza entro trasfusa
parte penetra onde il desio germoglie,
tosto ragion ne l'arme sue rinchiusa
sterpa e riseca le nascenti voglie.
L'una coppia riman vinta e delusa,
l'altra se'n va, né pur congedo toglie.
Essi entrar nel palagio, esse ne l'acque
tuffarsi: la repulsa a lor sì spiacque.

(While thus she sung, her sister lur'de them nie
With many a gesture kinde and louing show,
To musicks sound as dames in court applie
Their cunning feet, and dance now swift now slow;
But still the knights vnmoued passed bie,
These vaine delights for wicked charmes they know,
Nor could their heau'nly voice or angels looke
Surprise their harts, if eie or eare they tooke.

For if that sweetnes once but toucht their harts,
And profred there to kindle *Cupids* fire,
Straight armed reason to his charge vpstarts,
And quencheth lust, and killeth fond desire;
Thus scorned were the dames, their wiles and arts:
And to the pallace gates the knights retire,
While in their streames the damsels diued sad,
Asham'd, disgraste, for that repulse they had.)[69]

The seventeenth-century English translator interestingly renders Tasso's generic reference to music and dance in the first of the above stanzas with a more specific comparison of the nymphs to "dames in court," giving it a touch of social verisimilitude, and also emphasizing how their apparently angelic siren-voices and looks had indeed some effect on the men's eyes and ears. But as the Italian text makes clear, ear closure here is not actual, as in Boiardo, but a metaphor for their "hardened and deaf souls."

Allegorical interpretation of the different ways of resisting the sirens' song continued well into the seventeenth century. An original reader of mythology like Francis Bacon (1561–1626) individuated degrees in the challenge to sirens as symbols of voluptuousness, according to the different sorts of "listeners." For him, too, stopping the ears is the easiest but less noble antidote, as it does not involve any inner conflict or real commitment: the Sirens can be better silenced by opposing to their profane music the Orphic song of meditation and prayer. In the following passage, concluding Bacon's mythographic treatise, Orpheus, saving the Argonauts from the Sirens by covering their music with his own song (following the versions of Apollonius Rodius and of the *Orphic Argonautica*),[70] is exalted not as an embodiment of the power of philosophy but of religion:[71]

> The first meanes to shunne these inordinate pleasures is, to withstand and resist them in their beginnings, and seriously to shunne all occasion that are offered to debauch & entice the mind, which is signified in the stopping of the Eares; & that remedie is properly vsed by the meaner and baser sorte of people, as it were, Ulisses followers or Marrineres; whereas more heroique and noble Spirits, may boldly conuerse euen in the midst of these seducing pleasures, if with a resolued constancie they stand vpon their guard, and fortifie their minds; And so take greater contentment in the triall and experience of this their approued vertue; learning rather throughly to vnderstand the follies and vanities of those pleasures by contemplation, then by submission. . . . But of all other remedies in this case, that of Orpheus is most predominant: For they that chaunt and resound the praises of the Gods, confounde and dissipate the voices and incantations of the Sirenes; for diuine meditations doe not onely in power subdue all sensual pleasure; but also farre exceed them in sweetnesse and delight.[72]

From a more traditional religious perspective, the mariners' remedy was found particularly proper by the Jesuits as an image of utter refusal of sensuality. In a seventeenth-century emblem book that is mainly a monument of self-celebration of their religious order, the virtue of Chastity is illustrated by a fine engraving showing a new Ulysses tied to the mast of the ship and at the same time stopping his ears to the Sirens, one in the foreground provided with a woman's legs, apostrophized by the daring motto, "You sing to the deaf and you sing to the bound" (fig. 4.4).[73]

Far from the prescriptions of Catholic faith or the manly commitment of wars and chivalric enterprises, resistance is not always effective. In the realm of courtly love, where subjection and surrender to the lady is the rule, Petrarch himself had sometimes used the comparison between Laura and the Sirens as temptresses, complaining about his inability to apply the antidote of being blind to her beaming beauty and deaf to her words/ songs. This puts his other reference to Laura as an angelic siren in a rather different light, reinterpreting her song as "sweet poison":

> Così di ben amar porto tormento,
> et del peccato altrui cheggio perdono -
> anzi del mio, che devea torcer li occhi
> dal troppo lume, et di sirene al suono
> chiuder li orecchi, et ancor non me pento
> che di dolce veleno il cor trabocchi.

Caftitas Religiofa voto adftricta.

Canitis furdis, canitifque ligatis.

Figure 4.4. *Imago Primi Saeculi Societatis Jesu* (Antwerp: Ex Officina Plantiniana Balthasaris Moreti, 1640), 181. By permission of the Biblioteca Nazionale Centrale, Rome.

(Thus from loving well I gain torments, and I ask to be pardoned for another's crime; rather for my own, for I should have turned my eyes away from the excessive light, closed my ears to the siren song; and still I do not repent that my heart is overflowing with sweet poison.)[74]

Similar self-reproach inspires a comparison with the varied version of the Ulysses and the Sirens episode in a love poem by Boiardo, where the distinction between looking at and listening to the lady is totally blurred:

> Così avess'io ben li ochi chiusi in prima,
> Come Ulisse le orecchie a la sirena,
> Che se fie' sordo per fugir più male.

> (Oh would that I had shut my eyes back then,
> just as Ulysses sealed his ears to the Sirens' song,
> becoming deaf to flee a greater evil!)[75]

The parallel is still at work in the seventeenth century, as can be seen in Marino, who concludes another poem for a female singer with an invitation to close manly ears that is bound to failure:

> Chiudete il varco à l'armonia di foco.
> Mà di fral cera à si possente ardore
> L'orecchio armar che val, s'anco val poco
> Armar di smalto adamantino il core?

(Close the way to the fiery harmony. But what is the use of arming the ear by frail wax to such a fierce heat, if there is little use in arming the heart with adamantine enamel?)[76]

These lines, with their mock-heroic imagery of battle, remind readers by contrast of Tasso's knights and of their success in arming their hearts, but the obliged defeat is here motivated by the overt encomiastic intent of the poem. In fact it may have been written for a famous Neapolitan singer of the seicento, Adriana Basile, who was often compared to a siren in eulogistic poems by other writers. The legendary link between Naples and the mythical Parthenope made the analogy between female singers of that city and sirens a particularly happy and pregnant one.[77]

Conclusion

The siren in early modern literary imagery, even considered only in the context of female musicians, continued to be a polyvalent symbol. In fact, the name "siren" could be applied to women belonging to different social and geographical contexts: noblewomen or courtesans, amateur or professional singers. In works drawing on the tradition of Western love poetry, based on the praise and courtship of an angelic lady, the image often recurs in the variant of the heavenly Sirens of Platonic origin, later merged with the figure of Christian angels, and women's song is seen as an instrument of spiritual elevation for the worshipping poetical persona. Nevertheless, the theme of the rhetorical power of music, particularly strong in sixteenth- and seventeenth-century culture, touched on its physical as well as spiritual effects, so that the female musician was soon connected with the idea of music as a stimulus to love, in its material as well as spiritual, Neoplatonic aspects. If read in the light of contemporary social prescriptions for women, as well as of the current moralization of the myth of the Homeric Sirens in literature and the visual arts, many poems, including those apparently praising a woman dedicatee, end up by revealing an anxiety about female music, perceived as a threat, through sight and hearing, to "manly" rational behavior. This attitude, having roots in the ancient and medieval negative consideration of female musicians, found further grounds to develop in the contemporary practice of music within allegedly immoral contexts, such as the Renaissance courtesans' milieus. Significantly, it was often expressed through the frequent recurrence or indirect reference to a varied and lesser-known version of the Homeric episode, by which Ulysses turned literally a deaf ear to the Sirens' song.

Yet female music never ceased to be an irresistible attraction, and at least in literature a way out of the dilemma between surrender and refusal could come from an ideal reconciliation of opposites, as in one of the oxymoric images, again provided by Marino and so typical of Baroque poetry, of a "new" singer who is at the same time worldly prostitute and heavenly angel, mermaid and celestial Siren, hurting at a glance to heal by song:

> Hor apra à l'armonia soaue, e vaga
> Il varco Amor, che frà dolcezza e pena,
> Per gli occhi offende, e per l'orecchie appaga.
> Sì direm poi, questa celeste Maga,
> Questa del nostro mar noua Sirena
> Sana col canto, se col guardo impiaga.

(Now let Love open the way to the sweet and lovely harmony that offends by the eyes and satisfies by the ears, in sweetness and pain. So then we will say: This heavenly enchantress, this new siren of our sea heals by song, even if she wounds by her glance.)[78]

NOTES

I would like to thank Leofranc Holford-Strevens and Donato Mansueto for their helpful suggestions. Unless otherwise indicated, translations from the Italian are mine.

1. Leonard Forster long ago noticed that "almost all petrarchist ladies can sing or play an instrument or both," *The Icy Fire: Five Studies in European Petrarchism* (Cambridge: Cambridge University Press, 1969), 12. For the praise of musicians in English verse see John Hollander, *The Untuning of the Sky: Ideas of Music in English Poetry 1500–1700* (Princeton, N.J.: Princeton University Press, 1961), 332–79.

2. Plato, *Republic* 10.617; Homer, *Odyssey,* 12.

3. See Ruth Kelso, *Doctrine for the Lady of the Renaissance* (Urbana: University of Illinois Press, 1956), 52–53; Karin Pendle, ed., *Women and Music: A History* (Bloomington: Indiana University Press, 1991), 32–36; and Linda Phyllis Austern,

"'Sing Againe Syren': The Female Musician and Sexual Enchantment in Elizabethan Life and Literature," *Renaissance Quarterly* 42 (1989): 420–48.

4. *Rerum Vulgarium Fragmenta,* 167; *Petrarch's Lyric Poems: The "Rime Sparse" and Other Lyrics,* trans. and ed. Robert M. Durling (Cambridge, Mass.: Harvard University Press, 1976), 313.

5. *Republic* 10.617.

6. For this and other ideas developed in poetical allusions to music see James Hutton, "Some English Poems in Praise of Music," *English Miscellany* 2 (1951): 1–63; now chap. in *Essays on Renaissance Poetry,* ed. Rita Guerlac (Ithaca, N.Y.: Cornell University Press, 1980), 17–73; and Gretchen Ludke Finney, "Music and Neoplatonic Love," chap. in *Musical Backgrounds for English Literature: 1580–1650* (New Brunswick, N.J.: Rutgers University Press, 1962), 76–101.

7. Francesco da Barberino, *Reggimento e costumi di donna,* ed. G. E. Sansone (Rome: Zauli Editore, 1995), 11. Cf. this passage with the one from Castiglione's *Book of the Courtier* quoted later, and with another treatise by Federico Luigini da Udine, *Il libro della bella donna,* quoting Petrarch as an authority on female music, in *Trattati del Cinquecento sulla donna,* ed. Giuseppe Zonta (Bari: Laterza, 1913), 296.

8. Pietro Bembo, *Prose e Rime,* ed. Carlo Dionisotti (Turin: UTET, 1960), 518, no. 16.

9. See Hutton, "Some English Poems in Praise of Music." The standard study of ideas of world harmony in literature is Leo Spitzer, *Classical and Christian Ideas of World Harmony: Prolegomena to an Interpretation of the Word "Stimmung,"* ed. Anna Granville Hatcher (Baltimore: Johns Hopkins Press, 1963); see also Hollander, *Untuning of the Sky.*

10. *La Seconde Sepmaine de Gvillavme de Salvste, seigneur du Bartas* (N.p.: Iaques Chouët, 1593), 559, *Les Colomnes,* 2. 691–96; *The Divine Weeks and Works of Guillaume de Saluste Sieur Du Bartas,* trans. Josuah Sylvester, ed. Susan Snyder (Oxford: Clarendon Press, 1979), 1:487; *The Columnes,* 2: 711–16. The idea of human music as an imitation or prefiguration of heavenly music is also the ground for the widespread association of Italian singing nuns with the heavenly Sirens or with angels, see some of the documents quoted by Robert L. Kendrick, *Celestial Sirens: Nuns and their Music in Early Modern Milan* (Oxford: Clarendon Press, 1996), app. A and app. C, passim.

11. *Stanze di Messer Pietro Aretino in lode di Madonna Angela Serena,* no. 15, in Pietro Aretino, *Poesie Varie,* ed. Giovanni Aquilecchia and Angelo Romano (Rome: Salerno Editrice, 1992), 1:230. See also a sonnet for the same dedicatee that refers both to the Petrarchan "del ciel Sirena" and to an "angelico suon ne le parole" (1:247).

12. The first edition, now rare, was published in Venice in 1537 by Francesco Marcolini, who later reused the same woodblock for an illustration in the 1552 edition of Doni's *I Mondi* (see fig. 4.1). Angelic Sirens as part of the "Harmony of the Spheres" are also in a drawing by Buontalenti, designed for the Florence *intermedi* of 1589, see Roy Strong, *Art and Power: Renaissance Festivals 1450–1650* (Woodbridge, Suffolk: Boydell Press, 1973), pl. 88.

13. See Finney, "Music and Neoplatonic Love." In poetry the same effects of music are sometimes applied to female words, see, e.g., Tasso: "ché mi fu per le orecchie il cor ferito, / e i detti andaro ove non giunse il volto" ("because my heart was wounded through my ears, and her words went where her face did not reach"), Torquato Tasso, *Le Rime,* ed. Bruno Basile (Rome: Salerno Editrice, 1994), 1:7, no. 3, "Su l'ampia fronte il crespo oro lucente," 13–14.

14. Guido Casoni, *Della Magia d'Amore* (Venice: Appresso Fabio & Agostin Zoppini Fratelli, 1592), fol. 31v. See also Marsilio Ficino's commentary on Plato's *Symposium, Sopra lo Amore ovvero Convito di Platone,* ed. Giuseppe Rensi (Milan: SE, 1998), 50–52. On Casoni's work see Don Harrán, "Guido Casoni on Love as Music; A Theme 'for All Ages and Studies,'" *Renaissance Quarterly* 54 (2001): 883–913; on Ficino and music see Daniel Pickering Walker, "Ficino's Spiritus and Music" and "Le chant orphique de Marsile Ficin," chaps. in *Music, Spirit and Language in the Renaissance,* ed. Penelope Gouk (London: Variorum Reprints, 1985), unpaginated; and Gary Tomlinson, *Music in Renaissance Magic: Towards a Historiography of Others* (Chicago: University of Chicago Press, 1993), 101–44.

15. Baldassar Castiglione, *The Book of the Courtier,* trans. Sir Thomas Hoby (London: J. M. Dent & Sons; New York: E. P. Dutton & Co., 1928), 75.

16. Ibid., 313. The theme is elaborated at length in the second book of Bembo's treatise on love, *Gli Asolani.*

17. Castiglione, *Courtier,* 318.

18. The reference is to a series by Jan Saenredam after Hendrick Goltzius, see Sylvia Ferino-Pagden, ed., *I cinque sensi nell'arte: immagini del sentire* (Milan: Leonardo Arte, 1996), 118. For the treatment of the five senses in literature see, among others, Louise Vinge, *The Five Senses: Studies in a Literary Tradition* (Lund: CWK Geerup, 1975) and Frank Kermode, "The Banquet of Sense," chap. in *Shakespeare, Spenser, Donne: Renaissance Essays* (London: Routledge & Kegan Paul, 1971), 84–115.

19. The words are from John Dowland's *Come again: sweet loue doth now inuite* (1597), treated in connection with the theme of the "stair of love" in Robin Headlam Wells, "The Ladder of Love: Verbal and Musical Rhetoric in the Elizabethan Lute Song," chap. in *Elizabethan Mythologies: Studies in Poetry, Drama and Music* (Cambridge: Cambridge University Press, 1994), 83–112.

20. "The Fair Singer" in *The Poems and Letters of Andrew Marvell,* ed. H. M. Margoliouth (Oxford: Clarendon Press, 1952), 1:31.

21. "Alle intelligenze in lode d'una bella Cantatrice," in *La Lira: Rime del Cavalier Marino . . . Parte Prima* (Venice: Presso Gio[vanni] Pietro Brigonci, 1667), 15. Marino was probably inspired by one of Giovan Battista Guarini's madrigals, opting for the earthly Siren, see *Rime del molto illustre Signor Cavaliere Battista Gvarini* (Venice: Presso Gio[vanni] Battista Ciotti, 1598), fol. 58ᵛ, madrigal no. 2.

22. For the changing interpretations of the Sirens from the antiquity to the Middle Ages, see Edmond Faral, "La Queue de Poisson des Sirènes," *Romania* 74 (1953): 433–506, and the recent, well-documented study by Jacqueline Leclercq-

Marx, *La Sirène dans la pensée et dans l'art de l'Antiquité et du Moyen Âge: Du mythe païen au symbol chrétien* (Bruxelles: Académie Royale de Belgique, 1997). See also Leofranc Holford-Strevens's chapter in this collection (chapter 1).

23. For female music in Italy in the sixteenth and seventeenth centuries, see Pendle, ed., *Women and Music,* 31–93; see also Howard Mayer Brown, "Women Singers and Women's Songs in Fifteenth-Century Italy"; Anthony Newcomb, "Courtesans, Muses, or Musicians? Professional Women Musicians in Sixteenth-Century Italy," in *Women Making Music: The Western Art Tradition, 1150–1950,* ed. Jane Bowers and Judith Tick (Urbana: University of Illinois Press, 1987), 62–89, 90–115; On nuns' music in early modern Italy see also Craig A. Monson, *Disembodied Voices: Music and Culture in an Early Modern Italian Convent* (Berkeley: University of California Press, 1995); and Kendrick, *Celestial Sirens.*

24. The dualistic view of female musicians emerged even in this case: the particular status of musical nuns would often cause a tension between the vision of them as members of angelic choirs and as disguised opera singers, that is earthly sirens, see Kendrick, *Celestial Sirens,* 165.

25. Bembo exhorts his daughter to be content with literature and needlework in particular, see the letter "Ad Elena," dated 10 December 1541, in Pietro Bembo, *Opere in volgare,* ed. Mario Marti (Florence: Sansoni, 1961), 877.

26. Castiglione, *Courtier,* 194. See also Kelso, *Doctrine for the Lady of the Renaissance,* 52–53.

27. Some examples of this theme and its iconographic tradition are discussed in Emanuel Winternitz, "The Curse of Pallas Athena," chap. in *Musical Instruments and Their Symbolism in Western Art,* 2d ed. (New Haven, Conn.: Yale University Press, 1979), 150–65.

28. See also Kelso, *Doctrine for the Lady of the Renaissance,* 44, quoting a passage from an English translation of a sixteenth-century Italian conduct book for women: "when it behoves her through request to recite any Psalme, or other Spirituall song, or godlie sentence, she shall set forthe to doe it with a milde refusall, yet altogether voide of undecent affectyng."

29. *Artis Amatoriae* 3.311–28; Ovid, *The Art of Love, and Other Poems,* trans. J. H. Morley (London: William Heinemann; Cambridge, Mass.: Harvard University Press, 1969), 141.

30. For this interpretation of Orpheus and Amphion, see, e.g., Horace, *Ars Poetica,* 391–401. Ovid elsewhere emphasized Arion's control over nature through music, see *Fasti,* 2.83–90.

31. Among the many works on Renaissance courtesans see Rita Casagrande Villaviera, *La Cortigiana Veneziana del Cinquecento* (Milan: Longanesi, 1968); Georgina Masson, *Courtesans of the Italian Renaissance* (New York: St. Martin's Press, 1975); and Margaret F. Rosenthal, *The Honest Courtesan: Veronica Franco Citizen and Writer in Sixteenth-Century Venice* (Chicago: University of Chicago Press, 1992). On their possession of musical instruments, see Cathy Santore, "Julia Lombardo, 'Somtuosa Meretrize': A Portrait by Property," *Renaissance Quarterly* 41 (1988): 58–60.

32. See the letter "A Franceschina," dated May 1548, in Pietro Aretino, *Lettere,* ed. Paolo Procaccioli (Rome: Salerno Editrice, 2000), 4:347. On Venier's role as a literary and musical patron see Martha Feldman, "The Academy of Domenico Venier, Music's Literary Muse in Mid-Cinquecento Venice," *Renaissance Quarterly* 44 (1991): 476–512.

33. *De le rime di diversi nobili poeti toscani, raccolte da M. Dionigi Atanagi, Libro secondo* (Venice: Appresso Lodouico Auanzo, 1565), fol. 11ʳ.

34. "Alla virtvosa Madonna Gasparina Stampa," in Girolamo Parabosco, *Lettere Amorose. Libro Primo* (Milan: Appresso di Giouann'Antonio de gli Antonij, 1558), fol. 19ᵛ. On Stampa's personal response to Petrarchism see Fiora A. Bassanese, "Gaspara Stampa's Poetics of Negativity," *Italica* 61 (1984): 335–46; modern critics have alternatively seen the poet as "'onorata cortegiana' . . . redeemed sinner, emancipated woman, suicide for love, and musical *virtuosa*" (ibid., 344, n.1).

35. See Thomas Coryat, *Coryats Crudities* (London: Printed by W. S., 1611), 266. In the sixteenth-century educational treatise *The Scholemaster* Roger Ascham had already described the dangers for young English gentlemen traveling to Italy of running into Sirens and Circes, see Roger Ascham, *English Works,* ed. William Aldis Wright (Cambridge: Cambridge University Press, 1904; reprint, 1970), 225. For further information on this type of early modern English fantasy of Italy see Linda Phyllis Austern, "'Forreine Conceites and Wandring Devises': The Exotic, the Erotic and the Feminine," in *The Exotic in Western Music,* ed. Jonathan Bellman (Boston: Northeastern University Press, 1998), 26–42.

36. See *La Talanta* 2.2. The association of music and prostitution can be also found outside Italy: as regards Northern Europe, Richard Leppert notices that "Dutch prostitutes even carried lutes with them into taverns as a sonoric-visual advertisement of their profession" and that "Numerous Dutch paintings connect the lute to prostitution via the subject of the procuress" (*The Sight of Sound: Music, Representation, and the History of the Body* [Berkeley: University of California Press, 1993], 238, n.14). For similar views in early modern England, see Julia Craig-McFeely, "The Signifying Serpent: Seduction by Cultural Stereotype in Seventeenth-Century England," in *Music, Sensation, and Sensuality,* ed. Linda Phyllis Austern (New York: Routledge, 2002), 299–317.

37. Francesco Pona, *La Lucerna,* ed. Giorgio Fulco (Rome: Salerno Editrice, 1973), 108. See also Nanna's words in Aretino's *Ragionamento,* day 3.

38. John Rupert Martin, "Immagini della virtù: The Paintings of the Camerino Farnese," *Art Bulletin* 38 (1956): 91–112, and Jennifer Montagu, "Exhortatio ad Virtutem: A Series of Paintings in the Barberini Palace," *Journal of the Warburg and Courtauld Institutes* 34 (1971): 366–72, treat of some significative examples in frescoes decorating two Roman palaces. On this subject see also Bianca Candida, "Tradizione figurativa nel mito di Ulisse e le Sirene," *Studi classici e orientali* 19–20 (1970–71): 212–51 and Marco Lorandi, *Il mito di Ulisse nella pittura a fresco del Cinquecento italiano* (Milan: Jaca Book, 1995), 95–120.

39. On the tradition of moral exegesis of mythology, see Jean Seznec, *The*

Survival of the Pagan Gods: The Mythological Tradition and Its Place in Renaissance Humanism and Art, trans. Barbara F. Sessions (New York: Pantheon Books, 1953; reprint, Princeton, N.J.: Princeton University Press, 1981): 84–121; and Don Cameron Allen, *Mysteriously Meant: The Rediscovery of Pagan Symbolism and Allegorical Interpretation in the Renaissance* (Baltimore: Johns Hopkins Press, 1970).

40. The standard study of this motif is Erwin Panofsky, *Hercules am Scheidewege und andere antike bildstoffe in der neueren Kunst* (Leipzig: B. G. Teubner, 1930). The painting by Carracci in question is *Ercole al bivio,* executed for Palazzo Farnese in Rome and now kept in the Capodimonte Museum in Naples. For the choice of Hercules in emblem books see for example George Wither, *A Collection of Emblemes, Ancient and Moderne* (London: Printed by A.M. for Robert Allot, 1635), 22, drawing on a Continental example by Gabriel Rollenhagen; the meaning of the lute in the *pictura* of this emblem is considered in Headlam Wells, *Elizabethan Mythologies,* 52–53; Linda Phyllis Austern, "The Siren, the Muse, and the God of Love: Music and Gender in Seventeenth-Century English Emblem Books," *Journal of Musicological Research* 18 (1999): 115–18 and Elena Calogero, " 'Lo, Orpheus with his harpe': La musica nei libri di emblemi inglesi, 1565–1700" (Ph.D. diss., University of Florence, 2001), 113–16.

41. See the frontispiece to Richard Brathwait, *The English Gentleman* (London: Printed by Iohn Haviland, 1630) and the explanation following; sirens are again associated with youth and lust on 30. A similar choice of Hercules between personified Virtue and Voluptuousness is in an edition of a popular fifteenth-century illustrated work, Sebastian Brant, *Stultifera Nauis,* trans. Iacobus Locher (Basel: Johannes Bergman, 1498), fols. 130v–133v: in one of the engravings Voluptuousness, represented as a naked woman, is accompanied by two players of harp and lute (fol. 131v).

42. Among the wide literature on the subject, see the groundbreaking studies by Mario Praz, *Studies in Seventeenth-Century Imagery,* 2d ed. (Rome: Edizioni di Storia e Letteratura, 1964); and Rosemary Freeman, *English Emblem Books* (London: Chatto and Windus, 1948; reprint, New York: Octagon Books, 1966); for more recent criticism, see Peter M. Daly, *Emblem Theory: Recent German Contributions to the Characterization of the Emblem Genre* (Nendeln, Liechtenstein: KTO Press, 1979); Michael Bath, *Speaking Pictures: English Emblem Books and Renaissance Culture* (London: Longman, 1994); and John Manning, *The Emblem* (London: Reaktion Books, 2002).

43. *Sirenes,* in Andrea Alciato, *Emblemata* (Lyons: Macé Bonhomme, 1550), 116; this emblem is also in most earlier and later editions of the same work.

44. For Continental emblems on sirens see *Emblemata: Handbuch zur Sinnbildkunst des XVI. und XVII. Jahrhunderst,* ed. Arthur Henkel and Albrecht Schöne, 2d ed. (Stuttgart: J. B. Metzlersche, 1976), cols. 1697–99. Other symbolic meanings of sirens are collected in Pierio Valeriano, *Ieroglifici, overo Commentari delle occulte significationi de gli Egittij, & d'altre Nationi* (Venice: Appresso Gio[ranni] Antonio, c Giacomo de' Franceschi, 1602), 307–308 and particularly

in Filippo Picinelli, *Mondo simbolico* (Milan: Per lo Stampatore Archiepiscopale, 1653), 81–82.

45. Vincenzo Cartari, *Le Imagini dei dei de gli antichi* (Venice: Presso Marc'Antonio Zaltieri, 1592), 246.

46. See "Bellezza feminile" in Cesare Ripa, *Iconologia* (Siena: Appresso gli Heredi di Matteo Florimi, 1613), 69–70; the first unillustrated edition of this work was published in 1593; Henry Peacham, *Minerva Britanna or a Garden of Heroical Deuises* (London: Wa. Dight, [1612]), 58.

47. On visual representations of Sight see Ferino-Pagden, ed., *I cinque sensi nell'arte*. The mirror in Renaissance art and literature was also associated both with Venus and with courtesans, see Cathy Santore, "The Tools of Venus," *Renaissance Studies* 11 (1997): 179–207.

48. On medieval bestiaries see Florence McCulloch, *Medieval Latin and French Bestiaries,* rev. ed. (Chapel Hill: University of North Carolina Press, 1962). For Richard de Fournival, see *Master Richard's Bestiary of Love and Response,* trans. Jeanette Beer (Berkeley: University of California Press, 1986). For the use of animal similes in medieval love poetry see Milton Stahl Garver, "Sources of Beast Similes in the Italian Lyric of the Thirteenth Century," *Romanische Forschungen* 21 (1907): 276–320.

49. John Swan, *Speculum Mundi or a Glasse Representing the Face of the World* (Cambridge: T. Buck and R. Daniel, 1635), 375.

50. The basilisk was used by Petrarchist poets as a conventional comparison for the lady (Forster, 37–38); the sixteenth-century French poet Scève included an emblem of the basilisk and mirror in his peculiar sonnet sequence, see *The "Délie" of Maurice Scève,* ed. I. D. McFarlane (Cambridge: Cambridge University Press, 1966), 221. For the association of the beloved with the basilisk in love poetry see also Sergei Lobanov-Rostovsky, "Taming the Basilisk," in *The Body in Parts: Fantasies of Corporeality in Early Modern Europe,"* ed. David Hillman and Carla Mazzio (New York: Routledge, 1997), 205–207.

51. Picinelli, *Mondo simbolico,* 238.

52. Michael Drayton, *Works,* ed. J. William Hebel (Oxford: Shakespeare Head Press, 1961), 1:113.

53. "To *Thavmantia* singing," in William Drummond of Hawthornden, *Poetical Works,* ed. L. E. Kastner (Edinburgh: William Blackwood and Sons, 1913), 1:109.

54. See Florence McCullogh, "The Metamorphoses of the Asp in Latin and French Bestiaries," in *Studies in Philology* 56 (1959): 7–13; *Master Richard's Bestiary of Love,* 10–11. The asp, besides the sirens and the basilisk, can be also found in sixteenth- and seventeenth-century emblems, see, e.g., Joachim Camerarius, *Symbolorum & Emblematum ex Aquatilibus et Reptilibus Desumptorum Centuria Quarta* ([Nuremberg,] 1604), fols. 63v–64r, 79v–80r, and 85v–86r.

55. *Sirenes,* in Geffrey Whitney, *A Choice of Emblemes, and Other Devises* (Leyden: Christopher Plantin, 1586), 10; see also another emblem on the dangers of love, *In Amore Tormentum,* 219: "Then stoppe your eares, and like VLISSES

waulke, / The SIREENES tunes, the carelesse often heares." A few other English emblems on sirens with different applications are considered in Calogero, " 'Lo, Orpheus with his harpe,' " 87–108.

56. Whitney first give a different manuscript collection of emblems as a gift to Robert Dudley, Earl of Leicester, the leader of the campaign, and the 1585 printed collection seems to have been wanted by the latter. See John Manning's introduction to Geffrey Whitney, *A Choice of Emblemes* (Aldershot: Scolar Press, 1989); and ibid., "Whitney's *Choice of Emblemes*: a reassessment," *Renaissance Studies* 4 (1990): 155–200.

57. Coryat, *Coryats Crudities*, 268. A previous passage warns the foreign traveler "to beware of the Circæan cups, and the Syrens melody" of Venetian gondoliers taking him unawares to the courtesans' houses, where "he may afterward with *Demosthenes* buy too dear repentance for seeing *Lais*, except he doth for that time either with *Vlysses* stop his eares, or with *Democritus* pull out his eyes" (168–69).

58. This subject was studied by Harry Vredeveld, " 'Deaf as Ulysses to the Siren's Song': The Story of a Forgotten Topos," *Renaissance Quarterly* 54 (2001): 846–82.

59. Leclercq-Marx, *La Sirène*, 58. On Christian interpretations of the episode see also Hugo Rahner, *Greek Myths and Christian Mystery* (London: Burns & Oates, 1963), 328–86.

60. *Metamorphoses* 5, 551–63.

61. Gabriello Simeoni, *La Vita e Metamorfoseo d'Ovidio* (Lyons: Jean de Tournes, 1559), 85. When Ovid's passage is interpreted morally, the equivalence sirens=prostitutes recurs again, see *Le Metamorfosi di Ovidio ridotte da Gio[vanni] Andrea Dell'Anguillara in ottava rima* (Venice: presso Bern[ardo] Giunti, 1584), 182: "Solo Vlisse fugge dalle loro insidie, perche la sola Prudenza fa spreggiare le dannose arti delle Meretrici, chiudendo l'orecchie a i canti loro." ["Only Ulysses escapes from their snares, because only Prudence makes one disregard the dangerous arts of prostitutes, blocking one's ears to their song."]

62. *Metamorphoseon sive Transformationum Ovidianarum Libri Quindicem* (Amsterdam, [1606]), pl. 50. For this motif in paintings see Lorandi, *Il mito di Ulisse*, 118, and ibid., pl. 12, showing a fresco in the Ducal Palace in Mantua, evidently based on Tempesta's pattern.

63. For the presence of sirens in this genre see also Siegfried de Rachewiltz, *De Sirenibus: An Inquiry into Sirens from Homer to Shakespeare* (New York and London: Garland Publishing, 1987), 188–221. For early Italian poetry the obliged reference is to the siren trying to allure Dante in *Purgatorio* 19; on related criticism see Robert Hollander, "Purgatorio XIX: Dante's Siren/Harpy" in *Dante, Petrarch, Boccaccio: Studies in the Italian Trecento in Honor of Charles S. Singleton*, ed. Aldo S. Bernardo and Anthony L. Pellegrini (Binghamton, N.Y.: Medieval & Renaissance Texts & Studies, 1983), 77–88; Nancy A. Jones, "Music and the Maternal Voice in *Purgatorio* XIX," in *Embodied Voices: Representing Female Vocality in Western Culture*, ed. Leslie C. Dunn and Nancy A. Jones (Cambridge: Cambridge

University Press, 1994), 35–49; Naomi Yavneh, "Dante's 'dolce serena' and the Monstrosity of the Female Body," in *Monsters in the Italian Literary Imagination*, ed. Keala Jewell (Detroit: Wayne State University Press, 2001), 109–36.

64. *Orlando Innamorato* 2.4.34–36.

65. On the early modern gendered contrast between nature and culture see Linda Phyllis Austern, "Nature, Culture, Myth, and the Musician in Early Modern England," *Journal of the American Musicological Society* 51 (1998): 27–38.

66. *Orlando Innamorato* 2.4.37–39.

67. *Gerusalemme Liberata* 14.61–68. For the association of Armida with music see Walter Moretti, "Le 'Contrarie tempre' ovvero l'anima musicale d'Armida," *Studi e problemi di critica testuale* 1 (1970): 106–11.

68. *Gerusalemme Liberata* 15.57; Edward Fairfax, *Godfrey of Bulloigne,* ed. Kathleen M. Lea and T. M. Gang (Oxford: Clarendon Press, 1981), 445.

69. *Gerusalemme Liberata* 15.65–66; Fairfax, *Godfrey of Bulloigne,* 447.

70. For the episode of Orpheus and the Sirens see Apollonius Rhodius, *Argonautica* 4.891–919; *Orphei Argonautica,* 1264–90; it was also referred to by Natalis Comes [Natale Conti], see *Mythologiæ* (Venice, 1567), fols. 224r–v.

71. Orpheus is interpreted as philosophy in another chapter specifically dedicated to him, see Francis Bacon, *De Sapientia Veterum London 1609 and The Wisedome of the Ancients (Translated by Sir Arthur Gorges) London 1619* (New York: Garland Publishing, 1976), 40–45 of the Latin text and 54–60 of the English version.

72. Bacon, *Wisedome of the Ancients,* 173–74. Bacon's interpretation circulated even through emblem books in the adaptation made in Jean Baudoin, *Recueil d'Emblemes Divers* (Paris: Jacques Villery, 1638–39), 1:268, where the picture is a copy of Tempesta's engraving. Bacon too was indebted to Continental mythographers, see Charles W. Lemmi, *The Classical Deities in Bacon: A Study in Mythological Symbolism* (Baltimore: Johns Hopkins Press, 1933); and Barbara Carman Garner, "Francis Bacon, Natalis Comes and the Mythological Tradition," *Journal of the Warburg and Courtauld Institutes* 33 (1970): 264–91.

73. *Imago Primi Saeculi Societatis Jesu* (Antwerp: Ex Officina Plantiniana Balthasaris Moreti, 1640), 181. See also Claude-François Menestrier, *L'Art des Emblemes* (Paris: Chez R. J. B. De la Caille, 1684), 70–71; and Picinelli, *Mondo simbolico,* 82–83.

74. *Rerum Vulgarium Fragmenta* 207; *Petrarch's Lyric Poems,* 360. The ambiguities of this double frame of reference are discussed in Sara Sturm-Maddox, "Petrarch's Siren: 'Dolce Parlar' and 'Dolce Canto' in the *Rime Sparse,*" *Italian Quarterly* 27 (1986): 5–19.

75. *Amorum Libri* 113; *Amorum Libri: The Lyric Poems of Matteo Maria Boiardo,* trans. Andrea di Tommaso (Binghamton, N.Y.: Medieval & Renaissance Texts & Studies, 1993), 195.

76. "Canto," in *Rime del Caualier Marino Parte Terza* (Venice: Presso Gio[vanni] Pietro Brigonci, 1667), 36. Cf. the first madrigal by Guarini, *Rime,* fol. 58r.

77. Of the eight consecutive poems dedicated to female music by Marino in the third part of the *Rime*, only the first, preceding the one that contains the lines quoted here, is explicitly dedicated to Basile, but some critics have taken the whole group to be connected with her. Marino also associated Adriana's voice with that of siren-like *Lusinga* ("Flattery") in *L'Adone*, 7.88. Other poems in honor of this singer alternatively exploit the positive and negative connotations of siren imagery, see Alessandro Ademollo, *La bell'Adriana ed altre virtuose del suo tempo alla corte di Mantova* (Città di Castello: S. Lapi, 1888), passim. See also Dinko Fabris, "La città della Sirena: Le origini del mito musicale di Napoli nell'età spagnola," in *Napoli viceregno spagnolo: Una capitale della cultura alle origini dell'Europa Moderna,* ed. Monika Bosse and André Stoll (Naples: Vivarium, 2001), 2:478, 483.

78. "Nel medesimo soggetto" ["Alle intelligenze in lode d'una bella Cantatrice"], in *La Lira*, 15. Laura Peperara, one of the singers of the celebrated *concerto delle donne,* was already for Tasso a "nova sirena" ("Vaghe Ninfe del Po, Ninfe sorelle," 54).

The Sirens, the Epicurean Boat, and the Poetry of Praise

Stephen M. Buhler

Poets in early modern England were keenly aware of their precarious and potentially dangerous place in the cultural and political economy of their times. Such concern was not always defensive, voiced in reaction to criticism from early Puritans (such as Stephen Gosson in his *Schoole of Abuse*), among others. Poets themselves regularly confronted and explored the possibility that poetic expression could be harmful to the commonwealth. Their most vehement critics called attention to the supposed power of poetry to corrupt individuals and societies. The poets, however, took a different approach in their self-critique, worrying that the act of praising patrons, rulers, and nations could inspire complacency in their readers and hearers. The poetry of praise was intended to encourage virtuous action; poets acknowledged that the actual effect of its celebration of what had already been achieved could be a disinclination to achieve anything else. Recent scholarship, such as that of Melinda Gough, has called attention to early modern poetry's responses to accusations of prompting sensual debility, and Peter C. Herman has astutely identified texts by poets that essentially agree with such criticism.[1] Along with the sweetness of sensuality, the sweetness of self-regard was also admitted, explored, and (it was profoundly hoped) checked. When poets of the era addressed such concerns, they often invoked a lesser-known tradition surrounding the classical sirens, one that acknowledges that the sirenic temptation could have little to do with Eros, but plenty to do with Fama and Sapientia, both true and false.

Early modern writers could effectively deploy critiques of poets and their patrons for reasons other than sensuality by working from behind the erotic associations surrounding the sirens. The pervasive cultural view of the sirens as emblematic of poetry's allegedly effeminizing effects—encouraging an emphasis on sound, rather than sense; on otiose pleasure, rather than stern business or negotiation—provided a cover, in effect, for writers to offer sharp criticisms of unduly definitive claims to being sensible or practical in matters of state. In this tradition, an interesting twist is given to the Lucretian analogy of serious poetry with honey placed on the lip of a cup containing medicinal wormwood (see *De rerum natura* 1.936–42). Originally, it is the honey-like sweetness of verse that may provide sufficient distraction to allow the medicine of its instructive message to be ingested and to do healthful work upon the reader; here, the perceived *danger* that such sweetness presents distracts the reader from dismissing too quickly or too warily a harsh message. Writers could question the validity or permanence of announced achievements worthy of Fame or demonstrating Wisdom under partial cover of ideas about sirenic sensuality. They could more openly question the utility of poetic celebrations of supposed achievement by directly invoking the nonerotic significances of the sirens.

The basis for this countertradition resides in the Homeric source text itself and the specific temptations of the sirens' song: "Renowned Odysseus" is praised as the "great glory of the Achaeans" and is promised joy and wisdom from hearing the sirens, who claim to know all that occurs on earth, including what the Greeks and Trojans endured through the will of the gods (*The Odyssey* 12.184–91).[2] The two sirens, with their oracular acuity, know that only Odysseus can hear them and therefore they sing *his* praises. They address Odysseus as the glory of the Greek nation and promise wisdom as a product of their continuing to sing about what transpired at Troy and about events present and future. Odysseus responds powerfully and only the ropes that tie him to the mast of his ship keep him from meeting his own destruction. The siren-song that elicits this response, even in the astute and cunning hero of the *Odyssey*, presents itself as both encomiastic and vatic: it promises to celebrate in loving detail and sweet harmony its hearer's exploits; it asserts the power of prophecy, along with an understanding of the divine perspective and purpose. In short, the song of the sirens resembles bardic song as depicted throughout the *Odyssey* and, to a considerable extent, Homer's own verse. Robert Lamberton has noted the identification of the sirens with other bards, including Homer, in the epic and in the commentary inspired by them: he is particularly struck by a passage in the *Certamen* where the unknown author presents his reader with "an oracle [who] calls Homer himself an 'ambrosial Siren.'"[3]

Readers of the *Odyssey* in early modern England were well aware of these self-referential implications. The verse translation by George Chapman, published in 1614–1615 (and later celebrated by John Keats in a justly famous sonnet), highlights the messages of deserved praise and secret knowledge in the sirens' song:

> Come here, thou, worthy of a world of praise,
> That dost so high the Grecian glory raise.
> Ulysses! stay thy ship, and that song heare
> That none past ever but it bent his eare,
> But left him ravishd and instructed more
> By us than any ever heard before.
> For we know all things whatsoever were
> In wide Troy labour'd, whatsoever there
> The Grecians and the Troyans both sustain'd
> By those high issues that the Gods ordain'd:
> And whatsoever all the earth can show
> T'informe a knowledge of desert, we know. (12.272–83)[4]

In Chapman's rendering, Ulysses himself describes sirenic verse as consisting of "sweete accents" giving voice to "learn'd numbers" (12.270–71), paying tribute to the sirens' skill in harmony and in poetic craft; Homer's original specifies only that their song is "clear-toned" (12.183). Chapman's sirens conclude their incantation with a promise that the listener will be strengthened in his conviction that he is deserving of praise ("a knowledge of desert"); this explicit connection between knowledge and worthiness does not occur in Homer. Everything in Chapman's version points to the potentially debilitating and destructive effects of even the most finely crafted of encomia, which irresistibly draw those so honored toward the rocks.

The temptation offered by the sirens is sensual only in audition, then, while its deepest dangers are those implicit in the poetry of praise. Any poet dependent upon the support of the mighty must constantly balance any educative impulse, which implicitly critiques the hearer (since he or she is thought to need education), with ingratiation, which usually involves an account of worthy deeds already accomplished. The sirens, then, dramatize dilemmas faced on all sides in the cultural practice of civic verse: their song praises the hearer and promises enlightenment; the consequences of their song are evident in their own monstrous form and in the doom that awaits those drawn to their shores. Poets and their audiences alike suffer when the pleasurable praise of abilities, whether in artistic creation or in governance, completely displaces the harder task of sharing insight.

Much of the interpretive tradition tended to read additional sensuality into the sirens' song; in response, some ancient commentators insisted on pointing out the song's more intellectual attractions. This more complex understanding of sirenic verse was later revived by writers in early modern England, who would directly cite their literary forebears. In his *Memorabilia*, Xenophon depicts Socrates as a perceptive reader who can apply the Homeric episode to the problem of forging friendships:

> "But how does friendship come?"
>
> "There are spells, they say, wherewith those who know charm whom they will and make friends of them, and drugs which those who know give to whom they choose and win their love."
>
> "How then can we learn them?"
>
> "You have heard from Homer the spell that the Sirens put on Odysseus. It begins like this: 'Hither, come hither, renowned Odysseus, great glory of the Achaeans.'"
>
> "Then did the Sirens chant in this strain for other folk too, Socrates, so as to keep those who were under the spell from leaving them?"
>
> "No, only for those who yearned for the fame that virtue gives."[5]

While Xenophon's Socrates invokes the sirens in a fairly benign context, he does not purge them of their darker associations. Their song is described as a spell—as enchantment as well as chant, as charm as well as *carmen*. The would-be friend who imitates their craft may intend no ill, but the calculation involved in the flattering campaign and the dire effects of the sirens' song in the Homeric source are nevertheless worrisome. The same worries confront any principled poet who seeks favor from the great.

In his *De finibus bonorum et malorum*, Cicero has Piso, one of his interlocutors, read the call of the sirens as the appeal of promised knowledge to *innatus cognitionis amor*, the "innate love of learning" found in humankind:

> *Neque enim vocum suavitate videntur aut novitate quadam et varietate cantandi revocare eos solitae qui praetervehebantur, sed quia multa se scire profitebantur, ut homines ad earum saxa discendi cupidate adhaerescerent.*

(Apparently it was not the sweetness of their voices or the novelty and diversity of their songs, but their professions of knowledge that used to attract the passing voyagers; it was the passion for learning that kept men rooted to the Sirens' rocky shores.)[6]

Piso serves as the spokesman for the teachings of Antiochus, a contemporary proponent of what he termed the Old Academy or "authentic" Platonic tradition. But Piso is also something of a poet himself, having translated the sirens' song into Latin ("among other passages of Homer," he claims). His version offers subtle shadings of the original, especially in the concluding lines:

> *Nos grave certamen belli clademque tenemus,*
> *Graecia quae Troiae divino numine vexit,*
> *Omniaque e latis rerum vestigia terris.*

> (We know the grievous struggle and losses of war
> With which Greece shook Troy, by divine will,
> And all things that happen on the wide earth.)[7]

The conversation in Book 5 of *De finibus* is set in Athens, in the year 79 BCE; the historical Marcus Piso would go on to become a consul in Rome in 61 BCE, shortly after the time of Cicero's own consulship. A hint of Roman attitudes toward conquest appear in his slight rewriting of the last lines of the song: where Homer's sirens present the gods as allowing the horrors of war to be visited upon Greece and Troy alike, in Piso's version, they describe what Greece *does to* Troy as the will of the gods. In this recollection of youthful discussions of philosophy, composed soon before the events of 44 and 43 BCE that would lead to the end of the Republic and of his own life, Cicero quietly and casually documents the impact that politics can have upon poetry.

The problems of patronage during the nascent empire may have prompted Virgil's avoidance of any direct encounter with the sirens in *The Aeneid,* his grand appropriation of Homeric epic in service to the burgeoning Augustan regime. Even so, the beguiling and destruction of Palinurus by Somnus, the god of sleep, is intended as a parallel to the episode with the sirens in Homer. The god, we are told, assumes the appearance of a Trojan comrade and offers to take Palinurus's place at the ship's tiller. He counsels that *"datur hora quieti"* (5.844); in Thomas Phaer's rendering in English, first published in 1558, Palinurus is told that "an houre of rest to take is meet" (5.900).[8] Somnus urges Palinurus: *"pone caput fessosque oculos furare labori"* (5.845); Phaer's version is "Lay downe thy head, and steal thy painfull [that is, taking pains or weary from care] eyes one nap of sleepe" (5.901). Palinurus resists the temptation, but he is ultimately overcome by the god and falls into the sea. The pilotless craft and the other ships then approach the sirens' cliffs, ever dangerous, and white with the bones of their many victims: "*iamque adeo scopulos Sirenum advecta subibat / difficilis quondam multorumque ossibus albos*" (5.864–65); "And now they entring were the straytes, *Sirenes* rockes that hight [were named], / A parlous place sometime, and yet with bones of people whight" (5.920–21). Virgil concedes that the sirens' song—and its bardic equivalents—might lure its hearers to dereliction of duty, to a premature sense of arrival and fully earned rest; he discreetly transfers blame in this instance to Sleep itself, allowing another kind of pleasure to take the place of both eroticism and complacency.

Plutarch, in one of the earliest of his *Moralia*, applies the story of sirens to the question of poetry's effect specifically on the young, but also on the state as a whole. Part of his argument in "How the Young Man Should Study Poetry" is directed against Plato's banishment of poets from the ideal Republic, but another part of his argument counters Epicurus's repeated strictures against enculturation into civic society. In the Epicurean view, poetry serves the social function of preserving and transmitting myths across generations. This function has two deleterious consequences: first, mythic explanations for natural events perpetuate superstition; second, superstitious observance of the duties of civic religion encourages other forms of involvement in the affairs of the *polis*. Neither consequence is conducive to the kind of detached calm—tranquility or *ataraxia*—that Epicurus thought to be the highest state of existence and the true goal of philosophy. According to Diogenes Laertius, Epicurus famously (or infamously) gave his devotee Pythocles this advice: "Hoist all sail, my dear boy, and steer clear of all culture";[9] the term Epicurus uses for culture is *paideia,* with its connections to preparation for civic life. There may well be, in the Epicurean fragment, a witty subversion of Homeric verse: just as Odysseus endeavored to avoid Scylla, Charybdis, and the sirens, so too must the wise man avoid the pitfalls of myths preserved by the likes of Homer. Plutarch readily saw a connection between the texts and exploited it in his rebuttal to Epicurus's teaching. The English translation by Philemon Holland, first published in 1603, titles the essay "Reading and Hearing of Poemes and Poets" and renders the passage in this way:

> What is then to be done? Shall we constraine our youth to goe aboord into the Brigantine or Bark of *Epicurus,* to saile away and flie from Poetry, by plastring and stopping their eares with hard and strong waxe,

as *Ulisses* sometimes served those of *Ithaca?* or rather by environing and defending their judgement with some discourse of true reason, as with a defensative band about it, to keep and guarding them, that they be not caried away with the allurements of pleasure, unto that which might hurt them.[10]

Two traditions about the sirens' song are reflected in this passage. One, seen near the end, is the association of their song with distracting and, in time, destructive pleasure. But the other is the association with public and civic verse—especially the aspects of poetry and other forms of culture that provoked Epicurus's suspicion and scorn. The latter association has not received sufficient notice by scholars: even those who quote the Plutarchan passage in full have passed by the Epicurean boat with no comment. Over time, Epicureanism's own (and inaccurate) reputation as the philosophy of sensual pleasure would help to overshadow the latter significance of the sirens. But Plutarch, one of Epicurus's most well-informed critics, has both significances in mind.

A misreading of Plutarch, as well as the sirens' association with Circe (who, however, warns Odysseus about them), likely influenced such allegorical readings as Fulgentius's identification of the sirens with what he asserts is the threefold allure of love through the beauties of song, appearance, and manner.[11] Fulgentius, then, is certain that there were *three* sirens. The mention of Epicurus's boat came to suggest a hedonic and erotic orientation, rather than the anti-poetic, anti-paideiac, and anti-politic campaign originally intended by Epicurus and acknowledged by Plutarch. In contrast, Boethius, early in his *De consolatione Philosophiae*, sustains the connection between sirenic song and political life when the figure of Philosophy herself banishes the muses that have inspired his poetic laments. Boethius had begun his meditations mourning the loss of power and position—once consul under Theodoric, he came under the emperor's suspicion and was thrown into prison—and the passion with which he expresses his grief prompts Philosophy's appearance and rebuke. She berates his previous muses, who "with their sweet poison" (*dulcibus venenis*) only "accustom a man's mind to his ills, not rid him of them" (*hominum mentes assuefaciunt morbo, non liberant*). Finally, she dismisses them: *"abite potius Sirenes usque in exitium dulces"*—"Begone, sweet Sirens, who everywhere cause destruction."[12] Boethius's initial verse betrayed ongoing attachment to affairs of state and the favor of the powerful; such political concerns, as well as the poetry's "sweetness," mark the inspiration as sirenic. Philosophy's teaching will instead provide a cure for all such distractions. Queen Elizabeth herself tried her hand at translating

Boethius in 1593. In Elizabeth's version, the "Sirenes swite [sweet]" do not only inure their victim to sufferings, but also "with swit venom nourris [nourish] them."[13] Perhaps her own experience as a recipient of praise led the monarch to read Boethius's Philosophy as asserting that false poetry could actively contribute to problems in governance, as well as simply masking them.

Throughout the moralizing traditions of medieval allegory, the sirens were almost exclusively read as figures of sensual and erotic temptation. Dante, in *Purgatorio* 19, describes a prophetic dream in which a siren symbolizes the seductive varieties of *malo amor* of which he will be purged. If this passage, Beatrice's reference to the siren in *Purgatorio* 31, and the encounter with Ulysses in the *Inferno* are actually indebted to Cicero's *De finibus*,[14] they demonstrate starkly the power of a negative tradition over a positive source text. In the wake of the Renaissance's recovery of classical culture, however, the sirens' significance as poets of praise slowly reemerged. Natalis Comes, in his highly influential *Mythologiae*, asserts that the song of the sirens should be interpreted as *adulatorum voces*, the voices of flatterers: Comes compares their effect on princes to the deepest sleep—borrowing from Virgil's sirenic parallel—in which they are led at last into peril.[15] In the *Moriae Encomium* of Erasmus, Folly herself describes the hope for *"inanis gloria,"* an empty glory, as *dulcissima Siren:* the sweetest siren of all.[16] The terms are used as Folly alludes to the story of "Quintus Curtius," who reportedly rode his horse into a chasm so that he might fulfill a prophecy that the sacrifice of Rome's greatest strength would ensure the preservation of the Republic. That way he could be revered as the preeminent pillar, martyr, and savior of Rome. As it turns out, the story involves *Marcus* Curtius, not Quintus; the error is likely a strategic one, since it denies Marcus any kind of fame, even the notoriety of being a fool. The passage in Erasmus immediately follows one in which Folly dismisses *"Amphionis et Orphei cithara,"* the lyre of Amphion and Orpheus, as signifying nothing more than *"adulatio,"* flattery.[17] In this developing context, several poets saw again in the sirens the pitfalls of their efforts to combine both counsel and praise ("Criticism and Compliment" in Kevin Sharpe's apt formulation), to serve as both prophets and courtiers. English poets of the early modern period evince a high level of sensitivity—and perhaps anxiety—over the often subtle differences between laudatory verse and flattering lines, between exhortation to continued good works and invitation to rest on the laurels that poets themselves had awarded their patrons.

What might distinguish the early modern English approach to the sirens is not only poetic awareness of the contrary traditions about sirenic verse but also a poetic willingness to acknowledge the contradictions in order to consider the value of poetry itself. As we have seen, many of the texts that reflect the complexity of the sirens' significance were already being translated into English or were increasingly available in other vernaculars; yet other treatments, ranging from those by Cicero to those by Erasmus, were well known in their original languages, thanks to their status as—or their being mentioned in—school texts.[18] This academic orientation will be especially evident in Abraham Fraunce's explorations of the mythology surrounding the sirens; even so, Fraunce's approach to sirenic song also enjoyed more immediate literary contexts.

Edmund Spenser revisits the Odyssean voyage in Book 2 of *The Faerie Queene* as Sir Guyon, the Knight of Temperance, is lauded by the sirens while en route to the Bower of Bliss. In Spenser's retelling (canto 12), the sirens themselves are guilty of ambition, specifically of the poetic sort: "They were faire Ladies, till they fondly striv'd / With th' *Heliconian* maides for maistery."[19] The lower halves of their bodies have been changed to non-human form ("th' one moyity / Transform'd to fish," says Spenser's narrator) as punishment for attempting to displace the true Muses. A part of their beauty and all of their skill in song survive: "But th' upper halfe their hew retained still, / And their sweet skill in wonted melody" (stanza 31, lines 6–7). They now use such abilities "T' allure weake travelers"— and Spenser here wittily deploys a play on the words *traveler*, one who journeys, and *travailer*, one who labors or strives. Both terms aptly fit Guyon and his prototype, Odysseus; Spenser's version of the sirens' song is indebted to Homer's original. The sirens address Guyon as his vessel passes their "still / And calmy bay" (stanza 30, lines 2–3) and invite him to draw nearer:

> O thou faire sonne of gentle Faery,
> That art in mightie armes most magnifide
> Above all knights, that ever battell tryde,
> O turne thy rudder hither-ward a while:
> Here may thy storme-bet vessell safely ride;
> This is the Port of rest from troublous toyle,
> The worlds sweet In from paine & wearisome turmoyle. (2.12.32.3–9)

The implication, borrowed in part from Virgil's Palinurus episode, is that Guyon has already proven himself, that he need not "travel" any more or any further. Spenser deftly synthesizes various traditions about the sirens into an example of flattering, destructive bardic song—even as he attempts to produce the first unquestioned epic in English verse. His sirens praise

Guyon for his ancestry, his abilities, and his fame; at the same time, Spenser himself is celebrating the same attributes of Elizabeth I, his monarch and hoped-for patron, in *The Faerie Queene*.

Sir Philip Sidney, in *The Defence of Poesy*, may have influenced Spenser's treatment of the sirens. Sidney admits that poetry appears to its detractors as "the nurse of abuse, inflecting us with many pestilent desires; with a siren's sweetness drawing the mind to the serpent's tail of sinful fancies."[20] But, he argues, these dangers may be offset if "they that delight in poesy itself should seek to know what they do, and how they do; and especially look themselves in an unflattering glass of reason."[21] Margaret Ferguson has detected a subtle allusion to Plutarch's young man,[22] who uses reason as Ulysses used the mast of his ship; I would also call attention to Sidney's use of the term "unflattering," which draws upon both Xenophon's and Comes's readings of the power of sirenic verse to flatter its hearers. Making these connections all the stronger are intervening passages stressing the welcome and support that warriors and statesmen— "Alexanders, Caesars, Scipios, all favourers of poets" (240)—have granted poetry.

The interconnections between awareness in the Sidney circle of such traditions surrounding the sirens and the practical problems surrounding the search for patronage may be best illustrated in Abraham Fraunce's *The Countesse of Pembrokes Yvychurch*, which is dedicated to Sidney's sister, Mary Sidney Herbert. The third part of the work bears the title *Amintas Dale* and was published separately in 1592; the title page promises "the most conceited tales of the Pagan Gods in English Hexameters: together with their auncient descriptions and Philosophicall explications." The descriptions and explications overwhelm Fraunce's verses (and translations from other sources), but they also provide evidence that the full complexity of the sirens' significance was available to English writers and readers in the latter part of the sixteenth century. In addition, they show a writer carefully negotiating his way among the various dangers presented by attempting to praise without flattery (the learned Countess deserves a learned work) and by daring to teach a patron (the learned Countess would benefit from additional learning). Fraunce's initial commentary on the sirens reflects the tradition of reading them as sensual temptresses:

> Allegorically they signifie the cosning [cozening, deceitful] tricks of counterfeit strumpets, the undoubted shipwrack of all affectionat yonkers [young gentlemen or noblemen]: and therefore is it said by *Virgil*, that the Mermaydes rocks are all overspread with bones of dead men, whose destruction their deceaveable allurements had procured.[23]

Fraunce demonstrates not only how thoroughly the sirens' original song—and temptation of Odysseus—could be forgotten, but also how strongly Virgil's avoidance of the sirens had shaped their interpretation. He immediately follows this passage, however, with one that restores the bardic and political resonances found in the *Odyssey:*

> *Xenophon* is of this minde, that the *Sirenes* did learnedly and sweetely extoll the famous acts of renowned men: and that therefore *Homer* maketh them entertain *Ulysses* with their pleasing voyce, who indeede was for politick strategems the chiefe ornament of *Greece:* and no doubt, these sweete and glorious commendations of great mens exploites, are the most effectuall charmes to worke any impression in an heroicall mind, and with this conceite [idea] of *Xenophon, Cicero* doth also agree.[24]

Borrowing and extrapolating from the *Memorabilia,* Fraunce establishes the interpretive context for poetic depictions, such as Spenser's, of the sirens as cautionary examples of harmful public verse. So while he later compares the sirens' longing for the abducted Proserpina to the way in which "strumpets and wanton huswives folow riches & aboundance,"[25] he also associates the sirens' song with incitements to specious honor. Several of Odysseus's men, he notes, "drawne away with ambition and vaynglorie, would have yeelded to the deceiptfull sweetnes of the *Syrenes*" if their leader had not kept them from hearing the fatal song.[26] The assertion that Cicero's Piso (speaking for Antiochus) "doth also agree" with Xenophon's Socrates is not quite accurate, but it is true that neither speaker considers the temptation of the sirens to be primarily sensual.

Samuel Daniel, in *Ulysses and the Syren* (published in 1605), follows Spenser to some degree. The Siren invites the hero to "Possesse these shores" with her, where they can "sit, and view their toile / That travaile on the deepe" (2, 5–6).[27] But while Daniel's Siren initially dissuades from any additional striving toward honor, urging rest and sensual recreation as the rewards for both endeavor and rule, she ultimately chooses to join Ulysses on his journey. In this retelling, Ulysses successfully resists the Siren's temptation and wins her and her art over to his service: "For beauty hath created bin, / T' undoo, or be undonne," she explains in the poem's final lines. Since her song and physical attractiveness were unable to "undo" the hero, they must be "undone" by him—not, as in some traditions about the sirens, driven to destroy themselves (in imitation of the Sphinx), but instead transformed from forces destructive of honor into ornaments of true praise. As does Spenser, Daniel effectively conflates the erotic and encomiastic temptations of verse, demonstrating how an emphasis on the former can provide something of a shield for addressing the latter.

In the same year that Daniel suggested this possible resolution to the conundrums presented by the poetry of praise, Ben Jonson insisted on alluding to the sirens in the very first text he contributed to a masque performed at the court of King James. The masque form was inherently encomiastic, offering through verse, music, dance, spectacle, and drama an idealized representation of the persons and events each individual masque was intended to honor. Even so, the texts of several masques include passages of counsel—usually nothing so severe as critique—made possible, in part, by the context of high praise.[28] So Jonson made sure to warn against "*Syrens* of the land" in his first collaboration with Inigo Jones, *The Masque of Blackness*. While the primary meaning of the phrase might suggest male counterparts to Fraunce's "counterfeit strumpets," the general context of the masque form and the immediate context of the event's first dances with men and women together also suggest Comes's flatterers. Queen Anne and her noblest female attendants have just danced in pairs:

> *Their owne single* dance *ended, as they were about to make choice of their men: One, from the sea, was heard to call 'hem with this* charme, *sung by a* tenor *voyce.*

SONG.
Come away, come away,
We grow jealous of your stay:
If you doe not stop your eare,
We shall have more cause to feare
Syrens of the land, then they
To doubt the *Syrens* of the sea.[29]

Before they choose their rightful (dance) partners, Jonson's script calls for a male voice to cast a benign spell, a "charme," that will bring the ladies out of their self-sufficiency and that will soothe the men's fears—and perhaps the poet's own, as well—over the blandishments of flattering rivals.

William Browne in *The Inner Temple Masque* (presented in 1614) takes the Virgilian passage and its interpretive traditions for his starting point. The "Description of the Firste Scene" makes reference to "a cliffe of the sea done over in parte white according to that of Virgill, lib. 5," upon which one of two sirens offers a song "beginninge as that of theirs" in Homer. Even though Browne provides the quotation, in Greek, from the *Odyssey*, his siren sings an exclusively sensual and erotic invitation: "Here lye Loves undiscovred mynes, / A prey to passengers; / Perfumes farre sweeter than the best / Which make ye Phoenix urne and nest."[30] Not surprisingly, these sirens are allies to Circe. In a similar vein and a similar setting, Thomas Carew's masque *Coelum Brittanicum* (staged in 1633) presents Pleasure itself in the figure of Hedone as a "bewitching Syren," whose "*Circean* charmes" can dissuade the mighty from the paths of glory and honor.[31] By way of contrast, Michael Drayton's *The Shepheards Sirena* (published in 1627) sustains the connection between the sirens' song with the poetry of praise by virtue of its nearly obsessive topical allusions and its laments for lost patronage. Dorilus, the primary figure in the pastoral poem, has been separated from his beloved Sirena, who longs for his company and for his "faithfull counsel"[32] in distress but finds herself unable to join him. The shepherd would have to leave his flock even to attempt to lend her aid. As Dorilus muses over his predicament, he reflects the problems presented by the poetry of praise:

> Hard the choise I have to chuse,
> To my selfe if friend I be,
> I must my Sirena loose,
> If not so, shee looseth me. (lines 121–24)

Fidelity to one's pastoral vocation can lead to estrangement from those who once trusted in one's song. Making the link between shepherding and song all the stronger in this pastoral setting, Drayton puns on "swains" and "swans" when well-meaning "joviall shepheards" try to lift Dorilus's mood by singing one of the songs he had composed in Sirena's praise. The song's chorus goes:

> On thy bancke,
> In a rancke,
> Let thy swanns sing her,
> And with thy musicke,
> along let them bring her.

Drayton, at the time, was not involved (much to his sorrow) in the task of producing an inherently encomiastic work like a masque; the lack of generic constraints permitted his engagement with the more self-reflexive and self-critical associations of sirenic verse.

The tradition of self-critique culminates in John Milton, whose two experiments in the masque form (both written in praise of the Egerton family) are irresistibly drawn to the sirens. In *Arcades,* an entertainment given in honor of Alice Spencer Egerton, the Countess Dowager of Derby, Milton invokes the eight sirens of Plato's *Republic* 617b, who represent cosmic order. The "Genius of the Wood," who keeps watch over the family estate at Harefield, finds recreation and inspiration in the song of these divine sirens:

> But else in deep of night, when drowsiness
> Hath lockt up mortal sense, then listen I
> To the celestial *Sirens'* harmony,
> That sit upon the nine infolded Spheres
> And sing. . . .
> And keep unsteady Nature to her law,
> And the low world in measur'd motion draw
> After the heavenly tune, which none can hear
> Of human mold with gross unpurged ear. . . .[33]

Despite the loftiness of the music of the spheres, the Genius nevertheless finds it the most appropriate setting for any just tribute to Alice Spencer Egerton. He declares that "such music worthiest were to blaze / The peerless height of her immortal praise" (lines 74–75). While Milton is careful to identify these singers as heavenly sirens, there had often been confusion and conflation between Homer's and Plato's singers: Lamberton[34] has found instances in the interpretive tradition from commentaries by such late classical authors as Plutarch and Philo. Ambivalence over the poetry of praise leads Milton to think in sirenic terms.

The association is even more keenly felt in *A Maske Presented at Ludlow Castle* (also known as *Comus*) in honor of the installation of Sir John Egerton, the Earl of Bridgewater, as the Lord President of Wales in 1634. The tempter in this entertainment is the courtly, flattering Comus—the son, in Milton's telling, of Bacchus and Circe. After hearing the song of the masque's protagonist, known only as "the Lady" and played by the Earl's daughter, Comus contrasts the "raptures" of her voice with those of other singers:

> I have oft heard
> My mother *Circe* with the Sirens three . . .
> Who as they sung, would take the prison'd soul,
> And lap it in *Elysium; Scylla* wept,
> And chid her barking waves into attention,
> And fell *Charybdis* murmur'd soft applause:
> But they in pleasing slumber lull'd the sense,
> And in sweet madness robb'd it of itself,
> But such a sacred and home-felt delight,
> Such sober certainty of waking bliss,
> I never heard till now. (lines 252–53, 256–64)

Milton has his villain distinguish between the Lady's song and that of the Homeric sirens (even if the number is that provided by Fulgentius rather than Homer), who appear in the full context of Odysseus's voyage and its hazards. Attempting to reform the masque itself, Milton sets up a confrontation between the Lady's powerful purity on the one hand and, on the other, the insincerity and self-serving rhetoric that Comus will utter in his attempt to win the Lady (and the power of her song) over to his Circean crew. Milton confronts the dangers implicit in the masque and in the poetry of praise by addressing the dangers of flattery—and of flattering song—explicitly in his masque's dramatic action.

In "At a Solemn Musick," he hopes to reconcile all the traditions surrounding the poetry of praise by directing sirenic song "to him that sits" upon "the sapphire-color'd throne" seen in Old Testament prophecy (lines 7–8, based on *Ezekiel* 1. 26). His speaker addresses a "Blest pair of *Sirens,*" Voice and Verse, returning to the Homeric number and stressing the message of their song as well as the "divine sounds" that communicate it to our hearing and which suggest "to our high-rais'd fantasy" (line 5) the music of the spheres and universal concord with God's will. Even here, though, Milton resists flattering his secondary audience: those reading the poetic text or those attending a concert of religious works (the "Solemn Musick" of the title). The members of such audiences might be tempted to equate their glimpses of cosmic harmony with positive participation in the divine plan in order to identify the music they hear or create with the "celestial consort" (line 27). The poet reminds them that humankind has not yet been able to "rightly answer that melodious noise" (18): much more must be done before "we soon again renew that Song" (25).

Through classical times and through early modern English encounters with classical culture, the sirens have served not only as figures of sensual and aesthetic attraction but also as figures of poetry itself. By 1632, George Sandys could expand on Ovid's brief mention of the sirens in his *Metamorphoses* (as attendants of Proserpina and searchers after her) by noting their association with learning and eloquence, all of which was "intimated by *Homer,* who attributes unto them the endowments of the Muses; as harmony, and absolute knowledge both in Philosophy and history."[35] Sandys, providing commentary for his translation of Ovid, follows the lead of Comes; he observes that some readers in the tradition "interpret the songs of these *Sirens* by the flattery of *Sichophants:* a poyson that takes from a man the knowledge of himselfe, and kills by delighting."[36] The hazards of engaged poetry, that which seeks both to serve a public function and to gain patronage, continued to be expressed and explored by means of the sirens and the traditions surrounding them. Poets in English variously addressed these hazards as personal interest—both intellectual and economic--and as expectations determined by genre and by audience affected them; as they did so, they variously described the power of flattery in sirenic song and, by extension, in their own work.

NOTES

1. Melinda Gough, "Jonson's Siren Stage," *Studies in Philology* 96, no. 1 (Winter 1999), esp. 73–76 on Stephen Gosson, whose *Schoole of Abuse* (1579) regularly invokes the myth of the sirens in its condemnation of poetry in general and the stage in particular; Peter C. Herman, *Squitter-Wits and Muse-Haters: Sidney, Spenser, Milton, and Renaissance Anti-poetic Sentiment* (Detroit: Wayne State University Press, 1996), esp. 66–72 on Sidney.

2. I have used the edition and translation of *The Odyssey* by A. T. Murray for the Loeb Classical Library (Cambridge, Mass.: Harvard University Press, 1984).

3. Robert Lamberton, *Homer the Theologian: Neoplatonist Allegorical Reading and the Growth of the Epic Tradition* (Berkeley: University of California Press, 1986), 7, quoting *Certamen* 38.

4. George Chapman, *Chapman's Homer*, ed. Allardyce Nicoll, 2 vols. (New York: Bollingen Foundation/Pantheon Books, 1956).

5. Xenophon, *Memorabilia* 2.6.10–12. I have used the edition and translation of E. C. Marchant, in *Xenophon*, vol. 4 for the Loeb Classical Library (Cambridge, Mass.: Harvard University Press, 1979).

6. Cicero, *De finibus bonorum et malorum* 5.18. I have used the edition and translation of H. Rackham for the Loeb Classical Library (Cambridge, Mass.: Harvard University Press, 1967).

7. Cicero, 5.18. The translation here is mine, based on that of Rackham.

8. I have used the edition and translation of *The Aeneid* by H. R. Fairclough for the Loeb Classical Library (Cambridge, Mass.: Harvard University Press, 1935). Also Thomas Phaer and Thomas Twynne, *The Aeneid*, Steven Lally, ed. (New York: Garland, 1987). Phaer published his translation of the first seven books of Virgil's epic in 1558; this was expanded to nine books in a posthumously printed version in 1562. Twynne would complete the translation, often revising Phaer's verse to reflect his own interest in approximating classical meter; this version was republished five times after its initial appearance in 1573.

9. Diogenes Laertius, *Lives of Eminent Philosophers* 10.6. I have used the edition and translation of R. D. Hicks for the Loeb Classical Library (Cambridge, Mass.: Harvard University Press, 1979).

10. Plutarch, *The Philosophie Commonlie Called the Morals*, trans. Philemon Holland (London: Printed by Arnold Hatfield, 1603), 19. The passage is *Moralia* 15d; I have also consulted the edition and translation of F. C. Babbitt in vol. 1 of

the *Moralia* for the Loeb Classical Library (Cambridge, Mass.: Harvard University Press, 1949).

11. Fulgentius, *Mitologiarum* 2.8. In *Opera*, ed. Rudolf Helm (Leipzig: G. Teubner, 1898).

12. Boethius, *De consolatione Philosophiae*, prose 1. I have used the edition and translation of S. J. Tester in *Boethius* for the Loeb Classical Library (Cambridge, Mass.: Harvard University Press, 1973).

13. Queen Elizabeth, *Queen Elizabeth's Englishings*, ed. Caroline Pemberton (London: Early English Text Society, 1899), 3.

14. J. A. Mazzeo, "A Note on the 'Sirens' of *Purgatorio* 31.45," *Studies in Philology* 55 (1958): 457–63.

15. Natalis Comes, *Mythologiae* (Venice, 1567), fol. 226r–v.

16. Desiderius Erasmus, *Moriae Encomium*, ed. Clarence H. Miller, in *Opera Omnia*, series 4, vol. 3 (Amsterdam: North-Holland, 1979), 102.

17. Erasmus, *Moriae Encomium*, 100.

18. On Erasmus and Cicero, see Joan Simon, *Education and Society in Tudor England* (Cambridge: Cambridge University Press, 1966), 102–23. John Milton recommends Xenophon's moral writings in his treatise *On Education;* see his *Complete Poems and Major Prose*, ed. Merritt Y. Hughes (New York: Odyssey Press, 1957), 635.

19. Edmund Spenser, *The Faerie Queene* 2.12.31.1–2. I have used the edition of Thomas P. Roche Jr. (New Haven, Conn.: Yale University Press, 1981).

20. Sir Philip Sidney, *The Defence of Poesy*, in *Sir Philip Sidney*, ed. Katherine Duncan-Jones (Oxford: Oxford University Press, 1989), 234.

21. Sidney, *The Defence of Poesy*, 242.

22. Margaret Ferguson, *Trials of Desire: Renaissance Defenses of Poetry* (New Haven, Conn.: Yale University Press, 1983), 150.

23. Abraham Fraunce, *The Third Part of the Countesse of Pembrokes Yvychurch* (London, 1592), fol. 22 v.

24. Fraunce, fol. 22 v.

25. Fraunce, fol. 30 v.

26. Fraunce, fol. 48r.

27. Samuel Daniel, *Ulysses and the Syren*, lines 2, 5–6, in vol. 1 of *The Complete Works of Samuel Daniel*, ed. A. B. Grosbart (London: Hazell, Watson, and Viney, 1885).

28. Important studies of the Masque in Early Modern England include Enid Welsford, *The Court Masque* (Cambridge: Cambridge University Press, 1927), esp. 168–216; Kevin Sharpe, *Criticism and Compliment* (Cambridge: Cambridge University Press, 1987), 179–264; and Hugh Craig, "Ben Jonson, the Antimasque, and the 'Rules of Flattery,'" in *The Politics of the Stuart Court Masque*, ed. David Bevington and Peter Holbrook (Cambridge: Cambridge University Press, 1998), 176–96.

29. Ben Jonson, *The Masque of Blacknesse*, lines 291–300, in vol. 7 of *Ben*

Jonson, ed. C. H. Herford, Percy Simpson, and Evelyn Simpson (Oxford: Clarendon Press, 1941).

30. William Browne, *The Whole Works of William Browne,* ed. W. Carew Hazlitt (London: Roxburghe Library, 1869), 2:243.

31. Thomas Carew, *Coelum Brittanicum,* lines 174–75, in *The Poems of Thomas Carew,* ed. Rhodes Dunlap (Oxford: Clarendon Press, 1949).

32. Michael Drayton, *The Shepheards Sirena,* line 73, in vol. 1 of *Poems of Michael Drayton,* ed. John Buxton (Cambridge, Mass.: Harvard University Press, 1950).

33. John Milton, *Arcades,* lines 61–65 and 70–73. For Milton's works I have used Hughes's edition of the *Complete Poems and Major Prose.*

34. Lamberton, *Homer the Theologian,* 37, 52.

35. George Sandys, *Ovid's Metamorphosis: Englished, Mythologized, and Represented in Figures,* ed. Karl K. Hulley and Stanley T. Vandersall (Lincoln: University of Nebraska Press, 1970), 257.

36. Sandys, *Ovid's Metamorphosis,* 259.

"Longindyingcall"

Of Music, Modernity, and the Sirens

Lawrence Kramer

—bewitching fatal singers, the nixies and naiads, the Lorelei and (combers of combers and of hair in waves) the mermaids singing each to each, all the undulant forms of femininity calling from across the spray or under the wave, of the Rhinemaidens and the fair Melusine and Undine, the aspiring little mermaid of Hans Christian Andersen and the down-drifting one of Edward Burne-Jones, the one longing after the world of culture in the guise of love but struck dumb and no more able to walk on land, really, than she was underwater, the other rejecting the world of culture in the same guise, blank-faced and simpering, her arms tightly enwrapped about the naked man doubly castrated (loins and arms effaced) by her grasp and brought down to a cavern that contains, precisely, nothing:

Of these strange beings and their stranger spheres of being transvalued as means of making alternative worlds, home of lost continents, strange treasures, and sunken cathedrals, of shipwrecks and the dice of drowned men's bones that never abolished chance and of course those pearls that were his eyes, each and all scattered and changed yet purified and recognizable in the iris of the undulant watery lens, enhanced with the fluidity of the imaginary yet still contained within the gyres of the symbolic, dangerous, to be sure, but also emancipatory, revealing the possibility that ordinariness may yet be bathed in wonder and desire:

Of watery forms as a mode of philosophizing, a condensation and dream displacement of Hegel's proposition that the ocean gave humanity its original idea of the infinite, an *Aufhebung* in reverse whereby the high epic masterplot of civilization-building is destroyed yet invaluably preserved in a lower register, hard-headed and hard-hearted masculine aspiration both softened and fantasticated by immersion in the opalescent translucent medium identified with the feminine, the origin, and the end.

But perhaps it's time to break the surface of the waves and reason of these things more slowly.[1]

Loreleis, naiads, sirens, mermaids, and other undulant forms of dangerous femininity return in the nineteenth century to the waters from which the Enlightenment had banished them. They ply their seductive trade thereafter as projections—so the standard explanation goes—of masculine anxiety in a world of changing gender roles. The more women want, the more they demand access to public spheres and private pleasures, the more men worry about being lured by them into a fatal immersion:

> A mermaid found a swimming lad,
> Picked him for her own,
> Pressed her body to his body,
> Laughed; and plunging down
> Forgot in cruel happiness
> That even lovers drown.
> W. B. Yeats, "The Mermaid"[2]

This explanation cannot be gainsaid, especially with regard to the flood tide of fin-de-siècle paintings epitomized by Edward Burne-Jones's famous *The Depths of the Sea* (1887; fig. 6.1).[3] But fatal attraction is not the whole story. Burne-Jones's painting pretends nothing else is involved by the simple device of showing exactly that. It gives us virtually nothing but a male form in the fatal grip of a female one. Yeats's little poem does much the same. But this nothing is not a mere absence; it signifies. The loving but mindless grip of the mermaid's femininity effaces not only her victim's masculinity but also the symbolic foundation of his identity, his whole familiar world of signs, projects, and possessions. The painting makes this explicit in the bareness of the cavern to which its couple sinks, and it all but explicitly presents this effacement as a double castration—his arms gone, his loins a slot for the crook of her elbow. But far more is being

Figure 6.1. Edward Burne-Jones, *The Depths of the Sea*. Watercolor. Courtesy of the Fogg Art Museum, Harvard University Art Museums. Bequest of Grenville L. Winthrop. Photo: Katya Kallisen. Image copyright © 2004 by the President and Fellows of Harvard College.

effaced here than simple masculinity. Culture itself is stripped bare. Perhaps that's the point of the Venus de Milo arms: man is no longer *homo faber*, man the maker. The painting's mode of representation exceeds—but thereby also expands—its mythic content.

Numerous literary and, especially, musical treatments go even further in this direction. Not confined to or by seductive visualization, these media can suggest the rhythm, the timbre, the melodious strangeness of the sirens' song; they can listen better, be heard better. On that basis many of them suggest that post-Enlightenment sirens represent more than the *reductio ad absurdum* of the standard modern forms of gender construction, and more, even, than an alternative to them. To be sure, both the *reductio* and the alternative do matter; they can matter a great deal. But they matter as they do in the painting: in a form that exceeds, and thereby also expands, their mythic content. They range over the full field of ideology while pretending to inhabit only its fissures and edges. With alterative gender construction as a symbolic basis, the sirens, along with their watery sisters, represent an alternative to the standard modern forms of world construction. The sequence of evocations in Debussy's *Nocturnes for Orchestra* (1899) got the rhythm of it exactly right: a continuum runs from the cloud-world of shape-shifting fantasy ("Nuages") to the festive play of antinomian energy ("Fêtes") to the uncharted pursuit of the sirens' song ("Sirénes")—to which Debussy adds a wordless women's chorus, the undulant line of which literalizes the metaphor in the listener's ears. Fixed in his seat at the concert hall, the listener becomes the modern form of Odysseus tied to his mast, for whom the enchainment of the body makes possible the enchantment of the mind.

The sirens were called back to life in the nineteenth century not simply to help cope with modern forms of identity and desire, but to help cope with the form of modernity itself. In a multiplicity of versions and variants, the sirens and their song represent precisely what modernity and modern subjectivity have lost, precisely that which they must lose or alienate from themselves to become modern. For that very reason, the sirens also represent that which the modern must fantasize about regaining, even only in treacherous glimpses, and why, as Kafka tells us in his parable "The Silence of the Sirens," they are closest to the modern subject when he thinks he knows no more of them.[4]

These tropes are far from exhausted. As recently as 2000, Joel and Ethan Coen's film, *O Brother, Where Art Thou?*, made a loose transposition of *The Odyssey* to Depression-era Mississippi. Here one Ulysses Everett McGill and his companions are diverted from the road where they're driving—the archetypal action of modern American odysseys—to a wooded stream where the sirens, country girls in white shifts, sing while they wash their clothes. The soft-focus landscape bears no trace of the modern except the invisible presence of the camera that renders it. Shot in slight slow motion to accord with the singing, the scene might almost be imagined as set in the depths of the song, as if under water.

Or take the show planned for Las Vegas by *Cirque du Soleil* in 2003, as reported by the *New York Times*. The underwater scene here is not imaginary:

> The contortionist perched at the edge of a transparent basin like a nymph on the rim of a cocktail glass. She peeled off her bra and slid into the water, followed by a woman who was her near mirror-image. The two began a submerged dance less acrobatic than erotic: their backs arched, their arms twined, their legs moved in anatomically improbable ways. . . .
>
> Then, abruptly, the women shot to the surface and gulped at the air. "That will give you an idea of where we're going," explained Lyn Heward, the creative president of *Cirque du Soleil*, matter of factly.[5]

The leap from fantasy to, and as, the business of modernity could hardly be clearer. It is like a splash of cold water—in reverse.

The world below or beyond the waves, to which the sirens' or the mermaid's song beckons the voyager, is typically represented as the Nether Nightmare of misogynist fantasy, home of the subject as devoured or drowned. Stéphane Mallarmé's "Un Coup de dés" (A Throw of the Dice, 1895), a poem whose lines are strewn irregularly across successive pages in imitation both of the look of an orchestral score and the spread of debris after a shipwreck, plays darkly on Shakespeare's famous "Of his bones are coral made; / Nothing of him that doth fade / But doth suffer a sea-change / Into something rich and strange" (*The Tempest*, I.ii.398–401). The drowned master mariner, for whom "une stature mignonne ténebreuse / en sa torsion de sirène" (a delicate shadowy shape with the twist of a siren) has lodged within the plume of the fatal wave, finds

> son ombre puerile
> caressée et polie et rendue et lavée
> assouplie par la vague et soustraite
> aux durs os perdus entre les ais
> his childish shadow
> caressed and polished and rendered and washed
> suppled by the wave and withdrawn
> from the hard bones lost between the timbers[6]

In "Death by Water," the fourth section of *The Waste Land* (1922), T. S. Eliot displaces the sirens' song into the cry of gulls and describes the process of dissolution in a phrase packed with echoes of Shakespeare and Mallarmé both: "A current under sea / Picked his bones in whispers."[7]

But the water that thus transforms substance into shadow, leaving only the hard bones behind, also serves as a medium that jumbles, blurs, and transforms the constituents of the world above while still preserving their intelligibility. The preservation is both dangerous, because irrational —fluidity here belongs as much to categories as to bodies—and transfiguring. Borne on the sea swell, Eliot's drowned sailor enters a new mode of reflective awareness: "As he rose and fell / He passed the stages of his age and youth / Entering the whirlpool."[8] The dissolution of Mallarmé's mariner is followed by

> Fiançailles
>
> dont
>> le voile d'illusion rejailli leur hantise
>> ainsi que le fantome d'un geste

> [a] Betrothal
>
> whose
>> illusory veil splashed up its obsession
>> like the ghost of a gesture.

Betrothal as the upper world knows it finds its ghostly equivalent in betrothal to a siren, the play of whose illusory bridal veil is like the splash of a cresting wave. To trace such undulations across the page as both verbal music and visual image is the work of the poem's modernity. For Homer's Odysseus, the sirens' song is a lure to simple dissolution; for his modern descendants, the dissolution is the sirens' song itself, the pleasure of which is its own fatality. As Rilke puts it in his poem "Die Insel der Sirenen" (The Island of the Sirens, 1907), there is no defense against the knowledge that "es dort auf jenen / goldnen Inseln manchmal singt" (there on that golden island it sometimes sings).[9] "It" sings: just what or who does the singing scarcely matters. Whoever hears is immersed in the sea of fantasy.

Such immersion recalls an overrationalized modern mundanity to the fabulous time of legend and marvel. For Robert Schumann, Mendelssohn's concert overture *The Fair Melusine* (1834) should evoke a fairytale world in every listener, especially with the shimmering siren song that seems to immerse both the listener and the tale in an imaginary depth that restores a chastened reality to the condition of romance: "Here might grow vivid to everyone those happy images with which youthful fantasy delights to linger, those legends of life deep down on the ground of the waves, full of darting fish with golden scales, of pearls in open shells, of buried treasures that the sea has taken from men, of emerald castles towering up one atop another."[10] The depths of the sea systematically shift nature (the darting fish), art (those are pearls that were his eyes), commerce (the sunken treasure), and architecture (the emerald castles) into the register of enchantment. The multiplication of emerald castles is both comprehensive and climactic; it gives the suggestion not just of world-fragments, but of an alternative world with its own logic. To paraphrase in terms of a later, similar depiction, a great building—say a cathedral—in a modern city is a tourist site, an anachronism, and a familiar landmark. But a great building like the one evoked by Debussy's piano prelude "La Cathedral engloutie," the "engulfed cathedral" rising out of the waves and sinking beneath them again in a long, slow, endless rhythm—Mont-Saint-Michel as it looks, not as it is: a cathedral of which the musical image is built from processions of parallel chords rising or sinking over basses that plumb the depths of the keyboard in hollow resonant tones or murky undulations, occasionally relieved by splashes of high treble: a cathedral in the sea is a wonder.

This construal of the siren/mermaid trope in the modern era appears at its most explicit in two famous segments of Theodor Adorno's and Max Horkheimer's *Dialectic of Enlightenment* (1947). In the pages that follow, I will read backward from this text through its precursors in Kafka and Nietzsche, then forward through a series of musical instances of the modern siren from Mendelssohn through Wagner to Ravel. This sampling, in the shape of a wave that in breaking releases the siren within its plume, will survey the form taken by the watery trope in response to the rationalizing demands of modern enterprise culture, as Mary Douglas calls it.[11] Typically for the music of this era, this response embodies a reversion to an allure that has apparently been refused or at least contained. That reversion appears in its most restricted, resentment-laden form in Horkheimer and Adorno. With each step backward in textual time, it becomes looser and more rewarding, in alliance with musical imagery and a musicalized style. This retrospective tendency intensifies and plays forward when the narrative shifts to actual music and the image of the sirens' song becomes a symbolic rendering of its sound. What impels the tendency toward reversion is not just nostalgia for a beauty or pleasure not yet denuded of mystery, but the still more seductive call of critical intelligence: the exposure as ideological illusion of the need to resist such beauty or pleasure.[12]

In no case, however, will I suggest a comprehensive reading of any of these texts or pieces, and not just because of space constraints. As I've suggested elsewhere, "meaning, hermeneutically regarded, is not diffused evenly throughout a work of music (or anything else) but distributed unevenly in peaks and valleys. The peaks are the points of endowment"—installed by explicit sense-giving gestures, semantic performatives—"from which meaning extends to 'cover' the work as a whole."[13] My aim here is to trace the wavering course of the siren trope from peak to peak; to profile the trope by noting a series of open, obvious points at which its potentials for meaning are activated. The result should suggest an interpretation of the trope, at least within the limited horizon of my examples, while leaving the interpretation of the examples themselves incipient and underdetermined. In some cases what the work actually "says" or represents will be less important than the allure of a detail, a way of proceeding, a shift of expressive focus. This approach seems particularly appropriate for the sirens, whose paradigmatic effect is to appropriate all meaning and value to their song, so that the traveler who hears them wants—like Odysseus tied to his mast—only to leave the depleted shell of a world behind and deliver himself up to whatever the song portends.

Horkheimer and Adorno take Odysseus as the prototype of the alienated, overrationalized subject of Enlightenment, and the sirens episode of *The Odyssey* as his prototypical moment.[14] The allure of the sirens is the prospect of losing oneself in a past prior to the social and technological domination of nature; the sirens' song inevitably destroys the alienated subject who hearkens to it by promising, falsely, a "happy return" to the pre-enlightened state. Odysseus ratifies his identity as a—the—modern subject by creating a triple distance between himself and the beckoning song. First and foremost, he mobilizes the force of social domination, plugging his crew's ears with wax so that they can row him past the island of the sirens without themselves being touched by their singing. He is the master; he alone will be the hearer (*der Hörende*) who avoids bondage (*die Hörigkeit*). Second, he uses his famous wiliness to find the technical means to listen unharmed. He will be chained to the mast of his ship, unable to move, unable to order his deafened crew to turn back. With his arms bound, his ears will be free. His faith in this device comes from the third mechanism of distance, the use of his reason to find "a loophole [Lücke] in the contract [of his subjection], which enables him to fulfill the statute while evading it. The primeval contract does not anticipate whether the passing traveler listens bound or unbound to the song."[15] Purely a creature of instrumental reason, Odysseus feels entitled to heed the letter and break the spirit of the "contract" with neither regret nor scruple.

Horkheimer and Adorno are not impressed. Odysseus, they argue, degrades the sirens' song with the means he finds to hear it: "Odysseus recognizes the sublime archaic power [*archaisiche Übermacht*] of the song even as, technically enlightened [*technisch aufgeklärt*], he has himself bound. He yearns towards the song of pleasure and thwarts it as he does death [*Er neigt sich dem Liede der Lust und vereitelt sie wie den Tod*]."[16] Recognizing the song's primordial power is not the same as feeling it, and Odysseus can find no more in it than entertainment, a proto-bourgeois reduction of the song's unique enchantment to the "longing of the passerby [*Sehnsucht desser, der vorüberfärt*]". Or, as they also put it, he reduces the song from a compelling immediacy to "a mere object of contemplation, to art"; he treats the sirens' song like a casual concertgoer.[17] Worse yet, this fortunate-unfortunate (*glücklich-misglückten*) encounter has sickened (*erkrankt*) all subsequent song, so that "the whole of Western music labors against the contradiction of song in civilization, that nevertheless again proclaims the emotional power of all art music."[18] What we know as music is at best a parody of the sirens' song, a defensive appropriation of what we dare not hear.

Kafka's parable "The Silence of the Sirens" (ca. 1920) is less stringent. Like Horkheimer's and Adorno's, his Odysseus, here called Ulysses, is a technocrat proud of his wiles, a figure too competent for his own good, an allegorical embodiment of modern enterprise and concurrent lack of spirit. Perhaps because Kafka made an error, perhaps because he didn't, this Ulysses differs from Homer's original. He not only has himself bound to the mast, but also stops up his own ears with wax, not those of his crew; he does not want to hear the sirens at all. The parable puts a series of ironic spins on the fortunate-unfortunate results. The sirens know that "though admittedly such a thing has never happened, still it is conceivable that someone might possibly have escaped from their singing; but from their silence certainly never."[19] So they do not sing at all. Ulysses, hearing nothing, but not knowing that there is nothing to hear, mistakenly believes that his trick has worked. Yet he may not be wrong, because the look of bliss on his face seduces the sirens; it makes them forget their singing.

The ironies do not stop here, but cutting across their proliferation is a classic moment of epiphany that belongs both to the content of the parable and to its language. Ulysses sees for a moment the siren song he cannot hear, and the parable turns for a moment from detached reflection to absorbed lyricism: "For a fleeting moment he saw their throats rising and falling, their breasts lifting, their eyes filled with tears, their lips halfparted, but believed that these were accompaniments to the airs which died unheard around him."[20] Regardless of what Ulysses believes, the text presents the "accompaniments" as surrogates for the absent airs, the music of which sounds in the lyricism of the prose and underwrites the images that depict the moment as rhythmic, erotic, affecting, and enraptured. Admittedly, this is not the last word. Ulysses sails away and the ironies resume. Besides, the moment is an illusion. But so is Ulysses's triumph, even if we accept a "codicil" stating that he knew the sirens were silent and only pretended to mute the song they only pretended to sing. Either way, the sirens win as well as lose. Their silence, which is equivalent to the modern condition, is also the condition of possibility for imagining their song. As Rilke put it, the song is only the other side of the silence.

Silence is also the condition of the sirens' appearance in a key passage from Nietzsche's *The Gay Science* (1888). Acting in his own person as a modern subject rather than through a mythical deputy, Nietzsche comes too late to encounter the sirens themselves. But he can still find allegorical value in the material and symbolic forms that would once have made up such an encounter. He finds them in displaced bits and pieces of the imagery traditionally associated with them, or with their cousins the mermaids. And in displaced form, too, he hears them, even though, like their sisters in Kafka, they do not sing.

The passage begins with questions of hearing posed as Nietzsche wades amid the "burning of the breakers" [*inmitten des Brandes der Brandung*]: "Do I still have ears? Am I all ears and nothing else?" Then a ship sails by, mantled in "ghostly beauty":

> When a man is in the midst of his noise [*Lärm*], in the midst of the breakers of his plots and plans [*Würfen und Entwürfen*], perhaps he sees there calm enchanting beings glide past him, for whose happiness and retiringness [*Zürückgezogenheit*] he longs—*they are women.* He almost thinks that there with the women dwells his better self; that in these calm places even the loudest breakers become as still as death and life itself a dream of life. Yet! yet! my noble enthusiast, even in the most beautiful sailing ship there is so much noise, and so much petty, pitiable noise! The enchantment and the most powerful effect of woman is, in philosophical language, an effect at a distance, *actio in distans;* but there belongs thereto first and foremost—*distance.*[21]

Distance, it might be said, is the essential medium of the sirens' song. What is at stake in it here?

Overtly the passage seeks to reject the sirens, to affirm the Odyssean life of plots and plans regardless of the noise it makes. With Nietzsche, of course, the plots and plans are not willingly those of modern enterprise but those he requires to overcome it. The sirens represent an alternative that he would like to regard as regressive. But he cannot make the charge stick. The exclamatory "Yet! yet" that marks the turning point of his effort also marks its futility. The more pervasive effort of the passage is to enact the impossibility of rejecting the sirens, an action that cannot be carried out no matter how hard one tries, not least because one never tries as hard as one might. The sirens are still enchanting, too enchanting to let pass; they can be rejected only in terms that preserve their enchantment. This is implicit in Derrida's important reading of the passage:

> Woman's seduction works from a distance, the distance is the element of her power. But from this song, from this charm, it is necessary to keep one's distance, it is necessary to keep at a distance from distance, not only, as one might think, to protect oneself against this fascination, but also very much to succumb to it. It's *wanted,* this distance (which is wanting). *Il faut* la distance (qui faut).[22]

Derrida's comments are notable for restoring the sirens to Nietzsche's text, which makes no mention of their song or its charm, and for adding the implicit suggestion that for Nietzsche "siren" and "woman" are essentially synonyms. But they are not so much synonyms for each other as for the failure of critical reflection to unravel their enchantment. If distance enchants, then keeping one's distance from distance can only enchant the more.

But why do these sirens not sing? Their silence is not a stratagem like that of Kafka's sirens, but part of a broader pattern of reversal, or reversion, that endows the Odyssean quester with the sirens' own character. The quester in this passage is a centered figure, not a voyager; a figure of the shore, not of the ship; and a figure who does not hear, but sees, the object(s) of his desire. In each of these respects, the quester trades places with the sirens. Their song is his dream of silence, a dream that can never be fulfilled and that can be dreamed at all only amid the noise, the plots and plans, of the dreamer. The song is enchanting precisely because it must thus be dreamed. It is not the sailor who must elude the sirens, but the sirens who must elude the beached sailor—but who do so precisely so that, paradoxically, in their distance he can be moved by them, in their silence he can hear their song, and more, can, in the very texture of his prose, sing their song.[23]

A similar reversal underlies Mendelssohn's *The Fair Melusine,* a musical recounting of the legend of a mermaid who can assume human form and even marry, but only if she revisits her true shape by submerging herself once a week. According to Schumann, the overture consists of three types of music, representing in turn the "charming, yielding Melusine," her "proud, knightly" husband, Lusignan, and the rippling water, represented by a "magical wave figure" [*zauberischen Wellenfigur*], which alternately seems to envelop and divide the embracing couple.[24] All of these elements form complete sectional units, which the overture weaves into something like a sonata form. But this is a form that sounds the way a submerged object looks, drawn, so to speak, into a mermaid's "delicate shadowy shape" by the expressive allure of its topic. Form and expression continually vie with each other; the sections are arranged so as increasingly to problematize the impression of sonata, eventually to the point of dissolution. It is as if the archaic identification of music with feeling—that siren song—were drawing the ear away from the modern enterprise of reconciling feeling with form.

(Here the reader stops to hear the music. Failing that, to hear its silence.)

The overture begins tranquilly with reiterations of the justly famous wave figure; these apparently constitute the "first theme" of a standard sonata form in F major. The turbulent knightly music follows in F minor, at which point the formal trouble begins—in triplicate. In the standard form, energy precedes lyricism, not the other way around; the second theme is virtually never in the minor; and the two themes belong to different keys, not the different modes of the same key. The situation seems to right itself when Melusine's lyrical music subsequently enters in A-flat major, the key appropriate for a second theme when the first is in F minor. It now appears that the knightly and lyrical themes make up such a pair, expressively as well as tonally in the right order. They really do make a couple, with the music of the "charming, yielding" siren in her secular, domestic form presented as an adjunct to her husband's knightly pride, or knightly bluster, which returns to envelop the lyrical theme before the ensuing development. The wave music seems in retrospect like an introduction. Expressively primary, its evocative texture is formally secondary, setting the scene for a process it can adorn but not control.[25]

The development, where more knightly hubbub drives the lyrical theme to assume a turbulent form, would seem to confirm this impression were it not prefaced by a return of the wave music. This, the music of Melusine's other form—the form of her otherness—not only mimics the rippling of waves but also sets up a wavelike rhythm that ripples across the entire overture. Each time it appears the music seems self-sufficient, serenely unaffected by either the mood or the formal drama of the music around it. It next arises when the recapitulation flatly declines to bring back the supposed first theme with its knightly regalia, and puts a full restatement of the "introductory" wave music in its place. One result is to juxtapose this music with the return of the lyrical "Melusine" theme in its original "yielding" form, as if Melusine and her proper element were blissfully reuniting. The knightly music tries to intervene but washes harmlessly away. The scene of formal resolution dissolves the logic of the couple into the charm of the singular being who escapes all logic but her own. As if in protest, the knightly music makes one last appearance in the guise of a coda. But it is only a *faux* coda, or a failed one; the real coda belongs to the wave music, which returns yet again, expands to form a frame for the whole overture, evolves a group of exquisite farewell gestures, and quietly ebbs away.

In the end the siren prevails. Her song, the music of her element, sluices through and over the elements of a sonata form until the form blurs and fades. Yet it does not entirely fade; it does not even threaten to. The overture wants to overturn Odyssean illusions about the shipwreck of form, not to perpetuate them. Like the silence of the sirens in Kafka, the framing effect of the "magical wave figure" becomes significant only in relation to the form it eludes, the submerged and finally the absent presence that never stops mediating it. The wave-figure increasingly opens a utopian space outside the modern, progressive narrative embodied in the sonata-form couple, but, like a freshet, it takes its shape from sluicing along the contours of that narrative. The form is not destroyed; it is transformed. Polished and suppled, it suffers a sea-change.

Mendelssohn thus issues the claim that modern cultural anxieties about fluidity are groundless, or rather too earthbound. They are, he suggests, tied to a defensive sense of pragmatic rationality masquerading as an outdated nobility. The contrast between the wave figure and the knightly theme encapsulates this point. The wave figure varies but does not develop; mutable but continuous, it leads only to itself and luxuriates in its own presence. Its "magical" quality is the first thing we hear in it, as its throaty warble on solo clarinet becomes the murmuring of the strings in a collective dream. The knightly figure develops but does not vary. For all its motivic and developmental activity, it is rigid in its gestures and unable to escape the rigid codes that govern it. In context, its trumpet-and-drum rhetoric sounds in part like a proclamation of its own conventionality. The change of mode that unites and divides it from the wave music is something like a fall into modernity from a timeless or primordial realm. This is a modernity diminished by the transparency of its codes and techniques, the noise of its knightly enterprise. But the noise leaves the wave music undisturbed as, magical as ever, it calls from and recedes into the distance later celebrated by Nietzsche and Derrida.[26]

The opening of *Das Rheingold* (1854) is often thought to owe a resentful debt to the opening of Mendelssohn's overture. Wagner seems to recompose Mendelssohn's magical wave figure in order to invert its values; his version will be ambivalent, not merely attractive; complex, even tortuous, rather than simple; and deep where (from Wagner's fraught ideological perspective) Mendelssohn's is superficial.[27] These differences are particularly pointed with respect to the fall into modernity, which in Wagner cannot be divided neatly between masculine purpose and feminine temptation. To be sure, when the Nibelung dwarf Alberich renounces love in favor of the gold cared for by the Rhinemaidens, he embodies— among other things—the heartless spirit of modern enterprise as Wagner conceived it. But his action also reenacts a fall already traversed by the Rhinemaidens themselves, and in the place one would least expect for such sirens: in their song.

The action of the *Ring* cycle begins with that song. More exactly, it begins with the Rhinemaidens' transition to song from amid a rippling stream of soft, undulant nonsense syllables. Voice emerges from the instrumental Prelude to initiate the drama by progressing into speech. But to venture a reading of this event we need to immerse ourselves in the time before voice.

According to Wagner himself, the *Rheingold* Prelude is based on an evocation of "rapidly flowing water" represented by "the musical sound of the E-flat major chord, which continually surges forward in a figured arpeggiation; these arpeggios appear as melodic figurations of increasing motion, yet the pure E-flat triad never changes, and seems through its persistence to impart infinite significance to the [watery] element."[28] The music unfolds slowly in a continuous additive pattern that begins with a single E-flat at the bottom of the orchestra and ends with what Warren Darcy calls "a collage of six different ostinati" swirling simultaneously.[29] The evolution from a single, murky, unmeasured tone, reinforced by audible overtones, to a complex, transparent, measured texture suggests a passage from the static condition of primordial harmony to the rhythm of historical time. This movement, however, is not yet that of a fall or alienation, as the unchanging harmony, with its "infinite significance," affirms. Each new phase in the music reinscribes the primordial unity at its origin. The rupture that designates modernity has not yet occurred.

That begins to change when a Rhinemaiden's voice enters the scene, bringing with it the first change of harmony. Woglinde makes the pivotal utterance, mingling her nonsense syllables with phonetically similar words so that, for a moment, there is little distinction to be made between articulate speech and pure vocalic wave motion without meaning:

> Weia! Waga! Woge, du Welle!
> Walle zur Wiege! Wagalaweia!
> Walala weiala weia!

> Weia! Waga! Well up, you wave!
> Waft to a womb-bed! Wagalaweia!
> Wallala weiala weia![30]

The mingling of liquid utterance with lyrical melody creates a new form of magical wave figure that leaves any sense of rupture with the origin unacknowledged. To make it so is perhaps the very definition of a siren song. But when the Rhinemaidens thereafter move from voice to speech, when they begin to discuss who they are and what they ought to do, they introduce at a stroke all the elements of modernity that have so far been held in suspension: narrative, history, responsibility, law, the possibility of transgression, the seeds of retribution. When Alberich comes along, as he does all too quickly, an inevitable intruder, he simply initiates the repetition as action of the alienated condition that informs the siren song as irony. The one is as implicit in the other as the E-flat triad is implicit in the overtones of the originary tone.

Wagner thus gives a dark new turn to an old idea. The identification of the transition from voice to speech as the mark of the human dates at least back to Aristotle and had been revived by Jakob Grimm as recently as 1851.[31] The wave music of Mendelssohn's Melusine can also be heard as a revival of this idea; the rippling phrase that flows through it is heard most often passing between solo instrumental voices, primarily the two clarinets and first flute, before spreading to the strings, as if it were a wandering voice whose domain is the liminal space between the vocally articulate and the verbal.[32] The siren in this context represents the original power and pleasure of voice apart from the speech to which voice is drawn as powerfully as it draws the desire of those who speak.

But this is very far from the end of the story. For Wagner the origin and its echo in the siren song do not so much belong to the past as to the depths beneath the present, represented by the depths of the Rhine. That the Ring ultimately returns to those depths, ending where it began, is one of the most famous things about it. That this ending involves an extended reprise of the "Weia! Waga!" melody suggests that the reinscription of the origin, or at least the smallest of departures from it, is a permanent pos-

sibility even when the consequences of the fall into modernity are cata-
strophic. "Yet! yet"—and here the weight of Wagner's ambivalence can be
felt—that the melody returns only in the orchestra, not in a Rhinemaiden's
voice, suggests that to voice it, to realize the perennial possibility of re-
inscribing primordial harmony in historical time, would be to risk catastrophe all over again. It is only, Wagner seems to say, in the fleeting
moment of its first—or last—utterance that the siren song can keep the
promise it cannot keep from making.

This implication is perhaps anticipated in the first act of Wagner's
Tannhäuser (1845), which begins by representing the song of the classical
sirens themselves: an unaccompanied, and quite ravishing, lyric for a
small group of women's voices. This instance is exceptional with respect to
the trope described in this essay, thanks to a contradiction between the
dramatic and musical "plots" of the opera. Tannhäuser's relationship to
modernity is conceived along lines current among the German Romantics
around the turn of the nineteenth century: he is caught between the
finitude of the classical world and the Christian discovery of the infinite.
His antithetical beloveds, Venus and the saintly Elisabeth, personify the
choice between these alternatives, which he is never unequivocally able to
make; the sirens represent the essence of what holds him back. Musically,
however, the sirens are seductive precisely for their modernity, which
offers the hero—who is also, of course, a minstrel—a different mode of
infinity: the infinite ambiguity of a five-note chord that resolves only to a
discord and has no fixable identity, and which, perhaps for that very
reason, is possessed of an extraordinary sensuousness and sweetness. This
allure, like that of the women on Nietzsche's passing ship, depends on
action at a distance. Once heard, the sirens' voices recede into the "far
distance," presumably offstage, from which they are heard again later in
the act in a fragmentary reprise, thereafter to be heard no more. Fading
away is their mode of being. Proximity would destroy the promise of these
voices, as the events set in motion when Alberich accosts the Rhinemaidens will later prove. The Ring concludes by receding into the distance
of the sirens' song—and of their silence. It returns to the space of promise
apart from fulfillment.

German composers, of course, were not the only ones interested in
that promise, as my earlier references to Debussy acknowledge. Like their
counterparts in Debussy's slightly earlier Nocturnes, the three movements
of Ravel's piano suite Gaspard de la nuit (1908, based on poems by Aloys
Bertrand) form an allegorical sequence, one reading of which turns on the
wish to escape the stringencies of modernity.

As its title suggests, the central movement, "Le Gibet" [The Gallows], evokes a scene of punishment, fatality, the imposition of reason by law; the inexorability of these constraints finds its musical correlative in an ostinato on a single note that tolls throughout the piece. The outer movements lie beyond the boundaries of law and reason. The first, "Ondine," is the siren song. Although the associated poem represents a failed temptation—the narrator, betrothed to a mortal woman, rejects the water-nymph's call to rule in her moonlit palace beneath a lake—the music concentrates entirely on evoking the temptress. Ravel's Ondine is a creature of shimmering impalpability. She is associated primarily with high-treble tremolos, glissandi, and arpeggios that swirl around the melodic line and, at climactic moments, obliterate it, releasing more turbulent wave figures that span the keyboard. The process is continuous, and in its continuity seems completely unmoralized; the charm and the turbulence simply come and go, inextricably folded into each other.[33]

Neither, however, seems a match for the *Grand Guignol* horrors of the gibbet. For that the third movement is required, a portrait of the malicious imp known as Scarbo. A kind of punk Puck, Scarbo is a figure of pure antinomian energy; the music that depicts him is spiky, burly, scurrying, and belligerent. His special affinity is for the deep, growling bass, in pointed contrast to Ondine's shimmering treble; the depths he comes from are visceral, not glassy. And yet—another yet!—even Scarbo is susceptible to the charms of Undine. At about its two-thirds point, after a protracted spell of deep-bass growling, the imp's musical profile reverts to the siren's. Despite some efforts to turn the reversion to parody, the music clears and softens, evoking Ondine's rippling texture and slipping for a moment into a distant paraphrase of the wave-caressed melodic tracery of the earlier movement. There is nothing so definite—nothing so crude—as a quotation; the moment is already dissolving even as it forms; but its effect, imbued with a Mallarméan aura of precise but nebulous suggestiveness, is just for that reason the perfect reminiscence of a siren song.

The impalpability of this reminiscence may stem not only from Symbolist aesthetics, but also from the kind of anti-narrative impulse already noted in Mendelssohn and Wagner. After all, sirens exist to interrupt a voyage, the most ancient of templates for narrative. By avoiding literal quotation, Ravel can have Ondine interrupt Scarbo's narrative without regressing to a counter-narrative. The siren song thus defines itself by, or as, music's reflective withdrawal from the narrativity that is one of its chief links to the work of culture.

For the listener who yields to its charm, the song's action at a distance casts a shape-shifting spell. The apparition of Ondine in "Scarbo" turns

Gaspard de la nuit into a reflection on the grim consequences of rejecting Ondine and her world, or rather of trying to reject them, since the rejection proves impossible. "Scarbo," to be sure, moves on from this moment of reversion and reflection and finishes with its raw, vital energy intact. But the reversion cannot be undone, only ignored, and the ignoring of it may seem to give Scarbo's rampages an edge of panic that is harder to ignore. Where the energy of Debussy's "Fêtes" seems to liberate a responsiveness to the sirens' song, the energy of Ravel's "Scarbo" tries and fails to compensate for the song's receding. To the charms of the watery world, it can oppose only a great deal of Nietzschean noise: for Scarbo, too, is a creature of plots and plans, even if only in travesty. In him the bullying of Mendelssohn's Lusignan, the grasping of Wagner's Alberich, and the violence that Horkheimer and Adorno saw in instrumental reason, all find their inverted image. Ondine tells us so, the phantoms of her siren song and magical wave figure still acting at a distance, in the voice of another reason.

The watery world is attractive as a liminal medium because the boundaries of the masculine body and body-ego, the appointed vehicle of the modern subject, Odysseus updated, must continually be reaffirmed, traced against the solid impalpability of water as by the spindly figure of the stooped, sickly Nietzsche wading an imaginary Mediterranean, willing his way into the water or the thought thereof because the masculinity he inherits is defined as the will and the willingness to risk the mixing, the improper existence signified and enacted by fluidity, in order to become once more unmixed, a process that is also a political economy because water has no proper, observes no propriety, cannot be property, a dispossession that is the constant theme, the melos and melody, of the siren song that he both hears and ventriloquizes, song and wave and woman alike signifying and enacting the pleasures of mixing (Melville's Ishmael and Queequeg in the slippery union of squeezing lumps of whale sperm into fluid, the shoppers at Zola's department store The Ladies' Paradise drifting away on the liquescent fantasies induced by their softing silks), melting pleasures that in the masculine libidinal economy must (but can't) be disavowed because they are the pleasures (yes, of course, the pleasures, since we are speaking here of imaginary bodies, no more capable of being wounded than an animated cartoon) of castration (which must not, lest we honor the fantasy too much, be the last word, from the absence of which the sirens may infer that there should be no last word at all, absolutely no la

NOTES

1. Evocative language or no, academic protocol requires the identification of several of the allusions in these paragraphs. The mermaids calling and combing allude to T. S. Eliot's poem "The Love Song of J. Alfred Prufrock" (1909) and "the dice of drowned men's bones" to Hart Crane's "At Melville's Tomb" (ca. 1926), which itself may allude to Eliot's *The Waste Land* (1922) and to Stéphane Mallarmé's "Un Coup de dés jamais ne abolira le hasard" (A Throw of the Dice Will Never Abolish Chance, 1895), also alluded to (and subsequently discussed) here. G. W. F. Hegel's statement about the sea is from the Introduction to his *The Philosophy of History* (1830–1831), trans. J. Sibree (New York: Dover, 1956), 90. The allusions to Herman Melville and Emile Zola in the final paragraph of this essay refer to chaps. 94 and 4, respectively, of their novels *Moby-Dick* (1851) and *The Ladies' Paradise* (1883). The "Longindying call" of the title is from the "Sirens" chapter of James Joyce's *Ulysses* (New York: Random House, 1961), 256, an epitomizing phrase that is also an homage to a text too complex to be discussed in these pages.

2. No. III of "A Man Young and Old" from *The Tower* (1928), in *Collected Poems of W. B. Yeats* (London: Macmillan, 1967), 250.

3. For a comprehensive survey, with illustrations, see Bram Djikstra, *Idols of Perversity: Fantasies of Feminine Evil in Fin-de-Siècle Culture* (New York: Oxford University Press, 1986), 35–271.

4. The literature on modernity is too vast for citation. Classic starting points for its definition (especially for the tradition canvassed by this essay) include Max Weber, "Science [Wissenschaft] as a Vocation" (1917) and "Religious Rejections of the World and Their Directions" (1915) in *From Max Weber: Essays in Sociology,* ed. H. H. Gerth and C. Wright Mills (New York: Oxford University Press, 1958), 129–58 (esp. 138–49) and 323–59 (esp. 333–57); see also Charles Taylor, *Sources of the Self: The Making of the Modern Identity* (Cambridge, Mass.: Harvard University Press, 1989); and Anthony J. Cascardi, *The Subject of Modernity* (Cambridge: Cambridge University Press, 1992).

5. From Guy Treblay, "After Nice, a Return to Vice," from *The New York Times,* Sunday, June 8, 2003, sec. 9, 1.

6. Translation of this and the subsequent passage modified from Mallarmé, *The Poems: A Bilingual Edition,* trans. Keith Bosley (Harmondsworth: Penguin, 1977), 272.

7. T. S. Eliot, *Collected Poems, 1909–1962* (New York: Harcourt, Brace and World, 1963), 65.

8. Compare Arthur Rimbaud, "Le Bateau ivre" (The Drunken Boat), ll. 21–24: "je me suis baigné dans le Poème / De la Mer . . . ou, flottaison bléme / Et ravie, un noyé pensif parfois descend" (I bathed in the Poem / Of the Sea . . . where, flotsam pale / And enraptured, a pensive drowned man sometimes sinks); from Rimbaud, *Complete Works, Selected Letters,* trans. and ed. Wallace Fowlie (Chicago: University of Chicago Press, 1966), 117; translation modified.

9. From Rainer Maria Rilke, *New Poems, The German Text with a Translation, Introduction, and Notes by J. B. Leishman* (New York: New Directions, 1964), 168, my translation.

10. From Georg Eismann, ed., *Robert Schumann: Ein Quellenwerk Über Sein Leben und Schaffen* (Leipzig: Breitkopf und Härtel, 1956), 77, my translation.

11. Mary Douglas, "The Person in an Enterprise Culture," in *Understanding the Enterprise Culture: Themes in the Work of Mary Douglas,* ed. Shaun H. Heap and Angus Ross (New York: Norton, 1992), 41–62.

12. On reversion and music in the post-Enlightenment era, see chap. 2 of my *Classical Music and Postmodern Knowledge* (Berkeley: University of California Press, 1995), esp. 43–51. It is worth noting that the most explicit theorization of reversion and its troubles, Horkheimer and Adorno's rereading of the Homeric sirens, is also the latest. An implicit part of my argument here is that, in a typical effect, the belated theorization crystallizes a discourse that has already circulated for a long time, and that in this case—and this is *not* exceptional—all but begins in actual music. It might even not be going too far to speculate, given Adorno's preoccupation with Wagner, that the mythography of the sirens in *Dialectic of Enlightenment* is in part a response to Wagner's *Ring* cycle, to which this essay will turn at an important juncture.

13. From my "Yesterday's Moonlight: Chopin, Beethoven, and the Hermeneutics of Resemblance," in *D'une herméneutique de la musique,* ed. Christian Hauer (forthcoming).

14. On the relation of these paradigms to the general project of Horkheimer and, especially, Adorno, see Richard Leppert's Introduction to Theodor W. Adorno, *Essays on Music,* selected, with introduction, commentary, and notes, by Richard Leppert (Berkeley: University of California Press, 2002), 27–31.

15. Max Horkheimer and Theodor W. Adorno, *Dialektik der Aufklärung: Philosophische Fragmente* (1947; reprint, Amsterdam: Verlag de Munter, 1989), 76; my translation.

16. Horkheimer and Adorno, *Dialektik,* 76.

17. Horkheimer and Adorno, *Dialektik,* 48.

18. Horkheimer and Adorno, *Dialektik,* 76.

19. "The Silence of the Sirens," trans. Willa and Edwin Muir, in Franz Kafka, *The Complete Stories,* ed. Nahum N. Glatzer (New York: Schocken, 1971), 430–32.

20. Kafka, "The Silence of the Sirens," 431.

21. From section 60 of *The Gay Science;* the translation here is adapted from that of Barbara Harlow in Jacques Derrida, *Spurs: Nietzsche's Styles / Eperons: Les Styles de Nietzsche* (Chicago: University of Chicago Press, 1979), 47. Derrida begins his discussion of this section with the provocative observation that "All of Nietzsche's investigations, and in particular those which concern women, are coiled in the labyrinth of an ear" (43).

22. Derrida, *Spurs,* 48, my translation.

23. In section 310 of *The Gay Science,* "Will and Wave," another marine encounter reanimates the mermaids much as section 60 does the sirens. Nietzsche

again represents himself as standing amid the breakers, but this time his interest goes to the bodies of the waves themselves. The result is the creation of a sub-aqueous world in which erotic-romantic energy is indistinguishable from uncon-strained enjoyment of the will to power: "arch your dangerous green bodies as high as you can, raise a wall between me and the sun—as you are doing now! Truly, even now nothing remains of the world but green twilight and green lightning. Carry on as you like, roaring with overweening pleasure and malice [Übermut]—or dive again, pouring your emeralds down into the deepest depths, and throw your infinite white mane of foam and spray over them: Everything suits me, for everything suits you so well, and I am so well-disposed toward you for everything." From *The Gay Science,* trans. Walter Kaufmann (New York: Random House, 1974), 247–48.

24. Eismann, *Quellenwerk,* 1956), 77, my translation.

25. For a more detailed account of the formal design of the movement, together with information about the genesis of the overture, see Thomas Grey, "The Orchestral Music," in *The Mendelssohn Companion,* ed. Douglass Seaton (Westport, Conn.: Greenwood Press, 2001), 475–83.

26. The expressive contrasts of Mendelssohn's overture might be said to return, on a larger scale and with an infusion of a postwar melancholy, to organize Hans Werner Henze's romantic ballet *Undine* (1957). Here the plot takes a siren's twist and celebrates the hero's death by water as a triumph of love that unites him with the water nymph.

27. Wagner might be said to treat Mendelssohn himself here as a kind of siren, but one who can, so to speak, be outsung by the Odyssean artist-voyager whom he tempts. In the background of this song contest (shades of *Tannhäuser,* of which more below), Wagner chose to resist Mendelssohn's siren song by identify-ing it as Jewish within an anti-Semitic discourse, most pungently in the infamous pamphlet *Judaism in Music* (1850). But Mendelssohn for that very reason remains a presence in this music, while a figure such as E. T. A. Hoffmann—whose opera *Undine* (1816), based on the novella of that name by Friedrich de la Motte Fou-quet, is another of Wagner's sources—does not.

28. From Wagner's *Mein Leben* [My life], 1869; translated by Warren Darcy in his "*Creation ex nihilo:* The Genesis, Structure, and Meaning of the *Rheingold* Prelude," *19th-Century Music* 13 (1989): 79–100, at 79. I have changed the tenses here from past to present.

29. Ibid., 97.

30. To preserve the alliteration, I've fabricated "womb-bed" as a translation of "Wiege," cradle.

31. Aristotle's formulation appears in the *Politics,* 1253a, 10–18; for a discus-sion, see Giorgio Agamben, *Homo Sacer: Sovereign Power and Bare Life,* trans. Daniel Heller-Roazen (Stanford: Stanford University Press, 1998), 7–8. Grimm's statement is in his "On the Origin of Language," trans. Ralph R. Read III in *German Romantic Criticism,* ed. Leslie Willson (New York: Continuum, 1982), 262–69.

32. On the trope of wandering voice, see the Epilogue, "Voice and Its Beyonds," to my *Opera and Modern Culture: Wagner and Strauss* (Berkeley: University of California Press, 2004).

33. In her playful self-sufficiency, Ravel's Undine may look forward to the narrator of Laurie Anderson's *Blue Lagoon* (from Anderson's album *Mister Heartbreak,* 1984), a figure who, instead of attracting men, merges the traditionally masculine persona of the castaway into the figure of the mermaid. This is a woman's mermaid—one of the few. My thanks to Paul Attinello for calling my attention to the song.

SEVEN

Russian *Rusalka*s and Nationalism

Water, Power, and Women

Inna Naroditskaya

The Russian *rusalka*—a cousin of sirens, lorelei, naiads, undines, and mermaids—is specific to Russia's history and culture.[1] There are two siren-like creatures in Russia, the terrestrial woman-bird *sirin*,[2] and the water-inhabiting *rusalka*. Carved at the base of columns on St. Basil's Bridge near the St. Petersburg Admiralty and leading sailors seaward from the prows of Russian vessels, the fishtailed *rusalka*,[3] not the landlocked *sirin*, became a symbol of military expansion to the seas in the eighteenth century.

Opening a window to the West (via the Baltic Sea), the Russian empire emerged as a European state, its aristocracy rapidly acquiring a taste for Western art and fashion, its society molded by a drastic reformation advanced by four female monarchs whose reign of nearly two-thirds of the eighteenth century defined and redefined gender. In the next century, marked by the restoration of patriarchal leadership, Russian male authors repeatedly invoked images of the *rusalka*, exploring, commenting on, and constructing links between gender and power, metaphorically connected with femininity and water.

Water

Images of water—rivers, lakes, seas, clouds, and fountains—pervade the poetry of Gavrila Derzhavin (1743–1816), a forefather of Russian classical literature: "steppes floating like seas," "streaming rivers of delightful tears," "swimming golden moon," the "last day of nature that spilled into a river of stars," and love that "poured into the soul."[5] Though the turbulence and randomness of water imagery appealed to romantic poets elsewhere in Europe, bodies of water were especially reflective of the historical particularities of eighteenth-century Russia, whose military campaigns provided enormously important access to the Baltic, Black, and Azov Seas.[6] The establishment of the Russian empire as a naval power was manifested in the erection of one of the youngest European capitals, St. Petersburg. The city, built on a swamp bordering the Neva River, carried the name of its founder and embodied the aspirations of his successors, especially Catherine II, who was venerated by Russian poets linking water with royalty and power.

In Russian narratives of the late eighteenth and nineteenth centuries, water also became associated with female suicide. The gallery of heroines dying by throwing themselves into water includes Nikolai Karamizin's Liza (*Poor Liza,* 1792), Alexander Ostrovsky's Katerina (*The Storm,* 1859), Nikolai Leskov's Grusha, "swallowed up" by water ("The Enchanted Wanderer," 1873), and also Leskov's Katerina, who, "without removing her gaze from the dark waters," pulled herself and her rival into a river (*Lady Macbeth of Mtsensk,* 1865). Leo Tolstoy's Anna Karenina (*Anna Karenina,* 1878), stepping in front of an approaching *steam* train, has a feeling "like that she had experienced, when preparing to enter the water in bathing."[7]

Ippolit Bogdanovich's "Dushen'ka" (1783) and Karamzin's *Poor Liza* exemplify early Russian female suicide plots connected with water. In the Bogdanovich work, the sacrificial act ends unsuccessfully—animated singing pikes (actually naiads[8]) save the heroine and carry her to shore. Suicide is completed in Karamzin's story, when Liza, a peasant girl, seduced and promised eternal love by an aristocrat, throws herself into a river. Alexander Pushkin (1799–1837), of the next literary generation, creates a character reminiscent of Karamzin's unfortunate heroine Rusalka in his drama *Rusalka.*[9] In his version, the tragic suicide is not the end of the story; in the afterlife, the peasant girl becomes the tsarina of a water kingdom, a powerful and merciless *rusalka.* The traditional legend of Rusalka connects sacrifice with vengeance, reality with magic, classical poetry with folklore, and Christian Orthodoxy with paganism.[10]

The interplay of water, power, feminine sacrifice, and *volshebstvo* (fairytale magic)[11] became a major theme in Russian nineteenth-century operas. Although as dangerous to men as Homeric sirens, powerful magical heroines in some of these works perform self-sacrificial rituals—turning into a river (Rimsky-Korsakov's *Sadko*) or melting and evaporating into clouds (Rimsky-Korsakov's *Snow Maiden*) for the sake of their romantic lovers. Love and suicide turn Pushkin's and Dargomyzhsky's mortal heroine Natasha into a magical water sprite endowed with a desire to avenge men. Rusalka belongs to a "particular brand" of heroine that Susan McClary analyzes, a nymph "fixated on memories of a lover who has abandoned her—who has awakened her sexually and has left her with no outlet for that excess."[12] She also matches what Ralph Locke identifies as a "primary [female] stereotype: the dangerous woman who holds no allegiance and thus disturbs the placid world of good bourgeois wives and husbands."[13] Locke ponders whether such dangerous women disturb or reinforce social morality—an issue I will revisit in the analysis of two *Rusalkas,* Pushkin's dramatic poem (1832) and Dargomyzhsky's opera (1855), which echoed and simultaneously moved away from the ideals of eighteenth-century Russia toward the nationalistic, patriarchal nineteenth-century state. In the opera a "discursive space" between narrative and music has the paradoxical effect Abbate describes in Western European opera of the same period: the simultaneous empowerment and defeat of women.[14] Another discursive space can also be observed between Dargomyzhsky's opera and Pushkin's poem, on which the opera is based. Untangling the hermeneutic complexity that occurs within these spaces requires a study of many contextual facets[15] of the *Rusalkas*—the relationship of the poem and the opera to both European and Russian narratives; the poetic and musical conventions that reveal the interplay of gender, Russian history, and nationalism; and the dichotomies between drama and opera, opera and ballet, fire and water, female voice and muteness.

Who Is Rusalka?

The Russian *rusalka* is "light like a nocturnal shadow, white like early snow" (Pushkin), dazzling like the "twinkle of a serpent" (Lermontov), with "shining eyes looking through dark-*rusye* [blond hair] . . . woven with seaweed" (Gogol). A beautiful maiden, she "plays, splashing in the waves, laughs and cries like a child" (Pushkin), is "joined by her sisters in a dancing-circle," and sings a lullaby to her knight forever sleeping on the bottom of the sea. Rusalka's complexity begins with her very name.

The word *rusalka* is related to "Rus," the old name for Russia, and also to the singular noun for a Russian person (*russkii*). Some associate *rusalka* with *ruslo* (riverbed). In the literary world of Pushkin, Rusalka can be seen as a female counterpart of *Ru*slan, a legendary figure who represents Russian masculinity, heroism, bravery, and strength. Another possible source of the word *rusalka* is *rusii*, "reddish blond," often the color of mermaid hair.[16] The image of the *rusalka* occupies an important place in the ancient traditions of various Slavic tribes and groups. The term is also linked to pre-Christian rituals called *rusalii*, which included celebrations, offerings, and exorcisms intended to remove the powers of a *zalozhnaya* woman (*zalozhnaya* means prematurely dead from suicide).[17]

The *rusalka* is closely connected with European mermaids—amazing, passionate creatures, half-fish and half-woman, who rise from dark water to play dangerous games with men, and whose power is linked to their voices. Through centuries of Christianity, these water sprites came to represent unrestrained and irresistible sexuality, illicit paganism, and the chaos of creation. Despite her kinship to European cousins, the *rusalka* is a distinct creature. Unlike many mermaids and undines, who yearn to exchange their voices, hair, and kingdoms for human feelings, *rusalka*s are half-magic and half-human—once-earthly women inflamed by love and burned by betrayal. Though in their afterlife, vengeful *rusalka*s are commonly associated with water, they also inhabit the forest, where they merge with another relative, the Wila, "a spirit known all over Russia and other Slavonic lands, . . . the bride [that] continued to seek after death the joys of which she had been deprived."[18] Like a Wila, the *rusalka* may wear a bridal dress and flowery tiara. Or not. She may also appear naked, wrapped in her wet hair, or she may wear royal garb, turning into a mighty tsarina.

The dreadful and playful *rusalka*s despise live women; mesmerize or tickle men to death; kidnap children; steal clothes, milk, and bread; and swing by their hair in the depths of the forest, terrifying villagers and travelers with their laughter. At the same time, *rusalka*s may capriciously save children, and some believe that grass and wheat grow better in places where they dance.[19]

The versatile singing and dancing *rusalka* was attractive to poets and musicians. Her ability to draw on Western European, Slavic, and Russian mythologies, and to mediate between folk and classical literature, made her a poignant image for nineteenth-century artists searching for a nationalist narrative. At the same time, her sensuality unleashed the male sexual imagination—the splashing waves of her hair, "waves tickling curved shoulders," the "dazzling emerald of her eyes" (Mai), "her feverish lips and flashing cheeks, eyes luring [men's] souls . . . herself burning with passion" (Gogol). This image of the *rusalka* or *zalozhnaya* suggests that

eroticism, malevolence, and metamorphosis are inherent to female nature, a notion nourished beyond the tales of *rusalka*s by many romantic
artists.[20]

Literary Rusalkas

The water sprites and *rusalka*s Pushkin created in several poems and
three major works are closely related to other watery European heroines:
Fouqué's Undine (1811), Goethe's Melusine, Heine's Loreley (1823), Andersen's Mermaid (1836), and Hoffman's Undine (1813–1814). In Russia,
Fouqué's *Undine*[21] was read in French—the mother tongue of the native
nobility—and in the poetic translation of Zhukovsky,[22] who issued his
verse translation of *Undine* in 1830, a year before Pushkin began his
Rusalka.[23] German counterparts were likewise well known. The operatic
Undine, by German romantic E. T. A. Hoffmann, was not staged in Russian theaters, but, according to Norman Ingham, the "remote Russians"
were among the first (as early as 1822) to print Hoffmann's works in
translation. Ingham reflects that "from several sources we know that
Hoffmann had a vogue in the circles of Petersburg which Pushkin frequented, and that a manifestation of it was the improvising of fantastic
tales."[24]

Though Pushkin is glorified for bringing native mythology and folk
characters into the domain of Russian classical literature,[25] his heroine and
his story echoed the singspiel *Das Donauweibchen* [The Woman of the
Danube] by the Viennese composer Ferdinand Kauer and writer Karl
Hansler (1798). Successful in Austria, the opera was adapted by Russians
who, following common practice of the day, russified the names of the
main characters,[26] relocated the story from the Danube to the Dnepr, and
accordingly changed the title to *Dneprovskaya Rusalka*.[27] Throughout the
first half of the nineteenth century, this four-sequel soap opera[28] remained
a theatrical hit, with one or more sequels shown annually, further stirring
the imagination of poets and musicians.[29]

Pushkin owned three volumes of *Dneprovskaya Rusalka* and knew it
well enough to refer to it in *Eugene Onegin*.[30] The parallels between Pushkin's *Rusalka* and its Austrian-Russian predecessors are apparent—the
birth of Rusalochka, the wedding, the appearance of the *rusalka* in the
middle of the grand wedding celebration, and the depiction of the underwater kingdom. Using elements from European popular culture, Pushkin
fed the Russian fascination with native tales and myths, which from the
end of the eighteenth century were intensely collected and, as in Western

Europe, aligned with national identity. Unlike her various European counterparts, Pushkin's heroine is mortal; although she possesses enormous magic power, she is driven by a woman's feelings and desires. In this, Pushkin and his contemporaries followed the same literary path, including Orest Somov[31] in his short story "Rusalka" (1829) and Gogol in his portrayal of a *rusalka* as a *zalozhnaya* in *Evenings on the Farm near Dikanka* (1831).

Pushkin's Rusalkas

Pushkin frequently referred to water sprites in his poems and wrote three major works about *rusalkas*. In his short poem "Rusalka" (1819), Pushkin describes encounters between an old monk and a *rusalka* who comes from the bubbling waters and sits on the shore, gazing at the monk, brushing her wet hair, and luring him into deep water.[32] In 1819, the same year that Pushkin wrote his *Rusalka*, his friend and rival Zhukovsky issued a poetic translation of Goethe's "Fisherman" (1779), in which "the water rushes, the water swells" and "the gurgling waves arise; a maid, all bright with water drops" lures an old fisherman to "the misty heaven-deeps."[33] Five years later, a water sprite again emerges from the bottom of the river to meet the hero in another short poem "Kak schastliv ia" [How Happy I Am] (1824). Nearly five more years passed before Pushkin began his drama *Rusalka*, finished three years later. The heroine Natasha, the daughter of a miller,[34] is drawn into a romance with a *Kniaz* (Prince). She is deaf to the shrewd advice of her father, who wishes for a wedding or at least for some compensation from the daughter's wealthy lover. Natasha, faced with her pregnancy and the *Kniaz*'s decision to marry someone else, is driven mad by despair. After the *Kniaz*'s departure, she throws herself into the river Dnepr. The ritualistic wedding of the *Kniaz* and *Kniagina* (Princess) in the following scene is interrupted by a sad song performed by an invisible Natasha—the *Kniaz* recognizes her voice. As the years pass, the *Kniaz*, estranged from his wife, finds himself lured to the bank of the river and to the old oak where he used to meet his little "shepherdess." Meanwhile, Natasha, who in her afterlife has become Tsarina of the *rusalkas*, masters a plan of revenge and retribution, enlisting the aid of her little daughter Rusalochka. In the last scenes of Pushkin's drama, the poet portrays the bottom of the Dnepr river where Rusalka recalls herself as a "foolish and irrational girl" who turned into a "cold and mighty *rusalka*" dreaming of the vengeance to come. The *Kniaz*, drawn by his memory of "free, burning love," approaches the shore, where he is suddenly stunned by the sight of the daughter he never knew: "Otkuda ty, prekrasnoe ditye?" [Where are you from, beautiful child?]. The poem ends with this question, leaving the fate of Rusalka and the *Kniaz* unresolved.

Though the dramatic *Rusalka* is considered unfinished, Pushkin later retold the same story in *The Song of Western Slavs* (1834).[35] The setting is changed from the shores of the Dnepr to Moravia; the main characters are adapted to a new locale: the Russian *Kniaz* is replaced with Prince Yanysh, the *Kniagina* with the Czech Princess Lubusya, Natasha with a local beauty Yelitza, and Rusalka with Vodanitza (from *voda*, "water"), who "rules over all rivers and lakes."[36] The abridged version of the dramatic *Rusalka* has a slightly altered outcome: here Pushkin moves a step further than in his dramatic *Rusalka* by beginning to narrate the encounter of the *rusalka* and her mortal lover; Vodanitza does not look forward to retribution, and it is the Prince who seeks reconciliation.

Dargomyzhsky's Rusalka

In poetry, the water sprite's dancing and singing are mimicked by water, itself full of sound and motion—"waves run, waves roar" (Zhukovsky); "racketing and whirling, the river quivered" (Lermontov);[37] and "boiling waves pacified suddenly" preparing for the *rusalka*'s entrance.[38] Composers created images of sprites using musical conventions associated with water—wavy accompaniment, broken arpeggios, and cascades of rising/descending passages that referred, aurally and visually, to "splashing, veiled, and caressingly smooth" [waves] (exx. 7.1a, 7.1b, 7.1c).[39]

Many songs and instrumental pieces, virtuoso solos, and symphonic compositions were dedicated to the water sprite.[40] But the artistic domain most suitable to her "natural" talents was musical theater.[41] Among the many operas based on Pushkin's drama[42] is a classic of the nineteenth-century Russian operatic repertoire, *Rusalka* by Dargomyzhsky.

Like Pushkin, Dargomyzhsky created several works featuring a water sprite, including the little song "Pesn' Rybku" [Song of the Fish] (1860), based on Lermontov's poetry and the musical sketches of Prince Yanysh.[43] In Dargomyzhsky's opera *Rusalka*, the heroine undergoes a metamorphosis, appearing in three different forms. In the first act, the peasant girl Natasha—a mortal woman and a sympathetic victim of betrayed love—commits suicide. In the second act, as in Pushkin's, she arrives at her lover's wedding as an invisible bodiless spirit. Absent in the third act, where dancing and singing *rusalka*s prepare for her entrance, she appears in the fourth act as a powerful tsarina of the water kingdom accompanied by her little daughter Rusalochka. The character of the heroine is thereby

Example 7.1a. Balakirev/Golenischev-Kutuzov, "Nad ozerom" [Over the Lake].

fragmented into contrasting images: naive peasant girl, passionate mistress, desperate woman, invisible spirit, and vengeful queen of *rusalkas*.

The human Natasha, appearing only in the first act, remains largely undefined as a character—having no solo, she sings two duets and a trio with the main male characters, the *Kniaz* and the miller. Her expressive melodic lines in the dialogues with her "noble" lover and her father do not create a coherent portrait; instead, her musical episodes resemble unassembled puzzle pieces. In Natasha's first ten-measure solo episode, "Alas, passed the golden time" (ex. 7.2), the descending vocal line is framed by a lilting, waltz-like accompaniment.

At the departure of the *Kniaz*, she is stunned, disoriented, driven mad. In a duet with her father, irony ("You know, a *Kniaz* is not free to choose his wife following his heart's desire") gives way to sorrow ("O God, he

Example 7.1b. Borodin/Lermontov, "Morskaya tsarevna" [The Sea Princess].

left, forever abandoned me") in a swift 6/4 episode reminiscent of Lucia di Lammermoor's "Spargi d'amaro pianto." In this scene, Russian critic Serov finds the same mismatch between music and text that McClary described in Lucia:[44] the poetic text and music of the heroine's solo do not cohere, and the spectator does not perceive the "dreadful jealousy" in her vocal line.[45] Natasha's mad scene, like those in *Lucia di Lammermoor*, Vincenzo Bellini's *Il Pirata*, and Adolphe Adam's ballet *Giselle*,[46] is public, witnessed, commented upon by the chorus. Beginning with a folk song, the chorus deplores Natasha's denunciation of her father, then, learning about the cause of Natasha's despair, expresses first sympathy with her,

Example 7.1c. Rubinstein, "Ondine."

then fear mixed with a desire to help her.[47] Natasha's frenzied appeal to the Tsarina of the River Dnepr is expressed in short, repeated melodic gestures matched by ostinato rhythmical figures and scale-like sequences in the orchestra, devices conventional in European music for portraying madness.[48]

According to Uryi Keldish, at the moment when the heroine asks the Tsarina to embrace her and to teach her vengeance, the composer employs a short Russian folk tune.[49] This song signifies her farewell to the folk and her departure to a new world—magical, pagan, and feminine. Natasha's physical separation from everything human and Russian is fully revealed in the lavish wedding scene. As an invisible spirit, she sings a short song— "Above the gravel and yellow sand the fast river springs"—in which two small fish talk about a young maiden who killed herself, cursing her unfaithful lover. While the words and metaphors of the song are reminiscent of Russian folklore, the short teary motifs with intense coloratura ornamentation echo European *bel canto* conventions (ex. 7.3). Contrasting with the massive chorus praising the *Kniaz* and his new wife the *Kniaginia,* the spirit's lonely song forebodes catastrophe. It powerfully expresses, musically and dramatically, the separation between the *zalozhnaya* woman and the choruses that represent the folk.[50]

In the beginning of the fourth act, the heroine receives a scene and an aria, a solo at last—her siren's song, in which she promises vengeance. However, the *Kniaz* is not even present, and the best she can do is to teach Rusalochka how to lure the *Kniaz* to the riverbank, even though the girl does not sing (this is a speaking role) and thus lacks the very instrument of a *rusalka*'s power—a singing voice. This is the point where Pushkin's

Alas, the time has passed, the golden time
When you loved me with your heart and your soul

Example 7.2. Natasha's solo from Trio of Natasha, *Kniaz*, and Miller, act 1, no 2. "Alas, passed the golden time."

drama ends; Dargomyzhsky completes the remaining scenes. After her only solo in the opera, Rusalka once again becomes invisible—her last vocal lines are marked in the score as "Rusalka's Voice."

While the heroine provides the title for Dargomyzhsky's opera, it is the *Kniaz* who receives a memorable and lyrical musical part. Like Natasha, he has no solo in the first act, and the second act wedding celebration reveals little of his musical character. The intimate but uneventful third act, in the absence of both Rusalka and the mass choruses, establishes his presence as the male protagonist. In the cavatina "Unwillingly

Above the gravel and yellow sand the fast river springs
In this fast river the two fish strolled

Example 7.3. Voice of Natasha, act 2, no. 12. "Above the gravel and yellow sand the fast river springs."

to this sad shore I am lured by a mysterious force" ["Nevol'no k etim grustnym beregam," Pushkin's verse], the *Kniaz* remembers the ruined mill, garden, and tree where he once met with Natasha. The hero mourns his forever-lost love in a graceful, beautiful melody (ex. 7.4a).

The wavy, melodic line has a balanced sequential rise and fall and light nostalgic intonation, which leads, at the end of the first part, to recognition ("Here is this memorable oak tree! Here she embraced me . . .") and an emotional awakening. But soon his expressive, wide-ranging vocal line and sequences—rising as he recalls the delight of their meetings and falling

To this sad shore I have been lured by an unknown power,
To familiar dolorous places!

Example 7.4a. Cavatina of the *Kniaz*, act 3, scene 2, no. 16 (beginning). "To this sad shore I have been unwillingly lured."

when he grieves, "the delightful days passed with no return"—lead to increased melodic agitation, which culminates in his recognition of guilt: "Did not I myself, a madman, lose my happiness!" Starting as a dreamlike cantabile in 3/4 with soothing accompaniment that further intensifies the poignancy of the *Kniaz*'s part, the cavatina turns into a dramatic (and thus operatically victorious) solo given additional energy by a series of orchestral passages (ex. 7.4b). Emotional regret and lament are revealed in his duet with the mad miller, in which the *Kniaz* declaims repeatedly: "My heart is broken, my soul is full of pain. . . . Alas, it is I who am guilty of all these disasters." According to Abram Gozenpud, "the image of the *Kniaz* is ennobled and poeticized—he himself appears as a sufferer of the fated (unavoidable) separation from his beloved."[51]

Sacrificing the hero, the composer throughout the opera undermines his main heroine—by providing the live Natasha with no distinct musical characteristics, then isolating her, a peasant girl, from the folk, repeatedly disembodying her, and musically failing her even as a *rusalka*. The separa-

Mne vse-zdes' na pa-miat' pri-vo-dit bi
lo - e i u - no-sti kras-noi pri-vol' - ni - e dni.

Everything here reminds me of the past and the beautiful days of careless youth.

Example 7.4b. Cavatina of the *Kniaz*, act 3, scene 2, no. 16 (cont).
"Grief is in my heart! Isn't it I who destroyed our happiness?"

tion of voice and body suggested by Pushkin in the wedding scene is repeated in the operatic finale and becomes a major dramatic device in Dargomyzhsky's version.

This Dangerous Game: Pushkin's and Dargomyzhsky's Finales

In Pushkin's *Rusalka,* the surface of the water is a passage into a world of shifted powers and mixed realities. At the end of the seemingly unfinished drama, the divide between the real world and the supernatural is about to be broken, mixing the two irreconcilable worlds. At that moment of high suspense, Pushkin drops the curtain. What is the resolution? It is conceivable that Pushkin, the author of *Gavriliada,* famous for its explicit sexuality and for mixing the angelic and satanic worlds, lead his characters and his readers across the boundary between acceptable norms and unrestrained, hazardous pleasures. But would the hero's *quick wet death* justify the appetite of the underwater tsarina?[52]

Dargomyzhsky, drafting the conclusion of his opera, thus faced several possibilities. Perhaps Rusalka could liberate the *Kniaz* from her spell and bless his mortal union. Natasha's suicide, forbidden by Russian Orthodoxy, might then be justified by the fact that her death makes possible a Christian marriage. Or Rusalka could sexually embrace the live *Kniaz,* making him the tsar of the water kingdom. Or she might follow through with her plan for revenge—the traditional *rusalka*'s role.

Example 7.5a. Scene and Aria of Rusalka, act 4, scene 1, no. 19. "I call on him and I wait!"

At the beginning of the final act, Pushkin's *rusalka*s debate whether to frighten the strangers with their splashes, laughter, and whistles; Dargomyzhsky replaces this verbal exchange with a divertissement, an elaborate dance episode that ends with the entrance of the tsarina, who, after a brief instruction to the *rusalka*s, is left alone with her daughter. Their dialogue is colored by the harp, and a 6/8 waltz-like rhythm reinforces the association of the *rusalka*'s realm with dance. Little Rusalochka does not sing, but speaks—her voice has not yet developed a siren's perilous qualities. When teaching her daughter how to cuddle her father, *rusalka*'s vocal line is curvy and melodious, but ends with powerful, wide leaps: "I call on him and I wait!" (ex. 7.5a).

A long arpeggio on the harp signals the departure of Rusalochka and the beginning of Rusalka's most important solo in the opera. The opening recitative, Rusalka's recollection of herself as a foolish girl, is shaped into a peculiarly angular vocal line. In the following aria, long vocal lines give the singer no time to breathe, almost choking her. These extended vocal stretches alternate with short melodic sentences. The orchestra interrupts the vocalist's line, accentuating the weak beats, especially while she is holding long high pitches (ex. 7.5b). The vocal part and orchestral accompaniment are filled with chromaticism.

Serov describes the aria as "difficult in intonation and not very melodious, . . . requiring an exceptionally strong mezzo soprano."[53] He com-

Dav - no zhe lan - - nyi chas na -

stal! Zhar mes - ti i lub-vi ki - pit v kro - vi!

Long ago the desired hour came!
The fire of vengence and love is burning my blood!

Example 7.5b. Aria from Scene and Aria of Rusalka, act 3, scene 1, no. 19.

ments that Rusalka's music does not correspond to the dramatic task.[54] Similarly, McClary, commenting on *Lucia di Lammermoor*, writes about "the discrepancy between her [Lucia's] morbid text and her ecstatic dance music,"[55] Abbate's "discursive space." What is the meaning of this discordance between the text, the dramatic situation, and Rusalka's vocal part? Keldish suggests that Dargomyzhsky was more successful portraying his heroine as a suffering and tormented victim than as a merciless *rusalka*.[56] Yet it seems unlikely that Dargomyzhsky, praised by Keldysh, Serov, and other critics for his talent as an operatic dramatist and for his expressive arias, recitatives, and melodic lyricism, failed in the portrayal of his heroine throughout most of the opera. Could the discursive space between Rusalka's words and their musical realization be attributed to the composer's intent to contest and undermine the heroine's power? Not the cold and mighty *rusalka* of Pushkin's drama, she is rather a jealous, madly loving, devastated woman. Dargomyzhsky uses Pushkin's words in the recitative, but he writes different lyrics for the aria in which Rusalka's burning jealousy and love make her repeat again and again: "Alas, my proud, desired Kniaz you are mine forever, yes, forever!" (ex. 7.5c). The *Kniaz*, entering the stage singing the already familiar melody from his cavatina, is mesmerized by his little water daughter, who intersperses his melodious lines with her spoken sentences. The *Kniagina*, following her husband, now reveals her pain and despair, and she is soon joined by her compassionate companion Olga. As the *Kniaz* is torn between his wife and

Example 7.5c. Aria from Scene and Aria of Rusalka, act 3, scene 1, no. 19, "Alas, my proud desired Kniaz you are mine forever, yes, forever!"

little Rusalochka, the girl announces that if he does not believe her story, he must surely recognize Rusalka's voice. Invisible, Rusalka recites a melodic sequence with sentences gradually shortened and the tempo accelerated. The voices merge in a discordant ensemble, as another character joins the company: staccato dance-like steps precede the appearance of the miller, who calls the *Kniaz* his son-in-law. At the climax, the miller, inviting everyone to join the wedding of the *Kniaz* and his daughter, pushes the *Kniaz* into the river. The whole scene turns into a distorted replay of the wedding so lavishly performed in the second act. Providing no emotional release, the final scene shifts to the movement of silent *rusalkas* who carry the *Kniaz* to the feet of their tsarina in her watery kingdom.

Is the *Kniaz*'s death in the *wetness* of the night a complete ending? Does this death satisfy the heroine? Or does the ending proclaim the lovers' reconciliation in some other world? Serov, asserting that the dancing *rusalkas* impoverish the opera, noted that in some second-rate productions, this final scene became a series of banal divertissements and harlequinades, where the lovers reunite in cupid's temple. But Pushkin's Rusalka is a symbol of power, and whatever dangerous game one imagines beyond the frame of Pushkin's unfinished drama, it is governed by the capricious mind of a female monarch with unbounded power to play, to please, or to kill. By contrast, in the opera, it is not Rusalka but her father who reunites his daughter with the *Kniaz*. The sexual desire of the heroine, suppressed for twelve years, leads the hero to his death, but the final point comes too quickly to provide her with much satisfaction. Not much satisfaction—and not much singing. Throughout the whole scene, she is heard but not seen and, in the end, she is visible but mute. Her victory is silent and thus anti-operatic. Dargomyzhsky overshadows the actual resolution of the drama with a mesmerizing picture of floating, shadowy, mute *rusalkas*.

The Romantic Context: Supernatural Female Dancers

From the very beginning of the romantic age, water sprites sang and danced in both opera and ballet. The same year Alyabiev completed his operatic *Rusalka* (1838), Russian audiences were introduced to another incarnation of the Danube water maiden in the ballet *La Fille du Danube* by French composer Charles Adam and choreographer Filippo Taglioni.[57] Indeed in France as in Russia, in the first decades of the nineteenth century, opera and ballet—two not yet divorced genres—recycled the same stories,[58] with ballet employing operatic musical forms and dance "belonging comfortably with sung drama."[59] In Dargomyzhsky's *Rusalka*, ballet performs various roles, including ethnic tableaux—Slavic and Gypsy dances in the second act as well as the collective imagery of supernatural *rusalkas*.

In early ballets, ethnic and historic themes, referred to as "local color," coincided with the cult of the supernatural.[60] Cyril W. Beaumont suggests that the marriage between dance and the supernatural began in Meyerbeer's opera *Robert Le Diable* (1831), where in the third act Duke Robert, visiting the ruined abbey of St. Rosalie, finds himself surrounded by the ghosts of nuns emerging from their tombs in a mystical mimed scene.[61]

(The realm of the supernatural in ballet was limited to women—male leads were rarely associated with magic.) Within a decade, the musical theater stage, according to Theophile Gautier, was occupied by Wilis who "fluttered here and there," by Péri "skimming the ground without touching it," by supple, sensual Bayadera with "sorrowful languorous gestures," and by the daughter of the Danube, "a shade, intangible."[62] In no time, ballets such as *Les Sylphides, La Peri,* and *Giselle* were added to the core repertoire in Saint Petersburg and Moscow. *Robert Le Diable* and *Les Huguenots,* both including large dancing scenes, were well known and widely discussed by Russian musicians and musical critics.[63]

Despite the closeness of the two genres, opera, with its emphasis on singing and literary text, was considered more sophisticated than ballet, which was centered on the female body—moving, flying, fluttering, exposing and offering itself to the eyes of spectators.[64] Felicia McCarren suggests that "in the course of the nineteenth century the dance becomes an art form uniquely attached to the female form, an art . . . in which the female body, feminine sexuality, and thus femininity itself, become the essential subject of the dance."[65] The costumes themselves, gauzy and revealing, with raised hemlines, were designed to inspire male patrons' daydreams and erotic reveries. Describing the Parisian ballerina Marie Taglioni, Gautier writes about her "slender legs . . . beneath billowing clouds of muslin, the rosy shades of her tights plunging you into dreams of the same hue."[66] The Russian critic Yurkevich, observing Marie Taglioni on the Russian stage, claims that "thoughts passionate and tender, which destroy and elevate the soul before us, wordlessly flash in her expressive, burning eyes. A winged, fascinating dream, elusive and undefined, plays and sports before your eyes."[67]

On the ballet stage, the female dancer, simultaneously veiling and revealing her body, was cultivated as an emblem of both sexuality and otherworldliness. The silent, ethereal ballerina seemed to combine innocence and eroticism, reality and the supernatural. Gautier, for example, commented on Giselle as "a paradigm for poetry; her dance can be seen not simply as the stuff of poetry, but as an image for the movement of poetry between realms."[68] Gautier claimed that "out of four lines of Heine"[69] he produced the libretto of *Giselle,* whose triumph and endurance on the Russian stage have been equaled by only a few spectacles.[70] *Giselle* conquered the Russian stage in the years preceding Dargomyzhsky's *Rusalka.*[71] While "the original *Giselle* behaved like opera,"[72] Dargomyzhsky's opera incorporated elements of ballet.

The plot lines of the Russian opera and the French ballet are strikingly similar: the romance between a young peasant girl and a nobleman, and a betrayal[73] that leads the heroine to madness and death. In both *Rusalka* and *Giselle* the mortal heroines are rapidly introduced, loved, maddened, and crushed in the two first acts. In the afterlife each re-emerges as a supernatural woman endowed with magic destructive power. Like Rusalka, Wila in her afterlife remains an eternal bride who will chase, seduce, tickle, and dance her male victims to death.

In both *Giselle* and *Rusalka*, the ghostly brides appear late in the spectacles. In Dargomyzhsky's opera, the *rusalkas* emerge from the water singing in the second half of the third act and become absorbed in their dancing in the fourth. An orchestral interlude in the fourth act with wave-like rolling octaves and "splashes" on the strong beats echoes the *Scène des Wilis* from the second act of *Giselle*. In *Rusalka* the "watery introduction" has a melodious rather than a dancing character; in the following section the movement gradually gains energy and the speed increases, leading to the Allegro Vivace in 6/8 that explores syncopations reminiscent of *Giselle*'s Wilis. During this orchestral interlude, the *rusalkas*' voices are raised only in laughter.

Choruses and Nationalism

In both *Giselle* and *Rusalka,* mass scenes portraying peasants and hunters appear in the first acts. In the opera, they represent the *narod* (folk), an image inseparable from Russian nationalism, a three-part concept: God, tsar, and *narod,* the latter worshiping, obeying, and praising the first two.[74] Russian folk tales as mythology stress the role of the *narod* as the basis for the creation of national identity. (Indeed the authors who romanticized and politicized the *narod* in their literary works were barely acquainted with their low-class compatriots.) To be separated from the *narod* is to be exiled from God and nation.

Though absent from Pushkin's intimate poem, the folk chorus plays an important part in Dargomyzhsky's opera. For example, the folk choruses are interspersed with the duets of the two lovers. The choruses are important to the wedding scenes, which echo the weddings in Glinka's *Ruslan and Ludmila* (1838) and several French productions, such as Meyerbeer's *Les Huguenots*.[75] The wedding rituals in Dargomyzhsky include two ethnic vignettes, one of them a "Gypsy Dance."[76] The massive choruses, dances, and special characters portrayed by Dargomyzhsky function as "genuine" rituals with a pan-Slavic and particularly *boyar* or noble character.[77]

Traditionally the operatic mass scenes, choruses, folk or folk-like songs, and the figure of the victorious hero (the *Kniaz* is an exception) typify the political, nationalistic spirit of Russian opera, which corresponds to Smith's association of opera with "public political" matters and ballet with "private affairs of the heart."[78] Dargomyzhsky's mass scenes explore elements of ritualistic, urban, and popular culture. Active participants in the drama, the choruses anticipate and comment on operatic events. For example, at the beginning of the first act, after the peaceful trio of the momentarily happy heroine, her noble lover, and the miller, the chorus sings, on a sorrowful note, "Why are you, my willful heart, in such pain?" Similarly, a folk song and a *khorovod* (circle dance) with a mock fight contrast with and yet anticipate the troubled duet of the main characters before the tragic finale of the first act.

Not only is each choral scene significant by itself, but the sequence of scenes supports the dramatic process—the distribution and density of the choruses gradually decreases. The first act is replete with choruses representing peasants, and choral singing remains central to the wedding celebrations. After the end of the second act, however, there are no more massive folk choruses. In the third act, gender-segregated hunters (men) and *rusalka*s (women) replace the massive folk scenes. No choral singing takes place in the last act. At the same time, dances grow in importance, progressing from the women's *khorovod* song in the first act to the female Slavic and Gypsy dances in the second, to the *rusalka*s who conquer the stage in the fourth, framing the finale of the opera with their mute dance.

The reduction of the folk choruses coincides with the gradual disintegration of the main characters. At the same time, the increasing role of dancing is associated, especially in the fourth act, with the establishment of the magic realm. The operatic chorus and folk dances are linked with public male territory while ballet represents an intimate, private, supernatural female realm. Moreover, choral singing is associated with the live world, folk songs, the folk itself, and thus Russianness. Ironically, the nobleman whose class prejudice caused the downfall of the peasant girl becomes allied with the folk chorus in the second act and with the hunters in the third. It is the *Kniaz*'s downfall, not the betrayed heroine's, that coincides with the gradual disappearance of the folk, who vanish completely at the death of the male lead, leaving the stage to the female dancers.

Though the *rusalka*s emerge from the water singing (third act), they soon dive back into the river and thereafter dance silently or laugh. The finale, with ghostly *rusalka*s floating across the stage, strongly contrasts with Russian operas before and after *Rusalka*. After Glinka's *Life for the Tsar* and *Ruslan and Ludmila*, nearly all operas, despite differences of plot and genre, culminated in a massive final choral *Slava* (glory) glorifying the bravery and victory of Russians led by a national (male) hero. What moti-

vated Dargomyzhsky to conclude his opera with an unquestionably negative feminine ending, reversing the dynamics of gender and genre?

What Serov criticizes as the "weaknesses" of the score—an overabun-
dance of folk choruses at the beginning, "too much counterpoint and too
many voices" contrasted with the "cold and almost boring character of
[the *rusalkas'*] ballet scenes"—is perhaps the essence of Dargomyzhsky's
dramatic intent.[79] The replacement of Russian folk choruses with deadly
female nymphs perhaps constitutes a clear warning about the dangers of
being loved, controlled, and manipulated by powerful women—a bad
omen expressed by the folk, from whom Natasha, the character most
associated with native mythology and folk rituals, is separated by her
suicide and her transformation.

The Historical Context:
Pushkin's Precursors and Catherine the Great

Like their fellow European writers, Russian romantic authors were infatuated with the search for the feminine and for *volshebstvo* (magic); but for
Russians, unlike Europeans, the idea of female power was not an abstrac-
tion. For three-quarters of the eighteenth century the country was ruled
by female tsars; moreover, all noblewomen enjoyed legal rights and control over property unequalled elsewhere in Europe. In her study of "the
significance of separate property in practice" and the "the real scope of
women's control of their fortunes,"[80] Marrese discusses the emergence of
formidable women in public life, "peaking in the eighteenth century but
dwindling after the reign of Catherine the Great."[81] Could it be that the enthrallment of early-nineteenth-century Russian writers, including Pushkin, with dangerous and destructive *rusalkas* reflects the historical circumstances of the preceding era?

Considering Russian historical and cultural particularities, one might
compare Pushkin's Rusalka with Dushen'ka, the title heroine of Bogdanovich's poem *Dushen'ka* and his lyric comedy *Joy of Dushen'ka* (1786). In
the poem, Dushen'ka is portrayed as a pastoral heroine whose magical
encounters with an invisible lover are associated with water.[82] The first
time she appears, Dushen'ka is guided to her bath by forty nymphs, with
amurs (cupids) bringing her dew instead of water. Bogdanovich's detailed
poetic description of her bathing and her beauty is pregnant with sensuality.[83] A "little brook calls and guides her" along the "crystal water" of
its clear streams to a grotto where she spends "hours and days with her
beloved spouse."[84] Losing her lover, the desperate heroine finds drowning

to be the most "convenient" (*udobnyi*) method of suicide. Throwing herself into the water, she is miraculously saved by pikes—"in whom [she] recognized naiads"—and who lead the heroine to her beloved.

The two Bogdanovich Dushen'kas are dedicated to and modeled on Catherine the Great—the impoverished German princess who, marrying into the Russian crown and disposing of her husband (Peter III), ruled Russia for the last third of the eighteenth century (1762–1796). Writers such as Derzhavin, Bogdanovich, and Karamzin, seeking favors from one who, even during her life, was known as Catherine the Great, venerated her strength and femininity.

Pushkin, who does not make Catherine the protagonist of any of his works, nevertheless continuously refers to her era, her rule, and her persona. While the poet writes with nostalgia about the age of Catherine and recalls her marvelous palaces and parks, Catherine often appears as a formidable woman who, like Rusalka, eradicates men.

> Catherine supported the enlightenment, but Novikov, spreading its first rays, was transferred from Shishkovsky's hands (the domestic persecutor of shy Catherine) to a prison cell, where he remained till his death. Radishev was exiled to Siberia; Kniazin died under the whips, and Fonvizin, whom she feared would not avoid the same destiny were it not for his outmost popularity.[85]

Analyzing the obsession of Russian writers with history, Andrew Wachtel compares Pushkin's notes on eighteenth-century Russian history (1822) with his novel *The Captain's Daughter,* the first a work based on archival materials and the second a fictional first-person memoir of an accused traitor saved by a young woman who seeks forgiveness from Catherine.[86] Wachtel's analysis of the two works leads him to define a "multiplicity of ways in which historical material could be codified" in the "intergeneric dialogue" that occurs "across the boundaries of separate texts."[87] The Russian literary scholar Berezkina, employing a similar approach to investigate Pushkin's language, claims that expressions such as "kartiny, mostik, luzhok" (pictures, bridges, meadows), used to describe scenery in *Eugene Onegin,* were references to the Tsarskosel'skii park that surrounded Catherine's palace[88] and thus invoked the image of the tsarina herself.[89] Berezkina points out that on the margins of his manuscript of *Onegin,* next to the description of this scenery, Pushkin sketched the poem "Mne zhal' velikia zheny" (I pity the great wife) about the aged empress.

How far can one go searching for historical and literary cues, codifications, and commentaries employed in Pushkin's text? Though there is indeed no apparent connection between powerful Catherine and the tsarina-*rusalka* in Pushkin's tale, the story line of Pushkin's *Rusalka* parallels the queenly *Dushen'ka*. In Pushkin's drama, pikes do not save the heroine, as in the Bogdanovich story; but the song about two fish interrupts the flow of the wedding, signaling Natasha's mystical metamorphosis into an immortal queen, forever wedded to water. While Bogdanovich's poem playfully explores the connection of the royal Dushen'ka with water, magic, and sensuality, Rusalka, transformed from a peasant girl into a tsarina, accesses the magic power associated with water and sexuality.

It is intriguing that Pushkin, referring to Bogdanovich in his draft of "I pity the great wife," calls Catherine "tsarina dushen'ka," and paints her in the company of Derzhavin, who created an image of Catherine as the magic Felitza, the navigator of an invincible fleet, an explorer, ruler, and voluptuous woman. In Derzhavin's verses, cited above, the sound of the harp, the sirens' songs, and the *khorovods* the nymphs and cupids play all serve to "please the Goddess' eyes." (The Goddess is Catherine herself.)[90]

Writing his tale of Rusalka, and elevating his *zalozhnaya* into a tsarina, Pushkin comments on and revises the image of the monarch nourished by his literary predecessors—a formidable woman with an uninhibited appetite and will for power and sexuality. Considering the great attention paid to Catherine by the poet's predecessors, Pushkin's frequent references to and commentaries on their works, his strong interest in Catherine, and the rising fashion of literary tales, one might interpret Pushkin's Rusalka as an allusion not to historical Catherine, but to a rich literary tradition related to her imagery.

The Literary Context: Gender in Russian Skazka

Dargomyzhsky's *rusalka* is removed by several generations from the historical tsarinas—no female monarchs would again be admitted to power in Russia—*and* she is equally distant from Bogdanovich's and Derzhavin's royal heroines.[91] Dargomyzhky's rendition of the *rusalka* story reveals not only his adherence to Pushkin but also his great interest in the folktales that the French-speaking and foreign-educated Russian nobility saw as a revival of "the ingenuity and vehemence of the Russian soul."[92] At the end of the eighteenth century, the *skazka* or tale, a genre not yet fully defined, encompassed historical episodes and characters, events of real life, imaginary domains, and the magic world.[93]

In the mid-nineteenth century the fairy tale, recorded or created, represented a national mythology, with figures like *rusalkas* linking folk tales, pagan rituals, and Western mythology with romantic ideals. Rusalka, first as a mortal girl and later as a mythological figure, existed in two worlds, one real and the other ritualistic and fantastic—the two kingdoms that Vladimir Propp finds necessary for the composition of a magic tale. Dargomyzhshky's Rusalka resembles the character described by Propp in his typology of characters: "tsarina—*dusha* (dushen'ka) as a beautiful and faithful maiden, but also a wicked, vengeful, and nasty creature, always prepared to kill, to drown, and to harm her male partner, and the hero's main task is to suppress her." In Propp's typological plot, the aim of the male lead is "to remove her power. Then she is defeated and obeys the husband."[94]

Dargomyzhsky's Rusalka is affected by gender conventions developed in European operas and ballets. Female heroines were often destroyed: the stronger they were, the more intense and promising was the prospect of their subjugation to male power.[95] As shown above, Dargomyzhsky's opera celebrated the separation of the female voice from the body, manifested in the singing of the frequently invisible heroine and the dancing of the mostly silent *rusalka*s. When the male protagonist dies in the end, the heroine is victoriously mute. Her destructive power remains—she receives the body of her former lover from the arms of her fellow immortals. However, according to the national mythology examined by Propp, while her submission would bring happiness to both female and male protagonists, the *Kniaz*'s defeat gives Rusalka no satisfaction. And thus her victory makes impossible the traditional celebratory operatic ending with the heroine either surrendering to male authority or dying. Whether surrendering or dying, the operatic heroine should be a diva, but instead Rusalka is vocally weak. The most romantic part is given to the *Kniaz* and the rounded melodious lines to Rusalka's rival, the *Kniagina*. While Pushkin's *rusalka,* transformed into a tsarina, ascends to magic power, Dargomyzhsky's tsarina gradually fades away.

Conclusion

In nineteenth-century Russian narrative, the *rusalka* became an emblem useful in the creation of nationalistic mythology. As a folk-tale heroine, she was a bearer of the "ingenuity of Russian soul." She was closely associated with ancient rituals, and her image as *zalozhnaya* endowed her with spiritual power. Living in different waters—from the Dnepr (*rusalka*s in Somov and Gogol), the Dnestr, and the Volhova (Rimsky-Korsakov, *Sadko*) to the Aragva and the Kura in the Caucasus (Lermontov, *Msyri*) and the Bashkirian lake Aculu (Dal', "Bashkirslaya Rusalka")—the Russian *rusalka* served as a territorial marker of Russian imperialism and embodied a broad pan-Slavic identity.

On the other hand, Rusalka's paganism pitted her against Russian Orthodoxy. Pushkin in his tale warns his fellow men about the frightening potential of women to control and to destroy. Dargomyzhsky's Rusalka, created a quarter-century later, embodies both the qualities of Pushkin's water creature and a nineteenth-century European gender paradigm. Like Dargomyzhsky's formidable but finally muted heroine, some other heroines were destroyed by nationalistic Russian operatic composers. In Rimsky-Korsakov's *Sadko*, a successful version of the *Kniaz* is married to two women—the water spouse Tsarina Volhova and a mortal wife Lubava. While Lubava spills rivers of tears throughout the opera, at the end the tsarina Volhova turns herself into a river, benefiting Sadko and his city. This submission of women is celebrated in the finale of the opera by a massive choir glorifying the hero and the nation.

The *rusalka*, from whom writers and composers borrowed ritualistic power in the name of nationalism, is, by contrast, estranged from everything that is folklike and Russian. In her study of the connection between the image of women and national politics, Meyda Yegenogli argues that in different times and cultural contexts a woman "becomes the ground upon which nationalism builds its discourse."[96] The image of *rusalka*, repeatedly invoked in Russian literary works from the late eighteenth and into the second half of the nineteenth century, shows the transformation of discourse about women and power—discourse that converges the processes of continuous Westernization, masculinization, and rising nationalistic extremism. Once a formidable woman, a threat to men's physical existence and memory, Rusalka was turned into a magical otherworldly creature whose singing and dancing codified her sexual and social challenge for the Russian romantic man.

NOTES

I would like to express my gratitude to several musicologists and archivists of the Moscow Conservatory, Svetlana Sigida, Irina Brezhneva, and Galina Malinina, as well as the director of the Library of the Moscow Conservatory, Emma Rassina, for their assistance with my research. I appreciate the encouragement of Andrew Wachtel, who read parts of my research and gave me useful suggestions, and the influence of Richard Taruskin, whose revisionist approach to Russian musical history served me as an inspiration. Most of all I am thankful to James Borland for encouraging, reading, discussing, and editing this work.

1. See Dmitri K. Zelenin, *Izbrannye trudy: ocherki russkoi mifologii: umershie*

neestestvennoiu smert'iu i rusalki [Selected works: Essays of Russian mythology: Those who died of unnatural death and rusalki] (Moscow: Indrik, 1995). Joanna Hubbs discusses *rusalka* in relation to Mother Russia and Great Russian Goddesses in *Mother Russia* (Bloomington: Indiana University Press, 1993), 27–36. Linda J. Ivanits writes on *rusalka* as a sorcerer and a nature spirit in *Russian Folk Belief* (Armonk, N.Y.: M. E. Sharpe, 1989), 75–82, 185–89.

2. The *ptiza raiskaia sirin* [bird of paradise], symbolizing unearthly beauty and joy, often appears with another female bird, Alkonost, representing sorrow. See woodcut in *The Lubok* (Leningrad: Aurora Art Publishers, 1984), 58, 59. Rimsky-Korsakov composes a duet of Sirin and Alkonost in his *The Legend of Invisible City of Kitezh and Maiden Favronia* (1903–1905).

3. The *rusalka*s on St. Basil's Bridge had wings as well as a fishtail.

4. Russians shared European fascination with female water creatures, which was inflated by the increasingly frequent "discoveries" in the eighteenth and nineteenth centuries of mermaids and exhibitions of their supposedly preserved bodies. See Jan Bondeson, *The Feejee Mermaid* (London: Cornell University Press, 1999), 38–58.

5. Gavril Romanovich Derzhavin, "Tam stepi, kak mora struatsa," *Sochinenia* [Works] (St. Petersburg: Academic Prospect, 2002), 80. The expressions in parentheses exemplify Derzhavin's poetic language. Throughout the essay, texts cited from sources in Russian are translated by me, unless otherwise indicated. The excerpts from Derzhavin's poetry are cited below:

"Stremyatsa slez prozrachnyh reki" (78);
"Predstav' poslednii den' prirodyz
"Shto prolilasya zvezd reka" (98);
"Zlataya plavala luna" (84);
"Vlivayu v serdze ei lubov'" (75).

On the subject of Derzhavin and water see A. A. Levitskii, "*Obraz vody u Derzhavina i obraz poeta*" [The image of water in Derzhavin and the image of the poet"], *XVIII Vek* [18th century] 20 (St. Petersburg: Nauka, 1996), 47–71.

6. See Tom Lutz, *Crying: The Natural and Cultural History of Tears* (New York: Norton, 1999), and Lawrence Kramer, "Little Pearl Teadrops," in *Music, Sensation, and Sensuality*, ed. Linda Phyllis Austern (New York: Routledge, 2002), 59–60.

7. Leo Tolstoy, *Anna Karenina*, trans. Louise and Aylmer Maude (Oxford: Oxford University Press, 1995), 760–61.

8. Ippolit Bogdanovich, *Dushen'ka* (Moscow: V tip. N. S. Vsevolodskii, 1815), 89.

9. Svetlana Slavskaya Grenier also suggests kinship between Karamzin's Liza and Pushkin's Lizaveta Ivanovna from *Pikovaya Dame* (*The Queen of Spades*). Grenier, *Representing the Marginal Woman in Nineteenth-Century Russian Literature* (Westport, Conn.: Greenwood Press, 2001), 23.

10. When using the word *rusalka* as a generic term, it is lower-case and italic; referred to as a title, *Rusalka* is capitalized in italics; as the name of a heroine, "Rusalka" is capitalized, but not italicized.

11. See Vladimir Propp, *Morphology of the Folktale* (Austin: University of Texas Press, 2003, reprint of 1968), 3–18. Propp writes on the history and classification of folktales. Ivanits comments on the importance of magic healers in Russian countryside, where healers were perceived as capable of providing assistance and "curing with the aid of God and the saints," and at the same time were suspected of "dealing with the devil." See Ivanits, *Russian Folk Belief,* 111.

12. Susan McClary, *Feminine Endings* (Minneapolis: University of Minnesota Press, 1991), 86.

13. Ralph P. Locke, "What Are These Women Doing in Opera?" *En Travesti: Women, Gender Subversion, Opera,* ed. Corinne E. Blackmer and Patricia Juliana Smith (New York: Columbia University Press, 1995), 62.

14. Carolyn Abbate, *Unsung Voices: Opera and Musical Narrative in the Nineteenth Century* (Princeton, N.J.: Princeton University Press, 1991), ix.

15. Arthur Groos, "Madame Butterfly: The Story," *Cambridge Opera Journal* 3, no. 2 (1989): 125–58.

16. The connections with both riverbed and hair color are emphasized in Zelenin, *Izbrannye trudy,* 39, 142.

17. Despite these Russian cognates, the *Ethnagraphya Belarusi: Encyclopedia* (Minsk: N.p., 1989), 433, claims that the word is derived from the Latin phrase *dies rosae,* associated with ancient rites surviving in various cultures. See also Phyllis Ann Reed, "The Rusalka Theme in Russian Literature" (Ph.D. diss., University of California in Berkeley, 1973), 3–4; and Max Vasmer, *Etimologicheskii slovar' russkogo yazyka* [Etymological dictionary of Russian language], trans. Trubacheva (Moscow: Progress, 1971), 520.

18. Heine also suggested that "she is not, by any means, invariably a deceased bride, but a being corresponding to the *fata, fay,* or life-size fairy, or to the peri of the East." Heinrich Heine, "Elementary Spirits," *Collected Works,* trans. Charles Godfrey Leland (New York: Crosup & Sterling Company, 1906), v. 11, 107–211, 139–40.

19. Zelenin, *Izbrannye trudy,* 207.

20. See Marcia J. Citron, *Gender and the Musical Canon* (Cambridge: Cambridge University Press, 1993).

21. In the 1831 *Telegraph* (St. Petersburg), Frederich de la Motte Fauque is named among the most prominent European writers. See Norman W. Ingham, *Hoffmann's Reception in Russia* (Würzburg: Jal-Verlag, 1974), 88.

22. Vasily Zhukovsky translated tales from several European languages. His original tales, such as *Sleeping Beauty,* were modeled on German fairy tales. See P. Lupanova, *Russkaya narodnaya skazka v tvorchestve pisatelei pervoi poloviny XIX veka* [The Russian folk tale in the writing of authors of the first half of the nineteenth century] (Petrozavodsk: Gosudarstvennoe izdatel'stvo, 1959), 299.

23. Mikhail Shemiakin comments on their common interests and competition in the correspondence between Pushkin and Zhukovsky during the time they created their works on *rusalkas* and undines. See Vladimir Retsepter and Mikhail Shemiakin, *The Return of Pushkin's Rusalka* (Saint Petersburg: Pushkin State The-

ater Center, 1998), 84. Shemiakin suggests that Zhukovsky published fragments from his *Undine* between 1835 and 1837. Shemiakin also believes that Pushkin wrote his "Prince Yanysh" in 1833–34 before the drama *Rusalka* (84, 62).

24. Ingham, *Hoffmann's Reception,* 9, 139.

25. Propp, *Russkaya Skazka* [Russian tale] (Leningrad: Leningrad University Press, 1984), 71.

26. For example, the nixie Hulda became the *rusalka* Lesta.

27. The text of the original *Das Donauweibchen,* turned into *Dneprovskaya Rusalka,* was translated and revised in Russian fashion by N. Krasnopolsky. C. N. Davydov added several musical numbers. Like *Das Donauweibchen,* the *Dneprovskaya Rusalka* was followed by three Russian sequels. The second and third sequels, in 1804 and 1805, were generated by Catterino Cavos and Davydov. The fourth opera of the cycle was created by in 1807 by Davydov (music) and Shahtinsky (text).

28. Retsepter and Shemiakin, *Return of Pushkin's Rusalka,* 74.

29. Between 1804 and 1825, *Dneprovskaya Rusalka* was shown in Moscow theaters every year. Three of the operas were performed in 1807, and all four operas in 1824. After a hiatus of nearly ten years, the operas were reproduced in 1845, remaining a consistent part of the nineteenth-century repertoire. Vasily Fedotov, *Repertoire of the Bol'shoi Theater 1776–1995* (New York: Norman Ross Publishing Inc., 2001), v. 1.

30. Alexander Sergeevich Pushkin, *Eugene Onegin,* 2:213.

31. Somov, in his critical writing, repeatedly encouraged writers "to search for their romantic plots in native folklore." See Irina Semibratova, "Afterwards," in Orest Somov, *Oboroten': Russkie fantasmagorii* [Oboroten: Russian phantasmagorias], ed. Irina Semibratova (Moscow: Book Tent, 1994), 327–35, 330. Accordingly his "Rusalka" emphasized the folkloristic element more than the romantic plotline.

32. Pushkin, "Rusalka," *Collected Works* (Moscow: Hudozhestvennaya Literatura, 1985), 1:203–205.

33. Zhukovsky, "Rybak" [Fisherman], *Pesn' Lubvi: Lyrika russkih poetov XIX i XX vekov* [Love songs: Lyrics of Russian poets of the 19th and 20th centuries] (Moscow: Pravda, 1988), 44.

34. According to Ivanits, "in the case of the miller, the proximity to water, an element commonly used in magic rituals," led to the suspicion that he cast spells, or "whispered" over it, and that he lived in friendship with the water sprite (*vodianoi*). Ivanits, *Russian Folk Belief,* 111.

35. Curiously, though, Pushkin himself wrote that he borrowed most of his *Songs* from Mérimée, "the anonymous author" of *La Guzla, ou choix de Poésies Illyriques, recueillies dans la Dalmatie, la Bosnie, la Croatie et l'Herzégowine.* Pushkin, "Rusalka," 1:530. Also see Iosif Eiges, *Muzyka v zhizni i tvorchestve Pushkina* [Music in the life and works of Pushkin] (Moscow: Muzgiz, 1937).

36. Pushkin, "Rusalka," 1:554.

37. I shumya i krutyas', kolebala reka—Lermontov, "Rusalka."

38. "Zakipeli volny/I prismireli vdrug opat'."

39. "Pleshchut, tayatsya laskatel'no nezhnye"—Mily Balakirev's song, lyrics by Arsenii Golenishcev-Kutuzov, "Nad ozerom" [Over the Lake].

40. Anton Rubinstein, study for piano, *Ondine,* 1842; cantata *Svitezianka* by Nikolai Rimsky-Korsakov on the text of Mitskevich, and Lyadov's orchestral piece "Volshebnoe ozero" [The Enchanted Lake] (1909). Many songs were based on Lermontov's poems: Alexander Borodin, "Morskaya tsarevna" [The Sea Princess], text by Lermontov; Rubinstein, "Rusalka"; Mily Balakirev, "Pesnya zolotoi rybki" [Song of the Little Golden Fish], text by Lermontov; Mikhail Ippolitov-Ivanov, "Pesnya rybki," text by Lermontov; Arensky, "Pesn' rybki" [Song of the Little Fish]. Both Arensky and Balakirev composed songs called "Nad ozerom" [Over the Lake] based on Golenishchev-Kutuzov; and Rimsky-Korsakov created "The Nymph."

41. Russian operas featuring a water sprite include Alexander Alabiev's music for drama *Rusalka* (1838); Dargomyzhsky's *Rusalka* (1858); Alexei Lvov's opera *Undine* (1848); and Tchaikovsky's *Undine* (1869); also Alexander Serov's *Undine* (1858) and *Maiskaya noch* [May Night] (1850); Rimsky-Korsakov's *May Night* (1879) and *Sadko* (1897).

42. The operas and music dramas based upon Pushkin's *Rusalka* include works by A. Alabiev (1825), Dargomyzhsky (1856), Mestr de Mexur (1870), and A. Alexandrov (1913). See Valerii Kikta, *Pushkinskaya muzikal'naya panorama XIX–XX vekov* [Pushkin's musical panorama in the 19th and 20th centuries] (Moscow: Muzyka, 1999).

43. According to Mikhail Pekelis, a major biographer of Dargomyzhsky, though the existing fragments of *Prince Yanysh* were written as chamber music, the composer's remarks in the score indicate that it could be envisioned as an orchestral cantata.

44. McClary suggests that "Donizetti's music and his librettist's text do not match her "morbid text and her ecstatic dance." McClary, *Feminine Endings,* 92.

45. Alexander Serov, *Izbrannye stat'i* [Selected articles], ed. G. N. Khubova (Moscow: Gosudarstvennoe Muzykal'noe izdatel'stvo, 1957), v. 1, 302–304.

46. *Il Pirata* by Bellini (1827) was shown in Moscow's Bol'shoi Theater in 1837, *Lucia di Lammermoor* by Donizetti (1835), and the ballet *Giselle* (1841) by Adam in 1843.

47. Mary Ann Smart writes about Lucia di Lammermoor's Mad Scene that "at least as important as Lucia's appearance is in fact that she is *observed* by the chorus throughout the mad scene." Smart, "The Silencing of Lucia," *Cambridge Opera Journal* 4:2 (1991): 119–41, 125. McClary suggests that "the chorus of wedding guests . . . attempt in vain to lead her into a more suitable key. . . . Indeed, the wedding guests respond to and accompany Lucia very much as the trio of men did Monteverdi's nymph (*Lamento della Nimfa*)."

48. McClary writes: "Whether in the semiotic service of grief, erotic transport, or madness, the ostinato is always associated with some with some obsessive conditions." McClary, *Feminine Endings,* 192. On the subject of musical portrayal of women's madness, see selection of essays in *Embodied Voices,* ed. Leslie C. Dunn

and Nancy A. Jones (Cambridge: Cambridge University Press, 1994) and Catherine Clément, *Opera, or The Undoing of Women* (Minneapolis: University of Minnesota Press, 1988).

49. See Keldish, *Istoriya russkoi muzyki* [History of Russian music] (Moscow: Nauka, 1948), v. 1, 456. Also see Pekelis, who suggests that this folk song was also introduced abroad in Benjamin Beresford's anthology *The Russian Troubadour,* published in London in 1816. Mikhail Pekelis, *Dargomyzhskii i narodnaya pesnya* [Dargomyzhsky and folk song] (Moscow: Gosudarstvennoe Izdatel'stvo, 1951), 122.

50. This song is the heroine's most intimate and individualized number in the opera. No longer connected with her people and recognized only by the *Kniaz,* she leads a bodiless existence that depends entirely upon the male lead.

51. Abram Gozenpud, "Pushkin and Russian Operatic Classics," in *Pushkin: Issledovaniia i materialy* [Pushkin: Research and materials], 200–217 (Leningrad: Nauka, 1967), 200–217.

52. Even in Pushkin's short poetic stanza "Rusalka," the voluptuous little water sprite plays with the old monk for three days before luring him to the water.

53. Alexander Serov, *Rusalka* (Moscow: Governmental Musical Press, 1953), 147.

54. Ibid., 304, 330.

55. McClary, *Feminine Endings,* 92.

56. Keldish, *Istoriia russkoi muzyki,* 451.

57. See John Roland Wiley, *A Century of Russian Ballet* (Oxford: Clarendon Press; New York: Oxford University Press, 1990), 90–105.

58. For example, Glinka's first opera *Ivan Susanin* was preceded by the opera of the same title by Cavos/Shahovsky (1822), which was also adapted to ballet (1826). Two decades before Glinka's second opera, *Ruslan and Ludmila,* Schultz composed a ballet pantomime, also based on Pushkin. Dargomyzhshky's opera *Esmeralda* (1841) was based on Hugo's *Notre Dame de Paris.* Several years later, Pugni and Perrot created the ballet *La Esmeralda.* Dargomyzhsky was also familiar with hybrid genres. Between 1843 and 1848 he created *Torzhestvo Vakkha* [The triumph of Bacchus], an opera-ballet.

59. Marian Smith, for example, writes about the "verbal aspect" of the music for ballet that was "imitating the human voice in various ways and using so-called *airs parlants* (short snippets of melodies from folksongs or opera arias, which could introduce actual explanatory words into the viewers' minds)." Marian Elizabeth Smith, *Ballet and Opera in the Age of Giselle* (Princeton, N.J.: Princeton University Press, 2000), 6, 58.

60. Cyril W. Beaumont, *The Ballet Called Giselle* (London: Dance Books, 1988), 13.

61. Tenor Adolph Nourrit, after experiencing the "accidental spiritualism" of the ghostly dance in his performance of Robert in Meyerbeer's opera, wrote the scenario for *Les Sylphides.* Within a decade, opera theater became populated with

ephemeral but powerful creatures that, according to Marian Smith, "fared particularly well in ballet pantomime."

62. See Theophile Gautier's reviews of ballets in Parisian Opéra in *Gautier on Dance,* trans. Ivor Guest (London: Dance Books Cecil Court, 1986), 49, 119. See also Smith, *Ballet and Opera,* 67.

63. Serov, *Izbrannye stat'i,* 2:445.

64. Ibid., 1:311.

65. Felicia M. McCarren, "The Female Form: Gautier, Mallarmé and Celine Writing Dance" (Ph.D. diss., Stanford University, 1992), 3.

66. *Gautier on Dance,* 37.

67. P. Yurkevich, "Bol'shoi Theater: Debut of Mlle Taglioni," *Severnaya pchela* [Northern bee], 1837, as quoted by Wiley, 84.

68. McCarren, *The Female Form,* 20.

69. *Gautier on Dance,* 13.

70. *Giselle* remains in the core repertoire of the Bol'shoi Theater in 2001, 2002, 2003, and 2004.

71. Those were the years approaching the golden age of Russian ballet that culminated in the works of Tchaikovsky and Marius Petipa. Before the legendary Petipa moved to Russia, his older brother Lucien appeared on the stage of the imperial Russian theater as the first Albrecht in the premier of *Giselle.*

72. Smith, *Ballet and Opera,* 167.

73. In *Giselle* he is already married, "not for the heart, but for social reasons." This line of Pushkin's *Kniaz* (v. 2, 491) reflects on male characters and situations in both plotlines.

74. See Richard Taruskin, *Defining Russia Musically: Historical and Hermeneutical Essays* (Princeton, N.J.: Princeton University Press, 1997), 26.

75. In Meyerbeer's opera (1836, first premiered in St. Petersburg around 1837–1838?), a Catholic wedding procession in the third act is interrupted by a Gypsy Dance.

76. The two gypsy dances are idiomatically related and play similar roles in the dramaturgical plan of the operas. Though apparently a French fashion, musical references to gypsies were also reflective of Russian urban culture, in which gypsies played a vital role. Pushkin himself traveled with a gypsy tabor (tribe), wrote a poem entitled *Gypsy,* and developed a particular fascination for the singing of the real Gypsy Tanya in 1831, the year he was completing his *Rusalka* (Eiges, *Muzyka v zhizni i tvorchestve Pushkina* [Music in the life and works of Pushkin] (Moscow: Muzgiz, 1937), 228, 232–33; Aleksandr Nikolaevich Glumov, *Muzykalnyi mir Pushkina* [Musical world of Pushkin] (Moscow: Gosudarstvennoe Muzykal'noe Izd-vo, 1950), 185.

77. Keldish, *Istoriia russkoi muzyki,* 451.

78. Smith, *Ballet and Opera,* 59–60.

79. Serov (1853) 78, 102.

80. Michelle Lamarche Marrese, *A Woman's Kingdom: Noblewomen and the*

Control of Property in Russia, 1700–1861 (Ithaca, N.Y.: Cornell University Press, 2002), 71–72.

81. Ibid., 1.

82. Bogdanovich, *Dushen'ka,* 55–57 and 36–38.

83. Ibid., 37–38.

84. Ibid., 55–56.

85. Pushkin 1950, 19. Historically, the vengeance against the named authors did not take place: writer and publisher Nikolai Novikov (1744–1818) died over two decades after Catherine's death (see Levitskii's famous portrait of Novikov, 1797); Kniazhin (1742–1791), serving as an adjutant of the tsar's general, was punished for financial misconduct, but soon forgiven. See *Poets of the Eighteenth Century,* ed. I. S. Serman (Leningrad: Soviet Writer, 1958), 233; Denis Fonvizin (1745–1792) throughout his life kept attacking the Russian imperial rule and the empress. See Marvin Kantor, *Dramatic Works of Fonvizin* (Frankfurt: Herbert Lane and Co. Ltd, 1974), 22.

86. In *The Captain's Daughter,* on the other hand, Catherine reveals surprising benevolence.

87. See Andrew Baruch Wachtel, *An Obsession with History: Russian Writers Confront the Past* (Stanford: Stanford University Press, 1994), 71, 81.

88. Pushkin studied at the Tsarskoe Selo Lyceum, where he met his best friends and associates.

89. In 1814, as a young graduate of the Lyceum, Pushkin created the poem "Vospominanya v Tsarskom sele" [Memory of the tsar's village] in which every step through the majestic palace reminds him of Catherine:

> . . . so vzdohom Ross veshchaet:
> Ischezlo vse, Velikoi bol'she net!
> With hindsight Russia proclaims
> Everything has vanished with the Great One gone!

In the *Captain's Daughter* the meeting of the heroine and Catherine also takes place in the tsar's village.

90. Also, in the poetic tale *Tsar'-Deviza* (1812), based on a collected folk tale and one of the early examples of the convergence between Russian folklore and literary tradition, Derzahvin not only invoked an image popular in folk tales, but created a vision of the "ideal monarch" (Lupanova, *Russkaya narodnaya skazka,* 61–62).

91. Nineteenth-century authors recast folk tales as "magic-knight poems." Savchenko commented on figures such as the Tsar-Maiden as *prishlezy* ("comers" or "aliens") long ago assimilated in Russian tales. See S. V. Savchenko, *Russkaia narodnaia skazka* [Russian folk tale] (Kiev: N.p., 1914; reprint, Cleveland: Bell & Howell, 1967), 278.

92. Alexander Turgenev as quoted by Lupanova, *Russkaya narodnaya skazka,* 7. Late-eighteenth-century collections of tales and folk songs include M. D. Chulkov, *The Anthology of Russian Songs,* 4 vols. (1770–1774); Chulkov, *Slavic Tales*

(1766–1768); M. V. Popov, *Slavic Antiquity, or the Adventures of Slavic Knights* (1770–1771); V. A. Levshin, *Russian Tales* (1780–1783); and *Evening Hours, and Ancient Tales of Ancient Slavs* (1787). By the mid-nineteenth century, among many published compilations were a significant anthology of V. I. Dal' in two volumes (1832 and 1846); A. N. Afanas'ev, *Folk Russian Tales* (1855–1864); as well as E. A. Avdeeva, *Essays on Maslenitsa in Europe, Russia, and Siberia* (1849); Avdeeva, *Russian Tales for Children, Told by Nanny Avdot'a Stepanovna Cherep'eva* (1844); B. Bronnizyn, *Russian Folk Tales* (1838); and *Tales Russian Told by Ivan Vanenko* (1838). Several scholarly works about the tale included a dissertation by Bodanski, "About Folk Poetry of the Slavic tribe" (1837), and Kostomarov's *About the Historic Importance of Russian Folk Poetry* (1847). According to the folklorist Vladimir Propp, only two European languages, Russian and German, have a special term denoting this genre. See Vladimir Propp, *Russkaya Skazka,* 35.

93. Karamzin's "Poor Liza," for example, was considered a *skazka*.

94. Propp, *Russkaya Skazka,* 182, 239.

95. See Clément, *Opera, or The Undoing of Women*.

96. Meyda Yegenogli, *Colonial Fantasies: Towards a Feminist Reading of Orientalism* (Cambridge: Cambridge University Press, 1998), 126.

Rheinsirenen

Loreley and Other Rhine Maidens

Annegret Fauser

In the film *Gentlemen Prefer Blondes,* young Henry Spofford III spots Lorelei Lee stuck in a porthole as she is trying to escape from private detective Malone's cabin. He explains why he is helping her: "The first reason is, I'm too young to be sent to jail. The second reason is, you've got a lot of animal magnetism."[1] Throughout the film, blonde and beautiful Lorelei Lee (Marilyn Monroe) shows herself in the possession of magic power, turning all men but one into helpless victims. Although her brunette friend Dorothy Shaw (Jane Russell) shares Lorelei's clothes, her music and, in one scene, even her blonde hair, the mysterious charm of Lorelei is never within her reach.[2] Lorelei's inexplicable spell over men becomes most obvious when she is seducing and singing; but even her simple entry into a room can create uncontrolled male responses.

Lorelei Lee does justice to her first name, which makes us understand where her seductive power comes from. It identifies her as a "siren"—and not just any siren, but as the dangerous Loreley. This beautiful sorceress combs her blonde hair with a golden comb, sitting on a rock high above the Rhine, where she sings her songs, captivating the attention of passing sailors and thus causing their deaths in the swirls of the river. Even our first visual impression of Lorelei Lee in the opening song, "We're Just Two Little Girls from Little Rock," is linked to this siren image through the sparkling, sequined red dress that fits Monroe's body as if she had a fishtail. And as the finishing touch, the number ends in front of a shimmering, dark-blue curtain, which adds to the marine impression. For the robust Dorothy, "a horse used to be my closest pal," while Lorelei's seductive voice tells us about her broken heart; they are different beings, not just different women. This siren image became so strongly identified with the role of Lorelei Lee, that we find it even in a recent collector's "Marilyn Monroe" Barbie doll, while the visual link between Monroe and Loreley as the "American siren" was never stronger than in her famous rendering of "Happy Birthday, Mr. President" a decade later, sparkling sequins included.[3] Lorelei Lee's affinity to music was present already in the literary source for the film. Anita Loos's novel *Gentlemen Prefer Blondes* shows Lorelei Lee as a woman with only two talents, for music and for seduction, but given that music-making demands practice, the heroine—a "professional lady"—decides to rely on her seductive charm alone.[4]

The Siren of the "Lurley Rock"

Sirens feature in many an ancient legend and have repeatedly been "associated with the enchanting, inspirational and prophetic quality of music."[5] Sirens are related also to knowledge, seduction, and danger, most famously in Homer's *Odyssey*. As a result of the nineteenth century's fascination with sexuality, nature, and culture, the siren became a trope for the alluring threat of female seduction, in particular the *femme fatale*. Countless paintings show beautiful women holding a lyre and singing. Their victims either are the spectator or the painter lured into the scene, or are represented as doomed or already dead male bodies. We encounter sirens in operas such as E. T. A. Hoffmann's *Undine* (1816) and Antonín Dvořák's *Rusalka* (1901), and we hear their wordless song in Claude Debussy's nocturne, *Sirènes* (1901). In this context, it is not surprising that the mechanical sound that warns us from danger—the siren—takes the name of its female embodiment.

Loreley, the siren of the Rhine, is rather young for a mythical creature. We even know her year of birth, 1802, and her genealogy as the main character in a long ballad by Clemens Brentano, which was included in his novel *Godwi*. The ballad told of a beautiful young fisherman's daughter, betrayed by love, who was transformed into the sorceress Loreley.[6] Brentano introduced "this magical Rhine seductress as an incarnation of the landscape where her fatal song and body guarded the Nibelung

Example 8.1. Friedrich Silcher, *Lorelei,* poem by Heinrich Heine, mm. 1–8; transcription of autograph score, Silcher Museum.

treasure for Father Rhine."[7] Loreley was named after the "Lurley" or "Lorle" Mountain, a rock formation above the Rhine near Goarshausen, which had featured in various texts about the Rhine Valley and its geography since the thirteenth century. The presence of a "spirit" in the rock was first mentioned in the early seventeenth century in the *Origines palatinae,* and by the mid-eighteenth century, local folklore started gendering the spirit as female.[8] The first literary text that turned the spirit into a woman and thus fixed the local narratives into a quickly and widely accepted pan-German legend was, however, Brentano's *Lorelei* ballad. Through it, the modern Rhine Siren was born, and the landscape was transformed into its female embodiment by naming the siren after the rock. Within a short span of time, Loreley became a widely appropriated legend, and her transformations—of which Marilyn Monroe's Lorelei Lee is but one of the more recent—provide a fascinating case-study of the cultural tropes involving the alluring but ultimately fatal seduction attributed to sirens in the nineteenth and twentieth centuries.

The Loreley myth played an important role in the forging of German national identity in the nineteenth century, particularly through Friedrich Silcher's 1837 setting of Heinrich Heine's *Loreley* (ex. 8.1). The strophic song in a lilting 6/8 barcarole rhythm was conceived as a folk-like melody, appropriate for a poem that depicted an "old fairy tale."[9] Silcher's version acquired the status of a popular national hymn, which traveled with immigrants to the shores of the United States of America and to the German colonies in South West Africa.[10] The iconic power of the Silcher song becomes evident at the beginning of the 1979 television drama *Holocaust,* when a wedding party, comprising a wide range of the political and religious strands of 1930s Germany, unites in singing "Ich weiß nicht, was soll es bedeuten." Loreley had become the symbol for German "Rheinromantik," invoking patriotic nostalgia and nationalism in all its colors.

While European writers were fascinated with various female spirits in general, the Rhine Siren continued to represent German Romanticism in European literature, from Gérard de Nerval's enraptured evocation in *Loreley, souvenirs d'Allemagne* in 1852 to Maurice Genevoix's ambiguous novel *Lorelei* from 1978,[11] in which Genevoix's hero Julien refers to Romanticism's dark but seductive side: "Romanticism? . . . That is dangerous. More so than the dazzling golden adornment and the song of the Loreley above the crags of the Rhine."[12] English travelers and readers encountered the romantic Loreley as well, as for example in the nineteenth-century compilation *Legends of the Rhine:*

> It is no wonder, that there are so many popular tales about the rock of the 'Lurley' for there is not a mountain so romantically situated and so interesting. In times of yore a charming 'undine' had selected this rock for her abode; every evening she sate [*sic*] at the top of it, combed her golden hair or accompanied her pathetic and melodious songs on a golden lute. Every one, who saw and heard her, was charmed and felt in his heart a deep and passionate love, so that for the purpose of seeing the lovely enchantress, a great many boats, approaching too near the rock, were dashed on it and hurled into the foaming waves.[13]

The enchantress with her lyre is visible right at the outset of this book, on the engraving opposite the title page.

We also encounter Loreley in engravings that decorate sheet music and vocal scores. Thus even before we hear her music, we see its effect. Hans Pfitzner recalled his first encounter with the Rhine Siren when he opened the vocal score of Max Bruch's 1863 opera *Die Loreley* (fig. 8.1):

> Ich war noch ein Schulbub, höchstens elf bis zwölf Jahre alt . . . da fand ich . . . eines Tages in dem Notenschrank meines Vaters einen großen Klavierauszug. Er war dunkelgrün geheftet, das Titelblatt zeigte folgendes Bild: Ein Strom, von hohen Felsen begrenzt. Im Vordergrunde ein Baum mit breiten Ästen, in deren Schatten ein Liebespaar sich umschlungen hält—ein Jäger, an ihn geschmiegt ein Mädchen. Auf einem der hohen Felsen im Hintergrunde eine Frauengestalt in fliegenden Gewändern, mit der Harfe im Arm, am Fuß des Felsens im Nebel undeutlich ein Geisterreigen. Auf dem Grunde des Stromes die Leiche eines Mannes. Das war die 'Loreley' von Max Bruch.

> (When I was still a schoolboy, no more than eleven or twelve years old . . . I found . . . one day in my father's music library a large vocal score. It was bound in dark green, and the title page showed the following picture: A stream, surrounded by high cliffs. In the foreground a tree with large branches, in the shade of which a couple embraces—a young hunter, a girl nestled against him. On a high rock in the background, a woman in floating dress, with a harp in her arm; at the foot of the rock, blurred in the mist, a round of ghosts. On the bottom of the river the body of a man. This was the *Loreley* by Max Bruch.)[14]

Figure 8.1. Title page of Max Bruch, *Die Loreley,* text by
Emanuel Geibel (Breslau: Verlag Leuckart, 1863). By
permission of the Staatsbibliothek Berlin Stiftung Preußischer
Kulturbesitz.

Indeed, so quickly did the image of the harp- or lyre-playing beauty on the
rock become the familiar manner of representing Loreley that it could
serve as a clear iconographic reference even in caricatures, as in a title page
of *The Wasp* from 1883 that shows the American president Grover Cleveland as "the new Lorelei" whose song caused the shipwreck in the background (fig. 8.2).

The magic power of Loreley's singing is often echoed in the legend's
non-German reception, from the British musical play *A Royal Exchange* to
George and Ira Gershwin's *Pardon My English* from 1933.[15] In *A Royal
Exchange,* one of the hero's refrains begins "Your melody haunts me like a

Figure 8.2. *The New Lorelei*, cartoon, title page of *The Wasp*, August 11, 1883. Hawai'i State Archives, Honolulu. Kahn Collection. Corner note: "We are glad to hear evidences that the monumental fraud called the Kingdom of the Sandwich Islands, which has been maintained for the past twelve years at the expense of the people of the United States, is ready to fall to pieces. We presume that England will then step in and assume a protectorate."

Figure 8.3. Leonard Emil Bach, *Die neue Loreley,* opus 28, text by Siegmey (Berlin: C. A. Challier & Cie, 1878), title page. By permission of the British Library.

Lorelei." In *Pardon My English,* the Gershwins clearly combine the image of both political and sexual danger in the song *Lorelei*: in its refrain, the (German) female character describes herself as treacherous, lecherous, and full of passion, while interpolating this statement with the German "Ja, ja." Her love had overtones of both Wagner's Valkyries and yodeling:

> She used to love in a strange kind of fashion,
> With lots of hey! hodeho! hidehi!
> And I can guarantee I'm full of passion
> Like the Lorelei.

This number continued to refer to the famous Rhine song, for the "satiric tag finish of the printed music . . . echoed Silcher's familiar setting of the Heine poem."[16] Given the political situation, it is not surprising that the song was republished in London in 1944 or that, in a novel set toward the end of World War II, the "mission Loreley" would take the heroes into occupied Lorraine and the Rhine Valley.[17] But Loreley had already served as a German national symbol in the Franco-Prussian War of 1870, where Germans evoked her in a traditional siren's or mermaid's role as guardian of rivers, streams, wells, and oceans.[18] A striking example of this chauvinist literature is Siegmey's *Die neue Loreley* (1878), a reworking of Heine's poem in which Loreley is credited for alerting the German "knights" to the attack of French soldiers with her songs.[19] The cover of the sheet music (fig. 8.3) offers a fair-haired and imperial Loreley in front of a German army, warding off a fleet of French soldiers crossing the Rhine. Siegmey's poem turned Heine's opening phrase, "I don't know what it means," into "Now I know what it means," and he went from there to proclaim the new Loreley as victorious, with the imperial crown on her golden locks.[20] At the beginning of World War I, the same poem—to be sung to Silcher's well-known melody—was distributed by Emil Freiherr von Mirbach as a morale-boosting song text to the German troops.[21]

It was the conflation of universal archetype and national, if not "Teutonic," icon that, combined with her dangerous sexual allure, turned Loreley into such a modern siren. Right from the outset, the Rhine Siren was trapped within the opposing tensions of German Romanticism, which tried to create a German national identity through a universalist, *allgemein menschliche* culture.[22] As Cecilia Hopkins Porter has put it: "The appearance of the Romantic Loreley image in the work of Brentano and the Heidelberg Romantics illustrated the process whereby a culture's need to rediscover its mythic past resulted in the formulation of a new mythology based on an object of nature's beauty and its surrogate symbols."[23]

The Music of a Siren

Once Brentano had given birth to the romantic Loreley, the Rhine Siren ignited the fantasy of poets and composers. Poets reveled in descriptions of the effects of her singing. Heinrich Heine, for example, called it "a weird refrain / that steeps in a deadly enchantment / the listener's ravished brain."[24] In his 1840 novella, *Irrungen der Liebe*, Carl Matzerath's retelling of Heine's "old fairy-tale of Lorelei, the siren of the Rhine" portrayed her music as that of "a ghost voice singing a song of magic euphony."[25] Karl Geib described her song as "wondrously beautiful," like "the sound of a flute in the evening gold."[26] And the romantic poet Wolfgang Müller von Königswinter tried over and over again to capture the siren's music in his poems, culminating in his *Rheinfahrt,* which only throws in her name at the opening and continues by describing the result:

Die Lorelei!—Der Schiffer schaut und lauscht,
der Fahrt vergessend. Weh, am Felsenriffe
Zerschellt der Kahn! Die nasse Woge rauscht
Verderbend ob dem Jüngling und dem Schiffe!—

(The Lorelei!—the sailor looks and listens, / Forgetting the voyage. Woe!
On the crags / The boat is wrecked! The wet wave rushes / Fatally over the
youth and the ship!—)[27]

Composers, however, faced a mighty challenge, especially in dramatic settings that would take up Brentano's story line of a beautiful woman being transformed into a nymph or sorceress because she was betrayed by her beloved and then sold her soul for magic power. As with Orpheus, composers were confronted with musically representing a being whose expressive force lays within music itself, but not just any music. Loreley embodies the dangerous, seductive side of music, its sensual *jouissance,* its feminine part, its fatal attraction. In the nineteenth century—and based on it, in the twentieth—musical conventions offered composers a rich tool-box to represent feminine seduction and sensuality, which included lush instrumentation and chromaticism.[28] The musical representation of Lore-ley, however, needed more than just these musical signifiers in order to signal the difference between mere female guile and the magic attraction of a being both feminine and eternal. In dramatic compositions, another problem occurs as well: when do we hear Loreley simply communicate and when do we hear her siren's song? A look at some nineteenth-century compositions might help answer this question.

In 1854, Ferdinand Hiller—a well-respected German composer active in the middle of the nineteenth century—set out to compose his version of the Loreley legend in a dramatic cantata, a popular genre, in particular with amateur choruses. He collaborated on it with Wolfgang Müller von Königswinter. A letter that Hiller wrote to the poet at the outset of their project allows us a glimpse into his reasoning:

[I]ch habe nachgedacht, warum man sie auf alle Weise in Musik gesetzt hat, nur nicht auf die *eigentlichste* — ich bin zu keinem andern Resul-tat gekommen als zu dem Entschluß, es selbst zu thun, wenn Sie mir dabei helfen wollen. Der Moment nämlich, wo die schöne Hexe durch ihren Gesang den Schiffer dem Untergang weiht, die eigentliche Quint-essenz der Sage, ist nicht komponirt und doch eigentlich so musi-

kalisch, dass man höchstens ihm vorwerfen könnte, er sei es zu sehr.
[emphasis Hiller]

(I have thought about the fact why so far, one has set [Loreley] to music
in all sorts of ways, but never in the *truest*—I came to no other result
than the resolution to do it myself if you would agree to help me with it.
Namely the moment, in which the beautiful sorceress dooms the sailor
through her singing, the real quintessence of the legend, has not been
composed and is yet so musical that one could reproach it at best as
being too musical.)[29]

After outlining the scene, Hiller continued:

Was Details anlangt, so würde es vielleicht gut sein, *vor* dem Gesang der
Loreley nur *männliche* Geister auftreten zu lassen, um auch den Effekt
der weiblichen Stimme der Hexe aufzubewahren. . . . Das Lied des
Schiffers muss ein Strophenlied sein — wo hingegen der Gesang der
Loreley eine gewisse ungebundene phantastische Wildheit bewahren
müßte. [emphasis Hiller]

(In as far as details are concerned, it might be good to have only *male*
spirits *before* the song of the Loreley in order to reserve the effect of the
female voice for the sorceress. . . . The song of the sailor has to be
strophic, whereas the singing of Loreley would need to retain a certain
unbound fantastical wildness.)[30]

In the finished composition, Hiller kept to his plan to set the sailor's song
strophically, but Loreley's is far from the "unbound fantastical wildness"
to which he referred. Hiller represented the alluring song in a closed
bipartite setting with a coda, with harp accompaniment and chromatic
passages in the melodic line, while the general harmonic structure remained firmly grounded in a diatonic frame.[31] It appears that the harp
accompaniment and the closed musical form were part of the sign system
that composers used to represent Loreley's songs. Paul and Lucien Hillemacher, in their *Loreley* cantata from 1883 on a text by Eugène Adenis,
employed similar means as Hiller to render the siren's music.[32] This cantata opens with Loreley's ballad set as a separate piece, like Silcher's setting
in a barcarole rhythm, accompanied by the harp (ex. 8.2). The siren's song
thus becomes diegetic music, a "song" performed by Loreley. But this song
proves deadly to the sailors on the river. The scenic description that accompanies her ballad in 6/8 informs us about its effect:

Plusieurs navires descendent le fleuve . . . les voix se rapprochent . . .
tout à coup, un chant triste s'élève: c'est la Ballade de Lore.

(Several ships descend on the river . . . the voices approach . . . all at once a sad song begins: it is the ballad of Lore.)

After the ballad:

Le fleuve s'entr'ouvre et les navires, entraînés vers le rocher de Lore, se brisent et disparaissent dans l'abîme. . . Peu à peu les eaux se referment et le calme reparaît.

(The river opens itself, and the ships, pulled toward Lore's rock, crash and disappear in the abyss. . . Slowly the waters close again, and the calm returns.)[33]

Both Hiller and the two Hillermachers use diegetic song as the element of seduction and the tool of destruction.[34] Hiller's Loreley tells the story of her pain and transformation as the source of her fatal power while destroying by way of her song the young man approaching on the river, collapsing narration and dramatic action into one theatrical moment. Even in its apparent simplicity, her song thus seems to fit into the characteristic topos of dramatic narration in nineteenth-century operas. As Carolyn Abbate has shown, such narrative song often represents reflexive instances within the dramaturgy of an opera.[35] It is usually reserved for a unique moment, whether as revelation of a person's history or through informing the characters and audience about events that take place outside the scene. But in Hiller's cantata, and in contrast to Abbate's view, Loreley's narration of her history becomes a never-changing performance "on demand" whose effect is already a foregone conclusion, turning the uniqueness of narration within a dramatic context into an absurdity: every time Loreley repeats her story a man drowns.[36] In the later cantata by Paul and Lucien Hillemacher, however, Loreley does not even narrate her life in her destructive song, but rather she alludes to a "sleeping past" and "dark silence" (ex. 8.2), yearning for eternal sleep "under roses." The absence of narration within a song designated as "narrative" through its generic title as a "ballad" creates tension between text and music. The sailor should hear the sad tale but the text offers only fragments and relies on the audience's memory of the Loreley myth. Thus both Loreley narrations differ from the habitual narrative song in operas such as Meyerbeer's *Robert le Diable* (1831) or Wagner's *Der fliegende Holländer* (1843) in that they take an operatic trope and mould it into a siren's song, where music rather than text becomes the dramatic agent. Neither Hiller's nor the Hillemachers' Loreley creates narration as a "composing singer" in the way Tannhäuser does in his Rome narrative, where "Tannhäuser in effect

Example 8.2. Paul and Lucien Hillemacher, *Loreley, légende symphonique en trois parties*, text by Eugène Adonis. Paris: Tresse Editeur, 1883, 10, mm. 1–7.

begins to make music as a translation for the events that he narrates."[37] Instead the sirens are imprisoned in the act of performance, in an endless loop of repetition, performing music disguised as a narrative song, whose text is inconsequential in a plot whose quintessence, as Hiller's letter (cited above) indicated, was if anything only "too musical."

Indeed Loreley's act of seduction consists in the act of musical performance. What kind of music she performs will depend on the context of composition, but the seductive song needs to be different from other music in the piece, and the composer has to set a sign for the beginning of the magic song. In his opera *Loreley* (1890), Alfredo Catalani used, like Hiller and the Hillemachers, a change of instrumentation, especially the harp arpeggios, and the alluring call "come, come, come to my heart" to indicate the beginning of the siren's song, which he set as a closed musical form. The opening verses of Loreley's magic song allude even to another enchantress, Armida, with her:

Vieni! sul Reno, ho un' isola
tutta profumi e fior. . . .
(Come! On the Rhine, I have an island / all perfumed and flowering. . . .)[38]

However, unlike the representation of other sorceresses such as, for example, Massenet's Esclarmonde, it is not the virtuosic and alluring female vocalize that indicates Loreley's seductive singing in these nineteenth-century compositions, but a song accompanied by the harp. Indeed, the iconographic link of Loreley to her golden harp is so strong that composers make us listen to it even in a miniature such as Schumann's setting of Eichendorff's *Waldesgespräch* (1840), a dialogue between Loreley and a knight. The beginning of Loreley's seductive song is marked—as in dramatic settings—by a different harmony, melody, and "instrumentation": here the piano's contrasting arpeggios after the chordal first strophe clearly invoke the harp (ex. 8.3). The harmonic shift to C major in mes. 15 creates enough tonal distance to suggest another musical world, while Loreley's lilting and diatonic melody plays on musical signifiers of well-bred femininity.[39]

Example 8.3. Robert Schumann, *Waldesgespräch*, poem by Joseph von Eichendorff, mm. 11–20.

It is surprising that Loreley's magic music in nineteenth-century compositions lacks virtuosity, especially if compared to the prototype of all magic vocal music: Monteverdi's "Possente spirto," the lyre-playing Orfeo's showpiece.[40] It may reflect the siren's ancestry as a fisherman's daughter from the Rhine turned siren—therefore someone simple in her expression. She is not the highly trained male singer, the composing poet such as Orpheus or Tannhäuser. Loreley is just a woman with a sweet, bewitching voice that complements her beauty. Although, in literature and painting, we find her represented as a *femme fatale,* in music she sings almost like a bourgeois daughter in the parlor. The simplicity of her music might also reflect the overwhelming influence of Silcher's *Loreley* and of the folk-tone tradition that stems from it. But there may be more. It could well be the "grain" of her female voice that creates such fatal attraction, not the elaborate "science" of her musical art; thus what a composer makes us listen to in Loreley's diegetic songs is music whose simplicity allows us to admire without distraction "the grain, that is the body in the singing voice."[41]

Rhine Maidens

The centrality of the "grain" of the seducing female voice, and also the oedipal desire toward the alluring sound that stands at the beginning of consciousness, becomes more obvious in a different nineteenth-century incarnation of Loreley. Richard Wagner's version of the enchantress in the guise of three "mermaid Rhine Maidens"[42] in *Der Ring des Nibelungen* combines the sexual allure of Loreley plus her mermaid role as the protector of the river and its treasures with the Platonic concept of the sirens as figures that were part of the origins of the world.[43] The very first appearance of the Rhine Maidens in *Das Rheingold* (1869) offers a multiplicity of roles for these three creatures. The most obvious and traditional is that of three mermaid-guardians. Wagner's stage directions have them floating gracefully around the treasure that they are guarding, and the first performance in Bayreuth in 1876 tried to convey this visual impression with the means of the time, including "swimming cars" (*Schwimmwagen*). The barcarole rhythm in 6/8 and the periodic structure of Woglinde's "Weia! Waga! Woge du Welle!" ("Weia! Waga! Undulate you wave!"), with its arpeggiated accompaniment, takes up the familiar pattern of representing Loreley's diegetic song in nineteenth-century music, and Woglinde's is also a song containing the sexual allure that brings Alberich into the drama. We hear Woglinde over the *pianissimo* orchestra, the grain of her voice almost touchable in the simple triadic music whose onomatopoeic text does not distract from the sound (ex. 8.4).

But Woglinde's music is more than the short diegetic song of a Wagnerian Loreley. It is also a siren's contribution to the development of theories of music and language, in particular of the Wagnerian drama. In a famous passage in *Opera and Drama* from 1851, Wagner tried to describe his notions of music, language, and drama in gendered terms echoing contemporary theories of femininity and masculinity, such as the burning issues as to whether women did have a soul.[44] Wagner wrote:

Example 8.4. Richard Wagner, *Das Rheingold,* act 1, scene 1.

Die Musik ist die Gebärerin, der Dichter der Erzeuger. . . . *Die Musik ist ein Weib.* Die Natur des Weibes ist die *Liebe:* aber diese Liebe ist die *empfangende* und in der Empfängnis rückhaltlos *sich hingebende.* Das Weib erhält volle Individualität erst im Moment der Hingebung. Es ist das Wellenmädchen, das seelenlos durch die Wogen seines Elementes dahinrauscht, bis es durch die Liebe eines Mannes erst die Seele empfängt. [emphasis Wagner]

(Music is the child bearer, the poet, the procreator. . . . *Music is a woman.* Her nature is *love:* but this love is the *conceiving* kind, which in conceiving *gives itself* without restraint. Woman only receives full individuality at the moment of self-abandonment. She is the mermaid who swims, soulless, through the waves of her element, until she receives her soul through the love of a man.)[45]

The metaphor stands for the relationship of text and music in the generating of the drama. Wagner, as Reinhart Meyer-Kalkus puts it, composed in the song of the Rhine Maidens a myth of the genesis of language.[46] Woghilde's first words were derived by Wagner from the old German *Heilawac* ("holy water"). The procedure of forming Woghilde's verses, Wagner explained to Nietzsche, was similar to the way in which nursery rhymes such as "eia popeia" function.[47] But Wagner did not stop with the onomatopoeic derivations for the text. Woghilde's first utterance offers a—what one might call Wagnerian—"nursery rhyme" in musical terms, undulating up and down the triadic structure of an A flat major chord that floats over the E flat pedal like the mermaid in the water, while her nonsense sounds of "Weia waga" become words of invitation to the listener to approach the cradle: "Walle zur Wiege." These few bars encapsulate the moment when text emerges from music, when—to take on Wagner's metaphor—the drama is born. Thus the Rhine Maidens seem to represent a mythical but also human original state, the return both to the mother and a mythical past. They float in what Wagner called the "It"—the water—in dancing movement, communicating in an archaic sung language—a mythical *Ursprache*—where the "signified" has not yet been become alienated from the signifier.[48] Woglinge's *Stabreime* emerge out of the triadic sounds of the *Rheingold* prelude, shaping knowledge from the "mother element, the musical tone."[49] Therefore Wagner's multiple versions of Loreley in his Rhine Maidens turned the fisherman's daughter into the symbol of the power of music not only through their effect on the men present in the story (such as Alberich) but also through their alluring appeal to the listener today longing for an ideal state of being.

The mythical words that Woglinde evokes in her onomatopoeic lullaby "Weia! Waga!," however, belong not to a universal but to a particular language: German.[50] Thus the claim to universality of Wagner's myth is curbed by the specificity of its location within the heritage of German culture. If Brentano's and Heine's incarnations of Loreley, "the Rhine Siren," are embodiments of a landscape invested with national significance, Wagner's Rhine Maidens take this form of nationalizing a step further. The specificity of the landscape and her elementary spirits in the form of his Rhine Maidens nationalizes the myth of creation of humanity as culture. Indeed, by superseding the traditional Germanic landscape of the Teutonic forest—epitomized in Carl Maria von Weber's *Der Freischütz* (1821)—with the more universal water flowing down the Rhine, Wagner shifted, in one fell swoop, the location of national identity from the specific to the universal by invoking, in Wagner's words, the "lullaby of the world."[51] No other incarnation of Loreley took so far the romantic German-national notion of establishing national identity through universal cognition.[52]

But Loreley's modest ancestry as a fisherman's daughter and her fusion with the "Rheinromantik" seems to have triggered a further strand of reception in popular novels, tourist souvenirs, and other forms of triviali-zation.[53] They were as much part of the Loreley reception as were satire, irony, political reference, and music drama. Indeed, few sirens have been appropriated so widely as Loreley in the Western world of the nineteenth and twentieth centuries. She served not only as a social and artistic sign for the dangerous woman in all her colors but also as a political symbol both in creating a national myth and in identifying political danger. She devel-oped from the simple fisherman's daughter to a first-rate *femme fatale*, and she still seems to continue her transformations according to the needs of our time. When surfing the Internet, I came across a variety of refer-ences, of which the most dire was probably the pornographic "Bedroom Bondage—Lorelei's Diary," in the tradition of Loreley's *femme fatale* im-age, and of which the most pathetic may well be the homepage of a student from the University of Oregon, "Lorelei's Love Page," where we learn that

> [Lorelei's] beauty was her undoing. Lorelei was not willfully seductive, but men could not resist her charms, and she could not resist their advances. She was bringing scandal and disgrace to the respectable town of Bacharach-on-the-Rhine.[54]

The student has echoed the soppy kitsch of the popular nineteenth-century reception of the Loreley myth, particularly in trivial novels.[55] Indeed, the Mills & Boon list of romance novels bears witness to its on-going popularity with books such as Lucy Gordon's *Song of the Lorelei* (1993). "Reading Loreley" has become a popular activity of which "sing-ing Loreley" constitutes only a small part. It is the imaginary voice of the siren more than the actual sound that continues to seduce us. We do not even need to hear the sound of her voice—the simple reference to her best-known incarnation in Silcher's *Loreley*-setting might be enough to create a web of intertextual references, as for example in the installation *Autour de la Lorelei* by the Belgian symbolist Marcel Broodthaer, or in the poster for the Oberhausen Theater production of *Die Loreley* in 1984.[56] Neverthe-less, we not only see or read, but we still hear Loreley sing, not only when we see Wagner's *Das Rheingold* in the opera house but also even in popular music such as the Pogues' Irish hit "Lorelei" or Eagle-Eye Cherry's song "When Mermaids Cry."

Whereas the musical means and materials changed during the twen-tieth century, the notion of creating musical difference when setting Lore-ley's siren song remained a constant factor as regards her sonic representa-tion. In *Gentlemen Prefer Blondes*, Lorelei Lee has only one solo number. It is the piece which—according to Dorothy—shows the "true" Lorelei. It is a diegetic piece, a performed song aiming to seduce men both onstage and in the audience. As in the other compositions discussed earlier, the composer begins the piece with musical signs to alert us to the fact that this is the film's siren-song. Difference in a Broadway musical can mean the use of traditional operatic elements. In "Diamonds Are a Girl's Best Friend" we find as the opening sequence a ballet-style dance instead of a show number and operatic coloratura instead of the usual, straightforward text setting. The subsequent song presents us with a "composite" Loreley image: simple, witty lyrics in a strophic setting with refrains, but rendered by a sexually alluring blonde with a voice whose grain promises everything that a siren can offer: seduction, danger, and knowledge.

NOTES

I have presented versions of this text at scholarly meetings from Cambridge and Dublin to Malta, Zaragoza, and Chapel Hill. I am grateful for the fascinating contributions in discussions by colleagues and friends, of whom several were generous enough to offer me their time reading drafts. I wish to thank Juan José Carreras, Tim Carter, Jon Finson, and Anne MacNeil for their help and time.

1. *Gentlemen Prefer Blondes,* Twentieth Century Fox Film Corporation, 1953; directed by Howard Hawks; screenplay by Charles Lederer, based on Anita Loos's and Joseph Fields's successful Broadway version (1949) of Loos's novel (1925).

2. I do not agree with Lawrence Kramer's reading of the film, in particular with his understanding of both women as sirens. If anything, Dorothy is shown as an unsuccessful siren. Her song "Ain't There Anyone Here for Love"—what he calls a "poolside extravaganza" (174)—does not attract the attention of the Olympic team that she woos; they ignore her invitation for love. In the double numbers with Lorelei she serves as the background (her gesture urging Monroe to dance in "When Love Goes Wrong" plays on this difference). The closest Dorothy comes to being a siren is in her impersonation of Lorelei in the courtroom; but this scene reveals her as a cunning actress, not a seductive siren. See Lawrence Kramer, *After the Lovedeath: Sexual Violence and the Making of Culture* (Berkeley: University of California Press, 1997), 174–76.

3. The Internet advertisement informs us: "Marilyn Monroe's role of Lorelei Lee in the musical Gentlemen Prefer Blondes. Barbie wears a glittering sequin gown with a v-neck and high slit." See "Gentlemen prefer Blondes #1 Barbie." http://www.newbarbie.com/marilyntop.htm. Meyer's Toy World New Barbie Center: "Marilyn Monroe Barbie® Series," accessed July 2, 1998.

4. "[M]y family all wanted me to do something about my music. Because all my friends said I had talent and they all kept after me and kept after me about practising. But some way I never seemed to care much about practising. I mean I

simply could not sit for hours and hours at a time practising just for the sake of a career. So one day I got quite temperamental and threw the old mandolin clear across the room and I have really never touched it since." Anita Loos, *Gentlemen Prefer Blondes: The Illuminating Diary of a Professional Lady* (Harmondsworth, U.K.: Penguin Books, 1992), 20.

5. Daniel Chua and Henry Stobart, announcement for the international symposium "Knowledge, Seduction and Danger: Music and the Sirens," Cambridge, U.K., 1998.

6. See Elisabeth Frenzel, *Stoffe der Weltliteratur: Ein Lexikon dichtungsgeschichtlicher Längsschnitte*, 8th ed. (Stuttgart: Alfred Kröner Verlag, 1992), 467. For an excellent and concise overview of the development of the Loreley subject in the nineteenth century, see Heinrich Heine, *Historisch-kritische Gesamtausgabe der Werke*, 1:2. *Buch der Lieder: Apparat*, ed. and annotated by Pierre Grappin (Hamburg: Hoffmann und Campe Verlag, 1975), 878–86.

7. Cecilia Hopkins Porter, *The Rhine as Musical Metaphor: Cultural Identity in German Romantic Music* (Boston: Northeastern University Press, 1996), 112.

8. Heinrich Heine, *Historisch-kritische Gesamtausgabe der Werke*, 1:2, 881.

9. Ibid., 1:1. *Buch der Lieder: Text*, ed. Pierre Grappin (Hamburg: Hoffmann und Campe Verlag, 1975), 206: "Ein Mährchen aus alten Zeiten."

10. The song was published in many adaptations and translations all over the world. One early example for this is C. Everest's translation, published in Philadelphia in 1859, of which the first eight bars are reproduced in Hopkins Porter, *The Rhine as Musical Metaphor*, 127. Other publications include, for example, a song collection published in Boston in 1848, and a version from 1870, *That Fatal Lore Ley!* (London: Augener & Co., 1870).

11. Marcel Genevoix, *Lorelei* (Paris: Editions du Seuil, 1978). On Genevoix's ambiguous relation to Germany, see Klaus Heitmann, "Deutschland als Bezauberung und Bedrohung: Maurice Genevoix und sein Roman *Lorelei*," *Zeitschrift für französische Sprache und Literatur* 92 (1982): 9–27.

12. " . . . le Romantisme? . . . c'est dangereux. Plus que l'éblouissante parure d'or et le chant de la Lorelei au-dessus des écueils du Rhin." Given in Heitmann, "Deutschland als Bezauberung," 20.

13. A. H. Bernard, *Legends of the Rhine*, trans. Fr. Arnold, 11th ed. (Wiesbaden: Gustav Quiel, 1900), 233.

14. Hans Pfitzner, *Meine Beziehungen zu Max Bruch* (Munich: Albert Langen/Georg Müller, 1938), 5–6. Bruch's opera was based on a libretto that Emmanuel Geibel had written in the mid-1840s for Felix Mendelssohn Bartholdy. It was the only operatic project Mendelssohn ever took beyond discussion toward actual composition, but only some fragments survive. See R. Larry Todd, "On Mendelssohn's Operatic Destiny: *Die Lorelei* Reconsidered," in *Felix Mendelssohn Bartholdy: Kongreß-Bericht Berlin 1994*, ed. Christian Martin Schmidt (Wiesbaden: Breitkopf & Härtel, 1997), 113–40.

15. Frederick Herendon and Edward Horan, *A Royal Exchange*, "a romantic

musical play at His Majesty's Theatre" (London: Chappell & Co., 1935). The song entitled "Lorelei" starts with hummed broken chords and the lyrics: " I hear you call / From the clear blue, / And when I hear you, / I must be near you. / And when I'm near you / I fear you, / You're such a dear, / You mean more than all." George and Ira Gershwin's *Pardon My English* was first performed on January 20, 1933 at the Majestic Theatre, New York.

16. Lawrence D. Stewart, "Words upon Music," in the booklet for *Ella Fitzgerald Sings the George and Ira Gershwin Song Books* (Verve 1998), 19–65, at 61.

17. Charles Gilbert, *Mission Loreley en Lorraine occupée, 5 novembre–24 décembre 1944* (Les Sables d'Olonne: Cercle d'Or, 1985).

18. Hopkins Porter, *The Rhine as Musical Metaphor*, 110.

19. Leonard Emil Bach, *Die neue Loreley*, opus 28, text by Siegmey (Berlin: C. A. Challier & Cie, 1878).

20. Bach, *Die neue Loreley*, 1: "Nun weiss ich, was soll es bedeuten." Inna Naroditskaya, in her contribution to this volume, shows that both the Russian Rusalka (in Dargomyzhsky's 1858 opera) and Hansler and Kauer's *Donauweibchen* (1798) are crowned sirens who serve as national emblems.

21. Heinrich Lindlar, *Loreley-Report: Heinrich Heine und die Rheinliedromantik* (Cologne: Verlag Christoph Dohr, 1999), 135.

22. See in this context Siegfried Oechsle, "Nationalidee und große Symphonie: Mit einem Exkurs zum 'Ton,'" in *Deutsche Meister—böse Geister? Nationale Selbstfindung in der Musik*, ed. Hermann Danuser and Herfried Münkler (Schliengen: Edition Argus, 2001), 166–84; Carl Dahlhaus, *Die Musik des 19. Jahrhunderts*, vol. 6: *Neues Handbuch der Musikwissenschaft* (Laaber: Laaber-Verlag, 1980), 29–34.

23. Hopkins Porter, *The Rhine as Musical Metaphor*, 108.

24. The translation cited is by Mark Twain [Samuel L. Clemens], *A Tramp Abroad*, 2 vols., Stormfield ed. (New York: Harper & Brothers, 1929), 126. Heine, *Historisch-kritische Gesamtausgabe*, 1:1, 208: "Und singt ein Lied dabei; / Das hat eine wundersame, / Gewaltige Melodei."

25. Carl Matzerath, *Irrungen der Liebe* (1840), given in Heine, *Historisch-kritische Gesamtausgabe der Werke*, 1:2, 880: "Nun erhebt sie die Geisterstimme zu einem Liede zauberischen Wohllauts; sehnsuchtsatmend verschweben die Töne über Berg und Thal."

26. "Wie Flötenklang im Abendgold / Durch Auen und den Hain / Tönt eine Stimme wunderhold / Von Lurleis Fels am Rhein," given in Gerhard Bürger, *Im Zauber der Loreley: Eine kleine Monographie* (St. Goarshausen: Loreley-Verlag, 1952), 39.

27. Given in Dr. Nicolaus Hocker, *Rhein-Album* (Berlin: in Commission bei Mitscher & Röstell, 1873), n.p.

28. The literature on musical representation of gendered voices has grown significantly over the past decade. One of the key texts is still Marcia J. Citron, *Gender and the Musical Canon* (Cambridge: Cambridge University Press, 1993).

29. Letter by Ferdinand Hiller to Wolfgang Müller from September 6, 1854, given in Helmut Loos, "Wolfgang Müller von Königswinter und die Musik," in *Musikalische Rheinromantik: Bericht der Jahrestagung 1985,* ed. Siegfried Kross, vol. 140, *Beiträge zur rheinischen Musikgeschichte* (Kassel: Merseberger, 1989), 113–24, letter on 115–16.

30. Ibid., 116.

31. Ferdinand Hiller, *Lorelei,* opus 70, poem by Wolfgang Müller von Königswinter (Leipzig: Fr. Kirstner, 1857). See also Reinhold Sietz: "Die musikalische Gestaltung der Loreleysage bei Max Bruch, Felix Mendelssohn und Ferdinand Hiller," in *Max Bruch-Studien,* ed. Dietrich Kämper, vol. 87, *Beiträge zur rheinischen Musikgeschichte* (Cologne: Arno Volk Verlag, 1970), 14–45, here 44–45.

32. Paul and Lucien Hillemacher, *Loreley. Légende symphonique en trois parties,* text by Eugène Adenis, "Ouvrage couronné au Concours Municipal de la Ville de Paris" (Paris: Tresse Editeur, 1883).

33. Hillemacher, *Loreley,* 1, 2.

34. See Carolyn Abbate, *Unsung Voices: Opera and Musical Narrative in the Nineteenth Century* (Princeton, N.J.: Princeton University Press, 1991), 62.

35. Abbate, *Unsung Voices,* 70.

36. The naiads demand "Komm herbei, Lorelei . . . O singe, süsse Lorelei," to which Lorelei responds: "Ach! sie fordern meine Lieder und des neuen Opfers Gaben!" See Hiller, *Lorelei,* passim.

37. Abbate, *Unsung Voices,* 117–18.

38. Alfredo Catalani, *Loreley,* text by Carlo D'Ormeville and Angelo Zanardini, piano-vocal score (Milan: Ricordi, n.d.), 198.

39. Opera criticism has shown how these musical signifiers have an almost standardized reception field within the context of European nineteenth-century music. An obvious example for such nineteenth-century use of signifiers could be the contrasting musical representation of Carmen and Micaëla in Georges Bizet's opera *Carmen* (1875).

40. See John Whenham, *Claudio Monteverdi: "Orfeo,"* Cambridge Opera Handbooks (Cambridge: Cambridge University Press, 1986), 68–69.

41. Roland Barthes, *L'obvie et l'obtus. Essais critiques III* (Paris: Editions du Seuil, 1982), 243: "Le 'grain', c'est le corps dans la voix qui chante, dans la main qui écrit, dans le membre qui exécute." For an interpretation of Barthes' notion of the "grain" of the voice, see Reinhart Meyer-Kalkus: "Das 'Korn der Stimme'— Sprachtheoretische Voraussetzungen der Kritik Roland Barthes am Liedsänger Dietrich Fischer-Diskau," *Germanisch-Romanische Monatsschrift,* n.s., 42 (1992): 326–40.

42. Hopkins Porter: *The Rhine as Musical Metaphor,* 108.

43. Plato, *[πόλιτεια] / Politeia,* ed. Dietrich Kurz, Greek text established by Emile Chambry, trans. Friedrich Schleiermacher (Darmstadt: Wissenschaftliche Buchgesellschaft, 1990), §617c, 862–63.

44. Silke Leopold, "Von der Allgewalt vollsten Hingebungseifers: Weibs-Bilder in Wagners 'Ring,'" in *Richard Wagner "Der Ring des Nibelungen": An-*

sichten des Mythos, ed. Udo Bermbach and Dieter Borchmeyer (Stuttgart: Metzler, 1995), 59–74.

45. Richard Wagner, *Oper und Drama,* ed. Klaus Kropfinger (Stuttgart: Reclam, 1984), 118.

46. Reinhart Meyer-Kalkus, "Richard Wagners Theorie der Wort-Tonsprache in 'Oper und Drama' und 'Der Ring des Nibelungen;' *Athenäum: Jahrbuch für Romantik* 6 (1996): 153–95, 187: "Wagner dichtet im Gesang der Rheintöchter einen Sprach-Entstehungsmythos."

47. Richard Wagner: "An Friedrich Nietzsche" (1872), quotation given in Meyer-Kalkus, "Richard Wagners Theorie der Wort-Tonsprache," 184–85: "Dem Studium J. Grimms entnahm ich einmal ein altdeutsches 'Heilawac', formte es mir, um für meine Zwecke es noch geschmeidiger zu machen, zu einem 'Weia-waga' (eine Form, welche wir heute noch in 'Weihwasser' wiedererkennen), leitete hiervon in den verwandten Sprachwurzeln 'wogen' und 'wiegen' endlich 'wellen' und 'wallen' über und bildete mir so, nach der Analogie des 'Eia popeia' unserer Kinderstubenlieder, eine wurzelhaft syllabische Melodie für meine Wassermädchen."

48. Dietrich Borchmeyer, "Wagners Mythos vom Anfang und Ende der Welt," in *Richard Wagner "Der Ring des Nibelungen,"* ed. Bermbach and Borchmeyer, 1–25, at 5.

49. Wagner, *Oper und Drama,* 288: "sein Mutterelement, den musikalischen Ton."

50. See Meri Lao, "Un feminile musicale possibile," in *Les Symbolistes et Richard Wagner—Die Symbolisten und Richard Wagner,* ed. Wolfgang Storch (Berlin: Edition Hentrich, 1991), 29–31, at 29: "Cantano parole farcite di onomatopeie e allitterazione, come se dovessero richiamare il linguaggio dei primordi, ma si tratta pur sempre di lingua tedesca."

51. Cosima Wagner, *Die Tagebücher,* ed. Martin Gregor-Dellin and Dietrich Mack, vol. 1, 1869–1872 (Munich: Piper, 1982), 129: "Von der Wellenbewegung im Rheingold sagt R., 'es sei gleichsam das Wiegenlied der Welt.'" The association of forest and German nationality dates back to Tacitus's *Germania.* See Simon Shama, *Landscape & Memory* (London: HarperCollins, 1995), 75–134.

52. Wagner's Rhine Maidens did, however, have another mermaid ancestress in addition to Loreley in the figure of Melusina as she was portrayed in Felix Mendelssohn's 1833 concert overture *Zum Märchen von der schönen Melusine,* op. 32, and Mendelssohn's static arpeggiated wave motif found its echo in the *Rheingold* opening. Melusina, the mermaid emerging from (and returning to) the waves, shares traits also with Loreley (in the Brentano version) in that her mermaid existence was tied to betrayal in love. I am grateful to Jon Finson for pointing me to this connection. See also Thomas Grey, "The Orchestral Music," in *The Mendelssohn Companion,* ed. Douglass Seaton (Westport, Conn.: Greenwood Press, 2001), 395–568, esp. 475–83.

53. For an example of nineteenth-century Loreley tourism, see the entries for July and August 1878 in *Mark Twain's Notebooks & Journals,* vol. 2 (1877–1883),

ed. Frederick Anderson, Lin Salamo, and Bernard Stein (Berkeley: University of California Press, 1975), esp. 116, 125, and 212; Mark Twain, *A Tramp Abroad,* "An Ancient Legend of the Rhine," 119–29.

54. http://gladstone.uoregon.edu/~cek/@.html, accessed June 12, 1998.

55. See Heine, *Historisch-kritische Gesamtausgabe der Werke,* vol. 1:2, 878–86.

56. Julia Schmidt, "Jetzt lockt die Sirene in den sicheren Hafen der Ehe," *Frankfurter Allgemeine Zeitung,* April 28, 1998, 45. I wish to thank Eva Rieger for sharing this article with me.

NINE

The Mermaid of the *Meyhane*

The Legend of a Greek Singer in a Turkish Tavern

John Morgan O'Connell

This article concerns a Greek living in Turkey during the early republican period (1923–1938).[1] In particular, it concerns the story of a Greek singer (called "the Mermaid"), who performed in a Turkish tavern (*meyhane*) during a tumultuous moment in Turkish history.[2] By manipulating the legend of the mermaid (*deniz kızı*) for strategic effect, the vocalist was able to circumvent the ignominy attached to her position as an ethnic minority surviving in a newly established nation-state and to her status as a female artist performing in a disreputable locale. In this respect, the life story of the Greek singer, known as Deniz Kızı Eftalya Hanım (1891–1939), in many ways emulates the tale of Hans Christian Andersen's "The Little Mermaid" (1836). That is, her musical career replicates the emergent (the pre-human), the transformational (the human), and the transcendental (the superhuman) progression evident in Andersen's account, an account where the audible and the visible attributes of the mermaid story intersect with the sonic and the social dimensions of the artist's life.[3] Further, the tale provides an ideal medium for explaining the emergence of a national consciousness among Greek subjects in the Ottoman Empire. Not only does it help to illuminate the evolution of a pan-Hellenistic ideology during the nineteenth century, but it also helps to clarify a larger issue concerning ethnic identity. In this matter, the mermaid occupies a subordinate position in Turkish mythology, a subaltern voice persisting at the deepest registers of the Turkish subconscious. As an enduring reminder of a glorious maritime past (centered upon the Aegean), the mermaid at once calls into question the terrestrial core of Turkish hegemony (centered upon Anatolia) and offers instead a Greek reading of ethnic awareness. While this reading is European (rather than Asiatic) in orientation and Christian (rather than Islamic) in character, it exists in apposition (rather than opposition) to a dominant Turkish perspective. In this way, the Mermaid was able to transcend the historic schism that separates Greek from Turk, a schism that is articulated in divergent conceptions of the mythical and the mystical.

The Mythical Mermaid

For the Turks, mermaids are not mythical. Representing a maritime conception of folklore, the mermaid is not consistent with a Turkish interpretation of mythology, a mythology that emerged in the terrestrial heartland of Central Asia diffusing subsequently to the maritime shores of West Asia in the wake of Turkish military expansion. With the fall of Constantinople (1453), a new political order (the Ottoman Empire) replaced an older imperial system (the Byzantine Empire) in the Eastern Mediterranean. Initially, this Turkish conquest of Greek territory had a profound influence upon the regional balance of power, resulting in a dramatic reorientation of political interests away from a sea-based conception of economic exchange (that looked to Europe) toward a land-based notion of military control (that looked to Asia). In mythology, this new geopolitical alignment is evident in the legends of the colonizers, whose narratives (generally speaking) are set in terrestrial rather than aquatic spaces and whose protagonists (broadly speaking) are endowed with bird-like rather than fish-like features. While a seamless distinction between the East and the West is hard to validate, the gradual colonization of the region's subconscious with the mythological symbols of Turkish derivation finds a conscious expression in the performing arts. On the one hand, the magical symbols of a distant nomadic past are apparent in the folk traditions of the rural peripheries. On the other hand, the mystical symbols of a more recent sedentary past are manifest in the courtly traditions of the urban centers. From an ornithological perspective, the crane (*turna*) and the nightingale (*bülbül*) represent two distinctive but related readings of Turkish folklore, the former indicative of a pre-Islamic Turkic legacy (embodied in dance) and the latter indicative of a post-Islamic Persian inheritance (inscribed in music). In this way, the distinctive symbols of Turkish difference find a visible and audible expression in music and dance respectively.

For the Greeks, however, mermaids are mythical. Related to—yet different from—the Sirens legend, the mermaid represents the gradual colonization of maritime folklore with the myths of modern European extraction.[4] In this respect, the mythological tales written by romantic authors in Europe during the nineteenth century found a receptive audience among subject peoples in the Ottoman Empire. In particular, the Greeks, who were eager to acquire Western patronage and to adopt Western customs, identified with the maritime context (as mariners) and the liberating ethos (as nationalists) of the mermaid legend. For them, the legend operated as a subaltern voice, a voice that was increasingly audible in the form of subversive publications and revolutionary debates. Emerging from the Aegean but invisible as yet in Anatolia, the mermaid offered the possibility of a new political order. Assisted by European support (the sea witch of lore), Greek resistance was at first nurtured from within (the emergent stage), a resistance that was expressed in complex ways through the auspices of a semiautonomous religious community (the *millet*). Following the foundation of the Greek State in 1830 (the transformational stage), a pan-Hellenic principle (the *megali* idea) enflamed the Greek diaspora throughout the Mediterranean. Conforming to the transcendental stage, this *megali* idea sought to recover a mythical *Hellas* from the remnants of a decaying empire. Yet, this discordant interpretation of the mermaid myth is not fully consistent with the concordant resolution to be found therein. In this respect, Turkish apologists have proffered an alternative reading of Greek identity. This reading emphasizes the complicit rather than the antagonistic nature of Turkish-Greek relations. It shows how Turks and Greeks co-existed in Anatolia, sharing a common ethnic, political, and cultural heritage. Further, it demonstrates how the multiple textures of Ottoman society were sonically inscribed and socially maintained within certain institutions. In this matter, the *meyhane* played a significant role both within the secular and the sacred realms.[5]

The Mystical Meyhane

For many Greeks, the *meyhane* was not mystical.[6] It was a secular establishment where the consumption of alcohol and the smoking of tobacco were tolerated (most of the time) by a conservative Islamic elite. Recognized throughout Ottoman history as a site for subversion, the *meyhane* was an underworld refuge where professional singers (usually male) and

dancers (sometimes female) provided musical entertainment for an ine-
briated audience and furnished sexual favors for a price in certain locations (if tradition is to be believed).[7] Generally situated in the Christian
quarter of Ottoman cities but frequented by a cross-section of Ottoman
citizens, the *meyhane* provided a unique space for transcending the ethnic,
religious, and political distinctions characteristic of Ottoman society. This
social complexity had its sensible correlate. That is, the *meyhane* witnessed
the flowering of a heterogeneous music culture, a culture that celebrated
both Turkish and non-Turkish musical influences and that championed
both Muslim and non-Muslim musical performers. In this respect, the
meyhane was a place of ritual subversion. It was a subterranean world
dominated by the dominated, a world where good Muslims were symbolically shipwrecked upon the bedrock of Christian aberrance, enticed
into the murky depths of alcoholic excess by means of heterodox musical
sounds. This interpretation has a sirenic dimension. During the Tanzimat
period (1839–1908), female vocalists defied contemporary convention by
singing onstage and in taverns. Performing a new popular genre (the
kanto), these artists (called *kantocu*s) were admired as much for their
physical beauty as for their musical artistry and were celebrated both for
their sensual presentation (through dance) and their suggestive interpretation (through song) of *kanto* numbers. By attracting customers to the
tavern, *kantocu*s explicitly reinforced the profligate status of the *meyhane*
and implicitly perpetuated the seductive theme of the Sirens legend. Significantly, many *kantocu*s were Christian.[8]

For some Turks, however, the *meyhane* was mystical. As a sacred trope
in Ottoman poetry, the *meyhane* represented a sublime space where the
divine intersected with the mundane in an unequal dialogue between
spiritual domains. In this matter, wine (*mey*) acted as a catalyst. Signifying amorous intoxication, wine was distributed by a beautiful cup-bearer
(*saki*) who poured the alcoholic beverage into a receptive vessel (*bade*), a
poetic metaphor for the mystical union of the beloved (God) and the lover
(man) in mutual adoration. By invoking the profane in art, Turkish mys-
tics (called Sufis) were able to transcend the legalistic restrictions of Islamic orthodoxy and to proffer instead an alternative reading of religious
experience, a reading that was personal (rather than impersonal) and
active (rather than passive). Music played an important role in this exis-
tential search for the divine. Believed by Sufis to exist in an intermediary
zone (*berzah*) that separated heaven and earth, music operated both as a
means to and as an expression of transcendence. In the former, music
framed the mystical rituals that promoted trance, rituals that were often
characterized by energetic chant (*zikr*) and ecstatic dance (*sema*). In the

latter, music represented the mellifluous conjunction of the breath and the body, a mystical union expressed in the symbiotic exchange between musical performer and musical instrument. Like much of mystical lore, the *meyhane* suggests the symbiosis of a pre-Islamic and a Neoplatonic strand, an intersection of Asiatic and European philosophies articulated in writing and performed as ritual. In this respect, music and wine possibly indicate an older distinction, a distinction between two elements (air and water) and between two mythologies (Turkic and Hellenic). While some authors have presented alternative interpretations of the *meyhane*,[9] these interpretations confirm the secular and the sacred polarities of the analysis presented above, an analysis that conforms to the emergent and the transcendental stages of the mermaid myth.

Mermaid as Mediator

Deniz Kızı Eftalya Hanım was able to mediate this mythical divide. As a Greek living in Turkey at the dawn of the Turkish Republic,[10] this female vocalist embodied in many respects the myth of the mermaid. That is, her life story closely replicates the tripartite structure of Andersen's narrative, demonstrating stages to be found therein: the emergent (becoming a legend), the transformational (living a legend), and the transcendental (recognizing a legend). In this respect, the artist's own account of her fabled past is instructive. In a rare interview with Hikmet Feridun for the popular journal *Yedigün* (Feridun 1933, 10–12), she describes the origin of her mythological name (the emergent stage). Performing on the Bosphorus as a young child with her father near her home in Büyükdere (a coastal suburb of Istanbul), her enchanting voice echoing through the night air was admired by passing revelers who were enjoying moonlight excursions upon the sea (*mehtâbiye*).[11] Invisible yet audible to this appreciative audience, she was nicknamed "the Mermaid." This fabulous story manifests a number of fantastic themes. In particular, the Mermaid's home has a mythical register. Located toward the northern end of the Bosphorus, Büyükdere (in Greek, *Kalos Agros*) is situated at the juncture between the land and the sea, a place inhabited both by Turks and Greeks and situated strategically between Asia and Europe. That a mermaid should emerge from the depths of the Bosphorus in this location is not insignificant. Further, the context of the legend is itself legendary. Moonlight excursions upon the Bosphorus during hot summer nights are celebrated in a number of expressive media, especially poetry and music.[12] Translating a natural pastime into the supernatural realm, these media explore the mystical significance of place showing the interface between the night sky (the moon) and the still water (the moon's reflection) and demonstrating the propensity of humans (as helmsmen) to disturb but not to destroy the mystical equilibrium.[13]

Deniz Kızı Eftalya Hanım was unable, however, to mediate a more mundane divide. Living as a Greek in Turkey during a period of major political turmoil, her life story helps to articulate (audibly) but does not attempt to resolve (visibly) the major social disruptions that attended the foundation of the Turkish State. Consistent with the mermaid narrative, her home in Büyükdere provides a locus for understanding contemporary events. Following the Turkish victory in the War of Independence (1918–1923), Büyükdere lost most of its Greek residents under the complex provisions of the Treaty of Lausanne (1923), provisions that required the exchange of Greeks living in Turkey (estimated at 1.3 million) for Turks residing in Greece (estimated at 0.5 million). While the Municipality of Istanbul was allowed to retain most of its Greek population (estimated at around 100,000), it too witnessed a Greek exodus due to labor discrimination, communal violence, and unfair taxation. In this climate of inter-ethnic hostility, the artist was probably able to evade deportation by moving to Istanbul (ca. 1925), by marrying a Muslim (ca. 1926), and by remaining anonymous (until 1930). However, not consistent with the legend's mystical context, the balance between sky (symbolizing Turkey) and water (symbolizing Greece) was disturbed by a new and determined helmsman, Mustafa Kemal Atatürk (1881–1938). Steering Turkey toward a modern, secular, and Western nation-state, he advocated a revolutionary ideal that celebrated pristine Turkic values and that denigrated degenerate Byzantine traditions. While Atatürk maintained cordial relations with Greece, his introspective internal policies had important consequences for expressive culture. That is, the state no longer supported non-national (especially Greek) and non-secular (especially Sufi) expressive forms. By performing an acceptable Turkish repertoire and by hiding an unacceptable Greek identity, Deniz Kızı Eftalya Hanım was able to fulfill the audible and the invisible terms of her mythical destiny and to avoid the turbulent waters of ethnic discord.

Becoming a Legend

Deniz Kızı Eftalya Hanım became a legend by disguising her ethnic identity using the myth of the mermaid. During the formative years (the emergent phase) of the Mermaid's career, the singer remained nameless and dateless. That is, the singer is rarely acknowledged on sound recordings, and the history of her career is rarely documented in relevant musical sources. According to Ünlü (1998a, CD Notes, 2–6), the Mermaid recorded under a variety of names ranging from "soprano" to "madam" (*hanım*), names (where they exist) that give little clue as to the identity of the principal performer. He interprets this apparent anonymity in terms of the artist's ethnic identity, an identity that was problematic in the aftermath of the War of Independence when anti-Greek sentiment was deeply felt throughout Turkey. Since the singer recorded for Columbia definitive versions of Turkish folk songs in association with the Turkish music conservatory (the conservatory was then called the *Darülelhan*), she (or more likely the record company) may not have been eager to declare her non-Turkish background for political and commercial reasons. Further, the anti-Greek sentiment that was prevalent in artistic circles may also reflect a wider contemporary xenophobia amongst musicians, a distrust of foreigners dating back to the nineteenth century when non-Turkish musicians performing Western art music were granted preferential treatment at court. This favored position was repeated during the first years of the Turkish Republic (see Zimmermann-Kalyoncu 1980).[14] However, an interpretation that implies ethnic discrimination by commercial interests is probably simplistic. It disguises the anonymous status ascribed to Turkish vocalists (usually women) who performed Turkish music in public places and in recording studios for commercial gain.[15] It also disguises the promotion and acknowledgement of non-Turkish musicians (especially men) performing in the same venues. While there are a number of other reasons why Turkish artists wished to remain anonymous or wished to change their names,[16] it is noteworthy that the Mermaid became "the Mermaid" during the transformational stage of her career.[17]

Deniz Kızı Eftalya Hanım became a legend by concealing her turbulent past through employment of the myth of the mermaid. That is, a chronological account of the singer's life is hard to provide precisely because she remained anonymous during the formative period of her musical career. She probably reinvented her past during the transformational stage to suit the aesthetic expectations of her audience. In this matter, the extant secondary sources are deficient. For instance, Ünlü (1998a, CD Notes, 7–11) offers the following chronology of her life. First, he suggests that the singer went to France (1923–1926) with her husband, Sadi Işılay (1899–1969), to record for Pathé and to give concerts. This is unlikely given that Sadi Işılay was working as a teacher in Izmir between 1922 and 1926 (see Öztuna 1990, 1: 373–374). Further, it is more likely that she signed a contract with Pathé in Istanbul (rather than in Paris), visiting the recording studio administered by the İpekçi Brothers in Beyoğlu (ca.

1925–1926). Second, Ünlü maintains that the singer returned to Istanbul (1927) and performed as a soloist for Columbia in association with the *Darülelhan* (1927–1930). While her return from Paris at this moment is doubtful, Ünlü's description of her recording commitments is about correct (that is, during the period 1927–1929). Third, Ünlü argues that the artist obtained professional recognition following an audience with Atatürk in 1929. Quoting the partisan authority of Okur (1955), he suggests that the artist acquired public visibility and used her full professional name in commercial contexts after this date. However, the timing of this audience is problematic. The artist was in Paris for most of the time between 1929 and 1932, returning briefly to Istanbul in 1930 for the summer season.[18] As Cengiz (1993, 83) shows, the event could not have occurred before 1931. Further, another artist who was present at the occasion, Safiye Ayla (1907–1998), said that she herself did not appear before Atatürk until 1931 (Güngör 1996, 8).[19] Piecing together the extant secondary sources,[20] it is most probable that the Mermaid secured official sanction after her second trip to Paris (1930–1932). Returning to Istanbul in 1932, she probably performed for the Turkish president in that year, a year when she came of age as "the Mermaid" after her victory in the contest of the muses.

The Contest of the Muses

The Mermaid's audience with Atatürk is a moment of personal transformation. Invited to the presidential palace (*Dolmabahçe Sarayı*) overlooking the Bosphorus on an exquisite summer evening, she was asked to participate without warning in a musical competition with her professional adversary, Safiye Ayla. Seated on either side of the president, both artists were requested to perform their favorite songs in sequence. Contrary to the modernist expectations of contemporary taste, each vocalist chose to sing a classical composition composed by a minority composer (Bimen Şen 1873–1943) and by a mystic composer (Dede Efendi 1778–1846), respectively. Upon completion of their presentations, Atatürk asked other guests to recommend a winner by vote. Urged along perhaps by the playful machinations of his childhood friend Nuri Conker (1882–1937), he found in favor of the Mermaid, a result that did not please some of the musical connoisseurs present. Although not mentioned in other sources, Atatürk is said to have asked his principal vocalist, Hâfız Yaşar Okur (1886–1966), to provide a professional assessment of the result (Cengiz 1993, 81–84). As in other instances where non-Muslim performers were involved,[21] Okur showed his preference for the Muslim nightingale over the Christian mermaid. This veritable contest of the muses has a mythical dimension. Invoking one popular variant of the sirenic legend, the contest is reminiscent of a legendary encounter between the sirens (here represented by a nightingale) and the muses (here represented by a mermaid). Moderated by the goddess Hera (here represented by the president), the muses were triumphant in garnishing their crowns of victory with the feathers of their adversaries. Invoking one popular version of Sufic lore, the contest may also have a mystical dimension. Occurring on a moonlight night at a juncture between the land and the sea, the event symbolizes a wider conflict between two historic opponents, expressed in terms of cultural difference but endowed with mystical significance for discursive affect. Like Aphrodite, however, Hâfız Yaşar comes to the rescue of his native siren, adding a Turkish codetta to this transnational exposition of unequal subjects.

The Mermaid's audience with Atatürk occurred at a critical moment of national transformation. After the foundation of the Turkish Republic, Atatürk instituted a set of social and political reforms that altered profoundly Turkish culture.[22] Conceived as a dramatic break with tradition, these reforms were modeled upon a Western precedent where the legal system, the economic system, the educational system, and the linguistic system were modernized in accordance with contemporary European principles. As part of this process, Atatürk arranged private competitions between competing specialists in areas about to undergo reform. As Volkan and Itzkowitz show (1984, 303–16), these areas were not always confined to the executive branch of government. In particular, Atatürk viewed musical change as a touchstone of progress (Saygun 1965, 44), a veritable new art for a new society (*yeni sosyete, yeni sanat*). Often preoccupied in his later years with the westernization of Turkish music, he invited contemporary performers to participate in musical competitions for the purposes of refining his own modernist ideas. According to contemporary accounts, musicians were usually summoned to his presence in the middle of the night, at best uncertain of his intentions and at worst afraid of his wrath. While the written descriptions of these occasions follow a certain convention, they show remarkable factual divergences, discrepancies that reflect the mass production of republican memorabilia written in retrospect and tailored to suit the professional aspirations of individual authors.[23] In this respect, Hâfız Yaşar Okur's account of the musical contest between the Christian and the Muslim vocalists must be understood not only in terms of contemporary Greek and Turkish relations but also in terms of Okur's own search for social respectability, a respectability founded upon the twin tenets of Islamic proprietary and artistic excellence. Invoking the authority of Atatürk, he was able to vali-date his own aesthetic prejudices with ethical impunity (see O'Connell 1996, 172–222).

Living a Legend

The Mermaid was now visible in the public domain. Consistent with the mermaid legend, she had to endure a life-changing ordeal at the hands of the sea witch before emerging triumphant into the world of humans. For Deniz Kızı Eftalya Hanım, this ordeal was experienced in front of a critical Turkish president and this triumph was expressed in front of an admiring Turkish audience. In professional terms, the Mermaid began to perform in the most select nightclubs (*gazino*s), at first as a chorus member (named "Madam Eftalya") in an entertainment troupe but subsequently as a solo-ist (named "Deniz Kızı Eftalya Hanım") accompanied by her husband and by her own musical retinue. Appearing with and performing composi-tions by the most celebrated musicians of the period, she acquired celeb-rity status in a highly competitive professional world. Her aforementioned interview in *Yedigün* was itself probably strategic. Hoping to discard her reputation as a mere *meyhane* performer, she appeared in the same popu-lar media with respected Turkish classical vocalists (like Münir Nurettin Selçuk 1899–1981) (see Sait 1933, 10–12), wishing to acquire artistic validation but also commercial success in the process. In the former in-stance, her artistic ambitions were soon realized when she gave concerts in the same venues as her artistic rivals (for instance, at Belvü in association with the Red Crescent on May 26, 1933). Earlier, she even sang alongside her nemesis, Safiye Ayla, in a joint performance at Glorya Sineması, ac-companied by an ensemble of thirty-five professional musicians on March 29, 1933. In the latter instance, her interview had a beneficial economic impact. Although considered vulgar at the time (interview with Fahire Fersan, February 1994), her discussion of personal finances is illuminat-ing. Earning approximately 1200 Turkish lira (about $800) per month from public performances alone, her takings far exceeded those of her rivals who usually earned between 150–300 Turkish lira per month (about $100–$200). Simply put, the Mermaid was now conspicuously rich as well as ostentatiously successful.

The Mermaid was now visible within the private domain. Responding to a public interest in the lifestyles of prominent artists, the article in *Yedigün* gives a revealing insight into the personal life of the Mermaid. Pictured ironing a dress in one photograph and presenting a snack in another, the interview visibly portrays a modern domestic scene in a contemporary Turkish household. In these pictures, her conventional role as a submissive housewife serving her husband and his male guest seems to confirm the traditional status quo and not to challenge the chauvinistic norms of Turkish society. Ünlü (1998a CD Notes, 10–11) does not contest this tangible representation of unequal gender roles and argues that the photographs disclosed a mature artist (at the time aged forty-two) wishing to display marital stability and seemly decorum to a Turkish readership. Such decorum, however, is probably intentional. The text reveals a very different situation. The Mermaid dominates the conversation throughout the interview, leaving little room for her husband's commentary. Where it exists, his remarks seem to track hesitantly the cadential formulae punctuating his wife's ongoing discourse. The Mermaid dominates the domestic space, supervising her husband in culinary matters and monitoring her husband throughout the course of social interaction. Admitting frankly that she is only able to iron (hence the photograph), she proudly claims that her spouse does the cooking and "that he makes a wonderful house husband" (*gayet iyi bir ev erkeği, imiş*). The Mermaid dominates the economic arena, emphasizing her financial superiority over her husband and providing specific details of this disparity in the article. The Mermaid even dominates the visual space, pointing explicitly to pictures of contemporary Turkish vocalists on her wall and displaying French artists hanging there for a cosmopolitan impression. Smoking a cigarette and drinking cognac, the Mermaid orchestrates the course of the interview, demonstrating her ability to negotiate the patriarchal structures and the nationalist prejudices of republican Turkey. In this matter, she is evidently supremely capable.

Air Waves

Yet, the Mermaid is inaudible in the audible realm. That is, the Mermaid's individual voice is hard to discern in her sonic legacy, sound recordings. Tracking hesitantly the legend of the mermaid for intellectual effect, it is noteworthy that the mythical mermaid obtained human form by losing her enchanting voice, a voice that was unable to articulate her fundamental desires in the social arena. Conforming to this tale, Deniz Kızı Eftalya Hanım also had to relinquish her intrinsic identity to acquire public recognition. During the emergent phase, the artist had to suppress her Greek identity through anonymity and to contain her career aspirations through invisibility. Despite achieving public acclaim during the transformational stage, the artist repressed her social aspirations in favor of a commodified identity, an identity that is fashioned by commercial interests and packaged to suit a national audience. In this respect, recording companies played a significant role. For instance, His Master's Voice (*Sahibinin Sesi*) emphasizes the enigmatic qualities of the Mermaid's personality in a brief biography detailed in its *Supplement No. 7* (1934–1935). Here the record company describes (in a short text) the mythical circumstances of the Mermaid's past and reveals (in a small plate) the aesthetic attributes of the Mermaid's present. Significantly, the artist is represented here by her full marital name "Deniz Kızı Eftalya Sadi Hanım." Although an earlier catalogue exists (*Sahibinin Sesi* 1932), no biography is appended even though the publication is exclusively devoted to the recordings of the artist (here simply called "Deniz Kızı"). Also evident in other media (especially film and radio), this disparity in biographical information can be explained by the remarkable success of the artist after 1932, a success that is dependent in part upon her mythical standing and in part upon her marital status. In each case, her success is framed by a male agent who formulates her professional image for economic gain (her manager) and for social sanction (her husband).[24]

Is the Mermaid fully inaudible in the audible realm? That is, is it possible to detect personal agency in the groves of this mediated world? On the one hand, the Mermaid performs a musical repertoire that indicates professional conformity and personal sublimation. In this respect, the artist sings a standard repertory of Turkish folk and classical numbers suited to the national tastes of a bourgeois elite and indifferent to the personal interests of the artist herself. Hoping perhaps to bypass the discredit attached to her minority status by adopting the cultural capital of a hegemonic group, she performs a conservative repertoire with classical distinction in the conservatory and she does not perform musical genres (such as *kanto*) associated with the *meyhane*. Unlike other Greek artists of Turkish extraction, she does not record Greek songs,[25] not belonging to the pantheon of *rebetica* artists and not featuring significantly in contemporary Greek catalogues even in the relevant Turkish sections.[26] On the other hand, the Mermaid does include a number of songs that indicate a personal inclination toward social criticism. In particular, her rendition of the popular hit *Daktilo* ("Typist") suggests a subtle but critical reading of Turkish working conditions from a feminist perspective. As Hagopian suggests (1994, CD Notes, 3), the song represents a dialogue between a secretary and her typewriter on one level and between a lover and her untrustworthy partner at another. Written and produced by the Armenian Artaki Candan (1885–1948), the song also represents a wider interrogation of male and female (and possibly Muslim and non-Muslim) relations in early republican Turkey. While it could be argued that the Mermaid's performance is doubly framed by the same male intermediary (through composition and technology), she is able to transcend the controlling strictures of authorial intention and editorial control respectively by taking ownership of an expressive form through performance. That is, her satirical rendition of this popular number suggests a female ability to subvert male control in song and in life. In this way, the Mermaid recovers her voice and her agency in the mediated realm of the airwaves.

Recognizing a Legend

Recently, the Mermaid was audible but not visible. That is, her immortal sound has survived her mortal soul, despite the artist's untimely demise in 1939. Conforming to the transcendental stage of Andersen's narrative, Deniz Kızı Eftalya Hanım has been transported into the ethereal realm of the airwaves where her extant sound recordings operate as an enduring reminder of her mythical status. Yet her legend is not always acknowledged. When I conducted relevant field research (1991–1994) among artists still alive from the period, I was struck by a pervasive silence concerning the life of this artist. Asking Safiye Ayla (interview, March 1994) about her performance with (in Glorya Sineması) and her contest against (in Dolmabahçe Sarayı) the Mermaid, she stated emphatically that she could not remember either occasion. Showing her a newspaper advertisement of the former event (*Cumhuriyet*, March 23, 1933, 4), she retorted that journalists were inclined to misrepresent the truth and directed me toward her own version of events significantly documented by a reporter (Tanju Cılızoğlu) in the newspaper *Güneş* (April 8, 1987). Another artist, Fahire Fersan (1900–1996), was equally evasive (interview, March 1994). When questioned about the Mermaid, she huffed visibly and would not comment further. Inquiring somewhat indelicately about her own earnings from public performances and sound recordings, I showed her the article from *Yedigün* detailing the Mermaid's favorable financial position and her business acumen. Predictably, Fahire Fersan was cordial but indignant saying that she never inquired (as a woman) about monetary affairs, leaving such matters to her husband (Refik Fersan, 1893–1965). In both instances, the life story and the lifestyle of the Mermaid were consciously forgotten, a collective amnesia founded upon ethnic difference and social distinction. In both instances too, the Mermaid was acknowledged but not remembered, still audible in the sighs of intolerance but invisible in the signs of atonement. This invisibility has now changed.

Today, the Mermaid is both audible and visible. That is, recordings of Deniz Kızı Eftalya Hanım have been featured in a number of commercial compilations reissued from the early republican era. In particular, the Turkish label Kalan (Ünlü 1998a) has devoted an entire CD (entitled *Kadıköylü*) to the memory of the artist. Bringing together an impressive collection of 78s from a number of private archives in Turkey, the publication provides a useful overview of the vocalist's repertoire and career. It also presents valuable discographic information (in the form of an appendix) and includes substantial liner notes (in Turkish, Greek, and English). However, the document is not authoritative, showing a number of significant musical omissions (especially from the early period) and historical errors (especially in terms of chronology). Further, the quality of the recordings represented is often variable. That being said, the authors must be congratulated for attempting to reconstruct the life story of this enigmatic performer. Other collections have also included works by this artist. For instance, Traditional Crossroads (Hagopian 1994) and Yapı Kerdi (Yurttan Sesler 1998) both contain recordings and analyses of the popular hit *Daktilo*. However, it is surprising that the American label, Traditional Crossroads (Hagopian 1998), does not contain a recording by the Mermaid in its impressive collection *Women of Istanbul,* this despite featuring tracks by Jewish (Roza Eskenazi), Armenian (Necmiye Hanım), and Greek (Küçük Nezihe Hanım) singers. This may indicate in part the limited availability of extant original recordings outside Turkey and in part a continued antipathy toward the artistic contribution of the Mermaid. Yet, this snobbery is probably misplaced. As the Kalan recording demonstrates, the Mermaid not only was matched with the best musicians of the period but also was commemorated by them in a special composition written by the Greek instrumentalist Aleko Bacanos (1888–1950) after her death (see Ünlü 1998a, Track 21). In this way, the soul of the Mermaid lives on in the sound world of the airwaves.

A Legendary Legacy

The legacy of the Mermaid is still audible. Like the Little Mermaid of mythical fame, the sound of the singer has a wider social significance. At a national level, the reissue of her recordings must be understood as part of a recent local interest in the production of nostalgia, a development that allows for a postmodern engagement with tradition unencumbered by the modernist strictures of republican orthodoxy. That is, the sounds of the past permit the audiences of the present to experience practically another history. Experienced sonically (as music) and practiced visibly (as dance), this embodied history at once calls into question the singular version of Turkish identity proffered by a dominant nationalist elite and offers instead the possibility of an alternative reading of Turkishness, a reading where the multicultural fabric and the multidenominational texture of Ottoman society are once again acknowledged. In this matter, Deniz Kızı Eftalya Hanım provides a unique insight into this process. As a Greek living in Turkey, she was able to transcend an ancient cultural divide and to continue bravely a long-established tradition of "togetherness" (Greek, *tourkokratia*) inherited from an imperial past but questioned in a national present. At the international level, the reissue of her recordings must be understood as part of a recent rapprochement between Greece and Turkey. Following the tragic Istanbul earthquake (1999), there was a visible shift in Turkish and Greek relations. Long soured by territorial disputes (in the Aegean) and sovereignty debates (especially in Cyprus), the natural disaster rekindled a common cultural bond made impossible by nationalist intolerance on both sides. In this respect, Deniz Kızı Eftalya Hanım provides a sound model for reconciliation. Moving across major ethnic (Greek to Turkish), religious (Christian to Muslim), institutional (*meyhane* to conservatory), and aesthetic (popular to classical) boundaries, she demonstrates sonically how an individual is able to manipulate social distinction to good personal advantage.

The legacy of the Mermaid is still visible. As a woman, Deniz Kızı Eftalya Hanım was one of the first Turkish female vocalists to manage her own personal finances and to promote her own performance career. In this respect, her interview with *Yedigün* is illuminating (Feridun 1933). Here she publicly displays her professional success and her business acumen. She also displays, more subtly, her ability to control the discursive realm in a world traditionally dominated by men. In this world, she strategically avoids male prejudice by remaining anonymous (in her formative years) and by becoming enigmatic (in her transformational years). In both instances she manipulates a male preference for female invisibility in the public domain to good effect. While it could be argued that the myth of the Mermaid was fashioned by a dominant male interest framing both her public (her agent) and her private (her husband) lives, Deniz Kızı Eftalya Hanım herself explains the origin of her legendary past in the same interview. In this matter, she not only describes how she was named "the Mermaid" but also how she (and nobody else) came to use this name in the *meyhane*. This public display of female agency is evident in her visible defiance, a defiance that is represented here by her smoking and her drinking in a public disclosure of privacy inevitably highlighted by editorial scrutiny (perhaps eager to satisfy a male gaze). I suggest that it was precisely this visible display of difference that engendered consternation. As a vocalist, "Deniz Kızı" competed successfully with the best classical artists recently released from the nurturing seclusion of Ottoman pa-tronage. As a Greek, "Eftalya Hanım" competed successfully with the best Turkish artists by performing a traditional musical repertoire principally associated with a pristine nationalist past. As a woman, "Madam Eftalya" competed successfully not only with the best female artists but also with notable male vocalists who sometimes followed her artistic lead. While her legacy was once audibly invisible, "the Mermaid" is now both audible and visible.

The Mermaid of the Meyhane

In this article, I have examined the mythical transformation of a musical legend. In particular, I have looked at the metamorphosis of a Greek singer in a Turkish tavern according to the tripartite structure of a maritime legend, Hans Christian Andersen's "The Little Mermaid." By demonstrat-ing the ways in which the mythical tale intersects both audibly and visibly with the musical life of Deniz Kızı Eftalya Hanım, I show how a subaltern voice is able to manipulate the patriarchal norms and the purist ideals of Turkish society to good personal advantage. In this respect, the Mermaid is submerged within an invisible abyss, an unnecessary absence serving to define national identity and distill ethnic difference. Positioned strate-gically within the dialectic that moderates Greek and Turkish discourse, the artist configures a sound resolution to a social problem. By transcend-ing intracultural distinctions that are endemic within Turkish society, she offers the possibility of an intercultural solution to an ancient conflict. Founded upon the principal of "togetherness" (Greek, *tourkokratia*), this solution is clearly audible in the cultural realm where a shared musical system nurtures social cohesion and where a distinctive musical dialect exists in apposition (rather than opposition) to the aesthetic norm. Ex-ploring the polyphonic textures of Turkish taste in this way, the Mermaid exists in harmony with the dominant order. On the one hand, she submits to the concordant expectations of societal convention, being different nei-ther within the audible nor the visible realms. On the other hand, she demonstrates a subtle inclination toward resistance, a discordant register that expands the range of musical opportunities without subverting the fundamental structures of her tradition. For it is her tradition, a tradition that melds diverse cultural influences into a bricolage of stylistic differ-ences making agency possible in a world of systematic control. It is for this reason that the legend of the mermaid is important. It is for this reason that the legacy of "the Mermaid" is and has to be recognized.

NOTES

1. The distinction between Turk and Greek is not always easy to decipher. As Volkan and Itzkowitz (1994, 176–96) note, this definition is based upon divergent conceptions of identity resulting from different understandings of state. In both countries, a precise definition of national identity is difficult and complex. For the purposes of this article, it is important to distinguish between a Greek national (*Yunanlı*) and a Turkish citizen of Greek ethnicity (*Rum*), a citizen who is identifiable by religious (Orthodox Christian rather than Muslim) and linguistic (speaking Greek rather than Turkish) differences.

2. The Turkish language adopted a Latin alphabet in 1928. For the purposes of transliteration, I have followed Shaw's example by using the modern standard Turkish spelling system for all technical terms (including religious and literary terms) and place names (where no English equivalent exists). See Stanford Shaw, *History of the Ottoman Empire and Modern Turkey,* vol. 2 (Cambridge: Cambridge University Press, 1976–1977), ix. These spellings can be found in the New Redhouse Turkish-English Dictionary (Sir James Redhouse, *Redhouse Türkçe/Osmanıca-İngilizce Sözlük: Redhouse Turkish/Ottoman-English Dictionary* (Istanbul: Redhouse Yayınevi, 1999). I have also followed the modern Turkish convention of supplying family names (where relevant) and European dates. However, I do not employ the Turkish plural suffixes (-ler, -lar), choosing to append the English form instead.

3. The original version of "The Little Mermaid" (Andersen, *Fairy Tales* (New York: Henry Holt and Co., 1913) is divided into three stages: the maritime, the terrestrial, and the atmospheric stages. These stages mark distinctive narrative themes in the legend, themes that correspond to the pre-human, the human, and the superhuman states of the mermaid's existence and that replicate the emergent, the transformational, and the transcendental structuring of mythological forms founded upon a structuralist reading of binary oppositions. In this respect, the mythical and the mystical dimensions discussed here neatly correspond to the primordial and the immortal classes outlined above. Further, the audible and the visible registers in "The Little Mermaid" provide a mythical precedent for explaining the life story of "the Mermaid." In this respect, this paper replicates the threefold plan of the original legend and it alludes to relevant mythological events within that frame. For literature on the national production of folklore in Greece and Turkey, read Herzfeld (1982) and Öztürkmen (1998) respectively. For a useful analysis of Turkic cosmology in Central Asia, see Żerańska-Kominek (1997). I would like to thank Shiela Hogg for recommending the following standard reference on myth classification, Thompson (1955–1958).

4. Educated Greeks were familiar with the philosophical and the artistic traditions of Europe. As Herzfeld (1982) shows, this familiarity had a profound influence upon the development of a national consciousness. Usually able to read French, they had access to contemporary Western literature and ideas through

local print culture, probably being familiar early on with a published version of "The Little Mermaid." During the 1920s, the popularization of Western folk tales impacted upon the dominant Turkish population eager, perhaps, to escape the trauma of contemporary events. In 1921, Tevfik published a version of the mermaid myth.

5. A representative overview of different approaches to Greek and Turkish relations can be found in the following publications: Kasaba (2002), Millas (2002), Strauss (2002), and Volkan and Itzkowitz (1994). I would like to thank Engin Akarlı for recommending these sources. For general references on Turkish history read Lewis (1968), Quataert (2000), Shaw (1976–1977), and Zürcher (1993). For general references on Turkish mysticism read Rouget (1985), Trimingham (1998), and Trix (1993). For general references on Turkish music read Feldman (1996), Greve (1995), Jäger (1996), O'Connell (2003), and Wright (2000). For general references on Turkish customs, dance, and poetry read Lewis (1971), Lewis (1976), and Andrews (1985), respectively.

6. Literally meaning "the house of wine," the *meyhane* was predominantly a Christian concern usually owned by Greeks but sometimes run by Armenians or Jews. As Hezarfen demonstrates (1994), the tax receipts from income generated by *meyhane*s in Istanbul show details concerning the distribution and ownership of relevant establishments before tax reform (1829).

7. The promotion of illicit activities in the *meyhane* is well documented. As Refik Ahmet Sevengil shows (*İstanbul Nasıl Eğleniyordu* [Istanbul: İletişim Yayınları, 1985], 42–45), drinking and smoking were prohibited at various moments during Ottoman history. Further, he also describes illicit sexual activities in the context of the *meyhane* involving (historically) male dancers (*köçek*s) (ibid., 83–90) and (more recently) professional prostitutes, both of whom were usually Christian (ibid., 170–172). Vivid accounts of subversive practices in Turkish taverns can be found in both Turkish (including Tevfik 1991 and Hiçyılmaz 1992) and non-Turkish sources (for instance, Hobhouse ca. 1810 and Lewis 1971).

8. See Duhanî (1990), Hiçyılmaz (1999), Rasim (1958), and Sevengil (1961, 1985) for an overview of the *kanto* and the *kantocu*. Listen to Kantolar (Ünlü 1998b) for an excellent introduction to the music and the culture of *kanto* performance.

9. See Racy (1991) for a ritualistic analysis of nightclub performances in Arab music. See Silay (1994) for a sociological interpretation of Ottoman literature. See, also, Andrews (1985) for a polyvalent analysis of Turkish poetry emphasizing both the secular and the sacred dimensions of expressive culture.

10. Deniz Kızı Eftalya Hanım is described as *Rum*. However, her situation is slightly different in that she married a Muslim and she spoke perfect (although colloquial) Turkish. Further, Aksoy acknowledges (Bülent Aksoy, *Lale-Nerkis Hanımlar*, Notes in English and Turkish by Bülent Aksoy [Istanbul: Kalan Müzik, Arşiv Serisi, CD 101, 1997], 40) that her Turkish diction in performance is faultless. This may indicate that the singer was a Turkish-speaking Greek of Anatolian extraction, Karamanlı. According to Alexis Alexandris, *The Greek Minority of*

Istanbul and Greek-Turkish Relations 1918–1974, 2d ed. (Athens: Centre for Asia Minor Studies, 1992), 142, this group comprised about 3 percent of the total Greek population in Istanbul (1923). A journalist, Naci Sadullah, reporting for the popular serial *Aydabir* 1 (1936): 12, implies that the Mermaid was a Gypsy (*çingene*), probably repeating a popular misconception.

11. The term *mehtâbiye* refers specifically to a terrace upon which the moon can be enjoyed. See Sir James Redhouse, *Redhouse Türkçe/Osmanıca-İngilizce Sözlük: Redhouse Turkish/Ottoman-English Dictionary* (Istanbul: Redhouse Ya-yınevi, 1999), 748. However, the term is also used to signify moonlight excursions upon the Bosphorus in summer, usually involving music. In this respect, the legend of the mermaid repeats a long-established trope in the Ottoman imagination, celebrated in mystical poetry (where the moon symbolizes the face of the beloved) and ritualized in festive activities.

12. Related to the maritime festivities of an earlier period and similar to a later tradition of daytime outings to Göksu (Göksu alemleri), the *mehtâbiye* was a subject of literary interest during the late Ottoman period. This interest is expressed in the contemporary memoirs of court musicians: see Saz (2000) and Tel (1947). It is celebrated in the poetry of contemporary authors (such as Yayha Kemal Beyatlı 1884–1958), whose poems were adapted to music by classical vocalists (such as Münir Nurettin Selçuk 1899–1981).

13. It is noteworthy that the references to *mehtâbiye* occur at a time of cultural instability, generating a contemporary longing for an idealized Ottoman past. The production of nostalgic memorabilia during the 1920s is also evident in the realm of folklore. In this respect, see Calâl (1992), Deleon (1989, 1990), Duhanî (1990), Giz (1990), Rasim (1958), Saz (1996), Sema (1991), Sevengil (1961, 1985), and Tevfik (1991).

14. Of course the contemporary labor situation was more complex, with foreign companies hesitating to employ non-Turkish citizens for political reasons. See Alexis Alexandris, *The Greek Minority of Istanbul and Greek-Turkish Relations 1918–1974,* 108–12, for an analysis of anti-Greek discrimination in the workplace (1923–1929). See Shaw, *History of the Ottoman Empire,* 2:394 for a description of relevant labor legislation (1932) that adversely affected non-Turkish employees including musicians.

15. Many female artists appear anonymously in Turkish recordings before 1928. On occasion mistakenly cataloged but more often not directly named, this omission is significant. On the one hand, female vocalists were sometimes not identified on commercial Turkish classical recordings and in public concert programs, not wishing to be equated with professional *meyhane* singers (*kantocus*). On the other hand, female singers were not named on commercial Turkish folk recordings since anonymity was considered to be consistent with traditional Anatolian values. However, female performers are named in amateur contexts (see Gönul Paçacı, ed., *Cumhuriyet'in Sesleri* (Istanbul: Tarih Vakfı, "Bilanco '98" Ya-yın Dizisi, 1999). Following relevant legislation (1925), public performances by women were sanctioned. After this date, both Muslim and non-Muslim per-

formers openly and actively pursued professional careers. In this matter, Deniz Kızı Eftalya Hanım was one of the first female performers in this category.

16. Many Turkish artists changed their professional names during the course of their careers. Most were obliged to invent and to adopt second names after the institution of the family name reform (June 1934). Generally speaking, vocalists either adopted titles to enhance their reputations even when these were not always justified (such as the popular use of the religious designation, Hâfız). Or, they changed their names to avoid recognition. See Ali R. Sağman, *Meşur Hafız Sami Merhum* (Istanbul: Ahmet Sait Matbaası, 1947, 13–14).

17. Deniz Kızı Eftalya Hanım probably adopted the name "Deniz Kızı" for commercial reasons, employing this title on recordings (in 1932) even before using her full name (in 1934). After family names were required (1934), she appended her husband's first name to her title, becoming "Deniz Kızı Eftalya Sadi Hanım." Significantly, she never took on her husband's second name (Işılay) or used her own Greek family name.

18. A reasonably precise chronology of the Mermaid's career can be ascertained from contemporary newspapers (1929–1930). Early in 1929, the artist and her husband went to Paris to record with Pathé and to provide musical backing for at least two films. They probably appeared anonymously in an event organized by French Radio (*Son Saat*, April 14, 1929). Finishing the first film (shown in Istanbul in March 1930), the couple returned to Istanbul due to the sudden destruction of the Pathé studio (see *Cumhuriyet*, June 29, 1932). During 1930, the artist performed as "Madam Eftalya" in the backing chorus of a nightclub troupe led by Hâfız Burhan Sesyılmaz (1897–1943) (*Cumhuriyet*, August 8, 1930, 6).

19. The precise dating of Safiye Ayla's presidential début is unclear. All sources agree that her first public performance came after her initial recording sessions. According to Karl Signell and Richard Spottswood (editors of *Masters of Turkish Music*, vol. 2, notes in English by Münir Nurettin Beken [Cambridge, Mass.: Rounder CD 1111, 1996, 1990, CD Notes], 4), Safiye Ayla made her first recording by 1930 (Polidor V 51615, 1930), a fact corroborated in contemporary commercial notices (*Cumhuriyet*, July 19, 1930, 6). Her début in Mulen Ruj occurred the following year. See Nalân Seçkin, *Musalladan Şöhrete Safiye Ayla* (Istanbul: Bilgi Yayınevi, 1998), 20–21. Since the Mermaid was abroad until 1932, it is unlikely that either artist performed together in front of Atatürk before 1932. This is corroborated in Seçkin, *Musalladan Şöhrete Safiye Ayla*, 21. Understandably, Safiye Ayla does not mention a contest between the two vocalists in her published memoirs (Cılızoğlu 1987; Güngör 1996; Seçkin 1998) perhaps reticent to remember a public humiliation.

20. In 1930, the Mermaid returned to Paris with her husband (Sadi Işılay, 1899–1969) and with her two Greek accompanists (Yorgo Bacanos, 1900–1977 and Aleko Bacanos, 1888–1950). According to Yorgo Bacanos's testimony quoted in Nazimi Özalp, *Türk Musikisi Tarihi*, 2 vols. (Ankara: Müzik Dairesi Başkanlığı, 1986), 235, the Mermaid not only recorded and performed in the French capital, but also toured with her husband in Europe, the Middle East, and possibly in

India (ibid., 126). This is confirmed, for the most part, in her published interview. See Hikmet Feridun, "Deniz Kızı Eftalya," *Yedigün* 4 (1933): 19. Upon her return to Istanbul in 1932, she appeared regularly with her husband in the best night-clubs, on radio programs, and in film productions. This hectic career was short-lived. After a sea excursion on the Bosphorus in recognition of her mythical career (August 4, 1936), she caught a cold and never properly recovered (Ünlü 1998a, CD Notes, 11). In this respect, her poor health is already apparent in 1934 when her photograph appeared again in *Yedigün* (Tevfik 1934, 61)

21. See Halil Erdoğan Cengiz, *Yaşanmış Olaylarla Atatürk ve Müzik: Riyâset-i Cumhûr İnce Saz Hey'eti Şefi Binbaşı Hâfız Yaşar Okur'un Anıları (1924–1938)* Ankara: Müzik Ansiklopedesi Yayınları, 1993), 76–80, for Hâfız Yaşar Okur's disparaging account of a performance by the Jewish cantor, İzak Elgazi (1889–1950), in front of Atatürk (ca. 1932). See John O'Connell ("Alaturka Revisited: Style as History in Turkish Vocal Performance" [Ph.D. diss., University of Califor-nia Los Angeles, 1996], 323–27) for an analysis and an interpretation of this interesting encounter. Significantly, Seroussi (1989) does not mention this occa-sion in his biography of Elgazi.

22. See O'Connell (1996) for a description of relevant musical reforms during the early republican period (1923–1938). See also O'Connell (2000) and O'Con-nell (2002) for an analysis of institutional reform and stylistic change during the period respectively.

23. See Itzkowitz and Volkan (1984) for a challenging critique of republican memorabilia.

24. At this time, Artaki Candan (1885–1948) functioned as the Mermaid's agent.

25. The Mermaid is not featured in the standard literature on rembetica, even though the style is reputed to have emerged in the *meyhanes* of Anatolia. See Holst (1983) for a standard introduction to the genre. See Pennanen (1999) for a musi-cal analysis of Turkish influences in the tradition. See also Greve (1995), Manuel (1989), Petropoulos (2000), and Shand (1998). Listen to Schwartz (1991) and Spottswood (1996) for representative sound recordings of contemporary rem-betica musical styles in Greece. For a general bibliography on Greek sources in Turkish music read Bardakçı (1993), Beaton (1980), Brandl (1989), Feldman (1996), Gazimihal (1927a, 1927b), Plemmenos (2001), Popescu-Judetz (2000), Yekta Bey (1899a, 1899b), and Zannos (1990, 1994). Listen also to Dalgas and Sesyılmaz (1997) and Ünlü and Beberis (1999).

26. The Mermaid is mentioned in the Turkish section of a Greek catalogue published by His Master's Voice (1936, 53–54). She also features anonymously in relevant Columbia catalogues in Turkey (1928), Egypt (1928), and in the United States (1930) in association with the Darülelhan. However, she does not appear in the Turkish section of ethnic recordings found in Spottswood; Richard Spotts-wood, *Ethnic Music on Records: A Discography of Ethnic Recordings Produced in the United States, 1893–1942*, vol. 5 (Urbana: University of Illinois Press, 1990), 2521–32.

TEN

Siren Serenades

Music for Mami Wata and Other Water Spirits in Africa

Henry John Drewal with Charles Gore and Michelle Kisliuk

Introduction—Henry John Drewal

Mami Wata" (pidgin English for "Mother Water" or "Mistress Water," sometimes rendered as "Mammy Water") is the name for a beautiful, seductive water spirit worshipped widely in Africa. Often depicted as a mermaid, Mami Wata brings enormous wealth and good fortune to those she favors and poverty, impotence, insanity, or death to those she does not. Her creolized/pidgin English name reflects the fact that many devotees regard Mami Wata as a hybrid creature, an exotic, powerful, water-spirit stranger from "overseas," yet one who, for different reasons, has been fully incorporated into ancient and widespread indigenous African beliefs and practices honoring water spirits.

The name "Mami Wata" has other complex connotations as well. As *mami wata*, it is a generic (and generative) term used to talk cross-culturally (both within and beyond Africa) about a vast and uncountable "school" of African water spirits. These spirits have specific local names, histories, and distinctive personalities and are honored in complex systems of beliefs and practices that may or may not be shared with the deity

Mami Wata. There is Mami Wata and there are many *mami watas*. Their identities are as fluid and as amorphous as water itself. Only the frames of history, society, arts, cultures, and the agency of individuals/groups can contain them, give them shape, contour, substance, and specificity. And as these frames change so do the attributes, personalities, identities, and actions of these enigmatic, fascinating water spirits.

This essay presents a series of case studies about music in the beliefs and practices surrounding Mami Wata and various *mami wata*s from different parts of the continent. Some are from my own fieldwork and others are excerpts from the research of colleagues who have investigated Mami Wata and other water spirits in specific eras and locations and are contributors to my forthcoming edited volume in conjunction with a major traveling exhibition on arts for water spirits in Africa and the Afro-Atlantic world.

Individually, these case studies demonstrate the inventive uniqueness and diversity of devotees and their practices. Taken together, they also reveal certain striking similarities in Mami Wata/*mami wata* beliefs, practices, and arts resulting from interpersonal, intracultural, intercultural, and international social networks. Some may be the result of diffusion from a common source. Others may be creations of independent invention and convergence, or sometimes combinations of such processes. Both micro and macro perspectives help illuminate this widespread phenomenon of water spirit/mermaid music as it reflects and shapes cultures and the lives of individuals.

Whether as Mami Wata or one of the *mami watas,* she epitomizes and embodies hybridity. She is a transcendent, transformative, transcultural, transnational, transgendered, and trans-Atlantic being. She straddles both land and water, culture and nature (being half-human, half-fish). While most often female, she/he may also manifest in the body of a devotee as one of various male water spirits known as *papi/dadi watas.* Her visual culture draws upon many sources—ancient indigenous African images of serpents and aquatic creatures; fourteenth- and fifteenth-century European mermaids; nineteenth-century German prints of exotic snake charmers; twentieth-century Indian films and prints of Hindu gods and goddesses; contemporary photos of Nastassja Kinski with a boa; or movie posters advertising Disney's *Splash.* The music associated with MamiWata/*mami wata* is equally hybrid, combining primarily African and European (but also other non-African) instruments, melodies, and rhythms.

In their worship of Mami Wata/*mami wata,* devotees often study, interpret, and re-present in inventive ways data from both local and imported imagery, literature, trade goods, and music. They also interpret and re-present the "ways" of these spirits, either from personal experiences with Africans from different cultures, from encounters with non-African foreigners, or from diverse representations in films, TV programs, print media, and other sources. Inspired by these myriad sources and then processing them further in dreams and visions, Mami Wata/*mami wata* devotees create their spirits' attire, construct their watery world in shrine spaces, and impersonate them during rituals that frequently include possession trance, music, and dance. Worshippers select local and foreign images, arts, ideas, and actions, interpret them according to indigenous precepts, invest them with new meanings, and then re-present them in novel and dynamic ways to serve their own specific aesthetic, devotional, social, economic, and political needs. By these means they continually fashion and re-fashion themselves, their lives, and their communities.

Visual History

The early visual culture and history of Mami Wata/*mami wata* remain conjectural. Some have suggested an origin among Africans in the New World and a return to Africa.[1] A dance known as "Watur Mama," "Water Mother," or "Mere d'Eau" that existed among enslaved Africans in Surinam and the French Antilles in the Caribbean was first recorded in the mid-eighteenth century.[2] However, it seems more likely that its sources pre-date the massive dispersal of Africans to the Americas and come from ancient, indigenous African beliefs in water deities that were then juxtaposed with European myths and images from the era of first direct Euro-African contacts at the end of the fifteenth century. According to some of the earliest European travelers' accounts, many African peoples associated Europeans with the water and water spirits.[3] Elizabeth Isichei discovered a mid-nineteenth-century African song recorded by a European traveler in Central Africa that explicitly linked Europeans with the realm of water:

> In the blue palace of the deep sea,
> Dwells a strange creature:
> His skin as white as salt,
> His hair long and tangled as the seaweed,
> He is more great that the princes of the earth.
> He is clothed with the skins of fishes, Fishes more beautiful than birds.
> His house is built of brass rods;
> His garden is a forest of tobacco.
> On his soil white beads are scattered
> Like sand-grains in the sea-shore[4]

Figure 10.1. The earliest African depiction of this exotic hybrid aquatic creature was carved on an Afro-Portuguese ivory by a Sapi sculptor between 1490 and 1530 in what is today the coastal area of Sierra Leone. The National Museum of Denmark, Copenhagen—Saltcellar, lid missing, ivory, 16 cm (6.3″), Inv. No. ED c67a, Ex coll; Gottorp Kunsthammer, Gottorp Castle, Schleswig-Holstein. Photograph courtesy of Henry John Drewal.

Given these ideas, Africans would have regarded European icons, especially marine sculptures like ships' figureheads, as representations of those spirits. Several marine sculptures have been documented in African water-spirit shrines in widely dispersed places in Africa, and one was known to have been called Mami Wata/ *mami wata*.[5] One European icon in particular, the mermaid, became the primary image of Mami Wata/ *mami wata*. The earliest African depiction of this exotic, hybrid aquatic creature was carved between 1490 and 1530 on an Afro-Portuguese ivory by a Sapi sculptor on the coast of what is today Sierra Leone (fig. 10.1). Though the mermaid was most probably copied from a European model supplied by the Portuguese, the Sapi sculptor immediately "Africanized" her. He surrounded her with two crocodiles—ancient, indigenous symbols for water spirits. As their familiarity with European mermaid lore (including music) increased, Africans interpreted, adapted, and transformed the concept of the mermaid into Mami Wata/ *mami wata,* evolving elaborate systems of beliefs and sacred arts, both visual and musical.

Map 2. Map of Africa showing cultures and places metioned in the text.

Sometime between 1885 and 1900, Mami Wata/*mami wata*'s mermaid representation was joined by another exotic image, one that combined elements of the mermaid with allusions to indigenous African water-serpent deities. It was a popular German chromolithograph of an exotic "Oriental" female snake charmer (fig. 10.2). The original chromolith was printed in Hamburg circa 1885. It quickly reached Africa (possibly with African seamen working on German/European ships sailing from Hamburg), where by 1901 it had already been translated into a low-relief sculpted wooden image set in the center of an African water spirit headdress, which was photographed in the Niger River Delta town of Bonny, Nigeria.[6] Its influence spread to other areas and in many cases supplanted the earlier image of Mami Wata as a mermaid, or it led to depictions of her as a mermaid with snake(s). In 1955 the chromolith (presumably the ca. 1885 Hamburg original) was sent by an Indian merchant in Kumasi, Ghana to the Shree Ram Calendar Company in Bombay, India, and was reprinted in large numbers "without changing a line from the original."[7] This Indian edition (of 12,000 copies) was sent back to

Figure 10.2. The 1955 Indian edition of the nineteenth-century popular German chromolithograph of an exotic "Oriental" female snake charmer, printed in Hamburg circa 1885. Photograph by Henry John Drewal.

Ghana and sold in large numbers. The 1955 Indian edition is shown here since the original has not yet been found. This and other more recent editions (printed in London and copied in many places since the 1960s) have inspired Mami Wata icons in more than twenty African countries and fifty cultures as of 2003. Note the diamond-shaped inset in the lower right depicting a male figure playing a bifurcated flute to charm four writhing snakes. While I have never seen such a flute used in Mami Wata rituals, it was sometimes mentioned as one of her musical instruments.

Between the fifteenth and nineteenth centuries, the vast majority of foreigners from overseas seen by Africans came from Western Europe, followed by Lebanese and Indian traders. They were all associated with commerce, that is, wealth brought from overseas. Many of the same cluster of ideas associated with mermaids were also associated with this more recent image of a beautiful female snake charmer, first obtained from Europeans and later from Indians.

Another phase in Mami Wata imagery began in the 1940s–1950s. The popularity of the snake charmer lithograph and the presence of Indian merchants (and films) in West Africa led to a growing fascination with Indian prints of Hindu gods and goddesses, which people began to interpret as representations of a host of male and female Mami Wata/*mami wata* spirits associated with specific bodies and levels of water, like one *papi wata* called "Densu" in Togo and elsewhere (fig. 10.3). Using these prints as guides for rituals and for the preparation of altars known as "Mami Wata tables," devotees expanded the pantheon of spirits, fostering a growing complexity in Mami Wata/*mami wata* worship that includes elements of Christian, Hindu, Buddhist, astrological, and European spiritualist/occult beliefs and practices.[8]

While enormous diversity exists in Mami Wata/*mami wata* beliefs and practices in Africa, certain elements persist widely. Mirrors and other items like combs, jewelry, and perfumes, because of their prevalence in mermaid lore and imagery, are ritual instruments and shrine furniture for attracting and controlling the spirit. Dreams and visions are primary sources for communication between spirit and follower. Besides dreams and possession trance, people employ other means to communicate with Mami Wata/*mami wata* that reflect novel ways of worship. They read and write messages, speak with her on the telephone, and sing to her. These various modes play a crucial role in shaping ritual actions.

Mami Wata/*mami wata* worshippers perform their constructions of their spirit(s) in the ways they create sacred spaces and perform rituals. Shrines may range from environments that often evoke an aquatic world or rooms dominated by a cloth-covered table carefully arranged with "beautiful," sweet-smelling items. Both are a fusion of dreams, experiences, and the imagery in prints and other documents constructed to attract and please the spirit, making her feel at home. In possession performances, devotees swim with their arms and speak in pidgin tongues as they relate their long journeys by boat, canoe, or car to come from distant waters like the Indian Ocean. Among the Ewe and Igbo, priests write notes, speak with Mami Wata/*mami wata* on the phone, dance in

Figure 10.3. A popular Indian print of a Hindu god that
Africans interpret as a representation of one of a host of male
Mami Wata/ *mami wata* spirits associated with specific bodies
and levels of water. This *papi wata* is called "Densu" in Ghana,
Togo, and Benin among coastal peoples such as the Ga, Mina,
and Ewe. Photograph by Henry John Drewal.

a European-influenced ballroom style, play guitar or harmonica, sing
hymns, and prepare lavish Western-style banquets in her honor. All of
these acts are ritual bridges to Mami Wata/ *mami wata,* bringing her into
the world of her followers for their well-being by enacting/embodying
certain kinds of behavior in order to get in touch with the spirit(s). It is
this inventiveness that transforms beliefs and practices and forges new
ideologies that shape the lives of devotees and those around them.

Musical Culture

The musical arts for Mami Wata/*mami wata* exhibit the same kinds of hybridity as the visual arts, combining many different African and non-African elements. Although we may never know for certain, the earliest musical forms may have been those of sailors on the first European ships to reach the West African coast in the late fifteenth century. Some of this music may have been perceived as songs for mermaids/sirens, that is, for Mami Wata/*mami wata* from the perspective of those Africans who heard such songs. Many Ewe, Mina, and Igbo devotees explained to me that their spirits love music that is "sweet"—the sound equivalent of the sweet-smelling shrines and altars filled with perfume, incense, and talcum powder.

At Atakpame, Togo, Ewe devotees described to me Mami Wata's preference for slow "blues," Highlife, and especially "sweet" guitar music. They have devised a European-style performance as part of their rituals known as *Gran'bal* (French for "Grand Ball"). It combines romantic and melodic tunes with gentle, smooth "ballroom" dances performed by couples that occur, following European/Western mode, on Friday and Saturday evenings. Worshippers often said her most popular instrument was the guitar, followed by the harmonica, both possibly sailors' instruments. The popularity of the guitar (and violin) may have been partially inspired by European images of mermaids playing lyres or other stringed instruments.[9]

Mami Wata/*mami wata* encounters can be dangerous but also profitable. Her legendary beauty is awesome and frightening because, in the words of Chinua Achebe, it is a beauty that is "too perfect and too cold."[10] If you come under her seductive spell, you might be doomed. Yet if you have courage to meet her and capture one of her possessions, like a comb or mirror or guitar, you might be able to control her and reap fabulous riches as a result.

As one Senegalese friend told me,[11] Mami Wata is regarded as a *djinna muso* or "female spirit." His mother had a picture of her in her house. He told me Mami Wata is widely known in Senegal and Guinea-Conakry and associated with the success of artists such as the singer Abubakar Demba Camara of the orchestre Bembeya Jazz National of Guinea. Camara sang a song to Mami Wata in the early 1970s. It was believed that "he had a deal with Mami Wata." Some people said he had married her and she had given him his beautiful voice.[12] Others said that he would become rich if he promised not to reveal her as the source of his success. But he forgot his promise, sang her praises, gave her thanks in a song, and soon after died in a terrible car accident near Dakar, Senegal.[13]

Mami Wata: Rituals and Songs in Benin City—Charles Gore

Charles Gore[14] provides a wonderfully rich and detailed account of the diverse ways urban charismatic priests/priestesses (*ohen*) in Benin City, Nigeria, have "appropriated and changed [Mami Wata] to local contexts of significance and representation." Several of his case studies focus on the role of music as an important marker of these priests' individuality, agency, and different intentions.

The first case involves an early Highlife song celebrating Mami Wata, the hit tune "Guitar Boy" (1967), composed by the Nigerian musician Sir Victor Uwaifo. Charles Gore[15] writes:

> Benin City is the birthplace and home of Sir Victor Uwaifo who composed the hit song Guitar Boy (his nickname) in 1967 in which he tells how he encountered Mami Wata with the lines "Guitar Boy! Eeh, if you see Mami Wata, never you run away." He is a committed Christian and was brought up in the Benin Baptist church but he was inspired to write the lyric (and based the melody on the sounds he heard) after an experience he had at Bar Beach in Lagos when a strange figure, walking towards him, was transformed into a Mami Wata.

Gore quotes from Uwaifo's autobiography:[16]

> Could nature be making a mistake? I said to myself. "A mama" with a flowing hair, nimble hands and from the waist down like a fish with a tail? My heart almost jumped into my mouth. My stomach rebelled against me as my intestines rumbled against themselves as if to warn me to take to my heels. The guitar was almost frozen in my hands. And I heard a voice so shrill calling out guitar boy! My reply which was unrehearsed came out of my mouth spontaneously and it was gliss, like a sound with fluctuation in a crescendo. "Eh! If you see Mami Wata, never you run away." I stood motionless, sang it all over while she floated away in a heavy tide.

The song brought Uwaifo sudden wealth and regional fame. Although this was his only encounter with Mami Wata, Uwaifo became, as Gore explains,[17]

> an agent in promulgating ideas about Mami Wata over a wide region through the mass-marketing medium of the music industry. However the lyric is often interpreted at the sites of its consumption as a narrative of an encounter with a beautiful but strangely autonomous woman that evokes the space of urban encounters and possibilities so providing the context for other alternative appropriations/constructions of Mami Wata. This example of Victor Uwaifo's lyric highlights that popular

notions of Mami Wata are not unitary but are used to constitute various significances in different contexts.

Besides the guitar, another foreign instrument—the harmonica—seems to have become the instrument of choice in Victor Uwaifo's hometown. In a second case study, Charles Gore recounts the example of *ohen* Nomayisi. He was initiated by his father into Olokun, the deity of seas and rivers who brings wealth and fertility, but as a young man he became an active participant in the Jehovah's Witnesses. In 1975, while attending a meeting at Bar Beach, Lagos (where Victor Uwaifo had his Mami Wata encounter), he was swept out to sea. Nomayisi described to Gore how he spent "the next year as a servant of the deities in the water spirit world after which time he appeared at the river Adagbassa near Sapele, a small town to the east of Benin City. When he returned to his father's house he found he had healing powers and had acquired many different Olokun attributes including Mami Wata which in this case is conceptualised as one of Olokun's servants."[18] Gore describes how "during possession by Mami Wata he plays the harmonica to call out the deity in onlookers and sometimes lyrics are sung in the Itsekiri language which is spoken in the riverine areas to the south east of Benin City. . . . He greets all the guests playing the harmonica, spraying perfume and offering talcum powder."[19]

In a third case study Gore describes the initiation, musical instruments, and songs of the Mami Wata priestess Okperuanogbume:[20]

The variety of sources from which Mami Wata has been obtained by *ohens* and its multiple linkages to urban life has provided many different ways of constructing significance and practices associated with her. *Ohen* Okperuanogbume described how she first initiated into Olokun when she was sixteen in the mid-fifties. However the oracle warned her to placate *igbakhuan,* spirits from the water spirit world, with sacrifices each time she gave birth. After having several children she went to Koko, a notable river settlement, to offer sacrifice when she was called by Mami Wata. For three months she visited Olokun and Mami Wata under the sea finally returning from the water spirit world with a guitar and harmonica. She was then initiated by an Itsekiri woman into Mami Wata. During her public performances on the day of weekly worship, at her annual festival and other occasions when she is possessed by Mami Wata, she performs with a guitar.

This performance with the guitar in July 1991 incorporates popular notions about Mami Wata, underlining its involvement in contemporary urban life and especially in contrast to the musical instruments associated with the other deities. However she also underscores this performance by singing popular songs in pidgin English during possession by Mami Wata about relations between the sexes which highlight the deity's linkages to gender relations, sexuality and economic wealth.

> "Oh my wife! Oh my wife!
> Can't you remember me again
> I roll the truck one year,
> I tap a rubber so many years
> When money go, woman go."

> "Don't say da, da, darling
> Don't say da, da, darling
> When money no dey
> Oh darling, don't say da, da, darling."

The first song describes a man's efforts to make money by pushing a handcart in the city and then graduating to rubber tapping which is considered well paid and cosmopolitan by village standards. Despite all this hard work and the progress made in his life, when the money runs out his wife leaves him, suggesting a generalized interdependency of economic and gender relations. This theme is again re-iterated in the second song that follows directly after. In the context of ritual possession it also emphasizes the role of Mami Wata in the gaining of wealth and in defining gender relations. However, not only are these popular songs but the first song was also featured in a popular television drama series *De Hotel Jordan* of the 1980s. The song became a household by-word among television viewers in Benin City. *Ohen* Okperuanogbume has appropriated lyrics from television drama (a tradition or genre with particular associated conventions within the medium of mass-communication) but these are now sung by the *Ohen* while possessed by the deity which legitimates their usage during ritual performance. This appropriation situates the *Ohen* (and Mami Wata) as part of contemporary urban life both in its associations to the cosmopolitan space evoked by the hotel but also in the popular issues raised in the drama in which the redefining of gender relations had a prominent place (particularly in the roles of the young unmarried women characters in the drama who are often seeking an autonomy of action in relation to male social and economic dominance). This example draws upon popular notions of Mami Wata and other traditions of ideas and practice, combining the use of Highlife songs and references to popular television drama in order to construct an individuated ritual performance within the configuration of the cults and shrines of Benin City.[21]

In the final case studies from Benin City, Gore[22] describes the career of Chief Osula, a hereditary chief of the *Oba* (king) of Benin and a prominent musician:

Chief Osula along with other musicians have started to produce records that depict and acknowledge many aspects of Edo social life such as *Happy Marriage Life* and *Edo Music for the Dead*. . . . In February 1997 Chief Osula produced a new record devoted to Mami Wata with all the lyrics sung in the Edo language. The first track starts by introducing lullabyes sung to children by their mothers without musical accompaniment:

> When you maintain me, I will be beautiful
> Child of the pawpaw tree that has smooth skin

> Only one husband I shall marry
> The pigeon never marries two husbands

The first lullabye is concerned with beauty while the second compares staying married to the pigeon's propensity to stay with one mate. Chief Osula uses these lullabyes in the context of Mami Wata to suggest the power that beauty confers on women. The second lullabye also suggests that the devotee is married to Mami Wata in the spirit world and who must be given priority over any human relationships. Chief Osula then introduces the first song which has the title "Mami Wata":

> My Mami Wata is at the bottom of the sea
> Bring my wealth to me from the bottom of the sea
> Mami Wata the beautiful one
> Olokun who owns money
> Bring me my wealth
> Mami Wata the beautiful one
> I will follow you to the seashore
> Mami Wata I will follow you home

However this lyric was not created by Chief Osula but rather is a very popular song of the 1990s sung at shrines. . . . Its dominant context is a ritual one which introduces Mami Wata as she possesses the *ohen* and links her as a consort to the sea deity Olokun (giving Mami Wata a determinate status as this tradition has developed within the shrine configurations in the 1990s). The next song is titled "The Iyeye of Benin" [the most powerful priestess, seen as the spiritual mother of Benin] to whom it is dedicated and continues without break the tune and much of the lyrics of Mami Wata:

> I greet, I greet
> My Iyeye of Benin
> Child of the Oba of Benin
> Iyeye of Benin that is our proud daughter
> Mami Wata of Olokun

> Mami, Mami, Mami Wata the great one
> Iyeye the great one
> [In English] Important Mummy
> [In English] Expensive Mummy
> [In English] Mummy is Good
> My Mami Wata is at the bottom of the sea
> Bring me my wealth from the sea bottom

This song praises the Iyeye of Benin and celebrates her great spiritual powers, associating her directly to the previous song of Mami Wata. The interjections in English are some of her praise names that devotees call out when she is possessed by her powerful deities. The song evokes directly through these means the ritual contexts of possession at the shrine configurations. This song merges directly into the next one entitled "Ohen Adigbe of Benin":

> I thank you, I thank you,
> Osawaru the son of Amayo,
> The mermaid priest in Benin,
> Ohen Adigbe that is our son,
> [In English] Daddy is good,
> I will follow you to Benin, O Mami Wata
> Mami Wata the beautiful one,
> Bring me my wealth from the bottom of the sea!

Ohen Adigbe acquired Mami Wata in the 1990s but is already well-known for his abilities as an *ohen*. The sequence of songs places Mami Wata both as a ritual context and situates it socially within Benin City with two of its distinguished exponents. The use of the genre of praise songs by chief Osula allows him to create a specifically Edo sense of identity that distinguishes his music form from that of Yoruba and Ibo musicians through this process of reification of Edo culture. However it has not been the popular and generalised notions of Mami Wata which have been the impetus for lyrics and music as was the case in the 1960s with Sir Victor Uwaifo or the Highlife songs appropriated by Ohen Okperuanogbume. Instead, in the 1990s in Benin City, there has been the appropriation of songs and music directly from the ritual contexts of Mami Wata worship articulated in urban contemporary shrine configurations. The advent of multimedia capabilities including video in the 1990s, with its relatively small capital outlay, has enabled Chief Osula to set himself up as a multimedia publishing business in 1997.[23] He has further extended the profile of Mami Wata through the media by producing on audio tape of Ohen Adigbe's ritual performances of Mami Wata at his shrine marketed as "Adigbe special, MammyWata: Chief

Priest Osawaru Amayo and his Adigbe Spiritual Missionaries of Benin Kingdom." This is to be followed by the release of an accompanying video cassette of the performance by Ohen Adigbe onto the market. The use of the mass media to proselytize (and market their religious product) is no longer the uncontested domain of the Independent and Evangelical churches that have followed the example set by American evangelizing churches.

Mami Wata Music among Igbo People—Henry John Drewal

Sounds are a key element of rituals for Mami Wata/*mami wata* among certain Igbo devotees. Several priestesses manifest her presence through their voices. One devotional group is called the "Harriet Vocal Mermaid Society." Among the neighboring Ibibio, many worshippers described their communications with her by telephone.[24] And it is with the voice and song that devotees contact their spirit. In one encounter in 1978, a Mami Wata priestess told me she had trained seven years to "invoke Mami Wata's voice." When she did so, she took a small amount of clay from her altar, sprinkled it and perfume on the ground, put some perfume on her forehead, and entered her shrine while ringing a small bell and a wooden gong. Once inside the curtained enclosure, she began to sing a song in mixed Igbo/English that was modeled on a Christian hymn. In fact the priestess told me later that Mami Wata was a Christian and that she "beat" those who did not go to church. Then I heard a large bell and soon after the voice of Mami Wata filled the room—the bells and hymn had summoned the spirit to that sacred space. During the course of my conversation with Mami Wata, translated by the medium's sister because I could not follow the spirit's tongue—a combination of Igbo and English—she asked me if I wanted to see her "face to face." When I answered yes, the priestess's sister asked me, in the words of the famous Victor Uwaifo song, "If you see Mami Wata, won't you run away?"

Despite the fact that this Mami Wata priestess told me Mami Wata was a Christian, since the 1980s many Pentecostal/Evangelical Christian groups have demonized Mami Wata and those who honor her. Elizabeth Isichei[25] cites an Igbo pamphlet warning people of the evils associated with Mami Wata. It gives the story of a young girl who was taught a song by Mami Wata in "mixed Igbo" which reminded her that because of the contract she had with Mami Wata and the gifts received, she was the property of the sea and must return to the sea. This is typical of Mami Wata's "contracts"—in order to get wealth and rewards, one must give up something precious like family, friends, children, or longevity/life.

Mami Music in Centrafrique—Michelle Kisliuk

In central Africa, Mami Wata and her songs are also the site of debates and ideological battles between Evangelical (Apostolic) Christians and those who follow traditional faiths. The ethnomusicologist Michelle Kisliuk, who has worked in Bangui, Central African Republic (Centrafrique), tells the story of a very popular song (1993) by Thiery Yezo, composer and lead singer of Musiki, entitled "Mami Wata." [26] The song was sung in a mixture of French and Sanga, the lingua franca of Centrafrique. Instrumentation included electric guitar, traps, and keyboard with vocals by Yezo, creating a sweet sound in a Congo-Rumba style:

"Mami Wata"
by Thiery Yezo (1993), leader of Musiki (died 1995)
Bangui, Central African Republic (Centrafrique)
[Translated from French and Sango by Michelle Kisliuk and Justin Mongosso]

[French:]

Mami Wata tu viens a moi,	Mami Wata you come to me,
tu m'aimais, tu t'en vas	you love me, you go away
chêz toi la-bas	to your home over there
dans ton pays loin de moi.	to your country far from me.
Mon coeur battrait contre le tien,	My heart would beat against yours,
notre amour est trop beaux.	our love is too good.
Mami revient,	Mami, come back,
belle sirène qui est des eaux.	beautiful siren from the waters.

[Sango:]

Oh, Mami ka a yeke tonga na gne?	Oh Mami, how is it over there?
Na gbe ti ngou mo goué na mbi.	From the watery depths you come to me.
Belle sirène ka na mo ka eh	Beautiful siren, there with you
mbi yeke wende mbeni ape	I won't have to hide
bolingo ti y.	our love.
Oh Mami kiri mo mou mbi,	Oh, Mami, come back and take me,
la vie ti mbi na sese	my life on this earth
a ke ye oko ape	means nothing
tongana mo yeke ape, eh.	if you are not here.
Si non Mami,	If you do not come, Mami
Mbi gwe ba nganga, si	I'll go see a diviner,
bolingo so a yeke winzi	and if I learn this love is over

a to mbi kwi
a sala ye oko ape eh.

I'll die,
and it won't matter anymore.

[Spoken in French, then Sango:]
[Spoken:]
J'ecoute toutes les nuits,
les sons de sirènes.
J'ecoute a travers elles
ta belle voix qui m'appelle.
Guifono ngo na yanga ti ngou,
Ga mou mbi, maaaaa. . . .

Every night I hear
the sound of sirens.
I hear through them
your beautiful voice calling me.
I walk out to the water's edge
Come take me, please. . . .

[Sung in Sango:]

Aah, ti mbi wali ni, Mami Wata.

Aaa, this woman of mine, Mami
Wata.

Oh, oho oh . . .
Azo a lango kwe
si lo yeke ga eh.

Oh, oho oh . . .
Only when everyone is sleeping
does she come.

Oh, Mami ka a yeke tonga na gne
Na gbe ti ngou mo goué na mbi.

Oh Mami, how is it over there?
From under the water you come
to me.

Belle sirène ka na mo ka eh
mbi yeke wende mbeni ape
bolingo ti e.
Oh Mami kiri mo mou mbi,

Beautiful siren, there with you
I won't have to hide
our love.
Oh, Mami, come back and take
me,

la vie ti mbi na sese
a ke ye oko ape
tongana mo yeke ape, eh.

my life on this earth
means nothing
without you.

Si non Mami,
Mbi gwe ba nganga, si
bolingo so a yeke winzi
a to mbi kwi
a sala ye oko ape eh.

If you do not come, Mami
I'll go see a diviner,
and if I learn this love is over
I'll die,
and it won't matter anymore.

Aah, ti mbi wali ni, Mami Wata.

Aaa, this woman of mine, Mami
Wata.

Oh, oho oh . . .
Azo a lango kwe
si lo yeke ga eh.

Oh, oho oh . . .
Only when everyone is sleeping
does she come.

[French, then Sango:]

Je te suivrai ou tu iras,
je veux vivre avec toi,
Kiri mo mou mbi. . . .

I'll follow you wherever you go,
I want to live with you,
Come back and take me. . . .

Kisliuk recently offered the following description of the sound of this song, which feels at once slow and fast:[27]

> The most widely circulated recording of "Mami Wata" opens with the metallic, plinking tones of a *sansa* (a small *mbira* or thumb-piano) as the high tenor begins the plaintive, ephemeral melody in French (another recording begins with the sound effect of lapping water). Against the text in Sango, the beat becomes more urgent and polyrhythmic, shifting from what began as a reggae-like underfeel to a fast rumba. The final phrase, in French, returns to the plaintive style that floats over the rhythm of the band, and the song ends ("come back and take me. . . ."), holding the beat in suspension just as the band shifts into the Musiki dance groove.

Yezo died of HIV/AIDS in 1995, which shocked and saddened the entire country. For more than two decades he had been the leader of the longest-lived Bangui *orchestre* (pop band) and mentored many new and innovative urban musicians. But he, along with other musicians, came to be regarded by the evangelicals as "sons of Satan" and associated with sorcery. When Yezo died, *Mami Wata* was "playing ceaselessly on tape players all over the country" in the months following his death. The country was "in deep mourning and the song epitomized the poignancy of his death."[28]

According to Kisliuk,[29] in the years following Yezo's death, musicians have been able to find "ways to use the evangelical fervor to their positive advantage. . . . Musiki . . . put out an album of current hymns set to their characteristic dance beat. That cassette has been wildly successful, and they have so far staved off social censure of their other music, which might otherwise have been fodder for evangelists' critique."

Kaïda, another musician and former friend of Yezo, has adopted a similar strategy with his recent song called "Sambela" ("Pray"), a lively dance tune in the "traditional modern" rhythmic/harmonic/melodic style. Kisliuk writes:[30]

> This song calls upon people of diverse affiliations—Muslim, Apostolic, Baptist—to get up and go pray. The song can thereby appeal to a wide range of affiliations, be a popular tune, yet still espouse piety. Another, more longstanding songwriting strategy of Kaïda's has been to adapt popular myths and legends to an urban dance band style. He had a big hit in 2000 called "Dawili," about a young boy who studies hard and makes his father proud. The song is sung in the first person voice of the father. Children in Bangui who see him in the street now call him "Dawili." Kaïda tells us that, along these lines, he has also recently com-

posed a song on the theme of Mami Wata. He says he chose this topic, "because this kind of title, like "Mami Wata," attracts a lot of international attention. For example, in Centrafrique, the name "Dawili" is used in over 15 ethnic groups. It's a very popular name. Mami Wata is an English name that means the queen of the water. Anyone who hears the name Mami Wata in a song listens carefully and asks themselves what they are talking about in the song."

Kisliuk goes on to explain:

Kaïda makes sure to note that in his case the song is a fiction, a "sung legend, a fairy tale," and therefore not evidence of a relationship between himself and Mami Wata, which would place his use of "tradition" in the realm of what the evangelicals equate with sorcery and therefore condemn. "I took that subject on purpose, to get the attention of the public," Kaïda stipulates. Then he sings us a few lines in the traditional *motengene* rhythm, "Je suis allé a la source, je suis allé me beigner dans un ruisseau, j'ai trouvé une Mami Wata, je suis allé me beigner, j'ai trouvé une belle fille, une Mami Wata. J'ai fait la toilette en vein." ("I went to the spring, I went to bathe in a stream, I found a Mami Wata, I went to bathe, I found a beautiful girl, a Mami Wata. My bath was forgotten.")

Kaïda, so long passed over in terms of fame and fortune, here seems to be trying his hand at jumping on the bandwagon of an overwhelming hit by Theiry Yezo ten years earlier. Yezo's "Mami Wata" is still played by Yezo's band, Musiki, and reprised on thousands of private tape players. When I first heard the song in 1995, Yezo had just died, and I credited the song's wide popularity to public fascination with Yezo's purported liaison with Mami Wata, the fact that he had died of AIDS (which locally is thought to have crossed the water from America), and that he was a popular musician who traveled and toured Europe with his band. This interpretation is in keeping with the discussion of Mami Wata as a symbolic and practical negotiation with the "other" of colonial or post/neo-colonial encounters, as discussed by Drewal. To me in this song Mami Wata represented death itself calling Yezo. The foreign lures he loved and caused his death were all Mami Wata. But now when I ask Kaïda his perspective on this, he outlines a somewhat different interpretation of the song and its popularity, linking it more directly to the simultaneous appeal and suspicion of Yezo's success, in that this success is seen as being owed to Yezo's mystical pact with Mami Wata. In other words, his supernatural machinations were understood to have enabled his fame. In the climate of evangelical fervor, this attribution of a musician's success to a spirit entity held special interest. That Yezo died of AIDS was further proof of the devilish path that Yezo took, as Kaïda explained. The combination of music and imagery in this song, and the rumors about this prolific and long-beloved musician himself, kept the public transfixed.

Envoi—Henry John Drewal

The sensuous sight and sounds of mermaids continue to seduce and inspire artists across Africa and around the globe. In Zimbabwe, mermaids and their music are well known. The ethnomusicologist Christopher Berry has documented a Shona thumb-piano (*mbira*) song about mermaids (*njuzu*). *Njuzu* may have no direct historical connection to Mami Wata or the *mami wata*s of West Africa, yet it is interesting to note that several thumb-pianos from Calabar, Nigeria are decorated with images of mermaids.[31] Perhaps it is the "sweet" sound of a thumb-piano that links it with mermaids. Shana Dressler, a music historian who has been collecting mermaid music in Africa and the African diaspora, told me about the night in 2001 when she heard Stella Chiweshe, "The Queen of Mbira," sing at Joe's Pub in New York City: "She spent half an hour talking about mermaids and singing a song to them. . . . She said that the *mbira* represents water. . . . Zimbabwe mermaids are alive and well!"[32]

David Hecht (1990)[33] discussed and showed Madonna on a beach playing with an African boy with dreads and a fishtail, which appeared in her music video *Cherish* (1989). In 2001, the internationally renowned Senegalese singer Baaba Maal composed a song in her honor called "Fanta," which is included in his CD entitled *Missing You (mi yeewnii)*:

Did you have a nice day, Penda?
Did you have a nice day, Penda?
[Chorus in Mandinka—praising hope and trust]
Holele fanta
Aaah fanta
[Chorus in Mandinka—praising hope and trust]
In Congo they call her Fanta
In Guinea she is called Mami Wata
But I call her Penda Musa from the riverside
The woman who went to Ndar Gej river
And showed white people Africans do not know what they share . . .
     [meaning unclear]
Penda, it is dark/night
The stars are shining, Penda
Baby don't cry, it's Penda.
(translated by Amadou Fofana)

In July 2003 I happened to rent a Japanese film. In the middle of it, I suddenly heard a song and the name Mami Wata. This is what I wrote at the time:

I have just seen the film *Warm Water under a Red Bridge* (2001)—a funny, quirky tale of a woman who gushes water whenever having sex . . . well, in the midst of this odd story in runs an African athlete (being trained for the Olympics by a Japanese coach) singing about Mami Wata!—I could not believe my eyes and ears . . . Mami Wata has claimed many spaces, including Japanese cinema!

No telling where she might surface next. . . .

Mami Wata/*mami wata* followers articulate their devotions by selecting fragments from both local and foreign cultures and investing them with new meanings in order to create sacred symbols and sounds to honor their spirit. Musicians from all parts of Africa (and the African diaspora) continue to be inspired by mermaids and other water spirits. Their songs, whether for Mami Wata or a host of different *mami watas,* celebrate their unique understandings of these deities for specific reasons. At the same time, they often share similar ideas, attitudes, and actions. Such an array of perspectives attests to the power and presence of mermaids in human imaginations as devotees and artists seek to exploit a supernatural force that promises wealth and well-being in an Africa where local, but especially neocolonial, global forces play a considerable role.

NOTES

I want to acknowledge with sincere gratitude the contributions of colleagues whose extensive research and writing about Mami Wata/*mami wata* or other African water spirits have made possible this essay on mermaid music in Africa. Mami Wata/*mami wata* is a topic that is too vast and complex to be explored by a single person—a vast collaborative scholarly network, a "fishing net" of enormous proportions, is required to capture the richness and diversity of Mami Wata/*mami wata* arts and histories. In this essay I have selected specific examples that discuss Mami Wata/*mami wata* musical culture and history from my own work over thirty years, references to the work of several colleagues (cited in the essay), and, especially, the extended excerpts from two excellent essays by Charles Gore and Michelle Kisliuk that will appear in my forthcoming edited volume on Mami Wata/*mami wata* arts—a publication being done in conjunction with a major traveling exhibition and catalogue about arts for Mami Wata and other water spirits in Africa and the Afro-Atlantic being organized by the UCLA Fowler Museum of Cultural History.

1. Barbara Paxon, "Mammy Water: New World Origins? *Baessler-Archiv,* Neue Folge 31 (1983): 407–46.

2. Alex Stripiaan, "The Ever-Changing Face of Watermama in Suriname: Wotar Goddess in Creolization Since the Seventeenth Century," in *Sacred Waters: The Many Faces of Mama Wata/mami watam and Other Water Spirits in Africa and the Afro-Atlantic World,* ed. Henry John Drewal (Bloomington: Indiana University Press, forthcoming).

3. Henry John Drewal, "Performing the Other: Mami Wata Worship in West Africa," in *The Drama Review,* T118 (1988): 160–85; Henry John Drewal, "Interpretation, Invention, and Re-presentation in the Worship of Mami Wata," *Journal of Folklore Research,* 25, nos. 1/2 (1988): 101–39. (Reprinted in R. Stone, ed., *Performance in Contemporary African Arts* (Bloomington: African Studies Program, Indiana University, 1988), 101–39, 103–104.

4. Elizabeth Isichei, "Mami Wata, Water Spirits, and Returners in and near the Igbo Culture Area," in *Sacred Waters,* 2, quoting the song by Ananga and translated by Mafuk in Winwoode Reade, *Savage Africa* (London: Smith, Elder and Co., 1863), 228.

5. Drewal, "Interpretation, Invention, and Representation," 104.

6. Drewal, "Performing the Other," 171.

7. Drewal, "Performing the Other," 169, 183, n. 6.

8. Drewal, "Performing the Other"; Dana Rush, "Eternal Potential: Chromolithograph in Vodunland," *African Arts* 32, no. 4 (Winter 1999): 60–75, 94–96.

9. Not surprisingly, these same instruments (and a "blues" sound) are used to honor African water deities in the Americas—Yemoja, Oshun, Olokun, La Sirene, Erzulie, and others. John Mason, personal communication, 2003.

10. Chinua Achebe, *Girls at War and Other Stories* (London: Heinemann, 1972).

11. Amadou Fofana, personal communication, October 27, 2003.

12. Edouard Vincke, "Le Corps de la Sirene—Analyse Semiologique," forthcoming in *Sacred Waters,* ed. Drewal, 3.

13. Fofana, personal communication, 2003.

14. Charles Gore, "Mami Wata: An Urban Presence or The Making of a Tradition," in *Sacred Waters,* ed. Drewal, 1.

15. Ibid.

16. Victor Uwaifo, *Origins of the Highlife and the Nigerian Music Industry* (Benin City: Toromi Publishing Co., 1995), 46

17. Gore, "Mami Wata," 10–11.

18. Ibid., 12–13.

19. Ibid., 13.

20. Ibid., 14–16.

21. Ibid., 25–30.

22. Ibid.

23. Charles Gore, "Ritual, Performance and the Media in Contemporary Urban Shrine Configurations in Benin City, Nigeria," in *ASA Monograph,* no. 35 (London and New York: Routledge), 1998; Charles Gore, "Popular Culture in

West Africa," *Encyclopedia of Sub-Saharan Africa,* ed. J. Middleton (New York: Charles Scribner's Sons, Macmillan, 1998), note.

24. Salmons 1977:11.

25. Isichei, "Mami Wata, Water Spirits," 5.

26. Michelle Kisliuk, personal correspondence, 2003; Kisliuk, "The Intersection of Evangelism, AIDS, and Mami Wata in Popular Music in Centrafrique," in *Sacred Waters,* 4.

27. Kisliuk, Personal correspondence, 2004.

28. Kisliuk, personal correspondence, 1995.

29. Kisliuk, "The Intersection of Evangelism," 4.

30. Ibid., 4–5.

31. I documented these in the Nigerian National Museum in 1978.

32. Shana Dressler, personal communication, February 13, 2003.

33. David Hecht, "Mermaids and Other Things in Africa," *Arts Magazine* (Nov. 1990): 82–86.

The Navel, the Corporate, the Contradictory

Pop Sirens at the Twenty-first Century

Thomasin LaMay and Robin Armstrong

> Women, for all their apparent gains, still grapple with the prospect of marginal lives, with the commodification of their spirit, their bodies. Isn't Britney Spears just a singing toy marketed by jaded and cynical men? It's one of our culture's deep secrets, but women are still second-class citizens, more readily accepted when heeled to pornographic submission and so often vilified at any hint of ambition.
>
> —*New York Times*, August 13, 2000[1]

> That's one of the challenges I'm going through right now. I just cut my hair very short and I'm letting it grow back its natural color. I'm not going to be this red-headed siren any more. I might never sell a record because I'm not what they want me to be, this beautiful woman who wears makeup or whatever, but it's so liberating.
>
> —Inger Lorre, *Rockrgrl*, December 30, 1999[2]

> LA told me, "You'll be a pop star. All you have to change is everything you are." Tired of being compared to damn Britney Spears. She's so pretty, that just ain't me.
>
> —Pink, "Don't Let Me Get Me," from her album *Missundaztood*[3]

> Wouldn't the worst be, isn't the worst, in truth, that women aren't castrated, that they have only to stop listening to the Sirens (for the Sirens were men) for history to change its meaning?
>
> —Hélène Cixous, *The Laugh of the Medusa*[4]

Women have always held a tenuous position within the western world's sphere for "professional musician." Any level of accomplishment above polite amateur has been deemed deviant because it seems too sexually enticing ("she" luring "he"), and paradoxically at the same time it is seen as too unfeminine because it makes women behave like men ("she" can do it as well as "he" can).[5] In twentieth- and twenty-first-century popular music, women have continuously faced discrimination in the workplace, and the content of musical lyrics is so frequently misogynistic that it is a trademark of our culture.[6] Sometimes the texts are actually hateful toward women, but most commonly they objectify women as purely male fantasies rather than as real people.[7] When women have created their own musical works, they have had to at least grapple with, if not adopt, the masculinist formats so contrary to feminist teachings.[8] For our purposes here, it is instructive to look at those changes occurring during the close of the twentieth century that allowed women greater entry into the popular music arena. Most particularly we focus on the phenomenon of the corporate-designed "megastar" figure.[9] One of the more fascinating ways women have merged with this contradictory creation is by appropriating and exploiting the siren's image: they lure through music, sex, and a sense of danger. The level of danger is determined by the genre of music they explore.

Historically, women's limited access to the role of professional musician has been through singing. The avenue exists because singing as a feminine activity has been considered natural rather than skilled. "Moreover," as Mavis Bayton suggests, "the singer's only 'instrument' is her body. This both confirms and reinforces the long-standing association of women with the body and nature which runs through our culture and contrasts with the image of men as controllers of nature via technology."[10] So whether or not she is a trained singer, her art is deemed of nature, natural to her femaleness, and part of her body. Indeed, the megastar's body is more important than her sound to her success, and it is this melding of body/nature to a proscribed male fantasy that defines the twenty-first-century pop music siren. We would like to examine the paradoxical relationship between the female pop-singing siren and the corporate (male) fantasy who creates her, despite her claims for independence. We term this phenomenon "the corporate siren."

Women singers from antiquity to the present have been labeled sirens, a problematic yet commonplace epithet which seems able to describe at the new millennium a wide variety of performing females. She could be a rock diva, a classical violinist, or the corporate adjective for those performing at Lilith Fair. She is smoky siren, pop siren, sultry siren, disco siren, and in that capacity she is also sometimes the transvestite, the cross-dresser, the "other" siren. If she sings in movies she is not an actress, but a film siren.[11] If she appears on MTV she is often a nymphomaniac whose sexual appetite is unquenchable and sometimes dangerous. She is eager to put her body on the line.[12]

Whether or not she wants the label, women's singing in Western culture has been inextricably linked to her sexualized body, a body whose ambition is to seduce, and this relationship is what can denote her as siren. Early modern theorists contrived that the female vocal chords, or uvula, were simply an oral variation of her vulva, another entrance point for the phallus.[13] Her throat was likened to her uterus, and the clitoris was partner to the uvula on the grounds that both pieces of flesh controlled the heat of the "neck" to which they provided entry. When her uvula was undulating in the act of producing song she was considered especially "hot," her mouth open in an explicit invitation for sex, and her uvula in a rapturous state of "excessive jouissance."[14] She has had no say in this perception: it is simply because she has wanted to sing that she is thought to be the seductress, and this is virtually a trans-historical reality for her. The result is that she must choose to play the image, or reject it, but we would argue that she cannot (and has never been able to) unhinge the siren's legacy completely.[15]

Our early-twenty-first-century siren can be many kinds of musical woman, and indeed *Rolling Stone*'s Anniversary Issue for 1997 proclaimed the nineties as the decade that introduced a healthy diversity for women in the music industry. An "era of alternatives," young listeners craved female voices from the "lyric-driven lilt of singer/songwriters to the stark, slashing guitar chords of queercore bands," and there was a lively "middle-ground" that offered a wide variety of role models for women.[16] The subtext was that women no longer needed to conform to any one stereotype in order to sell. This was in sharp contrast, they suggested, to the 1980s, which welcomed in MTV on August 1, 1981; the result was a "post-feminist lapse that set even committed sirens' teeth on edge."[17] These "committed sirens" (Tina Turner was among the names invoked) were those who had always veered toward the "steamy," but had not gone quite as far as the sexually aggressive women of MTV. But things had changed, we were assured, and as they peered toward the twenty-first century, women musicians could aspire to a wide variety of looks and still anticipate artistic and financial success.

But is this actually the case for women in the music business at this writing, 2004? Or has the millennium ushered in yet a more insidious kind of siren: are the sirens really men as Hélène Cixous would have us think? In our modern world, the corporate male and men's fantasies have long stood behind the images women were allowed to portray in music. The corporate male acts as another kind of siren, luring women to performance roles with promises of fame and fortune. In turn these power figures expect to manipulate her completely: the megastar pop siren would not exist in our popular music culture today without the enabling corporate siren. But previously these "He's" have been out front, clearly visible, readily accepted, for better or worse, into the cultural mainstream.

The current notion that women have gained considerable freedom from patriarchal restrictions might imply that they have ready access to new self-images on (and off) stage.[18] Yet at least some of those freedoms exist in theory only. In her recent book, *Sex and Power,* Susan Estrich offers some alarming statistics about middle-class, college-educated women, and one of the most extraordinary is that 98 percent of corporate executives in America are male.[19] The corporate siren is still very much who he has always been. That he has been confined by a new "political correctness" to a murky backwater may make his lure all the more dangerous. As noted in the *New York Times* at the head of this essay, women are still second-class citizens but it is, unfortunately, a well-kept secret. Why must Inger Lorre refuse to be the corporately created siren, a move which seems to have halted her career? In an interview, partially quoted at the top of this essay, she continued to explain that "I wasn't ready for the industry to turn me into this sex thing. What usually happens is the execs tell you, 'You're not this enough, you're not that enough, not pretty enough.' "[20] And why does Pink rail against the standardized vision for beauty which seems required of those women who want to be (shall we say) "On Top?" Why did she need to refuse her record label's suggested media training: "He was trying to change me, change my whole thought pattern and I almost felt violated. One thing the guy told me was, 'if it's a guy, flirt.' "[21]

We would like to examine this paradoxical interrelationship between the corporate siren and the popular music siren, for we do see multiple sirens at work. We have located our questions in the careers of Mariah Carey (pop), Shania Twain (country), and Lil' Kim (rap), because they are highly visible, extremely successful women who claim to make their own choices, but they have also, and wholeheartedly, adopted the siren's persona. They acknowledge that they use this image to sell, and essential to their successes are the music videos, or mini movies, they make to accompany and advertise their CDs. Indeed, they *have* come a long way: they own their own copyrights, write and produce many of their texts and recordings, dictate the terms of their contracts, and have their own labels. But the siren they produce is the male fantasy, the megastar sex siren, and her image is remarkably alike across different musical genres. "She" is slim with cleavage, physically active, and most often blond (lots of long, blow-ing hair is essential). The exposed navel is central to her physical presentation, as is what we have dubbed her mermaid butt; the mermaid-shaped body is a modern cultural ideal. She might wear jeans or a bathing suit, but frequently the bottom half is in some way opened up, complemented by suggestive posturing and parted lips, a body poised for sex. Tellingly, though all three of our women identify ethnically as other than white, the siren they currently project is the white siren. Their musical languages differ, but Carey, Twain, and Lil' Kim aggressively want to be, and are, number one's. They are all astute businesswomen who run their own shows, yet they got their starts, have been backed, and still work with important corporate sirens who are central to their careers.

Finally, these women in particular lure us in, but often only to do what sirens of old were most feared for doing. They undermine the system by producing texts that put women—her needs, passions, feelings, and stories—in the foreground. They put themselves on top, place the critique of traditional music/text narrative at the center, and "write beyond the ending"[22] with these transgressive strategies. As such, these sirens represent for us an ultimate contradiction. They readily buy into the sex siren, lured by that corporate siren, and they make no apologies to those women musicians trying to buck that system. Their videos show the siren story, and their CD covers explicitly open up for us their bodies as we move from front to interior of the package. Yet in the end they will have us know that they are in control of it all. Therein, for us, lies the contradiction: who *is* the siren for us now?

Mariah Carey: The Siren on Top

> One day I woke up right in front of the siren rock. The sirens would sit there and lure in the men. They gave them this rock because women were considered less important than men, and that's their revenge: They sexually entice men with their voices to come to this rock. And I happened to wake up in front of the siren rock, and I just fell in love with that.
> —Mariah Carey[23]

> We don't look at her as a dance-pop artist. We look at her as a franchise.
> —Don Ienner, president of Columbia Records, to Rob Tannenbaum, *Rolling Stone*, August 23, 1990[24]

Mariah Carey's take on the siren rock has a modern, quasi-feminist twist to it. Classical mythology did not always make clear the sirens' motive or the music they played/sang, and ancient sirens incorporated many physical shapes and musical abilities.[25] Most consistently, however, the old stories recount that these women lured sailors to their deaths with exquisite sounds that men could not resist. Carey's notion for power inequities and *sexually* enticing capabilities (for classical sirens actually *had* power, and sometimes lured men in order to kill and eat them, rather than to have a sexual encounter) reflects much more of her own reality. Sirens of antiquity lured before they were seen, lured through their sounds; Carey recognizes the need to be a visual as well as a sonic apparition. It is a frank testimony to the kind of power reversal that now leaves the siren in a second-class position, manipulated rather than manipulative, reckoning her voice as a sexual object. Her image, as Don Ienner commented, is now a "franchise," and her artistic value matters primarily because it brings home the pay packet, both for herself and for her corporate sponsors.

Mariah Carey was *the* top-selling female artist of the 1990s, with more than 140 million albums and singles sold. She exploded onto the pop music scene in 1990 with her first CD, *Mariah Carey*, which topped the *Billboard* chart for nearly six months, spawned four number-one singles, and earned her Grammy Awards as best pop female vocalist and best new artist. Intensely driven, she has produced new CDs and videos almost yearly since her first album.[26] She has had more number-one hits than any female performer (only the Beatles and Elvis Presley have actually exceeded her in sales). Perhaps the most innately gifted vocalist of the three sirens we offer, she has an astounding vocal range that encompasses at least five octaves. Although rarely heralded as a songwriter, she has written thirteen of her fourteen bestselling songs herself.[27] Her lyrics are often about the traditional woes of love, for which she has sometimes been criticized, but she is an intensely personal singer whose appeal comes, as noted above, from her exposed navel as well as her willingness to share something autobiographical. She can be quite intentional in invoking those she cares for, but also those for whom she does not.

Mariah's self-chosen image as siren is now central to her career. As she strolled onto the stage for the Divas 1998 performance, she asked the audience suggestively how they liked the package, the outfit, the look, for she was there to give them "all the accessories."[28] This image follows her offstage as well, the tube dress with emphasis on her curvaceous backside being one of her favorite outfits. It is not the image with which she began, however, or the one chosen for her by her first corporate sirens. It has evolved with her as she has claimed more control over her career and she specifically nurtures it as her own vision. She tells us clearly in an interview included with her recent video, *No. 1 Hits,* that she alone is responsible for her image and her current career trajectory.[29]

Born in 1970, and showing precocious musical talent, she began voice studies with her mother, a vocal coach and soloist with the New York City Opera, at age four. Important to her self-identity, her mother is Irish American and her father is African American and Venezuelan.[30] She often visited her African American grandmother's large family. Biracial families were not always well received, and Mariah always struggled to be heard as "Black, Venezuelan and Irish, because that's who I am," though she has felt pressed to be "just one of them."[31] She started writing her own songs at age thirteen, and in high school she commuted to Manhattan to work with her friend and later professional musician, Ben Margulies. Schoolwork mattered not to her, but she worked hard at music, and three days after graduation she moved into the city to take odd jobs and peddle her demo tape.

Talent, hard work, and a mighty determination definitely got her to the door, but the door did not open without the help of the corporate siren. She eventually won an audition as backup vocalist for Brenda K. Starr, a Columbia Records pop recording artist, who in turn introduced Mariah at a record industry party to Tommy Mottola, president of Sony Music Entertainment (Columbia Records' parent company). She gave him her demo tape, and the Cinderella story has it that he listened to it on the way home, went back to the party to track her down, and offered her a contract. At the time, Columbia Records lacked a major female pop star on the order of Madonna or Whitney Houston. Mottola and Don Ienner, newly selected president of Columbia, saw Carey as the ideal candidate to become that "franchise." They were Mariah's corporate sirens.

The album *Mariah Carey* included eleven songs from the demo, and since Carey and Margulies had co-written and produced the tape, Mariah proposed to Columbia that they also co-produce the album. Ienner decided otherwise and hired the producers who had crafted Whitney Houston. Several months before the scheduled release of the album (in June 1990), Columbia implemented a carefully planned publicity campaign with a video presentation and several live performances.[32] They continued the publicity blitz after the album came out, buying full-page ads in *Billboard* as well as window and floor displays in record stores. Columbia had not introduced an artist with such fanfare since Bruce Springsteen in 1975, and the result was a highly produced album featuring Mariah as a young ingénue singing ballads. The cover of the CD offers a slightly quizzical but enticing woman, her naturally curly auburn hair blown gently across her face, while the back of the cover offers a tightly wrapped but contained figure who makes no eye contact with us as viewers.[33] Mariah made it clear in an interview that the control Columbia exerted over the production—even if it "made" her—was not her way of doing things. "I'm sure she wants to do a lot more on her next album," remarked Mottola.[34]

Carey's star was launched by a corporate vision, and during the making of the CD she also became romantically involved with Mottola, whom she married in 1993. She was given more say in her next album, *Emotions*, produced in 1991. The album was not as successful as the first, but the cover features her with flying hair (still auburn and curly, however) and a tight-fitting tube dress. Inside we meet her gazing at us with a youthful, somewhat shy, sexiness. *Music Box*, from 1993, offers an image that suggests Marilyn Monroe on the front cover, which opens out to a bare-shouldered pose. *Daydream*, produced in 1995, shows on the front a dark, straight-haired woman who on the back is wearing a black suit, a breast and the navel just slightly exposed. All of these albums were made with her husband as executive producer, so though she had gained some space from Columbia, this was only because she was still very much Mottola's product. She is suggestively sexy, but the image is honed, controlled and controllable. As many writers noted, he preferred her singing ballads and he packaged her accordingly.

The marriage was not a peaceful one, and as it began to unravel a curious thing happened to Mariah's persona. As one of many popular writers noticed, "Carey forged her stardom with a wholesome image and soaring ballads that highlighted her multi-octave voice. But over the past few years, her image has changed. After her divorce [which became official in 1998 after a year of separation] . . . she became sexier in her concerts and videos. She also switched musically, using more hip-hop beats."[35] The public got its first look at this freer Mariah when the video for "Honey" premiered on MTV in September, 1997. As her unofficial biographer wrote, "Suddenly Mariah was very grown up, Agent M, very sexy, showing a lot more of herself—in more ways than one: in action escaping from a mansion, riding a jet ski while evading pursuing thugs, and ending up on a beach safe in the arms of a hunk. This was, for the first time, Mariah as a babe."[36]

The video for "Honey" actually shares much more than a listener would glean from hearing the CD alone. The words might be heard as fairly standard love fare: "Honey you can have me / When you want me / If you simply ask me to be there / And you're the only one who / Makes me come running / Cause what you got is beyond compare." Yet the video begins with Mariah in handcuffs and tied to a chair as various men in business suits visit one at a time to ask things from her. They are portrayed as guards, but are only thinly veiled projections of the corporate sirens

Mariah longed to escape. She manages to unshackle her hands (outsmarting them!) and—running in very high heels—she dives out of the house into the ocean.[37] She grabs a jet ski and roars off, the "thugs" in business suits in hot pursuit on their own water machines. It is only after she has escaped into the arms of a waiting "hunk" that she teasingly sings "Honey you can have me when you want me." The music, with rapper Sean "Puffy" Combs at the helm, included strong hip-hop sections, something she had always wanted to do but which had not been permitted. Evidently Mariah's corporate sirens had not wanted her rubbing noses with her African American side. Mariah said in an interview that "I don't really think the video is overtly sexual, but for me—I mean people used to think I was the nineties version of Mary Poppins."[38] For Mariah, the video may have been less about "sexy" and much more about "power," even if the image she employed was the seductress. As viewers, too, we cannot escape the imageries of sea, of men in hot pursuit of a siren they cannot attain but whose voice taunts them, and of the siren's ultimate control.

Her album *Butterfly* appeared shortly after "Honey" and the cover offers us her new image (again we refer the reader to the Mariah Carey Web site). "This album is definitely something I've wanted to do for a long time. There were songs I wanted to do in the past. I recorded them, but they never got on the album. That happened even on the first album because some people felt they were too R & B. It's been a gradual process of my being able to say that this is what I'm going to do at this point. People owe it to you to let you express yourself."[39] She took all the credit but also lots of criticism for the R & B sound. People also noticed that many of the stories in the album were about divorcing Tommy Mottola, the husband who had been referred to as her Svengali, and "Honey" is the lead song on the CD. She promoted the album herself, without much input from Mottola or Columbia, and with a rare public appearance at Tower Records in New York

It was after *Butterfly* that Mariah left for Capri, to visit the siren rocks and to produce *Rainbow,* an album that "chronicles my emotional roller coaster ride of the past year," but a ride which has a "happy ending."[40] The CD features guest appearances from rappers Jay-Z, Snoop Dogg, Da Brat, and Missy Elliot, and the title derives from her own racial heritage as a "rainbow" of ethnicities. If Carey found inspiration from the sirens in Capri, it was to learn to claim the power of herself, to become her own lure: she would seduce and manipulate, rather than be manipulated by her corporate sirens. The album cover features her in delicate white underwear, bathed in a rainbow light, and opens to a full-color spread of her lying in bed on silk sheets, looking at us and inserting a red lollypop just to the tip of her mouth. One glass slipper is off, the other still on, a reference perhaps to her own Cinderella story, but also suggesting that the right prince *could* come in and put it on for her (see the Carey Web site). She is also now blond. She is waiting, she is inviting, and she is in control. When we enter, we hear a fluid admixture of pop and rap, along with texts like the following, from the song "Petals": "I gravitated toward a patriarch / So young predictably / I was resigned to spend my life / With a maze of misery / I stayed so long but finally / I fled to save my sanity."

There are songs about other relationships, her family, and the final song, "Thank God I Found You," provides the happy ending in that it looks forward to a new boyfriend. But there are many pointed moments such as "They Can't Take That Away, Mariah's Theme," where she declares flatly that "They can say anything they want to say. . . . They can do anything they want to you if you let them in, but they won't ever win." The opening piece, "Heartbreaker" (which immediately went No. 1), talks about the trap of a lost relationship: "Boy if I do the things you want me to / the way I used to do / would you love me or leave me feeling used." The video for this song again lends multiple meanings that are not heard in the lyrics themselves. It opens as Mariah and four female friends arrive at a movie theater (the women are an interesting "rainbow" of four different ethnicities). They encourage Mariah to reclaim her man, and their breakdancing is punctuated by Jay-Z's raps as they prepare to "kick butt." This Mariah is blond and as she and her friends enter the theater they see her guy with the "other Mariah"—Bad Mariah—who has very black hair. It is clear that the guy is infatuated with Bad Mariah, but she is much more interested in herself and her little dog, whom she inserts between them when the fellow tries to proffer a smooch. Bad Mariah leaves to primp in the restroom and Good Mariah follows her. When she tries to speak, Bad Mariah whirls and throws a punch. A wild fight ensues, punctuated by several humorous moments as her guy back in the theater is watching a movie about another blond Mariah at a pajama party (and we cannot escape the prepubescent fantasies of adolescent boys). Evidently victorious, Good Mariah comes back to sit next to him and while teasing seductively, she pours a large cup of cold water slowly into his lap (not seen, but understood as his penis). As she does so, she looks straight out at us, the viewers, in delicious triumph. Brett Ratner, who directed the video, wrote about working with Mariah that "she's really really smart. She does everything. She writes, she produces. People think she's writing these songs just to sell records, but these songs come right from her heart."[41] Indeed, this one came perhaps straight from her siren's heart, who would seduce now in order to seek the her "revenge."

When Mariah returned from Capri, she produced a video and album of her number-one hits. The cover features her as a take-charge, fully sexed woman who looks at us straight on (see Carey Web site), a photo that garnered for her the "sexiest woman's legs" award.[42] She also purchased the first piece of furniture she reportedly ever acquired, a white baby grand piano formerly owned by Marilyn Monroe and auctioned for $662,000.[43] She decided to tour widely, including a trip abroad to entertain troops in Kosovo, another homage to Monroe's earlier wartime efforts. Carey's visit was widely publicized, and she generally appeared in military fatigues that nonetheless revealed a serious amount of cleavage as she batted her eyes and flung about her now-straight blond hair. In February 2000 she appeared on the cover of *Rolling Stone* and there can be no doubt, as she pushes her body toward us and holds open the bottom of her bathing suit, that she sees herself fully capable of the ultimate seduction. But is it really to give away, or is it offered only to deny, to have the power to self-create, and then to do whatever she wants with that creation? Is it to seduce in order to do precisely what she does in "Heartbreaker" and emerge on top? Mariah may not push society's buttons in a Madonna-like fashion, but she *has* appropriated a powerful and, for her, empowering image of the siren in order to put herself back on top, in the position of manipulator, one who cannot be lured again.

There is much more to Mariah's story than this summary can supply. She was released from her Sony obligations before completing her last contracted album,[44] and immediately signed a megadeal with competitor Virgin. Her first work for them was the music and film for *Glitter*, but just before the film was to have been released Mariah suffered a much-publicized breakdown due to her exhausting schedule. The film was delayed, and then had the misfortune to be released on September 11, 2001. It was not a success, and Virgin then gave her $28 million to walk away from the contract. She was truly on her own, and asserted that she would mold her own future. But the corporate siren, ever lurking about, seemed remarkably available. As reported in the *New York Times* about her new contract negotiations: "One issue that has been a sticking point in the talks with Ms. Carey is how much say the label will have in molding her image . . . the question is, 'what does she want and is she prepared to listen?' She's got to find that certain executive she can truly work with to help her with her career."[45]

She took her time and a few vacations, and in May 2002 she got a new deal with the world's biggest music company, Universal Music Group. She is currently working with two of the industry's largest power brokers, Universal chief Doug Morris and fast-rising music executive Lyor Cohen, who heads Universal label Island Def Jam. In the deal she also got her own label. Mariah has gone back to the corporate siren, but is this a contradiction, or a power stroke? The *New York Times* recently noted that, "having signed Ms. Carey, Mr. Cohen and some Island Def Jam colleagues are off to Italy. He said that as they signed the contract, she said: 'I guess you have to come to Capri now. That's where I'm making the next album.' "[46] Mr. Cohen is taking twenty-five executives (all men) and their wives to visit the siren rocks.[47]

Shania Twain: The Siren Next Door

> I applaud the way she changed how videos are made. Loretta Lynn and Tammy Wynette and all those women were very sexy, but in country there's always been a problem with crossing the line and revealing too much of what you are. In pop music, it's okay to be a woman.
>
> —Faith Hill[48]

> Even on the sex symbol side of things, I'm very careful not to be sexual. And I think [this approach] rubs off in a healthy way for young women. I wish I had someone when I was 13 say "You can wear things that are flattering. You don't have to be afraid your body is changing. But do it on a comfortable level."
>
> —Shania Twain

A summary look at the covers of Shania Twain's most successful CDs gives us no indication that she is anything but a multiplatinum pop siren. Her long, loose hair, curvaceous (mermaid) butt, and cleavage leave no doubt as to who she might be, but again there is a contradiction. For Twain's *whole* public image is not just the pop siren, but a combination of the downhome girl next door from country music and the sexy pop siren, merged into a skimpily clad, yet somehow clean-cut woman who likes wholesome sex. "Shania Twain has carved out her own place in country," says one Nashville country correspondent for *Billboard*. "Until she came along, there was no job description for what she is—a pop femme fatale in country, for want of a better term. She's playing by her own rules. And she's changing the audience."[49]

This image has worked extremely well for her, as she has appealed and sold to a broadly based country, and ultimately crossover, pop audience.[50] With her second album, *The Woman in Me* (Mercury, 1995), produced only a few years after she arrived in Nashville, she broke the sales record it had taken Patsy Cline forty years to set. When her third album, *Come On Over* (Mercury, 1997), sold seventeen million units, Twain broke Whitney

Houston's record for bestselling female vocalist in any type of popular music.[51] As of March 2002, this CD had sold nineteen million units, and Twain remains the bestselling female vocalist of any type of music at any time.[52] She is, like Carey, a Woman on Top.

While she is unequivocally a talented singer and songwriter, Twain's "femme fatale" image is central to her appeal. She is, noted one writer, "a country singer who looks like a supermodel. . . . She is country's *Cosmo* girl, a fantasy that works for both men and women."[53] (Twain is in fact a Revlon model.) She is one of the few country singers who has sold platinum by making music videos before touring on the road, and no country singer has used video to promote herself with as much audacity. Like Mariah Carey, Twain has also claimed for *herself* the siren image. Luke Lewis, Nashville president of her Mercury label, noted that "a lot of people are accusing her of being packaged [by her management]. . . . But I don't think this is a marketing-driven artist. It's been *her* vision from the beginning—all the clothes, all the looks, all the concepts."[54]

Image has always been important in country music, and it has been crafted carefully since the first radio shows of the 1920s. Those programs evolved from the commercial success of recorded Anglo-American folk songs marketed as "old-time music." They especially appealed to rural and Midwestern farm audiences by reiterating "old-fashioned," conservative, and thus comfortable values. Texts of the folk songs, parlor songs, and hymns from which country music developed emphasized nostalgia for the good old days, the moral righteousness of the past, a sense that hard times were today's lot, and also love, both romantic and familial. There was a strong sense of pride in belonging to the poor but pure rural working class.

Country music singers have always needed to project this homespun model of purity and familiarity. They had to come from the lowest working classes and remain accessible to them through image, language, and texts; this has also meant strong connections to Christian-based "family values." Country musicians must be one of "us," the kid next door, highly approachable with no air of superiority. They must relate to their audience on a very personal level, an ideology that led to the annual country music event Fan Fair, organized solely to allow audiences to meet their favorite singers and get their autographs.[55]

Female country singers have especially needed to embody the idealized nineteenth-century woman: the pure young virgin and the perfect mother. Clothes and hairstyles were conservative, while texts and stage demeanor stressed goodness and wholesomeness. Songs by both men and women perpetuated traditional gender roles, even as they served to illus-

[329]

trate that canon's double standards. Texts sung by men described and even idolized women as sexy and alluring, but in sharply held contradistinction a female singer could not succeed in country music as a siren onstage since that image did not fit the genre's strict moral code. There have been a few exceptions, but women singers who have teased the rules in one way have done so by holding on strongly to them in others. Kitty Wells, an early country singer with a feminist bent, fought the double standards of country texts when she declared "It wasn't God who made honky-tonk angels," but she did so from the vantage point of feminine goodness and domesticity.[56] Dolly Parton has always exuded sex appeal with her buxom figure and flamboyant costumes, but she has also retained the country vernacular, maintains her home in rural Tennessee, and projects herself as happily married and therefore, essentially, harmless.

Shania Twain's pop siren image blatantly rejects long-held conventions, but she catapulted into country music through both her own untraditional venues and more "respectable" doors. Canadian rather than American, she identifies partly as Native Canadian. Her stepfather—also her adoptive father and the one who raised her—was an Ojibwa. Her birth name was "Eileen," but she changed it to the Ojibwa "Shania," meaning "I'm on my way," at the start of her recording career (the name change was requested by her corporate siren). One reason she has been able to succeed so well with her sexualized image is that her beginnings resonate well with country audiences. Raised by working-poor parents, she was dragged from bed by her mother at age eight to perform at local late-night shows. She started her singing career right after high school, but returned home every summer to help with the family reforesting business. At age twenty-two, she had to return home permanently to raise her younger brothers and sister when her parents were killed in a car accident. With the help of a well-connected family friend she was still able to continue performing at a popular Canadian resort, and when her siblings were old enough she was able to parlay her musical experiences into a Nashville contract. These working-poor roots and her devotion to family give her "country" credibility, even if she now lives in a Swiss chalet.[57]

Also like Carey, Twain started within the system. Her first album, *Shania Twain* (1991), was controlled and produced by her Nashville Mercury label. The texts are fairly conventional, as was the image devised for her. The cover of the album shows her standing in the snow, bundled in warm, bulky clothes next to a husky dog. All pictures inside are the same except one, which shows her in a conservative sleeveless blouse, holding a jacket over one shoulder.[58] Her hair in these pictures is fairly typical of the country woman's "big hair" style, pulled back and out of her face. Like

Mariah, she allowed her label to "make her," *except* that she promoted the album through a video—a sexy midriff-baring depiction of the song "What Made You Say That," rather than by going on the country tour circuit. It was the video that caught the eye of South African rock producer Robert John (Mutt) Lange, now her husband, who called her on the spot, a Cinderella story not unlike Carey's. It was the siren in the video who launched Shania "on her way," for "she" had attracted her corporate siren counterpart.

The album had modest sales of about 100,000 copies, but it led to the romance with Lange, which started as a songwriting relationship over the phone. They eventually met in Nashville and married six months later. Lange financed her second album, *The Woman in Me,* a $700,000 work of studio finesse touted as the most expensive country album ever recorded.[59] While still brought out by Mercury, Lange, with his rock music connections, now had the controls. Curiously, though, a rather outspoken country siren emerged. The album immediately catapulted Twain to multi-platinum, even as it drew criticism from those who suggested she was "a studio Barbie created by a Svengali husband and a high-powered rock management."[60] The cover to this album does not necessarily take her out of the country genre, but much of the video material and her texts do.

The picture on the international version of her third album, *Come on Over,* has a headshot of her in a skimpy sleeveless shirt, with loose siren hair and a sultry look (see Twain Web site). Pictures inside show her in what might have been photo shoots for her Revlon advertisements. One shows her lying on a piece of fur on the floor, in a suggestively low-cut dress. Another offers her in a tight-fitting, strapless costume. In all of these pictures, she has long, free, flying siren hair which is completely inconsistent with the country woman image.

Twain has served up the siren but often in order to dish out blatantly feminist versions of traditional country themes. Unlike Carey's lyrics, which often need help from accompanying videos to tell the "real story," Twain's texts are often sufficiently blunt on their own terms, and herein lies her dangerous lure. They are country in that they emerge from the working-class life experiences and language, but they are told from the woman's point of view and demand her equality.[61] She is the "no-nonsense sex symbol, a take-charge woman, line-dancing down the middle of the road, splitting the difference between feminine compliance and feminist effrontery."[62] She knows she is treading a fine line with her siren, and she often deflects the siren's power with humor and the frequent use of accompanying wholesome country images. She bombards us from both sides, and essentially lets us choose whether to see the siren or the good country girl. Perhaps she sees them as potentially one and the same, and that, too, is inherently dangerous for a tradition that requires clear (comfortable) boundaries.

In the video for her second album hit "Whose Bed Have Your Boots Been Under," Twain tries to seduce every man she sees. The lyrics are in direct opposition to traditional country female stories, for she tells men up-front that their philandering is not acceptable and she cannot have the usual gendered "double standards." The video, directed by John and Bo Derek, cuts between the "real" Twain playing her guitar alone on her porch, and the "siren Twain" dancing atop a diner table (a traditional country prop) in a red-hot dress. She becomes the fantasy siren of her own imagination, as Twain appears to conjure "her" up while musing on her desk. The fantasy siren is less potent, however, since none of the men she approaches actually seems to see *or* hear her. It seems comic when she talks to the cook, who does not hear her, even as he lets his cigarette ash fall into the food he is serving. She pours coffee and lets it spill all over the counter, and as she leaves the diner even the dog in the truck window does not see her as she walks away and down the street. We can choose to believe that she was never really there at all; or we might also ask, if she was an illusion, *whose* fantasy she was, for the men about her are impotent in their inability to hear her song.

Some of Twain's videos present a more provocative siren who does claim attention. The video for the song "You're Still the One," from her third album *Come on Over,* shows Twain just after a swim on a moonlit beach, still wet and wearing only a robe. She returns home where a handsome man is taking a bath and watching her on a video screen, much in the way that men voyeuristically watch women in MTV videos. Also much like Carey's video "Honey," there is no escaping the visage of the woman coming from the sea, knowing she is being watched, pursued, desired. There is a palpable sexual energy about the scene, and the song finishes with Twain in bed as the gentleman drops his towel and joins her. This is utterly the pop siren, exploding the limits for women in country music both visually and musically. Yet Twain suggested that the piece was about her husband Mutt, and "the nice feeling we've made it against all odds."[63] While steamy, she has covered herself by enacting a very erotic "marriage scene" that might still fall within the country bounds of "family," and it certainly makes that rubric more exciting. Who would not want such a delightfully fantasized home life, a dream denied to traditional country women whose lives are often hard and whose choices are limited. Wholesome women, Twain seems to claim, could also be sirens; or, sirens could be wholesome women. Her boundaries are fluid, and even as she entices us we are again denied the "comfortable" boundaries for good and bad so important to country music.

Like Carey, Twain sometimes manipulates her siren to project strong-minded women on top, a very potent reference to the classical siren who was always in control, feared for the power of her voice to debilitate men. In these stories, too, the boundaries between characters are porous, but the message is not as much about sex as it is about women claiming their own power. This kind of imagery is what makes Twain especially dangerous to a genre that historically puts women on the bottom, and where women are notoriously well-behaved and domesticated. Twain evoked this kind of authority even in the first song of her own that she released, "God Ain't Gonna Getcha for That," where the woman plays the "man's" role as sexual protagonist. Her second and third albums are rife with such pieces. In the song "The Woman in Me," the text "Any man of mine better be proud of me / Even when I'm ugly he still better love me," directly contradicts the notion that only beautiful women deserve attention. After the question in "Whose Bed Have Your Boots Been Under" is answered with a list of female names, Twain concludes: "So next time you're lonely / Don't call on me / Try the operator / Maybe she'll be free." In "I'm Outta Here," she charges men not to be attracted to her (siren image) for sex only, but for genuine relationships, with the chorus "If you're not in it for love / I'm outta here!"

Come on Over offers "Black Eyes, Blues Tears," and "If You Wanna Touch Her, Ask," explicit and forceful directives that country women would never traditionally invoke. She teases guys who think too much of themselves in "That Don't Impress Me Much" and those who are too possessive in "Don't Be Stupid." In "Honey I'm Home" she talks about her day at work ("With all this stress I must confess / This could be worse than PMS") and then flips traditional country gender roles on their head with the chorus: "Honey, I'm home and I had a hard day / Pour me a cold one and oh, by the way / Rub my feet, gimme something to eat / Fix me up my favorite treat / Honey I'm back, my head's killing me / I need to relax and watch TV / Get off the phone, give the dog a bone / Hey hey Honey, I'm home." This is not country language, but the language of power, packaged in the siren's body, potentially unsettling and dangerous for listeners, especially men who want their women beautiful but "on the bottom."

Both country and pop music industry media have made much of Twain's enormous success, and she has received as much criticism as praise for her image. The country music traditionalists deplore her unprecedented showing of skin. Her background and authenticity were questioned just after her second album appeared, and the media claimed that she had exaggerated her impoverished childhood. She was accused of trying to exploit a Native American heritage by unfairly claiming an Ojibwa father.[64] Despite these criticisms, Twain's background has worked to her advantage by locating her in the class structure of the country genre, and it has hooked her in just enough to keep her siren country-based. She does indeed dance down the middle, yet we have to ask whether she would have been able to belt out her feminist messages with a typical country-woman image: who would have believed her then? Or even listened? As a siren, the body and voice compel audiences to hear her; as a domesticated country woman, her messages would be heard only as incongruent with the genre. Her image has assured for her megastar status and a large audience who will eagerly consume her feminist texts without really knowing it. Therein lie Twain's multiple contradictions, for she will let us take her as siren even as she critiques that image, and this can allow us as viewers/hearers a similar critical stance. Or, we can simply leave her as the girl next door.[65]

Lil' Kim: The Siren of the Street

> When I was younger all the men liked the same women: Those light-skinned European-looking girls. Being the rapper Lil' Kim has helped me to deal with it a little better because I get to dress up in expensive clothes and look like a movie star.
>
> —"Kim on Kim"[66]

> Guys always cheated on me with women who were European looking. . . . Really beautiful women that left me thinking. How can I compete with that? Being a regular Black girl wasn't good enough."
>
> —Lil' Kim[67]

> If Kim didn't rock the blond weave, blue contacts and barely-there outfits, she probably wouldn't garner press. . . . It's disturbing that we don't try to decipher how the media is, in part, responsible for Kim's myopic view of beauty. . . . Her statements about European-looking women with long hair who are "really beautiful" beg for more introspection.
>
> —"Mediawatch"[68]

The world of hip-hop does not simply reflect male domination of the music industry. The conventions of gangsta rap, the most popular and lucrative type of hip-hop, are predicated on male power over women, and female subjugation is an essential component of the genre. As Marla Shelton described in her 1997 article on women in rap videos, "Rap has become synonymous with a masculine 'core' culture."[69] Only women who can fit themselves into this structure as one of the characters of the ghetto world on male terms can survive for long. The most secure of these roles is the city sister to the siren, the street walker, prostitute, Ho.[70] The siren of the ghetto is a man's possession; she is all about sex, a bad girl who knows how to please her man in the explicit sexual terms that pervade rap lyrics. While "Ho" might refer to any woman, in rap culture it is especially associated with African American women, and herein lies the challenge that brings us finally to the rap artist Lil' Kim.

Lil' Kim not only realized the connection between the Ho and the siren of her pop-star peers, but she also determined which one of those siren images would ultimately give her the most successful career. She started as a Ho, as an African American woman within rap culture, but then very self-consciously recreated herself as a siren, specifically her own version of the white siren. In doing so she not only challenges the misogynist leanings of rap, but also and importantly forces us to contemplate race in relation to the corporate siren in ways that Carey and Twain do not. Carey and Twain both acknowledge their racial roots, but as viewers we see them unquestionably as white. Carey was actively discouraged by her corporate sirens from using hip-hop materials in her songs, but it was a sound and not an image issue for them. Lil' Kim seems to imply that even in an essentially African American musical genre, power for her comes only through the image of the white siren. This, to these writers, sends complicated and disturbing cultural messages.

When rap first emerged during the mid-1970s, women did play roles in the music and culture of hip-hop, albeit small ones. They MC'd, tagged, and danced in the hip-hop arts of rap, graffiti, and breakdancing. Women's roles in hip-hop paralleled their place in the music industry and the nation at large at the end of the 1970s: small but promising. Soul singer Sylvia Robinson helped to create the first rap record label, Sugar Hill Records, which in 1979 released the first rap album titled *Rapper's Delight*.[71] Rapper Queen Latifah was even able to inject feminist texts into the discourse with songs like "Ladies First." However, when the economic problems of the 1980s began to affect American inner cities disproportionately, the musical responses from the men feeling this disenfranchisement began to describe more and more only "his" life in the ghetto. In the world of gangsta, love does not exist, only those with real power survive, and power is based on the acquisition of money, cars, jewelry, and women, who become less human and more objectified. In rap videos women are commonly abused, and they often die.[72] This image of the street gangsta, which closely parallels previous stereotypes of African Americans originating in the minstrel show, also had a curious and significant appeal to America's affluent (white) youth in that they could experience vicariously the dangerous life they did not need to live. It was this gangsta subgenre of hip-hop that came to control the music market, and only a few women have been able to enter this domain as performers even at a low-budget level. Since rap's early days, Queen Latifah has made more movies and television appearances than music albums, and only a few younger women have emerged as rappers.

Lil' Kim lived the authentic rap life before she entered the performance world. Like successful male rappers, African American Kimberly Denise Jones grew up in urban poverty. Her parents were divorced and she lived with her father, who never approved of her. She dropped out of high school, ran away from home at age fourteen, and worked for drug dealers. This is how she met Christopher (Biggie Smalls) Wallace, a small-time drug seller who was soon to emerge as Notorious B.I.G., rap superstar. They became "an item" (though eventually he married Faith Evans), and Kim apprenticed with his Junior MAFIA. It was Biggie who produced her first album, *Hard Core* (Atlantic, 1996), which debuted on the chart higher than any other rap album by a female, and then went multiplatinum.

The cover for *Hard Core* offers Kim as a high-class black hooker waiting for her next client. She is on hands and knees, with legs far apart, looking expectantly at the viewer.[73] The flowers and champagne surrounding her leave little doubt as to what she expects, and what it will cost. Lil' Kim started with the only image available to her in gangsta rap, the traditional Ho. She is sexy, seductive, but she is still Ho: the appeal is whorish and not about the more complex allurement tactics of sirens like Carey and Twain. The rap-like braggadocio of her first manager, Lance Rivera, also demonstrates just how overtly she was perceived by him to be *his* (rather than her own) creation and indeed possession: "I'm going to show people I know how to create. . . . I'm making records. I need to show the music business . . . that I do women. Women rappers are more difficult to break as artists. I make women happen. . . . That separates me from a lot of people in this business."[74] Kim seemed to make no objection to this gangsta version of the corporate siren who placed himself in a very real sense "on top" of her.

A year after Lil' Kim's first album, Biggie was murdered.[75] This was devastating for Kim, who took four years to produce her next album, *The Notorious K.I.M.* (Atlantic Records, Queen Bee, 2000), whose title reflects her first sponsor and love. Between albums, however, she left Rivera, her original corporate siren, and fundamentally recreated herself:

Instead of fading into the background [between her two albums] like most other artists, Lil' Kim's persona grew. She used the time between albums to flaunt her personality and her body. She got breast implants, and began wearing blond wigs and blue contacts. She appeared at parties and awards shows wearing next-to-nothing and boasting that she was "the Queen Bee" of rap. People began to talk about her, and soon she became a sex symbol of sorts. And in the process, she became perhaps the only female rapper whose personality preceded her rhymes."[76]

This new blond-haired, blue-eyed, scantily clothed Kim took from her Ho heritage only the rap and the notion of a highly sexualized woman, but gone is the Ho who would lie down for her man. This woman, like Carey and Twain, claims to be in charge of herself and her image, which poignantly buys into the corporate siren's whiteness. "[Men] all liked the same women. They always like that light-skin, European-lookin' girl."[77] So she took up this European image and hyper-sexed her because, in her words, "sex sells. People have to understand that this is how I came into the game. This is *my* image."[78] Robert Sullivan, at Fashion Week 2000, asked Kim's hair stylist to describe her hair. " 'Oh, it's up. . . . It's tousled, of course. Very Blonde. Very free. Very open. Very Ivana.' "[79] The reference to Ivana Trump, a rather infamous New York City siren who snared a very wealthy man, securely connects Kim to the European beauty she seeks.[80]

To promote her new persona, Kim made frequent and very public appearances that were always timed to be filmed, on TV, and in the media. She was extraordinarily bold in using seduction to market her name and her music, and she knew she needed to be first. "I'm a trend setter. That's what I do. That's just me."[81] After making a considerable stir at the 1999 MTV awards, where she appeared with one breast bare except for a pasty over the nipple, she told *Jet* that "the MTV awards show helped me. . . . My name got even bigger. It is all about fashion and my creative style. Guys want something to look at and girls want some kind of inspiration and style."[82] Fans readily support her claim that she is inspiring for women. At one public event, a viewer came to her and said, "I just want to say God bless you . . . for doing what you do. . . . You come out here and every day you have a different look, and it's like you're giving something back."[83]

In addition to using the image to sell her music, she has also sold her image. She has been paid as a runway and photo model; she has promoted M.A.C. cosmetics, Candie's shoes, Iceberg jeans; she models for Calvin Klein, Dolce & Gabbana, and Louis Vuitton. Selling is important to her, for her goals are global. She has stated, "I want the world to know that I can do anything. I'm versatile. I want to own my own business. I want to be an entrepreneur and a household name. I want people in India to know me. I want people in China to know me."[84] And also: "I plan to be an entrepreneur for the rest of my life."[85]

As one journalist noted, " . . . when Lil' Kim arrives, she, of course, does not merely arrive. She *arrives.* This particular type of arrival is made possible by the presence of numerous public-relations people, by the presence of several of Lil' Kim's friends or acquaintances, by the presence of a stylist, a makeup person, and a hair person, and by the presence of Lil' Kim's bodyguard. . . . Lil' Kim punctuates each of her arrivals with an outfit that puts the X in sexy and a formidable-for-her-size . . . hands-on-her-hips stance."[86] The pictures taken for M.A.C.'s Viva Glam III campaign illustrate this point clearly.[87] She and Mary J. Blige are photographed together, both staring into the camera with their smiling mouths open in a very inviting manner. Blige sports a low-cut dress, and Kim wears a gold pantsuit unzipped to her navel; her body is turned a bit to the side, which gives the viewer a tantalizing glimpse of her entire left breast save the nipple. Both (African American) women have very straight, very blond hair. Behind them, naked men in profile are jumping for joy. All of the men are white. There appears to be no room in this European American world for the black male, whose associations with rap are of power over women, but also whose projections in American culture are of danger, violence, and death. We as viewers/listeners do not connect white men generally with that same meanness. Lil' Kim may also have wished to project herself as a sexual being who can and in fact does appeal to white men, just as she complained that black men always rejected her in favor of European-looking white women.

Kim's album *The Notorious K.I.M.* (2000) was produced by Sean "Puffy" Combs, who had done *Rainbow* for Mariah just a year before. The cover of the CD offers a powerful blond seductress. Kim wears nothing above the waist, but conceals her breasts (for now) with her arms (see the Lil' Kim Web site). Her jeans are unzipped and pushed down as far as they will go and still remain on. Her mouth is open, and her eyes seem both to challenge and invite. She might do anything with those arms, or those pants, but only if she wants. She no longer has to play Ho, but she can, like Carey, make the choices herself. She might give, she might just walk away, or she might really scare you. With this forcefully seductive image, Lil' Kim has out-sirened the white siren with rap attitude and raw Ho sexuality. She has brazenly appropriated white siren power, and that can scare on more than a sexual level in a culture that often sees its African American females as sub-women, power*less*, Aunt Jemimas. Kim's appropriation of white siren power may be a "myopic view of beauty,"[88] but it also tells us that this is where she sees empowerment, where the corporate siren leads. *And,* she is not afraid to wrest that power away from a white world and claim it as her own.

So what does this siren tell us? She raps about an active, sexually aggressive woman who will get what she wants and will give only when she wants. In her world, bitches and Hoes are not there merely to meet the all-powerful male's sexual needs. Kim aligns herself with the male rapper not only in storyline but also in musical style, rapping as he would. In a February 2002 cover story, *Jet*'s feature on women in rap described Kim as the "outspoken rap dynamo [who] won a following as one of the first female rappers to show that women can look feminine and dress sexy and still rhyme just as hard as the men."[89] "So guess who the bitch is, but for now I be the mistress" concludes her song "M.A.F.I.A. Land" from *Hardcore.* She adopts sexually aggressive language in her song "We Don't Need It" and juxtaposes her authority over a man's in the chorus duet with rapper Lil' Cease:[90]

> Cease: If you ain't suckin' no dick we don't need it, we don't need it. / Kim: If you ain't lickin' no clits, we don't want it, we don't want it. / Cease: If you ain't drinkin' no nut, we don't need it, we don't need it. / Kim: If you ain't lickin' no butts, we don't want it, we don't want it.

In "Not Tonight" she brags like the men about her sexual power and control. The chorus touts that since she has everything she needs, if the men will not do her *her* way, she will happily refuse them.

In *Notorious K.I.M.* we hear Kim on the offense and sometimes on the defense. In "Lil' Drummer Boy," Kim's character defends herself against a murder charge even as the "real" Kim defends her image to the public: "Pardon Me your honor / May I address the bench / They try-na assassinate me like they did to Larry Flynt / Excuse my persona / I may be hardcore but I'm not Jeffrey Dahmer / Ever since I killed 'em / I ain't been in trouble since / It wasn't my fault I acted out of self-defense." In the media, Kim in fact spends much time defending herself. Because of her reliance on men, she has had to assure her audiences that she is not just male-produced. After her first album she asserted that she, not Biggie, wrote her texts; after her second, she explained that while Combs produced it, they both worked on the music, and that Combs now respects her as a musician. "Everything everyone heard me on, I wrote. I write. [Biggie] helped me with a lot of shit, but how the fuck can Biggie give a person a personality?"[91]

That personality is most powerfully presented in her "take charge" songs such as "Aunt Dot" and "Hold On." In "Aunt Dot," Kim expounds the litany for ghetto power as her "cousin" Lil' Shanice describes what she wants in life: "C'mon please, I wanna be just like you / 600 Mercedes, and 380's in all my doll babies / Fuck Barney and Lambchops; I don't love them hoes! / But anything goes when it comes to bankrolls / Diamonds on my toes, X and O's / Versace hottie in designer clothes." In "Hold On," Kim exhorts her fellow ghetto women to do just that: "Don't you give up, be strong / Hold on, hold on / Things are gonna get better / Tough times, they last so long. . . . If you believe, they will get better." She identifies explicitly with her own background: "So to my ladies, don't think I haven't walked in yo shoes / you thought this was only happenin' to you, righ' / Here's my shoulder, you can lean on this / cuz trust me, I know exactly what you're going through."

Even if she has refashioned herself in European style, this siren has not disavowed her roots and aspires to empower change for women in gangsta's world. That could be radically upending for both African Americans and white Americans, since being on the bottom is a mutually and culturally affirmed condition for those women: who would "go down" to replace them? This really has nothing to do with sex, even if the CD covers seem everything to do with it. Like Mariah, this claim is about acquiring ultimate power and complete control over situations that previously have been elusive, particularly for black women. This lure is dangerous: a black siren (Ho) posing as a white siren (to use Kim's word, "mistress" rather than slave) putting black women on top. With her image, Kim almost seems to suggest that in fact she *can* be white, that it is only on the surface, so our European American culture may also be only on the surface, a creation of the corporate siren, and all a fantasy. Perhaps Lil' Kim is the most dangerous of our three sirens, for her song would have us swim toward rocks that could ground us completely on the shores of an upside-down world. Here corporate sirens lose control of their creations, black and white meld into one, difference is only a matter of who is in control, and women are always on top.[92]

Who Is the Siren for Us Now?

Mariah Carey felt pressured to be "just one" of her ethnic possibilities, and Kim's siren forces us to look at that Medusa head-on, for unless we do not want to see her we must know that the siren is a many-headed one. She is multiracial, with all that implies, but she thinks that to have staying power she needs to be white. In order to be empowered to speak her mind, she needs the corporate siren to be there, both to get her started and also, ultimately, in order to reject him. She sees power as the ability to be On Top. She has strong feminist messages, but she thinks that to be heard she must seduce, play the male fantasy siren, and use her body as well as her voice. She has created *herself* in this image because this is where she thinks power lies, so she makes her body her ticket to freedom. She seduces, but in the end it is to tell us that she lures in order not to be lured. She wants to be feminine and also outspoken in the same body, epitomizing the centuries-old cultural penchant for opposing those characteristics. She critiques the corporate sirens who create her even as she wears their clothes. She is full of contradictions, and her very existence tells us much about ourselves at the new millennium. Despite the complex mesh of contradictions that bring her into being, however, the siren still does what she did of old. Because she is a woman who has found through her musical voice an access to power, she scares many who would seek to keep her as only a sexual, voiceless being on the page. She is embodied, three-dimensional, and even if we disagree with her we cannot ignore her, so we swim on, not quite knowing whether she is fact, fantasy, or—most dangerously—both at once.

NOTES

1. *New York Times,* August 13, 2000, 2: 27.

2. Desiree Guzzette, "Inger Lorre: Punk Rock's Renaissance Woman," *Rockrgrl* 30 (December 30, 1999): 13.

3. Pink, *Missundaztood* (Arista, 2001).

4. The complete article, originally published in *Signs* 1 (1975), can be found in *Feminisms: An Anthology of Literary Theory and Criticism,* ed. Robyn R. Warhol and Diane Price Herndl (New Brunswick, N.J.: Rutgers University Press, 1997), 347–62.

5. See, e.g., Thomasin LaMay, "Paola Massarenghi" and "Vittoria Aleotti/ Raphaela Aleotta," and Donna G. Cardamone, "Lifting the Protective Veil of Anonymity: ca. 1300–1566," in *Women Composers: Women Through the Ages,* vol. 1, ed. Martha F. Schleifer and Sylvia Glickman (New York: G. K. Hall, 1995), 127–59; and 110–19. Susan McClary also tackled this issue in several provocative essays, but perhaps especially in "The Undoing of Opera: Toward a Feminist Criticism of Music," in Catherine Clément, *Opera, or the Undoing of Women* (Minnesota: University of Minnesota Press, 1988), preface.

6. For further discussion of this phenomenon, see Mavis Bayton, *Frock Rock:*

Women Performing Popular Music (Oxford: Oxford University Press, 1988); Simon Reynolds and Joy Press, *The Sex Revolts* (Cambridge, Mass.: Harvard University Press, 1995); and James Dickerson, *Women on Top* (New York: Billboard, 1988).

7. See Reynolds and Press, *The Sex Revolts;* and Sut Jhally, *Dreamworlds 2: Desire/sex/power in Music Video* (Northampton, Mass.: Media Education Foundation, 1995).

8. See Clara Schumann's comments about her own compositional abilities in Nancy B. Reich, *Clara Schumann, the Artist and the Woman* (Ithaca, N.Y.: Cornell University Press, 1985).

9. For further discussion of the megastar mentality, see especially Reebee Garofalo, "From Music Publishing to MP3: Music and Industry in the Twentieth Century," *American Music* (1999): 318–53, esp. 347.

10. Bayton, *Frock Rock,* 13.

11. One could cite numerous examples for any of these categories. Typical are the following titles: "International Pop Siren Kylie Minogue Will Issue a New Single," *Billboard* 113 (August 4, 2001): 14; "Shaking it Up: Film Siren Jennifer Lopez Invades the Pop Scene," *People Weekly* 52 (September 13, 1999): 71; "Sirens of the Road," *Time* 9 (May 26, 1997): 101, which discusses the Lilith Fair tour, one dedicated to popular women performers and their music; k. d. lang is described in another *Time* article as the "smoky siren," a curious term for a woman who is an out lesbian and who eschews traditional siren garb or behaviors. See "It's a Cool, Cool Summer: Cowgirl? Pop Chanteuse? Smoky Siren?" *Time* 155 (June 19, 2000): 121. Finally, in a much newer venue, many classical women performers— especially string players—now attempt to market themselves as sexy sirens in order to sell. See for example Michael Walsh, "Siren Songs at Center Stage; Women Violinists of Talent and Temperament in the Male Preserve," *Time* 131 (April 11, 1988): 79, or Daniel S. Levy, "Seductive Strings, A New Crop of Alluring Young Women is Giving the Stodgy Male World of Classical Music a Dose of Sex Appeal," *Time* 146 (December 12, 1995): 86. Many of these women have Web pages and dust jackets to match those of the more culturally traditional pop sirens. Finally, the disco siren is often the diva of "Big Gay Followings," as noted in Anderson Jones, "Beautiful Dreamer: With a New CD and a Strong Slf-Vision, Gay-Loved Disco Siren Janice Robinson Is the Diva du Jour," *Advocate* No. 796 (October 12, 1999): 59.

12. This phenomenon has been well documented in the video *Dreamworlds 2: desire/sex/power in music video,* op. cit. MTV tried unsuccessfully to ban the production of this video.

13. For a lengthy discussion of this phenomenon, see Suzanne Cusick, "A Soprano Subjectivity: Vocality, Power, and the Compositional Voice of Francesca Caccini," in *Crossing Boundaries: Attending to Early Modern Women,* ed. Jane Donawerth and Adele Seeff (Newark, N.J.: University of Delaware Press, 2001), 80–98.

14. This term is further described by Renata Salecl in her essay, "The Sirens and Feminine *Jouissance,*" *differences: A Journal of Feminist Cultural Studies* 9

(1997): 14–28. She particularly focuses on the concept of the opera diva, another kind of siren, and suggests that the very enjoyment of opera resides in her voice alone. At its peak, she argues, the singer's voice assumes the status of the object detached from the body. Her mouth and voice become the "whole," and quite literally the "hole" of her, and the total focus of the collective audience's gaze. Salecl argues that especially in opera, the woman singer must succeed in this act of voice objectification in order to succeed at all.

15. This exemplifies the perception still prevalent in our culture that women in popular entertainment are somehow "bad girls," or at the very least, women who invite sexual relationships. It is still not possible for women simply to want to be popular musicians without confronting the "bad girl" label.

16. Gerri Hirshey, "Women Who Rocked the World," *Rolling Stone Magazine* 773 (November 13, 1997): 85.

17. Ibid., 80.

18. A survey of several female college students at Goucher College, Baltimore, suggested that most all of them felt they were as equally empowered as their male peers in all aspects of their lives. They certainly felt that they did not face the same patriarchal strictures their mothers or grandmothers did, and if they were to encounter such prejudice, they would readily be able to overcome it. Curiously, these same students also reported that they felt tremendous media pressure to conform to a certain kind of female body image, particularly in the wearing of pants, skirts, and tops which revealed a certain amount of navel.

19. Susan Estrich, *Sex and Power* (New York: Riverhead Books, 2000). Estrich, first woman president of the *Harvard Law Review,* gives us many other examples of inequality. Over 50 percent of law school and medical school students are women, but fewer than 10 percent of instructors are; 54 percent of the population is female but only 10 percent of elected officials are. The paradox she finds is that while at the new millennium women in America are richer, more educated, and more powerful than they have ever been, they account only for 2 percent of the nation's top executives.

20. Guzzette, "Inger Lorre," 13.

21. Mim Udovitch, "Pink Fights the Power," *Rolling Stone Magazine* 899/900 (July 4–11, 2002): 60.

22. A phrase borrowed directly from Rachel Blau Du Plessis's book of that title, *Writing beyond the Ending, Narrative Strategies of Twentieth-Century Women Writers* (Bloomington: Indiana University Press, 1985).

23. The quote is taken from an interview with Carey about the recording of her album *Rainbow.* She purposely traveled to Capri, Italy, one site of the mythological siren rocks, for the recording. See Mim Udovitch, "The Whirling Diva," *Rolling Stone Magazine* 834 (February 17, 2000): 47. Carey was featured on the cover of this issue.

24. In an interview given to Rob Tannenbaum, "Building the Perfect Diva," *Rolling Stone Magazine* 585 (August 23, 1990): 33.

25. For a detailed discussion of the variety of siren types and experiences from

antiquity through the middle ages, see Leofranc Holford-Strevens's essay, "Sirens in Antiquity and the Middle Ages," found in this volume.

26. Most artists wait about two years between CDs in order to allow for maximum sales, but also to tour and rest. Almost all who write about Carey note her self-imposed and extraordinarily demanding schedule.

27. As Bayton reports, journalists rarely discuss anything other than gender, sex, and image for female musicians: ". . . women are rarely discussed as musicians in their own right, in terms of playing an instrument, composing and arranging. Musicianship is not featured at all. . . ." Bayton, *Frock Rock,* 24.

28. *VH I Divas Live* (New York: Epic Music Videos, 1998).

29. *Mariah Carey's #1's* (New York: Columbia Music Video, 1999). This is a collection of videos that span her career to that point.

30. Her paternal grandmother is black and her paternal grandfather is Venezuelan. Her maternal grandparents are both Irish.

31. An interview given to Lynn Norment, "Mariah Carey," *Ebony* 49 (April 1994): 58.

32. Not happy with the first version, they completely remade the video at a cost of $450,000. Said Ienner, "if we're gonna take the time and effort that we did with Mariah, on every level, then we're going to image her the right way. If it costs a few extra dollars to make a splash in terms of the right imaging, you go ahead and do it." What is quite clear is that they were concerned far more with her image than her music. Quoted in Tannenbaum, "Building the Perfect Diva," 33.

33. We refer our readers to current URLs for all our illustrations. One of the characteristics of our culture's musical sirens is that they seldom grant permissions for reprints of their photos from albums. Getting permissions from magazines such as *Rolling Stone* is prohibitively expensive, since a fee goes not only to Mariah Carey but also to the magazine as well as the photographer. This is just another curious component to the megastar in relation to the power of corporate money. The exception among our sirens in this matter was Shania Twain, who did grant permissions. But we decided that including hers and not the other two would make for a less desirable outcome. Each of our sirens have Web sites that feature the covers to all their albums. For Mariah Carey we refer readers to www.monarc.com/mariahcarey/photos/index.las (accessed 2004).

34. Ibid.

35. "Mariah Carey Gets $49 million in Deal to Leave Virgin Records," *Jet* 101 (February 11, 2002): 46.

36. Chris Nickson, *Mariah Carey Revisited: The Unauthorized Biography* (New York: St. Martin's Griffin, 1998), 161.

37. Water imagery is an extremely important part of the male fantasy quotient of rock. Reynolds and Press dedicate the second major section of their book *The Sex Revolts* to the connection between women, water, and rock. See especially *The Sex Revolts,* 156–229. Jhally discuss water imagery as well in his *Dreamworlds 2.*

38. Reynolds and Press, *The Sex Revolts,* 162.

39. From an interview with Degan Pener, "Butterflies Aren't Free," *Entertainment Weekly* (September 26, 1997): 15.

40. The quote is found on the back dust jacket of the album *Rainbow* (Sony, 1999).

41. Udovitch, "The Whirling Diva," 47.

42. "Michael Jordan and Mariah Carey Voted Sexiest Celebrity Legs," *Jet* 95 (February 22, 1999): 33.

43. Udovitch, "The Whirling Diva," 49. Mariah read several books about Monroe as a child, "which was maybe not reading material for an eight-year old kid." She acknowledges a long fascination with the character, and she wanted the piano to have a home where it would feel "understood."

44. After her divorce from Tommy Mottola, Mariah made it clear that she wanted out of her Sony contract. She got her wish with an unlikely assist from Jennifer Lopez, another interesting siren. A piece of music Carey had licensed for herself mysteriously appeared on Lopez's *J.Lo* album, also released by Sony, and Carey astutely used the incident to speed her exit without producing the last album she had contracted to do. See "How Mariah Escaped Sony," *Time* 157 (June 18, 2001): 18.

45. *New York Times,* March 8, 2002: C1 and C2.

46. *New York Times,* May 21, 2002: B2.

47. One of the difficulties in writing about popular figures is that their careers are ongoing. Since the initial completion of this article, Carey has had a major role in the movie *Wisegirls* (2002). She has also released two albums, one of remixes, and a new album titled *Charm Bracelet.* The latter continues her mixture of soulful ballads with songs more aligned with R & B, and once again she markets her work with siren images. The video for the first song, "Through the Rain," features Carey as narrator singing in the rain. While her clothes are not particularly revealing, the rain metaphor is common siren water imagery. The video for the second cut, "Boy (I need you)" opens with a much more seductive siren waiting on her bed for her man.

48. Quoted in *Entertainment Weekly* (December 10, 1999): 56.

49. From an interview with correspondent Chet Flippo, cited in Brian Johnson, "Shania Revealed: The Queen of Country Wants to Step Out of the Packaging to Prove Herself on the Stage," *Maclean's* 111(March 23, 1998): 50.

50. Soundscan, the music business marketing tool that keeps track of sales, reports that Twain was the top seller in the early part of the 1990s. A crossover audience in popular vernacular is one that typically listens mainly to one genre, but will "crossover" to listen to someone in another venue if that artist has something that appeals to their preferences.

51. Jill Pesselnick, "Twain Breaks Records, Santana Soars in March Certifications," *Billboard* (April 22, 2000): 18.

52. "RIAA Certifications For March," *Billboard* (April 20, 2002): 22.

53. Johnson, "Shania revealed," 50.

54. Ibid.

55. See, for example, Troy Carpenter, "Music City's Fan Fair Grows," *Billboard Daily News* (April 30, 2002).

56. This album was produced by Decca, No. 28232, 1952.

57. Peterson discusses the fact that all country singers need some easily identifiable trait to give them an authentic country voice. Because Twain was raised poor and had to raise her siblings, she has the required "country credentials." Richard A. Peterson, *Creating Country Music* (Chicago: University of Chicago Press, 1997), 218.

58. As we mentioned previously, Twain was the only one of our sirens who granted permission for reproductions of images from her albums. However we decided to be consistent and refer to Web sites for all three. The Web site for Twain is www.musiciansclubs.org/shania/shania.

59. Johnson, "Shania revealed," 52.

60. Ibid., 50. Twain is managed by Jon Laundau, who also manages Bruce Springsteen.

61. We can still analyze these videos as Twain's own expressions despite male direction, because as Robin Roberts says in her article "Independence Day: Feminist Country Music Videos," *Popular Music and Society* 20 (1996): 140, "[While the] director, along with the performer's manager, undoubtedly has a hand in the final product . . . post-structuralist theory encourages the discussion of the performer as an equal participant, another voice, rather than as a puppet of a director. The performer's tone, gestures, and lyrics, in many cases written by her, strongly determine what will be presented in the video."

62. Johnson, "Shania Revealed," 50.

63. Ibid., 52.

64. Twain's mother divorced her father when she was young, and remarried an Ojibwa, Jerry Twain, when Twain was seven years old. From that time until her parents died, Twain lived on his Native Canadian reservation with his relatives almost as often as she resided in Timmins. Much was made in the press that she allegedly tried to hide the fact that he was not her biological father, claiming she wanted to cash in on the Native American ancestry. Twain maintains that she changed her first name rather than her surname when the label demanded she change her birth name (Eileen Twain). She wanted to keep the name Twain because to her mind Jerry Twain was her emotional father.

65. Since the initial writing of this essay, Twain has continued to expand her crossover appeal in both music and siren image; she has also maintained the feminist content of her lyrics. Her November 2002 album *UP!*—the first she produced after the birth of her son—includes two versions of each song on two different discs. The "green" version is mixed with country music accompaniments, while the "red" version features more rock-and-roll backdrop. She also made some of the songs available for downloading off her Web site in a "blue" version, which she calls a "global-pop" style. The dust jacket for the CD features her most siren-like poses yet, with a hole-filled, skimpy white tank top. Yet her live concert performances continue to be more along the wholesome, country-

oriented line, and she tends to wear more conventional and less revealing clothing. Some of her texts for *UP!* place her firmly in charge, as in "I'm gonna get you good," and "In my car (I'll be the driver)." Others such as "She's not just a pretty face" and "What a way to wanna be" are her most feminist texts to date, explicitly challenging our cultural obsession with the siren body image.

66. "Kim on Kim," *Essence* (October, 2000): 115.

67. Allison Samuels, "A Whole Lotta Lil' Kim," *Newsweek* 135 (June 26, 2000): 56. In the photo accompanying this article, the "o" in the word "whole" of the title encircles Lil' Kim's exposed breast with attached pasty.

68. "Mediawatch," *Source* 103 (September 2000): 102.

69. Marla L. Shelton, "Can't Touch This! Representations of the African American Female Body in Urban Rap Videos," *Popular Music and Society* 21 (1997): 107.

70. "Ho" is the rap vernacular for whore; frequently it is also used as a synonym for "woman" in general.

71. In 2000 she received a Pioneer Award from the Rhythm and Blues Foundation at their eleventh annual awards ceremony in New York. See "Rhythm and Blues Foundation Holds 11th Awards Gala in New York," *Jet* 89 (October 16, 2000): 36.

72. See Alvelyn J. Sanders, "From Video Hoes to Deathbed Divas," *Essence* 27 (February 1997): 160.

73. We refer the readers to Lil' Kim's Web site www.lilkim.com.

74. Paula T. Renfroe "The World According to Kim," *Source* 101 (February 1998): 122.

75. In March 1997, Biggie was shot; his murder has never been solved, but most people assume it was related to the shooting of rapper 2Pac Shakur and the rivalry between the two.

76. Kevin Chappell, "Is the Mainstream Ready for LIL' KIM?" *Ebony* 55 (October, 2000): 184.

77. Karen R. Good, "More Than a Lil' Bit," *Vibe* 56 (September, 1997): 176.

78. "Sexy Dress and Sassy Rap Make Lil' Kim a Big Star," *Jet* 98 (August 21, 2000): 58.

79. Robert Sullivan, "Diva Slam," *Vogue* (April, 2002): 318.

80. Kim is not the only non-white diva who currently adopts the white siren. Other popular singers to use the blond wig include African Americans Beyonce, of the trio Destiny's Child, and Mary J. Bilge, as well as South America's Shakira. So set is the image of the white siren that not only are the body types identical, but the poses are also identical: long, flowing, unkempt hair on a head which is slightly tilted, arms dangling limply, hips leaning out with weight on a single, long, bare leg. Clothes are low-cut with exposed navel, and either very tight or diaphanously loose.

81. Chappell, "Is the Mainstream Ready," 184.

82. "Sexy Dress," 58.

83. Sullivan, "Diva Slam," 318.

84. Chappell, "Is the Mainstream Ready," 184.

85. "Sexy Dress," 58.

86. Sullivan, "Diva Slam," 314.

87. M.A.C. cosmetics has created their Viva Glam makeup line to sell strictly for an AIDS benefit fund, and they use megastar celebrities to sell the products.

88. This was quoted at the head of this section.

89. "The Hottest Females in Rap Music," *Jet* 97 (February 21, 2000): 59.

90. She also turns the corporate tables on men with rapper Lil Cease; his first solo album was released on her Queen Bee label.

91. Good, "More Than a Lil' Bit," 176.

92. Since the initial writing of this essay, Kim has released a new album, *La Bella Mafia.* In a 2003 interview with *Ebony* she commented that this album was more her own work than previous albums, something which all our sirens progressively proclaim. She states that "Today, I am much more independent and in control of my own career, especially my music. Over the years, I worked with people who tried to influence my musical direction, but on my latest record . . . I followed my own vision. I stayed true to myself and the music I wanted to make, and I think this is why the fans have responded so well." "5 Questions for Lil' Kim," *Ebony* 58 (October, 2003): 22. For this album she no longer sports blond hair, but rather the straight and coifed look of the southern Europeans, reflecting the Italian language of the album's title. She has also moved toward film, with several cameo appearances and a major role in *Gang of Roses* (2003).

The Cocktail Siren in David Lynch's
Blue Velvet

Jeongwon Joe

The lovely voices in ardor appealing over the water
Made me crave to listen, and I tried to say
"Untie me!" to the crew, jerking my brows; . . .[1]
—Homer, *The Odyssey*

As this collection testifies, sirens have been a timeless and cross-cultural fantasy, incarnated and reincarnated in mythology, folklore, literary genres, visual arts, and music. Cinema is not an exception. As a deadly seductress and an embodiment of subversive sexuality, the cinematic siren has appeared in various embodiments, ranging from the vamp of Scandinavian and American silent films to the *femme fatale* of film noir.[2] "Draped across pianos, often in pouty poses and tight black dresses, they sang of lovemaking, hearts breaking, and sweet revenge" is how Joseph Lanza describes what he calls the "cocktail sirens" in film noir.[3] While the general usage of the term *femme fatale* in cinema includes nonsinging sirenic heroines, Lanza's cocktail sirens specifically refer to songstress seductresses such as Coral Chandler (Lizabeth Scott) in John Cromwell's noirish mystery *Dead Reckoning* (1974), Gilda (Rita Hayworth) in Charles Vidor's *Gilda* (1946), and many of the Marlene Dietrich characters, including Lola-Lola in Josef von Sternberg's *The Blue Angel* (1930).[4] Dorothy Vallens (Isabella Rossellini), a mysterious nightclub singer in David Lynch's scandalous noir thriller *Blue Velvet* (1986), is another celebrated cocktail siren.

[349]

Although *Blue Velvet* was (surprisingly) a commercial success and brought Lynch his second Oscar nomination for Best Director, it stirred a wide range of furious reactions. It was submitted to the Venice Film Festival but was eventually turned down on the grounds of its pornographic violence. In *Blue Velvet,* the noirish mystery starts when Jeffrey Beaumont (Kyle MacLachlan), a young college student, finds a severed human ear on the grass while strolling around town and takes it to Detective Williams. Although the detective asks him not to get involved in the case, Jeffrey journeys into the mystery, triggered by the detective's daughter, Sandy (Laura Dern), who provides him with information about Dorothy Vallens, who is suspected of being connected with the case. With Sandy's help, Jeffrey sneaks into Dorothy's apartment and witnesses the sadomasochistic sexual play between Dorothy and Frank Booth (Dennis Hopper), who has kidnapped her husband and son. The severed ear is revealed to be that of Dorothy's husband. Dorothy seduces Jeffrey into her erotic world of sadomasochism and because of their affair, their lives are endangered by Frank. After the young hero undergoes several adventures, he finally rescues Dorothy from her sadist lover by killing him.

Many of the previous studies of *Blue Velvet* focus on its Oedipal implications, the most visible of which is the film's (in)famous "primal scene" of Dorothy and Frank's sadomasochistic play witnessed by Jeffrey.[5] It is a widespread interpretation of the film that the entire mystery is Jeffrey's fantasy or journey into his Oedipal subconscious, which is structurally framed by the close-up of the ear: the camera zooms into the severed ear before Jeffrey visits Detective Williams's house, and the camera zooms out from Jeffrey's ear after Frank's death. This interpretation identifies Dorothy and Frank as Jeffrey's Oedipal mother and father, and in so doing, makes the Dorothy character highly evocative of the Homeric Sirens: if the Homeric Sirens' temptation of Ulysses is read as an invitation to *forbidden* pleasure or knowledge,[6] the Oedipal subconscious is the *forbidden* realm into which Dorothy seduces Jeffrey.[7] Dorothy's kinship with the mythological sirens is even stronger, perhaps stronger than any other cinematic cocktail sirens, from the perspectives of the psychoanalytic interpretation of sirenology that reads the siren figures as "none other than the beloved and incestuously desired mother."[8] Nevertheless, Lynch's songstress heroine takes a unique position among the cinematic sirens, ironically because of the primacy of her voice over her body.

In the original mythology and many of the literary works, the sirens' seduction is portrayed as an aural rather than a visual event: it is the ears, not the eyes, of Ulysses' crew that had to be covered. Some sirens are entirely devoid of visual charms: a "woman, stammering, with eyes asquint and crooked on her feet, with maimed hands, and of sallow hue," is Dante's siren.[9] For the cinematic cocktail sirens, however, the main weapon of their seduction tends to be their body rather than their voice, which is justifiable given the primacy of visuals over sound and the gaze over the voice in the standard practice of the cinematic medium. In the performance scenes of cinematic sirens, it is usually their bodily charm rather than their enticing voice that is foregrounded in the *mise-en-scène* and endows them with sirenic power. A testimony to this cinematic tradition is the fact that cinematic sirens' vocal performances often include dance, one of the most memorable of which is Gilda/Rita Hayworth's splendid striptease rendition of "Put the Blame on Mame."

Unlike most of the cocktail sirens, Dorothy's body is de-eroticized to the extent that it becomes the object of abjection near the end of the film. It is through her music, her embodied singing, that her abject body is normalized; it is her voice, not her body, that empowers her as a siren. This essay examines the way music contributes to the construction of Dorothy's character as a siren in spite of the ambiguity of her status as such at the visual and narrative levels of the film. I also discuss the gendered clash between Dorothy's *embodied* performance of Bobby Vinton's "Blue Velvet" and the *lip-synching* rendition of Roy Orbison's "In Dreams" by a drag-ish character, Ben (Dean Stockwell), Frank's friend. In relation to Dorothy's performance scenes, I reconsider the feminist critique of the embodied representation of the female voice from the phenomenological points of view of the singing voice, as explored by Carolyn Abbate.[10] I take up the issue of whether and how the phenomenal power of the live singing voice can be transferred to the technologically mediated medium of cinema.

Dorothy and Sandy 1: Siren Song versus Devotional Song

One of the most notable characteristics of classical film noir is the binary opposition between the two extremes of female archetypes—the whore and the Madonna, the siren and the redeemer—or, to use Kathryn Kalinak's distinction, "the fallen woman and the virtuous wife."[11] *Blue Velvet* also features these two female archetypes: innocent-looking, supposedly virginal, blond Sandy as opposed to the mysterious, dark-haired, and erotically subversive songstress Dorothy. Sandy verbally confirms her role as a Madonna, always forgiving and loving, when she condones Jeffrey, saying, "I forgive you, Jeffrey . . . I love you," after having found out about his relationship with Dorothy. The film ends with a suggestion of Jeffrey's union with Sandy, a "virtuous wife" to be: the camera shows the couple with their families, and a robin, Sandy's emblem of ideal love, enters into the frame. But as Michel Chion points out, *Blue Velvet* also demonstrates an intriguing confusion and collapse of the traditional noirish opposition between the Madonna and the whore.[12] Sandy's visual style is highly evocative of that of a sirenic character when Jeffrey first meets her: without seeing her image, one first hears her voice, a seductive and mysterious disembodied voice whispering to Jeffrey, "Are you the one who found the ear?"; then she slowly emerges from the dark shadow of the leaves, accompanied by ominous background music. As Christine Glendhill notes, this visual composition is a cliché for the typical noir *femme fatale*.[13] Sandy's elusive character is textually inscribed in the film script: after Jeffrey tells Sandy about what he has discovered at Dorothy's apartment, he says to Sandy almost out of context, "You're a mystery." From narrative points of view, too, Sandy's role is akin to a sirenic character, not as an aggressive seducer but as a catalyst who allures the hero to the siren call. For Sandy is the one who first invites Jeffrey to the murder mystery involving the severed ear by stimulating his curiosity about Dorothy and providing him with information about her. Furthermore, she takes Jeffrey to Dorothy's apartment and volunteers to be his sidekick for his first two journeys of adventure to Dorothy's apartment.

Dorothy's character is also elusive, deviating from the female archetype that she is supposed to represent. In contrast to the mysterious and powerful introduction of Sandy, Dorothy's first appearance is plain, casual, and undramatic when Jeffrey, disguised as a pest-control man, glimpses her through the crack of her chained door. Unlike typical noir *femmes fatales*, Dorothy's siren seduction is not for the purpose of pursuing her ambition and/or independence (compare Dorothy's ambiguity to Norma Desmond/Gloria Swanson's madness for her career in *Sunset Boulevard* or Phyllis/ Barbara Stanwyck's greedy desire for money in *Double Indemnity*).[14] Dorothy is perhaps most closely related to the noir *femmes fatales* of the post-1980s characterized by their insatiable and transgressive sexual appetite: one can think of the Sharon Stone character in *Basic Instinct* (1992) and the Kathleen Turner character in *Body Heat* (1981), although in Turner's case, her ambition takes priority over her sexual pleasure.[15] But in Dorothy's case, the pursuit of her own sexual desire is clouded and complicated by her involvement in sadomasochism, the complexity of which will be examined more closely later in this essay. Dorothy's image as a siren is further undermined by her motherhood, because classical noir sirens, like their mythological and literary ancestors, seldom appear in the domestic context; instead, they represent a threat to family and social order, resisting domestication.[16] Moreover, Dorothy is not just a mother but a suffering mother, because her son is kidnapped, evoking the blissful mother Jo Conway (Doris Day), who is also a singer, in Hitchcock's 1956 remake of *The Man Who Knew Too Much*. Dorothy's motherly image is verbally suggested when Sandy's ex-boyfriend asks Jeffrey, "Is that your mother?" when she is found naked around Jeffrey's house.

While her sirenic status is confused at the visual and narrative level of the film, Dorothy's music solidly registers her as a seductress, and, in so doing, restores the binary opposition of the two female archetypes. At the most simplistic level, the affective quality of Dorothy's and Sandy's leitmotifs contributes to the musical segregation of the two characters. Bobby Vinton's "Blue Velvet," Dorothy's theme, is obviously more sensual and seductive than Sandy's theme "Mysteries of Love," which is composed by Angelo Badalamenti, the composer of the film's original score, with lyrics written by Lynch. Badalamenti's tune is even evocative of sacred music to the extent that Paul A. Woods calls it a "devotional song."[17] Its celestial quality is reinforced by the angelic vocality of the singer (Julee Cruise) and the tune's visual anchoring with the image of a church when it first enters the soundtrack as an instrumental arrangement (it is heard as non-diegetic music[18] while Sandy is passionately recounting to Jeffrey her dream about robins, her emblem of ideal love, in front of a church). Before its full orchestration, the tune is introduced by the organ, which further imbues the tune with religious spirituality.[19]

Dorothy and Sandy 2: Diegetic Interiority versus Exteriority

The vocal version of "Mysteries of Love" is first employed at Sandy's prom party where she and Jeffrey are dancing. The diegetic status of this music is ambiguous: it is likely that the song is the music to which people are dancing, but the sound source is not visually presented. When the tune returns several more times later in the film, it is always employed as non-diegetic music. This diegetic exteriority of Sandy's theme is another element that separates Sandy from Dorothy, for Dorothy's "Blue Velvet" appears within the diegesis of the film as an embodied voice when she sings it at her two nightclub performances. The embodied-ness of Dorothy's theme and its diegetic interiority underscore her sirenic character from the two perspectives of sirenology as explored by Nancy Jones in her study of Dante's Siren.[20] First, Jones characterizes the Siren song first and foremost by its embodied-ness: "As an emphatically embodied form of vocality, the Siren's song stands at the opposite extreme from the singing of Angelic Love in *Paradiso* XXIII."[21] Second, the diegetic interiority of Dorothy's song is parallel to that of the Siren's song in Dante at the level of narratology. According to Jones's interpretation,

> the episode of the Siren, presented as a quasi-hallucinatory experience, represents a false dream narrative embedded within a true dream narrative. In narratological terms, the episode is relegated to a secondary level of the poem's diegesis.[22]

Jones describes this narratological status of the Siren song as "the diegetic interiority" and conceives it as a poetic counterpart of the typical discursive strategy of classical Hollywood cinema as explored by Kaja Silverman and Amy Lawrence, among others:[23] namely, the strategy that tries to confine the female voice to a "recessed area of the diegesis,"[24] a show within a show, such as Dorothy's performance scenes. Another musical difference between Dorothy and Sandy is the fact that Dorothy's theme is thoroughly vocal, while Sandy's "Mysteries of Love" appears mostly in its instrumental arrangement. Sandy is associated with other instrumental music: the orchestral music used for the opening credits accompanies Sandy several times throughout the film.

Dorothy and Sandy 3: The Gendered Dichotomy between Vocal and Instrumental Music in Film

The alignment of Dorothy with vocal music and Sandy with instrumental music can be discussed in the wider context of the gender ideology in cinematic tradition. Based on the fact that female classical musicians are not only uncommon in film but also tend to be presented in unprofessional, domestic contexts, Claudia Gorbman claims that cinema has coded high art as a masculine enterprise. She notes:

> The serious musician is a man who expresses the depth of his soul through consummate knowledge, skill, and passion. . . . Classical cinema reveals an anxiety about women as artists or musicians.[25]

Gobrman's claim, however, should be slightly modified given the privileged status of operatic film divas: they are not only prominent in number but also presented as no less accomplished professionals than male movie musicians. One can think of magnificent diva heroines in such films as Bernardo Bertolucci's *La Luna* (1978); Jean-Jacques Beineix's *Diva* (1981); Istvan Szabo's *Meeting Venus* (1991); Claude Miller's *The Accompanist* (1993), a French film about a diva named Irene Brice; and more recently,

Franco Zeffirelli's 2002 film *Callas Forever*, a fictitious story about Maria Callas. But in the films about instrumentalists, the protagonists are predominantly male; for instance, Glenn Gould in *32 Short Films about Glenn Gould* (1995), David Helfgott in Scott Hicks's *Shine* (1996), and, most recently, Wladyslaw Szpilman in Roman Polanski's 2003 film *The Pianist*. Female instrumentalists are not entirely absent, but, interestingly enough, their performances tend to appear in domestic and more privatized surroundings, such as practicing at home or in the recording studio, while the diva heroines are shown in splendid public concerts, flamboyantly displaying their enchanting singing, showered with thunderous applause.[26]

Even film musical, a genre that requires both female and male singers, confirms the gendering of vocal music as primarily a woman's domain by preferring a more natural, less refined voice for male singers. As Edward Baron Turk argues in his study of the dualistic attitude toward male and female voices in the American film musical, this preference reveals the patriarchal culture's anxiety about singing as a threat to masculinity. According to Turk, post–Civil War American ideology reinforced the suspicion of singing by males, especially classical singing, as testified by Hollywood's preference for the more natural voices of Al Jolson (the songster in the very first sound film *The Jazz Singer* [1927]), Fred Astaire, and Bing Crosby to the more trained, operatic voices of Dennis King, Lawrence Tibbett, and John McCormack.[27] This could be an excuse for the amateurish vocality of male singers in Robert Wise's *The Sound of Music* (1965): in this film, female singers overpower male singers, most prominently in the pairing of Julie Andrews and Christopher Plummer. The unbalanced vocal virtuosity between female and male singers continues in more recent film musical, such as Lars von Trier's *Dancer in the Dark* (2000), Baz Luhrmann's 2001 remake of *Moulin Rouge*, and Rob Marshall's Academy Award–winning film *Chicago* (2002). In *Dancer in the Dark*, the winner of the Palme d'Or and Best Actress Award at the Cannes Film Festival in 2000, the heroine Björk's splendid vocal power cannot be compared with any male singers. Neither *Moulin Rouge* nor *Chicago* features a diva as virtuosic as Björk, and both female and male singers are somewhat amateurish in these films, but male singers far exceed female singers in the unrefinedness of the voice: one can think of the pair of Satine (Nicole Kidman) and Christian (Ewan McGregor) in *Moulin Rouge* and that of Roxie (Renée Zellweger) and Billy (Richard Gere) and also the Billy and Velma (Catherine Zeta-Jones) pair in *Chicago*.

The cinematic coding of vocal music as a feminine domain can be situated in the wider context of the Western culture that has promoted the gendered dichotomy between vocal and instrumental music. Sirenology has made a contribution to this dichotomy. Although the most powerful weapon for Kafka's Sirens was their silence,[28] most of the siren episodes in Western mythology, literature, and folklore strongly foreground sirens' music as their main attraction and luring power; more importantly, it is not just any music, but vocal music. Although instrumentalist sirens are not entirely absent,[29] vocal music since the time of Greek mythology has been territorialized, if not stigmatized, as sirens' queendom and, by extension, a feminine prerogative.

The association of singing with women is an inevitable consequence considering the connection between the patriarchal construction and representation of woman first and foremost as a *bodily* entity and the presence of more *bodily* elements in singing than in instrumental music. To elaborate on the latter, there is literally more body in the singing voice—"more breath, more diaphragm muscles, a more open mouth"—because of the intensified and exaggerated vocalization when singing.[30] Furthermore, singing is inherently a more embodied, more carnal realm than instrumental music in that sound is produced *within* the performer's body, from her throat, whereas in instrumental music, the sound source, whether piano, violin, or others, is placed outside the performer's body.

While the sexual identity of vocal music has been fairly stable throughout the history of Western classical music, that of instrumental music has shown a complex history, oscillating between male and female. To put it in Daniel Chua's expression, instrumental music underwent "sex-changes" with a very "messy operation" performed during the Enlightenment.[31] The musical discourse at the beginning of the eighteenth century coded instrumental music as feminine, as "voluptuously soulless music," but it was finally reborn with a phallus after several sex-change operations. Since then, the gendered dichotomy between vocal and instrumental music became more or less stabilized.[32]

The privileged status of diva heroines among the male-dominated movie musicians is emblematic of this gendered musical biology constructed throughout the history of Western classical music. And this biology helps to illuminate the contrast between Dorothy's *vocal* leitmotif and Sandy's *instrumental* one in *Blue Velvet*. While Dorothy represents the extreme of femininity, Sandy's sexuality is more neutral: she is supposedly a virgin, and Laura Dern's slim lips and skinny body in contrast to Isabella Rossellini's full lips and voluptuous body make Sandy look far less feminine than Dorothy. This neutrality of Sandy's femininity can be compared to the ambiguous and androgynous sexuality of instrumental music, which, according to Chua, underwent a Tiresias-like oscillation before it was finally stabilized as masculine.

The Enchantment of the Embodied Voice and the Empowerment of Dorothy

Although the soundtrack of *Blue Velvet* conforms to the noir tradition, in which the two extremes of female archetypes are sharply differentiated from each other musically, Dorothy's music also shows a positive departure from the standard function of diegetic performance of female characters in general and cocktail sirens in particular. As briefly mentioned above in relation to Dorothy's diegetic interiority, performance sequences have been criticized because of their tendency to serve as a means to place female characters in the inferior position in the diegetic hierarchy by restricting their voices to a "recessed area of the diegesis," to use Amy Lawrence's description again. Lawrence argues that their diegetic interiority positions female characters as "sign rather than as signifying subject," deprived of their subjectivity.[33] It has become a classical theory in cinema studies that the diegetic interiority of the female voice is indicative of Hollywood's gendered politics of the voice. A testimony to this politics is the fact that voiceover narration, which is privileged to reside beyond and outside the diegesis, is conferred predominantly to male characters.[34] As Carolyn Abbate contends, the invisible speech of the male voiceover is an evocation of divine speech, in which "God's authority is predicated on the presence of his voice in the absence of his body."[35] This gendered dynamics between embodied voice and invisible speech, which represents diegetic interiority and exteriority, respectively, is especially visible in film noir, for male voiceover is one of the prominent characteristics of film noir.[36]

As explored by many feminist film scholars, embodied representation of female voice in cinema has another strategic purpose, which involves an ontological anxiety of the cinematic apparatus, that is, the anxiety about its irrecoverable separation between voice and body, sound and image, in the process of mechanical reproduction. Unlike live theater, in cinema, sound and image are separated in the process of recording and they are artificially reunited at the time of reproduction; unlike live theater's natural unity between voice and body, a technologically mediated unity between the two is the ontological condition of film. Drawing on psychoanalytic theories about subjectivity, sexuality, music, and voice, film scholars describe the lack of the natural unity between voice and body, sound and image, as cinema's "castration" anxiety, and have demonstrated how mainstream cinema has tried to disavow its lack by solidly anchoring the voices of female characters to their bodies.[37] In other words, embodied female voice functions as cinema's fetish, and diegetic performance, as being solidly embodied, best serves for this purpose.

Another problem involved in the female character's diegetic performance is that it is often staged to focus on the "grain" of the voice,[38] that is, its physicality, and, in so doing, it undermines the linguistic and discursive potency of the female voice. Borrowing the terminology used by Julia Kristeva and Roland Barthes, Leslie Dunn and Nancy Jones describe the female voice as "geno-song, purely sonorous, bodily element of the vocal utterance" rather than as "pheno-song," its verbal dimension.[39] The problematic representation of female vocality is not limited to the cinematic convention but has a long history. Ophelia's mad scene in *Hamlet* is an often-cited example in literature. Leslie Dunn contends that in this scene, Ophelia's psychological and sexual otherness is confirmed and reinforced by the discursive otherness of her singing. Ophelia is a woman, she notes, "who becomes even more 'Woman' when she sings."[40] And, I add, Ophelia is mad, and becomes even more mad when she sings.

Dorothy's nightclub sequences provide a counterexample to Ophelia's case and most of the diegetic performance numbers in film. Unlike Ophelia's singing, Dorothy's vocal performance de-otherizes her. While Dorothy's body, her face, and her emotional state appear extremely vulnerable and unstable for the rest of the film, she transforms into a confident and powerful professional singer at the nightclub, without bearing any sign of fear or suffering on her face. Her attire at performance is seductively elegant, perfectly illustrating Joseph Lanza's description of the cocktail sirens quoted above ("Draped across pianos, often in pouty poses and tight black dresses, . . .").[41] In contrast to this, she appears for the rest of the film in plain, casual, even untidy outfits, mostly in her blue velvet robe, to the extent that Michel Chion regards Dorothy's careless costume, except at her performance, as a "rare moment in cinema of providing scenes of genuine intimacy."[42] The visual composition of typical noirish sirens tends to fetishize their body parts, such as long hair (for example, Gilda/Rita Hayworth in Charles Vidor's *Gilda*) or lovely bare legs (for example, Phyllis/Barbara Stanwyck in Billy Wilder's *Double Indemnity*) as the source of their sexual power, although that power is almost always revealed to be evanescent. In *Blue Velvet*, Dorothy's body is presented differently. When she is found naked around Jeffrey's house near the end of the film, her body is presented as unattractive, undesirable, and even detestable, as her body is covered with bruises and other markings of beating. This "staggering naked abjection," to use Michael Moon's expression, is certainly not the body normally expected of the seductress.[43] It is at her nightclub performances that Dorothy's body becomes normalized.

While singing, Dorothy is overpowering everybody at the club, including Jeffrey and even Frank. Throughout the film, Frank is shown as Dorothy's oppressive "master" in their sadomasochistic relationship, but at the nightclub sequence, he appears as no more powerful than the ordinary *passive* listeners in the club. Like everybody else in the audience, he is immersed and enraptured in the power of Dorothy's enchanting performance; he is not even wearing his usual leather jacket, an allusion to the disappearance of his sadistic power. Given this visual *mise-en-scène*, Dorothy's performance sequences signify the moments when the complexity of the sadomasochistic roles is unveiled through Frank's passivity as a listener. Judith Bryant Wittenberg and Robert Gooding-Williams remark that Dorothy's status as a *femme fatale* is subverted by her "victimhood and her explicit role as mere sexual object."[44] But this view needs to be reconsidered, given the complex and paradoxical dynamics in sadomasochism, that is, the labile relationship between the subject and the object, the master and the slave.

According to Freudian theory, the role of the sadist and masochist, like that of voyeur and exhibitionist, are easily exchangeable and reversed. In masochism, "satisfaction follows along the path of the original sadism, the passive ego placing itself back in fantasy in its first role, which has now in fact been taken over by the extraneous subject," while the sadist enjoys himself "masochistically . . . through his identification with the suffering object."[45] As Alice Kuzniar points out, the interchangeability of the subject and the object of sadomasochism and voyeurism/exhibitionism is foregrounded in a "triadic structure" between Dorothy, Jeffrey, and Frank at the beginning of the film.[46] After Dorothy discovers Jeffrey in the closet, she takes the aggressive role of the sadist and expresses her voyeuristic desire by threatening him to undress, holding her phallic and castrating knife in front of his genitalia. She deflects Jeffrey's gaze by telling him what is to be revealed as Frank's refrain, "Don't you (fucking) look at me," and in so doing, confirms that she, not Jeffrey, is the subject of the gaze. In the following (in)famous sequence of Frank's perverse sexual play with Dorothy, she assumes Jeffrey's passive, masochistic, exhibitionist position and her previous role is projected onto Frank. This scene is not a "simple inversion" or a mere "re-enactment" of Dorothy's humiliating relationship with Frank with the positions reversed,[47] but rather it stages a fundamental condition of sadomasochism. Philosopher Giorgio Agamben argues not only for the interchangeability and reversibility of the sadist and masochist roles but also for those of shame and pleasure. Furthermore, he contends that the masochist is a master who controls the entire relationship, precisely and paradoxically through his/her own passivity.[48] Given this, Dorothy's (seemingly) oppressive relationship with Frank is not a mere "torment" to her, as James Maxfield construes,[49] but her pleasure as well.

Slavoy Žižek illuminates Dorothy's oscillation between what is normally conceived as the male position and female position, between subject and object, in terms of the crack in the causal chain, that is, the crack where the normal relationship between cause and effect is inverted.[50] Žižek approaches this complex philosophical inquiry through what he calls the "feminine depression." At the surface level, the causal link seems to be unambiguous for Dorothy's trauma: she is depressed because her child and husband have been kidnapped. But, Žižek asks, what if the depression comes first as a primordial malady and what would normally be regarded as the cause for the malady is in fact a therapy to protect Dorothy from her death wish? According to Žižek, this is the case for Dorothy's enigmatic suffering: "enigmatic," because Dorothy's whispering plea to Jeffrey, "Help me," is never clear throughout the film. As Michel Chion interprets, she is not imploring the young hero to rescue her son and husband held hostage: she strongly refuses the police's involvement, but the reason remains enigmatic throughout the film (there is no hint that her refusal is because she worries about the safety of her son and husband).[51] Dorothy's plea is not to help her with her sadomasochistic sexual frustration, either, as might be inferred from the alliterative relationship between her two recurring whispers to Jeffrey, "Help me" and "Hit me." In Žižek 's view, helping Dorothy involves understanding a human being's more primordial desire, that is, her death wish, as suggested several times at the verbal level of the film: for instance, Jeffrey's comment about Dorothy to Sandy, "I think she wants to die"; Frank asks Dorothy to stay alive and do it for "Van Gogh," meaning her husband with his ear severed. Žižek argues that Dorothy's depression, meaning her death wish, comes first, but the situation that her husband and son are kidnapped restrains her from committing suicide. This is where he locates the crack in the causal chain, the inversion of the normal relationship between cause and effect:

> The "effect" is the original fact, it comes first, and what appears as its cause—the shock that allegedly set the depression in motion—is actually a reaction to this effect, a struggle against the depression.[52]

Žižek 's theory about the "female" depression certainly invites a feminist reappraisal of the theory, but Žižek 's argument is not intended to create or re-create a degrading and despising link between depression and femininity. On the contrary, he professes that his theory is intended to renovate the most common prejudice about the female depression, namely, the notion of woman who can be aroused only by man's stimuli. The feminine depression that reverses the causal link, Žižek contends, is the "founding gesture of subjectivity, the primordial act of freedom, of refusing our insertion into the nexus of causes and effects." In conclusion, he claims, "woman, not man, is the subject par excellence."[53] Dorothy's role as the subject as well as the object of sexual desire and pleasure remains veiled throughout the film, and her subjectivity seems to be annihilated by the sadomasochistic violence. It is through the power of her embodied singing at her nightclub performances that Dorothy's shadowed subjectivity comes into view.

From feminist perspectives, Dorothy's performance sequences could be accused of being another example that confirms what Laura Mulvey identifies as a male scopophilic ideology, which has dominated the policy of gaze in classical cinema.[54] At her performances, Dorothy becomes the object of Frank and Jeffrey's *male* gaze. What solidifies this gendered policy of gaze is the fact that Sandy's *female* gaze is diverted from Dorothy; instead, she is looking at Jeffrey, as though she were worrying about his enraptured gaze at Dorothy.[55] However, as Carolyn Abbate illuminates, "listening to the female singing voice is a more complicated phenomenon" than the scopophilic ideology, which is largely, if not exclusively, based on the visual experience. Visually, Abbate contends, "the character singing is the passive object of our gaze, but aurally, she is resonant; . . . , and we sit as passive objects."[56] Here Abbate is theorizing the phenomenological experience of operatic voice, and it is a complicated question how and even whether this experience at a live theater can be transferred to the diegetic performance scenes in cinema. Cinema is a technologically mediated apparatus and its aesthetic effects are qualitatively different from those of opera or any live genres. However, some diegetic performance scenes in film are designed to produce the effects that approximate the phenomenal power of live performance. As Michel Chion contends, diegetic performance in general serves to expand the diegetic space of a film to the movie theater by encouraging the auditorium audience to identify with the on-screen audience.[57] Put another way, the movie theater and its audience are transported and deluded into the diegetic space and time of the film, and this process heightens an illusion that the film viewers are at the live performance by suturing them to the on-screen audience. By simulating the condition of live theater, diegetic performance in cinema serves to approximate the phenomenal power of live performance.

In certain films, the simulated effect of live theater is further enhanced through their *mise-en-scène*. *Blue Velvet* is among such films. Dorothy's nightclub sequences are distinguished from comparable performance numbers, such as Gilda's "Put the Blame on Mame" or Miss Sadie Thompson's "The Heat Is On" and "Blue Pacific Blues" in Curtis Bernhardt's *Miss Sadie Thompson* (1953). While in these performances, the audience is watching her in a distracted mood, actively responding to her both vocally and physically, Dorothy's audience is almost totally passive, evoking operatic theater as described by Abbate above. The absorbed and passive state of the listeners during Dorothy's performance is enhanced by the absence of dialog and the silencing of the diegetic noises. During the second nightclub sequence, Dorothy's voice is further privileged by obliterating her bodily and visual presence, for her singing is heard as voice-off without showing her image. Dorothy's performance scenes are the moments that unveil her veiled role as the master in the interchangeable roles of the master-slave relationship in sadomasochism. They are the moments when Jeffrey is bewitched by Dorothy, as his enraptured gaze confesses. But the object of his gaze is not her body but the sight of her voice. Dorothy is indeed a siren who is empowered by her voice, her music, her embodied song.

Sirens as Emblem and the Loss of the Real: Cinematic Anxiety

Dorothy's embodied performance sequences provide an intriguing and thought-provoking contrast to another diegetic performance by Frank's friend, Ben, an accomplice in their drug dealing. When Frank visits his place with Jeffrey, Dorothy, and his henchmen, Ben lip-synchs to a recording of Roy Orbison's song "In Dreams," with his drag-queenishly made-up face, grotesquely lit by a table lamp he is holding as if it were a microphone. "A candy-colored clown they call the sandman . . ." begins Orbison's song. This scene has largely been discussed in the context of the film's intertextual relationship with E. T. A. Hoffmann's story "The Sandman,"[58] but Ben's lip-synching performance also stimulates an inquiry related to the technological aspects of the cinematic apparatus. The pair of Dorothy's embodied performance and Ben's lip-synching, I propose, dramatizes cinema's inherent anxiety about its lack of the natural unity between voice and body, between sound and image. As discussed above, diegetic performance has been strategically employed to create an illusion of unity, since it solidly anchors the voice to the body. If Dorothy's diegetic, embodied performance stands for cinema's efforts to conceal its inherent lack, Ben's lip-synching embodies a reversed implication, namely a revelation of cinema's irrecoverable separation between voice and body.

Michel Chion argues that lip-synching, "assiduous but never perfect," is a manifestation of cinema's aspiration to achieve the "impossible unity" of voice and body.[59]

The concealment and the unveiling of cinema's impossible unity represented by Dorothy's embodied performance and Ben's lip-synching, respectively, can be illuminated in light of the conflict between Wagnerian theater and Brechtian epic theater. In Bertolt Brecht's view, Wagner's *Festspielhaus* is the apotheosis of the theater of illusion, where the spectator is seduced into believing that s/he is part of a timeless mythic world. "Witchcraft of this sort," contends Brecht, "must of course be fought against."[60] In his epic theater, Brecht pursued the alienation effect (*Verfremdungseffekt*) and used various devices, such as masks, placards, newspaper headlines, film, and puppets, in such a way that the spectator can be disillusioned from the Wagnerian witchcraft, that is, the masking of the theatrical artificiality. If we relocate the *aesthetic* opposition between Wagner and Brecht in the context of *technological* witchcraft, the Wagnerian theater of illusion can be aligned with Dorothy's embodied performance, which serves to conceal the artificiality of the unity between voice and body in cinematic apparatus. On the other hand, Ben's lip-synch sequence embodies the spirit of the Brechtian epic theater of disillusionment: when the camera discloses the boom box to the film viewer's sight and reveals that this machine, not Ben's voice, is the real sound source, its effect is surely Brechtian.

Cinema's castration anxiety, at least in mainstream cinema, about the loss of the natural unity between voice and body can be contextualized in the wider cultural anxiety about the loss of the real in the age of mechanical reproduction, which was a central issue of the much-explored debate between Walter Benjamin and Theodor Adorno.[61] As Siegfried de Rachewiltz suggests, this twentieth-century scholarly debate was foreshadowed by the siren trope developed during the Renaissance: namely, sirens as an emblem of the printed book.[62] Rachewiltz notes that during the Renaissance, printing technology was regarded as a diabolical invention since it served as a vehicle for the dissemination of profane books. Some great printers such as Gutenberg and Aldo Manunzio were suspected of their association with the devil, and Doctor Faust in the folklore tradition appears as the inventor of printing. Printing technology was further stigmatized, because the mechanical reproduction of the Bible endowed the general people with unmediated access to the Holy Scripture and in so doing, seriously undermined clerical power, which had assumed the role of mediator between laymen and God. Given these stigmas imposed on the art of printing, Rachewiltz expounds, it is not surprising that the sirens should emerge as an emblem of the printed book, as mere copies, counter-feits, and deceptions: sirens signified the death of the original, of the real.[63] If the Benjamin versus Adorno debate concerning the issue of mechanical reproduction was foreshadowed by this Renaissance siren trope, so was cinema's anxiety about its irrecoverable loss of the real in the process of technological mediation.

Postlude: ". . . And I Still Can See Blue Velvet Through My Tears"

If a siren is the emblem of counterfeit, forgery, and deception, so is Doro-thy's embodied performance, since it serves as cinema's masquerade to conceal its ontological lack of the natural unity between voice and body. However, Dorothy is not totally submissive to cinema's gendered policy of embodiment. Dorothy's voice is elusive and transgressive, for at the end of the film it is finally liberated from bodily imprisonment and transcends the confinement of the diegesis: when the silent image of Dorothy and her son comes into the final frame of the film, Dorothy's singing of "Blue Velvet" enters as a voiceover, non-diegetic music. The composition of image and sound in this concluding scene resembles that of music video in the sense that it is the music that begets the image, rather than the other way around as in the conventional orchestration of music and image in cinema. In other words, the music has the authorial power.

Perhaps the visual motif of the severed ear alludes to the dominance of the aural over the visual, voice over gaze, in the sensorial universe of *Blue Velvet*. Frank's refrain "Don't you fucking look at me," which signifies the deflected gaze in the film, can be read as a verbal motif to represent the impotence of the visual in contrast to the authorial power of the aural, that is, Dorothy's music, her voice. The film concludes with the memory of Dorothy's voice, which symbolically sings "And *I* still can *see* blue velvet *through my* t-*ears*"[64] (italics mine). This final disembodied appearance of Dorothy's singing voice is not an "emblem of her tormented relationship with Frank," as claimed by James Maxfield,[65] but an allusion to her veiled power as a siren and the primacy of her voice over her body, an unusual feature for a cinematic cocktail siren.

NOTES

1. Homer, *The Odyssey*, trans. *Robert Fitzgerald* (New York: Farrar, 1998), 216.

2. Mary Ann Doane, *Femmes Fatales: Feminism, Film Theory, Psychoanalysis* (New York: Routledge, 1991), 2.

3. Joseph Lanza, "Sirens of the Cold War," in *The Cocktail: The Influence of Spirits on the American Psyche* (New York: St. Martin's Press, 1995), 78.

4. Michel Chion's concept of the siren song in cinema is broader than its common usage as a seductress' song. See "The Siren's Song" in *The Voice in Cinema*, trans. Claudia Gorbman (New York: Columbia University Press, 1999), 109–22. Chion discusses several different dimensions of the siren song, ranging from the voice that entraps or ruins the protagonist to the voice (usually a female voice) that transgresses the boundaries of the screen. As example of this transgressive voice, Chion discusses the voice of an invisible soprano at the beginning of Jean-Luc Godard's *Sauve qui peut;* he describes this voice as "a voice summoned or indicated by nothing in the image, but which has its own life" (115). In Chion's view, this type of transgressive voice is related to the mythological Sirens in that they are the creatures who transgress the borderline between land and the sea (114).

5. Freud describes the primal scene as follows: "If children at an early age witness sexual intercourse between adults . . . they inevitably regard the sexual act as a sort of ill-treatment or act of subjugation: they view it, that is, in a sadistic sense." Quoted in James F. Maxfield, *The Fatal Woman: Sources of Male Anxiety in American Film Noir, 1941–1991* (London: Associated University Press, 1996), 149.

6. Siegfried de Rachewiltz, *De Sirenibus: An Inquiry into Sirens from Homer to Shakespeare* (New York: Garland Publishing, 1987), 14–15.

7. The ear motif creates a parallelism between Lynch's male protagonist and the Homeric hero: Ulysses literally becomes "all ears" when he alone was allowed to listen to the Sirens' song with his body tied to the mast, while his crew had to stop their ears with wax; as Homer's hero continued his journey beyond the divinely set limits of the Pillars of Hercules in pursuit of knowledge, Lynch's noirish hero pursues his investigation of Dorothy's mystery against the detective's exhortation to suspend his curiosity.

8. Henry Alden Bunker Jr., "The Voice as (Female) Phallus," *The Psychoanalytic Quarterly* 3 (1934): 429.

9. Quoted in Nancy Jones, "Music and the Maternal Voice in *Purgatorio* XIX," in *Embodied Voices: Representing Female Vocality in Western Culture*, ed. Leslie C. Dunn and Nancy A. Jones (Cambridge: Cambridge University Press, 1994), 37.

10. Carolyn Abbate, "Opera, or the Envoicing of Women," in *Musicology and Difference: Gender and Sexuality in Music Scholarship*, ed. Ruth A. Solie (Berkeley: University of California Press, 1992), 225–58.

11. Kathryn Kalinak, "The Fallen Woman and the Virtuous Wife: Musical Stereotypes in *The Informer, Gone with the Wind,* and *Laura*," *Film Reader* 5

(1982): 76–82. In this essay, Kalinak explores musical semiotics of these two archetypical female characters.

12. Michel Chion, "Welcome to Lynchtown (*Blue Velvet, The Cowboy and The Frenchman, Twin Peaks*)," in *David Lynch,* trans. Robert Julian (London: BFI Publishing, 1995), 83–99. Michel Chion is one of the few commentators who discuss the doppelgangerish relationship between Dorothy and Sandy, but he is not convincing when he argues that the church scene, in which Sandy recounts her dream about robins to Jeffrey, is an instance that links Sandy's character to that of Dorothy: he notes that the dream reveals a "hidden, depressive side to Sandy, linking her character to that of Dorothy" (87). What motivated him could have been the fact that when Sandy tells Jeffrey about her dream, her excited, exaggerated, ecstatic voice creates an impression of madness comparable to Dorothy's transgressive erotic madness. Indeed, there's something unnatural and a puzzling exaggeration in Laura Dern's acting. Another good source for the Dorothy-Sandy parallel is Robert Gooding-Williams and Judith Bryant Wittenberg's "The 'Strange World' of Blue Velvet: Conventions, Subversions and the Representation of Women," in *Sexual Politics and Popular Culture,* ed. Diane Raymond (Bowling Green, Ohio: Bowling Green State University Popular Press, 1990), 149–57.

13. Christine Glendhill, "*Klute* 1: A Contemporary Film Noir and Feminist Criticism" in *Women in Film Noir,* ed. E. Ann Kaplan, 2d ed. (London: British Film Institute, 2000), 32.

14. For more examples of typical noir *femmes fatales,* see Janey Place, "Women in Film Noir," in *Women in Film Noir,* esp. 53–60.

15. For more discussion about this type of sexually motivated sirenic heroine, see Kate Stables, "The Postmodern Always Rings Twice: Constructing the Femme Fatale in 90s Cinema," in *Women in Film Noir,* 164–82.

16. As Rachewiltz notes, it is interesting how Circe describes the danger of the Sirens essentially as a danger that threatens familial value and duty. Homer's original reads: "and that man . . . who . . . listens to the Sirens singing, has no prospect of coming home and delighting his wife and little children as they stand about him in greeting, . . ." quoted in Rachewiltz, 18.

17. Paul A. Woods, "Blue Velvet: America's Dark Underbelly," in *Weirdsville USA: The Obsessive Universe of David Lynch* (London: Plexus Publishing Ltd., 1997), 87.

18. E. Ann Kaplan defines "diegesis" (Greek for "recital of facts") as the "denotative material of film narrative including the fictional space and time dimensions implied by the narrative; the fictive space and time into which the film works to absorb the spectator, the self contained fictional world of the film." See E. Ann Kaplan, *Rocking Around the Clock: Music Television, Postmodernism, and Consumer Culture* (New York: Methuen, 1987), 187. Diegetic music can be defined as music whose sound source is visually presented on screen or narratively implied. Claudia Gorbman's definition reads, "music whose presence is motivated by something within the world of the story." See Claudia Gorbman, "Music in *The Piano,*" in *Jane Campion's The Piano,* ed. Harriet Margolis (Cambridge: Cam-

bridge University Press, 2000), 57 n. 2. Robert van der Lek provides an extensive discussion about the origin, concept, and usage of the term "diegesis," especially comparing its applicability to opera. See Robert van der Lek, "The Theory of Diegetic Music in Opera and Film," in *Diegetic Music in Opera and Film* (Atlanta: Editions Rodopi B. V., 1991), 27–62.

19. The musical polarity between Dorothy and Sandy is an evocation of the long-held tension between the sensuality of Sirens' music and the spirituality of Orpheus's. This tension was recently readdressed by the twentieth-century philosopher Vladimir Jankélévitch. See "Orpheus or the Sirens?" in *Music and the Ineffable,* trans. Carolyn Abbate (Princeton, N.J.: Princeton University Press, 2003), 3–7. Intriguingly enough, Linda Austern brings our attention to the fact that Orpheus's music, too, was sometimes linked to the deadly power of sensual love. See Linda Austern, "Love, Death, and Ideas of Music in the English Renaissance," in *Love and Death in the Renaissance,* ed. Kenneth R. Bartlett, Konrad Eisenbichler, and Janice Liedl (Ottawa: Dovehouse Editions Inc., 1991), 28–29.

20. Nancy A. Jones, "Music and the Maternal Voice in *Purgatorio* XIX," in *Embodied Voices,* 35–49.

21. Ibid., 36.

22. Ibid., 47–48.

23. Ibid., 48. For Kaja Silverman, see *The Acoustic Mirror: The Female Voice in Psychoanalysis and Cinema* (Bloomington: Indiana University Press, 1988). For Amy Lawrence, see *Echo and Narcissus: Women's Voices in Classical Hollywood Cinema* (Berkeley: University of California Press, 1991).

24. Lawrence, *Echo and Narcissus* 149.

25. Gorbman, "Music in *The Piano*," 44–45. Hollywood film's coding of high art as a masculine enterprise can be contextualized in the wider cultural context of the modernists' gendered (and elitist) discourse that stigmatized mass culture as feminine while advocating the "Great Divide" between high art and mass culture. One of the best sources for this topic is Andreas Huyssen, "Mass Culture as Woman: Modernism's Other," in *After the Great Divide: Modernism, Mass Culture, Postmodernism* (Bloomington: Indiana University Press, 1986), 44–62. For the discussion about film divas, see Susan J. Leonardi and Rebecca A. Pope, "Divas Do the Movies," in *The Diva's Mouth: Body, Voice, Prima Donna Politics* (New Brunswick, N.J.: Rutgers University Press, 1996), 175–96.

26. One chapter of my monograph-in-progress, *Opera at the Movies: What Can Opera Do for Film?* is dedicated to the gendered dichotomy between vocal and instrumental music in film. Among the films I examine are Claude Sautet's *Un Coeur en hiver,* in which the performance sites of the violinist heroine Camille Kassler (Emmanuelle Béart) are exclusively recording studios or private chambers, and Ingmar Bergman's *Autumn Sonata* (1978), where the performance scenes of the heroine, a celebrated concert pianist (Ingrid Bergman), are limited to domestic settings, such as her practicing room or her daughter's house (in both films, the heroines' public concerts are only verbally mentioned in dialog). I also discuss Joel Olinsky's *The Competition* (1980), a story about two young pianists,

Heidi Schoonover (Amy Irving) and Paul Dietrich (Richard Dreyfuss), and Anand Tucker's *Hilary and Jackie* (1998), a film based on the lives of the du Pré sisters, as exceptions to the cinematic tradition of the female instrumentalists' domesticity. This cinematic tradition signifies an intriguing twentieth-century resurrection of the Elizabethan sexual politics of music, which, as Linda Phyllis Austern illuminates, forced noble female musicians to use their music for private pleasure. See Linda Phyllis Austern, "'Sing Againe Syren': The Female Musician and Sexual Enchantment in Elizabethan Life and Literature," *Renaissance Quarterly* 42 (Autumn 1989): 420–48. It seems that unlike the film divas, who tend to be immune from the domestic confinement of the performance, female singers in renaissance England were not exempt from the imposition of privatized performance. Austern notes, "When women *sing* or play for themselves alone, the pure spiritual essence of their music remains untouched by feminine beauty or the passion of love and reaches their immortal souls simply and directly. But when they *sing* or play before men, knowingly or unknowingly, their music invariably unites with the equally powerful stimulus of feminine beauty to ravish their audiences twice over" [italics are mine] (436).

27. Edward Baron Turk, "Deriding the Voice of Jeanette MacDonald: Notes on Psychoanalysis and the American Film Musical," in *Embodied Voices,* 106.

28. "Now the Sirens have a still more fatal weapon than their song, Namely their silence. . . . And when Ulysses approached them the potent songstresses actually did not sing, . . ." See Franz Kafka, "The Silence of the Sirens," in *The Complete Stories,* ed. Nahum N. Glatzer (Franklin Center: Franklin Library, 1980), 363–364.

29. Apollodorus identifies three sirens, Ligeia, Leucosia, and Parthenope, who were adept in lute and lyre as well as singing. Also, on a page of the Arundel Psalter, illustrating Psalm LXXX, a bird-Siren is playing a portative organ. See Rachewiltz, *De Sirenibus,* 104.

30. Leslie C. Dunn, "Ophelia's songs in *Hamlet:* Music, Madness, and the Feminine," in *Embodied Voices,* 52–53.

31. Daniel K. L. Chua, *Absolute Music and the Construction of Meaning* (Cambridge: Cambridge University Press, 1999), 126.

32. Ibid., passim, especially chapters "On Women" (126–35) and "On Masculinity" (136–44).

33. Lawrence, *Echo and Narcissus,* 149.

34. As I discuss in an article in progress, the clash between the two voiceovers in Barbet Schroeder's film *Reversal of Fortune* (1990), one by Jeremy Irons and the other by Glenn Close, shows an intriguing reversal of the standard diegetic hierarchy between the male and female voice. While Irons's flashback voiceover resides within the diegesis, addressed to his onscreen audience, Close's voice speaks directly to the film viewers, transcending the film's diegesis.

35. Carolyn Abbate, "Debussy's Phantom Sounds," in *In Search of Opera* (Princeton: Princeton University Press, 2001), 148.

36. Glendhill, *"Klute* 1," 109.

37. A classical and pioneering study of this issue is Kaja Silverman's *The Acoustic Mirror*.

38. Roland Barthes, "The Grain of the Voice," in *Image, Music, Text*, trans. Stephen Heath (New York: Noonday Press, 1977), 179–89.

39. Dunn and Jones, *Embodied Voices*, 1.

40. Leslie C. Dunn, "Ophelia's songs in *Hamlet*: Music, Madness, and the Feminine," in *Embodied Voices*, 63.

41. See n. 3.

42. Chion, *David Lynch*, 87.

43. Michael Moon, "A Small Boy and Others: Sexual Disorientation in Henry James, Kenneth Anger, and David Lynch" in *A Small Boy and Others: Imitation and Initiation in American Culture from Henry James to Andy Warhol* (Durham, N.C.: Duke University Press, 1998), 23. In Kenneth Kaleta's view, Dorothy's nudity suggests "not eroticism but a medical victim." See Kenneth C. Kaleta, *David Lynch* (New York: Twayne Publishers, 1993), 127. Dorothy's nude scene reflects David Lynch's autobiographical experience. He said, "When I was little . . . I think it was in Boise, Idaho, I was with my younger brother, and we saw a grown woman walking naked on the street. And that was Dorothy, right there." Quoted in Woods, 86.

44. Robert Gooding-Williams and Judith Bryant Wittenberg, "The 'Strange World' of *Blue Velvet*: Conventions, Subversions and the Representation of Women" in *Sexual Politics and Popular Culture*, ed. Diane Raymond (Bowling Green: Bowling Green State University Popular Press, 1990), 155.

45. Sigmund Freud, *The Standard Edition of the Complete Psychological Works*, vol. 2, *Instincts and their Vicissitudes*, trans. and ed. James Strachey (London: Hogarth, 1953–1974), 128–29. Quoted in Alice A. Kuzniar, "Ears Looking at You: E. T. A. Hoffmann's *The Sandman* and David Lynch's *Blue Velvet*," *South Atlantic Review* 54 (1989): 20.

46. Kuzniar, "Ears Looking at You," 16.

47. Gooding-Williams and Wittenberg, "The 'Strange World' of *Blue Velvet*," 153–54.

48. Giorgio Agamben, *Remnants of Auschwitz: The Witness and the Archive*, trans. Daniel Heller-Roazen (New York: Zone Books, 1999), 107–108.

49. Maxfield, *The Fatal Woman*, 155.

50. Slavoy Žižek, "David Lynch, or, the Feminine Depression," in *The Metastases of Enjoyment: Six Essays on Woman and Causality* (London: Verso, 1994), 122.

51. Chion, *David Lynch*, 95.

52. Žižek, "David Lynch," 122. Chion finds this "inversion in the causality," although without using Žižek 's philosophical and psychoanalytic terms, in other female characters of David Lynch's films, such as Marietta Pace in *Wild at Heart* and Mary X in *Eraserhead*. See Chion, *David Lynch*, 95.

53. Žižek, "David Lynch," 122.

54. Laura Mulvey, "Visual Pleasure and Narrative Cinema" in *Visual and Other Pleasures* (Bloomington: Indiana University Press, 1989).

55. Abbate, "Opera, or the Envoicing of Women," 254. As Abbate points out, Laura Mulvey's inaugurating theory about the gaze policy in narrative cinema has raised an array of counterquestions, which include whether a female film viewer can be forced to take the position of the male gaze. (253). Mulvey herself pursued these follow-up questions in "Duel in the Sun: Afterthoughts on 'Visual Pleasure and Narrative Cinema,'" reprinted in her *Visual and Other Pleasures*.

56. Abbate, "Opera, or the Envoicing of Women," 254.

57. Michel Chion, *Audio-Vision: Sound On Screen*, trans. Claudia Gorbman (New York: Columbia University Press, 1994), 151.

58. See Kuzniar and Moon. In Kuzniar's interpretation, the lip-synching—its disjunction of sound and image—encapsulates the perceptual discrepancy between hearing and seeing in Lynch's film, which is also thematized in Hoffmann's story.

59. Michel Chion, *La Voix au Cinema* (Paris: Cahiers du Cinema, 1982), 125.

60. Bertolt Brecht, *Brecht on Theatre: The Development of an Aesthetic*, ed. and trans. John Willett (New York: Hill and Wang, 1964), 38. For a critical reexamination of Brecht's assessment of Wagner, see Hilda Meldrum Brown, *Leitmotiv and Drama: Wagner, Brecht and the Limits of "Epic" Theatre* (Oxford: Clarendon Press, 1991). She argues that Brecht's critique of Wagner is occasionally not only too simplistic but also erroneous.

61. See Theodor Adorno, "On the Fetish-Character in Music and the Regression of Listening," in *The Essential Frankfurt School Reader*, 270–99, ed. Andrew Arto and Eike Gebhardt (New York: Urizen Books, 1978); and Walter Benjamin, "The Work of Art in the Age of Mechanical Reproduction," in *Illuminations*, 217–51, ed. Hannah Arendt and trans. Harry Zohn (New York: Schocken Books, 1968).

62. Rachewiltz, *De Sirenibus*, 235.

63. Ibid., 222–37.

64. Alice Kuzniar also discusses the film's closing pun but in a different context, namely the perceptual ambiguity and deception of hearing and seeing in *Blue Velvet* (12). This pun reminds me of the reversed synesthetic interplay between eyes and ears explored by Žižek. See Slavoj Žižek, "I Hear You with My Eyes; or The Invisible Master," in *Gaze and Voice as Love Objects*, ed. Renata Salecl and Slavoj Žižek, 90–126 (Durham, N.C.: Duke University Press, 1996).

65. Maxfield, *The Fatal Woman*, 155. Kenneth C. Kaleta acknowledges a dualistic implication of the concluding scene. He notes, "the film's conclusion suggests that the close is not entirely painful; at least, that pain is not without its attraction for Dorothy." See Kaleta, *David Lynch*, 94.

BIBLIOGRAPHY

Abbate, Carolyn. "Debussy's Phantom Sounds." In Carolyn Abbate, *In Search of Opera*. Princeton, N.J.: Princeton University Press, 2001.

———. "Opera, or the Envoicing of Women." In *Musicology and Difference: Gender and Sexuality in Music Scholarship*, ed. Ruth A. Solie. Berkeley: University of California Press, 1992.

———. *Unsung Voices: Opera and Musical Narrative in the Nineteenth Century*, Princeton, N.J.: Princeton University Press, 1991.

Abercrombie, Thomas. *Pathways of Memory and Power: Ethnography and History among an Andean People*. Madison: University of Wisconsin Press, 1998.

Abraham, Lyndy. *A Dictionary of Alchemical Imagery*. Cambridge: Cambridge University Press, 1998.

Achebe, Chinua. *Girls at War and Other Stories*. London: Heinemann, 1972.

Ackermann, Hans Cristoph, and Jean-Robert Gisler, eds. *Lexicon Iconographicum Mythologiae Classicae*. 8 vols. Zurich: Artemis, 1981–1997.

Ademollo, Alessandro. *La bell'Adriana ed altre virtuose del suo tempo alla corte di Mantova*. Città di Castello: S. Lapi, 1888.

Adorno, Theodor. "On the Fetish-Character in Music and the Regression of Listening." In *The Essential Frankfurt School Reader*, ed. Andrew Arto and Eike Gebhardt. New York: Urizen Books, 1978.

Aesop. *Fables*. Trans. V. S. Vernon Jones and illus. Arthur Rackham. First published 1912. Reprint ed. New York: Franklin Watts, 1967.

Agamben, Giorgio. *Homo Sacer: Sovereign Power and Bare Life*. Trans. Daniel Heller-Roazen. Stanford: Stanford University Press, 1998.

———. *Remnants of Auschwitz: The Witness and the Archive*. Trans. Daniel Heller-Roazen. New York: Zone Books, 1999.

Aizenberg, Susan, and Erin Belieu, eds. *The Extraordinary Time: New Poetry by American Women*. New York: Columbia University Press, 2001.

Aksoy, Bülent. *Lale-Nerkis Hanımlar*. Notes in English and Turkish by Bülent Aksoy. Istanbul: Kalan Müzik, Arşiv Serisi, CD 101, 1997. Sound Recording. www.kalan.com.

Albertus, Magnus [Albert the Great]. *Man and the Beasts: De Animalibus*. Trans. James J. Scanlan. *Medieval and Renaissance Texts and Studies*, vol. 47. Binghamton, N.Y.: Medieval and Renaissance Texts and Studies, Center for Medieval and Early Renaissance Studies, 1987.

Alciato, Andrea. *Emblemata*. Lyons: Macé Bonhomme, 1550.

———. *Emblemata*. Paris: Jean Richer, 1608.

Alexandris, Alexis. *The Greek Minority of Istanbul and Greek-Turkish Relations, 1918–1974.* 2d ed. Athens: Centre for Asia Minor Studies, 1992.

Allen, Catherine. *The Hold Life Has: Coca and Cultural Identity in an Andean Community.* Washington, D.C.: Smithsonian Institution, 1988.

Allen, Don Cameron. *Mysteriously Meant: The Rediscovery of Pagan Symbolism and Allegorical Interpretation in the Renaissance.* Baltimore: Johns Hopkins University Press, 1970.

Allott, Robert. *Englands Parnassus: or the choysest Flowers of our Moderne Poets.* London: N.L. C.B. and T.H., 1600.

Andersen, Hans C. "The Little Mermaid." In *Fairy Tales.* New York: Henry Holt and Co., 1913.

Andersen, Hans Christian. *Fairy Tales and Stories.* N.p.: N.p., 1836.

Andreae, Bernard. "L'immagine di Ulisse." In *Ulisse: il mito e la memoria,* ed. Bernard Andreae and Claudio Parisi Presicce, 55–57, 141–47. Rome: Progetti museali, 1996.

Andrews, Walter. *Poetry's Voice, Society's Song: Ottoman Lyric Poetry.* Seattle: University of Washington Press, 1985.

Anguillara, Giovanni Andrea dell'. *Le Metamorfosi di Ovidio ridotte da Gio[vanni] Andrea Dell'Anguillara in ottava rima.* Venice: presso Bern[ardo] Giunti, 1584.

Aretino, Pietro. *Poesie Varie.* Ed. Giovanni Aquilecchia and Angelo Romano. Rome: Salerno Editrice, 1992.

Aretinus, Franciscus [Francesco Griffolino]. *Homeri poetarum clarissimi Odyssea de erroribus Vlyxis.* Strasburg: Übelin, 1510.

Arnold, Denise. "At the Heart of the Woven Dance Floor: The Wayñu in Qaqachaka." *Iberoamericana.* Special Issue: Native Literatures in Latin America, Jahrgang 3/4 (47/48) (1992): 21–66.

Arnold, Denise, and J. Yapita. *Río de vellón, río de canto: Cantar a los animales, una poética andina de la creacion.* La Paz: Hisbol, 1998.

Ascham, Roger. *English Works.* Ed. William Aldis Wright. 1904. Reprint. Cambridge: Cambridge University Press, 1970.

Atanagi, Dionigi, ed. *De le rime di diversi nobili poeti toscani, raccolte da M. Dionigi Atanagi,* Libro secondo.Venice: appresso Lodovico Auanzo, 1565.

Attali, Jacques. *Noise: The Political Economy of Music.* Trans. B. Massumi. Manchester, U.K.: Manchester University Press, 1985.

Austern, Linda Phyllis. " 'Forreine Conceites and Wandring Devises': The Exotic, the Erotic and the Feminine." In *The Exotic in Western Music,* ed. Jonathan Bellman, 26–42. Boston: Northeastern University Press, 1998.

———. "Love, Death and Ideas of Music in the English Renaissance." In *Love and Death in the Renaissance,* ed. Kenneth R. Bartlett, Konrad Eisenbichler, and Janice Leidl, 17–36. Dovehouse Studies in Literature 3. Ottawa: Dovehouse Editions, 1991.

———. " 'My Mother Musicke': Music and Early Modern Fantasies of Embodiment." In *Maternal Measures: Figuring Caregivers in the Early Modern Period,* 239–281. ed. Naomi J. Miller and Naomi Yavneh. Aldershot: Ashgate, 2000.

———. "Nature, Culture, Myth and the Musician in Early Modern England." *Journal of the American Musicological Society* 51 (1998): 1–47.

———. " 'Sing Againe Syren': The Female Musician and Sexual Enchantment in Elizabethan Life and Literature." *Renaissance Quarterly* 42, no. 3 (Autumn 1989): 420–48.

———. "The Siren, the Muse, and the God of Love: Music and Gender in Seventeenth-Century English Emblem Books." *Journal of Musicological Research* 18 (1999): 102–103.

Aykroyd, James, ed. and arranger. *The Siren: A Collection of Sacred Music.* Philadelphia: G. E. Blake, [1822].

B[ullokar], J[ohn]. *An English Expositor.* London: John Legatt, 1621.

Bach, Leonard Emil. *Die neue Loreley.* Opus 28. Text by Siegmey. Berlin: C. A. Challier & Cie, 1878.

Bacon, Francis. *De Sapientia Veterum London 1609 and The Wisedome of the Ancients.* Trans. Sir Arthur Gorges. 1619. Reprint. New York: Garland Publishing, 1976.

Bade, Patrick. *Femme Fatale: Images of Evil and Fascinating Women.* New York: Mayflower Books, 1979.

Banks, S. E., and J. W. Binns. *Gervase of Tilbury: Otia Imperialia.* Oxford Medieval Texts. Oxford: Oxford University Press, 2002.

Barberino, Francesco da. *Reggimento e costumi di donna.* Ed. G. E. Sansone. Rome: Zauli Editore, 1995.

Bardakçı, Murat. *Fener Beyleri'ne Türk Şarkıları..* Istanbul: Pan Yayıncılık, 1993.

Bartas, Guillaume du. *The Divine Weeks and Works of Guillaume de Saluste Sieur Du Bartas.* Trans. Josuah Sylvester and ed. Susan Snyder. 2 vols. Oxford: Clarendon Press, 1979.

———. *Seconde Sepmaine de Guillavme de Saluste, seigneur du Bartas.* N.p.: Iaques Chouët, 1593.

Barthes, Roland. "The Grain of the Voice." In *Image, Music, Text,* trans. Stephen Heath. New York: Noonday Press, 1977.

———. *L'Obvie et l'obtus. Essais critiques III.* Paris: Éditions du Seuil, 1982.

———. *The Pleasure of the Text.* Trans. Richard Miller. New York: Farrar, Straus and Giroux, 1975.

Bartholomeus Anglicus. *De proprietatibus rerum.* Trans. and ed. Stephen Batman. London: Thomas East, 1582.

Bassanese, Fiora A. "Gaspara Stampa's Poetics of Negativity." *Italica* 61 (1984): 335–46.

Baudelaire, Charles. *Les Fleurs du mal.* Trans. Richard Howard. Boston: David R. Godine, 1982.

Baudoin, Jean. *Recueil d'Emblemes Divers.* 2 vols. Paris: Jacques Villery, 1638–39.

Bayton, Mavis. *Frock Rock: Women Performing Popular Music.* Oxford: Oxford University Press, 1988.

Beaton, Roderick. "Modes and Roads: Factors of Change and Continuity in Greek Musical Tradition." *Annual of the British School of Athens* 75 (1980): 1–11.

Beaumont, Cyril W. *The Ballet Called Giselle.* London: Dance Books, 1988.

Beauvoir, Simone de. *The Second Sex.* Trans. and ed. H. M. Parshley. New York: Alfred A. Knopf, 1971.

Bembo, Pietro. *Opere in volgare.* Ed. Mario Marti. Florence: Sansoni, 1961.

——. *Prose e Rime.* Ed. Carlo Dionisotti. Turin: UTET, 1960.

Benjamin, Walter. "The Work of Art in the Age of Mechanical Reproduction." In *Illuminations,* ed. Hannah Arendt and trans. Harry Zohn. New York: Schocken Books, 1968.

Benton, Janetta Rebold. *The Medieval Menagerie.* New York: Abbeville Press, 1992.

Benwell, Gwen, and Arthur Waugh. *Sea Enchantress: The Tale of the Mermaid and Her Kin.* London: Hutchinson and Co., 1961.

Bernandt, Grigorii. *Dictionary of Operas.* Moscow: Soviet Composer, 1962.

Bernard, A. H. *Legends of the Rhine.* Trans. Fr. Arnold. 11th ed. Wiesbaden: Gustav Quiel, 1900.

Bertonio, P. Ludovico. *Vocabulario de la lengua Aymara* (facsimile). Cochabamba (Bolivia): CERES (Centro de Estudios de la Realidad Económica y Social), [1612] 1984.

Bertram, Colin. *In Search of Mermaids: The Manatees of Guiana.* New York: Thomas Y. Crowell Co., 1963.

Bessler, Gabriele. *Von Nixen und Wasserfrauen.* Köln: DuMont Buchverlag, 1995.

Best, Sue. "Sexualizing Space." In *Sexy Bodies: The Strange Carnalities of Feminism,* ed. Elizabeth Grosz and Elspeth Probyn, 181–85. London: Routledge, 1995.

Bigenho, Michelle. *Sounding Indigenous: Authenticity in Bolivian Music Performance.* New York: Palgrave Macmillan, 2002.

Blake, Cha[rle]s D. "The Mermaid's Evening Song: A Souvenir of the Great Lakes." Chicago: White, Smith and Co., 1881.

Blanckenhagen, Peter H. von, and Christine Alexander. *The Augustan Villa at Boscotrecase.* Deutsches Archäologisches Institut Rom, Sonderschriften 8. Mainz: P. von Zabern, 1990.

Bode, Georg Heinrich. *Scriptores rerum mythicarum tres Romae nuper reperti.* Zelle: E. H. C. Schulze, 1834.

Boer, Cornelis de. *Ovide moralisé: poème du commencement du quatorzième siècle.* 5 vols. Verhandelingen der Nederlandsche Akademie van Wetenschappen te Amsterdam, Afdeeling Letterkunde, nieuwe reeks 15, 21, 30/3, 37, 43. Amsterdam: Noord-Hollandsche Uitgevers-Maatschapperij, 1915–38.

Boethius. *De consolatione Philosophiae.* In *Boethius,* ed. and trans. S. J. Tester. Loeb Classical Library. Cambridge, Mass.: Harvard University Press, 1973.

Bogdanovich, Ippolit Fedorovich. *Dushen'ka.* Moscow: Press of N. S. Vsevolodskii, 1815.

Boiardo, Matteo Maria. *Amorum Libri: The Lyric Poems of Matteo Maria Boiardo.* Trans. with intro. and notes by Andrea di Tommaso. Medieval and Renaissance Texts and Studies, vol. 101. Binghamton, N.Y.: Medieval and Renaissance Texts & Studies, Center for Medieval and Early Renaissance Studies, 1993.

———. *Orlando Innamorato. Amorum Libri.* Ed. Aldo Scaglione. 2 vols. 2d ed. Turin: UTET, 1963.

Bondeson, Jan. *The Feejee Mermaid.* Ithaca, N.Y.: Cornell University Press, 1999.

Borchmeyer, Dietrich. "Wagners Mythos vom Anfang und Ende der Welt." In *Richard Wagner "Der Ring des Nibelungen": Ansichten des Mythos,* ed. Udo Bermbach and Dieter Borchmeyer, 1–25. Stuttgart: Metzler, 1995.

Borges, Jorge Luis, and Margarita Guerrero. *The Book of Imaginary Beings.* Rev., enl., and trans. Norman Thomas di Giovanni in collaboration with the author. New York: E. P. Dutton, 1970.

Boulanger, Lili. "Les Sirènes." New York: G. Schirmer, 1918; and Paris: Société anonyme des Éditions Ricordi, 1919.

Bowers, Jane, and Judith Tick, eds. *Women Making Music: The Western Art Tradition, 1150–1950.* Urbana: University of Illinois Press, 1987.

Boydell, Barra. "The Female Harp: The Irish Harp in 18th- and Early 19th-Century Romantic Nationalism." *RIdIM/RCMI Newsletter* 20 (1995): 10–16.

Brandl, Rudolf M. "Konstantinopolitanische Makamen des 19. Jahrhunderts in Neumen. Die Musik der Fanarioten." In *Maqam, Raga, Zielenmelodik: Konzeptionen und Prinzipen der Musikproduktion,* ed. Jürgen Elsner, 150–69. Berlin: International Council for Traditional Music, 1989. Conference Proceedings of the Study Group "Maqam."

Brant, Sebastian. *Stultifera Nauis.* Trans. Iacobus Locher. Basel: Johannes Bergman, 1498.

Brathwait, Richard. *The English Gentleman.* London: Printed by John Haviland, 1630.

———. *Essays Upon the Five Senses.* London: N.p., 1625.

Brecht, Bertolt. *Brecht on Theatre: The Development of an Aesthetic.* Ed. and trans. John Willett. New York: Hill and Wang, 1964.

Briquet, Charles Moïse. *Les Filigranes.* Ed. Allan Stevenson. Amsterdam: Paper Publications Society, 1968.

Brown, Hilda Meldrum. *Leitmotiv and Drama: Wagner, Brecht and the Limits of "Epic" Theatre.* Oxford: Clarendon Press, 1991.

Brown, Norman O. *Love's Body.* New York: Random House, 1966. Reprint ed. Berkeley: University of California Press, 1990.

Brown, Royal. *Overtones and Undertones: Reading Film Music.* Berkeley: University of California Press, 1994.

Browne, William. *The Whole Works of William Browne.* Ed. W. Carew Hazlitt. London: Roxburghe Library, 1869.

Brumble, David. *Classical Myths and Legends in the Middle Ages and Renaissance: A Dictionary of Allegorical Meanings.* Westport, Conn.: Greenwood Press, 1998.

Bulteau, Adeline. *Les Sirènes.* Puiseau: Éditions Pardès, 1995.

Bulteau, Michel. *Les Filles des eaux.* Monaco: Éditions du Rocher, 1997.

Bunker, Henry Alden. "The Voice as (Female) Phallus." *The Psychoanalytic Quarterly* 3 (1934): 426–27.

Bürger, Gerhard. *Im Zauber der Loreley: Eine kleine Monographie.* St. Goarshausen: Loreley-Verlag, 1952.

Burney, Charles. *A General History of Music from the Earliest Ages to the Present Period.* Vol. 1. London: N.p., 1776. Reprint. New York: Harcourt, Brace and Co., 1935.

Buschor, Ernst. *Die Musen des Jenseits.* Munich: F. Bruckmann, 1944.

Cahier, Charles. "Le Physiologus ou Bestiaire." In *Mélanges d'archéologie, d'histoire et de literature,* by Charles Cahier and Arthur Martin, vol. 2 (1851), 85–100, 106–233. 4 vols. Paris: Mme Vᵉ Poussielgue-Rusand, 1847–56.

Calogero, Elena. " 'Lo, Orpheus with his harpe': La musica nei libri di emblemi inglesi, 1565–1700." Ph.D. diss., University of Florence, 2001.

Camerarius, Joachim. *Symbolorum et emblematum ex Aquatilibus et Reptilibus Desumptorum Centuria Quarta.* Nuremberg: N.p., 1604.

———. *Symbolorum et emblematum centuriaetres . . . Accessit noviter Centuria IV. ex Aquatilibus et Reptilibus.* 2d ed. Nuremberg: Voegelin, 1605.

Campbell, Joseph. *The Inner Reaches of Outer Space: Metaphor as Myth and as Religion.* New York: Alfred van der Marck Editions, 1986.

Candida, Bianca. "Tradizione figurativa nel mito di Ulisse e le Sirene." *Studi classici e orientali* 19–20 (1970–1971): 212–51.

Capaccio, Giulio Cesare. *Delle imprese trattato.* Folio 23v. Napoli: Gio[vanni] Garlion & Antonio Pace, 1592.

Carew, Thomas. "Coelum Brittanicum." In *The Poems of Thomas Carew,* ed. Rhodes Dunlap. Oxford: Clarendon Press, 1949.

Carey, Mariah. *Mariah Carey's #1's.* New York: Columbia Music Video, 1999.

Carman Garner, Barbara. "Francis Bacon, Natalis Comes and the Mythological Tradition." *Journal of the Warburg and Courtauld Institutes* 33 (1970): 264–91.

Carmody, Francis J. *Brunetto Latini, Li livres dou tresor.* University of California Publications in Modern Philology 22. Berkeley: University of California Press, 1948.

———. *Physiologus Latinus: Éditions préliminaires, versio B.* Paris: E. Droz, 1939.

———. "Physiologus Latinus Versio Y." University of California Publications in Classical Philology 12:7, 93–134. Berkeley: University of California Press, 1941.

Carrington, Richard. *Mermaids and Mastodons: A Book of Natural and Unnatural History.* London: Chatto and Windus, 1957.

Cartari, Vincenzo. *Le Imagini dei dei de gli antichi.* Venice: Presso Marc'Antonio Zaltieri, 1592.

Casagrande Villaviera, Rita, ed. *La cortigiana Veneziana del cinquecento.* Milan: Longanesi, 1968.

Cascardi, Anthony J. *The Subject of Modernity.* Cambridge: Cambridge University Press, 1992.

Case, John. *Apologia musices.* Oxford: Joseph Barnes, 1588.

Casoni, Guido. *Della magia d'amore.* Venice: Appresso Fabio, & Agostin Zoppini Fratelli, 1592.

Castiglione, Baldassar. *The Book of the Courtier.* Trans. Sir Thomas Hoby. London: J. M. Dent & Sons; New York: E. P. Dutton & Co., 1928.

Catalani, Alfredo. *Loreley.* Text by Carlo D'Ormeville and A. Zanardini. Piano-Vocal Score. Milan: Ricordi, n.d.

Cavendish, Margaret, Duchess of Newcastle. *The Convent of Pleasure and Other Plays.* Ed. Anne Shaver. Baltimore: Johns Hopkins University Press, 1999.

Celâl, Musahipzade. *Eski İstanbul Yaşayışı.* Istanbul: İletişim Yayıncılık, 1992.

Cengiz, Halil Erdoğan. *Yaşanmış Olaylarla Atatürk ve Müzik: Riyâset-i Cumhûr İnce Saz Hey'eti Şefi Binbaşı Hâfız Yaşar Okur'un Anıları (1924–1938).* Ankara: Müzik Ansiklopedisi Yayınları, 1993.

Cereceda, Veronica. "Aproximaciones a una estetica andina: de la belleza al *tinku.*" In *Tres reflexiones sobre el pensamiento andino,* ed. T. Bouysse-Cassagne, O. Harris, T. Platt, and V. Cereceda, 133–231. La Paz: Hisbol, 1987.

Chance, Jane. *Medieval Mythography.* Gainesville: University Press of Florida, 1994.

Chapman, George. *Chapman's Homer.* Ed. Allardyce Nicholl. 2 vols. New York: Bollingen Foundation/Pantheon Books, 1956.

Chappell, Kevin. "Is the Mainstream Ready for LIL' KIM?" *Ebony* 55 (October 2000): 184.

Chaucer, Geoffrey. *The Romaunt of the Rose and La Roman de la Rose: A Parallel-Text Edition.* Ed. Ronald Sutherland. Berkeley: University of California Press, 1968.

Cherniss, Harold. *Plutarch's Moralia.* Vol. 13, part 1. Loeb Classical Library. Cambridge, Mass.: Harvard University Press, 1976.

Child, Francis James, ed. and collector. *The English and Scottish Popular Ballads.* 1882–1898. Reprint. New York: Dover Publications, 1965.

Chion, Michel. *Audio-Vision: Sound On Screen.* Trans. Claudia Gorbman. New York: Columbia University Press, 1994.

———. *David Lynch.* Trans. Robert Julian. London: BFI Publishing, 1995.

———. *The Voice in Cinema.* Trans. Claudia Gorbman. New York: Columbia University Press, 1999.

Chua, Daniel K. L. *Absolute Music and the Construction of Meaning.* Cambridge: Cambridge University Press, 1999.

Cicero. *De finibus honorom et malorum.* Ed. and trans. H. Rachman. Loeb Classical Library. Cambridge, Mass.: Harvard University Press, 1967.

Cılızoğlu, Tanju. "Unutamıyorum: Atatürk Dedicodudan Nefret Ederdi." *Güneş,* April 9, 1987.

Citron, Marcia J. *Gender and the Musical Canon.* Cambridge: Cambridge University Press, 1993.

Cixous, Hélène. "Laugh of the Medusa." In *Feminisms: An Anthology of Literary Theory and Criticism,* ed. Robyn R. Warhol and Diane Price Herndl, 347–62. New Brunswick, N.J.: Rutgers University Press, 1997.

Clair, Colin. *Unnatural History: An Illustrated Bestiary.* London: Abelard-Schuman, 1967.

Classen, Constance. "Creation by Sound/Creation by Light: A Sensory Analysis of Two South American Cosmologies." In *The Varieties of Sensory Experience,* ed. D. Howes, 239–55. Toronto: University of Toronto Press, 1991.

Clément, Catherine. *Opera, or The Undoing of Women.* Trans. Betsy Wing. Minneapolis: University of Minnesota Press, 1988.

———. "Through Voices, History." In *Siren Songs,* ed. Mary Ann Smart. Princeton, N.J.: Princeton University Press, 2000.

Clifton, Thomas. *Music as Heard: A Study in Applied Phenomenology.* New Haven, Conn.: Yale University Press, 1983.

Columbia Records: Catalogue général turc. Alexandria, 1928.

Columbia Records, New Process: Catalogue général no. 1. Istanbul, 1928.

Comes, Natalis [Natale de' Conti]. *Mythologiae, siue explicationum fabularum libri decem.* Venice: [Comin da Trino], 1567. Expanded ed. Venice: [same mark, but Comin was dead], 1581. Illustrated eds. Padua: P. P. Tozzi, 1616; Padua: P. Frambotto, 1637.

———. *Mythologiæ.* Venice: N.p., 1567.

Consoli, Silla. *La Candeur d'un monstre: essai psychoanalytique sur le mythe de la sirène.* Paris: Éditions du Centurion, 1980.

Cook, Albert Stansborough, ed. and trans. *The Old English Physiologus.* New Haven, Conn.: Yale University Press; Oxford, 1921.

Coryat, Thomas. *Coryats Crudities.* London: Printed by W. S., 1611.

Courcelle, Pierre. "L'interpretation evhémériste des Sirènes-courtisanes jusqu'au XIIe siècle." In *Gesellschaft—Kultur—Literatur: Rezeption und Originalität im Wachsen einer europäischen Literatur und Geistigkeit. Beiträge Luitpold Wallach gewidmet,* ed. Karl Bosl, 33–48. Monographien zur Geschichte des Mittelalters 11. Stuttgart: Hiersemann, 1975.

———. "Quelques symboles funéraires du néo-platonisme latin: Le vol de Dédale—Ulysse et les Sirènes." *Revue des études anciennes* 46 (1944): 65–93.

Courtney, Edward. *The Fragmentary Latin Poets.* Oxford: Oxford University Press, 1993.

Cowie, Elizabeth. "Film Noir and Women." In *Shades of Noir,* ed. Joan Copjec. New York: Verso, 1993.

Craig, Hugh. "Ben Jonson, the Antimasque, and the 'Rules of Flattery.'" In *The Politics of the Stuart Court Masque,* ed. David Bevington and Peter Holbrook, 179–96. Cambridge: Cambridge University Press, 1998.

Craig-McFeely, Julia. "The Signifying Serpent: Seduction by Cultural Stereotype in Seventeenth-Century England." In *Music, Sensation, and Sensuality,* ed. Linda Phyllis Austern, 299–317. New York: Routledge, 2002.

Curley, Michael J. Introduction to *Physiologus.* Trans. Michael J. Curley. Austin: University of Texas Press, 1979.

Cusick, Suzanne G. "A Soprano Subjectivity: Vocality, Power, and the Compositional Voice of Francesca Caccini." In *Crossing Boundaries: Attending to Early Modern Women,* ed. Jane Donawerth and Adele Seeff, 80–98. Newark, Del.: University of Delaware Press, 2001.

——. *Valerio Dorico: Music Printer in Sixteenth-Century Rome.* Studies in Musicology 43. Ann Arbor, Mich.: UMI Research Press, 1981.

Dahlhaus, Carl. *Die Musik des 19. Jahrhunderts. Neues Handbuch der Musikwissenschaft*, vol. 6. Laaber: Laaber-Verlag, 1980.

Dal', Vladimir Ivanovich. *Tolkovyi slovar' zhivogo velikorusskago iazyka* [Explanatory dictionary of Great-Russian language]. Moskva: Gosudarstvennoe izdatel'stvo inostrannykh i natsional'nykh slovarei, 1955.

Dalgas, Andonios, and Hafız Burhan (Sesyılmaz). *Great Voices of Constantinople, 1927–1933.* Cambridge, Mass.: Rounder CD 1113, 1997. Sound Recording. www.rounder.com, accessed March 22, 2003.

Daniel, Samuel. *The Complete Works in Verse and Prose of Samuel Daniel.* Ed. Alexander B. Grosart. 5 vols. Privately printed, 1885–1896.

Danielson, Virginia. *The Voice of Egypt: Umm Kulthūm, Arabic Song, and Egyptian Society in the Twentieth Century.* Chicago: University of Chicago Press, 1997.

Darcy, Warren. "*Creatio ex nihilo:* The Genesis, Structure, and Meaning of the *Rheingold* Prelude." *19th-Century Music* 13 (1989): 79–100.

Davies, Malcolm. *Poetarum melicorum Graecorum fragmenta.* Oxford: Oxford University Press, 1991.

Davies, Malcom, and Jeyaraney Kathirithamby. *Greek Insects.* London: Duckworth; New York: Oxford University Press, 1986.

Deleon, Jak. *Bars of İstanbul.* Istanbul: Labris, 1990.

——. *A Taste of Old İstanbul.* Istanbul: Istanbul Kütüphanesi, 1989.

Dennys, Rodney. *The Heraldic Imagination.* London: Barrie & Jenkins, 1975.

Derrida, Jacques. *Spurs: Nietzsche's Styles / Eperons: Les Styles de Nietzsche.* Trans. Barbara Harlow. Chicago: University of Chicago Press, 1979.

Derzhavin, Gavril Romanovich. "Tam stepi, kak morya struyatsya" [There are steppes flowing like seas]. In *Sochinenia* [Works]. St. Petersburg: Academic Prospect, 2002.

Descartes, René (Renatus Des-Cartes). *Compendium of Musick.* Trans. and ed. by a person of honour. London: Thomas Harper for Humphrey Moseley, 1653.

Desiderius Erasmus. *Moriae Encomium.* In *Opera Omnia,* series 4, volume 3, ed. Clarence H. Miller. Amsterdam: North-Holland, 1979.

Dickerson, James. *Women on Top.* New York: Billboard, 1988.

Dijkstra, Bram. *Evil Sisters: The Threat of Female Sexuality and the Cult of Manhood.* New York: Alfred A. Knopf, 1996.

——. *Idols of Perversity: Fantasies of Feminine Evil in Fin-de-Siècle Culture.* New York: Oxford University Press, 1986.

Dinnerstein, Dorothy. *The Mermaid and the Minotaur: Sexual Arrangements and Human Malaise.* New York: Harper and Row, 1976.

Diogenes Laertius. *Lives of Eminent Philosophers,* 10:6. Trans. R. D. Hicks. Cambridge, Mass.: Harvard University Press, 1966.

Doane, Mary Ann. *Femmes Fatales: Feminism, Film Theory, Psychoanalysis.* New York: Routledge, 1991.

Doni, Anton Francesco. *I Mondi del Doni.* Venice: Francesco Marcolini, 1552.

Donne, John. *The Complete Poetry.* Ed. John T. Shawcross. New York: New York University Press; and London: University of London Press, 1968.

Douglas, Mary. "The Person in an Enterprise Culture." In *Understanding the Enterprise Culture: Themes in the Work of Mary Douglas,* ed. Shaun H. Heap and Angus Ross. New York: Norton, 1992.

Douglas, Norman. *Siren Land.* London: J. M. Dent & Sons, 1911.

———. *Siren Land.* London: Secker and Warburg, 1923.

Drayton, Michael. "The Shepheards Sirena." In *Poems of Michael Drayton,* ed. John Buxton. Cambridge, Mass.: Harvard University Press, 1950.

Drayton, Michael. *Works.* Ed. J. William Hebel. 6 vols. Oxford: Shakespeare Head Press, 1961.

Drewal, Henry John. "Interpretation, Invention, and Re-presentation in the Worship of Mami Wata." *Journal of Folklore Research* 25 (1988): 101–39. Reprinted in *Performance in Contemporary African Arts,* ed. R. Stone. Bloomington: African Studies Program, Indiana University, 1988.

———. "Mami Wata and Santa Marta: Imag(in)ing Selves and Others in Africa and the Americas." In *Images and Empires: Visuality in Colonial and Postcolonial Africa,* ed. P. Landau and D. Kaspin. Berkeley: University of California Press, 2002.

———. "Performing the Other: Mami Wata Worship in West Africa." *Drama Review* (1988): 160–85.

Druce, G. C. "Some Abnormal and Composite Forms in English Church Architecture." *Architectural Journal* 72 (1915): 135–86.

Drummond, William, of Hawthornden. *Poetical Works.* Ed. L. E. Kastner. 2 vols. Edinburgh: William Blackwood and Sons, 1913.

Dryden, John. "King Arthur: or, the British Worthy." In *The Works.* Vol. 8. Edinburgh: William Paterson, 1884.

Du Plessis, Rachel Blau. *Writing beyond the Ending: Narrative Strategies of Twentieth-Century Women Writers.* Bloomington: Indiana University Press, 1985.

Duhanî, Said N. *Beyoğlu'nun Adı Pera İken.* Istanbul: İstanbul Kütüphanesi, 1990.

Dunn, Leslie C., and Nancy A. Jones, eds. *Embodied Voices: Representing Female Vocality in Western Culture.* Cambridge: Cambridge University Press, 1994.

Durkin, Jennifer. "The Iconography of Insurrection: The British Museum Tapestry No. 1913 3–11 and the Symbolism of Eighteenth-Century Peruvian Nationalism." M.A. thesis, Department of Art History and Theory, University of Essex, 1989.

Eden, P. T. *Theobaldi "Physiologus."* Mittellateinische Studien und Texte 6. Leiden: E. J. Brill, 1972.

Eiges, Iosif. *Muzyka v zhizni i tvorchestve Pushkina* [Music in the life and works of Pushkin]. Moscow: Muzgiz, 1937.

Eismann, Georg, ed. *Robert Schumann: Ein Quellenwerk Über Sein Leben und Schaffen.* Leipzig: Breitkopf und Härtel, 1956.

Eliot, T. S. *Collected Poems, 1909–1962.* New York: Harcourt, Brace and World, 1963.

Erguner, Kudsi. *Chants du harem: Ensemble des femmes d'Istanbul. Musique ottomane: Ottoman Music.* Notes in French by Ali Semizoğlu and Kudsi Erguner. Trans. Katherin Krieger. Nanterre, France: Al-Sur, ALCD 125, 1994. Sound Recording.

Estrich, Susan. *Sex and Power.* New York: Riverhead Books, 2000.

Ethnagraphia Belarusi: Encyclopedia. Minsk, 1989.

Fabris, Dinko. "La città della sirena. Le origini del mito musicale di Napoli nell'età spagnola." In *Napoli Viceregno Spagnolo una capitale della cultura alle arigini dell'Europa moderna (sec. XVI–XVII,* ed. Monika Boose and André Stoll. Vol. 2, Napoli: Vivarium, 2001.

Fairfax, Edward. *Godfrey of Bulloigne.* Ed. Kathleen M. Lea and T. M. Gang. Oxford: Clarendon Press, 1981.

Faral, Edmond. "La queue de poisson des Sirènes." *Romania* 74 (1953): 433–506.

Fauser, Annegret. "La guerre en dentelles: Women and the Prix de Rome in French Cultural Politics." *Journal of the American Musicological Society* 51 (1998): 83–129.

Fedotov, Vassily. *Repertoire of the Bolshoi Theater 1776–1995.* New York: Norman Ross Publishing, 2001.

Feldman, Martha. "The Academy of Domenico Venier, Music's Literary Muse in Mid-Cinquecento Venice." *Renaissance Quarterly* 44 (1991): 476–512.

Feldman, Walter. *Music of the Ottoman Court: Makam, Composition and the Early Ottoman Instrumental Repertoire.* Intercultural Music Studies, No. 10. Berlin: Verlag für Wissenschaft und Bildung, 1996.

Ferguson, Margaret. *Trials of Desire: Renaissance Defenses of Poetry.* New Haven, Conn.: Yale University Press, 1983.

Feridun, Hikmet. "Deniz Kızı Eftalya." *Yedigün* 4 (1933): 10–12.

Ferino-Pagden, Sylvia, ed. *I cinque sensi nell'arte: immagini del sentire.* Milan: Leonardo Arte, 1996.

Ficino, Marsilio. *Sopra lo Amore ovvero Convito di Platone.* Ed. Giuseppe Rensi. Milan: SE, 1998.

Finney, Gretchen Ludke. *Musical Backgrounds for English Literature: 1580–1650.* New Brunswick, N.J.: Rutgers University Press, 1962.

"Five questions for Lil' Kim." *Ebony* 58 (October 2003): 22.

Forster, E. M. *Collected Short Stories.* Harmondsworth, Middlesex: Penguin Books, 1947.

———. *The Story of the Siren.* Richmond, U.K.: Published by Leonard and Virginia Woolf, 1920.

Forster, Leonard. *The Icy Fire: Five Studies in European Petrarchism.* Cambridge: Cambridge University Press, 1969.

Fournival, Richard de. *Master Richard's Bestiary of Love and Response.* Trans. Jeanette Beer. Berkeley: University of California Press, 1986.

Fowler, Robert L. *Early Greek Mythography.* Vol. 1: *Texts.* Oxford: Oxford University Press, 2000.

Franco, Nicolò. *Le pistole vulgari.* Venice: Antonio Gardane, 1542. Reprinted in

Francesca Romana de' Angelis, *"Libri di Lettere" del Cinquecento.* Ferrara: Arnaldo Forni, 1986.

Fraunce, Abraham. *The Third Part of the Countesse of Pembrokes Yvychurch.* London: N.p., 1592.

Frenzel, Elisabeth. *Stoffe der Weltliteratur: Ein Lexikon dichtungsgeschichtlicher Längsschnitte.* 8th ed. Stuttgart: Alfred Kröner Verlag, 1992.

Freud, Sigmund. "Revision of Dream Theory." In *The Complete Introductory Lectures on Psychoanalysis,* trans. and ed. James Strachey. New York: W. W. Norton and Co., 1966.

Fulgentius, [Fabius Planciades]. "Mitologiarum." In *Opera,* ed. Rudolf Helm. Leipzig: G. Teubner, 1898.

———. *The Mythologies.* In *Fulgentius the Mythographer,* ed. and trans. Leslie George Whitbread. Columbus: Ohio State University Press, 1971.

Ganz, Peter F. *Geistliche Dichtung des 12. Jahrhunderts. Eine Textauswahl.* Berlin: Erich Schmidt, 1960.

Garofalo, Reebee. "From Music Publishing to MP3: Music and Industry in the Twentieth Century." *American Music* 17 (1999): 318–53.

Garver, Milton Stahl. "Sources of Beast Similes in the Italian Lyric of the Thirteenth Century." *Romanische Forschungen* 21 (1907): 276–320.

Gautier, Théophile. *Gautier on Dance.* Trans. Ivor Guest. London: Dance Books Cecil Court, 1986.

Gazimihâl, Mahmut. "Musiki: Avrupada Çeyrek Sesler." *Millî Mecmua* 91 (1927b): 1473–74; 94 (1927b): 1519–21; 95 (1927b): 1536–38; 96 (1927b): 1545–47.

———. "Musiki: Çeyrek Sesler." *Millî Mecmua* 85 (1927a): 1375–77; 86 (1927a): 1390–93; 87 (1927a): 1407–1409; 88 (1927a): 1423–26.

Genevoix, Marcel. *Lorelei.* Paris: Editions du Seuil, 1978.

Gentlemen Prefer Blondes. Twentieth Century Fox Film Corporation, 1953. Dir. Howard Hawks. Screenplay by Charles Lederer.

"Gentlemen Prefer Blondes #1 Barbie." http://www.newbarbie.com/marilyn top.htm. Meyer's Toy World New Barbie Center: "Marilyn Monroe Barbie® Series." Accessed July 2, 1998.

Gerstler, Amy. "Siren." In *The Extraordinary Tide: New Poetry by American Women.* New York: Columbia University Press, 2001.

Ghisalberti, Alberto M., ed. *Dizionario biografico degli italiani.* 61 vols. Rome: Istituto dell'Enciclopedia Italiana, 1960–[2003].

Gilbert, Charles. *Mission Loreley en Lorraine occupée, 5 novembre–24 décembre 1944.* Les Sables d'Olonne: Cercle d'Or, 1985.

Ginzberg, Louis. *The Legends of the Jews.* 7 vols. Baltimore: Johns Hopkins University Press, 1998.

Gisbert, Teresa. *Iconografía y Mitos Indígenas en el Arte.* La Paz (Bolivia): Editorial Gisbert y Cia. S.A., 1980.

Giz, Adnan. *Bir Zamanlar Kadıköy.* Istanbul: İletişim Yayınları, 1990.

Glumov, Aleksandr Nikolaevich. *Muzykal' nyi mir Pushkina* [Musical world of Pushkin]. Moscow: Gosudarstvennoe Muzykal' noe Izdatel'stvo, 1950.

Goethe, Johann Wolfgang. "Die neue Melusine." In *Three Tales,* ed. C. A. H. Russ. London: Oxford University Press, 1964.

Gold, Arthur, and Robert Fizdale. *Divine Sarah: A Life of Sarah Bernhardt.* New York: Albert A. Knopf, 1991.

Gollnick, James. *Love and the Soul: Psychological Interpretations of the Eros and Psyche Myth.* Waterloo, Ont.: Wilfrid Laurier University Press, 1992.

Good, Karen R. "More than a Lil' Bit." *Vibe* 56 (September 1997): 176.

Gooding-Williams, Robert, and Judith Bryant Wittenberg. "The 'Strange World' of Blue Velvet: Conventions, Subversions and the Representation of Women." In *Sexual Politics and Popular Culture,* ed. Diane Raymond. Bowling Green, Ohio: Bowling Green State University Popular Press, 1990.

Gorbman, Claudia. "Music in *The Piano.*" In *Jane Campion's The Piano,* ed. Harriet Margolis. Cambridge: Cambridge University Press, 2000.

Gore, Charles. "Mami Wata: An Urban Presence or The Making of a Tradition." In *Sacred Waters: The Many Faces of Mami Wata/mami wata, and other Water Spirits in Africa and the Afro-Atlantic World,* ed. Henry John Drewal. Bloomington: Indiana University Press, forthcoming.

———. "Popular Culture in West Africa." In *Encyclopedia of Sub-Saharan Africa,* ed. J. Middleton. New York: Charles Scribner's Sons, Macmillan, 1998.

———. "Ritual, Performance and the Media in Contemporary Urban Shrine Configurations in Benin City, Nigeria." In *ASA Monograph* 35. London: Routledge, 1998.

Gough, Melinda. "Jonson's Siren Stage." *Studies in Philology* 96, no. 1 (Winter 1999): 68–95.

Gozenpud, Abram. "Pushkin and Russian Operatic Classics." In *Pushkin: Issledovaniya i materialy* [Pushkin: Research and materials], 200–217. Leningrad: Nauka, 1967.

Graves, Robert, and Raphael Patai. *Hebrew Myths: The Book of Genesis.* New York: Doubleday, 1964.

Grebe Vicuña, María Ester. "Generative Models, Symbolic Structures and Acculturation in the Panpipe Music of the Aymara of Tarapaca, Chile." Ph.D. diss., The Queen's University, Belfast, 1980.

Greenblatt, Stephen. *Marvelous Possessions: The Wonder of the New World.* Oxford: Clarendon Press, 1992.

Grenier, Svetlana Slavskaya. *Representing the Marginal Woman in Nineteenth-Century Russian Literature.* Westport, Conn.: Greenwood Press, 2001.

Greve, Martin. *Die Europäisierung orientalischer Kunstmusik in der Türkei.* Berlin: Peter Lang, Europäischer Verlag der Wissenschaften, 1995.

Grey, Thomas. "The Orchestral Music." In *The Mendelssohn Companion,* ed. Douglass Seaton. Westport, Conn.: Greenwood Press, 2001.

Grimm, Jacob. "On the Origin of Language." In *German Romantic Criticism,* trans. Ralph R. Read III and ed. Leslie Willson. New York: Continuum, 1982.

Groos, Arthur. "Madame Butterfly: The Story." *Cambridge Opera Journal* 3, no. 2 (July 1991): 125–28.

Guaman Poma de Ayala, Felipe. *El Primer Nueva Corónica y Buen Gobierno* (ca. 1615). Ed. J. Murra and R. Adorno. Mexico: Siglo Veintiuno, 1980.

Guarini, Giovan Battista. *Rime del molto illvstre Signor Caualiere Battista Gvarini.* Venice: Presso Gio[vanni] Battista Ciotti, 1598.

Güngör, Necatı Ed. *Safiye Ayla'nın Anıları.* Istanbul: Milliyet Yayınları, 1996.

Guzzette, Desiree. "Inger Lorre: Punk Rock's Renaissance Woman." *Rockrgrl* 30 (December 30, 1999): 13.

Hagopian, Harold, ed. *Istanbul 1925.* Notes in English by Harold Hagopian. New York: Traditional Crossroads CD 4266, 1994. Sound recording. www.tradi tionalcrossroads.com.

———. *Women of Istanbul.* Notes in English by Harold Hagopian. New York: Traditional Crossroads CD 4280, 1998. Sound recording. www.traditional crossroads.com.

Hanchant, W. L. "The Truth about Mermaids: A Warning to Sailors." *Lilliput* (March 1945): 215.

Haraway, Donna J. *Simians, Cyborgs, and Women: The Reinvention of Nature.* London: Free Association Books, 1991.

Harrán, Don. "Guido Casoni on Love as Music: A Theme 'for All Ages and Studies.'" *Renaissance Quarterly* 54 (2001): 883–913.

Harris, Olivia. "The Dead and Devils among the Bolivian Laymi." In *Death and the Regeneration of Life,* ed. M. Bloch and J. Parry, 45–73. Cambridge: Cambridge University Press, 1982.

———. "Etnomúsica en el Norte de Potosí." *Jayma,* Año 6, nos. 26–27 (1988): 3–4.

———. "The Power of Signs: Gender, Culture and the Wild in the Bolivian Andes." In *Nature, Culture and Gender,* ed. C. McCormack and M. Strathern, 70–94. Cambridge: Cambridge University Press, 1981.

Harrison, Regina. *Signs, Songs, and Memory in the Andes: Translating Quechua Language and Culture.* Austin: University of Texas Press, 1989.

Hecht, David. "Mermaids and Other Things in Africa." *Arts Magazine* (November 1990): 80–86.

Hegel, G. W. F. *The Philosophy of History.* Trans. J. Sibree. New York: Dover, 1956.

Heine, Heinrich. "Elementary Spirits." In *Collected Works,* trans. Charles Godfrey Leland. Vol. 11, 107–211. New York: Crosup & Sterling Co., n.d..

———. *Historisch-kritische Gesamtausgabe der Werke.* Vol. 1, *Buch der Lieder: Appa-rat.* Ed. and annotated by Pierre Grappin. Hamburg: Hoffmann und Campe Verlag, 1975.

Heitmann, Klaus. "Deutschland als Bezauberung und Bedrohung: Maurice Gen-evoix und sein Roman *Lorelei.*" *Zeitschrift für französische Sprache und Litera-tur* 92 (1982): 9–27.

Helm, Rudolf. *Die Chronik des Hieronymus.* 2d ed. Eusebius Werke 7. Die griechi-schen christlichen Schriftsteller der ersten drei Jahrhunderte 47. Berlin: Akademie-Verlag, 1956.

Henkel, Arthur, and Albrecht Schöne, eds. *Emblemata: Handbuch zur Sinnbild-kunst des XVI. und XVII. Jahrhunderst.* 2d ed. Stuttgart: J. B. Metzlersche, 1976.

Henkel, Nikolaus. *Studien zum Physiologus im Mittelalter.* Hermaea, germanistische Forschungen, neue Folge 38. Tübingen: Niemeyer, 1976.

Herbert, Edward, Lord of Cherbury. *Pagan Religion.* Ed. John Anthony Butler. Ottawa: Dovehouse Editions; and Binghamton, N.Y.: Medieval and Renaissance Texts and Studies, 1996.

Herendon, Frederick, and Edward Horan. *A Royal Exchange.* London: Chappell & Co., 1935.

Heres, Gerald. "Odysseus und die Tritonin, zu einer Gruppe gefälschter Tonlampen." *Eirene* 12 (1974): 63–68.

Herman, Peter C. *Squitter-wits and Muse-haters: Sidney, Spenser, Milton, and Renaissance Anti-Poetic Sentiment.* Detroit: Wayne State University Press, 1996.

Herr, Cheryl. "Nature and Culture in the 'Sirens' Episode of Joyce's Ulysses." In *James Joyce's Ulysses: Modern Critical Interpretations,* 133–43. New York: Chelsea House Publishers, 1987.

Herzfeld, Michael. *Ours Once More: Folklore, Ideology and the Making of Modern Greece.* Austin: University of Texas Press, 1982.

Heywood, Thomas. *Gynaikeion.* London: Adam Islip, 1624, 364–65.

Hezarfen, Ahmet. "H. 1245'te (1829) Başmuhasebeye Gedik Olarak Kayıtlı İstanbul Meyhaneleri." *Tarih ve Toplum* 129 (1994): 36–39.

Hiçyılmaz, Ergun. *Eski İstanbul Meyhaneleri ve Alemleri.* Istanbul: Pera Orient Yayıncılık, 1992.

———. *İstanbul Geceleri ve Kantolar.* Istanbul: Sabah Kitapları, 1999.

Higgins, Jim. *Irish Mermaids: Sirens, Temptresses and Their Symbolism in Art, Architecture and Folklore.* Galway: Crow's Rock Press, 1995.

Hillemacher, Paul, and Lucien Joseph Edouard. *Loreley. Légende symphonique en trois parties.* Text by Eugène Adenis. Paris: Tresse Editeur, 1883.

Hiller, Eduard, ed. *Theon Smyrnaeus: Expositio rerum mathematicarum.* Leipzig: B. G. Teubner, 1878. Reprint. Stuttgart: B. G. Teubner, 1995.

Hiller, Ferdinand. *Lorelei.* Opus 70. Poem by Wolfgang Müller von Königswinter. Leipzig: Fr. Kirstner, 1857.

Hipkins, A. J. *Musical Instruments Historic, Rare and Unique.* First published 1888. 2d ed., London: A. & C. Black, Ltd., 1921.

Hirschberger, Martina. Gynaikōn Katalogos und Megalai Ēhoiai: Ein Kommentar zu den Fragmenten zweier hesiodeischer Epen. Beiträge zur Altertumskunde 198. Munich: K. G. Saur, 2004.

Hirshey, Gerri. "Women Who Rocked the World." *Rolling Stone* 773 (November 13, 1997): 85.

His Master's Voice. *En Son Çıkan Türkçe Plaklar: Deniz Kızı.* Trans. Sahibinin Sesi. Istanbul: N.p., 1932.

———. *Genikos katalogos diskon 1936: "His Master's Voice."* Trans. Sahibinin Sesi. Athens: N.p., 1936.

———. *Türkçe Plakların Esamısı.* Trans. Sahibinin Sesi. Supp. no. 7. Istanbul: N.p., 1934/5.

Hobhouse, John C. "Constantinople." Unpublished Manuscript, British Library Mss. 56529, ca. 1810.

Hocker, Dr. Nicolaus. *Rhein-Album.* Berlin: in Commission bei Mitscher & Röstell, 1873.

Holford-Strevens, Leofranc. "Tinctoris on the Great Composers." *Plainsong and Medieval Music* 5, no. 2 (1996): 193–99.

Hollander, John. *The Untuning of the Sky: Ideas of Music in English Poetry 1500– 1700.* Princeton, N.J.: Princeton University Press, 1961.

Hollander, Robert. "Purgatorio XIX: Dante's Siren/Harpy." In *Dante, Petrarch, Boccaccio: Studies in the Italian Trecento in Honor of Charles S. Singleton,* ed. Aldo S. Bernardo and Anthony L. Pellegrini, 77–88. Binghamton, N.Y.: Medieval & Renaissance Texts & Studies, 1983.

Holst, Gail. *Road to Rembetika: Music of a Greek Sub-Culture; Songs of Love, Sorrow and Hashish.* Athens: Denise Harvey and Co., 1975.

Homer. *The Odyssey.* Trans. A. T. Murray. Loeb Classical Library. Cambridge, Mass.: Harvard University Press, 1984.

———. *The Whole Works.* Trans. George Chapman. London: Nathaniell Butter, [1616?].

Hopkins Porter, Cecilia. *The Rhine as Musical Metaphor: Cultural Identity in German Romantic Music.* Boston: Northeastern University Press, 1996.

Horkeimer, Max, and Theodor W. Adorno. *Dialektik der Aufklärung: Philosophische Fragmente.* 1947. Reprint. Amsterdam: Verlag de Munter, 1989.

Hornblower, Simon, and Anthony Spawforth. *Oxford Classical Dictionary.* 3d ed. Oxford: Oxford University Press, 1996.

Horney, Karen. *Feminine Psychology.* New York: W. W. Norton and Co., 1967.

"Hottest Females in Rap Music." *Jet* 97 (February 21, 2000): 59.

Houwen, L. A. J. R. "Flattery and the Mermaid in Chaucer's *Nun's Priest's Tale.*" In *Animals and the Symbolic in Mediaeval Art and Literature,* ed. L. A. J. R. Houwen, 77–92. Mediaevalia Groningana 20. Groningen: Egbert Forsten, 1997.

"How Mariah Escaped Sony." *Time* 157 (June 18, 2001): 18.

Hubbs, Joanna. *Mother Russia: The Feminine Myth in Russian Culture.* Bloomington: Indiana University Press, 1993.

Hugh-Jones, Stephen. *The Palm and the Pleiades: Initiation and Cosmology in Northwest Amazonia.* Cambridge: Cambridge University Press, 1979.

Hutton, James. "Some English Poems in Praise of Music." *English Miscellany* 2 (1951): 1–63. Reprinted in *Essays on Renaissance Poetry,* ed. Rita Guerlac, 17– 73. Ithaca: Cornell University Press, 1980.

Imago Primi Saeculi Societatis Jesu. Antwerp: ex Officina Plantiniana Balthasaris Moreti, 1640.

INDICEP. "El Carnival en las Comunidades Aymaras del Departamento de

Oruro." INDICEP (Instituto de Investigación Cultural para Educación Popular). Doc. 10 Serie. A. Oruro, Bolivia. *Año* 4, no. 7 (Octubre 1973): 1–9.

Ingham, Norman. *W. E. T. A. Hoffmann's Reception in Russia.* Würzburg: Jal-Verlag, 1974.

Irigaray, Luce. *Speculum of the Other Woman.* Trans. Gillian C. Gill. Ithaca, N.Y.: Cornell University Press, 1985.

Isichei, Elizabeth. "Mami Wata, Water Spirits, and Returners in and near the Igbo Culture Area." In *Sacred Waters: The Many Faces of Mami Wata/mami wata, and Other Water Spirits in Africa and the Afro-Atlantic World,* ed. Henry John Drewal. Bloomington: Indiana University Press, forthcoming.

Isidore of Seville [Isidore de Séville]. *Etymologies.* In *Des animaux.* Book 4. Paris: Societé d'édition "Les Belles Lettres," 1986.

Ivanits, Linda J. *Russian Folk Belief.* Armonk, N.Y.: M. E. Sharpe, 1989.

Jacoby, F., ed. *Die Fragmente der griechischen Historiker.* Berlin: Weidmannsche Buchhandlung, 1923. Reprint. Leiden: E. J. Brill, 1957.

Jäger, Ralf. *Türkische Kunstmusik und ihre handschriftlichen Quellen aus dem 19. Jahrhundert.* No. 8. Münster: Schriften zur Musikwissenschaft aus Münster, 1996.

James, Jamie. *The Music of the Spheres: Music, Science and the Natural Order of the Universe.* London: Abacus, 1993.

James, Montague Rhodes. *The Bestiary: Being a Reproduction in Full of the Manuscript Ii. 4. 26 in the University Library, Cambridge, with Supplementary Plates from Other Manuscripts of English Origin, and a Preliminary Study of the Latin Bestiary as Current in England.* London: Roxburghe Club, 1928.

Jankélévitch, Vladimir. "Orpheus or the Sirens?" In *Music and the Ineffable,* trans. Carolyn Abbate. Princeton, N.J.: Princeton University Press, 2003.

Jhally, Sut. *Dreamworlds 2: Desire/Sex/Power in Music Video.* Northampton: Media Education Foundation, 1995.

Joe, Jeongwon. "Hans Jürgen Syberberg's Parsifal: The Staging of Dissonance in the Fusion of Opera and Film." *Music Research Forum* 13 (1998): 1–21.

Johnson, Anna. "The Sprite in the Water and the Siren of the Woods: On Swedish Folk Music and Gender." In *Music, Gender, and Culture,* ed. M. Herndon and S. Ziegler, 27–40. Wilhelmshaven: Florian Noetzel Verlag, 1990.

Johnson, Brian. "Shania Revealed: The Queen of Country Wants to Step Out of the Packaging to Prove Herself on the Stage." *Maclean's* 111 (March 23, 1998): 50.

Johnson, Buffie. *Lady of the Beasts: Ancient Images of the Goddess and Her Sacred Animals.* San Francisco: Harper and Row, 1988.

Johnstone, Tom, and Klaus R. Scherer. "Vocal Communication of Emotion." In *Handbook of Emotions,* 2d ed., ed. Michael Lewis and Jeanette M. Haviland-Jones, 220–35. New York: Guilford Press, 2000.

Jones, Gwyn. *William Browne: Circe and Ulysses, the Inner Temple Masque.* London: Golden Cockerel Press, 1954.

Jones, Nancy A. "Music and the Maternal Voice in Purgatorio XIX." In *Embodied Voices: Representing Female Vocality in Western Culture,* ed. Leslie C. Dunn and Nancy A. Jones, 35–49. Cambridge: Cambridge University Press, 1994.

Jonson, Ben. "The Masque of Blacknesse." In *Ben Jonson,* ed. C. H. Herford, Percy Simpson, and Evelyn Simpson. Oxford: Clarendon, 1941).

Joyce, James. *Ulysses.* New York: Random House, 1961.

Kafka, Franz. *The Complete Stories.* Ed. Nahum N. Glazer with a new foreword by John Updike. New York: Schocken Books, 1983.

Kaimakis, Dimitris. *Der Physiologus nach der ersten Redaktion.* Beiträge zur klassischen Philologie 63. Meisenheim am Glan: Hain, 1974.

Kaiser, Erich. "Odyssee-Szenen als Topoi." *Museum Helveticum* 21(1995): 109–36.

Kaleta, Kenneth C. "Lynch at His Best—*Blue Velvet.*" In *David Lynch.* New York: Twayne Publishers, 1993.

Kalinak, Kathryn. "The Fallen Woman and the Virtuous Wife: Musical Stereotypes in *The Informer, Gone with the Wind,* and *Laura.*" *Film Reader* 5 (1982): 76–82.

Kano, Ayako. *Acting Like a Woman in Modern Japan: Theater, Gender, and Nationalism.* New York: Palgrave, 2001.

Kantor, Marvin. *Dramatic Works of Fonvizin.* Frankfurt: Herbert Lane and Co., 1974.

Kaplan, E. Ann, ed. *Women in Film Noir.* 2d ed. London: British Film Institute, 2000.

——. *Rocking around the Clock: Music Television, Postmodernism, and Consumer Culture.* New York: Methuen, 1987.

Karlinsky, Simon. *Russian Drama from Its Beginning to the Age of Pushkin.* Berkeley: University of California Press, 1985.

Kasaba, Reşat. "İzmir 1922: A Port City Unravels." In *Modernity and Culture: From the Mediterranean to the Indian Ocean, 1890–1920,* ed. L. Fowaz and C. A. Bayly, 204–229. New York: Columbia University Press, 2002.

Kaster, Robert A. *Suetonius: De grammaticis et rhetoribus.* Oxford: Oxford University Press, 1995.

Kastner, George. *Les Sirènes.* Paris: Brandus and Dufour, 1858.

——. *Les Sirènes: Essai sure les principaux mythes relatifs a l'incantation.* Paris: Barthès et Lowell, 1885.

Keldish, *Istoria russkoi muzyki* [History of Russian music]. Moscow: Nauka, 1948.

Keller, Adelbert von. *Hans Sachs: Werke.* Vol. 7:2. Bibliothek des litterarischen Vereins in Stuttgart 115. Tübingen, 1873. Reprint. Hildesheim: G. Olms, 1964.

Kelso, Ruth. *Doctrine for the Lady of the Renaissance.* Urbana: University of Illinois Press, 1956.

Kendrick, Robert L. *Celestial Sirens: Nuns and Their Music in Early Modern Milan.* Oxford: Clarendon Press, 1996.

Kermode, Frank. *Shakespeare, Spenser, Donne: Renaissance Essays.* London: Routledge and Kegan Paul, 1971.

Kierkegaard, Søren. *Either/Or.* Part 1. Ed. and trans. Howard V. Hong and Edna H. Hong. Princeton, N.J.: Princeton University Press, 1987.

Kikta, Valerii. *Pushkinskaya muzykal'naya panorama XIX–XX vekov* [Pushkin's musical panorama in the nineteenth and twentieth centuries]. Moscow: Muzyka, 1999.

"Kim on Kim." *Essence* (October 2000): 115.

Kircher, Athanasius [Athanasii Kircheri, S.J.]. *Arca Noe.* Amsterdam: Apud Joannem Jansonium à Waesberge, 1675.

Kireevsky, Ivan. "On the Nature of Pushkin's Poetry." In *Literature and National Identity: Nineteenth-Century Russian Critical Essays.* Ed. and trans. Paul Debreczeny and Jesse Zeldin, 3–17. Lincoln: University of Nebraska Press, 1970.

Kisliuk, Michelle. "The Intersection of Evangelism, AIDS, and Mami Wata in Popular Music in Centrafrique." in *Sacred Waters: The Many Faces of Mami Wata/mami wata, and Other Water Spirits in Africa and the Afro-Atlantic World,* ed. Henry John Drewal. Indiana University Press, forthcoming.

Korinfskii Narodnaya Rus' [Folk Russia]. 1901. Reprint ed. Moscow: Laborer, 1995, 44–55.

Kramer, Lawrence. *After the Lovedeath: Sexual Violence and the Making of Culture.* Berkeley: University of California Press, 1997.

——. *Classical Music and Postmodern Knowledge.* Berkeley: University of California Press, 1995.

——. *Franz Schubert: Sexuality, Subjectivity, Song.* Cambridge: Cambridge University Press, 1999.

——. "Little Pearl Teadrops." In *Music, Sensation, and Sensuality,* ed. Linda Phyllis Austern. New York: Routledge, 2002.

——. *Opera and Modern Culture: Wagner and Strauss.* Berkeley: University of California Press, 2004.

——. "Voice and Its Beyonds." In *Opera and Modern Culture: Wagner and Strauss.* Berkeley: University of California Press, 2004.

——. "Yesterday's Moonlight: Chopin, Beethoven, and the Hermeneutics of Resemblance." In *D'une herméneutique de la musique,* ed. Christian Hauer. Forthcoming 2004.

Kremlev, Urii. *Russkaya mysl' o muzyke* [Russian thought on music]. Leningrad: Governmental Musical Press, 1954.

Kroll, Wilhelm. *Procli Diadochi in Platonis Rem publicam commentarii.* 2 vols. Leipzig: B. G. Teubner, 1899–1901.

Kuberski, Philip. *The Persistence of Memory: Organism, Myth, Text.* Berkeley and Los Angeles: University of California Press, 1992. Kulcsár, Péter. *Mythographi Vaticani I et II.* Corpus Christianorum. Ser. Latina 91C. Turnhout: Brepols, 1987.

Kuzniar, Alice A. "Ears Looking at You: E. T. A. Hoffmann's *The Sandman* and David Lynch's *Blue Velvet.*" *South Atlantic Review* 54 (1989): 7–21.

La Motte Fouqué, Friedrich Heinrich Karle de. *Undine.* Trans. Paul Turner. London: John Calder, 1960.

Lacan, Jacques. *Écrits: A Selection.* Trans. Alan Sheridan. New York: W. W. Norton & Co., 1977.

Laertius, Diogenes. *Lives of Eminent Philosophers.* Ed. and trans. R. D. Hicks. Loeb Classical Library. Cambridge, Mass.: Harvard University Press, 1979.

Lakoff, George, and Mark Johnson. *Metaphors We Live By.* Chicago: University of Chicago Press, 1980.

LaMay, Thomasin. "Paola Massarenghi," and "Vittoria Aleotti/Raphaela Aleotta." In *Women Composers: Women Through the Ages,* vol. 1, ed. Martha F. Schleifer and Sylvia Glickman, 127–59. New York: G. K. Hall, 1995.

Lamberton, Robert. *Homer the Theologian: Neoplatonist Allegorical Reading and the Growth of the Epic Tradition.* Berkeley: University of California Press, 1986.

Lampedusa, Giuseppe di. "The Professor and the Siren." In *Two Stories and a Memory,* trans. Archibald Colquhoun, intro. E. M. Forster. London: Collins and Harvill Press, 1962.

Lanza, Joseph. *The Cocktail: The Influence of Spirits on the American Psyche.* New York: St. Martin's Press, 1995.

Lao, Meri. "Un feminile musicale possible." In *Les Symbolistes et Richard Wagner— Die Symbolisten und Richard Wagner,* ed. Wolfgang Storch and Josef Mackert, 29–31. Berlin: Edition Hentrich, 1991.

———. *Sirens: Symbols of Seduction.* Trans. John Oliphant of Rossie in collaboration with the author. Rochester, Vt.: Park Street Press, 1998.

Lawrence, Amy. *Echo and Narcissus: Women's Voices in Classical Hollywood Cinema.* Berkeley: University of California Press, 1991.

Lebaud, Philippe. *Le Bestiaire[:] Reproduction en fac-similé des miniatures du manuscrit du Bestiaire Ashmole 1511 de la Bodleian Library d'Oxford.* Texte integral traduit en français moderne par Marie France Dupuis et Sylvain Louis. N.p.: Philippe Lebaud Éditeur, 1988.

Leclercq-Marx, Jacqueline. *La Sirène dans la pensée et dans l'art de l'Antiquité et du Moyen Âge: Du mythe païen au symbol chrétien.* Bruxelles: Académie Royale de Belgique, 1997.

Lemmi, Charles W. *The Classical Deities in Bacon: A Study in Mythological Symbolism.* Baltimore: Johns Hopkins University Press, 1933.

Leonardi, Susan J., and Rebecca A. Pope. "Divas Do the Movies." In Leonardi and Pope, eds., *The Diva's Mouth: Body, Voice, Prima Donna Politics.* New Brunswick, N.J.: Rutgers University Press, 1996.

Leopold, Silke. "Von der Allgewalt vollsten Hingebungseifers: Weibs-Bilder in Wagners 'Ring.'" In *Richard Wagner, "Der Ring des Nibelungen": Ansichten des Mythos,* ed. Udo Bermbach and Dieter Borchmeyer, 59–74. Stuttgart: Metzler, 1995.

Leppert, Richard. Introduction to Theodor W. Adorno, *Essays on Music.* Selected, with introduction, commentary, and notes by Richard Leppert. Berkeley: University of California Press, 2002.

———. *The Sight of Sound: Music, Representation, and the History of the Body.* Berkeley: University of California Press, 1993.

Levitskii, A. A. "Obraz vody u Derzhavina i obraz poeta" [The image of water in Derzhavin's and the image of the poet"], *XVIII Bek* [18th century]. St. Petersburg: Nauka, 1996.

Lewis, Bernard. *The Emergence of Modern Turkey.* Oxford: Oxford University Press, 1968.

Lewis, Raphaela. *Everyday Life in Ottoman Turkey.* New York: G. P. Putnam's Sons, 1971.

Lewy, Heinrich. *Die semitischen Fremdwörter im Griechischen.* Berlin: R. Gaertners Verlagsbuchhandlung, 1895. Reprint. Hildesheim: G. Olms, 1970.

Lifar, Serge. *A History of the Russian Ballet from Its Origins to the Present Day.* Trans. Arnold Haskel. New York: Roy Publisher, 1954.

Linche, Richard. *The Fountaine of Ancient Fiction: Wherein Is Lively Depictured the Images and Statues of the Gods of the Ancients, with Their Proper and Perticular [sic] Expositions.* London: Adam Islip, 1599.

Lindlar, Heinrich. *Loreley-Report: Heinrich Heine und die Rheinliedromantik.* Cologne: Verlag Christoph Dohr, 1999.

Livanova, Tamara. *Russian Musical Culture of the Eighteenth Century.* Moscow: Gosudarstvennoe Muzikalnoe Izdatelstvo, 1952.

——— and Vladimir Protopopov. *Opernaya kritika v Rossii* [Opera criticism in Russian]. Vol. 1. Moscow: Music, 1966.

Lloyd-Jones, Hugh, and Peter Parsons. *Supplementum Hellenisticum.* Berlin: Walter de Gruyter, 1983.

Lobanov-Rostovsky, Sergei. "Taming the Basilisk." In *The Body in Parts: Fantasies of Corporeality in Early Modern Europe,* ed. David Hillman and Carla Mazzio, 195–217. New York: Routledge, 1997.

Locke, Ralph P. "What Are These Women Doing in Opera?" In *En Travesti: Women, Gender Subversion, Opera,* ed. Corinne E. Blackmer and Patricia Juliana Smith, 59–98. New York: Columbia University Press, 1995.

Loos, Anita. *Gentlemen Prefer Blondes: The Illuminating Diary of a Professional Lady.* Harmondsworth: Penguin Books, 1992.

Loos, Helmut. "Wolfgang Müller von Königswinter und die Musik." In *Musikalische Rheinromantik: Bericht der Jahrestagung 1985,* ed. Siegfried Kross, 113–24. Vol. 140, *Beiträge zur Rheinischen Musikgeschichte.* Kassel: Merseberger, 1989.

Lorandi, Marco. *Il mito di Ulisse nella pittura a fresco del Cinquecento italiano.* Milan: Jaca Book, 1995.

"Lorelei's Love Page." http://gladstone.uoregon.edu/7Ecek/@.html. Accessed June 12, 1998.

Lucie-Smith, Edward. *Sexuality in Western Art.* London: Thames and Hudson, 1991.

Lupanova, Irina Petrovna. *Russkaya narodnaya skazka v tvorchestve pisatelei pervoi poloviny XIX veka* [The Russian folk tale in the writing of authors of the first half of the nineteenth century]. Petrozavodsk: Gosudarstvennoe Izdatel'stvo, 1959.

Lutz, Tom. *Crying: The Natural and Cultural History of Tears.* New York: Norton, 1999.

Maal, Baaba. *Missing You (Mi Yeewnii).* Palm Pictures, 2001, Music CD.

MacGregor, Arthur. "Collectors and Collections of Rarities in the Sixteenth and Seventeenth Centuries." In *Tradescant's Rarities: Essays on the Foundation of the Ashmolean Museum 1683,* ed. Arthur MacGregor. Oxford: Clarendon Press, 1983.

Madonna. *Cherish.* Music video directed by Herb Ritts. Hollywood: Warner Brothers, 1989.

Magnus, Hugo. *Lactanti Placidi qui dicitur Narrationes fabularum Ovidianarum. In P. Ovidi Nasonis Metamorphoseon libri XV,* 625–721. Berlin: Weidmann, 1914.

Mallarmé, Stéphane. *The Poems: A Bilingual Edition.* Trans. Keith Bosley. Harmondsworth, U.K.: Penguin, 1977.

Manuel, Peter. "Modal Harmony in Andaluzian, Eastern European and Turkish Syncretic Musics." *Yearbook for Traditional Music* 21 (1989): 70–94.

"Mariah Carey Gets $49 Million in Deal to Leave Virgin Records." *Jet* 101 (February 11, 2002): 46.

Mariño Ferro, Xosé Ramón. "*Muerte, religion y simbolos en una comunidad quechua.*" Universidade de Santiago de Compestella, Spain, 1989.

Marino, Giambattista. *La Lira: Rime del Cavalier Marino . . . Parte Prima.*Venice: Presso Gio[vanni] Pietro Brigonci, 1667.

———. *Rime del Caualier Marino Parte Terza.* Venice: Presso Gio[vanni] Pietro Brigonci, 1667.

Marrese, Michelle Lamarche. *A Woman's Kingdom: Noblewomen and the Control of Property in Russia, 1700–1861.* Ithaca, N.Y.: Cornell University Press, 2002.

Martin, Rupert. "Immagini della virtù: The Paintings of the Camerino Farnese." *Art Bulletin* 38 (1956): 91–112.

Martinez, Rosalia. "Musique et démons: Carnaval chez les Tarabuco (Bolivie)." *Journal de la Société de des Américanistes* 76 (1990): 155–76.

Marvell, Andrew. *The Poems and Letters of Andrew Marvell.* Ed. H. M. Margoliouth. 2 vols. Oxford: Clarendon Press, 1952.

Masson, Georgina. *Courtesans of the Italian Renaissance.* New York: St. Martin's Press, 1975.

Maxfield, James F. *The Fatal Woman: Sources of Male Anxiety in American Film Noir, 1941–1991.* London: Associated University Press, 1996.

Mazzeo, J. A. "A Note on the 'Sirens' of *Purgatorio* 31.45." *Studies in Philology* 55 (1958): 457–63.

Mazzotta, Giuseppe. "The Dream of the Siren." In *Dante's Vision and the Circle of Knowledge,* 135–53. Princeton, N.J.: Princeton University Press, 1993.

McCarren, Felicia M. "The Female Form: Gautier, Mallarmé and Celine Writing Dance." Ph.D. diss., Stanford University, 1992.

McClary, Susan. *Feminine Endings.* Minneapolis: University of Minnesota Press, 1991.

McCullough, Florence. *Medieval Latin and French Bestiaries.* University of North Carolina Studies in the Romance Languages and Literatures, no. 33. Chapel Hill: University of North Carolina Press, 1960.

———. "The Metamorphoses of the Asp in Latin and French Bestiaries." *Studies in Philology* 56 (1959): 7–13.

"Mediawatch." *Source* 103 (September 2000): 102.

Menestrier, Claude-François. *L'Art des Emblemes.* Paris: Chez R. J. B. De la Caille, 1684.

Mercado, Claudio. "Detrás del sonido, el mundo." *Takiwasi* (Tarapoto, Peru) 4 (año 2, 1996): 46–61.

Merkelbach, R., and M. L. West, eds. *Fragmenta Hesiodea.* Oxford: Clarendon Press, 1967.

Merriam, Alan. *Ethnomusicology of the Flathead Indians.* Chicago: Aldine Publishing Co., 1967.

Meyer-Kalkus, Reinhart. "Das Korn der Stimme—Sprachtheoretische Voraussetzungen der Kritik Roland Barthes am Liedsänger Dietrich Fischer-Diskau." *Germanisch-Romanische Monatsschrift,* n.s., 42 (1992): 326–40.

Meyer-Kalkus, Reinhart. "Richard Wagners Theorie der Wort-Tonsprache in 'Oper und Drama' und 'Der Ring des Nibelungen.'" *Athenäum: Jahrbuch für Romantik* 6 (1996): 153–95.

"Michael Jordan and Mariah Carey Voted Sexiest Celebrity Legs." *Jet* 95 (February 22, 1999): 33.

Michel, André. *La Sirène dans l'élemént musical.* N.p.: Éditions de la Diaspora Française, 1970.

Migne, J. P. *Patrologia Graeca.* 162 vols. Paris: Les Ateliers Catholiques, 1857–1866.

———. *Patrologia Latina.* 221 vols. Paris: Les Ateliers Catholiques, 1844–1864.

Millas, Hercules. "Non-Muslim Minorities in the Historiography of Republican Turkey: The Greek Case." In *The Ottomans and the Balkans: A Discussion of Historiography,* ed. Fikret Adanır and Suraiya Faroqhi, 155–191. Leiden: Brill, 2002.

Milton, John. *Complete Poems and Major Prose.* Ed. Merritt Y. Hughes. New York: Odyssey Press, 1957.

Monson, Craig A. *Disembodied Voices: Music and Culture in an Early Modern Italian Convent.* Berkeley: University of California Press, 1995.

Montagu, Jennifer. "Exhortatio ad Virtutem: A Series of Paintings in the Barberini Palace." *Journal of the Warburg and Courtauld Institutes* 34 (1971): 366–72.

Moon, Michael. "A Small Boy and Others: Sexual Disorientation in Henry James, Kenneth Anger, and David Lynch." In *A Small Boy and Others: Imitation and*

Initiation in American Culture from Henry James to Andy Warhol. Durham, N.C.: Duke University Press, 1998.

Moore, Thomas. *Moore's Irish Melodies.* Illustrated by D. Maclise, R.A. New ed. London: Longman, Brown, Green, Longman, and Roberts, 1866.

Moretti, Luigi. *Inscriptiones Graecae urbis Romae.* 4 vols. Rome: Istituto italiano per la storia antica, 1968–1990.

Moretti, Walter. "Le 'Contrarie tempre' ovvero l'anima musicale d'Armida." *Studi e problemi di critica testuale* 1 (1970): 106–11.

Morgan, Elaine. *The Descent of Woman.* New York: Stein and Day, 1972.

Morvan, Francoise. *La douce vie des fees des eaux.* N.p.: Actes Sud, 1999.

Moss, Ann. *Poetry and Fable: Studies on Mythological Narrative in Sixteenth-Century France.* Cambridge: Cambridge University Press, 1984.

Mulvey, Laura. *Visual and Other Pleasures.* Bloomington: Indiana University Press, 1989.

Novikova, N. "Vvedenye" [Introduction]. In *Russkie skazki v rannikh zapisyah i publikatsiyakh (XVI–XVIII veka)* [Russian tale in early collections and publications], ed. E. Pomerantzeva. Leningrad: Nauka, 1971.

Nauck, August. *Tragicorum Graecorum fragmenta.* Leipzig: B. G. Teubner, 1889.

Nickson, Chris. *Mariah Carey Revisited: The Unauthorized Biography.* New York: St. Martin's Griffin, 1998.

Nietzsche, Friedrich. *The Gay Science.* Trans. Walter Kaufmann. New York: Random House, 1974.

Norment, Lynn. "Mariah Carey." *Ebony* 49 (April 1994): 58.

Nosov, A. *The Chronicle of Russian Theater.* St. Petersburg: N.p., 1882.

Nuckolls, Janis. *Sounds Like Life: Sound-Symbolic Grammar, Performance, and Cognition in Pastaza Quechua.* New York: Oxford University Press, 1996.

Numerical Catalogue of Columbia Foreign Records. New York, 1930.

O'Connell, John M. "Alaturka Revisited: Style as History in Turkish Vocal Performance." Ph.D. diss., University of California Los Angeles, 1996.

———. "Fine Art, Fine Music: Controlling Turkish Taste at the Fine Arts Academy." *Yearbook for Traditional Music* 33 (2000): 117–42.

———. "From Empire to Republic: Vocal Style in Twentieth-Century Turkey." In *Garland Encyclopedia of World Music,* ed. Virginia Danielson, Scott Marcus, and Dwight Reynolds, 6:781–87. New York: Garland Publishers, 2002.

———. "Song Cycle: The Life and Death of the Turkish Gazel: Review Essay." *Ethnomusicology* 47, no. 3 (2003): 399–414.

Oechsle, Siegfried. "Nationalidee und große Symphonie: Mit einem Exkurs zum 'Ton.'" In *Deutsche Meister—böse Geister? Nationale Selbstfindung in der Musik,* ed. Hermann Danuser and Herfried Münkler, 166–84. Schliengen: Edition Argus, 2001.

Offermanns, Dieter. *Der Physiologus nach den Handschriften G und M.* Beiträge zur klassischen Philologie 22. Meisenheim am Glan: Hain, 1966.

Okur, Hâfız Yaşar. "1929 Yılında Deniz Kızı Eftalya Dolmabahçe Sarayında." *Yirminci Asır* (December 29, 1955): n.p.

Orchard, Andy. *Pride and Prodigies: Studies in the Monsters of the "Beowulf" Manuscript*. Cambridge: D. S. Brewer, 1995.

Ortner, Sherry B. "Is Female to Male as Nature Is to Culture?" In *Women, Culture and Society*, ed. Michelle Zimbalist Rosaldo and Louise Lamphere, 67–88. Stanford: Stanford University Press, 1974.

Ovid. *The Art of Love, and Other Poems*. Trans. J. H. Morley. London: William Heinemann; Cambridge, Mass.: Harvard University Press, 1969.

——. *De arte amandi, or The Art of Love*. Amsterdam: Nicholas Janz Vissher, n.d.

——. *Metamorphoses*. Trans. George Chapman. London: N.p., 1632.

Özalp, Nazimi. *Türk Musikisi Tarihi*. 2 vols. Ankara: Müzik Dairesi Başkanlığı, 1986.

Öztuna, Yılmaz. *Büyük Türk Mûsikisi Ansiklopedesi*. 2 vols. Ankara: Kültür Bakanlığı, 1990.

Öztürkmen, Arzu. *Türkiye'de Folklor ve Milliyetçilik*. Istanbul: İletişim Yayınları, 1998.

Paçacı, Gönul, ed. *Cumhuriyet'in Sesleri*. Istanbul: Tarih Vakfı, "Bilanço '98" Yayın Dizisi, 1999.

Page, D. L. *Poetae Melici Graeci*. Oxford: Clarendon Press, 1962.

Paglia, Camille. *Sexual Personae: Art and Decadence from Nefertiti to Emily Dickinson*. London: Penguin, 1992.

Panofsky, Erwin. *Hercules am Scheidewege und andere antike bildstoffe in der neueren Kunst*. Leipzig and Berlin: B. G. Teubner, 1930.

Parabosco, Girolamo. *Lettere Amorose. Libro Primo*. Milan: Appresso di Giouann'Antonio de gli Antonij, 1558.

Parke, H. W., and D. E. W. Wormell. *The Delphic Oracle*. 2 vols. Oxford: Basil Blackwell, 1956.

Pasquali, Gorgio. *Procli Diadochi in Platonis Cratylum commentaria*. Leipzig: B. G. Teubner, 1908.

Pavel, Thomas G. "In Praise of the Ear (Gloss's Glosses)." In *The Female Body in Western Culture: Contemporary Perspectives*, ed. Susan Rubin Suleiman. Cambridge, Mass.: Harvard University Press, 1986.

Paxon, Barbara. "Mammy Water: New World Origins?" *Baessler-Archiv*, Neue Folge, 31 (1983): 407–46.

Payne, Ann. *Medieval Beasts*. London: British Library, 1990.

Paz, Octavio. *The Siren and the Seashell*. Trans. Lisander Kemp. Austin: University of Texas Press, 1976.

Peacham, Henry. *Minerva Britanna or a Garden of Heroical Deuises*. London: Wa. Dight, [1612].

Peek, Werner. *Griechische Grabedichte, griechisch und deutsch*. Schriften und Quellen der alten Welt 7. Berlin: Akademie-Verlag, 1960.

——. *Griechische Vers-Inschriften I: Grab-Epigramme*. Berlin: Akademie-Verlag, 1954.

Pegg, Carole. *Mongolian Music, Dance, & Oral Narrative*. Seattle: University of Washington Press, 2001.

Pekelis, Mikhail Samoilovich. *Dargomyzhskii i narodnaya pesnya* [Dargomyzhsky and folk song]. Moscow: Gosudarstvennoe Izdatel'stvo, 1951.

Pendle, Karin, ed. *Women and Music: A History.* Bloomington: Indiana University Press, 1991.

Pener, Degan. "Butterflies Aren't Free." *Entertainment Weekly* (September 26, 1997): 15.

Pennanen, Risto P. "The Nationalization of Ottoman Popular Music in Greece." *Ethnomusicology* 48, no. 1 (2004): 1–25.

———. *Westernisation and Modernisation in Greek Popular Music.* Tampere, Finland: Acta Universitatis Tamperensis, 1999.

Pesselnick, Jill. "Twain Breaks Records." *Billboard* (April 22, 2000): 18.

Peterson, Richard A. *Creating Country Music: Fabricating Authenticity.* Chicago: University of Chicago Press, 1997.

Petrarch. *Petrarch's Lyric Poems: The Rime Sparse and Other Lyrics.* Trans. and ed. Robert M. Durling. Cambridge, Mass.: Harvard University Press, 1976.

Petropoulos, Elias. *Songs of the Greek Underworld: The Rebetika Tradition.* Trans. Ed Emery. London: Saqi Books, 2000.

Pfeil, Fred. "Home Fires Burning: Family Noir in Blue Velvet and Terminator 2." In *Shades of Noir,* ed. Joan Copjec, 227–59. New York: Verso, 1993.

Pfitzner, Hans. *Meine Beziehungen zu Max Bruch.* Munich: Albert Langen and Georg Müller, 1938.

Physiologus. *Physiologus Latinus.* Ed. Francis J. Carmody. Paris: Librarie F. Droz, 1939.

Picinelli, Filippo. *Mondo simbolico.* Milan: Per lo Stampatore Archiepiscopale, 1653.

Pierre de Beauvais. *Bestiare.* Ed. Guy R. Mermier. Paris: A. G. Nizet, 1977.

Pink. *Missundaztood.* Arista, 2001.

Plato. [πόλιτεια] / *Politeia.* Ed. Dietrich Kurz. Greek text established by Emile Chambry. Trans. Friedrich Schleiermacher. Darmstadt: Wissenschaftliche Buchgesellschaft, 1990.

Platt, Tristan. "The Andean Soldiers of Christ: Confraternity Organization, the Mass of the Sun and Regenerative Warfare in Rural Potosí (18th–20th Centuries)." *Journal de la Société des Américanistes* 73 (1987): 139–92.

Plemmenos, John. " 'Micro-music' of the Ottoman Empire: The Case of the Phenariot Greeks of Istanbul." Ph.D. diss., University of Cambridge, 2001.

Pliny [Plinius Secundus]. *The Historie of the World Called the Natural Historie.* Trans. Philemon Holland. London: Adam Islip, 1601.

Plutarch. *The Philosophie Commonlie Called the Morals.* Trans. Philemon Holland. London: N.p., 1603.

———. *The Philosophie Commonlie Called the Morals.* Trans. F. C. Babbitt. In *Moralia.* Vol. 1. Loeb Classical Library. Cambridge, Mass.: Harvard University Press, 1949.

Poché, Christian. *Turquie: Archives de la musique turque.* Vol. 1. Notes in French,

English, and German by Christian Poché. Paris: Ocora C 560081, 1995a. Sound Recording. www.eyeneer.com/labels/Ocora.

Poché, Christian. *Turquie: Archives de la musique turque*. Vol. 2. Notes in French, English, and German by Christian Poché. Paris: Ocora C 560082, 1995b. Sound Recording. www.eyeneer.com/labels/Ocora.

Pollard, John R. T. "Muses and Sirens." *The Classical Review* n.s., 2, no. 12 (1952): 60–63.

———. *Seers, Shrines and Sirens: The Greek Religious Revolution in the Sixth Century B.C.* Unwin University Books 21. London: Allen and Unwin, 1965.

Pomerantseva, E., ed. *Russkie skazki v rannikh zapisyakh i publikatsiyakh (XVI–XVIII veka)*. Leningrad: Nauka, 1971.

Pona, Francesco. *La Lucerna*. Ed. Giorgio Fulco. Rome: Salerno Editrice, 1973.

Ponsich, Michel. *Les Lampes romaines en terre cuite de la Maurétanie Tingitane*. Publications du Service des Antiquités du Maroc 15. Rabat: N.p., 1961.

Popescu-Judetz, Eugenia, and Adriana Ababı Sırlı. *Sources of 18th Century Music: Panayiotes Chalathzoglou and Kyrillos Marmarinos' Comparative Treatises on Secular Music*. Istanbul: Pan Yayıncılık, 2000.

Potter, Caroline. "Nadia and Lili Boulanger: Sister Composers." *The Musical Quarterly* 83 (1999): 526–56.

Propp, Vladimir Iakovlevich. *Morphology of the Folktale*. Austin: University of Texas Press, 2003.

———. *Russkaya Skazka* [Russian fairy tale]. Leningrad: Leningrad University Press, 1984.

Prusak, Bernard D. "Woman: Seductive Siren and Source of Sin? Pseudo-epigraphal Myth and Christian Origins." In *Religion and Sexism: Images of Women in the Jewish and Christian Traditions*, ed. Rosemary Radford Ruether. New York: Simon and Schuster, 1974.

Pushkin, Alexander. "Rusalka." In *Collected Works*, vol. 1, 203–205. Moscow: Hudozhestvennaya Literatura, 1985.

Quataert, Donald. *The Ottoman Empire, 1700–1922.* Cambridge: Cambridge University Press, 2000.

Queen Elizabeth. *Queen Elizabeth's Englishings*. Ed. Caroline Pemberton. London: Early English Text Society, 1899.

Rachewiltz, Siegfried de. *De Sirenibus: An Inquiry into Sirens from Homer to Shakespeare*. Harvard Dissertations in Comparative Literature. New York: Garland, 1987.

Racy, Jihad A. "Creativity and Ambience: An Ecstatic Feedback Model in Arab Music." *Asian Music* 33, no. 3 (1991): 7–29.

Radice, Betty. *Who's Who in the Ancient World*. London: Penguin, 1973.

Radt, Stefan, ed. *Tragicorum Graecorum fragmenta*. Vol. 4, *Sophocles*. Göttingen: Vandenhoeck & Ruprecht, 1977.

Rahner, Hugo. *Greek Myths and Christian Mystery*. London: Burns & Oates, 1963.

——. *Griechische Mythen in christlicher Deutung.* 3d ed. Zurich: Rhein-Verlag, 1957.

Randall, Lilian M. C. *Medieval and Renaissance Manuscripts in the Walters Art Gallery.* Vol. 3, part 2. Baltimore: Johns Hopkins University Press, 1997.

Rasim, Ahmet. *Fuş-i Atik.* Istanbul: İstanbul Matbaası, 1958.

Reade, Winwoode. *Savage Africa.* London: Smith, Elder and Co., 1863.

Real-Encyclopädie der classischen Altertumswissenschaft. 83 vols. Stuttgart: J. B. Metzler; Munich: Alfred Druckenmüller, 1894–1978.

Redhouse, Sir James. *Redhouse Türkçe/Osmanıca-İngilizce Sözlük: Redhouse Turkish/Ottoman-English Dictionary.* Istanbul: Redhouse Yayınevi, 1999.

Reed, Phyllis Ann. "The Rusalka Theme in Russian Literature." Ph.D. diss., University of California at Berkeley, 1973.

Regali, Mario. *Macrobio: Commento al "Somnium Scipionis."* 2 vols. Biblioteca di studi antichi 38, 58. Pisa: Giardini, 1983, 1990.

Reich, Nancy B. *Clara Schumann, the Artist and the Woman.* Ithaca, N.Y.: Cornell University Press, 1985.

Reid, Jane Davidson. *The Oxford Guide to Classical Mythology in the Arts, 1300–1990s.* 2 vols. New York: Oxford University Press, 1993.

Renfroe, Paula T. "The World According to Kim." *Source* 101 (February 1998): 122.

Retsepter, Vladimir, and Mihail Shemyakin. *The Return of Pushkin's Rusalka.* St. Petersburg: Pushkin State Theater Center, 1998.

Reynolds, Simon, and Joy Press. *The Sex Revolts: Gender, Rebellion, and Rock 'n' Roll.* Cambridge, Mass.: Harvard University Press, 1995.

"Rhythm and Blues Foundation Holds 11th Awards Gala in New York." *Jet* 89 (October 16, 2000): 36.

"RIAA Certifications for March." *Billboard* (April 20, 2002): 22.

Ridenour, Robert C. *Nationalism, Modernism, and Personal Rivalry in Nineteenth-Century Russian Music.* Ann Arbor, Mich.: UMI Research Press, 1977.

Rilke, Rainer Maria. *New Poems. The German Text.* Trans., intro., and notes by J. B. Leishman. New York: New Directions, 1964.

Rimbaud, Arthur. *Complete Works, Selected Letters.* Trans. and ed. Wallace Fowlie. Chicago: University of Chicago Press, 1966.

Ripa, Cesare. *Iconologia.* Siena: Appresso gli Heredi di Matteo Florimi, 1613.

Ritvo, Harriet. *The Platypus and the Mermaid and Other Figures of the Classifying Imagination.* Cambridge, Mass.: Harvard University Press, 1997.

Roberts, Robin. "Independence Day: Feminist Country Music Videos." *Popular Music and Society* 20 (1996): 140.

Robertson, Jennifer Ellen. *Takarazuka: Sexual Politics and Popular Culture in Modern Japan.* Berkeley: University of California Press, 1998.

Róheim, Géza. "Aphrodite or the Woman with a Penis." *Psychoanalytic Quarterly* 14 (1945): 350–90.

——. *The Gates of the Dream.* New York: International Universities Press, 1952.

———. *Psychoanalysis and Anthropology: Culture, Personality and the Unconscious.* New York: International Universities Press, 1950.

———. "The Song of the Sirens." *Psychiatric Quarterly* 22 (1948): 18–44.

Romano, Vincenzo, ed. *Genealogie deorum gentilium libri by Giovanni Boccaccio.* 2 vols. Scrittori d'Italia 200–201. Bari: Laterza, 1951.

Rosolato, Guy. "La Voix." In *Essais sur le symbolique.* Paris: Éditions Gallimard, 1969.

Rossetti, Dante Gabriel. *Collected Writings.* Selected and ed. Jan Marsh. London: J. M. Dent, 1999.

Rotroff, Susan L. *Hellenistic Painted Pottery: Athenian and Imported Moldmade Bowls.* The Athenian Agora 22. Princeton, N.J.: American School of Classical Studies at Athens, 1982.

Rouget, Gilbert. *Music and Trance: A Theory of the Relations between Music and Possession.* Chicago: University of Chicago Press, 1985.

Rousseau, Jean Jacques. *The Confessions.* London: William Glaisher, 1883.

Rush, Dana. "Eternal Potential: Chromolithographs in Vodunland." *African Arts* 32, no. 4 (Winter 1999): 60–75, 94–96.

Rutherford, Ian. *Pindar's Paeans: A Reading of the Fragments with a Survey of the Genre.* Oxford: Oxford University Press, 2001.

Sachs, Emanie Louise. *The Terrible Siren: Victoria Woodhull (1838–1927).* New York: Harper and Brother, 1928.

Sadie, Stanley, ed. *The New Grove Dictionary of Music and Musicians.* 2d ed. London: Macmillan, 2001.

Sadullah, Naci. "Çingene Gözü ile Biz ve Onlar." *Aydabir* 1 (1936):10–13, 78–79.

Sağman, Ali R. *Meşur Hafız Sami Merhum.* Istanbul: Ahmet Sait Matbaası, 1947.

Said, Edward. *Orientalism.* New York: Vintage Books, 1979.

Sait, Mekki. "Münir Nurettinin Yuvasında." *Yedigün* 30 (1933): 10–12.

Salecl, Renata. "The Sirens and Feminine Jouissance." *differences: A Journal of Feminist Cultural Studies* 9 (1997): 14–28.

Samuels, Allison. "A Whole Lotta Lil' Kim." *Newsweek* 135 (June 26, 2000): 56.

Sánchez, Wálter C. "Circuitos Musicales (Música Autoctona del Norte de Potosí)." Centro Pedagogico y Cultural de Portales/Centro de Documentacion de Música Boliviana. *Boletin,* no. 11 (Marzo 1989): 1–10.

———. "El Proceso de Creación Musical (Música Autoctona del Norte de Potosí)." Centro Pedagogico y Cultural de Portales/Centro de Documentacion de Música Boliviana. *Boletin,* no. 7 (Octubre 1988): 1–18.

Sanders, Alvelyn J. "From Video Hoes to Deathbed Divas." *Essence* 27 (February 1997): 160.

Sandys, George. *Ovid's Metamorphosis: Englished, Mythologized, and Represented in Figures.* Ed. Karl K. Hulley and Stanley T. Vandersall. Lincoln: University of Nebraska Press, 1970.

Santore, Cathy. "Julia Lombardo, 'Somtuosa Meretrize': A Portrait by Property." *Renaissance Quarterly* 41 (1988): 44–83.

———. "The Tools of Venus." *Renaissance Studies* 11 (1997): 179–207.

Saunders, Gill. *A Book of Sea Creatures.* London: Victoria and Albert Museum, 1992.

Savchenko, S. V. *Russkaya narodnaya skazka* [Russian folk tale]. Kiev: N.p., 1914. Reprint. Cleveland: Bell & Howell, 1967.

Saygun, Adnan. *Atatürk ve Musıki: O'nunla Birlikte, O'ndan Sonra.* Ankara: Ajans-Türk Matbaacılık Sanayii, 1965.

Saz, Leyla. *Şair Leyla (Saz) Hanım Anılar: 19. Yüzyılda Saray Haremi.* Istanbul: Cumhuriyet Kitapları, 2000.

———. *Solmuş Çiçekler.* Ed. Nezi Neyzi. Istanbul: Pera Yayınları, 1996.

Sbordone, Francesco. *Physiologus.* Milan: Società "Dante Alighieri-Albrighi, Segati, etc.," 1936. Reprint. Hildesheim: G. Olms, 1991.

Scarborough, Elizabeth. *Song of Sorcery.* New York: Bantam Books, 1982.

Scève, Maurice. *The "Délie" of Maurice Scève.* Ed. I. D. McFarlane. Cambridge: Cambridge University Press, 1966.

Schadewaldt, Wolfgang. *Von Homers Welt und Werk.* 4th ed. Stuttgart: K. F. Koehler Verlag, 1965.

Scheer, Eduard. *Alexandra Lycophronis.* 2 vols. Berlin: Weidmann, 1881, 1908.

Schmidt, Julia. "Jetzt lockt die Sirene in den sicheren Hafen der Ehe." *Frankfurter Allgemeine Zeitung,* April 28, 1998, 45.

Schueller, Herbert. *The Idea of Music: An Introduction to Musical Aesthetics in Antiquity and the Middle Ages.* Kalamazoo: Medieval Institute Publications, Western Michigan University, 1988.

Schuman, Amy. "Gender and Genre." In *Feminist Theory and the Study of Folklore,* ed. Susan Tower Hollis, Linda Pershing, and M. Jane Young. Urbana: University of Illinois Press, 1993.

Schumann, Robert. *Lieder.* Vol. 1. Ed. Max Friedlaender. Frankfurt: C. F. Peters, n.d.

Schwartz, David. *Listening Subjects: Music, Psychoanalysis, Culture.* Durham, N.C.: Duke University Press, 1997.

Schwartz, Martin. *Greek-Oriental Rebetica: Songs and Dances in the Asia Minor Style, 1911–1937.* Notes in English by Martin Schwartz. El Cerrito, Calif.: Arhoolie Folklyric, CD 7005, 1991. Sound Recording. www.arhoolie.com.

Seay, Albert. *Johannis Tinctoris opera theoretica.* 2 vols. Corpus Scriptorum de Musica 22. American Institute of Musicology, 1975.

Seçkin, Nalân. *Musalladan Şöhrete Safiye Ayla.* Istanbul: Bilgi Yayınevi, 1998.

Segal, Charles. *Singers, Heroes, and Gods in the Odyssey.* Ithaca, N.Y.: Cornell University Press, 1994.

Sema, Sadri. *Eski İstanbul'dan Hatıralar.* Istanbul: İletişim Yayınları, 1991.

Semibratova, Irina. "Afterword." In Orest Mikhailovich Somov, *Oboroten': Russkie fantasmagorii* [Oboroten: Russian phantasmagorias]. Ed. Irina Semibratova. Moscow: Book Tent, 1994, 327–35.

Serman, I. S., ed. *Poets of the Eighteenth Century.* Leningrad: Soviet Writer, 1958.

Seroussi, Edwin. *Mizimrat Qedem: The Life and Music of R. Isaac Algazi from Turkey.* Jerusalem: Institute for Jewish Music, 1989.

Serov, Alexander N. *Izbrannye stat'i* [Selected articles]. Ed. G. N. Khubova. Moscow: Gosudarstvennoe Muzykal'noe Izdatel'stvo, 1957.

———. *Rusalka.* Moscow: Gosudarstvennoe Muzykal'noe Izdatel'stvo, 1953.

Sevengil, Refik Ahmet. *İstanbul Nasıl Eğleniyordu.* Istanbul: İletişim Yayınları, 1985.

———. *Türk Tiyatrosu Tarihi IV: Saray Tiyatrosu.* Milli Eğitim Basımevi, 1962.

"Sexy Dress and Sassy Rap Make Lil' Kim a Big Star." *Jet* 98 (August 21, 2000): 58.

Seznec, Jean. *The Survival of the Pagan Gods: The Mythological Tradition and Its Place in Renaissance Humanism and Art.* Trans. Barbara F. Sessions. New York: Pantheon Books, 1953. Reprint. Princeton, N.J.: Princeton University Press, 1981.

Shama, Simon. *Landscape & Memory.* London: HarperCollins, 1995.

Shand, Angela. "The Tsifte-teli Sermon: Identity, Theology and Gender in Rebetika." In *The Passion of Music and Dance: Body, Gender and Sexuality.* ed. William Washabaugh, 127–32. Oxford: Berg, 1998.

Sharpe, Kevin. *Criticism and Compliment.* Cambridge: Cambridge University Press, 1987.

Shaw, Stanford. *History of the Ottoman Empire and Modern Turkey.* 2 vols. Cambridge: Cambridge University Press, 1976–1977.

Shelton, Marla L. "Can't Touch This! Representations of the African American Female Body in Urban Rap Videos." *Popular Music and Society* 21 (1997): 107.

Shepherd, John. *Music as Social Text.* Cambridge: Polity Press, 1991.

Sidney, Sir Philip. *The Defence of Poesy.* In *Sir Philip Sidney,* ed. Katherine Duncan-Jones. Oxford: Oxford University Press, 1989.

Sietz, Reinhold. "Die musikalische Gestaltung der Loreleysage bei Max Bruch, Felix Mendelssohn und Ferdinand Hiller." In *Max Bruch-Studien,* ed. Dietrich Kämper, 14–45. Vol. 87, *Beiträge zur rheinischen Musikgeschichte.* Cologne: Arno Volk Verlag, 1970.

Signell, Karl. *Makam: Modal Practice in Turkish Art Music.* Seattle: Asian Music Publications, 1977.

Signell, Karl, and Richard Spottswood, eds. *Masters of Turkish Music.* Notes in English by Karl Signell and Richard Spottswood. UMBC Center for Turkish Music. Cambridge, Mass.: Rounder CD 1051, 1990. Sound Recording. www.rounder.com.

———. *Masters of Turkish Music.* Vol. 2. Notes in English by Münir Nurettin Beken. UMBC Center for Turkish Music. Cambridge, Mass.: Rounder CD 1111, 1996. Sound Recording. www.rounder.com.

Silay, Kemal. *Nedim and the Poetics of the Ottoman Court: Medieval Inheritance and the Need for Change.* Turkish Studies Series No. 13. Bloomington: Indiana University, 1994.

Simeoni, Gabriello. *La Vita e Metamorfoseo d'Ovidio.* Lyons: Jean de Tournes, 1559.

Simon, Joan. *Education and Society in Tudor England.* Cambridge: Cambridge University Press, 1966.

Smart, Mary Ann. "The Silencing of Lucia." *Cambridge Opera Journal* 4, no. 2 (1991): 119–41.

Smith, Marian Elizabeth. *Ballet and Opera in the Age of Giselle.* Princeton, N.J.: Princeton University Press, 2000.

Solomon, Thomas. "Mountains of Song: Musical Constructions of Ecology, Place, and Identity in the Bolivian Andes." Ph.D. diss., University of Texas at Austin, 1997.

Somov, Orest Mikhailovich. "Rusalka." In *Oboroten': Russkie fantasmagorii* [Oboroten: Russian phantasmagorias], 24–30. Ed. Irina Semibratova. Moscow: Book Tent, 1994.

Sontag, Susan. "The Pornographic Imagination." In *Styles of Radical Will.* New York: Farrar, Straus, and Giroux, 1969.

Spek, Miranda van der. *The Devil's Horn: A Documentary about Brass Bands in the Andes of Bolivia.* 1994. Video recording.

Spenser, Edmund. *The Faerie Queene.* New Haven, Conn.: Yale University Press, 1981.

Spitzer, Leo. *Classical and Christian Ideas of World Harmony: Prolegomena to an Interpretation of the Word "Stimmung."* Ed. Anna Granville Hatcher. Baltimore: Johns Hopkins University Press, 1963.

Spottswood, Richard. *Ethnic Music on Records: A Discography of Ethnic Recordings Produced in the U.S. 1893–1942.* Vol. 5. Urbana: University of Illinois Press, 1990.

———. *Roza Eskenazi: Rembétissa.* Notes in English by Richard Spottswood. Cambridge, Mass.: Rounder Records, Rounder CD 1080, 1996. Sound Recording. www.rounder.com.

Stallbaum, Gottfried. *Eustathii archiepiscopi Thessalonicensis commentarii ad Homeri Odysseam.* 2 vols. in 1. Leipzig: J. A. G. Weigel, 1825–26. Reprint. Hildesheim: G. Olms, 1970.

Stanford, W. B. *The Ulysses Theme: A Study in the Adaptability of a Traditional Hero.* Oxford: Basil Blackwell, 1954.

Starnes, DeWitt Talmage, and Ernest William Talbert. *Classical Myth and Legend in Renaissance Dictionaries.* Chapel Hill: University of North Carolina Press, 1955. Reprint. Westport, Conn.: Greenwood Press, 1973.

Steadman, John M. *Nature into Myth: Medieval and Renaissance Moral Symbols.* Pittsburgh: Duquesne University Press, 1979.

Stewart, Lawrence D. "Words upon Music." Liner notes for *Ella Fitzgerald Sings the George and Ira Gershwin Song Books.* Verve, 1998: 19–65.

Stobart, Henry. "Bodies of Sound and Landscapes of Music: A View from the Bolivian Andes." In *Musical Healing in Cultural Contexts,* ed. P. Gouk, 26–45. Aldershot: Ashgate, 2000.

———. "Flourishing Horns and Enchanted Tubers: Music and Potatoes in High-land Bolivia." *British Journal of Ethnomusicology* 3 (1994): 35–48.

———. "Interlocking Realms: Knowing Music and Musical Knowing in the Bolivian Andes." In *Knowledge and Learning in the Andes: Ethnographic Perspectives,* ed. H. Stobart and R. Howard. Liverpool: University of Liverpool Press, 2002.

———. "The Llama's Flute: Musical Misunderstandings in the Andes." *Early Music* 14, no. 3 (August 1996): 470–82.

———. "Lo recto y lo torcido: La música andina y la espiral de la descendencia." In *Gente de carne y hueso: las tramas de parentesco en los andes,* ed. D. Arnold, 581–604. La Paz: ILCA/CIASE, 1998.

———. "Mediation and Transformation: Towards an Andean Musical Cosmology." M.Phil. diss., University of Cambridge, 1990.

———. *Music and the Poetics of Production in the Bolivian Andes.* Aldershot: Ashgate, in press.

Strathern, Marilyn. "Out of Context: The Persuasive Fictions of Anthropology." *Current Anthropology* 28, no. 3 (1987): 251–81.

Strauss, Johann. "Ottoman Rule Experienced and Remembered: Remarks on Some Local Greek Chronicles of the Tourkokratia." In *The Ottomans and the Balkans: A Discussion of Historiography,* ed. Fikret Adanır and Suraiya Faroqhi, 193–221. Leiden: Brill, 2002.

Strong, Roy. *Art and Power: Renaissance Festivals 1450–1650.* Woodbridge, Suffolk: Boydell Press, 1973.

Sugarman, Jane C. *Engendering Song: Singing and Subjectivity at Prespa Albanian Weddings.* Chicago: University of Chicago Press, 1997.

Sullivan, Robert. "Diva Slam." *Vogue* (April 2002): 318.

Swan, John. *Speculum Mundi or a Glasse Representing the Face of the World.* Cambridge: T. Buck and R. Daniel, 1635.

Sweet, Henry, and T. F. Hoad. *A Second Anglo-Saxon Reader: Archaic and Dialectal.* Oxford: Clarendon Press, 1978.

Sytova, Alla. *The Lubok: Russian Folk Pictures, 17th to 19th Century.* Trans. Alex Miller. Leningrad: Aurora Art Publishers, 1984.

Tannenbaum, Rob. "Building the Perfect Diva." *Rolling Stone* 585 (August 23, 1990): 33.

Tarrant, Richard J. "The Narrationes of 'Lactantius' and the Transmission of Ovid's Metamorphoses." In *Formative Stages of Classical Traditions: Latin Texts from Antiquity to the Renaissance,* ed. Oronzo Pecere and Michael D. Reeve, 83–115. Biblioteca del "Centro per il collegamento degli studi medievali e umanistici in Umbria" 15. Spoleto: Centro italiano di studi sull'alto medioevo, 1995.

Taruskin, Richard. "Chernomor to Kashchei: Harmonic Sorcery; or Stravinsky's 'Angle.'" *Journal of American Musicological Society* 38, no. 1 (1985): 72–143.

———. *Defining Russia Musically: Historical and Hermeneutical Essays.* Princeton, N.J.: Princeton University Press, 1997.

Tasso, Torquato. *Opere.* Ed. Bruno Maier. Milan: Rizzoli, 1963.

——. *Le Rime.* Ed. Bruno Basile. Rome: Salerno Editrice, 1994.

Taylor, Charles. *Sources of the Self: The Making of the Modern Identity.* Cambridge, Mass.: Harvard University Press, 1989.

Tel, Mesud C. *Tanburî Cemil'in Hayatı.* Ankara: Sakarya Basımevi, 1947.

Tempesta, Antonio. *Metamorphoseon sive Transformationum Ovidianarum Libri Quindicem.* Amsterdam: N.p., [1606].

Tervarent, Guy de. *Les Enigmes de l'art: l'heritage antique.* Paris: Les éditions d'art et d'histoire, 1946.

Tevfik, Mehmet. *İstanbul'da bir Sene.* Istanbul: İletişimYayınları, 1991.

Tevfik, Selim. "İstanbul Radyosunda Neyler Gördüm?" *Yedigün* 61 (1934): 14–16.

Tevfik, Süleyman. *Deniz Padişahının Kızı.* Istanbul: Orhaniye Matbaası, 1921.

Theophrastus von Hohenheim [Paracelsus]. *A Book on Nymphs, Sylphs, Pygmies, and Salamanders, and on the Other Spirits,* trans. Henry E. Sigerist. In *Four Treatises of Theophrastus von Hohenheim called Paracelsus,* trans. C. Lillian Temkim, George Rosen, Gregory Zilboorg, and Henry E. Sigerist, ed. Henry E. Sigerist. Baltimore: Johns Hopkins University Press, 1941.

Theweleit, Klaus. *Male Fantasies.* Trans. Stephen Conway in collaboration with Erica Carter and Chris Turner. Vol. 1, *Women, Floods, Bodies, History,* foreword by Barbara Ehrenreich. Minneapolis: University of Minnesota, 1987.

Thompson, Stith. *Motif Index of Folk Literature.* Bloomington: Indiana University Press, 1955–1958.

Todd, R. Larry. "On Mendelssohn's Operatic Destiny: *Die Lorelei* Reconsidered." In *Felix Mendelssohn Bartholdy: Kongreß-Bericht Berlin 1994,* ed. Christian Martin Schmidt, 113–40. Wiesbaden, Leipzig, and Paris: Breitkopf & Härtel, 1997.

Tolstoy, Lev. *Anna Karenina.* Trans. Louise and Aylmer Maude. Oxford: Oxford University Press, 1995.

Tomlinson, Gary. *Music in Renaissance Magic: Toward a Historiography of Others.* Chicago: University of Chicago Press, 1993.

Touchefeu-Meynier, Odette. *Thèmes odysséens dans l'art antique.* Paris: E. de Boccard, 1968.

Toulmin, Stephen. *The Return to Cosmology: Postmodern Science and the Theology of Nature.* Berkeley: University of California Press, 1982.

Treblay, Guy. "After Nice, a Return to Vice." *New York Times,* Sunday, June 8, 2003, sec. 9, 1.

Trimingham, J. Spencer. *The Sufi Orders in Islam.* Oxford: Oxford University Press, 1998.

Trix, Frances. *Spiritual Discourse.* Philadelphia: University of Pennsylvania Press, Conduct and Communication Series, 1993.

Turino, Thomas. "The Charango and the Sirena: Music, Magic and the Power of Love." *Latin American Music Review* 4 (Spring/Summer 1983): 81–119.

Twain, Mark [Samuel L. Clemens]. *A Tramp Abroad.* 2 vols. New York and London: Harper & Brothers, 1929.

———. *Mark Twain's Notebooks & Journals.* Vol. 2, 1877–1883. Ed. Frederick Anderson, Lin Salamo, and Bernard Stein. Berkeley: University of California Press, 1975.

Udovitch, Mim. "Pink Fights the Power." *Rolling Stone* 899/900 (July 4–11, 2002): 60.

———. "The Whirling Diva." *Rolling Stone* 834 (February 17, 2000): 47.

Ünlü, Cemal, ed. *Gazeller II: 78 Devirli Taş Plak Kayıtları. Ottoman-Turkish Vocal Improvisations in 78 rpm Records.* Notes in Turkish and English by Cemal Ünlü and Bülent Aksoy. Istanbul: Kalan Müzik, Arşiv Serisi. CD 072, 1997. Sound Recording. www.kalan.com.

———. *Kadıköylü: Deniz Kızı Eftalya.* Notes in Turkish, English and Greek by Cemal Ünlü, Bülent Aksoy, and Leonidas Asteris. Istanbul: Kalan Müzik, Arşiv Serisi. CD 089, 1998a. Sound Recording. www.kalan.com.

———. *Kantolar (1905–1945).* Arşiv Serisi. Notes in Turkish by Cemal Ünlü and Murat Belge. Translated into English by Brenna Mac Crimmon. Istanbul: Kalan Müzik CD 085, 1998b. Sound Recording. www.kalan.com.

———. *Seyyan Hanım: Tangolar.* Notes in Turkish by Cemal Ünlü and Murat Belge. Istanbul: Kalan Müzik CD 050, 1996. Sound Recording. www.kalan.com.

Ünlü, Cemal and Stelyo Berberis. *İstanbul Laternası.* Notes in Turkish by Cemal Ünlü. Translated into English and Greek by Sonia Tamar Seeman and Stelyo Berberis. Istanbul: Kalan Müzik CD 136, 1999. Sound Recording. www.kalan.com.

Underhill, Lois Beachy. *The Woman Who Ran for President: The Many Lives of Victoria Woodhull.* Bridgehampton, N.Y.: Bridge Works Publications, 1995.

Urton, Gary. *At the Crossroads of the Earth and the Sky: An Andean Cosmology.* Austin: University of Texas Press, 1981.

Uwaifo, Victor. *Origin of Highlife and the Nigerian Music Industry.* Benin City: Joromi Publishing Co., 1995.

Valderrabano, Enrriquez de. *Libro de musica de vihuela intitulado Silva de Sirenas* (facsimile). Geneva: Minkoff, [1547] 1981.

Valeriano, Pierio. *Ieroglifici, overo Commentari delle occulte significationi de gli Egittij, & d'altre Nationi.* Venice: Appresso Gio[vanni] Antonio, e Giacomo de' Franceschi, 1602.

Van der Lek, Robert. *Diegetic Music in Opera and Film.* Atlanta: Editions Rodopi B. V., 1991.

Vasmer, Max. *Etimologicheskii slovar' russkogo yazyka* [Etymological dictionary of Russian language]. Translated from German by Trubacheva. Moscow: Progress, 1964 or 1971.

Vega, Ángel Custodio. *El "De Institutione Virginum" de San Leandro de Sevilla.* Scriptores Hispano-Latini Veteris et Medii Aevi 16–17. Madrid: Real Monasterio de S. Lorenzo de El Escorial, 1948.

Vermeule, Emily. *Aspects of Death in Early Greek Art and Poetry.* Sather Classical Lectures 46. Berkeley: University of California Press, 1979.

Vermigli, Peter Martyr. *The Common Places.* Trans. Anthonie Marten. London, 1583.

VH 1 Divas Live. New York: Epic Music Videos, 1998.

Vincent of Beauvais. *Speculum quadruplex.* 4 vols. Douai: B. Beller, 1624.

Vincke, Edouard. "Le Corps de la Sirene—Analyse Semiologique." In *Sacred Waters: The Many Faces of Mami Wata/mami wata, and other Water Spirits in Africa and the Afro-Atlantic World,* ed. Henry John Drewal. Bloomington: Indiana University Press, forthcoming

Vinge, Louise. *The Five Senses: Studies in a Literary Tradition.* Lund: CWK Geerup, 1975.

Vinycomb, John. *Fictitious and Symbolic Creatures in Art with Special Reference for Their Use in British Heraldry.* London: Chapman and Hall, 1906.

Virgil. *The Aeneid.* Ed. and trans. by H. R. Fairclough. Loeb Classical Library. Cambridge, Mass.: Harvard University Press, 1935.

——. *The Aeneid.* Trans. Thomas Phaer and Thomas Twynne. Ed. Steven Lally. New York: Garland, 1987.

Volkan, Vamik, and Norman Itzkowitz. *The Immortal Atatürk: A Psychobiography.* Chicago: University of Chicago Press, 1984.

——. *Turks and Greeks: Neighbours in Conflict.* Huntingdon, U.K.: Eothen Press, 1994.

Vredeveld, Harry. " 'Deaf as Ulysses to the Siren's Song': The Story of a Forgotten Topos." *Renaissance Quarterly* 54 (2001): 846–82.

Wachtel, Andrew Baruch. *An Obsession with History: Russian Writers Confront the Past.* Stanford: Stanford University Press, 1994.

Wagner, Cosima. *Die Tagebücher.* Ed. Martin Gregor-Dellin and Dietrich Mack. Vol. 1, 1869–1872. Munich: Piper, 1982.

Wagner, Richard. *Das Rheingold.* New York: Kalmus, n.d.

——. *Oper und Drama.* Ed. Klaus Kropfinger. Stuttgart: Reclam, 1984.

Walberg, Emmanuel. *Le Bestiaire de Philippe de Thaün.* Lund: H. Möller, 1900. Reprint. Geneva: Slatkine, 1970.

Walker, D. P., ed. *Musique des intermèdes de "la pellegrina": Les fêtes de Florence— 1589.* Paris: Cente National de la Recherche Scientifique, 1986.

Walker, Daniel Pickering. *Music, Spirit and Language in the Renaissance.* Ed. Penelope Gouk. London: Variorum Reprints, 1985.

Warm Water under a Red Bridge. Nikkatsu Imamura Productions. VAP. Eisei Gekijo. Maru. Produced by Hisa Iino. Directed by Shohei Imamura, 2001.

Weber, Max. *From Max Weber: Essays in Sociology.* Ed. H. H. Gerth and C. Wright Mills. New York: Oxford University Press, 1958.

——. "Religious Rejections of the World and Their Directions." In *From Max Weber: Essays in Sociology.* Ed. H. H. Gerth and C. Wright Mills. New York: Oxford University Press, 1958.

Weicker, Georg. "Seirenen." In *Ausführliches Lexikon der griechischen und römischen Mythologie,* by W. M. Roscher. Vol. 4 (1909), 601–39. 6 vols. in 9. Leipzig: B. G. Teubner, 1884–1937.

Weicker, Georg. *Der Seelenvogel in der alten Literatur und Kunst. Eine mytholo-gische-archaeologische Untersuchung.* Leipzig: B. G. Teubner, 1902.

Weinmann, Karl. *Johannes Tinctoris (1445–1511) und sein unbekannter Traktat "De inventione et usu musicae." Historisch-kritische Untersuchung.* Rev. Wilhelm Fischer. Tutzing: Hans Schneider, 1961.

Wells, H. G. *The Sea Lady.* New York: D. Appleton and Co., 1902.

Wells, Robin Headlam. *Elizabethan Mythologies: Studies in Poetry, Drama and Music.* Cambridge: Cambridge University Press, 1994.

Welsford, Enid. *The Court Masque.* Cambridge: Cambridge University Press, 1927.

Werner, Hans. "A German Eye-Witness to Troia-Nova Triumphans: Is Dekker's Text a Reliable Description of the Event?" *Notes and Queries* 46, no. 2 (1999): 251–56.

West, M. L. *The East Face of Helicon: West Asiatic Elements in Greek Poetry and Myth.* Oxford: Oxford University Press, 1997.

———. *The Orphic Poems.* Oxford: Clarendon Press, 1983.

West, Stephanie R. "Lycophron Italicised." *Journal of Hellenic Studies* 104 (1984): 127–51.

Whenham, John. *Claudio Monteverdi: "Orfeo."* Cambridge Opera Handbooks. Cambridge: Cambridge University Press, 1986.

White, T. H., ed. *The Book of Beasts: Being a Translation from a Latin Bestiary of the Twelfth Century.* New York: G. P. Putnam's Sons, 1954.

Whitney, Geffrey. *A Choice of Emblemes, and Other Devises.* Leyden: Christopher Plantin, 1586.

Wilde, Oscar. *A House of Pomegranates.* London: Methuen & Co., 1891; 3d ed., 1909.

Wiley, John Roland. *A Century of Russian Ballet.* Oxford: Clarendon Press; New York: Oxford University Press, 1990.

Willink, C. W. "The Parodos of Euripides' Helen (164–90)." *Classical Quarterly,* 40, no. 1 (1990): 77–99.

Wirtjes, Hanneke. *The Middle English Physiologus.* Early English Text Society, orig. ser. 200. Oxford: Oxford University Press, 1991.

Wither, George. *A Collection of Emblemes, Ancient and Moderne.* London: Printed by A.M. for Robert Allot, 1635.

Wolkstein, Diane, and Samuel Noah Kramer. *Inanna: Queen of Heaven and Earth.* New York: Harper and Row, 1983.

Woods, Paul A. *Weirdsville USA: The Obsessive Universe of David Lynch.* London: Plexus Publishing, 1997.

Wright, Owen. *Demetrius Cantemir: The Collection of Notations.* Vol. 2, *Commentary.* Aldershot: Ashgate, 2000.

Wyatt, Sir Thomas. *The Poetical Works.* Boston: Little, Brown and Co., 1856.

Xenophon. *Memorabilia.* In *Xenophon,* ed. and trans. by E. C. Marchant. Vol. 4. Loeb Classical Library. Cambridge, Mass.: Harvard University Press, 1979.

Yavneh, Naomi. "Dante's 'dolce serena' and the Monstrosity of the Female Body."

In *Monsters in the Italian Literary Imagination,* ed. Keala Jewell, 109–36. Detroit: Wayne State University Press, 2001.

Yeats, William Butler. *Collected Poems of W. B. Yeats.* London: Macmillan, 1967.

Yegenogli, Meyda. *Colonial Fantasies: Towards a Feminist Reading of Orientalism.* Cambridge: Cambridge University Press, 1998.

Yekta Bey, Rauf. "Osmanlı Musiksinden Çeyrek, Salis, ve Nesif Sedalar." *İkdam,* no. 1972 (December 29, 1899) n.p.

——. "Rum Kiliselerinde Musiki." *İkda,* no. 1960 (December 17, 1899): n.p.

Yurttan Sesler. *Yurttan Sesler: Yeni Türkiye'nin Ezgileri* ("Voices from Across the Land: The Melodies of New Turkey"). 3 vols. Notes in English and Turkish by Cemal Ünlü. Istanbul: Yapı Kredi Kültür Sanat Yayıncılık, CD Ö-01, 1998. Sound Recording.

Zannos, Iannis. "Intonation in the Theory and Practice of Greek and Turkish Music." *Yearbook for Traditional Music* 23 (1990): 42–59.

——. *Ichos und Makam: vergleichende Untersuchungen zum Tonsystem der griechisch-orthodoxen Kirchenmusik und der türkischen Kunstmusik.* Bonn: Orpheus-Verlag, 1994.

Zelenin, Dmitrii Konstantinovich. *Izbrannye trudy: ocherki russkoi mifologii* [Selected works: Essays of Russian mythology]. Moscow: Indrik, 1995.

Zender, Hans. *Les Sirènes chantent quand la rasion s'endort.* Berlin: Boosey and Hawkes, Bote and Bock, 1966.

Żerańska-Kominek, Slowomira (with Arnold Lebeuf). *The Tale of the Crazy Harman.* Warsaw: Dialog Academic Publications, 1997.

Zhukovsky, Vasilii Andreevich. "Rybak" [Fisherman]. In *Pesn' Lubvi: Lyrika russkih poetov XIX i XX vekov* [Love songs: Lyrics of russian poets of the nineteenth and twentieth centuries]. Moscow: Pravda, 1988.

Zimmermann, E. Heinrich. *Vorkarolingische Miniaturen.* 5 vols. Berlin: Deutscher Verein für Kunstwissenschaft, 1916.

Zimmermann-Kalyoncu, C. *Deutscher Musiker in der Türkei im 20. Jahrhundert.* Frankfurt: Peter Lang Verlag, 1980.

Zizek, Slavoj. "David Lynch, or, the Feminine Depression." In *The Metastases of Enjoyment: Six Essays on Woman and Causality.* London: Verso, 1994.

——. "I Hear You with My Eyes; or The Invisible Master." In *Gaze and Voice as Love Objects,* ed. Renata Salecl and Slavoj Zizek. Durham, N.C.: Duke University Press, 1996.

Zonta, Giuseppe, ed. *Trattati del Cinquecento sulla donna.* Bari: Laterza, 1913.

Zorzetti, Nevio. *Le Premier Mythographe du Vatican.* Association Guillaume Budé, Collection des Universités de France. Paris: Les Belles Lettres, 1995.

CONTRIBUTORS

Robin Armstrong is Associate Professor of Music at McDaniel College in Westminster, Maryland, where she teaches, among other courses, African-American Heritage Music, Hispanic Music of Latin America, and History of Jazz.

Stephen M. Buhler is Professor of English at the University of Nebraska–Lincoln. He has published extensively on John Milton and William Shakespeare, and his most recent book is *Shakespeare in the Cinema: Ocular Proof*.

Elena Laura Calogero holds a doctorate in English from the University of Florence, Italy. She is author of articles on English and comparative literature and of a forthcoming book on musical imagery in early modern English and European emblem books and poetry.

Henry John Drewal is the Evjue-Bascom Professor of African and African Diaspora Arts at the University of Wisconsin–Madison. He is currently preparing an exhibition on arts representing Mami Wata and other African and African Atlantic water spirits to open at the Fowler Museum of Cultural History–UCLA in the fall of 2007.

Annegret Fauser is Associate Professor of Music at the University of North Carolina at Chapel Hill. Her most recent publications include a 2005 monograph, *Musical Encounters at the 1889 Paris World's Fair,* and a series of articles on such diverse topics as dance, body, and music; Wagner's Parisian *Tannhauser;* and modernism as a challenge to historiography. She is currently writing a monograph on women musicians in fin-de-siècle Paris.

Charles Gore is a lecturer in the History of African Art at SOAS, University of London who has conducted research in Benin City and southern Nigeria since 1986, with a particular focus on Edo religion and ritual at the grassroots level. His current interests are religion and ritual, African artist and photographers, and approaches to popular culture and its relations to locality and the processes of globalization.

Leofranc Holford-Strevens is Consultant Scholar-Editor at Oxford University Press, Oxford. He is a classicist whose other interests include calendars and Renaissance musicology. His publications include *Aulus Gellius: An Antonine Scholar; Achievement; The Oxford Companion to the Year* (with Bonnie J. Blackburn); and *History of Time: A Very Short Introduction*.

Jeongwan Joe is Assistant Professor of musicology at the University of Cincinnati's College-Conservatory of Music. She is co-editor of *Between Opera and Cinema,* and is currently working on a monograph entitled *Opera at the Movies: What Can Opera Do for Film?* Her publications have focused on the intersections between opera and cinema, film music, and twentieth-century music.

Michelle Kisliuk is Associate Professor of Music at the University of Virginia, teaching in the Critical and Comparative Studies in Music program. She has researched and written extensively on the music, dance, and daily lives of forest people in the Central African Republic, as well as on urban music in central Africa, bluegrass jam sessions in America, ethnographic writing, and performance theory.

Lawrence Kramer is Professor of English and Music at Fordham University, and co-editor of the journal *Nineteenth-Century Music.* He has written extensively on the interrelationships of music and culture. His recent books include *Franz Schubert: Sexuality, Subjectivity, Song; Musical Meaning: Toward a Critical History;* and *Opera and Modern Culture: Wagner and Strauss.*

Thomasin LaMay teaches in the Music and Dance departments at Goucher College, Baltimore. Her teaching and research focus primarily on women in diverse artistic communities. She recently edited a collection of essays entitled *Musical Voices of Early Modern Women: Many-Headed Melodies.*

John Morgan O'Connell is Senior Lecturer in Ethnomusicology at the University of Limerick (Ireland). He completed his Ph.D. at UCLA, specializing in the musical traditions of the Middle East. He was recently awarded a Senior Fulbright Fellowship to conduct research into Central Asian music at Brown University in association with the Aga Khan Foundation. In 2004, he hosted in Ireland the fifteenth ICTM Colloquium, and he was instrumental in founding a National Committee there.

Henry Stobart is Senior Lecturer in Ethnomusicology in the Music Department of Royal Holloway, University of London. His co-edited books include *Sound and Knowledge,* and *Learning in the Andes: Ethnographic Perspectives,* and his monograph, *Music and the Poetics of Production in the Bolivian Andes,* is forthcoming. As a performer, he has toured and recorded widely with the early/world music ensemble Sirinu.

INDEX

Abbate, Carolyn, 218, 231, 260
Achebe, Chinua, 302
Achelous, 18–19, 24, 35; River, 5
Achilles, 17
Adam, 5, 82
Adam, Adolphe Charles, 224, 233–234
Adenis, Eugène, 259
Adigbe (Ohen), 307–308
Adorno, Theodor, 9, 200–202, 211,
    213n14, 363–364
Aegean, 274–275, 287
aesthetics, 54, 106, 113, 147, 210, 363
Africa, 294–297, 300, 309, 314
Afro-Atlantic, 295
agriculture, 108, 113–115, 124–126, 128–
    131, 139n99
AIDS, 311–312
Alberic of London, 27–28, 35, 45n67
alchemy, 85
Alciato, Andrea, 36, 78, 152, 157
Aldhelm, 29
allegory, 24, 64, 66, 70, 75, 89, 151, 162,
    183, 202–203
Alyabiev, Alexander, *Rusalka,* 233
Ambrose, 26
Amphion, 149, 151, 183
Anatolia, 274–275, 293n25
Andersen, Hans Christian, 194, 288; *The
    Little Mermaid,* 61, 73, 83–86, 220, 273,
    277, 286
Anderson, Laurie, *Blue Lagoon,* 215
Andes, 105–106, 113, 115–116, 118, 123,
    125, 131–132
angel, 8–9, 69, 93, 110, 141, 143–144, 147,
    149–150, 162–163, 165, 167n12, 229–
    330, 353
Angela Serena, 143–144
Anguillara, Giovanni Andrea dell',
    173n61
Aphrodite, 18, 20, 42n26, 281

Apollonius of Rhodes, 9, 20, 23, 163
Aretino, Pietro, 143–144, 149–150
Argonauts, 162
Arion, 89, 149, 151
Aristotle, 68, 154, 208
Armida, 161, 174n67, 261
Ascham, Roger, 170n35
asp. *See* snake
astrology, 300
Atatürk, Mustafa Kemal, 10, 278, 280–
    282
Atlantic Records, 336
aulos, 18–19, 24, 28, 41n9, 148
Aulus Gellius, 21–22
Ayla, Safiye, 280, 282, 285, 292n19

ba, 41n18
Baaba Maal, 313
Babylon, 25, 32, 36
Bach, Leonard Emil, 256
Bacon, Francis, 162, 174n72
Balakirev, Mily, 223, 245n40
Bangui. *See* Centrafrique
Barberino, Francesco da, 142, 148
bard, 9–10
Bartholomeus Anglicus, 60–61, 70
Basile, Adriana, 165, 175n77
basilisk. *See* snake
beards, 39n5
beast, 9, 26, 29, 55, 59, 61, 66–67, 69, 71,
    75, 80, 82–83, 153–155, 161. *See also*
    bestiary
Beauvoir, Simone de, 12n1, 54–55
Bellamano, Franceschina, 149–150
Bellini, Vincenzo, *Il Pirata,* 224
bells, 308
Bembo, Pietro, 142–144, 148, 169n16
Benin, 301
Benin City. *See* Nigeria
Benjamin, Walter, 363–364

[413]

LINDA PHYLLIS AUSTERN is Associate Professor of Musicology in the School of Music, Northwestern University. She has written extensively on issues concerning music in western European intellectual culture, concentrating on sixteenth- and seventeenth-century England and Europe. Her previous books are *Music, Sensation, and Sensuality* (editor), and *Music in English Children's Drama of the Later Renaissance.*

INNA NARODITSKAYA is Assistant Professor of Ethnomusicology in the School of Music, Northwestern University. She specializes in music and culture in contemporary central Asia, in former Soviet republics, and in imperial Russia. Her most recent book is *Song from the Land of Fire: Azerbaijanian Mugam in the Soviet and Post-Soviet Periods.*